# EVROPA

MARE SEPTENTRIONALE

ASIÆ

ASIAE PARS

PONTVS EVXINVS

MARE ADRIATICVM

MARE MEDITERRANEVM

# THE
# FACES
# OF
# EUROPE

# THE
EDITED
## FACES
BY
# OF
ALAN
# EUROPE
BULLOCK

*Phaidon Press 1980*

to the memory of Jean Monnet

© 1980 Elsevier Publishing Projects SA, Lausanne, Switzerland,
except for "Workers" (Chapter 4) © 1980 Walter Kendall
and "Lawyers" (Chapter 27) © 1980 Ronald Graveson

Planned and Produced by
Elsevier Publishing Projects (UK) Ltd,
Oxford, England

Origination by MBA Ltd, Bucks, England

Typeset in Monophoto Van Dijck and
printed by Jolly & Barber Ltd, Rugby, England

Published by Phaidon Press Ltd,
Littlegate House, St Ebbe's Street,
Oxford, England

ISBN 0 7148 2094 6

# Foreword

## ALAN BULLOCK

The best way to introduce this book is to explain how the idea it expresses came to be developed.

I was invited by the publishing house Elsevier to edit a volume which would commemorate in 1980 the double anniversary of their imprint. The first dates to 1580, at the beginning of the Revolt of the Netherlands, when Louis Elsevier, who had worked for the famous Antwerp printer Plantin, fled to the north and settled at Leyden in the grounds of the university which William of Orange had founded five years before, becoming its librarian and first registrar as well as the founder of a family firm which achieved fame throughout the learned world as publishers, booksellers, printers and typefounders.

The original firm went out of existence in the 18th century but its name was revived by a new publishing company established in Rotterdam in 1880, the second anniversary. As well as the name, this company also took over the Elsevier device of "the solitary", a man standing under an elm tree which bears a fruitful vine, with the motto *Non solus*. From this new beginning the present company moved to Amsterdam and, after World War II, became the holding company of an international group publishing in many languages throughout the world.

The origins and character of the company suggested that the work should be devoted to a European theme, and it was given the provisional title *The Face of Europe*. I was asked to produce a plan which would provide a coherent framework for a collaborative work into which contributions by a number of writers (in the end 30) could be fitted.

This was a congenial task since I have been absorbed throughout my life by the history of Europe and its civilization and never cease to be fascinated by its variety and vitality. These were the qualities which I wanted the book to convey: the problem was how best to do this.

A strong historical consciousness seems to be one of the distinctive characteristics of European civilization, but another history of Europe was out of the question. So was a division of the book into national or regional sections instead of historical periods. The plan had to allow justice to be done to the conflicts and contradictions which have always marked Europe's history, without losing sight of the common elements which make it possible to distinguish European from Asian, American or African experience.

I found what I was after by looking at Europe as made up of a series of different worlds corresponding to the different professions and activities in which people spend their lives, from farming to scholarship, from sport to government, from the theatre to the factory. The doctor, the engineer, the banker, the soldier, the industrial worker, the sailor, the artist, the intellectual – each has a different picture of the Europe in which he lives, a different experience, a different set of associations. It is their sum total which constitutes Europe in all its extraordinary variety and is expressed by the simple alteration of the title of the work from *The Face* to *The Faces of Europe*.

Many of these "worlds" have a long history, sometimes going back to ancient times, which has had a powerful formative influence on them. Thus, the actor's world begins with the drama of ancient Greece, has its landmarks in the famous theatres of Europe, a pantheon of great actors and actresses and a repertoire of great roles – all very different from, say, the doctor's world, although this too goes back to ancient Greece, to the island of Cos and the Hippocratic Oath, has its landmarks in the famous hospitals and teaching schools and its roll of honour in the pioneers of medical science and treatment.

Even 30 essays do not exhaust the perspectives which this way of looking at Europe opens up. But if the volume has to be selective rather than comprehensive, the selection has been made as wide as possible, finding room for sportsmen and entertainers as well as writers and scientists; for the poor and the workers as well as Europe's rulers, its politicians and civil servants, its lawyers and bankers.

I was once, at a dinner in Brno, placed next to a professor of civil engineering who, on learning that I was a historian, said that European history could be written around the history of Europe's roads, a thesis which he expounded with wit as well as conviction. Expand this to take in the successive industrial revolutions from that of steam and iron to the microchips of today and one sees how much European civilization owes to its engineers. At the other extreme, there is no older or more permanent a feature of European life than "the underworld", a traditional name which fits naturally into the framework of this volume. The picture would not be complete, and quite a lot of the variety as well as the colour lost, without the thieves and vagabonds, the con men and counterfeiters, not to mention the accompanying army of drabs, tarts and *demi-mondaines*, who have strutted or whined their way across the stage of history from Greek times on.

Nor would Europe be Europe without its rebels, the subject of Friedrich Heer's chapter, the nonconformists who from Socrates to the Russian dissidents have asked awkward questions and refused to be impressed either by orthodoxy or by authority.

The greatest gap of all in the record, as we are only beginning to realize, is the world or rather worlds of women, a gap we have highlighted by making this the theme of a chapter by itself in the centre of the book and giving it the title "Women, Half of Europe's Population". In one of the most perceptive studies in the book, Naomi Griffiths goes on to ask the further question, how far the inadequacy of the historical record only reflects the one-sided character of Europe as a man's world.

In finding the authors and translating the plan into a finished text, I have had the great advantage of working with Graham Speake, senior history editor of Elsevier in the United Kingdom. All the essays we have included are aimed at stimulating the imagination rather than providing a systematic treatment. Necessarily so, since each could be expanded into a whole book, but at the expense of concentrating on only one of Europe's faces and losing sight of the others, the many varied worlds which it is the purpose of this book to bring together. I recall from the first memorandum I was sent by the publishers a remark of Emrys Jones (the author of the first chapter which follows this Foreword) which puts the same point in a graphic phrase: "The sections need the light and shade of an essay, and demand a broad assessment rather than a lot of detail, in short 'A View of Venice' by Bonnington rather than by Canaletto."

The pictures in this book represent an independent, complementary statement of the theme, and for this reason they have been grouped separately instead of as illustrations of specific chapters. It seemed to me that the chronological order of historical periods which we had avoided in planning the text could with advantage be used in arranging the visual evidence so as to establish that Europe, at each successive stage of its history, has always constituted a multiplicity of worlds, often with an unmistakable continuity between their ancient Greek or Roman and their contemporary versions. The resulting 128 pages do not pretend to be a history of art but aim rather to provide a visual evocation of the activities verbally described in the essays, for in the past painters, sculptors and other artists were as involved in capturing contemporary events, including portraits and people at work, as photographers are today. It is a pleasure to record how much of the success in carrying out this part of the plan is due to the skill of Polly Friedhoff.

Historically, as Charles Boxer's essay makes clear, Europe has had a great impact upon the rest of the world, through conquest and trade, emigration and the export of ideas. This role, which Europe continued to play as recently as the earlier decades of this century, has now been dramatically reduced. Europe is no longer the centre of the world politically: the proportion of its population to that of the other continents has shrunk; its empires have disappeared and the lands bordering on the Pacific, it can be argued, are on the way to replacing those bordering on the Atlantic in the same way that the Atlantic in its turn replaced the Mediterranean as the central theatre of human history. The rest of the world has emancipated itself, with much suffering and bitterness, from the hegemony which the European powers formerly exercised over it.

To many it seems natural to conclude from this that Europe is ceasing to be of interest, not only to the rest of the world, but even to itself. I do not myself accept this as self-evident, for two reasons.

The first is that a great part of the cultural, intellectual and spiritual capital of the human race is locked up in the currencies of European thought and art, literature and languages. At a time when, in a new Iron Age, the prospect is poor of such capital accumulation being resumed in the foreseeable future, I believe that European civilization will continue to exercise a powerful attraction on the imaginations of men and women similar to that which ancient Greece has done for two and a half thousand years since it ceased to count as a centre of power.

The second is that the extraordinary power of recovery which the European peoples have shown after the appalling losses of two self-inflicted wars suggests, as Edward Heath argues in the concluding essay, that Europe's vitality is far from exhausted.

There have been few decades in European history when any hope for the future appeared more implausible than the 1940s, a decade in which the destruction of war was followed by the division of Europe and the separation of its eastern half under a second occupation. Yet the astonishing fact is that, in the 20 years which followed 1950, western Europe staged a recovery which produced higher levels of general prosperity than ever before in its history and that, despite more than 30 years of indoctrination and forced rule, the peoples of eastern Europe – certainly the Poles, the Hungarians, the Czechoslovaks – perhaps one should add Russians too, though how many no one knows – have not abandoned their European identity and their claim to a share in European civilization.

No one can foresee what Europe will be like even 20 years from now; but I share Edward Heath's view that the future is not foreclosed, any more than it was at the beginning of the 1940s (though few believed so at the time), and that there are options open. Nor do I believe that what happens in Europe is unimportant, even in the changing context and scale of tomorrow's world. Even leaving aside what Europe has inherited as irreplaceable capital from the past, a world in which the peoples of Europe have no continuing role to play, and to which they are no longer capable of making a distinctive contribution, will be immeasurably poorer in everything which makes human life something more than a material struggle for existence.

November 1979

# CONTENTS

# CONTRIBUTORS

BOXER, Charles R. FBA. Member of the Royal Netherlands Academy of Sciences. Emeritus Professor of Portuguese, University of London.

BULLOCK, Lord (Alan L. C.). FBA. Master of St Catherine's College, Oxford. Vice-Chancellor of Oxford University, 1969–73.

CARTWRIGHT, F. F. President of the Section of the History of Medicine, Royal Society of Medicine.

ELKANA, Yehuda. Professor of the History and Philosophy of Science at the Hebrew University of Jerusalem and Director of the Van Leer Jerusalem Foundation.

ESSLIN, Martin J. Professor of Drama at Stanford University, California. Formerly Head of BBC Radio Drama.

FINER, Samuel E. Gladstone Professor of Government and Public Administration at the University of Oxford.

GARDINER, Stephen. Practising architect in London and architecture critic of the *Observer*.

GRAVESON, Ronald. CBE, QC. Professor Emeritus of Private International Law at King's College London. Bencher of Gray's Inn. Member of the Polish Academy of Sciences.

GRIFFITHS, Naomi E. S. Professor of History and Associate Dean of Arts, Carleton University, Ottawa.

HEATH, Rt. Hon. Edward R. G. MBE, MP. Prime Minister of Great Britain, 1970–74.

HEER, Friedrich. Professor of History at the University of Vienna.

HERRMANN, Luke. Professor of the History of Art at the University of Leicester.

HUFTON, Olwen H. Professor of Modern European History at the University of Reading.

JOHNSON, Douglas W. J. Head of Department of History and Dean of Faculty of Arts at University College London.

JONES, Emrys. Professor of Geography, University of London, at the London School of Economics and Political Science. Vice-President of the Royal Geographical Society.

KEEGAN, John. Senior Lecturer in War Studies at the Royal Military Academy, Sandhurst.

KEMP, Lt-Comdr Peter. OBE. Formerly Head of Naval Historical Branch and Naval Librarian, Ministry of Defence.

KENDALL, Walter. Formerly Senior Research Fellow at Nuffield College, Oxford. Currently associated with the University of Sussex.

KROCKOW, Christian Graf von. Formerly Professor of Political Science at the Universities of Göttingen, Saarbrücken and Frankfurt-am-Main.

LEVI, Peter. Fellow of St Catherine's College and Lecturer in Classical Studies at Christ Church, Oxford.

McMANNERS, The Revd. John. FBA. Regius Professor of Ecclesiastical History, Canon of Christ Church, and Emeritus Fellow of St Edmund Hall, Oxford.

OSBORNE, Harold. Former editor of the *British Journal of Aesthetics*. Editor of the *Oxford Companion to the Decorative Arts*.

POLLARD, Sidney. Professor of Economic History at the University of Sheffield.

POWELL, Dilys. Film critic, broadcaster and writer.

QUINTON, Anthony. FBA. President of Trinity College, Oxford.

ROLPH, C. H. Vice-President of the Howard League for Penal Reform. A former Chief Inspector of the City of London Police.

STEVENS, Denis. Musicologist and conductor. Artistic Director of the Accademia Monteverdiana.

SUTHERLAND, Dame Lucy. DBE, FBA. Honorary Fellow and sometime Principal of Lady Margaret Hall, Oxford.

THOMPSON, F. M. L. Director of the Institute of Historical Research and Professor of Modern History in the University of London.

VERLINDEN, Charles. Emeritus Professor, University of Ghent. Fellow of the Royal Belgian Academy.

VRIES, Johan de. Professor of Economic History at the Economics Faculty of the Roman Catholic University of Tilburg.

# LIST OF PLATES

# PART ONE

*Introduction:*
*Europe: Land, Peoples*
*and Languages*

# 1

# Europe: Land, Peoples and Languages

## EMRYS JONES

"For my part," wrote Herodotus, "I cannot conceive why three names, and women's names especially, should ever have been given to a tract which is in reality one." The tract was the known world, and to the father of history the world was one. It was the *oikoumene* which centred on Greece and which receded in all directions to vague uncivilized, unpeopled and fabulous parts, unknown except in fantastic travellers' tales and in the imagination of men. The Greeks identified three parts to this world, which they called Asia, Libya and Europe.

The division was perpetuated in the image of the medieval Christian world, and enshrined in the maps of that period. Medieval T-O maps are so called because they picture a world which is a disc containing a T. The east is to the top: the stem of the T is the Mediterranean and the cross piece is the Black Sea and the Red Sea. This conveniently produces a tripartite division, focused on a central point, which is Jerusalem: the upper half of the O is Asia, the lower left quadrant is Europe and the lower right is Africa (the Romans having changed the name from Libya to Africa).

The physical subdivision of the known world into three parts was given greater significance in Christian cosmography by the belief that the world's peoples might also be descended from the three sons of Noah. The philosopher Josephus, in the 1st century AD, suggested that Europe was peopled by the sons of Japhet, Africa by the sons of Ham, and Asia by the sons of Shem.

The picture was a neat one, but Europe itself did not mean much in a civilization in which Christendom embraced the entire world. An identity beyond that of a formal part of the symbolic world was not established until Europe emerged as the Christian world. Even so, it was still the concept of Christendom, not Europe, which was emotive until the 14th or 15th century. After that the word Europe was increasingly used in a secular sense, as new forces, like the economic links which were being forged from the North Sea and Baltic to the Mediterranean and from the Atlantic to Asia, were investing the territorial term with a new meaning. Moreover distance, direction and location were acquiring new and more "scientific" meanings. By the 15th century the adoption of the magnetic compass and the improvement of the astrolabe made navigation a more rational exercise. Portolano charts which guided navigators along compass points show that coastlines were now being drawn fairly accurately, and a new picture of the world was emerging. But the new Christian realm had now taken on the shape we know today, a series of promontories, little more than an appendage of Asia.

Knowledge of the real world revealed that in the east Europe merged imperceptibly into Asia. Was Russia in Europe or was it in Asia? Peter the Great did his best to show his allegiance by forcing Russia to look westward and by making St Petersburg a visible link to emphasize the symbolic one. But it was only after the Napoleonic Wars, and the great part played in these by Russia, that the concept of Europe was extended eastward. An atlas of the 1830s put the boundaries of Europe at the Ural Mountains and the Ural River. Europe, as we know it, was established.

Having disentangled some of the historical threads in the concept of Europe, we are only a little better equipped to introduce the continent. There is an inborn bias which makes an objective "setting of the stage" virtually impossible. The view is from within, written in a European language, the product of a European cultural heritage, reflecting European hopes. It is too much to expect a geographer to be able to stand outside a tradition and calmly examine the elements which make up Europe and the Europeans: the fact that he can see the whole as a map may give him Olympian heights, but not Olympian judgement; perspective, but not detachment; scale, but not value.

Its coasts and contours, rivers and basins can be described fairly easily. Geologically and geographically, Europe is an appendage of Asia, an extension of a much grander continent. The North European Plain is an extension of the West Siberian Plain; the steppe lands of Asia end only in the suburbs of Vienna; Europe's mountain system is part of the vast tertiary folded system centred on the Himalayas. Neither the Urals nor the Volga constitutes a marked physical divide. The political and cultural frontiers alone are significant.

There are features in the environment which are worth noting, not because they necessarily dictate human action, as some have argued, but because they are facts of life which society has to take into account. The world in which we live is the outcome of the way in which man has come to terms with his environment, the way he has perceived and used its resources, the way he has refashioned it. But however much he seems to rise above his habitat, man cannot ignore it.

For a continent which is only a little more than half the size of the USA and less than half the size of the USSR, Europe has a very varied topography. In the northwest, in most of Norway and Sweden, Scotland, north England, north Wales and parts of Ireland, are found some of the world's oldest rocks, paleozoic and pre-Cambrian, in complex mountain areas, where a strong and rugged relief is also the outcome of past glaciation. High, cold and bare, the poor soils of this region repel cultivation, and population is sparse and poor. To the south of this, most of north Europe is part of a great plain system, extending from Russia to the English Channel. Rarely over 300 metres in height, its hills are gentle and its terrain conducive to movement. Much of the northern part of this plain was affected by glaciation, which left extensive areas either of gravel and sands washed out of the glaciers, or of boulder clay. Both surfaces are infertile and make cultivation difficult. There are still vast natural areas here of grassland and forest. The southern part of the plain is fertile, and cereals and root crops flourish. This area is broken by great masses of Hercynian rocks, high plateaux rather than peaks, like the Massif Central of France, the Vosges, the Black Forest and the mountains of Bohemia. Movement through them is made easier by waterways like the Rhine, the Moselle, the Weser and the Elbe. Further south again are the great lines of geologically young Alpine rocks. These are massive, peaky, snow-clad mountains, typified by the Alps themselves, by the Pyrenees and the Apennines. They sweep southeastward into the Dinaric Alps and curve back into Europe in the Transylvanian Alps. These have usually been barriers to movement, and their passes have a significance of their own. The biggest gap in this line of mountains is made by the Danube, and the gateway so formed from Asia Minor to the centre of Europe has been of especial importance in the prehistory of the continent.

The southern shore of Europe looks to the Mediterranean, virtually an inland sea. To a lesser extent the Baltic looks inward and has tended to form a culture area since Neolithic times. More important is the Atlantic outlook of the westernmost fringes of Europe. Their location was turned topsy-turvy when the New World was discovered. Regions which had been so distant from the old centres of civilization became a link with the other half of the world: Ultima Thule became the centre of civilization. An intense interest in the sea, its economy, conquest, hazards and in what lay beyond the sea, has often been a common bond between the Atlantic-facing countries of Europe.

Although the whole of Europe can be called temperate, showing none of the extremes of cold or heat, of rain or of drought, nevertheless it has distinctive climate regions. The climatic influence of the Atlantic, for example, has played a part in identifying the northwest of Europe as a distinct region, subject to Atlantic depressions, to rain and gales, to winter maxima of rain, as well as to the warmer ocean current which has kept its shores ice-free. The interior, on the other hand, is subject to Asiatic climatic conditions: it is drier, has summer maxima of rain, and contrasts in summer and winter temperatures are sharper. South of the Alpine peaks the Mediterranean countries bask in a warmer, kinder, drier climate which the northerner so much envies.

Climatic differences are reflected in the natural plant cover, and in the alternating summer brown of the Mediterranean with its winter green, and the perennial green of the northwest. The grasslands of the drier interior and the deciduous forests of the west form very distinctive zones. The mixed forests further north and in Russia give way to the great pine forests of Scandinavia and north Russia and eventually to Arctic tundra.

The components of the habitat are comparatively simple compared with those of the people and their culture. In the broadest sense, a case could be made for some kind of homogeneity based on its people. It is the home of the white man, so called, and this gives the continent a homogeneity – but one that is shared: anthropologically Europe is part of a larger province. It could be claimed that Europe is linguistically one; but again there are Indo-European languages far beyond its boundaries. It could be argued further that Christianity has given it a moral-religious homogeneity, and Latinity its Classical antecedents. All this adds up to a considerable weight of common elements, though many are shared with other peoples. Perhaps a sociologist from another planet would not hesitate on the evidence of shared features to see strong common identity, particularly when comparing Europe with other major divisions, such as Africa or Asia. But this again is a view from above, and has surprisingly little bearing on the way people behave. Differences rather than similarities tend to dictate our actions. That our many languages have common roots means little in the face of the divisiveness, not only of languages, but of dialects within a single language, or even of accent. The bitterness of sectarian differences seems to make nonsense of the homogeneity of Christendom. At the very moment when the common elements in our cultures are being stressed politically, as in the Common Market, demands for separation seem to be increasing, on nationalistic terms as with the Basques, or on regional terms as in Britain.

The common heritage is hidden by a bewildering complexity, by the variety of ethnic groups, the many sects and the numerous tongues. It is this complexity which gives Europe its richness, and which now challenges description.

The picture is further complicated by time and change. For the patterns of peoples and cultures are not static. Ours is merely the latest stage of many in a very dynamic picture. It is rather like looking at a kaleidoscope being very slowly moved by history, the shapes changing with every move. The pattern today is a product of the processes of the past. We must hold the picture still for a moment in order to describe and analyse the elements in it.

Small though peninsular Europe is, it is richly endowed with the most important of all resources – people. The continent has a population of about 650 million, or one-sixth of the total population of the earth, but they are distributed very unevenly. The focus of concentration has shifted markedly over the last 500 years. In medieval times the Mediterranean was the home of the majority of Europe's people, as it had been since Classical times. From that period on, the west and centre became increasingly more important: first because of advances in agricultural techniques which raised the standard of living, and secondly because the Industrial Revolution transformed the economy first of England and then of the remainder of the northwest. The imprint of the Industrial Revolution is still there. A band of dense population extends from the Midlands of England, across north France and the Low Countries and north Germany into Russia, with an outlier in northern Italy. Throughout much of this area density is very high, over 80 people per square kilometre. Further north, however, there is a dramatic fall in density in Scandinavia and north Russia to 2 per square kilometre; here even farming peters out.

The difference in densities is also largely the contrast between rural and urban economies. In the United Kingdom and in the Netherlands about 80 per cent of the population live in towns and cities; the figure is 70 per cent in France and Sweden, and around 50 per cent in most other European states. But the growth of the super-city is the most striking modern feature. In 1800 London, with nearly a million people, was by far the largest city in Europe. By 1900 there were six one-million cities in Europe – London, Paris, Berlin, Vienna, St Petersburg and Moscow. Today there are 50. The impact of these cities on the areas around them is such that it is more pertinent to talk of metropolitan regions than of cities and there are six such regions in Europe. The London metropolitan region has eleven million people, the Rhine-Ruhr region ten million, Paris has eight million, Moscow eight million, Berlin four million and Randstadt-Holland four million. The traditional farmer-peasant economy has become numerically weak even though it still dominates the landscape. Even the industrial worker does not dominate the scene any more. More and more the urbanite, the creator of services, the entrepreneur of information, is emerging as the European of the future.

Urbanization seems also to be one of the social processes which is guiding Europe through a demographic transition. Throughout the last 150 years death rates have fallen dramatically, and while there was no corresponding fall in the birth rate, the resulting increase in total population was very marked. A decline in the birth rate in this century means that the population is stabilizing, with a low birth rate and a low death rate, although in the last decade growth has again increased a little. Compared with the rest of the world, Europe's growth is still relatively moderate, in most countries between 1 and 2 per cent per annum, although some are low (i.e. less than 1 per cent per annum), even the least industrialized countries like Romania, Spain and Hungary.

One of the main variables in population growth is migration. During the last century and the first decade of this, Europeans have virtually peopled two other continents. Population pressure would have been even greater in Europe had not some 30 million crossed the north Atlantic. The historical development of Europe is the story of movement, and the explanation of the present distribution of peoples, religions and languages lies in diffusion. Europe was first peopled from the east and its early cultural streams came from the Near East; the Mediterranean, the Danube and the North European Plain saw continual movements of peoples and cultures. Empires expanded and contracted; resources attracted and created concentrations of people. I referred above to what were the greatest movements of the last century, from the country to the town. Population was, and is, in constant flux, sometimes no more than modifying a larger and stable pattern, but sometimes great enough to institute a new major pattern and to have important political and social implications.

For example in the interwar period France, which had lost much of its manpower in World War I, welcomed migrant workers, and in 1931 its population included 2·8 million born outside its boundaries – 910,000 from Italy, 520,000 from Poland, 380,000 from Spain and 320,000 from Belgium. War is a great uprooter of people. By 1939 Spain, as a result of its civil war, was trying to cope with three million refugees, and about 300,000 of these crossed into France. World War II may well have caused the movement of 25 million peoples. Seven million forcibly drafted by Germany were moved across Europe. At the end of the war six million Germans were transferred from Poland and Czechoslovakia and Hungary, back to their own country. Exchanges between Poland and the USSR accounted for another 2·5 million. These are only a few figures to indicate the scale of the movements.

Since 1945 labour has again moved freely across most of Europe. In the mid-1960s, for example, nearly 4·3 million workers lived in countries other than those of their birth. The great suppliers of labour were the Mediterranean countries which accounted for over two-thirds of the total: Italy supplied 1·5 million, Spain 675,000, Greece 225,000, Turkey 180,000, Portugal and Yugoslavia 125,000 each. The receiving countries were mainly western European: Western Germany received 1,139,000, France over a million and Switzerland 775,000, and in each case the vast majority came from southern Europe. The second conspicuous element in the pattern of movement is the fact that the USSR takes no part in it. This has its own precise expression in Berlin where the wall is a physical barrier as well as a symbol of an ideological divide between two parts of Europe.

Older than any of the other differences is the variety of physical types in Europe's population.

To classify is a human trait, but it is also human to base our categories on differences rather than similarities. All Europeans belong to the major subgroup of the human race called Caucasoid, which merely means they are light in pigmentation – that is "white" – and that they usually have brown or fair hair, fairly fine in texture and tending to be wavy. Within this class there are considerable variations, and traditionally anthropologists talked about three subgroups which they located in north (Nordic), central (Alpine) and southern Europe (Mediterranean). But any scientific classification is a series of constructs, a product of the scientist's mind; and although the models they produce may be useful pointers to the origins of groups and their relationships, they are not very helpful in identifying people today. Even more important is the fact that movement, examples of which we have seen above, makes nonsense both of the purity of these types and of any great significance about their location.

For classification blood groups are much more satisfactory than measuring features which can change because they are mixed. Blood groups remain unchanged in inheritance, and they are useful indicators of older racial groups. Type O is by far the most common, but its distribution has a western predominance, highest in Scotland and Ireland. It seems ethnically quite stable, and it may represent an Asian substratum. Blood group B seems to have a nucleus in central Asia, so not unnaturally this type is predominant in eastern Europe; whereas type A is more common in the west with a very high incidence in Scandinavia.

For practical purposes in Europe, we can ignore "race". And yet we cannot ignore societies' ideas about race. For whereas an anthropologist will hesitate even to generalize about race, the layman will step in blithely and assert that he can recognize a Jew or a Russian, or an Italian or a Scot at a glance. In extenuation remember that human relationships often depend on decisions about other people which have to be immediate, however wrong. The layman does not hesitate either to add cultural and mental attributes to his "racial" class: in short, he deduces everything about a man from his appearance.

In the 1860s a German philologist, Max Müller, replaced the term Indo-European with Aryan, and unwittingly gave birth to a misconception which has bedevilled the problem of race in Europe ever since. Some saw Aryan as a description of a people, who came from an Asiatic cradle and who were the forerunners of the Germanic people, prototypes which were physically and culturally superior (*Arya* means noble). Comte de Gobineau compounded the error by claiming that Germanic tribes were the most "undiluted" in Europe, and this was largely the basis of the Nazi myth of the superiority of the so-called Aryan or Nordic peoples of Germany.

In fairness, French "Kelticism" at the end of the 19th century was equally convinced of the superiority of the French. Sadly, people think of themselves as superior to others, both mentally and physically, and consequently they belittle those whom they recognize as physically different. Ironically, the Jews who suffered the effects of the Aryan myth do not have a specific set of racial characteristics. Their dispersal meant that they took on the physical characteristics of the predominant types wherever they found themselves. A large number have physical features found most often in Mediterranean countries, but the great majority are physically akin to the Slavs of eastern Europe.

Although there are no clear composite "racial" types in Europe, there are variations in the key physical traits which tend to be more characteristic of some areas than of others. Tall people – by which we mean populations with men more than 173 centimetres in height – are characteristic of northwest Europe, from Iceland and Scandinavia to the British Isles, Germany and the Baltic, with outliers in parts of European Russia and in Bosnia and Albania. Short people, that is 163 centimetres and less, are more characteristic of the western Mediterranean, of France, Italy or Spain, although the Lapps share this characteristic. People with dark skins, eyes and hair predominate in the Mediterranean, the south of France, Italy and the Balkans, whereas fair persons are in a majority in Scandinavia and the Baltic countries, in Germany, in the Low Countries and in England, Scotland and Ireland. The shape of the face or the head also shows marked variations – long in Spain and in the northwest, roundish in mid-France and in the mountain regions of middle Europe. Anthropologists trying to include all these measurements produce ever more complex classes as the permutations increase. Somewhere in the midst of all this there is a kernel of truth which says that in the western Mediterranean you are more likly to meet people who are short and dark and long-headed; and in Scandinavia, tall people who are also long-headed, but fair; and in eastern Europe, shortish and round-headed, medium-coloured people.

Race has been defined as a physical peg on which people hang their prejudices. Societies face the complexities of identifying other societies by creating stereotypes. One of the classic stereotypes of European society is that of the Jew, in which all the social prejudices of European society are coupled with a distinctive physical type. But we have seen that, however homogeneous Jewish culture or religion is, there is no foundation at all for postulating a Jewish physical type.

Stereotypes are most likely to arise when there is a contrast between, say, migrants and a host society. If the hosts are fair and the migrants are dark, then the latter are very "visible", that is, identifiable and likelier to attract attention; any social characteristics, such as different language or religion or even habits, will confirm the stereotype. After the potato famine in the 1840s there was a tremendous influx of Irish labourers to London. They were visible mainly in a social sense, but they became an established stereotype which has persisted quite remarkably.

The oldest substratum of languages in Europe was probably more or less obliterated by others brought in from what is now southern Russia in the last two millennia BC. From a historical point of view, therefore, European languages are all grouped as Indo-Aryan, suggesting a common origin and consequent linguistic affinities. This is of little more than academic significance, for only when we come to the next stage in classification do we find familiar groups of languages with common elements. We can immediately recognize the common affinity of the Romance languages. They are not lineal descendants from Latin, but may be a mixture of vulgar Latin and pre-Latin elements. Europe has four such major families which are spatially more or less mutually exclusive. The Romance family occupies a western and Mediterranean bloc of land, and includes French, Italian, Spanish, Portuguese, Romanian, Sardinian and Rhaeto-Romanic (in Switzerland). The Germanic family occupies a northern bloc and comprises German, English, Flemish, Swedish, Norwegian, Danish, Frisian and Icelandic. These expanded westward in historical times to replace a formerly much more extensive family, the Celtic languages. The latter have been pushed to the Atlantic extremities of Europe, and the survivors are found on the westernmost promontories: Cornish and Manx have disappeared as mother tongues, Irish and Gaelic are numerically very weak, and only Welsh and Breton flourish, though both are hard pressed. The Slavic family occupies eastern Europe, a large group composed of Lithuanian and Lettish, Russian with Byelorussian and Ukrainian, Czechoslovakian, Polish, Slovenian, Serbo-Croat, Macedonian and Bulgarian. A more easterly family is the Ural-Altaic, found in the USSR and in Turkey and also represented by Lapp, Finnish, Estonian and Magyar. Finally there are, in addition to the large blocs, several smaller families represented by single languages, such as Greek, Albanian, Armenian and Basque.

Most European languages have been rooted for a thousand years, and so it is worth mentioning two which are not "territorial". Romani, the language of gypsies, has a vocabulary which is rich in words from a dozen languages, from Indian to Welsh, the range indicating the amount of movement of gypsies. Yiddish, based on a medieval Rhenish German, has many Slav elements together with much Hebrew. Again it has helped in retaining the identity of a group which is ethnically and culturally dispersed.

Linguistic affinity may be academically important, but when it comes to understanding one another we need to take our classification further. Languages within a family may be mutually almost unintelligible: q-Celts (Irish and Gaelic) and p-Celts (Welsh and Breton) can never hope to understand one another.

Even local variants of the spoken tongue – dialects – often create barriers to understanding. The Romance language of medieval France developed regional dialects and, although Charlemagne tried to reintroduce Latin as an official language, the local variants proved too strong and polarized into a northern *langue d'oïl* and a southern *langue d'oc*. Eventually a Parisian dialect prevailed over both, but remnants of the original dialect are still very evident.

Dialects rarely reach the stage of being used in literary form, but they are nevertheless extremely important because this is the way the majority of people communicate with one another, and complete understanding may depend on linguistically very small variations.

Language unites people within groups at the expense of separating them from other groups.

Language divides are often blurred. Political boundaries may change frequently, as in Alsace Lorraine, resulting in a bilingual population. Belgium's borders contain two major languages and an enclave of German-speaking population. As a result, in addition to monoglot French (2·9 million), monoglot Flemish (3·5 million) and monoglot German (59,000), there were in Belgium in 1947 1·3 million who spoke French and Flemish, 83,000 who spoke French and German, 23,000 who spoke Flemish and German, and 216,000 who spoke all three languages.

Languages which become "minority" tongues because state boundaries do not follow linguistic divides are fairly common, and sometimes single states have subsumed entire minority groups – e.g. the Celtic languages in the United Kingdom and Breton in France. Nevertheless the strength of feeling and emotion engendered by language cannot be over-estimated. Lingua francas rarely oust native languages, and invented languages, like Esperanto, have made virtually no headway, possibly because they enshrine no values. A mother tongue is inextricably bound up with beliefs and traditions, and can withstand great pressure for change. In the 19th century Polish was outlawed and officially replaced by German and Russian; but it survived to become a vital element in the emergence of a new Polish state after World War I.

The greatest problem facing the minority languages is coping with modern technology, and it is difficult to withstand the pressure of major languages which command the media of information. Bilingualism may be an immediate answer, but in the long term usually leads to the adoption of the major language. Language, more than anything, highlights the problems of cooperation and internationalization without destroying the rich heritage of smaller cultures.

In view of the origins of Europe one would expect religion at least to be homogeneous. The basic tenets are, of course, derived from one source, but once again fundamental variants have played a critical part in the foundation of national cultures.

We can dismiss the small enclaves of Islam in Albania and Yugoslavia which are all that remain of the Muslim incursion in the Mediterranean world. And the Jews do not occupy specific regions, being largely urban. The differentiating elements are variant beliefs within Christianity itself, and there are three religious areas, one dominated by Roman Catholicism, one by the Eastern Orthodox Church and one by Protestant sects. The beliefs are characteristics of areas rather than of people. Whereas everyone claims a language, not everyone claims a religion, and consequently it is one of the most difficult of cultural traits to record in those countries where orthodox belief has diminished.

The only full-scale census of religion in Britain took place in 1851, when religious observance was recorded, and since that time it has proved either too difficult or irrelevant, except in Northern Ireland where religious allegiance is a very live issue. Conflict sharpens edges. Whereas normally areas of overlap in religion are very blurred, where there has been – or there is – intransigence, boundaries are razor sharp.

A very generalized distribution reveals three major Christian realms, reminiscent of certain geographical regions which have emerged more than once: the Mediterranean, northwest Europe and continental Europe. But rather than reflecting regional differences as such, the three realms are really a product of history, a function of distance from an original core. Christianity originated outside Europe, and diffused into the Mediterranean world from the Middle East. The first split was east-west, reflecting a change of focus in the Roman world. The real schism came in 1054, and the Eastern Orthodox Church showed characteristics which were more territorially based and more national in type than the Roman: for example, Slav languages were used in liturgy rather than Latin. The largest single unit today is the Greek Orthodox Church, which is the state Church of Greece.

The second split was between southern and northern Europe. The Reformation succeeded only in that area of the former Western Roman Empire beyond the Rhine and Danube, with two exceptions – Poland and Ireland. New ideas may well be absorbed more easily on the periphery, where mere distance from the centre of authority may be conducive to change. The core retains the traditional elements. At times, certainly, as in Ireland, the periphery can be extremely conservative; but generally speaking new ideas sprang up north of the Alps, and

Calvinism spread west and Lutheranism spread north. The interplay of locational elements, centres of new thought and diffusion of ideas, and the cultural patterns which absorbed or rejected these ideas underlie the seeming simplicity of the broad threefold geographical pattern.

Interspersed with Christians ever since their dispersal from the Middle East in 70 AD were the Jews. Jews in Europe still number about four million, nearly a third of world Jewry. Virtually absent in Spain and Portugal, few in France and in the Mediterranean countries, and very few now in Germany, Jews are numerous in Britain, Poland, Romania, Hungary and west Russia. Their eastern concentration reflects the protection offered to refugees from Germany by Poland in the 14th century (when Poland included much of the Ukraine). But most of these Jews are city dwellers, whose efforts to retain orthodoxy at all costs often contribute to ghetto conditions. Consequently it is their concentration rather than their absolute numbers that makes them important as an ethnic group.

Disentangling some of the threads of European cultural history raises the question of whether they have been woven into a single easily recognizable pattern. One simple answer lies in the political map of Europe. Long-established state boundaries tend to reinforce the cultural characteristics of a national core; language tends to become uniform in a state because it is taught at schools, and is also the vehicle of taught behaviour. Consequently the whole pattern of state life, of tradition even, tends towards homogeneity.

The political divisions are not always an accurate reflection of the cultural, though there is in many cases a rough correspondence. There are classic instances of incongruence. A language divide cuts across Belgium separating the Flemings in the north from the Walloons in the south, and Brussels is the bilingual capital of a divided country. On the other hand Switzerland seems to have coped extremely well with straddling four cultural regions. The boundary between France and Spain seems an easily defined line along mountain crests, but in fact it cuts across a group of mountain-based cultures, which in this case include the politically thorny Catalan and Basque areas. Minority cultural groups – the Bretons in France or the Celtic groups in the United Kingdom – are also politically volatile, though Ireland alone has attained full statehood and that along strictly religious lines. Otherwise western Europe shows a fairly stable relationship between state boundaries and cultural boundaries.

Eastern Europe is a much more unstable area. Until comparatively recently this was largely undifferentiated within the pre-1914 imperial boundaries of Germany, Russia and Austria. On their dissolution eight new states were created which reflected ethnic groupings. Although largely successful, their creation did not add greatly to the stability of the so-called "shatter" zone, which includes fragments of many cultural realms, because these areas are open to alternating influences from Germany on the west and from Russia on the east. After 1945 there were changes in the allegiance of Lithuania and Estonia and Latvia, a dividing line was drawn through Poland, the Moldavian SSR was created and other minor boundary changes made; and most critical of all, the German Democratic Republic was created. The last is a reminder of what may be a fundamental cultural divide between east and west which reflects two ideological areas expressing themselves today in separate economic and political groupings, such as COMECON (Council for Mutual Economic Assistance) on the east and the EEC on the west.

Time and again scale seems to play an important part in deciding whether Europe can be thought of as one or as several distinctive regions. Although from a world point of view similarities outweigh differences, this chapter has revealed heterogeneity rather than homogeneity. Both views must be taken into account. Relative to the remainder of the world, Europe as a whole is highly industrialized and very urbanized. In fact the core of industrialization still lies in the northwest, in sharp contrast to the much less industrialized Mediterranean and Balkans; and urbanization is relatively low in the last two areas, particularly in the Balkans where it is often below 40 per cent. Within Europe, as we have seen, a complex combination of cultural, economic and political differences has produced distinctive regions. They are: (a) the northwest, (b) the Mediterranean and (c) the continental interior and eastern parts of Europe. The last is best thought of as a core region in Russia and an eastern European region whose orientation has vacillated in the past between east and west.

These same differences have been projected beyond Europe itself, as the expansion of people has taken the "western world" to other continents. Russia expanded eastward into Siberia, eventually to the Pacific. The maritime regions looked west: the northwest expanded to produce Anglo America, South Africa and Australasia, and the Mediterranean expanded to create Latin America.

There may well be a "common" European heritage, but its strength lies in the underlying richness and variety, both geographically and culturally, which make the whole.

# PART TWO

# 2

# Landowners and Farmers

## F. M. L. THOMPSON

Late 20th-century European man is an urban man on wheels, liable to take part in mass seasonal sorties into the countryside, which he expects to find neat, tidy, attractive and ready to provide him with amusement and recreation. The late 20th-century countryman, being no fool, does not disappoint him, and provides plenty of ice cream, cafés, piped music, cream cakes and cola at every rural stopping place to make the visiting townsman feel at home. Here and there an enterprising farmer may have organized guided tours around the farm, turning an honest penny out of the invasion by the picnicking masses. Forty years ago there were hundreds of thousands of city children who had never seen a grass field, or a cow, until they were evacuated from the danger of bombing. Today there can be precious few who cannot tell the back end from the front of a cow, for if they have not seen one in the flesh they will surely have seen one on the television, most likely taking part in some improbable advertisement for margarine. If town has been getting to know country, so too has the farming world been entering into the urban and industrial experience: machines, tractors, cars and television have brought farmers and farm workers into the same technological and cultural environment as that of the business man or factory worker. The divorce between town and country which started with the Industrial Revolution seems to have ended in joyous reunion, with the barriers of ignorance and misunderstanding tumbling down. And yet it is only a few years since millions of viewers failed to recognize as a hoax a film of spaghetti cultivation showing a whole bogus cycle from the planting of spaghetti seedlings in paddy fields to the gathering of the crop by lovely Italian girls who proceeded singing and laughing to a traditional spaghetti harvest carnival. Some factory workers, at least, did know that St Albans is the pasta centre of Britain. Many more millions, however, are indignant, bewildered or outraged by the butter mountains, beef mountains, wine lakes and powdered milk piles which are the most notorious props of the European farmer's existence, and which mock continuously at the housewife's purse. As town spills over the country, and the look and smell of the countryside become familiar to more and more people, the incomprehension of what goes on down at the farm in fact remains as great as ever.

The mounting surpluses of uneaten food and unappreciated drink are testimonies to the imperfections of the international economic system, the inequalities of the social distribution of incomes and the inability of governments to satisfy the conflicting interests of consumers and producers. They are also evidence that agricultural technology has outstripped and outgrown the social organization of farming, that great increases in output have taken place within a largely traditional, and increasingly unsuitable, structure of farm holdings and farming families: they are, indeed, the price which the rest of the European community pays for its peasant ancestry. The spectacle of the advanced countries — and Europe is not alone in this — accumulating enormous stocks of unwanted food while in the third world millions go hungry is profoundly shocking to liberal consciences, and to common sense; the probable alternative prospect, that the absence of the mountains would be accompanied by large pockets of impoverished and wretched peasants and marginal farmers within affluent industrial Europe itself, is certainly frightening enough to goad politicians and governments into protective action, and real enough to shock liberal consciences into agreeing that farming deserves specially favoured treatment.

The dilemma is paralleled by the paradox that the smaller the European agricultural sectors have become, in relative terms, the larger the apparent surplus they produce. The gluts have appeared in the second half of the 20th century when the proportion of total population which is engaged in farming has been moving rapidly down in western Europe towards the 10 to 15 per cent level, chasing (without expectation of catching up) Britain, where only 3 per cent of the population is directly involved in agriculture. A couple of centuries ago there was nowhere in Europe where less than a third of the people was occupied in cultivating the land, and in most countries it was well over one half; and yet there was no certainty that this massive work force would succeed in producing enough food. Shortage, dearth and famine were not everyday events, but they happened sufficiently often to show that pre-industrial Europe lived precariously near the limits of its capacity to feed itself. It is symptomatic that the nature of food protests has shifted from the bread riots of the 18th century, in which consumers hustled, intimidated or attacked corn merchants, millers and bakers, or helped themselves from farmers' stocks, to the farmers' demonstrations of the 20th century, in which producers block the roads by dumping unsaleable tomatoes, peaches or artichokes, trusting that the disruption will make the tariff makers, price fixers and quota regulators aware of their plight. Appealing to authority to impose a just price is a very old game, at which different groups can play: poor consumers expected it to lower prices, poor producers to raise them, and the comfortably off stood to gain whoever won.

If Europe, in very general terms, has moved in the last 200 years from scarcity to abundance, it should no more be supposed that no one was affluent in the earlier period than that everyone is prosperous today. In pre-industrial Europe the landowners were the wealthiest and most powerful group, well fed, finely clothed, comfortably housed, enjoying material luxuries and cultural refinements beyond the reach of any others except for a few merchants, financiers and ecclesiastical dignitaries, and living at a gentlemanly distance from the dirt and toil which produced their rents. In contemporary Europe many of the most primitive and poorest lives are led on undersized peasant holdings, where the hours of work are longer, the incomes lower, the material possessions scantier, the leisure less and the amenities and public services fewer than those of the lowest-paid town dweller. The farmers' ranks, however, contain many contrasts. Some farmers are extremely wealthy, keeping private airplanes, racing stables and Mediterranean villas, living in an aristocratic style only dimly remembered by many surviving aristocrats. On their way up they have passed many landowners on their way down, for whom industrialization, wars, taxation and political upheavals have meant loss of power, loss of position, loss of estates and in the end loss of any separate social identity. Agricultural Europe has always contained many grades and distinctions of wealth and status, and it is not surprising that it still does so. The surprise is that the cross-currents of change have carried the successful farmers to a life-style which is growing more and more like that of the surviving landowners, differentiating both groups from the dirty-boot farmers and small peasants. Where once an analysis resting on status and contract, on the differences between peasant and lord, or between labourer, tenant farmer and landlord was sufficiently illuminating, today it is necessary to grasp the distinctions between Mercedes and Volkswagen, or Range Rover and Ford to appreciate the gradations of rural society and their links with industrial symbols and urban values.

There is, however, an urban intellectual myth about the peaceful idyll of rural life, first fostered by the early critics of factories and industrial capitalism, and vigorously alive today in the enthusiastic hands of the ecological Jeremiahs. It sees in rural life a repository of traditional values of simplicity, honesty, pride and satisfaction in work, and wholesome integrity, persisting in defiance of the brittle, synthetic and superficial glitter of life under the city lights. There is, of course, an alternative rural myth couched in terms of the earthiness, dull-wittedness and crude sensuality of bucolic existence which is a good deal less flattering to countryfolk. Nevertheless belief in one form or other of the traditional country stereotypes is powerfully reinforced by the highly traditional appearance of the countryside itself. The most stable feature of the agricultural world has been the landscape, the place on which all the action takes place. It was remarked in 1850 that a 13th-century French peasant would have felt comfortably at home in the contemporary French countryside, so little had the basic tasks and rhythms of cultivation changed in the interval. It would be perverse to make the same remark today, for where in 1850 the medieval visitor would have seen familiar ox teams, wooden ploughs and flails still being widely used, he could now hardly fail to come across strange objects like tractors, combines or tall gleaming silos to startle him with their unfamiliarity. But although there are indeed unmistakably visible signs of agricultural change planted on any expanse of European country one might chance to view, it is still the case that the fundamental groundwork of the cultivated landscape, in the fields and the patterns which farm holdings draw among them, remains very much as it has been for centuries. This is most obviously so in the scene which is common in parts of France and Western Germany, of a wide expanse of farmland undivided by fences or hedges but cultivated in the long narrow strips that have endured from the time of early medieval settlement. Here, it has been said, it is possible to feel that one is looking at history in the landscape and taking in 15 centuries at a glance. There is a village, maybe, dominated by its feudal castle and its medieval church; and the brightly variegated pattern of the strips, with the different crops before harvest painting ribbons in different hues of yellow and green, carries with it the bonus of evoking the agricultural revolution of the early 19th century that swept away the three-field system of two crops and a fallow within which the strips had originally evolved, and which had imposed common cropping, and hence a uniform visual appearance, on the small, individually cultivated strips.

Elsewhere the visual impact may be less striking, and the historical roots of the landscape are certainly much younger. They are none the less vigorously alive on that account in, for example, the neat and trim Danish countryside of regular-shaped enclosed fields symmetrically grouped around individual farmsteads, which communicate the royal land reforms and consolidation of strips and holdings of the late 18th century clearly and directly to the 20th-century eye. In England, also, the imprint of 18th- and early 19th-century enclosures is clearly visible in the rectangular fields, the hedges and the uncharacteristically straight country roads of the Midland counties and much of East Anglia. The stone-wall country of the Yorkshire dales and hills, Cumbria and Northumbria is a country which was laid out in the great divisions of the commons and hill grazings 150 to 200 years ago; and the much more ancient landscape of the southwest, with its twisting sunken lanes and its thick-hedged fields of very varied shapes and sizes, has altered very little in recent times. It can be argued too that in crossing the modern frontier into east Europe one is, roughly speaking, crossing the very ancient frontier that divided the peasant-farmed west from the large estate-farmed east, along the line of the Elbe, and that the collective farms with their great expanses under single crops – a broad brush landscape in comparison with the west – are but echoing and continuing the physical features of the great grain-growing enterprises of Junker Prussia, Poland and the Danubian plain, however much they may have revolutionized the ownership arrangements.

To assert that the farming landscape has literally stood still over the centuries would be to establish yet another rural myth. In the last 30 years new farming methods, which have made it profitable and technically possible to move towards monoculture through massive use of chemicals and sophisticated mechanization of all stages in cereal growing, have indeed made their mark on the countryside. In parts of East Anglia or Lincolnshire, for example, hedges and windbreaks have been grubbed up in a large way as many farmers have concluded that chemical fertilizers enable them to dispense with keeping livestock, and hence with keeping enclosed and fenced fields, and liberate them to create vast open expanses across which teams of tractors and combines can advance in majestic echelons prairie-style, with never a tree, fence or ditch to impede their progress straight to the horizon. This indeed has produced a different landscape from the fenced and hedged fields of the sheep-and-barley farming of the 18th-century agricultural revolution in Norfolk; history is not indelibly scored on the land itself here, and much the same might be said about the bread basket of France in the Champagne country to the east of Paris. On a smaller scale, farming techniques which were new in the middle of the 19th century here and there rubbed out some of the older landmarks, perhaps as holdings were consolidated and fields were thrown together, perhaps as hedges were removed to make room for ponderous steam-ploughing tackle, or perhaps, moving in the opposite direction, as holdings in some continental countries became minutely subdivided and two fields were carved out of one.

These earlier changes, however, amounted to no more than tinkering with the landscape in very small patches; and the most recent changes have been too localized even within their regions to effect any sweeping transformation of the prospect. The farming landscape as a whole, therefore, although by no means entirely static or ossified, moves with glacier-like slowness and in its essentials displays a living record of the agricultural past, evoking farming systems and methods that stretch back, according to the particular viewpoint, to 18th-century crop rotations or to medieval strips, three-field systems and ridge-and-furrow ploughing. In this sense there is nothing illusory about the impression of history in the landscape. The chequerboard pattern of fields in one region, the random mosaic pattern in another, the striped fabric of crops here, and the plain-coloured blocks there, mean exactly what they seem to say: that the layout of the countryside was determined a long time ago. The illusion arises if one is tempted to jump from conclusions about the traditional and enduring character of the layout to conclusions about the traditional and unchanging character of the farming operations and the farming lives which go on within the layout. Permanence of the framework might indeed plausibly suggest conservatism in methods and life-styles; in fact it indicates that farming has been notably successful at pouring new wine into old bottles, and at accommodating new methods, new tools, new businesses and changing social and economic relationships within an unchanged outward husk of landscape features.

This entire view, however, is open to the objection that the landscape has apparently become frozen at quite different points in the histories of different countries. If the physical setting is so adaptable and capable of containing different systems at different times, why has the oldest setting of all, derived from early medieval settlements, failed to survive everywhere in Europe and to show impartially its capacity to cope with all the shifts from fallows and common grazing rights, through roots, clover and improved strains of wheat, to sugar beet, tractors and chemicals? It is at this point that questions of political power, social structure and economic opportunity enter into the picture and explain the different routes taken by different parts of Europe when, in the closing stages of the pre-industrial economy, agriculture was faced with the challenge and opportunity of rapidly increasing populations and demands for food. Broadly speaking, until some point in the 17th or 18th century agricultural Europe was very much of a piece. That is not to say that there were not pronounced differences between regions, between the close country of wood-pasture areas, the open country of the open-field districts, or the forest, hill and mountain areas; nor that amid a general sea of subsistence farming there were not large islands producing grain, cheese, wool or wine for distant markets. It is merely to say that these differences showed up regardless of national boundaries, determined largely by soil and climatic conditions and, within the variations of these conditions, demonstrating farming customs and rural social structures which were common to much of Europe. Then, in the 17th and 18th centuries, the great divergences in landscape forms set in. Britain and the Low Countries went one way, towards the landscape of enclosure and compact farms; Germany east of the Elbe, Poland, much of the Habsburg lands and southern Italy went another way, towards the landscape of latifundia and large farms directly run by the landowners; while the heart of western Europe, France, western Germany and northern Italy, on the whole conserved its medieval landscape along with the peasants who farmed it. The choice of directions was settled by the possession of power, the relative strength or degree of fusion of central governments and the landowning classes, the sizes of non-agricultural populations and the proximity and accessibility of markets.

The Low Countries were the first to experience the pressures of a fast-growing urban and commercial population, and of a specialized and concentrated cloth industry, outstripping the capacity of local resources and traditional farming methods to feed it. They responded by developing a reliance on imported Baltic wheat for their bread supply, and by breaking through

*1.* A rhapsode, or professional bard. Painting on a Greek amphora, c. 480 BC.

3. A scene from a Greek comedy: Achilles assists his aged tutor Chiron. Vase painting, c. 410 BC.

2. The Parthenon, Athens, erected 447–432 BC, viewed from the Propylaea.

4. A competitor in a chariot race. Decoration on an amphora given as a prize at a Panathenaic festival, late 5th century BC.

5. A form of ball game. From an amphora, c. 540 BC.

7. A noblewoman playing the cithara. Fresco from a villa at Boscoreale, near Pompeii, 1st century BC.

6. The apotheosis of Homer (enthroned, lower left-hand corner). Marble relief, c. 200 BC.

8. The Battle of Issus (333 BC), at which Alexander the Great defeated the Persians under Darius III. Part of a mosaic from Pompeii, 1st century BC.

*9.* Plato (third from the left) teaching in Athens. Mosaic from near Pompeii, c. 70 AD.

*10.* The Roman emperor Augustus. Statue, c. 20 BC.

*11.* A Pompeian representation of the Judgement of Solomon, modelled on a Roman magistrate's court. Fresco, c. 70 AD.

*12.* A ceremony of the cult of Isis. Detail of a fresco from Herculaneum, c. 70 AD.

13. A Roman schoolroom in Gaul. Sandstone relief, c. 200 AD.

14. Part of a pictorial record of the Roman emperor Trajan's military campaigns in Dacia.
Trajan's column, Rome, 113 AD.

*15.* An anatomy class of the 4th century AD. Fresco from the Via Latina catacomb in Rome.

the low output ceilings of medieval farming on their own land, held low by limited manure supplies and by weed infestation which primitive ploughing could not control, by developing crop rotations which increased the nitrogen available for plant growth, by careful husbanding of every scrap and drop of animal and human manure, and by laborious garden-like cultivation of the soil. Here, in a highly labour-intensive form, the elements of the classic agricultural revolution were created: the field cultivation of roots and nitrogen-fixing clovers and lucernes, the elimination of fallows and the control of weeds through intensive cultivations, harrowings and hoeings, and the increase in manuring by moving livestock around the fields, all performed on the small holdings which plentiful labour made viable. But it was England which provided the fertile soil for the application of these new techniques on an extensive scale, and it was in England that they were acclimatized and developed in a whole new structure of agrarian organization, which spawned its distinctive landscape, until eventually they were re-exported to Europe as the most advanced and most productive practices of the day in the early 19th century. This happened because in England the structure of power and of landownership, the growth of total population and the expansion of commerce and industry combined to produce a favourable environment for the commercialization of farming.

The key to the English agricultural revolution was production for the market. This in turn depended on the existence of a body of landless and non-agricultural consumers who had to purchase their food and their raw materials such as wool or leather from specialized producers; and it depended on the producers needing or wanting the cash incomes flowing from the sale of agricultural produce. All the other changes – technical, biological, cadastral and eventually mechanical and scientific – flowed from this. Until the 16th century most farming was subsistence farming, carried on by peasants on small holdings made up of many individual strips scattered around the large open fields of the village or manor, whose main aim was to grow enough to meet the needs of the family, with the hope that there might be a residual surplus left over for sale to satisfy the small cash demands of the peasant household. There are many qualifications to such a simplified generalization, from the great sheep runs or cattle ranches of early medieval ecclesiastical and lay lords onwards; but the general trend towards commercial farming, in which the prime object was to raise cash crops, and the supply of the farmer's family with food in kind became a secondary or even a non-existent purpose, set in strongly with the great inflation of the 16th century. This had a twofold effect. The larger peasants saw the openings for profiting from rising prices, laid strip to strip, consolidated holdings into more compact units that could be managed and cultivated more economically as farming businesses, studied the markets and enriched themselves. Landowners, where they could, raised the level of money rents in order to protect the real value of their own incomes. In doing so they converted their peasantry, who had been customary tenants paying nominal rents and accustomed in practice if not in law to hereditary occupation of their holdings, into tenant farmers paying something like full commercial rents for their farms, which meant that tenants had to grow an increasing proportion of their crops for the market in order to raise the cash to pay the rent. The process was in a sense self-fulfilling, since one important consequence of the tenurial and structural response was that the extra people who made up the 16th-century population growth, instead of fending for themselves through simple multiplication of traditional peasant-subsistence holdings, were excluded from occupation of the land and by becoming landless labourers or by moving into the towns or into industry became the means of increasing the absolute and relative size of the market for food.

The commercialization of farming, therefore, grew out of inflation and population growth, and was the only way in which a significant increase in the proportion of the people who were not fully occupied in raising their own food could be supported, short of developing dependence on imported food supplies – something the Dutch accomplished, but which the available techniques and resources of shipping and international trade would not have permitted for a population as large as the English. It should not be imagined that the change took place with such rapidity that it was completed within a generation. In an activity which has a social dimension larger than its economic one, in which there were not merely hundreds of thousands of separate production units, but in which the production units or holdings were also the family homes and the essence of status, social identity and membership of communities, change is inevitably slow and long drawn out. A subsistence sector, with small family farms, survived in English agriculture certainly until well into the 19th century; and elsewhere in the British Isles, in the crofts of the Scottish highlands or the peasant patches of western Ireland, for much longer than that. Nevertheless the commercial sector grew strongly from the 16th century and became the pace setter for farming techniques, and it was characterized by a greatly sharpened differentiation in the rural social structure. Some of the larger and more fortunate peasants moved upwards, became secure owner-farmers, perhaps began to employ hired labour, and maybe even entered the squirearchy; other peasants moved sideways and became tenant farmers; some kept a toehold on the land, and became part-time farmers of holdings too small to sustain a family, and part-time industrial workers, above all in one of the branches of the domestically organized, cottage-based, textile industry; many more sank into the ranks of landless farm labourers. Lords of the soil there had always been, barons, knights and esquires, owed allegiance, service or quit rents by the serfs or peasants on their lands, and managing directly the exploitation of the lord's demesne which was one part of their lands. They moved towards becoming modern landowners, owning not a bundle of rights over the inhabitants of a territory, but the land itself; this estate might be smaller than the feudal territory, as some customary occupiers escaped from the lord's control altogether and carried their land with them, but it was an estate over which the landowner had full property rights and whose tenanting and management lay in his control. Here, in essentials, was the landlord-tenant-labourer structure, the fundamental organizational basis of commercial farming in England, corresponding roughly to the functional divisions between capital, management and labour. Although not unknown outside England, this structure became as typically English as the peasant, or peasant-labourer, structure was typical of most of western Europe, and the landlord-serf, or landlord-labourer, structure was of eastern Europe.

Market forces encouraged the emergence of this three-tier structure in English agriculture, and sizeable and expanding commercial, industrial and urban sectors in the economy provided the cash flows to sustain the rural economy of rents, farmers' profits and labourers' wages. But it was permitted to develop, at the expense of the dissolution of the traditional peasant society, because royal governments were not strong enough to prevent it. Disruption of the accustomed fabric of rural society on this scale caused plenty of friction, discontent and unrest, erupting in periodic risings, and Tudor and early Stuart governments had ample incentives to try and preserve social stability in the interests of internal security. There was no lack of policies to prevent enclosures, to limit the exaction of excessive rents or entry fines, to conserve "houses of husbandry" each with its minimum supporting acreage or to prevent people leaving the land; but the crown lacked the power to enforce them. The landowning groups, magnates and gentry, were extremely powerful and influential, and although their power fell short of controlling government, for the crown towered above them in independent authority, it was more than sufficient to frustrate governmental acts of which they disapproved, for the crown was entirely dependent on their cooperation and goodwill as the unpaid royal servants who administered the counties. Hence, while it would be misleading to suggest that the landowners had everything their own way, or indeed that they were agreed among themselves what their own way should be, it was certainly true that the traditional peasantry and their ancient customary rights had no powerful champions.

By the time the dust had settled after the great Civil War and the Revolution of 1688 the landed classes were firmly in the saddle in Britain, their power tempered by the surviving authority of the crown and by the need so to conduct government that influential or important groups were not seriously offended. In spheres where law or political decisions affected farming, it was axiomatic that considerations of the rights of property owners would prevail. By this time, in the early 18th century, it was clear that the smallholding peasantry was well on the way to disappearance in Britain, and that it had survived largely intact in western Europe, in practice mainly personally free though in law still bound by many irritating and servile obligations; to the east lay the true serfs. It had survived, in spite of the fact that most European countries had landed aristocracies as grand and as wealthy as the English, partly because the pull of the non-agricultural consumer market was weaker, partly because governments were stronger and more determined to maintain their peasantries – because they were the main taxpayers, or the chief source of sturdy soldiers, or a useful counterbalance to prevent nobles becoming overmighty. In most of Europe outside the Low Countries and northern Italy urban centres were small and far apart. Given the difficulties and enormous cost of land transport, their food supplies were drawn from a localized hinterland, which did indeed respond to the market attractions as in England; in the great intervening stretches of countryside that were too remote to reach the consumer markets, the population when it grew – and in much of Germany it probably stagnated in the 17th century after the Thirty Years' War – had little choice but to support itself by replicating and extending the peasant subsistence culture. Where, as in east Prussia and Poland, and later on in Hungary, the prospect of distant markets for grain exports opened up, it required the large-scale operations of estate farming using compulsory labour to produce the grain surplus in sufficiently large consignments at low enough cost to stand the delays and expenses of overland haulage to river transport, for movement to Danzig or Memel and eventual shipment to Amsterdam, Antwerp, London or Hull. Over this economic situation brooded a political struggle in which monarchs sought to free themselves from the trammels of dependence on their nobility and involvement in their faction squabbles without provoking the social revolution of a complete overthrow of the landed order which the Reformation crisis in Germany had shown to be a distinct possibility. The French monarchy won the political fight with its nobility, through its centralized government, extensive bureaucracy and large army, and by using the weapon of protecting peasants against enclosing and engrossing lords: it settled on preserving an aristocracy shorn of effective power as an ornamental and privileged bulwark of the social order. The way was open for the Revolution to shred the charters and manorial rolls which gave rights and claims over many peasants to the lords, to reduce the aristocracy to a landed interest with only moderately large estates, to dispossess some altogether and to reveal France as in the main a country of peasant proprietors.

The power struggle between crown and nobility had different results elsewhere. In Prussia and the Habsburg Empire the monarchs, enlisting their nobles in the service of the state and its armies, did not convincingly reduce them to subordination; and the attempt by the Habsburg Joseph II to mobilize the lower orders to help in reducing the economic power of the aristocracy, through emancipation of the serfs by royal decree, backfired disastrously. In the event the Junkers survived in Prussia, and the Habsburg nobility in Bohemia, Austria and Hungary, with the means to steer through emancipation on terms which left them with by far the largest privately owned landed estates in 19th-century Europe, with castles, forests and hunting lodges of princely proportions. In Poland in the last days of its independent political existence in the 18th century the landed aristocracy and gentry were to all intents and purposes the nation and its government, with an elective king as their creature; the disappearance of the kingdom in the Partitions made no difference to the persistence of the landed estates. In this fashion the lines were already drawn between west and east, ready for that confirmation by the export of the principles of the French Revolution by the armies of Napoleon to the Low Countries, western Germany and Italy, which set the seal on their peasant complexion.

Peasant life was, and still is in many poor and backward parts of the Massif Central or the Dauphiné, or in entire regions like the Mezzogiorno, a primitive existence of unremitting toil and drudgery for scant rewards. The days may have passed when the family shared the single-roomed, earth-floored, home with the livestock, its dung conveniently at hand to furnish fuel; when baking could only be afforded twice a year, so that half a year's bread supply was strung up in the roof, preserved and hardened by the fire smoke; or when old peasant women at work looked to Arthur Young like beasts of the field. Wretched, dirty, hungry conditions were in any case never universal, and contented, well-fed, peasant families enjoying their home-cured ham or their home-made cheese washed down with their own wine or beer could no doubt always be found. But it was in the 1960s that the 20-year-old daughter of a peasant family in the Isère expressed in modern dress the traditional austerity and isolation of peasant life:

We are absolutely cut off from news. We have neither radio nor newspapers. We have few visitors we are so isolated . . . My mother has not even been to the capital of the département 60 kilometres away . . . The only girl in my class [from school] who is left lives at the other end of the village and works in the local factory . . . Her parents don't want her to be a farmer like themselves. They say she should not tire herself out farming for little gain at such a dirty job. Every summer she buys a new dress. She goes to the cinema, goes dancing, reads magazines, has her Sundays free . . . But I never go out . . . I have only been to the cinema three times. I never read a newspaper . . .

Subsistence farming was, and is, one long slog for the peasant, his wife and such of his children as are old enough to work, an unending round of ploughing, sowing, weeding, harvesting, feeding animals, milking, making cheese, wine, coleseed oil, all in small quantities and for meagre returns. Unless the harvest is poor, there is probably always enough to eat; but there is no leisure, and no luxuries, since the sale of the small surplus only covers the purchase of necessities like salt, soap and perhaps clothing, which cannot be produced on the holding or in the household. A serious drawback is that the peasant holding – which may only be a couple of hectares, though it could be as much as five or ten – is unlikely to be able to provide for many children once they are grown up. The traditional, and less traditional, answers to this problem were high mortality, which kept a community roughly in balance with its resources; creation of new holdings, subdivision of old ones and all the pressures of land hunger; or family limitation. The modern answer is to quit the land. As soon as the opportunity to move has appeared – with railways and transatlantic steamships in the 19th century, but more dramatically with motors and rapid industrialization in the second half of the 20th century – peasants and peasants' children in their millions have voted with their feet on the attractions of the subsistence version of country life.

All the same it was not merely the lack of opportunities for quitting which explains the delay in the onset of the great rural exodus, and it certainly cannot explain the continued presence of the peasantry today. Peasant life has its attractions as well as its hardships. It may well be that the distinctive vernacular styles of peasant communities, in costume, ceremonial finery, domestic architecture, humble furniture and household equipment, which have been so much admired and conserved since the city intelligentsia discovered their merits at the end of the 19th century, are not the evidence of the honest untutored craftsmanship and natural taste of simple peasants occupying their winter evenings which they seem to be, but rather the products of the skilled craftsmen to be found in every village. But if every peasant did not sit happily whittling away at his wood carving, every peasant could run the soil of his land through his fingers and look with passionate attachment on the land which was his holding, his security. The marriage of peasant and land, if in the long run not permanently indissoluble, is harder than granite to break. Where peasants clung to security and status, governments clung to peasants as guarantors of social stability, whose conservatism provided a shield from the awkward problems which any kind of social movement and economic development was bound to create. The mutual self-preservation of peasants and regimes has been one of the grand underlying themes of modern European history; long after the economic developments have in fact occurred that, despite the conservative alliance, have made the peasant way economically anachronistic, echoes of this theme persist in the efforts to shore up the way of life still widely regarded as the exemplar of the stable family and the foundation of social order, with props of high-cost beef and buttresses of butter.

The saving grace of peasant farming was that in spite of its great attachment to custom and tradition it could adapt to new ideas, new crops, new techniques, often painfully slowly and under the menace of increasing misery posed by land shortage, but sufficiently fast to support an urbanizing and industrializing population. Without this measure of flexibility and adaptability European countries would have been condemned to remain predominantly agrarian, unable to support more than tiny islets of urban culture with the small surpluses of food produced by the permanently low yields of traditional farming, and with populations held in check at less than a quarter, or even a tenth, of present-day levels by dearth, famine and disease. It is a fate which some critics of modern industrial society would regard as a blessing should they choose to ignore the poverty of diets and material conditions, the shortness of life and the cultural simplicity which accompanied it. The spur to industrialization came from a multiplicity of sources, which it is not important to analyse here. The lead in raising the productivity of farming came partly from the small sectors of larger farms and more commercial, capitalist farming which fortunate and enterprising landowners did create here and there in defiance of the general deadweight of custom, and partly from the market-conscious peasantry of the agricultural hinterlands of the existing towns. They were followed, with stubborn slowness, by the general mass of the subsistence-farming peasants, so that by the first half of the 19th century the process of infusing the husks and outlines of the ancient landscape with new crops and new methods was well under way. Clovers, sainfoins, new strains of wheat, maize, potatoes and sugar beet, strips and holdings in the sole control of the farmer through the abolition of common grazing rights over the stubble, the extinction of fallows, these were the means by which yields were raised and the surplus available for off-farm consumption was increased. The peasant-farming version of the agricultural revolution was reasonably effective in raising the productivity of the land, but it was highly labour-intensive and did not achieve much improvement in the productivity of men.

This was one of the decisive factors in holding back the rate of industrial expansion and economic growth. Peasant society held on to its people and did not release manpower easily or rapidly to industry. The small holdings with their continuing emphasis on self-sufficiency did not generate large money incomes for their owners, and with the continuing large size of the peasant sector this restrained the growth of the internal market for manufactured consumer goods, and hence the growth of industry. Peasant proprietors, anxious to avoid the impoverishment of excessive fragmentation of family holdings and to limit the effects of laws of partible inheritance, limited the size of their families and thus checked the rate of population growth. It is not without reason that ordinary English usage commemorates the pre-eminence of the French in the techniques of contraception. Nineteenth-century France, remaining largely self-sufficient in her food and drink supply aside from tropical products, and even becoming more so as home-grown sugar beet replaced imported sugar, certainly developed an important industrial sector. But she also retained a very large agricultural sector, still in 1900 five times larger than the British in terms of manpower although the total populations of the two countries were very similar, and her farming used nearly three times as many men per hectare as the British. Among the major continental countries, Austria-Hungary by 1900 had an industrial base comparable to the French, centred in Bohemia, and thanks to the great grain lands of Hungary remained a food exporter; Italy, with only a small industrial centre in the north, maintained considerable agricultural exports of wine, rice, olives, apples, oranges and tomatoes from the fertile lands of the Po Valley, the prosperous small farms of Tuscany and the wretched peasantry of the southern latifundia; while Russia coupled her efforts to make a rapid start on industrialization with retention of her position as one of the world's major grain exporters from a mixed agriculture of downtrodden peasants and large estate farms.

Germany alone of the major continental countries had experienced both rapid and massive industrialization by the end of the 19th century, her empire an *Industriestaat* outdistancing Britain and inviting comparison with the USA. The feeding of her fast-growing urban population was mainly the work of the cultivating squires and lords – *agriculteurs exploitants* – on the large estate farms of the north and east, who both switched their cereals from exports to the home market, and increased their acreages and output; but the peasant farmers of west and south Germany also made a contribution, perhaps responding to the call of the urban food market rather more readily than their French counterparts. Potatoes were more of a peasant than an estate crop, and the Germans grew and ate seven times as many as the British, for a population only 50 per cent larger. The Germans also remained great rye eaters, eating nearly twice as much rye as wheat, and they were still comfortably self-sufficient in rye in 1914; indeed they produced a small export surplus. The solid fare of rye and potatoes, however, was not sufficient to prevent Germany making a swift transition in the decade of the 1870s from a food-exporting to a food-importing country, with Russian grains pouring in from the east. World cereal prices were starting to fall steeply, more under the influence of massive exports from North America than from Russia, and the response of the Junker ruling class was to erect high protective tariffs designed to keep prices up and imports out. The tariffs were primarily intended to protect the wheat and rye economy of the Junker estates and thus preserve the landowning class which was regarded, by itself at least, as the essence of the *Agrarstaat* within the industrial economy, and the guardian of the social and political order. The *Agrarstaat*, however, also contained as junior partners the peasant farmers of the west and south, and protection – with the assistance of tariffs on livestock which had the effect of turning Danish pork for the German dinner into Danish bacon for the English breakfast – had the almost incidental effect of preserving them as well. Protection slowed down the growth of German reliance on food imports, but did not halt or reverse it; by 1914 one-third of her wheat, most of it from North America, half her barley and a quarter of her oats, most of them from Russia, Hungary and Romania, were imported. Neither did protection prevent German prices from falling; it simply kept them somewhat above the world price level and made German consumers pay more than they need have done. The result was that Germany entered the 20th century with an agricultural sector kept artificially large by protection, and one in which its peasant component in particular was kept up in numbers and down in fortunes.

While the German peasantry – and much of the middle European peasantry as well – was carried into the 20th century largely on the coat tails of the landed aristocracy, the reverse was true in France. There a landed class had survived the Revolution with considerable wealth and estates, and positions of local influence well entrenched in habits of deference to the châteaux, even though the majority of the land was in the hands of landowning peasants. This landed class, divided within itself politically, may have lost political power and importance as Orleanists followed Legitimists into the limbo of a self-imposed abstention from public life, to emerge again briefly on the national scene in dominating the National Assembly of 1871 when other notables were temporarily discredited; it may even have surrendered social leadership to the *haute bourgeoisie* and the 200 families which were said to control French finance and industry. But as individuals, landowners most assuredly continued to survive, owning sizeable estates and country seats, supporting hunting and horse racing, contributing to the glamour and glitter of *fin de siècle* high society, and no doubt well content that since political and social analysts no longer identified them as a distinct class attention was not focused on their existence. Their agricultural interests and incomes were well served by the high tariffs to which France also turned to meet the threat of floods of imports and the reality of falling prices after the 1870s; they were probably better served than the interests of the peasants whom these policies were primarily designed to protect. So in the decades before 1914 the French countryside began to lose landless labourers in considerable numbers to the towns; the landholding peasantry stood their ground in numbers and steadily lost ground in their living standards; and the aristocracy, despite some signs of neglect beginning to show in some of the châteaux, remained much in evidence at Longchamps.

In some such manner the traditional face of Europe was brought into the 20th century. Its least traditional features lay in Britain, where the chief contours of the farming landscape had been laid down in the course of the 18th and early 19th centuries as the consequences of the commercialization of farming and the primacy of landowners' rights over the claims of custom worked themselves out, in the extinction of common grazing rights, the rearrangement of strips, the consolidation of scattered holdings into compact farms and above all the enclosure of open fields and commons. Farming for the market stimulated and cajoled the tenant farmers, with encouragement and assistance from a few of the more agriculturally minded landowners, to raise their output through the techniques of sheep-and-corn husbandry to such effect that they were almost able to feed a population which grew threefold in the 100 years after 1750 and whose non-agricultural consumers grew from 55 to nearly 80 per cent of the total. The labour force that produced this great increase in the supplies of food did not increase very much in size itself, so that in effect the country folk released the major part of their own natural increase to industry. These were the major, perhaps the decisive, contributions of agriculture to the Industrial Revolution. They were achieved at some social cost: the displacement of many smallholding families, and the descent of many others into the ranks of agricultural labourers; the depression of labourers' wages and living standards well below the level of industrial workers and not much above bare subsistence; and, possibly, some decline in the diets which the mass of the urban population could afford. The price, from the point of view of British farming, was that a process of industrialization, urbanization and population growth had been set in motion which outran the capacity of British land to sustain it. The answer was growing reliance on imports of food, from 1846 under free-trade conditions which threw the British market open to the farmers of the world. By the 1870s half the wheat and half the wool consumed in Britain were imported, and it was above all in response to the appetites of British consumers and British industry that the vast new territories of North America, Australasia and later South America were opened up to agriculture and pastoral farming. Low-cost agricultural supplies from these new areas, and from the black earth region of Russia, triggered and sustained the great price fall of the late 19th century, and far from trying to put up the shutters against the imports British consumers welcomed the cheap food and became so attached to it that ever since it has been exceedingly hard to convince them that there are any sound reasons why the cheapest available food, wherever it happens to be grown, is not good for them.

By the early 20th century Britain relied on imports for over three-quarters of her wheat, nearly half her barley, half her beef and lamb, three-quarters of her cheese and 90 per cent of her butter, and was somewhere within sight of being self-supporting only in milk, potatoes, oats and hay. Such a staggering degree of import dependence was without precedent or parallel, and implied for British farming not its wholesale sacrifice, as is sometimes thought, but massive adjustments. These adjustments were in the direction of switching the emphasis from cereals to livestock; this has been done, at different periods, by increasing the stock kept in relation to arable acreages, within mixed farming operations; by reducing the cereal acreages and increasing the grassland; or by feeding more stock on feed grains grown at home and imported from overseas. The long-run movement in British farming since the middle of the 19th century has been towards reliance on milk and meat to produce the cash, and for the main purpose of cereal growing to be to feed the animals. For a generation after 1846 the adjustments went at a gentlemanly pace and were profitable rather than painful for farmers and landowners alike. After the 1870s they proceeded at a violent rate and were extremely painful for very many farmers who were forced out of farming altogether, and by no means painless for landowners who found their rentals slipping sharply. The main casualties, however, or perhaps one should say beneficiaries, were those agricultural labourers who left the land in their thousands in the first great rural exodus. By 1914 Britain had a much-slimmed agricultural community, but one still organized in its landlord-tenant-labourer structure and carrying on its farming with its greatly altered techniques and economic objectives within a stable frame of farms and fields.

Since World War I the differences between British and west European farmers have narrowed somewhat, even while the countrysides they cultivate have remained strikingly different. To the east, the great landed magnates have been swept away since World War II, Esterhazys, Schwarzenbergs, Radowitzes and Thuns survive, if at all, in exile far from their castles and hunting forests; and the farmers work for a collective, pouring out their peasant past in the care lavished on the market-garden plots they are allowed to retain in individual possession. Britain has experienced agrarian change of a less sudden variety. Landowners have sold their estates, under the pressure of death duties and in pursuit of the attractions of stock-exchange investments, on such a scale that the landlord-tenant relationship has ceased to be typical. Over half the farmland is now in the hands of owner-farmers, although these behave in the main as wealthy businessmen managing their farms as large-scale agricultural enterprises, keeping a sharp eye on costs and profits, and not in the least like peasant-owners. Even the family farms with no hired labour, of which there are considerable numbers in Britain, though reckoned small by British standards – 30 to 60 hectares maybe – are likely to be anything from three to ten times larger than their continental counterparts, and in social standing and life-style a European observer would consider their farmers to be closer to the *petit bourgeois* world of shopkeepers than to the rusticity of the small to middling peasants. It is in the adoption of protection that Britain has moved decisively closer to Europe; the differences in the aims and methods of providing protection to farming serve to make this underlying common approach a source of misunderstanding and friction rather than agreement. In Britain the motive has been primarily economic, to save imports when the balance of payments has been chronically unhealthy, and to protect employment; and to a much lesser extent it has been socio-political, to protect the interests of a very small minority group that happens to be dominant in a few rural constituencies. In Europe the motives have been primarily social and political, to look after the welfare of one of the major groups in society, and to a lesser extent economic, to reduce the drag of backward agricultural sectors on the growth of the rest of the economy. In Britain, until 1972, agricultural price support meant that the taxpayers supported the farmers by paying them the difference between a negotiated level of prices and the actual market price at which farmers managed to sell their produce on the open market, in more or less free competition with imports. In Europe of the Community protection means that taxpayers support the farmers by paying for their food at prices fixed to remunerate the less efficient, possibly the least efficient, growers, and by buying at those prices, through their governments, all that the farmers choose to produce. In the British system the market was by definition cleared of the total supply produced by British farmers, if necessary at comparatively low prices, and no obtrusive beef mountains could grow, although the size of deficiency payments to farmers might. In the Community system the consumers do not necessarily – or ever – buy at the comparatively high fixed prices all the supply which these prices encourage farmers to produce, and so the unsold surpluses pile up in the warehouses.

Either way the taxpayers pay. Either way farming has prospered since 1945 on a scale that has made the memory of the bad days of the interwar years fade into a bad dream. The prosperity which has made the farmlands look more healthy, cared for and productively used than at any time since the 1860s – though cared for by machines which give the hedges a mechanical crew cut rather than by men who lay them with skilful hands – has also made the countryside much less exclusively the preserve of agriculture. This is so in Britain, where villages near the great urban concentrations are thronged with commuters and those more remote and scenically attractive have been taken over by weekenders. It is perhaps even more so in western Europe, where in most villages which were almost wholly agricultural only a generation ago only a small minority of the inhabitants are today engaged in farming. These country villages support their commuting populations also, who work in factory jobs in the towns. But the most distinctively European result of the permeation of the country by the tractor, often hailed as the saviour of the peasantry, has been the rapid spread of part-time farming among the smaller landholding peasants. The tractor both permits the smallholder to hold a regular factory job and get through his farming work – such as his wife has not done – in his spare time, and obliges him to do so in order to raise enough income to pay for the tractor and its necessary implements. Alongside this phenomenon the impact of the industrialization of both agriculture and food processing is more commonplace: the supply and repair of machinery, the production and distribution of agrochemicals, and of feeding stuffs, and the factory processing and preservation of a whole range of foods from peas to pastries, and cheese to chickens, all these have brought industrial and business activities into the countryside. In this fashion town and country, which drew apart in the steam and coal phase of industrialization when urban factories crushed the traditional rural craft and cottage industries and made the country almost purely agricultural, have been drawn together again in the age of electricity and refrigeration. The industrialization of farming and of the countryside is in full swing, and is shaking the structure of peasant Europe to its foundations. Some peasants will survive the crisis of affluence, and in their survival will become more like British farmers, or perhaps less shockingly, more like the French capitalist farmers of the Paris region. The survivors may reduce the butter mountains; they will certainly give rural Europe a facelift.

# 3

# Sailors and Fishermen

## PETER KEMP

The growth and complexity of modern sea transport have seen a phenomenal, almost bewildering, increase in the past 30 years. A ship of 20,000 tons was still a big ship in 1948; today she is a comparative minnow among the monsters, particularly in the field of oil tankers and container ships which transport so much of the world's seaborne trade. Sophistication in the handling of cargoes, in the shapes of roll-on roll-off ferries, of containerization, of the stern fishing trawler, has revolutionized the traditional tasks of the sailor, making him perhaps more of a technician and less of a seaman in the older meaning of that word. In the same way, modern navigational systems, hyperbolic, inertial and satellite, the wide use of radar, the automatic helmsman and the worldwide prediction of weather changes have all eased the burden and anxiety of the navigator so that the world's cargoes can today flow faster and more surely along the great trade routes.

The same swift growth and complexity in the organization of Europe's ports, the traditional homes of the sailors, have matched those of the ships that use them. New deep-water docks to accommodate the huge ships of today, modern handling methods for bulk cargoes, vast marshalling yards to cope with the growth of containerization, new building and repairing yards to speed the building and refitting of ships, have transformed the major ports into new complexes geared to the vast growth in world trade and have called for an unparalleled degree of control to harness all the differing processes of efficient cargo handling into a compact, smooth-running organization.

It is largely the same story in the fishing industry, where modern organization and development have transformed what was until quite recently a very individual, almost a personal, vocation into a national industry. This revolution has been largely based on the substitution of the big stern trawler, built on the lines of the whale factory ship, for the smaller beam trawlers which had for so long borne the brunt of deep-sea fishing, their greater capacity and efficiency being geared to fish factory ships which process the catches on the spot and free the trawlers for yet more intensive effort. And to this must be added a new impetus in oceanographical research which studies the growth and habits of fish and predicts their movements, directing the modern, highly organized fishing fleets to the most prolific fishing grounds.

Against this picture of rapid change, modernization and growth, and the men who work it, it is difficult, perhaps, to accommodate that of the seamen and fishermen of Europe who lived and did their work in the less sophisticated centuries which preceded this modern explosion of technology. Yet basically they were the same sort of men doing the same sort of work in carrying their cargoes across the world's oceans; the same sort of men searching the seas for the richest fishing grounds; the same sort of men manning the ships of national navies. The modern seaman is more technically skilled today because he lives in a more technical age, but he sails the same trade routes which his ancestors pioneered centuries ago, uses the same ports that his ancestors used and needs the same skills of seamanship and navigation which brought his ancestors in safety across the oceans to their journey's end. The difference is one of degree only; the great common element which links them is always the sea itself, for it still demands today the same sense of dedication – a love of the sea – that it has done throughout the centuries.

It is towards the eastern Mediterranean that we must look for the cradle of European seamanship. There is enough evidence in the form of rock carvings and temple decorations to show that, as early as the third millennium BC, the Egyptians had built up an extensive seaborne trade in the Mediterranean, and had also built warships both to protect their trade and to do a little marauding on the side. They were perhaps unadventurous sailors in our modern idiom, for only inadvertently in those early years did a ship venture beyond sight of land or sail during the hours of darkness; their trade routes hugged the coasts and they anchored when the daylight failed at sunset.

Only one Mediterranean people of the pre-Christian era broke clear of the pattern of coastal voyages. The Phoenicians were notable workers in metal, and to make the bronze for which they were famous they needed both copper and tin. Copper was to be found almost on their doorstep in Cyprus, but for their tin they had to go further afield, to Spain and, eventually, to southern Britain and the Canary Islands. For these longer voyages they had not only to build bigger ships, "the great ships of Tarshish", but also to breed seamen who were not afraid of sailing into unknown waters, far beyond the edge of the then known world. Alone among the seamen of that age they used the windrose, forerunner by 2,000 years of the magnetic compass, to find their way across the oceans; they knew, too, that the sun at noon gave them the true south and that the pole star at night gave them a close enough approximation to the true north. They were the first real European navigators, in the sense that their navigation was mainly in European waters, and even the Greeks, their traditional enemies, had to admit that they were magnificent seamen. Ezekiel, prophesying the eventual destruction of Tyre, paints a picture of their greatness. "The inhabitants of Zidon and Arvad were thy mariners; thy wise men, O Tyrus, that were in thee were thy pilots . . . The ships of Tarshish did sing of thee in thy market; and thus thou wast replenished and made very glorious in the midst of the seas."

Greeks, Carthaginians, Romans fought in turn for the Phoenician trading empire when Alexander the Great razed Tyre to the ground and sold its 30,000 inhabitants into slavery in 333 BC, a long, grumbling sea war that spread and multiplied prodigiously the number of men who made the sea their career. Few names have come down to us from these dim centuries of Mediterranean navigation and sea battle. Jason and his crew of heroes in the *Argo* are perhaps the earliest. Odysseus, perhaps at first an unwilling or unlucky sailor, became the archetype of the Hellenic sailor race, representing the ideal of heroism and adventure as Greek sea power stretched from east to west across the Mediterranean. And we know that Aeschylus served as a marine in a Greek trireme at the battle of Salamis in 480 BC. Of the Romans, Gaius Duillius was the first of that race to gain a victory over the Carthaginians at the battle of Mylae and had a column erected in Rome in his honour and the attendance of a torch bearer and a flute player when he walked the streets of Rome in the evenings. But we get a better picture of a typical Roman sea captain from Lucian, writing in Athens in the 2nd century AD, when he visited a Roman grain ship lying in the harbour of Piraeus. "And the whole fortune of the ship is in the hands of a little old man who moves the great rudder with a tiller no thicker than a stick. They pointed him out to me, a little, white-haired, almost bald fellow. I think they called him Heron."

One other small facet of early seafaring life in the Mediterranean has come to light in a recent archaeological discovery of a warship sunk off Marsala during the First Punic War between Rome and Carthage in the 3rd century BC. In her hold she carried baskets of *Cannabis sativa*, and being a warship and not a merchantman, one wonders why. Could this be the equivalent of the sailor's rum ration of 17 centuries later, an evening solace for the hours of labour at the oars?

Yet the Romans, though the ultimate victors in the long struggle for Mediterranean sea power, were never real seamen. They fought their battles at sea in the same way as they fought their battles on land, and the extensive trade generated by the needs of their spreading empire still crept laboriously around the Mediterranean shores, unable to discover the means of making a voyage out of sight of land. They drew magnificent maps of their great land empire, these Romans, based on accurate surveys and measurements, but they never drew a map of the seas that surrounded it and brought it its nourishment slowly and unadventurously to port. The navigational knowledge of the Phoenicians had died with the death of Tyre and Sidon.

It was born again at the other end of Europe, along the shores of the Baltic Sea and of Scandinavia. For a thousand years following the Roman conquest of Gaul and Britain those waters were torn by piracy and battle, little port against little port, princeling against princeling, king against king. Kings became kings only by conquest, and in those days of sword and battle-axe, the battle was always to the strong. It was from this scene of continuous battle and attack that the longship was developed, the better to carry the princeling or the king, with his fighting men, to their next venture of aggrandizement. Today, somewhat loosely and evocatively, we are apt to give all these seafaring people the generic name of Vikings, but they were people of many different nations, Norwegians, Swedes, Danes, Angles, Jutes. The coastal settlements of Britain, France and Spain all felt the force of their marauding ventures, and Sicily and the Mediterranean were not beyond their reach.

It was all based on the longship, a magnificently simple design that could ride the strong waters of the North Sea and eastern Atlantic in comparative safety. Almost certainly it was the ship that developed the sailor. They already knew, of course, the single square sail which eased the rowers' burden when the wind blew from astern; under the human stresses of longer sea voyages they invented the *beitass* to extend the tack of the square sail and make the wind serve them even when it blew from before the beam. It was the *beitass* that made possible these longer voyages which, it is now reasonably well established, took them across the Atlantic as far as the coasts of Newfoundland 500 years before Columbus sailed to the New World. Many of their names, enshrined in the Norse sagas, have come down to us, most of them for their victories in battle, three for the length and endurance of their voyages. Eric the Red, forced to flee from Norway to escape a charge of murder, sailed his longship to Greenland and founded a Norse colony there. Biarni Heriulfsson, a sea trader on his way to Greenland, was blown off course to the westward in 986 AD and sighted an unknown land down to the southwest before the wind relented and he could claw his way home. Fourteen years later Leif Ericsson, son of "the Red", decided to investigate Biarni Heriulfsson's story and landed, we believe today, on the coasts of Labrador and Newfoundland or, as he named the places where he went ashore, Helluland, Markland and Vinland.

The seafaring urge of Europeans, for so many centuries centred on the Mediterranean, had by now moved up towards the north after the Muslims had stormed across that inland sea during the 9th century. Dominating the North African coast as far west as the Pillars of Hercules, and even establishing themselves in Spain, they turned that once open ocean highway into a nightmare of piracy that made seaborne trade too hazardous for most merchants to contemplate. The move to the north was at first based on fishing in the Baltic, where the huge shoals of herring offered a quick path to profit. And when the herring migrated to the North Sea in the 14th century, those waters too became equally profitable. As the fishery grew in importance, so did trade between the northern European nations. Europe was beginning to open up, and the Hansa ports of Lübeck and Hamburg set up a trading confederation which, joined later by five other Baltic ports, operated a virtual monopoly of seaborne trade along the coasts which bordered the Baltic, the North Sea and the Bay of Biscay. The trade was carried in a new type of ship, the first definite break away from the basic longship design of northern Europe, a broad-beamed sailing ship with a long, straight keel, admirably designed to carry a worthwhile cargo across waters more turbulent than those of the Mediterranean. This was the Hansa cog, which grew in size and multiplied in numbers prodigiously as the Hansa towns pursued their search for trade. And with its expansion in size, in numbers, in length of voyage, there began to grow up with the ships almost a new breed of men whose lives were dedicated to the sea and who were quick to learn the new skills which such a dedication demanded.

This burgeoning of trade was responsible for the huge step forward into the unknown which brought the European sailor into the forefront of world dominion. In spite of the teaching of the Church in Rome that the world was flat, seamen had realized for hundreds of years that it was a sphere and that if a ship sailed far enough to the west she would end her voyage in the east. The Muslim domination of the Mediterranean had effectively cut the existing trade routes, by overland caravan and trans-shipment in the Levant, by which Europe had enjoyed the spices, silks, carpets and jewels of the east, and the merchants who dealt in these desirable commodities were now prepared to listen to the theories of the seamen and to believe them when they said they could bring home the riches of the east by sailing to the westward.

So Europe entered its first heroic age of navigation and exploration, its seamen pushing out their small ships into waters not only unknown but often damned by legendary horrors. A great many European sailors believed the story that the sea near the Equator boiled and would melt the pitch with which the bottom of a ship was made watertight, thus letting in the sea and sinking her. Portuguese seamen, exploring down the west coast of Africa, for years refused to venture further than Cabo de Não (Cape Nun) on the bulge of Africa for fear of entering the boiling sea, and a free English translation of a contemporary Spanish couplet runs:

> When old Cape Nun heaves into sight,
> Turn back, me lad, or else – good night.

Yet by 1434 this particular fear had been proved groundless, and in succeeding years Portuguese sailors pushed steadily south until, in December 1488, Bartholomeu Diaz sailed his three caravels proudly up the Tagus, having successfully rounded the southernmost cape of Africa and sailed further to the south than any other man in the world. He had named the cape Tormentosa, because of the great storms he had encountered there, but the king changed the name to Bona Speranza, Good Hope, for the next expedition must surely reach India, the greatest prize of all. And so, indeed, it was, for in 1498 Vasco da Gama successfully navigated his squadron to Calicut, on the mainland of India.

Almost simultaneously the western route to the east was being opened, though it was for a few years stopped by the new continent which none of the world's geographers had thought was there. Indeed, when Columbus sighted land in the west on 12 October 1492, he thought it was India that he had reached and he gave the many islands he touched at the collective name of Las Indias. It was not until his third voyage to the west in 1498–1500 that the great navigator realized that what he had discovered was neither India nor China, and that it must be a new and unknown continent.

The names now fall thick and fast in the annals of exploration and navigation, almost like a peal of bells. To those of Bartholomeu Diaz and Vasco da Gama must be added Pedro Cabral, Ugolino and Sorleone Vivaldo, Antoniotto Uso di Mare and Alfonso d'Albuquerque; to that of Christopher Columbus those of Hernando de Alarçon, Vasco Nuñez de Balboa, Alvaro Nuñez and Giovanni Verrazzano. They were the first to establish recognized routes across the oceans, but they were followed by a host of others, equally famous, in these early years of European navigation. They came from France, England, Holland and Denmark, as well as from Spain and Portugal; Jacques Cartier and Jean Ribault, John and Sebastian Cabot, Humphrey Gilbert, Henry Hudson, John Davis and Martin Frobisher, Willem Barents, Jacob le Maire and Willem Schouten, Jens Erikson Munk. And, a year or two on, perhaps the greatest navigator of them all, Ferdinand Magellan, whose ship *Vittoria* circled the globe, though Magellan himself did not live to complete his voyage, being killed in a local squabble in the Philippines.

What drove these men to make these stupendous voyages in their tiny ships? It would be pleasant to be able to record that it was a curiosity to discover what lay beyond the horizon, or an urge to prove beyond all doubt that their theory of a spherical world was the true one. Perhaps it was true for one or two of them, but it was the dream of riches and of power that was ever the principal driving force of the great majority. Even Columbus, by repute a gentle man, drove a remarkably hard bargain with his royal patrons for his own enrichment and a patent of personal nobility in the event of his discovering a shorter sea route to the east. Most of them went armed to the teeth, determined to enforce their right to trade on their own terms, almost invariably by conquest, no matter how reluctant the inhabitants of the lands they reached might be.

Yet, perhaps unwittingly, they wrote the names of European seamen, their skill in navigation and seamanship, across the map of the world. They were the pioneers, the adventurers, the men who forced the nations of Europe to realize that the oceans were the only open highways to the world's trade and riches. Most of their voyages were contemporary miracles of endurance, hope and hardihood; of long battles against storm, hunger and the diseases peculiar to the sea which as yet defied diagnosis or cure. And these were conditions that bred in them a feeling of superiority over their stay-at-home neighbours, so that a man who could say "I was one who sailed with Diaz", or with Columbus, or Cabot, or Magellan or any other of the great navigators, was a man who could expect, and indeed demand, to be honoured in his home town or village.

Inevitably this opening up of the world led to increased national rivalries, a determination to enforce the nation's right to trade or to break another nation's self-declared monopoly of trade in new areas of the recently discovered world. Technology was catching up at sea; gunpowder and the cannon, for over a century the monopoly of land-based armies, were adapted to the ship, and a new type of vessel made her appearance in the world's oceans, the ship designed purely for fighting. National navies were formed to uphold or dispute the nation's rights or aspirations, and, in their turn, they bred a new type of sailor, the fighting seaman. Like the great navigators who preceded them, their names too are enshrined in national, and indeed in world, history. Dutch, English, French and Spanish fleets, led by their naval heroes of the time, disputed across the oceans to the east and the west, and their particular skills, adapted to the seas in which they fought, added yet another dimension to the art and mystery of European seamanship, and yet another cubit to the stature of the European seaman. Theirs, indeed, were names to conjure with. Francis Drake, Walter Raleigh, John Hawkins, Robert Blake, George Rooke, George Monck and Cloudesley Shovel, of England; Cornelis and Marten Tromp, Michiel de Ruyter, Piet Hein and the great fighting family of Evertsen, of Holland; Jean Bart, Louis de Rousselet, Abraham Duquesne and René du Guay Trouin, of France; Alvaro de Bazan, Alonso de Guzman and Antonio de Oquendo, of Spain; all were men who made seafaring history in their time. And they made themselves masters of the seas, extending the power of their individual countries across even the distant Indian and Pacific Oceans.

We know, too, that European fishermen date back into the mists of time, and that they thought nothing of taking their frail craft great distances out to sea in search of their catch. There were, without doubt, European fishermen long before Peter of Galilee came to Rome and made the outline of a fish the symbol of Christianity, for the bones of deep-sea fish excavated in a Stone Age site near Stavanger in Norway have proved that Scandinavian fishermen sailed long distances out into the Atlantic for their catch some centuries before the birth of Christ. In the year 879 King Alfred of England sent two seamen, named Oddr and Wulfstan, to discover how far to the northward the coasts of Scandinavia extended, and north of the Lofoten Islands they encountered the whale hunters of France, Denmark, Norway and Lapland at their work. Breton and Portuguese fishermen were crossing the Atlantic to fish the Newfoundland Banks nearly two centuries before John Cabot discovered in 1497 that, by lowering baskets into the sea, he could haul up more cod than his crew could eat. They must surely have sighted the western continent at least a hundred years or more before Columbus set foot on it. Herring and mackerel were being taken in the Baltic and North Sea with seine nets of which it is recorded that Dutch fishermen made them longer than any others in the world.

Life at sea was a hard and often a merciless one, and so it remained for the next three centuries during which the last and most distant corners of the earth were being opened up. In all these years it was the seamen of Europe who dominated world navigation and who stamped their names and national characteristics on the distant nations to which their ships brought them. Inevitably their knowledge and skill grew and prospered to an extent where a voyage to the far ends of the earth became more of a certainty than a problematic adventure. In the 17th and 18th centuries they mapped the world's oceans; they learned how to use astronomy to find their way across the oceans; and eventually they learned, too, how to measure time with an accuracy that gave them virtual exactitude of daily position along the pathless highways of the sea. These were the centuries during which the general pattern of seafaring settled down into a more or less fixed routine. They were the years of the East India Companies – English, Dutch, French, Danish, Scottish, Spanish, Austrian and Swedish – whose ships, captains and crews were considered the aristocrats of the sea. They made regular, fixed voyages to the east,

running them on a schedule almost as rigid as a modern steamship line. So great was their
prestige that, almost alone among shipowners of those years, they did not need to recruit crews before each voyage. Almost all their officers and seamen looked upon service with an East India Company as a career for life. In all other ships, and in all navies, a seaman was signed on for a single voyage in a merchant ship, for a commission in a warship. For some, their first experience of life at sea was discouraging enough to make them search elsewhere for a way of life, but a considerable majority, once they had taken the initial step, adopted the seafaring life for good, signing on again and again for further voyages or commissions. Looking back now at those centuries during which the pattern was set, it seems strange that they did so with such regularity. The work was generally hard and ill paid, the conditions of life on board still rudimentary in comparison with life ashore, the food atrocious, the discipline, in our modern eyes, ferocious, and the danger of death from the two killer diseases so prevalent in ships, scurvy and typhus, many times higher than anywhere else in the world. Yet return they did, and throughout these centuries of overall expansion there was rarely a shortage of men to man the ships as they were built, except in times of war when the rate of warship building always exceeded the number of men willing to serve. It was in those periods that compulsion had to be introduced to get the warships manned, and the sea fraternity was swollen by largely unwilling conscripts.

Virtually the whole of the world's trans-ocean trade was still in the hands of European merchants during these centuries. They were the years, too, when the maritime nations of Europe devoted many of their energies to the process of empire building, taking armies overseas to win new lands or to garrison existing colonies. It was a process requiring big ships, big fleets and big crews to man them, and the need for men bred and brought up to the sea was to be counted in the millions. It became a huge seafaring amalgam of fighting seamen and marines, trading seamen and fishermen, almost, one might say, a special breed of men who spoke the language of the sea, who dressed, even ashore, in the peculiar clothing adapted to life on board a ship, and who were at home with wind, tide and tempest. Their rolling gait, said to be induced by the perpetual movement of a ship at sea, their speech, their dress, even their food and drink, made them easily recognizable wherever they went, forming as it were a sort of individual brotherhood of men who served the same universal mistress.

The 18th century saw a small break in the general pattern, again European in its conception and dedication. This was the introduction of the scientific voyage, one designed not for trade or national aggrandizement but mainly to learn and record the anthropology, fauna and flora of far-off lands and to observe the earth's magnetic variations in various parts of the globe, vital knowledge in the perfection of navigation. They are best exemplified, perhaps, in the voyages of James Cook, Samuel Wallis, Francis Beaufort and Matthew Flinders of Britain, of Louis de Bougainville, Jean-François, Comte de la Perouse, Louis-Claude de Freycinet and Yves Kerguelen-Tremarec of France, of Adam Krusenstern, Yuri Lisiansky and Thaddeus von Bellingshausen of Russia. Their voyages were typical of many during this period, all designed to contribute to the spreading knowledge of the world and its various peoples. Frequently they were recorded in magnificently descriptive writing and fine, detailed drawings and paintings, so that the world of the sea became a powerful constituent of the world of literature and art.

If the great naval wars of the late 18th century tore Europe apart, at least at the same time they produced many of the giants of naval warfare, leaders of the stamp of Samuel Hood and Richard Howe, Horatio Nelson and John Jervis, François Brueys and the Comte de Villeneuve. These wars were the last fling of the sailing navies, manned by officers and men who took a fierce pride in their individual skills as prime seamen.

Behind the great naval fleets lay the ever-expanding merchant navies, breeding their own type of seaman. The world lay on the brink of a huge explosion of international trade as the 19th century, with its technical revolutions in methods of sea transport, took hold. The great majority of world trade still lay in the hands of Europe, and European ships and seamen still dominated the world of seaborne trade. Shipping was to become during this 19th century the fastest-growing industry in the world, drawing in new young men in great numbers to be trained as seamen, and some of the world's nations outside Europe were also being drawn into the expansion. But already the old picture of the sailor in all his aspects was beginning to change as the new technology spread to the sea. Just as the iron ship and the marine steam engine drove out the wooden hull and the tall sail rig, so the new technical skills they demanded drove out much of the old seafaring lore and habits which had made the deep-sea sailor so distinctive and recognizable a man amid his fellows. His was still a brotherhood of the sea, but the conditions of the brotherhood were changing. The fisherman now used an engine to take him to his fishing grounds instead of sail and oars, and he used steam power to haul in his trawls instead of his hands and arms. The upper yardman, always the aristocrat of any sailing ship's crew, now had no yard or sails on which to demonstrate his expertise. The gap between the sailor and his fellow worker ashore, although still distinctive, was beginning to narrow, since many of the technical skills required by the scientific expansion of the times were much the same afloat and ashore.

The old ways took a long time to die, and even after the new ships had established themselves beyond all doubt, there were many seamen who clung for as long as they could to the life they had known. The ships they had known and sailed all their lives had had an unbroken history of 400 years, and there was virtually no difference in design or in handling between a ship of England or France or Spain or Holland or Russia, or indeed of any of Europe's seafaring nations. Much the same could be said of their seamen. At the battle of Trafalgar in 1805 there were men from 12 different European countries, even including France and Spain, among the crew of H.M.S. *Victory*, the British flagship and as such surely the ship in which to expect an all-true-blue British crew. Yet this was nothing remarkable for the time; it was to be found in almost every ship of every nation, and was as true of the merchant ship as of the warship. It was in its way a measure of the universality of the seafaring life. Perhaps it was no wonder that the iron ships bred so much distrust among seamen when first they put to sea.

It was, of course, a losing battle. The riches to be gained in international trade, the rewards in freight money from carrying large numbers of passengers and big cargoes across the oceans, dictated the building of ships in a material stronger and more resilient than wood. In the late 19th century steel came in to take the place of iron, and the strength of this new material enabled yet larger ships to be built. For a time the sailor had to take second place to the ship designer, builder and engineer, as the new ships slid down their launching ways into the water. A new and different generation of seaman had to be trained in the new ways and new skills of the technical revolution at sea.

Most of the new design and new building of the 19th century still came from the shipyards of Europe, and most of the seamen and engineers who manned the new ships were still European. But the virtual monopoly of Europe was not to last. A natural result of earlier colonization was inevitably later independence, and the new nations so evolved, as well as more ancient ones as they developed industrially, were as quick to appreciate the importance of ships and the sea as had been the older ones of Europe. International competition has cut deeply into what was once a supreme European dominance.

The sailor had always been conditioned by the ships in which he served. In the simpler days of wooden hull and tall masts, the requirement of a prime seaman was an ability to "knot, reef and steer". He was, like his ship, a relatively simple man. Today, as ship development keeps pace with the technological revolution of the 20th century, he has to be much more of an expert technician than the simple sailor of past generations. He lives better on board than ever did his father or his grandfather. And in every way this is all to the good, no matter how much of a traditionalist the sailor may be. The only constant is the sea itself, a great leveller in all its varying moods. But this is still enough to set the sailor apart from those who spend their lives on land, and to make his world, as it has always been, a separate and distinctive one.

# 4

# *Workers*

## WALTER KENDALL

The world of work, the world of the workers within that circumscribing globe, is defined by external factors, on occasion changes as they change, changes too as a result of man's own innovations, or changes in that environment itself. Cities such as Ghent and Bruges, preserved as in aspic, give us a picture of what life was like in the Low Countries during the Middle Ages. Erected with the wealth generated by the wool trade with England, the native manufactures to which this gave birth, they died as living forces when the rivers giving access to the sea silted up, cutting them off both from source of supply and markets at the same time. Had Ghent and Bruges continued to prosper their face would have been altered beyond recognition today. Economic downturn has preserved them as testimony to the power and magic of a bygone age.

Small-scale iron production once flourished in the forests of the Sussex Weald. When the forests were cut down, the industry vanished altogether leaving scarcely a trace behind. Until the discovery of America and the east, the Mediterranean constituted the centre of life on our land mass. Britain was no more than a frontier post of civilization on the distant Atlantic. The discovery of America, 16th-century innovations in gun, sail and navigation, turned her into an imperial power with global pretensions. In such a fashion through all recorded history hitherto the workers have been for the work, never the other way about. That the working man all too often has come to see himself as object rather than subject, as the hapless victim of the whims of fortune, not at all the master of his fate, in such circumstances is not at all surprising.

The origin of a feeling of powerlessness in the worker thus has its roots in well-founded historical experience, not at all in social failings, or the innate characteristic of particular individuals. Such a feeling, finding much of its origin in man's relationship with nature, has been reinforced in reciprocal fashion by man's own relationship with man, by the unequal degrees of sovereignty which throughout recorded history have been allotted to separate individuals, groups and classes, living together in society.

Once man's labour could provide for more than his own subsistence, ownership of other men became a means to wealth, to power and thus to still further dominion. In paradoxical fashion the increase in wealth production involved in man's rise from the lower depths, from itinerant hunter and herdsman to settled cultivator of the soil, created the means not for his further liberty but for his enslavement. The Roman Empire grew out of the empty bellies of its slaves. The castles of feudal lords and crusaders, the majesty of the courts of the Middle Ages, the culture of chivalry, the splendour of abbeys, monasteries, cathedrals, all in the end found their origin in the unrequited labour of serf and tenant on ecclesiastical and manorial estate. The grandeur of the aristocracy, the squalor of the tenantry were the two sides of the same coin; the glory of Latin as a universal European language, the illiteracy of the nameless tiller of the soil, the inseparable components of the same social equation.

Industrial capitalism created new industries, new jobs, new men. Engine drivers, porters, signal-men, railwaymen, boiler-makers, stokers, crane drivers, mill-hands, lathe operators, fitters appeared for the first time. Industrial capitalism not only created new work tasks, it also changed the social situation of the worker in a number of different ways. It may well be, as has powerfully been argued, that the economic position of the white wage worker in the northern United States was far more insecure, far more harsh, his expectation of life often lower, his intensity of labour often greater, than that of the slaves in the better-run plantations of the South. The fact remains that his possibilities of social advance, economic amelioration and self-liberation were enormously greater than those of his counterpart under serfdom or under slavery. The situation of the wage labourer as against his ancestor in Europe changed in just the same way. Output, and with it social wealth, soared too, to an unprecedented degree. It was inevitable that to some extent the more skilled, more urgently needed, segments of the work force should benefit in line. The wage worker was at the mercy of the market, isolated, insecure, defenceless, in a fashion in which no man had ever been before. In the eyes of entrepreneurs, economists and their other self-serving apologists, the worker ceased to be a man, became a "factor of production", an inanimate object, innately no more worthy of consideration than a log of dead wood, a sack of beans. Since he might live only by labour, since labour was available not at all by his will, but only at the gift of others, if without employment he had no alternative but to starve and die.

The rapid urbanization which accompanied the Industrial Revolution made the working population, hitherto scattered across field and countryside, highly visible for the first time. In 1871, of the German population, 64 per cent lived in the countryside. By 1910 the population had increased by 24 million. The balance between town and country had been almost exactly reversed. In different degree the same phenomenon began to be observed all over Europe. The unproductive minority which lived off the labour of others, the "leisured class", from time immemorial, out of its own ranks, had devolved the task of maintaining its own dominion on to a "ruling class" and "aristocracy" of its own making. Now a clearly differentiated "*working* class*" appeared on the social scene and began to make claims of its own for the first time.

The Industrial Revolution which began in Britain in the 18th century transformed much of Europe and North America in the 19th, and continues still to advance across Asia and Africa today, took different forms according to the varied circumstances of the national states in which it got under way. In Britain and the United States the industrial and social revolution was conducted almost solely under the leadership of the entrepreneurial bourgeoisie. In other states, above all in tsarist Russia, but also in lesser degree in Germany, Austria-Hungary and Italy, the role of the independent native entrepreneur was assumed either by the state or else by large industrial banks, high finance, foreign *rentiers*, working independently or in collaboration. The Industrial Revolution gave birth to two social classes: one possessing the means of production, the other by its labour putting them to work. According to the degree of state intervention in the process so the entrepreneurial bourgeoisie was more or less liberal, the working class more or less free. The distinction continues to the present day, and reaches its fulfilment in the "communist" states of eastern Europe.

The "worker" in this social order was not characterized primarily by the nature of his work, rather by his social relation to its product. The artist and the sculptor after all "work", as does the author himself as he writes these lines, yet none of them customarily are categorized as members of the "working class". The explanation, if at first not apparent, is not far to seek. The artist, the author, the sculptor own the product of their labour whilst the member of the working class does not. The worker sells his power to labour, and in so doing loses all contractual right of ownership and control over the ensuing product. By a form of legal fiction he is regarded as an inanimate agent when carrying out his taskmaster's will, yet remaining a free man, liable for his acts, should he (as a truck driver committing a traffic offence) break the law whilst so doing.

The railway and the steam ship opened first our own continent, then the outside world, to Europe's more adventurous, more hard-pressed working-class inhabitants. Jews from the Russian Pale emigrated to London, Leeds, Chicago and New York. Serbs and Croats, modern-day Yugoslavs, crossed the Atlantic to Toledo on the Great Lakes, Akron in Ohio. Italians journeyed to Buenos Aires, Montevideo, also New York, and the other great cities of the United States. British workers travelled the length and breadth of their masters' empire, also to the United States. Germans and Czechs shipped out of Hamburg for the Mid-West, and there brewed the beer that made Milwaukee famous. Ukrainian farmers ploughed the prairies in Alberta, Hungarians helped man the steel mills in Pittsburgh, Welsh miners dug coal in Pennsylvanian pits. Wicklow and Galway men vied one with another to enhance the profits of the copper trust at Butte, Montana, swelled too the slums of Boston and New York on the eastern seaboard. Poles established their own enclave in the city of Hamtramck in Detroit. Scandinavians farmed Minnesota, elected their own as state governors in St Paul. Scots engine drivers exchanged their bowler hats, professional emblem of the "aristocrat" of labour, for the favours of the ladies of the high Andes, an item of headgear their descendants continue to wear with pride up to the present day.

If the great industrial cities of the United States drew their labour force from immigrant labour so the great cities of Europe drew their proletariat from native internal migration no less. Manchester, Liverpool, Birmingham, Glasgow, London include large specifically Irish contingents in their population up to the present day. The Welsh mining valleys, empty until the 19th century, were largely peopled by emigrants from outside. Much of the workforce of the Ruhr came from Poland, central and eastern Europe. On the vast estates of Prussian landowners the harvest until recent days was gathered in large measure by migrant labourers from abroad. France in 1931 included almost three million foreign workers within its borders; 900,000 from Italy, 500,000 from Poland, 400,000 from Spain. Some 25 million people were forcibly uprooted from their homes as a consequence of World War II. Mass internal migration continues to characterize Europe to the present day. Millions in post-war Italy have trekked from south to north, established themselves in Milan, Turin, gone further afield to work in Germany, France, Belgium, Britain or beyond. Spanish workers have travelled north in search of employment as have their counterparts from Yugoslavia, Greece and even Turkey. None of these, however, have chosen to cross the border between "East" and "West", to seek employment in Russia, elsewhere in eastern Europe. Nor have workers in the East been allowed to avail themselves of the job opportunities in the West, thus radically changing one aspect of the pattern of labour migration which had existed hitherto.

The life and life-style of the workers of 20th-century Europe, caught in the grip of the same industrial system, working with comparable technology, exposed to much the same intensity of advertising for consumer durables of a generally similar order, tend increasingly to become the same. Eastern Europe seems to differ here only in that the wage levels are lower, the right of the workers as citizens less, the consumption targets for the next decade those achieved by their counterparts in the West already in the 1960s, the 1950s, or even before. Cowley, Halewood, Bathgate in Britain are auto-dominated towns, just as the auto, personified by FIAT, dominates Turin; Ford dominates Ghenk in Belgium, and parts of Cologne in Germany; Volvo dominates Gothenburg in Sweden. Meanwhile in Russia, at Togliattigrad, a factory designed and installed under contract by FIAT builds a Russian version of an outdated Italian car. This specially designed, single-purpose auto city represents the Soviet version of a concept first originated by the Nazi Labour Front with their Volkswagen plant erected at Fallersleben 40 years before.

Millions of workers from Europe have travelled their own continent, journeyed abroad, in search of employment and a better life. Yet the outstanding fact remains that, left to themselves, the great majority have preferred not to move at all. Capital travels great distances, climbs mountain ranges, crosses vast oceans, at very little social cost. Labour moves much more slowly, as a rule only at the price of much personal inconvenience and dislocation to the individuals involved. Labour, of all the factors of production, is the least transportable. In Europe, separated as it remains by national frontiers, split by religious and cultural divisions, cut off one part from another by language barriers, separated East and West by a veritable wall against free communication set up by the self-chosen rulers of the "socialist" states in the East, this is especially so.

In Yugoslavia the income per head of Slovenia, the richest province, is six times that of Kosovo, the poorest. In Italy the wealth of the north markedly outweighs that of the

south, although in not so stark a manner. The existence of such great differences, not only
between nations, but also between specific regions within the same state, points to the degree
to which even late 20th century Europe fails to conform to the ideal model of the capitalist
economy in which perfect competition irons out all differences between different regions of
the economy. Regional differences remain, like national, religious and cultural differences,
and constitute a powerful factor maintaining separation between the workers of one part of
Europe and another.

All this apart, the working class in being is not, nor ever has been, an entirely homogeneous
unit. As industrial processes differ, so do worker tasks, the human requirements, and attitudes
essential to their proper fulfilment. Rail, road and air are all means of transport. The skills,
training, essential qualifications, the resulting outlook, of engine drivers, truckers and airline
pilots are hardly the same. Coal may be mined in *pits* deep below the earth's surface or
shovelled out by huge drag lines in open-cast workings. The mentality of the operators is not
the same. The outlook of face worker and maintenance man, surface worker and underground
collier, rarely coincides. Europe's auto industry now out-produces that of the United States,
and employs a labour force more than one million strong. Yet contrary to popular impression
scarcely one man in ten in the auto industry works on the assembly line. The outlook of
production worker and storeman, of skilled and unskilled worker in the auto plant, sometimes
conflicts, often with tempestuous results. The secret of success in some kinds of *mechanical
mass-production* industry seems to lie in large degree in *man management*. In industries such as
chemicals man management may be less important. Here the *flow production* largely manages
itself, leaving man only to fulfil maintenance tasks, to supervise a production process which,
once started, continues largely independent of human will.

Again some industries are highly urbanized. Others, like coal mining, frequently take place
in largely rural areas. Some plants tend to be very large. Others are predominantly small.
Garment manufacture until now has been a haven sheltering relatively small employers with a
predominantly female labour force. Textile workers in most countries have been more often
women than men. Women workers are the majority in many areas of retail distribution and
other sectors of the service trades. Nurses in most countries in the main have been women.
Hotel staff have been more mixed, but the nature of their employment has hardly been such, in
the past at any rate, as to encourage militancy of the same order as that found amongst coal
miners, metal workers or the man on the auto production line. Zenica, Bari, Sheffield and Essen
all produce steel, yet it would be foolish indeed to expect workers raised in Bosnia, Apulia,
Yorkshire and the Ruhr all to behave in exactly the same way. Oil is pumped out of the earth at
Ploesti in Romania, also out of the bed of the North Sea, 150 miles out from the Shetlands.
Neither the process nor the resulting outlook and attitudes of the work force are the same. The
lumber industry reaches across northern Europe, quite neglectful of national frontiers. Scandinavian lumberjacks, British Forestry Commission employees, the hapless forced labourers of
the Gulag Archipelago all approach their work, their leisure, of necessity in many different
ways.

Agriculture demands different skills, poses different problems, consequently is organized in
a different fashion, develops a different worker mentality, from that of more urban industry.
Climatic conditions, topographical features, vary greatly from one region of Europe to another.
Crop patterns, resulting labour force tasks, vary both in skill requirements and in intensity of
labour. Periods of peak labour demand vary in line. Patterns of ownership in Europe are by no
means identical. In our own century these have ranged from vast latifundia-type estates in east
Prussia, parts of Italy and Spain, through to small-scale peasant holdings operated by self-
employed family units in France, Germany, Austria and large areas of the Balkans. In Britain
neither model holds good. Here small capitalist entrepreneurs employ a wage labour force
analagous to that which exists in the cities, unionized in essentially a similar way. In specific
areas throughout Europe, in chicken, pig and certain other types of livestock production, the
"factory farm" begins to make its appearance. A hitherto exclusively urban form of factory
employment now arrives unexpectedly in the heart of the countryside. Yet whilst 21st-century
factory method now exists in some parts of the European rural environment, near prehistoric
sharecropping tenancies persist in others, notably in whole regions of Italy, up to the present

time. The latifundia meanwhile, largely abolished in Italy, continue to thrive under communist patronage in eastern Europe. Here the peasant gains the bulk of his income from a
private plot ("minifundia") whilst the latifundia, disguised as a "collective farm", reappear in a
new form under the Red Flag. Rural employment can prove as varied as that of the town, and
produce as many differences of outlook, interest and mentality amongst the individuals who
compose its workforce.

Not all workers in Europe work in the same region or in the same country. Nor do all work
in the same industry. Not all workers work at the same job within the same industry, or indeed
even within the same plant. In different plants, making comparable products, either in the same
state or in different states, job specifications for comparable tasks often vary greatly, leading the
worker to approach his productive role in a different fashion. "Management style" differs
greatly even amongst comparable giant multi-national corporations. It differs much more
amongst small employers, in different countries, with greatly different social, national,
linguistic and cultural traditions. Given these differences it has not yet proved possible to breed
a worker who will behave like a battery hen, neither under Hitler, Mussolini, Franco or Henry
Ford, nor indeed under Joseph Stalin, Matyas Rakosi or any of the infinitely less colourful
dictators of eastern Europe.

The workers in each country experience reality in a different way. In part this is because
their pre-existing culture conditions them to react even to identical stimuli in a dissonant
fashion. In part too, and more largely so, this is because the reality of employment, of industry,
of worker opportunity, varies greatly from one place to another. As I wrote in *The Labour
Movement in Europe* (London, 1975, p. 8),

> The nature of the economy . . . is both formed by and itself forms the nature, methods and
> behaviour of the entrepreneurial class . . . This process is conditioned by the particular strategic
> needs of specific states. The behaviour of the economy, the entrepreneurial class and the state
> establish the environmental conditions in which the modern urban working class is formed, the
> social pressures in response to which its own forms of consciousness, its own modes of
> organisation arise. It is here that we hold the key to the specific characteristics of the European
> working class and the working class in general. It was not after all formal rules and procedures
> which created the modern labour movement. Rather these rules and procedures were the
> outcome of ideas and attitudes already present in the minds of the working class.

Latin was the universal language of educated and leisured classes throughout western
Europe in the feudal era. As late as the 19th century the Russian aristocracy was accustomed to
converse in French rather than its native tongue. So frequently did its counterpart in countries
elsewhere. Working people remained largely illiterate, their intellectual horizons of necessity
bounded by the limited opportunities of local employment, the limited reach of the local dialect
of the national language in which as a rule they were entrapped. In its origin working-class
culture was remarkably local in character, and drew none of its inspiration from classical
models of Greek antiquity. Trade-union and socialist propaganda and activity did much to
widen working-class horizons. Yet it is only now, in the era of universal literacy, instant mass
communication, largely effortless low-cost long-distance travel, the global "pop" star, that the
gap between "upper" and "lower" classes begins to narrow, although not to disappear. The gap
remains. Working-class children, as a general rule, throughout Europe, do not go to university.
Nor do they expect to. The minority that bridge the chasm dividing the two cultures feel out of
place. On qualifying they are forced to choose between the values of their first friends and
parents and those of their new peers.

Brass and silver bands, whippet and greyhound racing, pigeon lofts, all-in wrestling, soccer,
rugby league, union banners, the Durham Miners' Gala, the massed choirs of Welsh miners,
Lancashire and Yorkshire mill-hands, Methodism, Congregationalism, the Salvation Army,
essential elements of one milieu, are not at all to be found in the other. What holds true of
Britain in differing degree holds true of all other nations of western Europe. This situation is not
limited to the capitalist "West". The party elite in the "East" nurtures its own members in an
even more exclusive, even more sharply divided fashion. The communist "apparat" reserves to
itself special schools, special apartments, the finest doctors and surgeons, the best-equipped
hospitals, special rest homes, special travel facilities, even special cut-price shops to which

access is totally forbidden to the general public. Under capitalism the workers over generations have been conditioned to think in terms of "them" and "us". The Durham miners have a saying, "Once a policeman, never a man." The class divide, in the mind at least, is very plain. To the social élite the policeman is little more than a uniformed body servant. The law courts are no more than the proper means of enforcing one's rights. To the "underman" the police officer is the representative of hostile dark forces beyond his control. The law is a dangerous and expensive mystery, recourse to which is to be avoided at all cost. The predilections of the dominant section of the ruling élite constitute the larger measure of what we accept as "culture". The predilection of the working majority we know by contrast only as "sub-culture". In eastern Europe the Communist Party apparat prides itself on the superior "consciousness" on which its "cadres" base their claim to rule, and looks with contempt on the inferior consciousness of the masses in much the same way. That workers in Russia, Poland, Bulgaria, Romania, Hungary, Czechoslovakia, Yugoslavia see their relationship with authority as a matter of "them" and "us", just like their counterparts in the West, seems certain. Indeed in these countries on occasion the extent of "alienation" goes even further. In London, Paris and Bonn we have no equivalent of the current Czech proverb which declares, "He who does not steal from the state robs his own family."

The working class in Europe was present at its own conception. The class in being was antecedent to the class as a category, as a philosophical notion. Intellectuals have always found difficulty in coming to terms with this fact, and continue to do so up to the present day. As a result the class in being is constantly contrasted with the intellectual's notion of what it ought to be. In eastern Europe today this view of the world has run riot. The intelligentsia, moulded into a caste through the Leninist party, rules over and above the working class, claims to act in its name, much as Vatican, pope, bishops and archbishops rule the Roman Catholic Church, acting as proxy on behalf of Almighty God. The aim of the class in being now, as always, diverges from that postulated for it by intellectuals, if only because it has a closer and more direct perception of its own needs. "What does the American worker want", Sam Gompers, spokesman for the American Federation of Labour, was asked many years ago. "More. Now!" came Gompers's reply.

If the practical working-class movement in Europe, its trade-union wing, has often diverged to some extent from the socialist, this, it will readily be seen, is not always without good reason. Trade-union gains at any given moment, it is true, are usually only marginal. Yet most working men live at the margin. Marginal increments frequently are all that realistically working men feel themselves quickly able to achieve. That apart, as the weight and power of the trade-union movement throughout western Europe today amply demonstrate, a series of marginal increments in living standards and "in-plant" sovereignty, over time, may aggregate imperceptibly into a highly visible shift of power, not only in factory and workshop, but also in society as a whole.

Already by the 1880s the forces of modern capitalism were making themselves felt throughout Europe. In 1880 the Scots herring fisheries were conducted with sail boats costing £60; by 1914 the industry ran on steam trawlers costing £3,000. Highland fishermen found themselves transformed from proud self-employed artisans to hapless wage slaves within a single generation. The same process, in other industries, took place at a comparable pace all over Europe. Norway's North Cape was no more immune than Izmir in Turkey. Galway in the west felt its impact, as did the Urals far away in the east. In certain states, notably in Britain, Belgium, France and Germany, capitalist industrialism became the predominant economic form. In others, as in Italy's "Iron Triangle" of Milan-Genoa-Turin, it existed as the dominant force in a whole region. In yet others, as in the Balkans and parts of central and eastern Europe, it consisted of a series of enclaves immersed in a basically pre-capitalist hinterland. This indeed was the case in Russia where much of the native capitalism that had been nurtured by the bureaucracy of the tsar was an excrescence on a form of Asiatic despotism rather than a predominant socio-economic-political system in its own right. From Danzig southwards towards Venice a line divided Europe. On the one side modern capitalism was predominant. On the other it had yet to come to rule. The boundary line remains with us, continues to separate capitalist from "socialist" societies up to the present day.

As was to be expected in such circumstances, the characteristics of the working-class movement varied greatly from one region, from one country, to another, in accordance with the circumstances in which the workers found themselves. Yet in every case, without exception, in every major city, the working class, oppressed, degraded, exploited, lived a life of its own, quite separate from that of the ruling élite. Jack London came to London in 1907, went to live in the proletarian quarter of the imperial capital, and wrote a terrifying account of his experiences under the title *The People of the Abyss*. The trade unionist James Connolly wrote that the "Irish Transport and General Workers Union found the workers of Dublin with no means of defence but the arts of the liar, the lick-spittle and the toady. It taught them the power of combination, made it possible for the first time that they assume the erect stature of the full man." The working-class movement fought everywhere in Europe that the average man might emerge in much the same way from the "abyss" to which industrial capitalism had consigned him.

In the United Kingdom where "bourgeois democracy" already existed as a fairly fully fledged political system, where capitalist industry was firmly entrenched throughout the nation, the trade unions, powerful organizations predominantly of skilled men, already one million strong in 1900, emerged at first as the predominant element. Tsarist Russia existed at the other pole, where workers and peasants were denied all political rights. Here serfdom had been abolished only in 1861. Here the first trade unions were prophylactic creations of the secret political police rather than independent organizations in their own right. As a result the socialists played a predominant role in the nascent working-class movement. The movement directed its main endeavour towards the overthrow of the tsar, the necessary precondition for the establishment of the most elementary civil rights. In this struggle socialists and workers were joined by many liberals, a large proportion of the intelligentsia, even sections of the bourgeoisie. In much this fashion, according to circumstance, the balance between socialist party and trade unions in the national labour movements varied greatly between country and country. In some states, as in Britain and Belgium, the unions at first were the predominant force; in others, as in Germany and Italy, the socialist party at first came to the fore. The International Working Men's Association, better known as the First International, founded in London in 1864, comprised both elements. Karl Marx acted as Corresponding Secretary for Germany. Just the same the core of the organization was composed of old-line English craft unionists, men like William Randolph Cremer of the Woodworkers, and George Odger, President of the London Trades Council.

The First International lasted only a few years, and disintegrated in an unedifying series of disputes following the suppression of the Paris Commune of 1871. In the next two decades the trades-union and socialist movements in Europe advanced at a considerable pace. At Paris in 1889, on the 100th anniversary of the French Revolution, socialists and trade unionists gathered to re-establish the International once again. The resulting Labour and Socialist, or Second International, has lasted without a break in continuity down to the present day. The most powerful single voice in the International during its first years was the Social Democratic Party of Germany. By 1914 this enrolled over one million members and polled more than four million votes.

Until the last quarter of the 19th century working people had never achieved more than a "walk-on" part on the stage of history. Their voice was heard episodically in the slave revolts of the Roman Empire, peasants' revolts such as those of Thomas Munzer and John Ball in feudal Europe, the apprentice riots and near-insurrections which erupted regularly in medieval cities, the demands of the "Agitators", the "Levellers" and "Diggers" which emerged from the ranks of Cromwell's army, in the demands of the sansculottes of the French Revolution. Such voices were rarely listened to for long. Once the moment of crisis passed, the puny armed force which gave them momentary recognition was all too easily suppressed. The *mass socialist party* of which the German SPD became the pre-eminent model enabled the voice of organized working people to be heard clearly and consistently for the first time. The socialist party forced its rivals to organize in a similar way in order to maintain their power, and forced them, even against their will, to give a voice, however muted, to the opinions of labour within their own ranks. Political affairs ceased to be the concern only of a leisured, moneyed, *propertied* élite, and became a matter of popular concern, of mass participation for the very first time.

The Labour and Socialist International, through debates at successive congresses held at regular intervals, Brussels in 1891, Zurich – 1893, London – 1896, Paris – 1900, Amsterdam – 1904, Stuttgart – 1907, Copenhagen – 1910, Basle – 1912, Berne – 1919, Hamburg – 1923, down to the most recent held at Vancouver in 1978, gradually came to create a worldwide body of opinion. The socialist movement in Europe as a result was always united around common aims, albeit frequently divided about tactics. The respective socialist leaders, Jaurès from France, Bebel and Liebknecht from Germany, Luxemburg from Poland, Plekhanov from Russia, Turati and Treves from Italy, Troelstra from the Netherlands, Vandervelde from Belgium, Tranmael from Norway, Hjalmar Branting from Sweden, Keir Hardie and Ramsay MacDonald from Britain, became figures of some international renown. Already long before 1914 the socialists possessed a delegation of measurable size in the parliamentary assembly of every European state. Even the tsarist Duma, after its establishment in 1906, contained a socialist delegation of importance too. The trade unions, although at first continuing to participate in international socialist congresses, after 1901 began also to meet separately on their own account and established the International Federation of Trade Unions. As the International Confederation of Free Trade Unions this body continues to exercise an important influence up to the present day. In 1889, on the motion of the American Federation of Labour, the International dedicated May Day to a worldwide demonstration of labour solidarity based on the universal demand for the eight-hour day. Well before the outbreak of World War I, the Labour and Socialist International and the IFTU mustered affiliates in every major European state. The larger parties, in Germany, France, Italy, Belgium and Austria-Hungary, possessed a dominant voice in the councils of the International. Yet the parties of other nations, Britain, Norway, Denmark, Sweden, Bulgaria, Serbia, the Netherlands, Poland, Romania, were forces of importance too. At first the subordinate partner, the trade unions over time came to assert equality and an increasing degree of independence from socialist leadership and control.

At the turn of the century the great majority of the workers of Europe lived under the arbitrary rule of kings, queens and emperors. Only to a most limited degree had parliamentary institutions been grafted on to the pre-existing autocratic regimes, and this only as a sop to rising, largely socialist-directed, popular discontent. Most working people were entirely disfranchised. Where they were not the authorities rigged the voting system, gerrymandered it Tammanny Hall fashion, as in Belgium and Germany, the better to deny the working man's vote its proper weight. Women as a general rule were without the vote altogether. After World War I, which the labour movement everywhere proved too weak to prevent, the socialist-directed mass upsurge of indignation, which followed its conclusion, brought this situation to an end. The emperors of Germany and Austria-Hungary were toppled from their thrones. The tsar was executed. A majority of the British people received the vote for the first time. Europe, Russia and minor Balkan principalities apart, became a continent of republics or constitutional monarchies. In these, first adult male suffrage, then, after World War II, *universal* adult suffrage became the rule.

At the outbreak of World War I, the central headquarters of the International, two men and a typist, lacked the resources, even had it possessed the will, to organize effective opposition. Nowhere in 1914 did the socialists form a government. Nowhere did they possess the power to dismiss by their parliamentary vote a government already in office. In many countries, notably in Belgium, the Netherlands and Italy, also in France, Germany and elsewhere, confessional political parties and trade unions, organized around one version or another of the Christian religion, challenged the socialist for working-class allegiance. Just the same the socialists had possessed a vastly exaggerated view of their own ability to prevent a war amongst the major powers, and were disproportionately disoriented as a result of their failure.

The collapse of the Russian autocracy, the abdication of the tsar, the end of the monarchy which came about in March 1917, were followed in October by a *coup d'état* conducted by a largely unknown faction of the hitherto quite unimportant Social Democratic Labour Party of Russia. Renaming their faction the "Communist" Party in March 1918, the Bolsheviks took the first steps towards the establishment of a world party, itself a facsimile of that now ruling in Russia, with the foundation of the "Communist" International, the so called "Third" International, in March 1919. Funded on a vast scale from its base on the territory of the former

tsarist empire, attracting many of a new generation of radicals formed by World War I, the
Comintern within a decade established a "national section", with all its activity under the day-to-day direction of the Executive Committee of the Communist International in Moscow, in every major nation of the world. Comintern publicists insisted that the dividing line between communist and "social democrat" lay between reform and revolution. Except perhaps in 1919–20 this was never true. Rather the divide lay between those who considered Soviet Russia the present image of the future ideal society in the West, its leaders above criticism, worthy of blind support; and those who continued, more wisely, to maintain independent criteria of judgement of their own. Convinced that the socialist parties were themselves the most dangerous enemies of the working class, the Comintern devoted the larger part of its considerable organizational energy to encompassing their destruction. The resulting dissension caused working people throughout Europe grave harm. The Comintern's original exaggerated and violent revolutionism caused grave concern to the threatened ruling élite and caused it to take countermeasures of its own. This was especially so in the territories bordering Russia. It was also true elsewhere. In Italy the offensive of militant fascism found the by now gravely disunited socialist movement quite unable to resist Mussolini's march to power. In Germany the communists from 1928 until some time after Hitler's victory regarded the Nazis as a lesser danger than the socialists, thus clearing the way for Hitler. In these years the Fascist and Nazi parties learnt the technique of mass organization from the labour movement, added their own techniques of mass agitation derived from commercial advertising, modelled their military-style party moving at the command of a single leader on that created by Lenin, changed only the verbiage, and kept the essential structure intact.

Before 1914 few socialists had been inclined to credit capitalism with a long life yet to live. William Morris in his Utopian romance *News from Nowhere* scheduled its demise for 1952. Few of his contemporaries, one imagines, expected "the Revolution" to be delayed so long. In fact slump, depression, the dissension caused by the artificially induced communist split, largely halted the socialist and trade-union advance in the inter-war decades. Fascism conquered first in Italy, Germany and Austria, then by armed aggression extended its dominion to the whole continent.

The 20th century did not introduce the promised millennium at all. Instead it proved the most bloody in human history. In addition to the many millions killed in the two world wars – principally in Europe – eight million Europeans, six million of them Jews, died in the Nazi gas chambers; perhaps 20 million more perished in Russia's "collectivization" or else died in the forced labour camps of the Soviet regime. In eastern Europe, once the war was over, communist activists who arrived in the baggage train of the Red Army were installed by the Russians in power. In the West by contrast communist partisans peacefully surrendered their arms, and communist leaders joined with Christians, Conservatives and Liberals to contribute the decisive force to the stabilization of the gravely shaken capitalist regime.

The post-war crisis of 1945–50 once surmounted, capitalism in western Europe, contrary to much radical prognosis, has proved surprisingly stable. Eastern Europe under "socialism" by contrast has undergone repeated convulsions. Outright armed revolution against communist one-party rule took place in Hungary during 1956. A new near-overturn, this time peaceful, came close to succeeding in Czechoslovakia during 1968. There were near insurrections in East Germany and at Poznan in Poland during 1953. A series of major convulsions in Poland during 1970, and again during 1976, resulted in much bloodshed and cost many lives. Only the threat of Russian invasion has until now ensured the survival of Poland's profoundly unpopular communist regime. The range and extent of these events far outshadow the riots in Paris during May 1968. Had they taken place anywhere in the West they would appear in popular memory as full-scale "revolutions".

In the post-war years, especially from the 1960s onwards, the advanced industrial nations have reached levels of affluence hitherto unimagined. Immigrant workers, old people, especially the unskilled with large families, continue to experience hardship and poverty. Just the same the routine suffering which throughout the centuries scarred the whole substance of working people's life has now become almost unknown. The welfare state, first introduced by the Labour Government in Britain during 1945–50, now, thanks to working-class pressure, finds its

counterpart in every major European nation. Television sets, motor-cars, hi-fi, package
holidays abroad, now become articles of mass consumption for the first time. Slums have remained and become increasingly the preserve of newly arrived immigrant workers. Nevertheless the housing stock has been renewed at an astonishing rate. German cities, formerly in ruins, were rebuilt well before the 1960s were out. In Britain low-rent council housing came to represent millions of dwelling units, a very large proportion of the total housing stock. Much of the character of working-class life changed almost beyond recognition. Full employment through the 1940s, 1950s and 1960s and the relatively high level of unemployment benefit thereafter have largely ended the terror of being "out of work" which haunted all previous working-class generations. The National Health Service in Britain, the systems of "socialized medicine" which now exist in most other advanced industrial societies, have brought reasonably satisfactory medical treatment within the reach of all working people, irrespective of income, for the first time. The scale and pattern of such benefits differ but overall their range tends to become more and more the same. Britain, formerly a leader in wages, conditions and social-service benefits, now increasingly falls behind. France, Germany and the Scandinavian countries blaze the trail ahead. The standards of living of many European workers begin to approach, even to pass, those of the United States for the first time.

Capitalism in western Europe has by far surpassed even the most right-wing socialist's past expectations. "Socialism" in Russia, Poland and Czechoslovakia, by contrast, continues to leave left-wing socialist hopes largely unfulfilled. The gap in living standards, East Germany only excepted, does not diminish, despite growth in overall output. If anything, it has probably increased. Liberty, long promised as the final forthcoming fruit of future economic development, fails to blossom too. Measured in simple monetary terms (Russia excepted) eastern European societies appear more egalitarian than their counterparts in the West. However the ruling communist oligarchy benefits from so many hidden non-monetary privileges that even here appearance is likely to prove profoundly deceptive. "Capitalism", it is true, in the main has been abolished. Yet that the workers in any meaningful sense control the means of production vested in the state is not worthy of reasonable belief. In Spain and Portugal fascist regimes of more than 40 years' standing have peacefully given way to forms of bourgeois democracy. In Europe today only the communist states continue to remain rigid and immobile, neither able nor willing to devolve political and economic power downwards towards their own working people.

The modern mass labour movement, the organized public expression of the worker's separate class interest, his distinctive social aspirations, has increased in power enormously since its birth around a century ago. No state in western Europe any longer can be governed without taking note of labour's will. In Scandinavia, Britain, Germany, Belgium, the Netherlands, increasingly also in France and Italy, the working-class parties are perceived less and less as parties of opposition, and increasingly as parties of government. There is no reason to suggest that this tendency will be reversed. All the evidence suggests that the process will advance still further in the years to come. Perhaps more important, although largely neglected in the respective canons of bourgeois and socialist thought, is the ever increasing power exercised by the trade unions and their members, both at the point of production and in the economy overall. Not only the government of the nation but also the management of economic enterprise, the elaboration and enforcement of a coherent economic policy, becomes increasingly impossible without the participation and assent of representatives of working people. The once disfranchised masses, having largely made good their claim to a proper share of sovereignty over the nation, are now making a long-overdue demand for an equivalent share of sovereignty over economic decision-making as well. In Britain over 12 million of the 22-million-strong work force are organized in trade unions; 300,000 individuals serve as shop stewards. There is one worker representative to every 40 members of the organized work force overall. In continental Europe the degree of unionization increasingly moves upwards towards a similar level. Works-council and shop-steward representation little by little begins to "encroach" on management prerogative to a similar degree. The horizon of the workers' world in each country is widening. The worker in Europe is demanding the right to be consulted, to have a voice in control, to an ever greater degree.

As the commodity market widens, and the obligatory level of advertising, basic research
and capital investment increases, so the scale of production must expand in line. The
phenomenon, to be observed in an ever wider range of products, is excellently typified by the
automobile. In post-1945 years auto production in Europe, at first negligible, has risen first to
challenge, then to surpass, that of the United States. In order to maintain their market share the
US giants, Ford, General Motors and Chrysler, have been forced to diversify into Europe (Ford;
Opel-Vauxhall; Chrysler-Simca). Renault, Volkswagen, FIAT, Volvo in turn have been driven
to diversify both inside and outside Europe, even to the extent of establishing their own
assembly operations in the USA. FIAT, under contract, has built Russia's largest auto plant at
Togliattigrad. Poland manufactures FIAT automobiles under licence, as do other eastern
European states. Peugeot has bought out Chrysler UK, thus extending its operations from
France to England. Meantime Chrysler has contracted to buy 200,000 auto engines a year from
Mitsubishi, Japan, in which it owns a 15 per cent share, from 1981 onwards. British Leyland will
have to negotiate its own version of the Chrysler-Mitsubishi or the Peugot-Chrysler deal with
one of its giant European rivals if it is to survive.

Hitherto, although socialist ideology has sought with some success to inculcate a *sentiment*
of international solidarity in the work force, worker *interest*, in consequence of the limited local
regional and national market size, has remained much more provincial. The new pattern of
production and marketing in auto makes it plain that industrial bargaining will be taking place
at international level in Europe well within the next decade. Where auto leads, other industries,
aerospace, chemicals, electronics, are likely to follow suit. The proposals for a common
European currency, the call for a coordinated European economic policy to end the slump, to
bring back work to the *six million* European workers currently unemployed, are likely to
enhance the pace of such multi-national development still further.

The multi-national corporation, as the FIAT case demonstrates, by no means restricts its
operations to the West. Pepsi-Cola now markets Russian vodka in the "imperialist" countries.
In exchange for this concession communist-controlled state agencies reserve to themselves the
monopoly on the distribution of Pepsi-Cola in Russia. The era of "Vodka-Cola Communism"
has already arrived. Failure successfully to innovate causes the communist hierarchs in the East
anxiously to seek to import high technology from its sole possessor, the capitalist multi-
national giants of the West. The oligarchs of communist and capitalist super-corporations speak
a common language and understand one another very well. Increasingly capitalist corporations
build their new manufacturing plants in the East and find their loans repaid by the supply of
low-cost commodities, which are then marketed under their own brands, through their own
agencies, in the West. These east European plants are strike-free. All attempts at worker
resistance are summarily quelled. The resulting unification of the productive systems must
cause trade unionists in the West increasingly to seek the establishment of free trade unions, of
genuine collective bargaining in the East. Their counterparts in the East, however tardily, will
seek to achieve, to consolidate, the gains their colleagues in the West have already made. This
will prove to be one of the inexorable consequences of *détente*.

The rulers of Russia and eastern Europe seek to convince their own subject populations,
and with them public opinion in the West, that their rule, like that of the Medes and the
Persians before them, will last for ever. The Apocalypse has arrived. In the East we are asked to
believe that "history" has ended, that there will be no more "time". In due course, sooner or
later, inexorably, capitalism will collapse. The "soviet" system will rule supreme.

In fact, far from "history" being ended, the regimes in eastern Europe remain so backward
that for them modern history has scarcely begun. The rulers of Russia in particular face such
problems that their survival much beyond the immediate future seems highly unlikely. Soviet
"socialism" is not at all the pattern of the "wave of the future". Well before the end of the
century it is likely to appear as an ephemeral, highly aberrant special case. When the Soviet
system disintegrates, the communist regimes in their present form in eastern Europe assuredly
will rapidly fall into ruins as well.

"Euro-Communism", to the extent that it is something more than a diplomatic manoeuvre, a multi-national communist corollary of the Helsinki Agreement, a passing counterpart
of *détente*, in itself represents a recognition that the Soviet experiment has failed and can no

longer be accepted as the obligatory universal model by the communist parties of the West. This in turn involves the belated recognition that the very decision to split the socialist movement in itself was an error. If Russia is not the embodiment of the socialist ideal, if revolution on the Russian model is accepted as a chimera, there is nothing left for the communist parties to do but disband. The decline and fall of communist rule in Russia inexorably must bring with it the disintegration of the communist parties in Europe as well.

During the 20th century the productivity of labour, the overall total of social wealth in Europe, has risen faster than at any time in history. Working-class living standards have increased to a degree that in an earlier age would have been deemed quite impossible. Just the same wide social differences, structural causes of class antagonism, still remain. Western capitalism in its present form assuredly will not last for ever. Private, corporate ownership of the means of production, however, is unlikely ever to be replaced by Party-Church ownership on the Russian state model. Instead, as educational levels rise, as worker horizons rise in turn, so union bargaining power is likely to encroach ever more deeply on managerial prerogative. Just as the First and Second Internationals raised the cry for the workers' right to vote in the state a full century ago, now the demand that sovereignty within the economic enterprise shall be transferred from owners to workers will begin to be heard in an exactly similar way. The voice indeed already achieves a certain resonance in the world of affairs and influences government and entrepreneurs in countries as diverse as Britain, the Netherlands, Norway, Germany, Belgium and France. As yet outside Yugoslavia it has won no gains in eastern Europe. Here the rulers with reason fear that to devolve significant economic authority upon their subjects would rapidly undermine, and in due course shatter, their present illegitimate monopoly of political power. In the end it is likely to triumph there just the same.

# 5

# *The Poor*

## OLWEN HUFTON

"A peste, fame et bello libera nos domine." We must respect the priorities of this medieval prayer for they tell us something of the fears which haunted the common people of Europe for most of recorded history. All were killers. The most spectacular and instant was pestilence, at its worst in the form of bubonic plague, transmitted by the fleas that prey on rats and men, which ravaged Europe at least three times: the first time in the final years of the Roman Empire when the population was probably cut back from 60 to about 27 million, the second in the 14th century when the Black Death eventuated in immense disruption, and for the last time in the late 17th and early 18th centuries. Famine, attendant upon chronic harvest failure, was a more constant visitor. Grain yields were low; communications, with few exceptions, were poor; and most communities, confronted with a reduced harvest, the product perhaps of freak weather conditions – excessive rain in the north and west, drought in the south – or of devastation by insects, grain weevil or locust, could expect little relief from outside until the mysterious disappearance of generalized famine in the opening decades of the 18th century. Of the ravages of war, little need here be said. War did not take civilian life on a massive scale. But the Viking or Hun of the Dark Ages, whose maraudings pushed the poor husbandman into a fortified village or caused him to seek the protection of some seigneur in return for the cession of his land, or the armies of Habsburg and Bourbon, locked in dynastic confrontation centuries later, were equally contemptuous of the peasant whose fodder and stores were seized by armies which lived off the land. "A peste, fame et bello . . ."

The poor of medieval Europe were people cognizant of their exposure to this triple threat. In the early Middle Ages lack of manpower and an abundance of land ensured ready employ for the able-bodied man and his family. There was perhaps no problem of endemic poverty but famine and pestilence could in any year eradicate entire communities. The violent conditions of the times precipitated the peasant in search of protection into a seigneurial relationship, and protection was meant to extend to more than immunity from Viking attack. The manorial economy was a collective one in which there was a speculative amount of protection – at least for the temporarily incapacitated – by communal effort, and domainal revenues were the surplus guaranteeing some buffer against harvest failure. It was, however, relatively easy to fall through the planks of manorial society. The lord was no philanthropist and to cope with those who did so there existed the fail-safe of monastic relief. Embodied in the Christian ethic was the concept of holy charity. Ecclesiastic revenues were according to canon law divided into two parts, *necessitas* and *superfluae*, the first for the upkeep of clerics, the second for the sustenance of the poor. Every monastic house made some provision found enshrined in monastic statute by which hosteler and porter were precisely instructed in how much bread and what shelter should be accorded. Let us take the statutes of the Abbey of Corbie founded in 822:

Each of the twelve poor people who shall pass the night shall receive his loaf, and in the morning another half-loaf as food for his journey . . . The five wheaten loaves must be divided between the travelling clerks who shall be taken to the refectory and by the sick who are fed here. This distribution of bread we entrust to the hosteler: he shall decide what is to be done if it should happen that the number of poor people increases . . .

There are two significant parts to this passage: one is the extent of relief envisaged, the other is the ambiguity reigning if the numbers demanding should be altered. Medieval relief was formulated to cope with small societies in which manpower was at a premium. This need not obscure medieval misery: malnutrition attendant upon diet deficiences – particularly fresh food, fruit and vegetables; the constant living with pain and deformity; and the virulence of quite minor epidemics among ill-nourished people, dwelling overclose to scrawny animals and huddled in shacks to defend themselves against cold winters. Yet what was radically to transform the lot of medieval man was demographic growth without the economic growth to support it. By the late 12th century, certainly by the 13th and most strikingly by the 14th, settled Europe knew a marked demographic upswing and the manifestations of population pressure. Land remained to be brought under control but the business of clearing forest and heath was expensive, work for an entrepreneur, who inevitably waited for demand to make his investment worthwhile. The old three-field system of crop rotation scarcely replenished the soil and, most significantly of all, demographic upsurge altered the relationship between man and lord. The seigneurial system had been evolved to protect the one and furnish a surplus for the other in an environment in which land had no value without the men to work it. But when men multiplied, lords adopted two dangerous attitudes. First, since manpower was abundant, there was little need to fix it by offering land in return for work: it could be hired and dismissed at will. Secondly, when bread grain was in demand, the surplus producer was placed in an economically advantageous position. Hence the juxtaposition of the increasingly rich and the progressively poor.

The protective nature of the manor was replaced by the concept of the landed estate run on businesslike principles. The emancipation of many European peasants reflected their weakness rather than their strength. Unable to make a living in the countryside, they drifted towards towns hoping that they might find work or that monasteries or urban authorities or overt begging would in some way assuage their plight. Poverty was born in the countryside, but it manifested itself in its most frightening form in towns. Undernourished people were fodder for epidemics, caught in what we have since come to call the Malthusian population-subsistence scissors: that is, given the problem of maintaining the precarious balance between population and supply, the only resolution was that of two natural checks, famine and disease, which rising at intervals applied ruthless shears to a growing populace whose demands were rapidly outstripping food production. In a 14th-century context the Black Death thus trimmed the fringes of society and gave us some of the earliest visual memorials of the lot of the poor, those who lived in rat-infested dwellings and hence were the principal victims of the disease borne by fleas. On a fresco of the Last Judgement by Orcagna in Santa Croce in Florence a number of cripples with dark sunken eyes await the onslaught of pestilence, hands outstretched for alms from passers-by who gave them a wide berth to escape the possible contamination of touch. Yet there is life in these degraded beings and they are no easy acceptors of imminent death. Moreover, each one knows all the ploys and stratagems needful to draw the attention of more affluent society to his plight. He can deceive, steal, cajole, coerce. Poverty, in spite of the evangelists, is a corrupting process and revulsion rather than pity secured more donors. By the onslaught of the Black Death, European thought distinguished several types of beggars and a hierarchy of worthiness. It knew deserving and undeserving poor; the one the sick, aged, crippled, weak or unemployed but emphatically worthy; the other the deceiver ready to use tricks and violence to achieve his ends.

Yet until the 16th century no fundamental onslaught was made upon the obligation of the Christian to help *all* his weaker brethren. In part this might reflect an "easy" 15th century in which the cutback achieved by famine and plague purchased a breathing space in which work was more easily obtained or the fact that the existence of a wealthy church with theoretical obligations to the poor obviated the necessity for the rest of society to formulate fresh provision and hence to dip into its pockets. Masaccio's frescoes in Santa Maria del Carmine in Florence

remind us that the crippled soldier and the one-eyed, the leper and the old man past work, did
not suddenly vanish from the 15th-century street, from church porch and marketplace. Yet for
a century their imprecations did not disturb the tenor of urban life. Two factors were
dramatically to reverse that situation. The first and most important was another demographic
upsurge. Far more obliquely, the second (in face of the first) comprised attempts radically to
restructure the principles on which charity was based, transferring it from a voluntary donation
to an obligatory levy. Perhaps the Italian wars, the French Wars of Religion and the Thirty
Years' War, by making ever increasing tax demands, by marauding armies and when peace
came by disbanded soldiers, also created localized problems. Notwithstanding, when in the
16th century the beggar, in Eileen Power's graphic phrase, leapt into literature, it was as a
victim of population growth unsupported by economic expansion. The period 1525–1660 is one
of agrarian disturbance in which one sees the subsistence farmer squeezed by the demands of the
state and seigneur, the latter no longer necessarily the owner of the peasant's land but the
owner of quit rents and obligations which encumbered that land and which, since they were
levied in kind, became a steady source of revenue in an inflationary situation. The same French
or German seigneur by encroaching upon traditional rights of commons and woodland, and the
English lord of the manor assuming control of common land and enclosing on his own account
erstwhile open fields divided into myriad strips, were essentially about the same business:
making money while produce prices were high. The participants in the peasant wars which
erupted in Germany in 1525 detailed in a manifesto the grievances they intended to redress:

> Game, wild fowl and fish are to be free as God created them. Woods, unless duly purchased, to
> revert again to the community.
> Fuel from the woods to be free to all. The next complaint is in regard to the excessive services
> demanded of us, which are increased from day to day . . . All services beyond the contract to be
> paid for in wages.
> Rents to be revised in accordance with the value of the land . . .
> Common pastures and fields to be restored . . .

But though the peasantry sought an immediate culprit for their plight, their real problem
was that of numbers and a primitive agriculture. In the mountainous regions of the Pyrenees
and Languedoc it is possible to trace the inching of communities up mountainsides and into
marginally productive lands during periods of pressure; in arid Italy and Spain such a palliative was out of the question because the logistics of irrigation were beyond the resources
of communities. The excess dispossessed of the countryside had no option but to throw
themselves upon the mercy of the towns and, confronted with these inflated numbers, 16th-
century cities (and ultimately governments) responded one after another with a policy for poor
relief which marked a radical point of departure from the medieval spirit of voluntary alms-
giving, and this even in countries where ecclesiastical wealth had not been distrained by the
Protestant state. Indeed the first of these was formulated and executed in Flanders at Ypres in
1520 working on a suggestion laid down by the Spanish humanist Juan Luis Vives and was
rapidly emulated by Flemish and French cities – the most noteworthy in the Aumône Générale
of Lyons founded in the 1530s. In these cities a tax was levied upon all citizens owning houses
and administered by a central organization specially created to assess the needs of the poor.
Protestant theologians perforce gave themselves over to the problem. The new national
churches were state-directed and the state must therefore assume functions hitherto the work
of the Church. This is not to say that they abandoned the vocabulary of Christian charity but
that the deflection of the wealth of monasteries and bishoprics to the state coffers shifted on to
the shoulders of the state the responsibility for the succouring of the needy. In *The Common Chest*
(1525) Luther specifically evolved the concept of a parish tax with lay administration on the
model of Juan Luis Vives. Calvin and Zwingli leant more towards a tax upon a particular
congregation organized by church elders to help the needy of that congregation, a model later
most specifically adopted by the Dutch. The fact that the onus of reorganization lay in the long
run with the state did not mean immediate state intervention: rather the state looked to the
parishes to make their own, but eventually, as the provisions of the Act of 1601 show in
England, the state tried to accelerate parish action.

The question of two kinds of charity, one religious and voluntary, one lay and obligatory, sparked off a significant debate which began in the 16th century and which in some instances was still going on at the turn of the 20th. This debate centred upon the rectitude of stripping the rich of the means of personal salvation by the exercise of freely undertaken charitable donations. If it is harder for a rich man to enter the kingdom of God than for a camel to pass through the eye of a needle, and if the one means of salvation for such an individual was to give freely to the poor, then it was of crucial significance to preserve the religious and voluntary aspects of giving. The Tridentine Councils admitted the failure of the medieval Church to cope with the problem of poverty and underlined the need to look afresh at the situation but refused to abandon the basic principle of voluntary rather than obligatory charity.

In the course of the great debate in Catholic Europe, and in the midst of municipal and parochial initiatives in Protestant Europe to formulate provisions for local relief, the concept of the deserving and the undeserving poor was carefully spelt out with unprecedented precision. In Spain, for example, a Benedictine monk Juan de Medina in a tract of 1545 drew a distinction between the "true" poor, who deserved help because of age, illness and other personal circumstances, and the "false" poor, capable of work but persuaded that it was easier to live on the alms of the faithful. Protestant towns like Aberdeen, concerned that a local tax should succour only the known (and therefore verifiable) needy and that the news of an established fund for the poor should not bring in hordes of beggars from the surrounding villages which would either push up the tax to unrealistic dimensions or nullify its effect, erected, as every other town did, provision specifically excluding the outsider from relief.

> The said day, the haill toun, burgessis and craftismen, etc., the mater concerning the prouision for the pure being opinlie decleirit to thame be the bailleis and minister ... and the puir being devydid in four rankis, to wit, in babis, decayit persones houshalderis, leamit and impotent persones, and in sic as war decrepit and auld, borne and bred within this burght, at the leist that hes maid their commoun resort and residence within the same be the space of thir sevin yeris bypast ...

The French evolved a vocabulary of extraordinary complexity – *pauvre, le vrai pauvre, le mauvais pauvre, pauvre valide ou invalide, pauvre honteux, indigent, misérable, nécessiteux, mendiant de profession, mendiant de bonne foi, mendiant volontaire, sédentaire* etc. – which sought to draw fine distinctions between those who had had their situation thrust upon them and those who had opted for a life of poverty-stricken idleness. Only the former merited help. Yet that such people truly did need help no one questioned: how, not if, was the major stumbling block. There was another. Both the great debate and attempts to define the deserving poor were conducted without reference to the socio-economic environment. Until well into the 18th century population movement was assumed constant, a birth replacing a death in perfect proportions, and until the mid-18th century the existence of sufficient work was taken for granted. The able-bodied beggar was hence regarded as work-shy, *unless* he was known to have dependent upon him children and aged relatives who made it impossible for him to live off his wage because nowhere in the conditions of the 16th, 17th, 18th or much of the 19th century was the wage earner or smallholder expected to be able to support more than himself and a couple of children by his own efforts. Indeed this was a significant aspect of mercantilist thought which believed men would only labour if forced to do so to remain alive and that the wage was allied with the costs of production and must be kept low if goods were to remain competitive. It was easy then to countenance need when dealing with the widow, the large family, the old and the sick, those unemployed because of slump, or hungry because of a diminished harvest, but no one looked beyond that. The lusty beggar, the vagrant, was a criminal. Even Catholic social thought could not in the main countenance him and was prepared to leave him to penal legislation.

From the 16th century, society converted the wandering poor into criminals but declared a responsibility towards its concept of the deserving poor. For example the empowering of magistrates to levy a parish rate ceded in England in 1601 and taken much further in Scandinavia in the 1680s when, in Denmark at least, the deserving poor were ceded a legal right to relief, expresses Protestant recognition of that responsibility – though *how* relief should be accorded was nowhere expressly laid down. In Catholic Europe the exhortations of the Council of Trent were taken up by the Jesuits in Spain, Portugal, France and Italy and in the early 17th century found their greatest disciple of all time in St Vincent de Paul, who was to provide the Church in France in particular with a seemingly comprehensive scheme of poor relief, one which was to have unexpected repercussions even upon Protestant Europe. St Vincent's starting point was an acceptance of "honest poverty" and a reiteration of the obligations of every Christian towards those who fell below a certain threshold because of age or infirmity. He envisaged those farmsteads with a little to spare helping the poor family by welcoming its children for simple repasts – bread, milk, a bowl of soup – and by allowing the old and tired to warm themselves by the kitchen fire. The spirit of St Vincent was captured in the paintings of the Le Nain brothers, where the meals, shared by substantial and lowly, of bread and wine recalling the eucharist, and the careful emphasis upon the beggar at the hearth, all encapsulated Tridentine principles. But St Vincent went further; in conceiving the idea of an incapacitated poor, old and infirm without families to support them, children abandoned by their parents, cripples unable to fend for themselves, he and his disciples moved on to the evolution of the *hôpital général*, an institution founded by pious bequests under the aegis of bishops, chapters and municipal authorities – it did not matter whether the management was lay or ecclesiastical – and run by a whole spate of new religious orders who responded to the call of the need of the poor, like the Sisters of Charity or those of St Joseph du Puy. The French government, attracted by the idea of clearing the streets of its poor, seized upon the *hôpital général* as a cheap way of coping with the problem of poverty but took matters in 1684 a stage further. Though it could not, because of the voluntary nature of donations, force the foundation of *hôpitaux*, it could enact legislation insisting that anyone caught in the act of begging should immediately be taken to an *hôpital général* where his needs would be assessed and work given to him if he was capable. The nursery of Cartesian rationalism, with remorseless logic, produced the idea of locking up its poor, *le grand renfermement des pauvres*, a principle to be adopted throughout Europe and which in England gave rise to the workhouse.

Needless to say, no institution was in 17th-, still less 18th-century conditions, capable of performing the miracle of removing the pauper from the public gaze or of assuaging the overall problem of poverty. In Catholic Europe, constantly beset by the problem of wresting funds from a progressively unresponsive populace, in Protestant England, directed with scandalous parsimony by parish officials concerned with keeping the rates as low as possible, neither *hôpital général* nor 18th-century workhouse enjoyed any chance of realizing the government's fantasies. They merely underscored the hopelessness of the lot of the man, woman or child condemned to seek public relief. Moreover, from the second decade of the 18th century, Europe as a whole embarked upon steady if unspectacular demographic growth (in some cases less than an annual rate of 1 per cent), the product perhaps of the dying out of plagues and of generalized harvest failure, or perhaps of improved communications permitting speedier relief to areas with localized disasters, but growth which without cutback was to broaden the base of the social pyramid more widely than ever before and to result in the proliferation of people experiencing difficulty in making ends meet. These might be smallholders whose farms were fractionalized by each generation, or day labourers condemned to sell their labour in a bloated market – in either instance the smallholding and labouring families formed the bulk of the poor who had to look to the generosity of the more affluent for survival. Where entire communities shared a common poverty, this might mean moving out, seeking in temporary or permanent migration a palliative in the form of work, begging or petty crime and hence emphasizing the futility of a workhouse relief founded on the principle of a lengthy residence in a particular parish. The poor did not sit back and wait for famine to overtake them. They shifted, singly or *en masse*, into towns and cities, towards areas offering temporary work, like the grape harvests of Languedoc and Gascony. They went on foot, begging their way, and, if back home lay a fragile holding, they returned in the same manner but, with luck, bearing a remittance which made it possible for those who had remained behind to hold on to life. Thus the Irish crossed the Irish Sea and made for the navvy's world of Whitechapel, Clerkenwell and Bermondsey-Southwark. Hated by every Londoner for their willingness to work for less, a hatred which erupted in every city riot and which Gordon and Wilkes alike knew how to exploit, their lodestar was a return to an oat or potato patch, a pig and a filthy mud-floored cabin. Thus the smallholder of the Campine

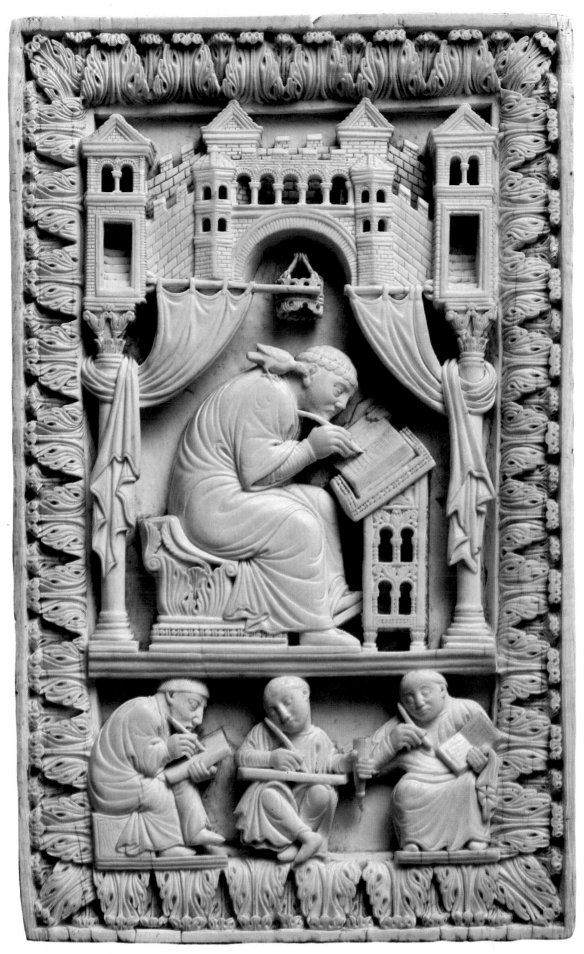

*16*. Gregory the Great (pope 590–604) and his monastic scriptorium. Ivory book cover, 10th century.

ET·HIC·EPISCOPVS·CIBV·ET·POTV·BENEDICIT·

17. An English banqueting scene. From the Bayeux tapestry, 11th century.

18. A page from the *Domesday Book*, a census compiled by order of William I of England in 1086.

1

DOVERE tempore regis Edwardi
reddebat .xviii. libras. de quibus
denarius habebat rex .E. duas partes.
& comes Goduin' tercia. Contra hoc
habebant canonici de sco Martino medietate alia.
Burgenses dederunt .xx. naues semel in anno ad .xv.
dies. & in una quaq; naui erant hoes .xx. & uii. hoc
faciebant pro eo qd eis pdonauerat sacca & soca.
Quando missatici regis ueniebant ibi: dabant pro
caballo transducendo .iii. denarios in hieme. 7 ii. in
estate. Burgenses u inueniebant sturemannu 7 unu
aliu adiutore. & si plus opus esset: de pecunia eius
conducebat. A festiuitate s Michaelis usq; ad
festu sci Andree: treuua regis erat in uilla. Siquis
eam infregisset: inde pposito regis accipiebat co
mune emendatione. Quicunq; manens in uilla
assiduus: reddebat regi consuetudine: quietus erat
de theloneo p tota Anglia. Omes he consuetudi
nes erant ibi. quando Witts rex in Angliã uenit.
In ipso pmo aduentu eius in Angliã: fuit ipsa uilla
cobusta. & ideo pciu eius non potuit coputari quantu
ualebat quando eps baiocensis eã recepit. Modo
appciatur .xl. lib. 7 tam ppositus inde reddit .l.iiii.
lib. Regi .xxiiii. lib de denar qui sunt .xx. in
ora: comiti u .xxx. lib ad numeru.
In douere sunt .xx.ix. mansure. de quib; rex pdit consue
tudine. De his habet Robt de romenel duas.
Radulf de curbespine .iii. Witts fili redaldi .i.
Witts fili ogeri .i. Witts fili redaldi 7 Robtus
niger .vi. Witts filius goisfridi .iii. in quib; erat
gihalla burgensiu. Hugo de montfort .i. domu.
Durand .i. Rannulf de columbels .i. Wadard .vi.
filius modbti una. Et in omib; de his domib; retio
cant epm baiocense ad ptectore 7 liberatore.
De illa masura quã tenet Rannulf de columbels que
fuit cuidã Galli: cordant qd dimidia tra est
regis. 7 Rannulf ipse habet utrunq;. Hunfridus
tenet .i. masura. de qua erat forisfactura dimidia
regis. Roger de Ostreha fecit quandã domu sup
aqua regis. & tenuit huc usq; consuetudine regis. Nec
dom' fuit ibi T.R.E. In introitu portus de douere
est unu molendin. qd oms pene naues confringit
p magnã turbatione maris. 7 maximu damnu fa
cit regi & hominib;. 7 non fuit ibi T.R.E. De hoc dicit
nepos herbera. qd eps baiocensis concessit illi
fieri auunculo suo herberto filio Iuonis.

Has infra scriptas leges regi cordant hoes
de .iiii. lastis. hoc e Stormarlest. 7 Estrelest.
7 Limuuarelest. 7 Wiuuarelest. Si quis fecerit
sepe uel fossatu pro quo strictior fiat publica
uia regis. aut arbore stante extra uia intra pro
strauerit. & inde ramu uel fronde portauerit:
pro una quaq; haru forisfacit' soluit regi .c. sot.
Et si aperte domu non apphensus uel diuadi
atus: tamen minister regis eu sequet 7 c. sold
emdabit. De gribrige u si quis ea fecerit & calu
niat' aut diuadiat' fuerit: .viii. lib regi emda
bit. Sin aute: quiet' erit erga rege. non erga
dnm cui homo fuerit. de aliis forisfacturis sicut
de gribrige. sed .p.c. sot emdabit. Has forisfac
turas ht rex sup oms alodiarios totã comitatus
de chent. 7 sup hoes ipsor. Et quando mortu
alodiarius: rex inde habet releuatione tre.
excepta tra s kuilricis 7 s Augustini. 7 s mar
tini. 7 Exceptis his. Godric de burnel. Godric
carlesone. 7 Alnod cilt. 7 Esber biga. 7 Sirei de
chilleha. 7 Turgis 7 Norman. 7 Azor. Sup istos
ht rex forisfactura. de capitalis eor tantu.
Et de terris eor ht releuamen. qui hnt suã saca
7 soca. Et de his tris scilicet: Gosthes. 7 Boche
land. 7 aliu Bocheland. 7 trciu Bocheland. 7 hec ste.
.i. tutiu de ora. 7 i. rutu de herce.
Schildricheha. Macheheue. Ernulsitone. Osta
dunnone. piriu. 7 alia piriu. Brulege. Ospringes.
horcone. ho rex has forisfacturas. hand soca.
Gribrige. forisfel. De adulterio u p totu cheil
ht rex homine. 7 archieps muliere. excepta
tra s kuilricis. 7 s Augustini. 7 s martini. de
quib; rex nichil ht. De latrone qui iudicat' est ad
morte: ht rex medietate pecunie ei. Et qui quale re
ceprt sine licentia regis: inde ht rex forisfactura.
De terris supnominatis Alnodi 7 similiu el: ht rex
custodia .vi. dieb; apud cantuaria. uel apud saniuic:
7 ibi hnt de rege cibu 7 potu. Si non habuerint: sine
forisfactura recedunt. Si fuerint pmoniti ut cueniant
ad seruitu: ibunt usq; ad pinnedenna. non longius. Et si
non uenerint: de hac forisfactura de aliis omib; rex
.c. sot habebit. excepta Gribrige que .vii. lib emdat.
7 de callib; sic supius scriptu e.
In Limuuarelest in brisceua ht rex consuetudine scilicet:
.iii. caretas. 7 ii. sucas anguillar. p uno snewiardo. 7 in
tra sophis ht .xii. den p uno snewiardo. 7 de uno iugo
de norchburia. xii. den aut unu snewiard. 7 de deia.
xviii. den. 7 de cara unu snewiard. He tre iacent in Wi:
7 hoes de his tris custodiebant rege apud cantuaria
l apud sanuuic p iii. dies. si p eos illuc uenisset.

uobis Beatus uir Quoamplius Beatus uir

rum amen Hec est Ecce concipies Secul

amen Cum ezro tuff & iob Sapiencia TR

OFAGIS

m & filio

sancto Sic

principio & n

20. A flautist from an 11th-century liturgical manuscript in Paris.

19. The poor and afflicted. Detail from the fresco *The Triumph of Death* (1349) by Andrea Orcagna, in Santa Croce, Florence.

*21.* The law school at Bologna, one of Europe's earliest universities. Detail from the tomb of Cino da Pistoia (1272–1337) in Pistoia cathedral.

*22.* Joan of Arc on trial for heresy in 1431. Illumination on a contemporary document.

*23. Overleaf:* A Portolano chart made by Freducci d'Ancona in 1497.

# In nomine domini amen ⸿

Incipit processus in causa fidei contra
quandam mulierem Johannam vulgariter dictam la
pucell...

**Univ**ersis presentes
litteras inspecturis peto... re-
vocatio... divina beneditio
... sit... Johannis magni
... festorum... divina hono...
... magnis religiosis... et... cura
... inspecturis... magistro
Johanni... in sacra pagina professore ...
... Inquisitore fidei de here... pravitatis
in toto Regno... simul explicata deputato in
diocesi... et ... speculator... ad presentem
processum in causa Domini Inquisitoris deputatus
... ... in ... fidei ... ...
fidei domini nostri Jesu Christi **placuit** ...
... mulierem ... Johannam vulgariter dictam
vulgo puella... ... ...
diversis de ... ... et ...
... mulier... ... rape de ...
... in licet ... mulierem
... ... ... Regni ... ...
... ... ... ... ...
...

24. Farming series in February. From *Les Très Riches Heures du duc de Berry* (1413).

25. Leisure pursuits in August. Ibid.

26. Craftsmen at work. Illumination from a 15th-century manuscript of the Jewish historian Josephus.

27. St Joseph portrayed as a medieval carpenter. Part of the Merode Altarpiece, a 15th-century triptych attributed to Robert Campin.

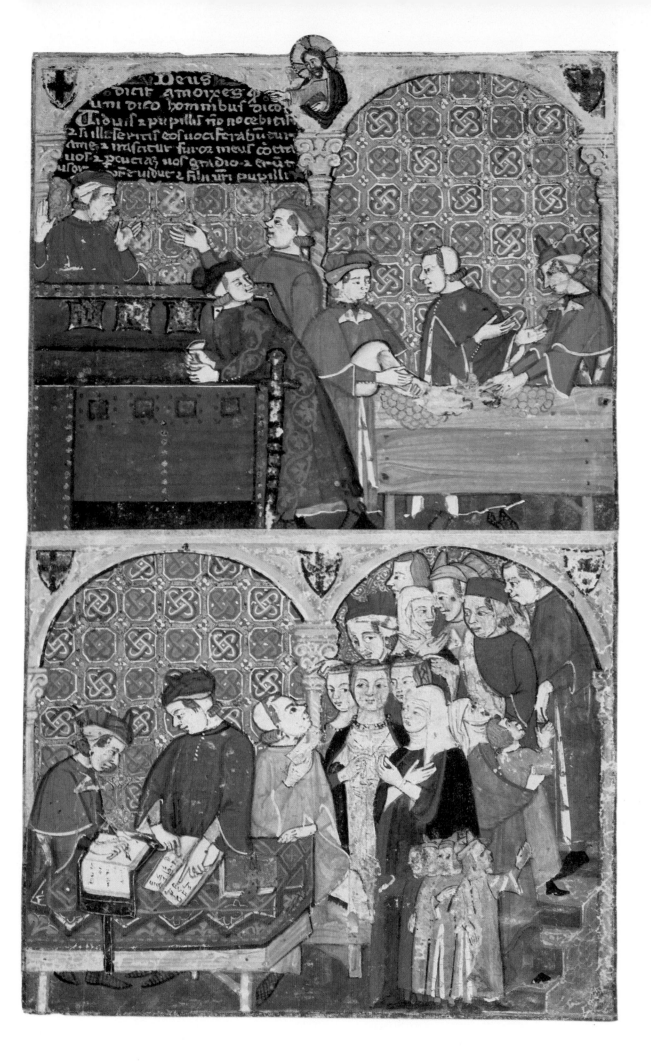

*29.* A 15th-century representation of merchants at Hamburg harbour.

*28.* Early banking scenes, probably at Genoa, from a 14th-century manuscript.

*30. Overleaf*: Self-portrait of the sculptor Adam Kraft. Detail from the Shrine of the Sacrament, begun in 1493, in the church of Sankt Lorenz, Nürnberg.

trudged to Hungary; the Cévennol spilled out on to the Mediterranean littoral, while the violent Auvergnat monopolized the coal-heaving and water-carrying jobs in Paris, and all to the same end. The Sicilian of our day, who in Common Market conditions digs tunnels and roads in the Swiss Alps and sends his solid francs back home, perpetuates sharecropping and the existence of minuscule holdings incapable of sustaining a family and is one of the few surviving bearers of a long European tradition.

In the history of poverty there is no more significant period than the 18th century. For not only did this emancipation from famine and plague create a larger number of poor than ever before and allow the European population to embark upon a remorseless upward move outstripping the pace of economic growth, but the very weight of numbers forced a radical reappraisal of the vital questions "who are the poor?" and "why are they there?" The 18th century was the age of counting heads and the census was progressively to make nonsense of the concept of a static population. Though Enlightenment thinkers despised the common people, they conceded that the wealth of nations depended upon their labour and hence that ideally government had obligations to ensure sustenance in exchange for labour. Knowledge was an uncomfortable experience for 18th-century administrators. The poor family leapt from litera-ture to swell crime statistics; the numbers of abandoned children doubled, tripled, quadrupled; the city ghettos were packed with rural immigrants visibly unemployed, and the monuments of private philanthropy could do nothing to contain them. Perhaps as much as 20 per cent of the French population lived constantly with hunger (and a further 20 per cent were exposed to that threat); the statistics available for Belgium suggest much the same pattern; for Great Britain a speculative figure of 10–15 per cent is offered. Moreover, we know exactly who these people were: they were the members of poor families, fathers, mothers, children, old people, temporarily or permanently infirm. The young man or woman unencumbered by family ties in good health had few problems. He or she might even put a little bit by to cushion some of the blows of marriage and a family. But for the smallholder or man dependent upon the work of his hands, this would never be enough. Debt would stalk him through his adult life: debt contracted when prices of vital commodities rose and wages lagged; debt contracted to counteract the effects of illness; debt which encumbered smallholdings yet further or which swallowed up the day labourer's wage when he regained his health. The road to indigence invariably lay through cumulative debt and through marriage and a family – yet if one did not marry and raise children, what shelter was there in sickness or old age?

The 18th-century working-class family was surprisingly small – 4·5 children. In con-tinental Europe the age of marriage was late, 28 for a man and 26 for a woman, and the menopause was probably relatively early, preceding 40. Yet three children could strain a restricted budget to an intolerable degree and in pre-industrial Europe a child was perhaps 10 or 12 before it could support itself by its labour. Hence for every adult man or woman on the lists of indigent, there were three or four times as many children and twice as many old and infirm. Whatever the conditions, anyone who created work which offered children a living was regarded as a philanthropist. The children of 18th-century Europe, without shoes on their feet or adequate clothing on their backs, touted their smaller brothers and sisters around fairs and markets to elicit pity in their supplications for a coin or a bit of bread; learnt the techniques of pickpocketing or salt smuggling; majored in metropolitan vices like the child prostitution of Mercier's Paris; scavenged the Thames and the seashore for driftwood; ran errands, hung around the dockland of Bordeaux, Marseilles, Amsterdam, Leghorn; climbed perilous chim-neys, peddled pins and needles and, only if fortunate, were apprenticed to tradesmen or textile workers. The silk industry of Lyons, a massive murderer of rural children who descended from the hills of Besse and Forez to be apprenticed to silk weavers, emptied and unwound cocoons, grew with limbs distorted by the loom, slept under the machinery and perished like flies from tuberculosis, was perhaps an indicator of the shape of things to come, though it is doubtful if a child's lot in pre-industrialized Europe was conspicuously better. The English establishment wallowed in Dick Whittington-type fairy stories wherein the industrious apprentice, however lowly his origins, could aspire to the highest social positions while the idle tended ineluctably towards Tyburn; but, at another level, the parishioners of Killem (Nord) in 1789 recognized philosophically, "il semble que c'est une chose décidée que le pauvre doit rester pauvre."

Moreover in 1791 the Comité de Mendicité set up by the French Constituent Assembly to replace voluntary charity by state assistance expressly recognized the inadequacy of the working man's wage to support more than himself and a couple of children and conceded the right of such an individual to apply for a subvention for subsequent offspring.

In the same vein the Berkshire magistrates, who in the aftermath of the worst winter in the annals of the 18th century, that of 1796, recognized the inadequacy of wage rates and used the parish rates to raise them to a minimum level in order to sustain the lives of the wage earner's dependants, stand out in the annals of poor-law history because the idea of a minimum standard to which every individual has a right is still today the basic premiss of social welfare provisions, albeit lent sophistication by the complications of the welfare state. In the conditions of the 18th century, given the numbers qualifying under such principles for relief, the French state did not have the means at its disposal to lend reality to its schemes. What Europe needed, like the third world today, was economic growth, and economic growth in two crucial directions: the first in supplying more food to feed more mouths – bread, grain or a carbohydrate substitute like potatoes or rice – the second in industrial growth to absorb the excess which could not be employed on the land. Both were obviously achieved in the course of the 19th and 20th centuries but the price of achievement for the poor of Europe in terms of human suffering was immense. The great reservoir of men, women and children who sought employment in the early factories (which more than any *hôpital* achieved *un grand renfermement des pauvres*), exploited in terms of hours of work, physical conditions and rates of pay to what would seem to be the limits of human endurance, have been described with graphic clarity by a venerable historical tradition. They were people without alternatives, responding like the medieval peasant in submitting to a seigneurial relationship to the sovereign imperative of the need to stay alive. What else drove the women who did the work of pit ponies down the mine or pushed parents into condemning their rickety children to the mercy of a cotton overlooker? Van Gogh's *Potato Eaters*, grey and dirty, have reached a basic rock bottom and to keep hunger away their labour must be unremitting. They are Zola's people. We should follow Maheude of *Germinal*, the miner's wife with a large family (pit fodder like Catherine, her eldest daughter) nourished on a mash of bread, potatoes, leeks and sorrel. Condemned to a perpetual borrowing here and there to ensure the next meal, trapped in the credit mesh of Maigrat the grocer upon whom the pit women eventually took their revenge, Maheude is ever ready to beg at the kitchen door of the gentry for her little ones, pushing anything extra on to Maheu's plate because of his labour in the mine and his leisure hours on the vegetable plot. Or we should be present when Annie, the Breton servant girl of *Dans Paris*, abused by entire regiments of impecunious employers, contemplates the baby she has herself delivered alone, before wrapping it in newspaper to leave at the foundling hospital and reflects that it is a girl whose fate can be no better than her own, because it perhaps demands literary genius to impress upon us the lack of alternatives in the lives of the poor.

From the medieval poor man's litany of famine, pestilence and war the last alone perhaps had truly receded by the 19th century, to be replaced by another bogeyman, slump. This could, overnight, lop off the earning power of men, women and children, leaving them resourceless. The great depression ending in the 1930s was the last and most generalized of such slumps. Plague had been replaced by other much less massive killers, waterborne diseases like Asiatic cholera and typhoid which were generated in the polluted water supplies of ramshackle dwellings and proved particularly deadly in cities. Carried by Irish immigrants even into the cities of the United States, cholera had an impact in recorded history second only to plague. Improvements in transport and the more generalized use of the potato until the mid-19th century in some way helped to keep the poor fed; but the potato famine of 1846–48, which took over a million Irish lives and precipitated a massive exodus to Liverpool and the New World, had its repercussions all over Europe. The year 1848 is significant in the annals of the poor as the last in which the poorest people of Europe (largely Irish) died in hunger on any significant scale. In other respects too the 1840s were an important turning point in the history of the European poor, though in terms of personal experience these hungry years must have seemed an all-time low. They were significant because, although an imbalance between demographic and economic growth still existed, the pace of the latter was accelerating and governments were stepping in to prevent some of the worst abuses of industrialization – long hours and the flagrant abuse of child labour. The first Factory Acts in Britain, France, Germany and Belgium emanate from the 1830s and 1840s. Public Health Acts rapidly followed. They were only a beginning and were without a proper inspectorate to enforce them, but they were a beginning.

By the 1850s real wages in Britain were rising, at least for textile workers, miners, transport workers, iron shipbuilders and engineers. Yet below them – and much more numerous – struggled agricultural workers and those in small, often partially domestic industries, hosiery, nail making, match makers, boot and shoe makers, tailors, dressmakers, ribbon makers, stay makers, embroiderers, straw plaiters for hats, pin makers, paper-flower makers – many of whom were women. Some of the most pitiful of these cases were found in capital cities. Let us take Haussmann's Paris in which many of the more insalubrious dwellings of the poor had been ripped down to construct the grand boulevards and where most women could earn a living only by doing the needlework that had given Paris its international reputation: on average, such labours averaged 2 francs a day. Rent, oil for light and charcoal for a footwarmer extracted, this left some 60 centimes, enough for bread and milk but nothing over to put aside say for a doctor's visit, or days without work. Small wonder prostitution comprised "the fifth quarter" of the seamstresses of the Rue Quincampoix and the Faubourgs. They belonged to the "sweated trades". Their English equivalents and the servant girls who joined them come to light as Dollymops in Mayhew and in Booth's London (1891) and Rowntree's study of York a decade later. These analysts posited that 31 and 28 per cent respectively of the total population of these cities fell below a poverty line whose criteria were a regular diet with a protein element, adequate shoes and clothing, housing which equalled something more than a damp cellar or attic, sufficient income to be able to afford a doctor's visit and all this without recourse to borrowing. These were of course criteria far more exigent than those applied by the Comité de Mendicité or the Speenhamland magistrates a century before. In short, an evaluation of poverty had changed as gross national income rose. The employer was no longer a philanthropist merely because he offered work since, for the first time in modern history, some kind of work was freely available. Moreover, the spectacle of two nations, one in want, drunken, violent, crime-prone, depraved and suffering, and another in ease, disturbed the conscience of the latter.

This is not to suggest that monuments of private philanthropy in the 19th century – like Octavia Hill's artisans' dwellings – made any more significant impact upon the lives of the poor than the *hôpital général* 200 years before. What changed the position of the poor in European society was economic growth and political realities: economic growth which lifted sufficient of them above the poverty line to make viable the assistance of the rest and the politicization of the skilled worker which lent weight to his demand for a bigger share of the national cake. Collective bargaining and the franchise were the sturdiest stepping stones to a more secure existence which came in the form of higher wages, rational working hours and social security for the sick, aged and the unemployed. But it was not an easy path as the heroes returning from World War I who were to enter a depressed economy were to discover.

There is no quick way to generalize about the history of the poor in the 20th century. Reference must be made above all to the evolution of the welfare state and the increasing ubiquitousness of the state in the economic life of nations. We must consider the complex implications of the state as a massive employer in welfare services, such as housing, medical provisions, education, and in nationalized industries and services and the ramifications of a hinterland of subsidiary industries upon which these industries repose. For the first time in the 20th century governments have been able at the stroke of a pen to opt for a full employment situation by injecting money into the economy and hence boosting spending on the lines Keynes explained so totally clearly. What governments have not been able to do is curb inflation at unprecedented levels, or, in the British case, solve the related balance of payment problems, and they have chosen as a means to deal with these bogies to allow unemployment to spiral, curbing spending power with the cold comfort of social security to sustain the workless and the promise of better days ahead. In the sense that Europeans no longer die with a few sorrel seeds in their stomachs or fall victim, through undernourishment, to minor epidemics, the 20th century marks a radical departure from the past. But there are many spectres too insistent to be put to rest. However innocent the unemployed, a society which has always historically defined a man's worth by reference to his work achievement can still contemplate them as second-class citizens, spongers on the public purse, like our *mendiants valides* or lusty beggars in 16th-century Aberdeen. We in the 1980s have devised no more comprehensive solution to the unemployed school leaver than government training schemes — thinly disguised successor of the 18th-century work project — involving in some instances public works like canal clearance which may, like the obelisks on Killiney Hill raised by the unemployed in the winters of the 1740s, or the "famine walls" of 19th-century Ireland in their time, remain as monuments to a confused post-Keynesian world.

British economic planning in the shape of pay policies is a direct inheritor of Speenhamland principles in which the lower-paid are shored up not by a living wage but by family allowances, rate rebates and free school meals. Even so their lot is perhaps easier and more dignified than that of an unemployed Black in the streets of Chicago or a "spic" in a New York barrio. Though conservative *laissez-faire* economies may no longer in the conditions of the mid-20th century permit men to die of hunger, there are evident victims like wetbacks or the Okies caught in Steinbeck's novels. It is, of course, possible to fall through the planks of the welfare state as the single-parent family, historically society's most vulnerable element, can still attest. Moreover, Europe's economic growth has been far from even. There are still *favellos* of tin and cardboard in Lisbon and the Portuguese are the European migrants of our day, the servant class of Paris, London, New York and Toronto. It is less than 20 years since Danilo Dolci drew attention to Sicily in which 47·1 per cent of the population were destitute or semi-destitute and the criteria for determining destitution those which might have been applied by Britain or France in the 18th century. The world's poorer nations now bring their problems into the developing world: Bangladeshi, Pakistani, Algerian, Turk, Mexican, Puerto Rican, West Indian, welcome enough as long as, as *Gastarbeiter*, they fill needed gaps in employment demands but resented, like the wandering poor of earlier centuries, at the first sign of recession. There are still signs of the existence of two nations but now more striking, as the kwashiorkor belly of the African or Asian child reminds us from the charity poster, is the existence of two worlds. The European may have passed a significant way-stage in his history but outside a world of poverty remains to be conquered.

# 6

# *Popular Entertainers*

## DILYS POWELL

On summer evenings the road from Athens to Epidaurus is busy with traffic – not simply the lorries which carry fruit and vegetables, tomatoes and fat green water-melons, from Argos to the markets of the capital, but private traffic, fast shiny cars with Athenians and tourists on a night out. They are on their way to a festival. In the ancient theatre at Epidaurus they will see a Classical play, perhaps a tragedy by Sophocles or Aeschylus; it was there I once saw the *Iphigenia in Tauris* of Euripides. The ancient text will have been translated into modern Greek; the Athenians as well as the tourists would have difficulty with the original, and so would the local people, the non-paying audience which has been known to appear outside the top rim of the semicircle of stone seats. The owls hoot softly in the darkness of the trees as the players declaim and the chorus circle and comment. It is an entertainment which has its roots in religious awe. The passage of history has bleached out the religion; this is a sophisticated evening. But in the vast, haunted setting the shadow of awe persists.

Leave the capital behind you and drive north or west to one of the provincial centres of Greece. You will find the relics of another tradition – the itinerant theatre. In one of the side streets of Jannina I have seen the vans waiting with the canvas scenery and the peasant costumes of folk drama. And for once the cinema, which has overlaid so much of Europe's historic entertainment, has become its celebrant. *The Travelling Players*, a major work of the Greek screen, has made a strolling theatre company the mirror of a terrible period. Through World War II, through Occupation, famine and the deathly upheavals of civil conflict, the players are shown performing a drama of tragic love. Their own lives are torn by private treachery, adultery, rage and revenge. But still they minister to the need for distraction. Their repertoire may lack the distinction of Hamlet's court theatricals. But what they have to offer is a fitting background for the political tragedy in which they are enveloped.

A gulf separates the Epidaurus Classical drama from the folk drama of the provinces. But both are alive, linked by the demands of an audience. To be puzzled or frightened, to laugh or weep, to be elevated, informed or dissolved in the pleasures of the absurd – the craving is always with us. The avalanche of the centuries has never extinguished the longing to be entertained and, conversely, to entertain. And in the gap before the Renaissance came to rekindle Europe, the Church, recognizing a basic human need, chose to present at the Christian festivals brief liturgical plays drawn from the drama of the Gospels.

Towns and villages enlarged and broadened what the Church had begun. The pageants which developed were themselves a kind of itinerant theatre, though their itinerary was limited; and the miracle plays which composed the programme were wheeled on movable stages through the city. Chester, for instance, presented a pageant of *The Deluge* and a pageant of

*Abraham, Melchisedec and Isaac*; Coventry had a Nativity play; Wakefield, which performed a Crucifixion, was famous also for *The Harrowing of Hell*.

The religious basis persisted. But the sacred and the profane have a habit of keeping company, and at times the religious theme was stood on its head. Pious, priest-ridden, the Middle Ages broke out in travesties of the sacred. Minor cathedral officials, especially in France, celebrated the Feast of the Circumcision by singing irreverent songs; they played dice on the altar; homage to the divine was translated into the Feast of Fools. No doubt *The Harrowing of Hell* was a popular draw. But one suspects that people liked the Feast of Fools even better.

At any rate one can already discern the easy coexistence of tragedy and farce, emotional drama and the undermining forces of satire. And looking back, one can see, here in medieval Europe and in the theatre of Europe's classical ages, the beginnings of all our entertainment, from Racine to stand-up comic.

Reading the historians on pre-Renaissance Europe one sometimes has the impression of a vast dangerous fairground, a Petrouchka ballet, grotesque, enshrining the whole of society. Of course one cannot know. One can only guess at the strands of that far-off web of life. But one thing strikes the modern reader: the change in the relationships between entertainer and entertained. The casts of the miracle plays were working people, members of a guild: masons, perhaps, or cordwainers, vintners or carpenters. *The Deluge*, appropriately enough, was the concern of the "Water-Leaders and Drawers of the Dee". *Abraham, Melchisedec and Isaac* was the business of the Barbers and Wax-Chandlers. The performers were not professionals, and so far as one can see no great barrier was set between them and their audience.

Today the classical actor, the popular singer or the variety star is segregated. We read about him. We think we know him, for his face, his gestures and his personality are daily exposed to us in the public prints. But we do not really know him. We live in an age of professionals, and he is not one of our lot.

Once I got into a train at a London terminus, found a seat, sat down – and was immediately aware of hostility. I looked across the carriage. Surely I knew those faces? They regarded me with curiosity, as if I were a specimen from a different branch of creation. And indeed I was. In my haste I had settled in a compartment reserved for a touring theatrical company. As, confused and apologetic, I bolted, I could feel their cold stares at my shoulder blades. It was not, I was sure, that I was an intruder in a private area. I was an alien who had no passport to their enclosed world.

The cinema has sharpened the alienation of the modern entertainer. The film star or the television actor is today's popular idol. We see him with an intimacy which the theatre never afforded. We see his wrinkles. We know about his toupee. We possess details of his dental equipment and his surgical history – for no public figure these days can have a private stomach. Nevertheless he is removed from us. He is doubly removed, for what we see is merely his shadow, black-and-white or coloured. And yet the bright shiners of the screen have often come from a medium which places the minimum of emphasis on the distance between performer and spectator. Charles Chaplin emerged from the English music hall; the variety stage it was that taught him the trick, so effective in the cinema, of the sudden brake on the full-tilt run. On a stage, after all, you can run only as far as the wings or the backdrop, then you must stop. In his old age Chaplin was to come back to Europe in clouds of glory, but it was in a knockabout music-hall team that he first went to the United States.

Again, Buster Keaton (to many of us greater than Chaplin) as a child took part in a family vaudeville turn; his father, he said, used to "wipe up the floor" with him. "When I gave no sign of minding this he began throwing me through the scenery, out into the wings, and dropping me down on the bass drum in the orchestra pit." Permissible, I think, to count Keaton as a European entertainer, for in a period of neglect and misfortune he resorted to the circus, and the European circus; it was in Paris that he performed until at the end of his career he returned to the cinema. Finally with *A Funny Thing Happened on the Way to the Forum* he adorned the British cinema.

To these great names one must add a pure European, Jacques Tati, who also came to the cinema via the music hall. A foreigner is apt to think of French variety as a matter of spectacle. The elaborate pattern of nudes on the Paris stage was a special treat to the English tourist –

until the human body ceased to be taboo, and naked figures of both sexes began to festoon what had once been the puritanical screen. But beside the spectacular one must set the individual performer. One must remember Mistinguett waving her famous legs at an idolatrous audience. One must remember Edith Piaf; once a street performer, she sang out her urchin heart to an audience which her recordings had made international. And one must remember Tati, the supreme pantomimist who took the essence of his music-hall turns and developed them into the wittiest, most observant and most humane of cinema comedy. And Tati brings another country into the catalogue, for Tati is part-Russian.

The famous comics, the elegantly acrobatic clowns (Tati says that comedy resides in the legs), even on the impersonal screen have to a certain extent preserved the intimate relationship with an audience which marks the music hall. For there intimacy is the secret. Think of the solitary figure on the stage projecting her voice to the dark high cavern at the top of the auditorium. "The boy I love", she sings, "sits up in the gallery." She has failed if every young man up there does not feel she is singing for him. But now something else, something as powerful as the cinema has intervened; something which may increase the size of the audience but which increases also the distance between the entertainer and the entertained. I mean the record album. Of course recording is a blessing for everyone living out of reach of the urban centres visited by the popular singer. But the alienation grows. In the cinema the shadow at any rate of the performer is present. With the growth of recording the performer has become merely a sound. Not always a true sound. For in the recording studio a performance can be recreated piecemeal. A high note can be clarified. A vowel sound can be sharpened, an intonation lifted; just as in the cinema a player can be given someone else's voice, and few in the audience will be any the wiser.

Many of the best of the European music-hall or variety or circus stars are long beyond recall; beyond the record album, beyond even the shadow images of the cinema. A few survive in the archives of the cinemathèques. There is a French film of Grock. *Au revoir, Monsieur Grock*, it is called; and since it was made with the cooperation of the distinguished clown and in the maturity of the cinema (the date is 1949) one may take it as a fair record. But for many of the famous British singers and dancers we have mere fragments of celluloid, blurred, faded, dead. Little Tich, for instance, who danced in boots with yard-long soles on to which he would suddenly leap and, perching, there balance himself – of Little Tich no more than a scrap of film exists, together with photographs – and memories. And drawings. England in the 19th century and the first decades of the 20th had artists in plenty to celebrate the figures of variety; for example one finds George Cruikshank illustrating a ditty sung by a popular performer.

Most of the illustrators, however, were of smaller calibre. The French did better, and one of their most brilliant artists it was who immortalized the café concert. People who might never have heard of Yvette Guilbert know what she looked like, know her profile, the curve of her neck and the long black gloves, worn as a measure of economy, which contrasted with her simple white dress. They have seen her through the eyes of Toulouse Lautrec. A whole era of Paris entertainment and Paris life is there in Lautrec: the dancers, the musicians, the onlookers. Just as Degas recorded without flattery the images of the ballet, so Lautrec and his fellows recorded the bold creatures of variety and the cabaret: Aristide Bruant, song writer as well as singer; Jane Avril in her wide black hat. And the images have a movement so powerful that the cinema, whose very name implies motion, has tried to recapture it. In the 1950s the American dancer Gene Kelly appeared on the screen in an impersonation of a grotesque and electrifying figure: *Chocolat*, Lautrec had called his original, *dansant dans le bar d'Achille*.

Not only the painters frequented the cafés and the theatres of Paris. Zola, describing his Nana appearing as Venus at the Théâtre des Variétés, presented an extraordinary scene of modish bad taste; one feels one could reconstruct from its entertainments the social history of the city. German cabaret spoke with a different voice, harsher, cruder – though perhaps one is judging it at a later period – the period reflected in the heartless cruelty of the Stroheim film *The Blue Angel*, or the dangerous days between the wars described in the witty, restless early novels of Christopher Isherwood.

Nevertheless German cabaret began by imitating the darker side of French cabaret. Aristide Bruant stunned his audience by singing the farewell of a condemned murderer to his sweetheart. At the turn of the century the German entertainers too were singing of murder, of whores and the street. Hitler's war was later to drive some of the composers and performers to the United States. But before that Germany had bred another kind of song, the ironical, political song with which Bertolt Brecht punctuated his dramas. With Kurt Weill's music these were to become widely known through the *Dreigroschenoper*, the bleak version of Gay's *The Beggar's Opera*.

Brecht is entertainment with a mission; it is alien from the music hall which enlivened 19th-century and early 20th-century London. Entertainment can be the image of a people; it can symbolize the French, the Germans, the operatic Italians, the gusty British. We are all changing, of course. In the 1880s, one reads, there were over 500 music halls in central London. Even between the wars a good many of them were still extant. I remember cheerful evenings spent at the Metropole in central London's Edgware Road, listening to the impudent exchanges of the comics. "What are your main means of support?" one of them would courteously inquire. "My main means of support", the answer cracked back, "is string and elastic." But by the 1970s nearly all these lively haunts have vanished, ousted in the first half of the century by the cinema. Now the cinemas too are dwindling, and families which used to go out twice a week to see a film now sit at home in front of the television set, watching American crime serials.

Not that the talent which once furnished the halls is extinct. The well-to-do clubs of working men in the north of England have their own entertainment and pay well for it. Again, gifted performers can make a reputation on the television screen. But the music hall proper has shrunk to a theatre or two in London and the provincial cities; variety has given way to pop music and the rock singers with their electric guitars. Sometimes there has been an attempt at revival. Music hall, growing out of miscellaneous and often outdoor entertainment, began its true life in the taverns: a chairman would announce the performers, often amateur. For some years London enjoyed – it was in the 1950s and later – a show of the sort, still with a chairman but now in a theatre. Then television took the programme over and presented it to a larger audience. But television involves a sharp separation of artist from public. And again one thinks with nostalgia of the days when the great stars of variety linked performers and spectators in a unity sometimes sentimental, sometimes boisterous, but always warm-hearted.

For in England, perhaps more than in the rest of Europe, the popular entertainers have come from the people and have belonged to the people. True that in France Yvette Guilbert began by making a living as a seamstress, selling her work to any shop which would buy it. Her theatrical skill was learnt in contact with popular, not intellectual, audiences. But there is a fundamental difference between Guilbert and, say, England's Marie Lloyd. To say that Marie Lloyd represented low comedy is not to denigrate the artist. It is simply to record her supremacy in a special and essential branch gf entertainment. Singing "The Boy in the Gallery" (for that was among her triumphs) or intimating with a flash of her rich vitality that "A little of what you fancy does you good" she was not only admired, she was at one with a popular and in particular a working-class audience.

There is a story that, summoned to appear before some censorious committee, she demonstrated the purity of her performance by singing her own songs absolutely straight. Then she gave a rendering of "Come into the garden, Maud" which filled the Tennyson lyric with innuendoes. It was her gift to speak to the heart. But she could speak also to the taste for a suggestive hint – and to the working-class love of disaster jokes. Perhaps her art was not exportable. She never, so far as one knows, made a hit in Paris or Berlin. Variety may be an international pleasure, and Yvette Guilbert succeeded in winning over her audience in London. But English music hall is probably too much a product of working-class English society to be understood and enjoyed elsewhere. And language intervenes. Since the early 1930s and the advent of the talkies, the cinema – and nearly all performers aspire to the riches of the screen – has urged on continental European players the importance of speaking English. The sophisticated stars – a Marlene Dietrich, a Maurice Chevalier – will learn the alien tongue and turn to advantage an incurable accent. One cannot imagine a Marie Lloyd translating her famous song "I'm one of the ruins that Cromwell knocked about a bit" into the idiom of French or German. Continental audiences may applaud Laurence Olivier as the failing music-hall comedian in John Osborne's *The Entertainer*. They would probably have greeted the real professional comic with incomprehension.

No doubt of it, the visual comedians suffer least in translation to another medium. That is why Tati with his expressive features, his ingratiating walk – and his long legs – has been a success with the British public. One thinks of George Robey, alone on the stage with a selection of musical instruments, his fingers ever straying towards some monstrous convolution of brass which he never plays. George Robey could have been funny in any language. And the circus: that is international in every sense of the word. Its performers may be Hungarian or Italian, German or Japanese. We follow through the air their terrible somersaulting flights. We tremble for the stability of some tall pyramid of bodies, feet balancing on shoulders, head inverted on head. Anxiously we watch the equestrian girls and the jugglers, the riders and the plate twirlers; their cries to one another sound strange, like the call of some unknown forest creature, the cry of some nameless jungle bird. No matter. We cannot hope to comprehend the interminable practice, the endless risks which have culminated in such precision of movement, such inviolable timing.

And we do not ask whether their families, for circus people often work in families, have grown up in Budapest or Hong Kong; they are altogether out of our range. The Russians, we say, have splendid circuses. But the performers from any country are always remote, divided from us by a gulf far greater than separates us from the stars in the firmament of the cinema. Film stars, after all, are known to live ordinary lives, perform ordinary human functions; they marry and divorce, gamble, play golf. But the circus people and the fairground people come from an enigmatic past. A man may sing to please himself. He may dance to please his gods. But what instinct can drive a man to let himself be fired from a gun?

And we are back with the mysterious desire not only to be entertained but to entertain. And that can be a devouring passion; it can destroy. It destroyed Dan Leno, probably the most celebrated of all the artists of the English music hall. I remember when I was a child, living in a provincial backwater, my grandmother would speak of Dan Leno with a mixture of reverence and pity. Why the pity? Now I know. The desire to make people laugh became an obsession with him. And he had delusions of another kind of glory. He really was the clown who wanted to play Shakespeare. At last he drove himself into madness; and at the age of 44 he was dead.

Reading of the stars of the past, learning at second hand or relying on faint memories, I wonder if the performers of today, those who still preserve something of the spirit of the music hall, are as good as their predecessors. Is the Frenchman Rufus, is Frankie Howerd the equal of the historic names? One cannot answer the question. One can only be thankful for the delight today's favourites afford. And one thinks of both the famous and the forgotten. One thinks of Gracie Fields and of the acrobat riding a recalcitrant bicycle across an empty stage. One thinks of Billy Bennett – "almost a gentleman", he called himself, his boiled shirt for ever bursting out of his trouser-tops; one thinks of the comedian – to my shame I am no longer sure of his name – who at intervals in his poker-faced patter would remark gloomily: "Joke over."

The list is endless, from the Paris cabaret couple greeting late arrivals with mischievous solicitude to the Punch-and-Judy show on the beach; from the bouzouki players, applauded and fêted, of the Piraeus cafés to the shadow theatre, the Karaghioz, which is still said to haunt the Athens streets; perhaps even to the old woman touching her harp in the darkness outside a Dublin playhouse. Occasionally a street performer will win acclaim. Carol Reed, looking for a musical background to his film *The Third Man*, found a Viennese zither player – and made him famous. On the other hand some of the familiar sights and sounds of the past are disappearing. In a London street you no longer hear a barrel organ or see a monkey sitting on top of it, holding out his leathery little hand for a coin. The Pierrots, singing and dancing on a temporary stage for the holiday crowds, are no longer a seaside draw. For with changing moods and tastes, with new technologies and greater freedom of choice for a young public, a more strident form of amusement has taken hold. The first decades of the 20th century brought jazz, dance bands, the Charleston. In the 1960s and the 1970s the pop-singer and the pop-group have reigned. Across Europe from London to Paris, from Berlin to Prague and beyond, one has seen the photographs and heard the choruses of the Beatles, the Rolling Stones and their successors.

And still the longing for some sort of relationship, some kind of intimacy with the sources of entertainment increases. When the disembodied voice, when the two-dimensional shadow takes on living form, when in fact the remote idol-entertainer appears in the flesh, the longing can lose control. It can turn to mass hysteria. In the 1920s a schoolgirl might cherish a picture postcard of an adored stage celebrity. In the 1970s the teenager becomes a Bacchante tearing at the body of her Orpheus. She wants to rip off the pop-artist's shirt. She fights at the funeral for a relic of the dead Elvis Presley.

Psychiatrists may deplore the excess, and it is fashionable to agree with them. Nevertheless one cannot help thinking that the communal expression of emotion has its value. It is a release of the tensions in which modern society lives. It is a homage to talent, though the homage (as well as the talent) takes a form different from the plaudits of the past. It expresses the same passion to acknowledge delight and give thanks for an experience as was manifested by the devotees of some great diva when after her performance they would harness themselves – or so we are told – to her carriage and drag it through the streets. Enthusiasm – in the 18th century the word was used in a derogatory sense. It could imply a lack of religious balance. To be enthusiastic was ill bred. The enthusiasm which greets the successful pop-singer may be ill balanced. Some might call it ill bred. But it has the warmth of popular feeling rather than the measured appraisal of intellectual judgement. Major entertainers may be admired by both the highbrow and the unsophisticated. Chaplin, before he allowed himself to pontificate, was everybody's favourite. He won the respect of Bernard Shaw, of Somerset Maugham. But the unlettered audience in the pit and the gallery recognized him first. Popular applause it is that makes the star.

A far cry from the Classical drama at Epidaurus or *The Harrowing of Hell* at Wakefield. And with every new set of idols, every change of medium – variety stage, cinema, television, record album – the unity of feeling once engendered by religious awe grows fainter. Or does it? I sometimes think it lives in the vast gladiatorial arenas of today. Paradoxical, I suppose, to claim a sense of awe for the most violent and vindictive of modern entertainments. All the same I think it is there, amid the shouting, the rage and the ferocious partisanship, that the element of submission to an overpowering idea, a superior force, still exists.

For all its dangerous savagery the football field is the inheritor of an evening at Epidaurus.

# 7

# *Sportsmen*

## CHRISTIAN GRAF VON KROCKOW

In 1826 the German aristocrat Prince Pückler-Muskau travelled to England in the hope of finding a wife to free him from his financial worries. That quest was in vain. One thing Pückler did bring back with him, however, was a new word, "sport", though the prince felt that the word denoted something specifically English and was therefore "as untranslatable as 'gentleman'".

And so it proved! It took decades before sport gradually began to conquer the continent. In Germany especially its first attempts encountered a powerful and determined adversary, the athletics movement, which loudly condemned sport as "outlandish" and "un-German", and denounced it as permeated by the "mercenary shopkeeping spirit" of the English. The game of football in particular was banned as an imported product. Even the Olympic idea was met with ostentatious coldness. Those were the days before World War I when anti-British feeling generally was steadily building up to the explosion of 1914. Perfidious Albion! God punish England! In the Weimar Republic the situation worsened still further. In 1923 the German Athletics Association decreed a complete and "absolute separation" of sport from athletics.

This is not so very long ago, and yet now seems almost incomprehensible. Starting from England, sport has conquered Europe and America, and from Europe and America the world. Like a corrosive acid, it has destroyed all other forms of games and competitions, regional and national, or transformed them in its own image. Basketball courts, for example, are to be found today in every corner of the globe, in Chinese kindergartens, schools, factories and housing estates, as a legacy of the YMCA no less than in out-of-the-way Mexican villages.

Why is this? What is the secret of this success? An obvious answer is to say that sport is a child or by-product of industrial development. It makes up for the privations imposed on people in modern society. This is true physically – we need only think of our extremely unbalanced occupations and relaxations, and in general of the lack of movement. It is also true socially, especially in the great concentrations of working-class population. The positions of the great football grounds in Glasgow, Liverpool, Manchester and London give the connections physical reality, and the social history of the German Ruhr is also totally inconceivable without the history of its clubs, especially its football clubs. Today the position of underprivileged minorities is an obvious example: one thinks of the pre-eminence of Blacks in the commercial spectator sport of the United States. A lad with no other opportunity can still perhaps fight his way to the top, literally with his fists. In brief, was England not the home of the Industrial Revolution and – for that very reason – also the home of sport? Is this not then the explanation of the triumphal progress of sport, since the history of the world since then has everywhere been a story of modernization and economic development?

But we should not be too hasty. Studies constantly show that most of those who practise a sport are not those who most need relaxation, but members of the upper and middle social strata, and young people and students before they embark on a career. The example of England is particularly puzzling. Here the beginnings of the development of modern sport appear as early as the late 17th and early 18th centuries, in other words before we can talk about the Industrial Revolution in the strict sense. This naturally does not exclude the possibility that economy, society and sport develop in parallel, but the assumption of a close, direct relation of cause and effect is misleading.

So what was the cause of sport's triumphal progress? And what are its characteristics? One distinctive feature is the growing tendency to regulate and rationalize sporting contests. This had a cause both simple and practical, though one which was embarrassing for Coubertin's disciples: competitions were the result of passions for gambling. To make possible clear decisions on wagers in which large sums may be at stake there is a need for standards. What is the distance? How much time should be taken? Who is the winner and under what conditions? In short, there has to be measurement. If the early modern period as a whole was typified by the development of a new exact sense of time and the progress of clockmaking, it is characteristic of sport that the first stop-watches were already ticking in the early 18th century.

The route was, of course, long and sometimes tortuous. At first it is an individual achievement which arouses admiration, such as Sir Edward Carey's Marathon ride in 1603 to bring the news of Queen Elizabeth's death to James VI in Edinburgh in only three days. Even earlier, in the time of Henry VI, a royal chaplain – the later Cardinal Wolsey – had laid one of the foundation stones of his career by making the journey to the Emperor Maximilian's residence in Flanders and back in what we would automatically call "record time", though in fact the term "record" for an outstanding sporting achievement did not come into use until much later.

The principle of the record, however, was soon established. Its basis is, of course, precisely verifiable conditions of performance which can therefore, in principle, be reproduced, and similarly accurate measurement of actual performance. This detaches a best performance from its uniqueness; it can be produced at different times and in different places – and it can be surpassed.

Such comparisons of performance became possible once "matches against time" had begun to come into fashion, especially after the Restoration of 1660. There were wagers, for example, about the possibility of covering the distance from London to York and back five times in six days. The elaborateness of such ventures made direct comparison of performances difficult, but this changed as races over shorter distances became popular. And since the speed of the horse was the most important factor, the breeding of racehorses became important. It is thus to the passion for gambling that horse-breeding owes the vital stimulus which finally led to the worldwide triumph of the English thoroughbred.

The possibilities are many. The important men of the 17th and 18th centuries kept "footmen", trained runners, and since every nobleman wanted to have the best footman, the obvious thing was to race them against each other and lay a wager. The principle was capable of infinite variation. There were toddler races, and races for men with wooden legs. But these were peripheral. In the main it was the performance of the trained horse or man that mattered, and there soon followed a further logical step towards the autonomy of sport, the laying out of special race tracks. Voltaire describes a development of this kind which he saw on his visit to England in 1727.

There are in all three features of modern sport which can be traced back to the needs of gambling and its pressure for results to be determined publicly and accurately.

The first of these is the search for the best performance. The second is the desire for comparability of performances, in other words competition. The two go together, since a best performance can only be discovered by being systematically compared with other performances in a contest. Conversely, competition would be meaningless unless it was related to performances which could be made intelligible and recorded in a universally recognized way by means of a common standard.

The third feature is the equality of the practitioners of the sport. The discovery of a best performance through the contest presupposes, not just technical comparability, equality of conditions, but also the principled, formal equality of all those who enter, or might enter, the contest. When, for whatever reason, someone is denied the opportunity of having his or her performance compared, the idea of the best performance is destroyed. There is no way of telling with certainty whether or not the person excluded could have produced an even better performance. However important, therefore, in "real" life, differences between human beings in religion, race, regional or national affiliation, wealth, status or class may be, sport presses, and must press, for these differences to be kept outside the competitors' enclosure. Sport is, through the mechanics of the particular game, a temporary shutting out of the world. Or, as the proverb says, "On the turf and under it, all men are equal."

This fact is particularly important, and deserves attention, because it cuts across tendencies which are, at first sight, characteristic of the early modern period, the pressures for an increasingly strict separation of the different ranks of society. One area in which this tendency appears is the right to wear a sword and fight a duel, a carefully guarded privilege of the higher orders, those who were "capable of giving satisfaction". The duel as a ritualized form of private single combat first appeared in the Latin countries in the 15th century, and spread like a plague throughout Europe. It did not reach England until later, making a gradual appearance in the 16th century, but by the reign of James I it was already so widespread that the English became notorious for their quarrelsomeness. But a change was on the way. It took place in England first – and at first only in England.

Towards the end of the 17th century and the beginning of the 18th, a new sport, boxing, came into fashion. At first sight there seems to be nothing very special about this. Boxing was better suited to betting than the earlier favourite, wrestling, because it was marked by drama and clear decisions, and it was also possible for the weaker contestant to win with a single lucky blow. But that is not the whole story, nor even its most important part.

First, boxing increasingly supplanted duelling with swords. Many reports testify to this. Typical is the story of the Frenchman Martin Nogué, who, in the 1720s, in ignorance of local customs, attempted to fight a duel in London with a fellow countryman. Passers-by fell upon the disputants, pulled them apart, broke their swords and threatened them with a beating. A quarrel should be settled fairly, with fists. This attitude was disconcertingly at odds with the continental view, based originally on Spanish and later on French practice. The wearing of swords soon went out of fashion along with duelling, and London "dandies" took to "arming" themselves with walking-sticks instead.

This is also a curious paradox: in highly aristocratic England equality is brought about by a general abandonment of weapons. In the land of the "common man", in contrast, the United States, the Second Amendment of 1789 confirms that "the right of the people to keep and bear Arms shall not be infringed." It is tempting to talk about the creation of equality through a general "ennoblement": everyone is allowed what in Europe remains the privilege of a minority and is, even as a privilege, increasingly disputed. The cult of the weapon has remained an American characteristic to this day. The contrasting developments in England and America have also had important consequences, affecting the equipment of the police and the forms taken by crime.

A crucial factor in the development of sport, however, was the early appearance of cracks in the structure of social privilege. "An Osborne, duke of Leeds, often amused himself by boxing in the streets of London with people of the lowest class, and he was not the only peer of England to be a terror to London coachmen and chair-bearers." And as early as the 1790s the Swiss Beat von Muralt reports with incredulity that gentlemen of rank, insulted by relatives of lower social classes, will take off their swords and fight with their fists. Not that this indicates a general breakdown of social distinctions. Prince Pückler can still describe English society as "Indian in its caste structure". This makes the specific development of sport as a "temporary shutting out of the world" all the more striking.

This specific development can only be understood if two factors are taken into account. The first has to do with the make-up of the English aristocracy. The strict application of primogeniture meant that younger members of aristocratic families continually passed into the bourgeoisie while, on the other hand, deserving bourgeois could be ennobled without the risk of an inflation of nobility. There is in addition the unique figure of the potential aristocrat, which Alec Guinness – since 1959 Sir Alec Guinness – brought to life even for non-Englishmen in his film *Kind Hearts and Coronets*. These gliding transitions made it possible for England to remain more aristocratic than all the other countries of Europe, which sooner or later had to undergo a revolutionary break, a violent abolition of aristocratic privileges. On the other hand it became easier for aristocrats and non-aristocrats to be educated together and cooperate in many areas of activity; sport is merely one particularly impressive illustration of the situation.

The second factor may be termed "religious forces". It is, on the face of it, strange that modern sport should have achieved its break-through in the one country above all in which puritanism and other, later forms of radical Protestantism have always shown themselves vehemently hostile to games and sport. At first, this made itself felt in politics too. Whereas under Cromwell all recreation and sporting activities had, as far as possible, been suppressed, after the Restoration they exploded back into life and Charles II ostentatiously played the part of the "thorough English sportsman" as which he was later revered.

Religious criticism, however, was directed chiefly at the traditional pleasures, especially those associated with the stages of the Church's year and the principal feastdays. These were often close – often enough obviously close – to originally pagan rituals. There was no need to wait for Sigmund Freud to see through, for example, the symbolism of frolics under the maypole. But by detaching games from their traditional contexts and, as it were, banishing them to the ghetto while at the same time proving unable completely to drive out the old Adam and leave no alternative to "prayer and work", Protestantism pushed the development of sport in a direction it was already taking; it helped to make it fundamentally secular, a rationalized and regulated "temporary shutting out of the world".

This development naturally also prepared the way for, and indeed made possible, the later universal triumph of sport. Activities which have firm ties with social and cultural situations are inevitably also limited by those ties. On the other hand, forms of activity which have been freed in principle from such ties are universally transportable. In modern sport first England and then Europe created one of the products which are marked by their worldwide transportability. This explains how the highly artificial game of basketball could become the most popular sport in revolutionary China, apparently without attracting objections even from the "Gang of Four": it could be completely separated from its former American Christian importers.

But the question is how far this explanation goes, and how far underlying influences were at work. Could the venerable mandarins of the past have been imagined playing basketball? Or the ladies of the imperial court with their crippled feet? Does a society remain the same once it has chosen to import transistor radios, penicillin and sport? And, where sport is concerned, must not at least the principle of formal equality be first accepted? In a society of slave-owners, masters and slaves could hardly take part in sporting contests against each other, since the possibility of the slave's winning would fundamentally break his chains, just as it would shake the rights of the masters. These are only two of the essential differences between modern sport and not only Roman gladiatorial games but also the Olympic games of ancient Greece.

There are indeed many ways in which it can be shown that modern sport has developed in parallel with modern industrialized society and is hardly conceivable without it. The importance of an exact sense of time, of measurement, or regulation and rationalization has already been mentioned. All this is, of course, found in economic activity just as much as in sport. The same is true of the principles of performance and competition, and of the interaction of competition and performance which creates a unique momentum, the constant "Forward" which seems to tolerate no stopping and above all no turning back.

This momentum can be illustrated from sport. Johnny Weismuller was the most famous and most outstanding crawl swimmer of the 1920s. He set up numerous world records and won gold medals at two Olympics. He later turned his gold into money as Tarzan. In Munich in 1972, however, his former records would not have allowed him even to qualify – or if he had, even the girls would have made him a laughing-stock. And the superstar of Munich, Mark Spitz

– seven gold medals and a total of 34 world records – would have had a hard time four years later in Montreal. His last world record has now been broken.

The situation is similar in the economy. The firm which stands still, which relies on the products, techniques, forms of organization and marketing strategies with which it has been successful in the past is already on the steep slope leading to the bankruptcy court. Thomas Hobbes, in the 17th century, gave the position general application in an elaborate and terrifying sporting image in which he describes human life as one great race of all against all. He says at the end: "But this race we must suppose to have no other goal, nor other garland, but being foremost . . . And to forsake the course, is to die."

A movement in the same direction can be seen in the specialization or division of labour which is becoming as much a feature of sport as it is of economy and society. Charles II may have been a model all-round sportsman, and the first prize boxers were also prize swordsmen. As the tendency to compare best performances gained ground, however, specialization became unavoidable: now you are no longer just a sportsman or woman, but a boxer or a swimmer, and if a swimmer, primarily a crawl swimmer, specializing in short distances. And the decathlete, on the other hand, becomes a specialist in diversity.

At the same time constant training becomes necessary as a long-term preparation for the record. To make the parallel with the development of the modern economy more exact, we may talk about a long-term investment perspective: everything depends on sacrificing the present for the goal anticipated in the future. In his famous studies on the connection between capitalism and the Protestant ethic Max Weber coined the phrase "worldly asceticism", and asceticism is also demanded in greater measure from the top-flight sportsman the further the process advances. If he wants to make it to the top and stay there, he must give up many enticing pleasures of the moment – just like the person who wants to rise in the hierarchy of industrial management and become a successful businessman. "The gentleman goes out by day", was a famous banker's lapidary and damning comment on a younger colleague. "The boy likes night-clubs and goes with women", must frequently be the nub of a trainer's reason for breaking with one of his protégés, "writing him off" as a businessman does a bad investment.

What applies to performance and competition is equally true of the principle of equality. The dismantling of legally sanctioned privileges and distinctions, the abolition of serfdom, slavery or mass forced labour, has everywhere been a feature of modern social development, once the economic and industrial process has got beyond its crude early stages. It was certainly not, at least not primarily, a sudden access of philanthropy on the part of the ruling classes which brought this about, but the pressure of economic logic. As work ceases to be limited to primitive processes and turns instead into a large-scale operation with many stages in a succession of ever more complicated organizational structures, it is less and less possible to supervise it directly and control it by pure force. The motivation for the work must instead be transferred within the person; it must at least appear to them to be their own "free", autonomous impulse, and this internalization of motivation is possible only on the basis of formal equality and freedom.

Radical Protestantism, with its anti-hierarchical outlook, did as much to establish the principle of equality as it did to bring about the related internalization of the motivation to produce. This was its main contribution to the development of the modern economy, and one which was incomparably more important and direct in its action than Max Weber's rather laborious construction from the Calvinist doctrine of predestination.

Sport shows the same pattern. The athlete too, and he above all, must internalize his motivation. One of the most important parts of the trainer's art is producing this motivation, keeping it alive during the slog of training and bringing it to a peak for the contest.

"Why is sewing mailbags work and climbing Mont Blanc sport?" Mark Twain once asked. The answer is already contained in the question. "Sewing mailbags" symbolizes the extreme of imposed work which can be forced out of a prisoner by the overseer's rod. A first-class sporting performance, on the other hand, and especially a great, perhaps extreme and highly dangerous feat, cannot be forced, but must be the product of a free choice, an inner motivation. To that extent it is almost a Utopia, a symbol of what ought to be universal but is not. It fascinates as a sign of human freedom, and provides a mark of dignity for a creature whom the iron pressure of providing for his material needs still binds all too tightly to sewing mailbags.

There will be more to say about sport's power to fascinate, but first a different question must be answered. How is it that sport can flourish in social systems as different from those of the West as those of the Soviet Union and other eastern European states? How, for example, has the little German Democratic Republic been able to establish itself as the third sporting power in the world alongside the USSR and the USA? Certainly perfect organization and the almost unlimited supply of material resources within a state-controlled undertaking may explain a lot. In socialism, too, the principle of performance is given as much recognition as that of equality, and to realize the latter, in the form of educational equality – especially for women – a very great deal of work, much of it exemplary, is being done. One pillar of the system, however, is missing, the principle of competition: for the socialist states' boast that they have reached a higher moral level than capitalism is based on the claim to have left behind this capitalist "wolf law".

Nevertheless this produces serious problems for the dynamic and logic of performance, and some competitive practices have therefore been smuggled in by the back door, the "principle of material interest" in the fulfilment or over-fulfilment of the plan, and "socialist competition". But because at the same time the foundations of the system, the claim to moral superiority, may not be touched, all this is done half-heartedly. Competition is forced to lead a twilight existence, and as a result the socialist states have so far stayed firmly in second place in the East-West race for economic progress.

In sport things are different, yet another indication of its relative autonomy as a sector on its own. In sport – and only in sport – competitive behaviour is fully acknowledged, especially when it can symbolically demonstrate the superiority of the "system" at international competitions and the Olympic games. This is, of course, a facade, since in sport the very things which normally attract condemnation are allowed and rewarded. And yet at the same time it becomes clear why such amounts of time and energy are devoted to sport, far in excess of the official norm. In sport young people can achieve and experience what is denied to them in other spheres, whereas their western contemporaries seem to have a dazzling, sometimes even depressing, variety of opportunities for finding adventure, success, risk and fulfilment.

Coming back now to our own society, we are faced finally with our question in even more urgent form. What is it about sport which continues to fascinate people when they apparently have so many other possibilities? To say it makes up for a lack of movement may be plausible and reasonable, but are people fascinated by what is reasonable? For health it would be enough to eat properly, not to smoke, to take regular walks and, at most, to do exercises in the morning by an open window. Is that sport? Bertolt Brecht once talked about the apostles of sport as an aid to health and hygiene:

> These sort of people like to operate with the slogan "Sport is healthy", and use it, in the schools and through popular literature, to try and ruin for all time any real sporting instinct which exists in younger people. Of course sport, that is, real, passionate sport, is not healthy. When it really has to do with struggle, records and risks, it in fact demands extraordinary efforts on the part of the person doing it to keep his health half-way up to scratch. I don't imagine Lindbergh prolonged his life by ten years by flying the Atlantic. Boxing for the purpose of encouraging bowel movement is no sport.

So where does that leave us? There is an important pointer in the origin of sport in England which we have already discussed, the passion for gambling. In some sports it may still be important – the best example is horse-racing. But betting is a means to produce excitement, and, as a rule, sport, in the course of its development, has been able to throw away the aid like crutches because it has enough sources of excitement in itself.

Take the case of football. It is hardly an accident that it is an attractive and popular sport. Football is a better sort of thriller. There are heroes and villains, "my" team and the others. But who will win is not determined in advance by this distribution of roles. It is an open question, a question of skill, effort and performance – and of luck too. An inch to one side, and that shot which shook the post could always have produced the all-important, redeeming goal. Of course, people want both, confidence born of the performance they credit themselves with, which others credit them with, and luck. We secretly long and dream that "things" will go for us, that the stars or fate will be kind to us, that we shall be chosen.

"Glorious uncertainty" and luck can never quite be rationalized out of the contest – just like the referee's mistake, which is always there to be blamed for the misfortune if need be – but this secret twist in the principle of performance only helps to increase the popularity of sport and of football in particular. It does not reduce, but increases, the excitement.

Excitement. Television, of course, shows us every day the sources of tension in our world – crises, conflicts, looming disasters wherever we look. But our ordinary life remains strangely untouched by all this, unexciting. No more jungles hide their secrets. The witches have been burnt and the dragons exterminated. Every patch of earth, the whole of existence, has been surveyed. We have average, statistically calculated life expectancies and careers, traffic signs, vaccinations and social security. Even the excitement of the relations between the sexes no longer seems to hold what it once promised now that the taboos have, like the dragons in the jungle, been dealt with. Where is there left to build up and release tension, to invest passion? Where can men still cry, if not on the field in the moment of victory or defeat?

A better sort of thriller. The action is real, not fiction like a film or novel; it is really happening here and now, before our eyes. And yet "real" life is still shut out. What is happening has no consequences for me. It is the same with identification. We win and suffer with our team. We are our team – and yet are not. We are only spectators, judging, condemning and switching allegiance with flags flying: the king is dead – long live the king!

Football, and sport in general, also has a crucial advantage over other spectacles of our age. Everyone can understand what is happening. Everyone can talk about it to everyone else. The business man's achievements, in comparison, are obscure and only to be judged by his success, which may rest on dubious practices – perhaps tax evasion. The artist's achievement is partly created by the managers of the market, and may be a confidence trick. The politician's rise may be due to his unscrupulousness, and at best is inseparable from his ability to sell himself. And even the scientist's achievement we must take on trust from the experts who selected him for the Nobel prize.

To put it briefly, modern man is permanently disoriented, and feels himself permanently deceived. But take Bob Beamon's jump of the century at the Mexico Olympics of 1968, checked three times, taken visually round the world. Everyone can understand it; no one can make any insinuations about it or take anything away from it – he jumped further than any man before or since. And so with football: everyone can feel himself an expert, everyone his own national trainer. In all the depressing, endless complexity of our lives sport, through the mechanisms of the different games, artificially creates clarity. It reduces the complexity to a human scale.

The cult of football and sport in general may, of course, seem plebeian to many, and some may find it boring. Nevertheless it is a notably tolerant cult; no one is forced to join in. And all societies have the cults they deserve, the cults they need to give them symbols to reflect themselves and recognize themselves in. We no longer have to conciliate the natural forces, to invoke the divinities of sun, rain and fertility. Nor are we caught in the conflict between human actions and the fate devised by the gods. In Marx's words: "All rank and permanence disappear, everything sacred is profaned, and men are finally forced to look at their position in life, their mutual relations, with sober eyes."

And yet even despite or just because of this cold sobriety, in the predictability, at the heart of the disenchantment, there still hides a magic. In the stone labyrinths of our cities we still carry inside us the hopes and fears of the Stone Age. The magic of the ground: the white pitch markings, the goal, the 90 minutes, all the rules. There are even taboos, infringement of which is denounced by the thousandfold shout of "handball" and incurs the ritual punishment of the penalty.

A masterpiece of choreography, ballet on the field, whose taut structure switches at every moment into new configurations: created in years of training, every possibility, all the movements, thought out, planned in advance, ceaselessly practised. But the ballet is in contest and so, in spite of all the planning, it is impossible to predict what will happen or what will have to be done. No game is like another. Seen from the point of view of choreography, games can succeed or fail, find their rhythm or lose it. Teams connect or fail to make contact; they stimulate each other or are paralysed. Football matches are artistic products of the moment, on a scale going from repulsive ugliness to captivating beauty.

And on top of everything else, excitement, drama. The fragile construction of skill and chance bears into the arena failure and success, despair and happiness, clad in the finery of the irrecoverable, accompanied by the agonized gasps of the ancient chorus in the broad circle or by its chants of contempt and triumph. Fascination by football, fascination by sport.

To sum up, sport is a product of the modern development which leads finally to industrial society. It is not, however, as it is so often presented, simply a child of this society, just a compensatory reaction. It can, in fact be clearly seen taking shape in Britain at the end of the 17th and beginning of the 18th century, so before the beginning of the Industrial Revolution proper.

At the same time sport is a characteristically British contribution to the development of modern society. It is impossible to understand its beginnings and the principles which have shaped it without taking into account various factors unique to England. These include the particular composition of English society and especially of the aristocracy. They also include religious forces such as Puritanism and other forms of radical Protestantism. The specifically British character of modern sport is also revealed by the initial attempts to resist its spread. Germany shows this continuing into the 20th century.

And yet, not the least typical feature of modern sport is its separability from the conditions which shaped its origins. It has proved itself to be universally transportable. It has conquered Europe and America, leaped all frontiers between political systems, and in our own time has permeated the world. This process shows its not merely British, but generally European character. This ability to create objects and ideas which can transcend all cultural barriers and be used by, and fascinate, the whole human race, has been a characteristic of Europe since the beginning of the modern period. Sport, therefore, in ceasing to be a European and still less a British monopoly, shows itself to be a symbol of Europe.

# PART THREE

*Writers*

*Architects*

*Artists*

*Musicians*

*Actors*

# 8

# *Writers*

## PETER LEVI

It is hard to say which gives the falser impression, the apparent unity or the apparent diversity of European literature. When they are published, all books become fellows on a shelf. When books come together, they breed; there is a book population problem. In Europe the invention and exploitation of printing led to the same books being available everywhere, and as books influence each other, the somewhat inbred discourse of European literature has become a forceful stream. The degree of individuality it permits has been now wider, now narrower, but in the whole area of distribution of European books, the collective soul of Europe has a massive energy. Even the notion of a book carries with it a certain morality about truth, about method, about integrity. But the liveliest springs that feed intellectual and academic and literary life are individual, and a long way from the bookshops.

The Europe of books has not always extended over the whole of geographic Europe. It first did so probably in the 19th century, when Pirandello was born the son of a station-master in one of the remotest Sicilian stations, and in Poland, in Greece, and in Serbia three powerful national movements expressed themseves in a new and liberated style, a reverse image of the Europe of Metternich. But in the 16th century parts of Europe were illiterate and isolated. There were druids in the forests of Lithuania, and bardic schools in Ireland closer in spirit to the Europe of 600 AD or 600 BC than to the London or even the Dublin of 1600.

As the mutual conversation of books has extended, it has spread far beyond geographic Europe. It makes no sense, for example, to speak of 19th-century European literature without including Russia, or of English literature without including America. Among modern poets Vallejo is as essentially European as he is essentially Latin American. But was the Alexandria of Cavafy part of Europe or not? And further afield what are we to say of French-speaking African poets like Senghor and Aimé Césaire? Césaire is surely very much not a European. His splendid, revolutionary verse takes its power from the refusal of Europe. And yet he published in Paris, he plays as crucial a role as Fanon in the intellectual history of Europe in this century, he can be placed in European terms as easily as the Russian Mayakovsky.

One of the comforts of a writer who moves about Europe today is that he discovers in his contemporaries a community of taste. It is hard to know quite how that has been generated, but the process has surely been gradual. I am not speaking of the shared admiration for Dante or Shakespeare or Ronsard, still less of the shared interest or disinterest in Marxism or Structuralism or the New Novel or the silent cinema. It is more a matter of like recognizing like by small, tell-tale symptoms. In the taste for new or for minor or obscure writers, the contemporaries one meets and admires all over Europe, and in Israel and the Arab countries, have a nose for the same qualities. They all accept what used to be called the modern movement in literature, but with similar reservations. They talk about Francis Jammes or Edward Lear or Trakl, not much about Goethe or Victor Hugo or Tennyson.

There are some interesting points to be made about this mysterious common direction in which writers move. It must depend on the availability of books, but writers more than other people go to great lengths for a rare text, and their taste is a long way ahead of publishers', who usually follow them 10 or 30 years later. I was introduced to Vallejo's importance, for example, when the only book in print was a poor French version of a few poems, and similarly to Mandelstam, to Paul Celan and to Trakl, by other writers. Critics of course have an influence, but usually by chance, and more often by a casual phrase in *Le Monde* or an English Sunday paper than by a full-scale essay or a book. It is probably true that most writers, at least most poets, get more than half their information about what to read from other writers. Academic training plays almost no part, and the books they read that universities teach are usually outside their own subject.

But Homer, Dante, Shakespeare are in common. It is also in common that writers in minority languages usually know some English and French, and explore in those meadows. But hardly one writer knows all the six necessary languages of modern Europe, which I take to be Italian, Spanish, French, English, German and Russian. Everyone uses translations and almost every poet makes and publishes translations. That is not only for obvious financial reasons, but to come to terms with the grit and bones and surface textures of another language, rather as a chicken eats grit to harden the shells of its own eggs. Sometimes a writer has a prolonged love affair with another language. To take English examples, Milton had one with Italian, Dryden with Latin, Eliot I think with French. But in the end, what most feeds poets is the vernacular and traditional speech which is native to them. When Milton is on his highest horse there is still a homely element in his language. Eliot never ceased to write like a New Englander.

It was the same at the earliest stage of European literature, at the time of the earliest texts which are still on our shelves. We begin with Homer. Elsewhere there was the Bible. Both are due to the early exploitation of adaptable alphabetic scripts. There are much earlier documents from elsewhere in the world, some of them of great literary merit, the epic of Gilgamesh, for example, and the ruined fragments of many religious writings, but the *Iliad* and the *Odyssey* are unique in their scale, and in the significant fact that they were written down when epic poetry was fully vigorous. It is not the existence of writing that brings the traditional vigour of epic poetry to an end, but a whole series of social circumstances. Different societies in Europe and elsewhere have reached the point of no return at different times, the French as late as the 12th century, the Serbians in the 15th or 16th, the native Irish in the 18th. Only in the *Iliad* and the *Odyssey* can we get some fuller conception of what epic poetry, altered in performance, transmitted by word of mouth, perpetually adapting and rationalizing itself through generations, must at one time have been like everywhere.

For the subtlety and breadth of its self-image of a whole society, as that society sees itself and its past, for the impersonal moral force of its procedures, for the intensity of its grief and the abundance of its language, Homeric poetry has hardly been equalled in later literature. But in Norse, in Anglo-Saxon, in French, in Serbo-Croat and in Russian, to mention only some examples which can be called European, there are similar traditions. Of course the societies and the poetry in which we read them are always, at the moment at which writing catches them, in the last hours of archaism, on the edge of headlong change. The poets themselves are conscious that life is appalling, and that traditional morality, with its basis in a boyish system of honour and shame, ramifying into economics and into the whole social structure, contains many contradictions. That is what gives the poetry its tension, and if I may use a term which is more apparently than really anachronistic, its tragic sense.

The Latin language, like the later Italian language, and like modern English, seems to have missed the moment for genuine epic. Virgil is an immensely great and skilful writer, but he is a literary imitator on a grand scale. His work was done at his desk, and he was conscious not only of great examples which he read and reread, but of generations of intervening poetry, and perhaps even more significantly, of acres of learned commentary on the poetry he was imitating. The *Aeneid* is a continuous dialogue with the scholars who had commented on Homer. There has been something false about European literary epics ever since. The skill of great poets like Spenser and Ariosto and Milton has been lavished on them, they contain wonderful passages and fascinating structures, but their bones are not alive. They are not the complete self-image of societies. The reality of experience and of society is outside them, and we read of it elsewhere in an attempt to bring them to life. What is humanly genuine is to be found in Latin, but rather in Catullus and Horace than in Virgil.

The most pliant, the most unstable of all the European literary forms, but the most able to cope with the most of reality, has surely been the theatre. In ancient Athens, to some extent in Republican Rome, in classical Spain and France, in Elizabethan England, in 19th-century Russia and Sweden and Italy, the theatre does something for semi-coherent societies that Homer did for a more coherent world. No great age of the theatre has lasted long. A single generation saw the plays of Marlowe and Shakespeare and the beheading of Charles I. Political comedy at Athens began to be trenchant when Aristophanes was a young man, but he outlived it by many years, and in his last plays the comedy was socio-moral, not socio-political, and the old amusing chorus had disappeared. There are those now alive who have seen the beginning and the end of Brecht's theatre.

It is tempting to suggest that all these movements died through the withering away of social hope. Social and political impotence is a blight of theatrical force. But the theatre, even when it seemed most pure and neoclassic, in the work of Corneille for example, has always been mixed at its best, and its existence depends on a fine balance of elements, one of which is the audience. The Athenian audience altered faster than Aristophanes did. Shakespeare's audience rather reverted than altered, and there are not many Shakespeares. Brecht's audience has sensibly abandoned the old rational hopes of the Communist Party. Impotence for Chekhov is an element in the texture of the air, nor am I personally at all certain that hope predominated in his own sense of his dramatic works. Lorca's tragedies are written at a time of hope, but their atmosphere is intensely black; the same might be said of Aeschylus. But ritual lamentation is deeply embedded in social structure, and hope of taking our future in our hands, though not the possibility of change, belongs to traditional societies as closely as spring belongs to the year.

It is worth stressing that drama has a ritual basis, and ritual dramatic forms have been part of the mixture that has fed the European theatre at more than one historical period. Aeschylus was closer to the ritual origins than Sophocles or Euripides, and disposed of the ritual elements in tragedy more majestically. The enormously long opening part of the *Agamemnon* is an only slightly dramatized adaptation of epic narrative. When that play was reproduced in the 4th century BC, the impresario added a spectacular procession of horses and chariots and the loot of Troy. The momentum of Aeschylus' conception was no longer understood, and a spectacular pseudo-ritual was invented. When Aeschylus took a modern, very nearly a contemporary subject, the Persian Wars, in which he and many of his audience had fought, his sense of the necessary form of tragedies, and of their ritual basis, made him tell the story from a Persian point of view, because it was a Persian catastrophe which only the Persians lamented. Of course he showed the Athenians as heroes, and his eyewitness account of the sea-battle of Salamis is one of the most impressively written pieces of history that we have from that dead world. But he is said to have been publicly prosecuted for showing sympathy with the enemy. No one prosecuted Homer for writing the *Iliad*, which ends with the lament for Hector.

Greek comedy is more obviously European than Greek tragedy. By the time of Aristophanes and the first complete plays we have, it was a heady and exhilarating mixture of forms. Socrates appears as a knock-about comic character, there are cheerful and nostalgic religious and ritual overtones, politics is sharply touched, the verses are full of parody and the plots imitate each other, institutions and social types are taken from anywhere to be grist to the comic mill. What followed after the collapse was less exciting, but longer-lived. It was a gentle comedy of manners, with everyday scenes about ordinary people, moral speeches, romantic plots and happy endings. At least the central, middle-class characters were shown as ordinary. These tamer performances were adapted by the Romans, and through Roman adaptations they were influential in the Renaissance, although the Greek originals of that style slept in the sands of Egypt, on rubbish-heaps and among the wrappings of the dead, until the 19th century.

It is hard to call ancient Greek literature European, because there was no Europe at that time, or if there was one it consisted of the Greeks. The La Tène Celts were as great artists in bronze as the Greeks or greater, but from a literary point of view they were pre-Homeric. Yet the dialogue with the dead that links us to Greek writers, and to their sense of reality, has never ceased. It was a noticeable murmur throughout the Middle Ages, and in the Renaissance it swelled to a noise like that of a crowded cocktail party. By the 15th century, educated Europe had a great deal in common. The inheritance was sidelong, transmuted, misunderstood, so that when attention was payed to original texts the results were startling.

The achievements of medieval European literature were very great, but not unified, not universally available, and with a few exceptions they left no aftermath. The intellectual inheritance of Thomism, and still more so the wilder inheritance of late scholasticism, took a long time to disappear. But the medieval writers we read as literature (a curious and often a misleading category) are isolated stars, they are not a constellation. The immense greatness of Dante lies partly in his intellectual seriousness, partly in his authority of language. From the first point of view he has never ceased to be admired, and read, and loved. From the second, his immediate influence was confined to Italian. Chaucer, for example, shows too little respect for lessons he could have learned from Dante. He can cope with courtly Boccaccio, not with that serious monumental plainness.

The lyrics of the Middle Ages, whether vernacular or Latin, exist in isolated worlds of their own. There is more in common between European ballads, which are at least all based on a similar social system, and related folklore. Villon stands on the brink of the Renaissance, but he belongs surely to the Middle Ages. He is perhaps the greatest, in a few poems, of all European poets from the Augustan age until now. The reality of his work is astonishing and moving. But how isolated he is as a poet. He is deeply rooted in popular life and language, utterly individual, as harmonious in his soul as the nine muses, with a cutting edge like a broken whisky bottle. Those who preceded and who followed him are as little able to achieve what he achieved as those excellent poets who preceded and followed Dante.

To take only the tradition I personally know best, Langland is unparalleled, the poet of *Sir Gawain* stands alone, Chaucer is a completely lonely monument. This odd phenomenon probably has to do with difficulties of dialect and language. We know for example that because the anomalies of the pronunciation of the final *e* in words had been settled in Scotland soon after Chaucer's time, but not in England, Chaucer had Scottish followers in the iambic pentameter, but not English. In England the metre had to be reinvented in the 16th century. With insignificant exceptions, it was first widely understood about 1580, when Shakespeare was a young man. What is usually meant by European literature began with the Renaissance, and with the first results of the invention of printing.

It is a curious and important question, why England of all barbarous places should have been blessed with the Elizabethan theatre. The Italian theatre was sophisticated and developed as early as Machiavelli, the vernacular theatres of the Venetian Empire flourished when Shakespeare was a schoolboy, the wish for literary glory and the pretensions of princely patronage were widespread, French was already exquisite in the mouth of Ronsard, Spanish was at a flowering point. So why on earth England? Whether the mixed audience of the new, mercantile London, or the mixed society and the national chauvinism of that period, or some other medieval or modern element in the constitution of 16th-century consciousness may have been a determining characteristic, I am not competent to say. But the literary traditions that Shakespeare inherited were certainly extremely mixed.

We have, for example, a play called *Horestes*, written shortly before Shakespeare wrote. It is based on the *Phoenissae* of Euripides, through an Italian adaptation of a Latin version. The English play starts with the stage direction, "Enter Rusticus and Hodge, upon the battlements of Mycenae." It ends with a hanging from the battlements, while the heroine howls and swoons. These two scenes are by no means Euripidean. It may be that the very misunderstandings and anachronisms, above all the mixture of comic and tragic scenes, gave a freedom and an unrivalled opportunity to Shakespeare, whose acid test of everything was how it worked in the theatre. The French theatre was neoclassic; its theories, wrong as they may have been in ancient Greek terms, were a rigid guide. The brilliant light of the focus of interest in Racine and Corneille brings off effects that never tempted Shakespeare, because he never understood their technical possibility. A comparison of Dryden's *All for Love*, a neoclassic adaptation of *Antony and Cleopatra*, with its Shakespearean original, even allowing for the intervening century, serves to underline what was at stake.

But Shakespeare read Montaigne, Voltaire came close to understanding Shakespeare, Milton produced, incredibly and with that learned passion which belongs to many great poets, the noise of fine Italian poetry in English. Moral ideas were in common, with some national differences, as much in 1700 as they were after the 1939 war. Movements of taste flowed this way and that. The greatest Italian contributions until this century were made early, the greatest German contributions perhaps in the 18th century, the last chapter of the European Renaissance. The English contributions have been sporadic, subject to a variety of foreign influences, and all owing a considerable debt to the utterly unsystematic and therefore unshackling nature of English literary education. Nowadays, of course, we have altered all that, and there may in future be fewer British contributions. But even in the dying away of literature since the Indian summer of the modern movement, the intransigent and unsystematized British have continued to write and to be read, more than most European countries outside Russia.

Literature is about reality, or if you like, the consciousness of reality. By this is meant any and every reality of which normal human beings can be conscious. If by some stroke of literature they could be made conscious of some new kind of reality, then that would be included; if not, not. The new possibilities of films, and the fulfilled possibilities of statistical studies, have taken over what used to be a large part of the area slowly colonized by European literature, rather as railways and railway-determined settlement patterns took over from canals, at the moment when canals had reached their maximum, and as improved road transport and air transport have taken over from railways. You and I may prefer to go by train, we may dream of going by canal, but we travel as we must. A film can show in three minutes of film time what a novelist would agonize to describe, and not be believed. Poetry, because its skill is so primitive, survives. But the bridge, which led from the fullest development of European consciousness into the sober art forms of this century, is undoubtedly the novel.

No one has read in their original languages all the great novels that exist, any more than anyone has read all the lyric poems. There is no European language, except perhaps in the Swiss mountains, without important novels. It is not so interesting to trace the development of the form as it is to observe its momentum. Everyone has learnt something from Dickens or from Balzac, from Manzoni or from Tolstoy, the greatest of novelists, let alone what we learn from those contemporaries on whose works we pounce, Pasternak, Solzhenitsyn, Camus, Sartre and so on. I am not an immensely wide reader of novels, except thrillers, but I recollect wonderful Hungarian, Greek, German, and Italian and Spanish novels that have taught me more about those countries than I could otherwise possibly have learnt. This, surely, is part of the community of Europe. In poetry one discovers only a human being like oneself, but in novels one senses the bulk of the differences.

The novel has its formal origins in romance literature. It starts at a time when the notion of literature, which I take to be a sort of egalitarianism of books, a consent to be housed on one shelf, produced in one workshop, reviewed in the same periodicals, has already been established. The idea of literature can even be ignored, since the needs of a reading public which is no longer well able to differentiate its own needs seem to indicate bulk and plot rather than any refinement of style. The novels of Balzac, an invaluable social document, and those of Dickens, a great literary corpus which is misleading as a social document, arose in this atmosphere. The novel is essentially as middle-class as late Greek comedy. Attempts to extend it into the whole of life have usually failed to alter the form, even when they produced masterpieces. The exception that proves this rule is the work of James Joyce.

The European novel, from Fielding through the vast achievements of the Russian and French 19th-century novelists, of whom Stendhal is still as relevant to our own world in prose as Baudelaire is in poetry, until the American and German and French novels of the last 20 years, has offered a uniquely broad field of expression. The trilogy, *Ungoverned Cities*, and its untranslated sequel, *The Lost Spring*, by Iannis Tsirkas in modern Greek, tell us more about Greece since 1939 than anyone, whether Greek or not, could otherwise learn. They do for modern reality what Walter Scott so brilliantly did for the imagined past. The thrillers of Simenon, read in bulk, tell us more about a France we know to exist than any grander writer could do. Hemingway's novel about the Spanish Civil War (I must count him as European) is truer to what we know from old friends as the atmosphere of that war than the orthodox

histories of it, though there are truer novels about what followed in Spanish, and George
Orwell's sober, autobiographic *Homage to Catalonia* is better than any novel.

How is it that we know truth in a novel, so immediately, even before the inevitable, careful checking? Why is it that we value novels for their truth, and autobiographies for their fictional power? We are hungry for reality, to make sense of the world, and the forms of literature tell us silently, at once, what we may expect of a new book. The attenuated supremacy of poetry is based there. So is the overwhelming force of realism in fiction, and of the social and the political novel. Many readers outside Paris, who would think Sartre a scholastic, theoretic, unconvincing writer, have been convinced by him in novels and in the theatre. There must still be readers like myself who are unable to take Saint-Simon as seriously as they take Proust, even though in the last analysis they prefer Saint-Simon. And why do we prefer Montaigne to anything modern? And why could the same be said, analogously, in other European languages? Is it not because in modern writing, with its abundant techniques of describing, each with roots in 19th-century intellectual history, but not all of which any one novelist can master, the stable prose picture of reality has dissolved? Which of us would not prefer Freud to a Freudian novelist?

What is unstable is our consciousness of reality, and in this century our potential has outrun our actual consciousness. The average European intellectual is still faithful to the broad stream of liberal common sense that stems from Erasmus and his friends. But writers must be extreme, they must explore the limits of their articulate reason and of their experience of life, and they must use their form, as Lorca has said of poets, to the marrow of its bone. At best, the form becomes something else, and recognized experience is vastly extended, as it was in Pasternak's great novel. Merely formal revolutions are trivial, and strange or extreme experience does not convince until it can be fully and powerfully imagined, and I think I must add until it has created its form. One should remember that the last work of Cervantes was a neoclassic pastoral romance. The form of *Don Quixote* was not repeated; maybe it was unrepeatable.

In the modern period prose writers and poets have been fighting almost consciously over the carcass of European reality. The great movements have taken place in great cities, but the admirable writers have often been provincials: Pessoa, Trakl, Hardy, Chekhov and their like. The impetus of surrealism is not to be assessed by the manifestoes of André Breton, but in painting by the work of the Belgian Magritte, and in writing by the work of Lorca, who combined an intellectual but not a Parisian grasp of that movement with his own deep roots in Spanish popular tradition. One might add Aimé Césaire, and the remarkable and pure masterpiece, *Amorgos*, a poem in modern Greek by Nikos Gatsos. In the process of filtering metropolitan movements to the serious children of the provinces, a necessary misunderstanding takes place. Something similar may be true of the whole modern movement in European literature. Isaac Babel is a writer of genius, no Russian metropolitan writer is comparable. Compared to him, Hemingway is a clodhopper. There is more of reality, and more important reality, in Babel's short stories, each one cut down in a period of months from 90 pages to nine or 60 pages to six, than there is in entire novels by other writers. Edmund Wilson has suggested that Dostoevsky's novels are poetry by other means. This is, on the face of it, nonsense; but it might be said of Babel, and even of Zamyatin at greater length, that their writings have the tense balance and the convincing mythology that poets long to have.

Saint-John Persse has written poetry which wins back a lost territory from prose writers. Eliot took at least temporary possession of what had belonged to novelists. Neither poets nor novelists nowadays are unconscious of Proust, an influence as pervasive now as that of Rousseau was in its day. These influences are liberating, but no literature completely liberates. In most, though not in all his works, D. H. Lawrence is an example of an apparently liberating influence which is now an expired balloon. It is worth noticing that his poetry still reads as purely and beautifully as ever; so do a few of his novels. The great novelists who have disputed the territory or condition of poetry have been Joyce and James and Proust and Pasternak. One might add Breton, Cendrars, and a tradition going back to Goethe. Pound, in the gigantic ruins of his epic attempt, in the *Cantos*, has attempted to win back for poetry the ground of economic and political textbooks, of wisdom literature, of religion, of narrative epic and of anthropology.

Such a supercharge has produced both a poetry and a detritus in some ways unequalled, but many readers may prefer clarity and separation of subject-matter.

In fact what has most characterized European writing has been its rationality. Novelists learnt to write not so much from romance writers as from philosophers and historians, and from the theatre with its conspiracy of common sense. Powerful epic poetry exists in many less rationalizing traditions than ours. The magic of theatrical performance is at least as wonderful elsewhere. But what is completely said, the full and level discussion of human behaviour, is more easily to be found in the ebb and flow of European writing. Diderot and Voltaire and Machiavelli, or to make the same point with a different colouring, Clarendon and Fielding and Gibbon, concentrate all the means of prose lucidly and soberly on their subject-matter. It is the rationality and the ease, something socially different from witty contrivance or rhetorical force, in the best prose stylists ever since Montaigne, that make possible their morally substantial discussions of reality.

That is true even of short collections of maxims in French and in German, and of the diaries and letters of some writers. Substance is not at all equivalent to length. Nor is it the same as overt earnestness. Buffon on nature and Brillat-Savarin on food are not simply charming; they are fully human and morally substantial writers. The late, unfinished work of Stevenson and I believe of Stendhal are no less important than literary offerings completely worked out. In the short stories of Isaac Babel it is precisely the small scale of the vignettes, the massive pressure of what is not said, that invests his writing with its extraordinary human and literary greatness. Among the young German critics who were at work around 1800, any big literary work could be called a novel, a *Roman*. Distinctions are more useful than extensions of the language of criticism, but it is true that there is something in common underlying all the activities of literature; there is an appetite for sharpness and control of the language, and always the same hunger, however sidelong or minimal, to express the reality of human experience.

Of course the position of the novel, at its fullest and strongest, is all-important in the history of our literature, and the development of the novel has altered all our consciousness of reality. That development is intimately bound to a social history in Europe which at the present time is altering itself completely. The development is subtle, it has by-ways and hidden elements, it has not yet been satisfactorily charted. The world in which it was possible for George Eliot or for Tolstoy or for Flaubert to write was a strange mixture, and its opportunities were unique, but at least it was less volatile than what made possible the wonderful political comedies of Aristophanes. One difference is the bulk of printed books and the massive popular audience that fed itself on 19th-century novels.

But what we most value now is not, in general, what has done most to transform our notions of reality. Edmund Wilson has pointed out that the mass of 19th-century prose could not be finely written. Most of those novels one reads once in a lifetime, but one may turn back many times to an obscure provincial diarist, to the same 20 pages of Proust, to the poems of George Herbert or Emily Dickinson. Being finer, and sharper, and crystallized in psychological distance, being also more immediate because so individual, they nourish a profounder personal need than Dickens nourishes. Since the reading of a book is such a personal matter, it ought not to be unexpected that most of us read many of the books we read for personal reasons. My judgement votes for Lope de Vega, but my hand reaches for Gongora. I read the notebooks of Seferis and of Camus more often than any great novel of this century.

There is some analogy with the old European expresses that ground their way under steam-power so thrillingly across France and Germany and the Balkans. When they stopped during the night at stations like Dijon, one woke to hear the heavy iron tapping as railwaymen tested the big wheels. That dislocated bang, bang, bang gave one a sense of security, and one imagined through one's sleep the whole vast train, the whole railway system of Europe, the amazing history of engineering. In this analogy, all but the greatest novels are read faster than poetry, their destination is distant and impressive, their noises are those of the train in motion, the steam and the lights and the passing countryside. But in the most individual works of European literature, particularly in poetry, the train is in an unnamed provincial station, and one can hear the banging on the wheels. It sounds very close.

Much of modern poetry, and a large minority of modern prose, has become so specific as to be fragmentary, baffling. I do not mind being baffled by poetry so long as I receive from it an immediate charge of human quality, and some promise that time and rereading will reveal more. Baffling prose is almost never worthwhile. *Finnegan's Wake* is enough, and I suspect, anyway, that its attraction is that of poetry; it is a *materia poetica* of language, a wonderful, flawed, unwritten poem. With poetry there are no general rules: no device is justified or unjustifiable except as some poet in a particular poem makes it so. Every individual poet alters the rules by his own understanding of them, inevitably and unconsciously. Each feels the pressure of his own language. Metropolitan movements reappear at the other end of Europe purged of folly, with a pure strength they never had until then. Seferis is even greater than Laforgue. The works of Russian or French or Polish provincial writers translate into English like the central stream of a great tradition. The same happens in the interchange of centuries. It is as Mayakovsky wrote:

> Centuries later metal expresses
> creep up and kiss your hard hands,
> poetry.

We are still trying, sometimes more and sometimes less consciously, to revive the conditions of Homer, when every phrase was finely written, when the range of literature was vast, when coherent values determined structure and perpetual questioning of those values and that structure kept it living, when the language of narrative was both special and popular, both unexpected and traditional. The traditions of European literature do in fact embody those ideals in one way or another. There is no going backwards, but there is a sense in which the whole of European literature is simply Homer, written out at greater length. Thank God for the length. It means that no one has read all the great books. Tomorrow I could read some new Stendhal, or some new Boccaccio.

# 9

# *Architects*

## STEPHEN GARDINER

Looking around at the 20th-century scene, it is sometimes difficult to see the architecture for the buildings, design today is generally so poor. This state of affairs, which is not, of course, confined to Europe, leads to considerable confusion about what is architecture and what is not, and to the widespread belief, which is more alarming, that architecture is not work of the imagination and has no meaning as art any more; for an art it still is, or should be – and not merely a past art as some may well feel it is when, for instance, they peer out between tower . blocks at the magnificent dome of St Paul's cathedral in London. The desecration of Wren's great work is one of the oustanding acts of aesthetic vandalism in Europe, and it provides a dreadful glimpse of contemporary values. In the foreground is a kind of computerized version of building, the form and appearance of which have been dictated by the requirements of the machine; in this section of the 20th-century picture the responsibility for design has been shifted from the architect to such methods as industrialized systems of prefabrication, and these exclude people as they exclude the contribution of the artist and craftsman, thus displaying a horrifying misuse of the machine. In the background there is a view of the past, made by people.

Modern architecture is also made by people; here is work by individuals, as Renaissance or ancient Greek architecture was, and it has nothing whatever to do with its awful commercialized imitations in which its outlines are copied and little else. However much the opportunities and aesthetics of modern architecture are influenced by mechanization, the individual, as artist and craftsman, survives to determine the direction of the style, as we see from the works of such varied architects as Le Corbusier, Frank Lloyd Wright, Mies van der Rohe and Alvar Aalto, all of whom were concerned with the imagination of architecture, and all of whom had an immense effect in determining the direction of the European modern movement – although American, Wright had a huge following among European students, as, of course, Le Corbusier did. In principle, their objective was the same – to reduce often highly complex problems to simple and immediately comprehensible forms and arrangements of space that would give the greatest possible pleasure to others. All fell in love with the freedom of modern architecture, and with the tremendous opportunities thrown up by new structural ideas – Wright with the cantilever, for example, Le Corbusier with the plasticity of concrete, as displayed in his masterly chapel at Ronchamp. What was more, of course, these architects were horrified to find such structural ideas, beautiful in themselves, dressed up, and covered up, in the drab, old-fashioned clothes of Neoclassical styles – the obsolete clothes had to be stripped off, it was essential to get back to first principles, to start with a clean sheet; a reason why architects liked white (and painted their buildings white), and why the aesthetic of the early days was simple and direct. Wright took his inspiration from nature, and his influence has been most felt through his passion for natural forms and materials; Le Corbusier, on the other hand, stepped off from the Parthenon, and his influence, one hopes, will continue to be felt through his insistence on the need for a human scale and a firm order in architecture. It is the work of these two architects, above all others, which separates, through their different phases, the multiple characteristics of the modern movement into distinct strands. In one, the spirit of nature seems to be uppermost; in the other, man is in the wings, controlling operations; and in their finest works, as with great art of any time, the germ of the one is contained in the other.

This presents a very different picture from the jet-age formula that spoils countries by ignoring national characteristics and customs. It is art and craftsmanship which isolate modern architecture in a world of dense populations and high technology – indeed, in the end, it may be craftsmanship that most clearly identifies the modern style, since the concern of the artist for his product places such very great emphasis on this aspect of his work. The attention architects like Le Corbusier and Aalto gave to detail is breath-taking: the perfection of their craftsmanship seems to belong to another age. And so, in a sense, it does because, of course, a very long, very rich history lies behind such architects, stretching far away into the remote past to ancient Greece, and reminding us that all the different periods of architecture are really stages in development where there are no specific beginnings and ends, every style being as much a part of the past as the present is of the future. We are a piece of a much larger story than we realize sometimes, or would perhaps care to admit; when we look back, European architecture since Pericles is like a huge plain in which the principles that were set down at the Acropolis have spread everywhere. In the middle of the plain, there is, of course, a hump – Gothic – studded with the fantastically beautiful jewels of great artists and craftsmen, which, like a sudden mountain range, appears to begin and end with almost equal suddenness, leading on to nothing except a total appreciation of aesthetic values, which is everything.

This diagrammatic picture suggests something of the scale of European architecture. While the cathedral was the portrait of the Gothic Age, and gigantic in size, the building that was subjected to influences from Classical sources was generally rather modest in appearance: one thinks of the Greek temple, the Roman villa with its airy peristylar garden, a Byzantine church, a Renaissance chapel by Brunelleschi, the Place des Vosges, the English domestic 18th-century style, the Corbusier Centre in Zurich, and one thinks too in more general terms of certain geometric disciplines and principles of proportion that ordered the aesthetic frame of this classically orientated architecture. Then, again, Europe is a story of immense upsurges of creative energy that show themselves in some stupendous architectural conclusions like the Acropolis, the Pantheon and St Peter's, Santa Sophia, Chartres, and Wren's City of London churches. After 300 or 400 years or so, these upsurges of energy are succeeded by immense collapses; and then there follows, or should follow, a period of renewal – we ought to be at the beginning of one now, although it is not always easy to believe this. The story of Europe is one of continuity where each supreme effort is in some way communicated to the next; it starts in southeast Europe, but 2,000 years elapsed before the entire and vast store of ideas that had built up from the Acropolis onwards showered out of the Renaissance to sweep through the continent and across the channel to England.

Several patterns recur in architectural history. Let us take one of these. The Romans were men of action; they were empire builders, and their technically sophisticated and highly organized way of life at home, which travelled with them on their conquests abroad, led to such astonishing advances in structure in the arch and the vault that it is sometimes exceedingly difficult to accept that they ever happened, and that they happened 2,000 years ago; yet they did, and the Renaissance, that age of thought and imagination, looked back at these developments and observed how an architecture of great elegance could be made out of them; feats of engineering thrown up by necessity and conceived for use were turned into art. Again, in the 19th century expansion was once more underway, and this in turn led to cast-iron bridge construction, railway sheds with enormous spans and framed structures of great size in steel and concrete; and like those of the Renaissance, 20th-century architects looked back at these leaps in technology and saw how they could be put together to make an ordered architecture. So too with the ancient Greeks: the early people made huts out of reeds for shelter, and the Greeks looked at those bundles of reeds and perceived what could be made of such forms – fluted columns and capitals. It is this, perhaps, which makes the Greek triumph at the

Acropolis – or at Paestum or Delphi – seem far more inconceivable than any Roman aqueduct or amphitheatre. The Greeks started with so little – primitive huts, bundles of reeds, a strange art and colonnaded tombs seen in Egypt, the earth coloured columns in Knossos and the old *megaron* form excavated from the depths of Tiryns – and from so little, from the muddled yet marvellously imaginative mind of the past, from, in particular, that naive *megaron* form struggling to surface, they accomplished in the Acropolis the greatest architectural conclusion ever reached. From confusion they discovered order, and this order then guided Europe for well over 2,000 years. The Greeks created architecture, and in the process they established, of course, beyond any possible doubt, the meaning of art.

Here is another pattern. A style starts out, as only it can, in the form of large buildings for government or similarly influential patrons, and it is these structures which determine certain basic principles of design. The style then contracts and finds a more universal range where these principles apply to everyday things – domestic building is an example. In the case of the Acropolis, however, the architectural principles embodied there have been in the process of being studied, understood and scaled down ever since. For instance, people need order; they must be able readily to comprehend their surroundings; they have always sought order – in life, in art. And the buildings at the Acropolis – the Parthenon, the Propylaea, the temple of Athena Nike and the Erechtheum – present an order, a structural order through the repetition of columns in which the Greeks observed aesthetic possibilities. This order solved problems with which the Greeks were particularly concerned. For one thing, it established human scale; for another, it created a background discipline and a firm relationship between buildings and with surroundings. The ancient Greeks started from man; for them, the accomplishment of human scale was perhaps the most important matter of all in building. Unlike Gothic, where architecture was seen as a manifestation of the spirit of God, the Greek view was concerned with the expression of an ideal through art that was a manifestation of the spirit of man. At the Parthenon, for instance, you have the old house form of the *megaron* surrounded with a peristyle, and thus the relationship between man and structure is communicated by the shape of the space made by the frame of columns and entablature which correspond to the shape and proportion of a man. But these peristyles, widely used in all kinds of public buildings in the centres of cities and towns, also performed the function of breaking down the conventional barriers of walls which separate insides and outsides; they introduced freedom of movement (most important to people), and connected, through the spaces between the columns, one building with the next, the one being like the mirrored image of the other. When we remember that much the same kind of order that was used at the Acropolis and elsewhere was being employed on a wide front and for the same aesthetic reasons – to determine a real human scale and establish a continuity of background – in vast 19th-century European planning developments, the achievements of the ancient Greeks seem as bewildering and as difficult to imagine as the idea of eternity.

The Greeks took immense trouble with proportion and detail – all had to be beautiful in the eye of the beholder. While on the one hand, for instance, the view through a peristyle located man's position in a town or landscape, on the other, details to do with optical illusions had to be adjusted to eliminate distortions. Slight curves, like the entasis to columns, were introduced, and innumerable subtle variations, and all arranged to obtain an exact balance between perfection and variety. Ictinus, the architect to the Parthenon, was, of course, a perfectionist, and in his attempts to perfect every detail he seemed to be reflecting the differences between people, even their imperfections. It is no wonder that over the centuries architects like Vitruvius, Alberti, Palladio and Le Corbusier, indirectly or directly, returned to the Acropolis for guidance and inspiration. But the Romans had a very different attitude to architecture, nevertheless; they took what they found useful in Greek architecture as they took what they needed from Etruscan engineering. And since their chief preoccupation, at least in the beginning, was with organization and with communications, their primary contribution to European architecture was their pioneering of amazing feats of engineering.

The Greeks, of course, showed no special interest in engineering, and this was because their interests lay elsewhere, with aesthetics, scale – perhaps most particularly with scale and proportion, and columns at close centres met their prescription for these; in their temples, they did not even use the wooden truss for a clear span, although they did investigate it; the clear span might have meant a loss of human scale. The Romans, on the other hand, developed Greek beginnings in the truss and achieved clear spans in their temples; the Romans were a practical, economical people. For example, they adopted the Greek plan for temples but generally eliminated the peristyle. They also took the Greek peristyle house and attached it to the Etruscan *atrium* – sunlight and leisure were married to water and its uses. The Romans were fascinated by any kind of gadget, structure or building system that would support their highly complex society. Like the Greeks, the Romans regarded man as being of supreme importance in the world, yet while the Greek outlook was directed towards art and philosophy, the Romans' was directed towards good management, the practicalities of living, and the family. Hence the importance of the house, but hence, too, those immense constructions that brought water across valleys to strengthen the lifelines of the family and communications with far distant lands. Again, it was from the Etruscans that the Romans learnt about irrigation, and the Etruscans also started them off with the arch and the vault. And when the Roman discovered the arch, all was arches: the aqueduct, for instance. Yet a glance at these fantastic skeleton constructions – the Pont du Gard and the aqueduct at Segovia are about the most dramatic – must make one wonder what inner strength has seen such slender structures through 20 centuries. And, of course, they did have an inner strength – the Romans' one contribution to architecture that was entirely their own: concrete.

Nevertheless, practical-minded as the Romans were, these developments in structure led to great works of architecture; as in Gothic, the structure was the architecture; the originality of the Roman style depended on structural invention, and it was from the conquest of structural problems, hitherto unresolved or unrecognized, that the inspiration of the Romans' truly original building forms and plans was derived. The Romans' comprehension of structure was compatible with their comprehension of nature; namely, an economic structure obeys certain natural laws, and if the design conflicts with these laws the structure will fail. The recognition of these laws became the spring-board for the Romans' creative ideas. The structural solutions, using the arch, at the triple aqueduct of Aqua Marcia in Rome of 144 BC, for example, gave the Romans the confidence to build their hot baths, palaces, basilicas and theatres. The interest in Roman architecture begins with the discovery of the arch which led on to the discovery of concrete, the material which made ambitious structures possible. Concrete led to brick and stone piers to eliminate walls; to coffered ceilings to reduce waste of material and weight; to aqueducts 30 metres high; to buttresses, and to vaults and domes with huge spans, and so the circular, dramatic and rich and rounded forms that make Roman architecture so memorable, seen at their most spectacular in the Colosseum and Hadrian's villa, and at their most conclusive in the Pantheon.

Thus the Romans completed the work on the foundations of European architecture. The arch and vault are as fundamental to its structural history as the Greek view of scale and proportion is to its aesthetic guidelines. The sphere, as demonstrated at the Pantheon, one of the oldest forms as well as the strongest, remained an equally positive influence in the future. In its use of the minimum surface area to cover any volume of space, the sphere focuses attention on the centre, which is why it makes so much sense in religious buildings: why, for example, it was central to the theme of Santa Sophia, and why Leonardo was working on the form in the early 1500s and Michelangelo returned to it at St Peter's. Santa Sophia, however, brought two great, and conflicting, themes together – the circle and the square. The Roman influence is indicated by the circle, the Greek influence by the square, and the dual theme is introduced by a totally new architectural form – the Greek cross. It is true that a cross of sorts, but of a much more elongated kind, had been developing in early Christian churches in central Italy since Christ's death and Constantine's recognition of Christianity as the state religion, but here, at Santa Sophia built for Emperor Justinian in 537, the cross became a decisive, near-symmetrical plan of great power that forced out a correspondingly powerful three-dimensional form. It is as though the architects – Anthemius of Tralles and Isodorus of Miletus – had seen in the symbol a remarkable architectural idea – one of those ideas that have the mark of immortality – and had seized it. That the architects were Greek is not all that surprising, and not merely because Greeks were poor at this time and on the lookout for work, as they undoubtedly were, but because they had centuries of knowledge behind them, and their wisdom and expertise were

*31.* The humanist scholar Desiderius Erasmus. Portrait by Hans Holbein the Younger, 1523.

*32. Overleaf*: The family of Ludovico Gonzaga, Francesco II of Mantua (1466–1519). Detail of a wall painting by Andrea Mantegna, 1474.

33. Niklaus Kratzer, astronomer to Henry VIII of England. Portrait by Hans Holbein the Younger, 1528.

*34.* Georg Gisze, banker and merchant. Portrait by Hans Holbein the Younger, 1532.

*35. Overleaf*: A landscape depicting the Fall of Icarus. Painting by Pieter Bruegel the Elder, 1550.

36. A map of Europe drawn by Gerhardus Mercator, c. 1590.

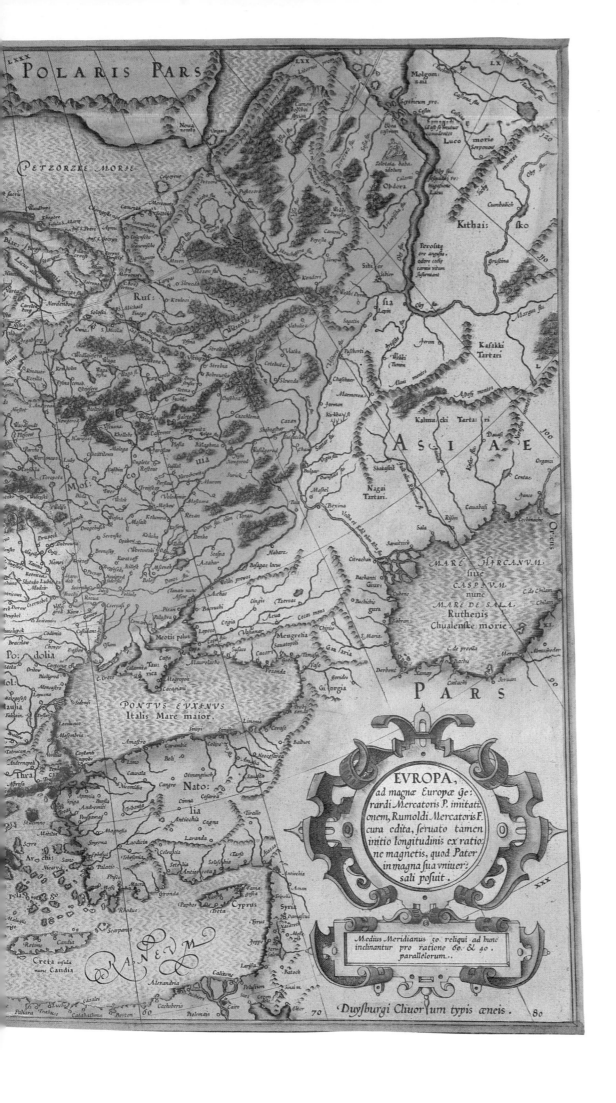

37. Lorenzo de' Medici, the Magnificent, of Florence (1449–92). A 16th-century painting, anon.

38. An Italian tailor. Portrait by Giovanni Battista Moroni, c. 1570.

*39.* A moneylender and his wife. Painting by Quentin Metsys, 1514.

*40, 41.* *The Alchemist* (1558) and *Summer* (1568). Engravings by Pieter Bruegel the Elder.

DEBENT IGNARI RES FERRE ET POST OPERARI     QVATVOR INSERTA NATVRIS IN NVBE REFERTA
IVS LAPIDIS CARI VILIS SED DENIQ₃ RARI     NVLLA MINERALIS RES EST VBI PRINCIPALIS
VNICA RES CERTA VILIS SED VBIQ₃ REFERTA     SED TALIS QVALIS REPERITVR VBIQ₃ LOCALIS

Iulius, Augustus, nec non et Iunius Aestas.    AESTAS    Frugiferas aruis fert Aestas torrida meßeis.

42. Tax collecting. Painting by Pieter Bruegel the Elder, 1556.

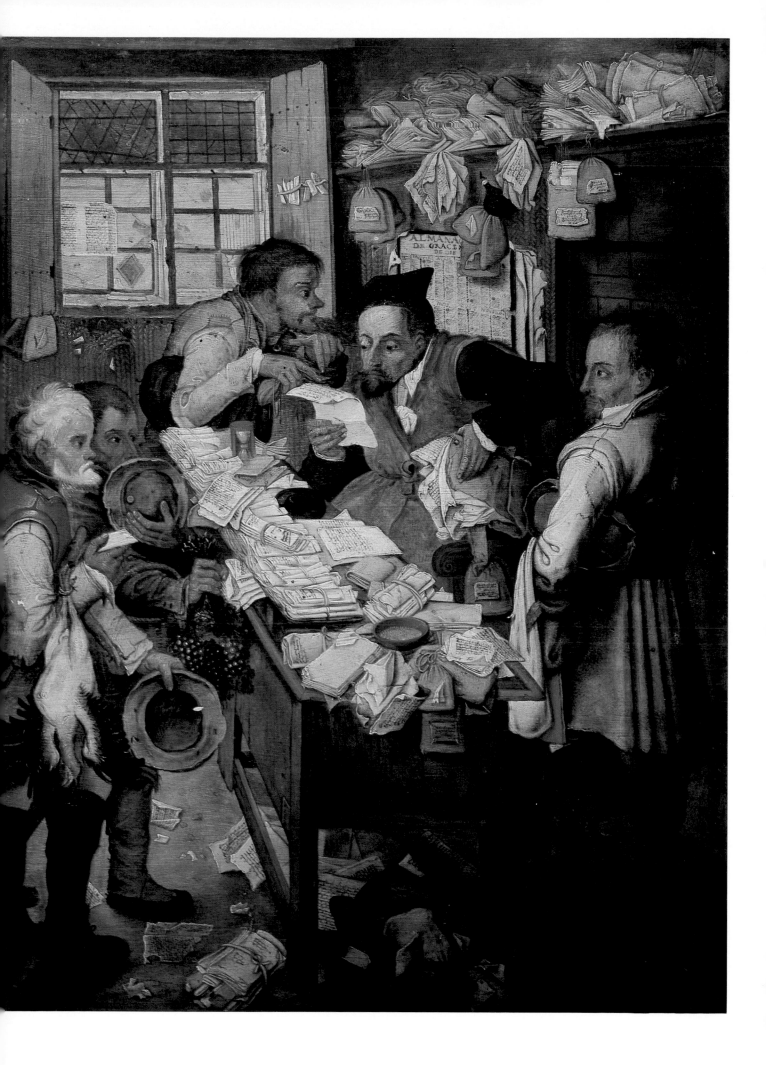

*43.* A musical gathering at the Bavarian court directed by Orlando di Lasso (extreme left). Miniature by Hans Mielich, c. 1560.

most needed when the Roman Empire was on the brink of crumbling. The conception, moreover, has an aesthetic purity that is utterly Greek. The architects' objective at Santa Sophia was to build a single space where people could gather, as a crowd; they wanted a focus on the centre. To make this space they employed a structure of gigantic piers which pegged out the plan of the Greek cross; backed up by knowledge from the Roman end, the Greek architects then completed the cross with the drum and the dome. Yet to do this successfully, they had to invent the pendentive, a structural device which resolved the awkward transition between the square base and the circular superstructure as a single, effortless curve. And so here, at Santa Sophia, was the prototype of Michelangelo's St Peter's and of the Baroque that followed, all of which happened 1,000 years and more later; behind this building, predictably perhaps, was the genius of the Greeks, superbly supported by Roman engineering.

Santa Sophia sparked off the Byzantine church forms, those richly modelled little buildings with the hand-shaped quality of pottery, where plans were derived from the Greek cross and drums, and domes were raised on pendentives from square bases, and which spread with the Byzantine Empire from the Greek mainland to the islands, into Italy and across to France. But Santa Sophia makes us think of something else: the tremendous importance of people – of the people who commission buildings and the people who create them, of the patrons and the architects, of how one man's inspiration can start a style or a movement. The course of art has so often returned to the genius of one man enlightened enough to see outside the limits of his own time, or whose conceptions had a life beyond the works made. Pericles, of course, was such a man; he chose Ictinus to design the Parthenon and it was from this building that the architects of the Propylaea and the Erechtheum took their inspiration; one thing leads to another – the Acropolis would have been a different place without Ictinus. The peristylar garden in Hadrian's villa has connections with the spirit of Palladio's colonnaded country houses, and the form of the Pantheon, for that matter, had an influence on the Villa Rotonda's. Then there was Justinian's choice of architect for Santa Sophia; and the Byzantine church form led to a branch of Romanesque. In the 11th century in the Burgundy district of France, the Abbey of Cluny had grown in power and influence to become the greatest church in Europe, and its enlightenment and inspiration were transmitted directly to architecture through the three churches that were built there. The abbey imposed severe design regulations to determine a pervasive style, and the plan of the second church spread all over Burgundy. The third church was completed in 1103, and its vast and simple plan inspired two of the most exquisite works of architecture in Europe – S. Madeleine at Vézelay and Autun cathedral, both completed in 1132. The patron was Hugh of Semur, at the end of his great period as abbot of Cluny; the artist most closely associated with all three buildings was Giselbertus; and the style was, of course, French Romanesque.

Vézelay and Autun are all that is left of this late and finest phase of the style; the Abbey of Cluny was demolished in the 19th century in a senseless piece of vandalism – and there went what must have been one of the great examples of Romanesque. Vézelay and Autun are, however, both mighty landmarks in architectural history that rise above their contemporaries as masterpieces, unmistakable and heroic. Their economy of plan and form is the essence of true Romanesque, the hall-mark of the Cluniac movement; no unnecessary decoration; functional, plain walls vaulted and cross-vaulted, the stone cut simply yet with great skill; an architecture of edges. Once more, the Roman arch and vault were the structural starting-point; but where the Romans saw the vault as an engineering solution to building problems, the French Romanesque architects saw the vault as a sculptural form which enclosed space, and they saw the space that lay between the supports; and with another visual jump, they saw the vault and the support as a single element – the one flowed into the other, and down to the ground as continuous ribs. It was this development, together with the pointed arch and vault, that made the transition between Romanesque and Gothic so easy and natural. At the St Denis Abbey in Paris, built eight years after Autun, the Abbot Suger, another magician with great influence and imagination, seems to have waved a wand: Romanesque vanished and Gothic appeared. The extraordinary art of space, flying buttresses, enormous structures climbing away into the sky, of cathedrals perched on precipices and of vaults plunging down columns to earth, of dark chapels hidden around corners and vast stained-glass windows and misty distances overhead

had arrived; a kind of architectural space age which threw up perhaps the most strangely
imaginative and unworldly monuments to an unearthly ideal the world has ever seen.

Every great cathedral in some way takes one completely by surprise – they are all amazing, huge, restless, marvellous spaces and silhouettes, yet each is an individual: Chartres, Bourges, Beauvais, Cologne, Durham, Lincoln, Wells, Léon. When the Romanesque cathedral was burnt down at Chartres, the stonemasons from St Denis went there, and somehow, via a bewildering chain of inspired minds, Romanesque metamorphosed as Gothic and this miraculous architectural pinnacle happened. The gigantic building was started in 1194, completed in 1260, and afterwards the style spread rapidly through Europe and to England. When you walk from the chapter house at Wells and take the stone flight of steps, fanning out as pure as ivory between the delicate vaults springing up around you, down to the nave where that singular arch does a remarkable handstand, you will probably think this is the most beautiful building you have ever seen. But then you remember the glass at Chartres, and the colours from it on the floor when the sun shines through, and the startling silhouette from the Paris road, and the figures around the west portal. Or you remember the overwhelming structure at Bourges, or Durham lit up on its rock at night from the Edinburgh express. There is, I think, no "greatest" cathedral, although I do think, individual wonders apart, that the last phase of Gothic in England – the Perpendicular style – was the most perfect of any. Gothic was a total art; untroubled by earthly matters of ordinary life, architecture, sculpture, frescoes and pictures on glass met in Gothic; here was a release of creative energy the like of which had never been seen before, and has never been seen since. And then this great period of European art ended, just 300 years after it had begun, with a last, flamboyant gesture in the north spire at Chartres. And so how extraordinarily ephemeral was the art of the cathedral. It started, and those armies of builders must have thought that Gothic would go on for ever; then it stopped – all of it happened in the space of three centuries. A vision had arisen, and was gone.

There is no record of the identity of the artists who created the cathedrals. All that is really known is that they were the work of teams of churchmen who were concerned with the expression of an ideal through God. The individual was unimportant; people were left out of the picture, as we see from the muddle of timber-framed and wattle cottages huddled around cathedrals and churches as though frightened of the outside world – no wonder the word "Gothic" was a term of abuse until the 18th century when the revival of Gothic art began. The view that God was beauty was regarded as narrow and probably barbaric by the Renaissance. But then the Renaissance invented the individual – this invention was the key to the Renaissance age of discovery. When we look at a Renaissance building – the Foundling Hospital by Brunelleschi, say – we are looking at the work of one man: that man, and no other, designed and drew *that* facade with its delicate columns and arches, working out the proportions to find the most perfect to give the maximum pleasure; you can see him with his pencil or his pen or compass; but Gothic is so huge and complex it is impossible similarly to discern the signature of an individual. On the other hand, through the work of someone like Brunelleschi, it is possible to imagine, and quite clearly suddenly, an architect like Ictinus at work, carefully making a drawing to full size of, perhaps, a channel cut in the marble at the base of a Doric column to get the water away, or working out, with a beam compass, the six-kilometre radius for the steps and entablature (to correct optical illusions in their line) at the Parthenon. There is, in fact, a mysterious affinity between the ancient Greek and the Renaissance man; so much so, that the Renaissance is like Roman ideas and inventions used by people as civilized as ancient Greeks; it is as though Renaissance architecture is precise, fastidious and humane because the Greeks had been given another chance to return and finish the job they had begun – this is the kind of quality that the buildings of the 15th century, in particular, convey. Here was an architecture by individuals with independent minds who examined the Roman past with the disinterested curiosity of archaeologists – Greek architecture under Pericles suggests a similar independence through its own assimilation of past material. And as in Greek architecture, Brunelleschi's geometry was of the purest kind – the square and the cube rather than the rectangle, the hemisphere and the circle rather than pointed domes and arches, were the ultimate aims: geometry was decisive in establishing the shape and form of a design. Alberti's definition of beauty as "a harmony and concord of all the parts, so that nothing could be added or subtracted except for the worse" is like another echo across the centuries from ancient Greece.

The Renaissance is a story of discovery, a search for the truth through art that led to a tremendous intellectual and spiritual upheaval; man and the Church were revalued in relation to each other; accepted dogmas were reassessed along with accepted theories of design; the scrutiny of Roman structural methods uncovered new methods, new ideas, a new spirit in architecture – Brunelleschi's examination of the Roman vault, for instance, led to his amazing double shell dome in Florence that was copied at St Peter's in Rome and St Paul's in London, while the invention of the printing press led to Alberti's translation of Vitruvius and to the publication of his own great book *De Re Aedificatoria*, in which he supplied a coherent theory of design derived from mathematical principles. Brunelleschi, Alberti, Leonardo, Donatello, Piero della Francesco, Masaccio, Mantegna and Bramante were all explorers; there seemed to be, in this golden moment of art, an endless chain of geniuses to carry the Renaissance into the 16th century and far beyond; as with the Renaissance, which was a universal art, these geniuses were universal artists; the barriers between the arts were broken down, or were removed, as if by the rediscovery of perspective. And here one may observe a mysterious link with the Gothic world: the armies of unknown artists who created great works of art from architecture, sculpture and painting seem to contract, sharpen into focus, and to become Renaissance men capable of more or less everything.

Leonardo was perhaps the most extraordinary case of all. There were his scientific discoveries, his *Mona Lisa*, his anatomical studies, his diagrams of Greek proportion as a square superimposed on a circle encompassing man, but there are also some very special sketches of plans made at the end of the 15th century and at the beginning of the next which look like thoughts for St Peter's; like his drawings of whirlpools, they are Baroque in feeling – the centralized space, the Greek cross turning into a circle, the perspective drawings projecting the plans as round and sculptural forms. Bramante was working on St Peter's at about that time – it was a building which seems to have been set aside, as though by some divine will, as the climax of the Renaissance. So many great minds contributed to it but only Michelangelo brought an immensely complex problem to a magnificent conclusion, and to a magnificently simple conclusion at that. His drawings for the building in ink line and wash – the plans, doors, studies of profiles – are masterly for precision and simplicity, beautiful just as drawings. In his design he reduced the Greek cross to the merest outline and found an exquisite balance in the ancient theme of the square and the circle. Although his conception was, of course, spoilt by Carlo Maderna who added the nave and facade, Bernini put everything right in the end with his magnificent colonnades. And so Renaissance and Baroque overlap at St Peter's; here was the beginning of the last movement of that Golden Age which cut loose from the sharply conceived, fastidious and intellectual architecture of a secure network of artists, and was swept off into an emotional, bubbling finale of circles, semicircles, ovals and domes. Baroque was a sensuous architecture, it reacted against the strict aesthetic rules imposed by the Renaissance and was released by a structural freedom that followed scientific advances: through the invention of calculus and projective geometry in the 17th century, architects had both the means to effect a far greater liberation of space than before, and the means to project complex spatial conceptions as drawings. Like Gothic, Baroque focused on the Church, and, like Gothic too, it was an international style that spread across Europe; unlike Gothic, it was, of course, disciplined by Classical principles and masses where every wall, apse and ceiling seems to dissolve into a gigantic curve.

As so often before, one man was at the centre of the movement: Bernini. Bernini's Rome, Bernini in Paris, Bernini at Versailles – he was the idol of his times, and his influence, like his energy, was vast. And because his range was also vast – architect, sculptor, painter, theatre designer, writer and composer – he inspired every aspect of Baroque art; in one way or another, Bernini and his contemporaries and followers completely changed central European architecture, the focus of Baroque finally shifting to Germany and Austria in the 18th century. There was, however, a parallel movement that was inspired by another man whose influence proved to be as great as Bernini's, but in a different way: this man was Palladio. The direction of the Renaissance seemed to divide after the completion of Michelangelo's St Peter's, taking two distinct routes – the one followed Baroque, the other followed Palladio's much more spare forms for private patrons. As it turned out, Palladio's influence spread throughout the world. Younger than Michelangelo, dead before Bernini was born, Palladio continued a theme of Grecian simplicity that had a mathematical order and a plain domestic scale which could be related to the size of a human being. He was interested in every aspect of life and took as much care over the design of a farm building as he did over the plan of a palace. He eliminated almost all decoration from his villas, stressing only the practicalities of living – the roof, the entrance, the structure, the foundations – pediment, portico, columns, piano nobile; he selected a firm form derived from the square and elaborated from it – the plan of the Villa Rotonda, for instance, is constructed from ten squares; and he recorded his theories in *I quattro libri dell'architettura*, a book which became a best-seller and spread them abroad. His following of architects around Venice, Vicenza and Verona (where he did so much of his work) was considerable – among them, Serlio and Sansovino – and in 200 years or so he had become the name of an international style: Palladian. Where Baroque, like drama, entertained and stimulated the emotions, Palladian reassured you when you got home again. Inigo Jones visited Italy in 1613, discovered the book, went overboard for Palladio, and, accordingly, the Palladian style came to England. Its secret was its humanity, and its flexibility. Palladio started from people – people in the country, on the farm, in the town – and, in consequence, the Palladian style could be adapted to suit any situation: the country mansion, the town house, the grand planning schemes of the 18th and 19th centuries – Bath, Edinburgh, London, Leningrad, Helsinki; it could look up to the scale of the community and of the house, simultaneously. The style's reticence, uncluttered order and domestic air had, and still have now, a particular appeal for the English who have, in any case, the knack of adopting the ideas of others and of interpreting them in a universally acceptable way. And the Georgian domestic style, as it evolved through the work of Jones, Wren and their contemporaries and followers, represents the last marvellous phase in the long process of scaling down Classical principles to meet day-to-day requirements of living.

And then, of course, in the middle of the 19th century, the influence of the Classical past finally broke up and collapsed, just about 400 years after the Renaissance had become established. Expansion, as in Roman days, was back, and this time with the help of mechanization, of the machine. William Morris, one of the last of the Renaissance universal men, saw the danger as we can see it today, 100 years later, for the machine has destroyed architectural values, excluded the individual and has swept away human scale in building. We have to remember these things when we come to consider the work of Le Corbusier who led the European modern architectural movement. When he started as an architect in the early 1920s there was no secure environment by which he could define his position – the most that existed, besides the works of a past age, besides new structures and materials, was a dying academicism – the fine values that inspire fine buildings had vanished away. He had to find his identity for himself. And his search for this began where the story of European architecture begins, with the Acropolis. He spent six weeks there (during a two-year journey around the continent) making drawings and notes, in exactly the same way that Brunelleschi and others had studied Roman remains; Le Corbusier, however, went to the source, to the Parthenon. And from then on his entire life's work was devoted to trying to put together the disciplines of design he had discovered there and the modern methods of construction that surrounded him, and so to find an architecture which suited both the highly complex times in which he was living and the nature of the place in which he was building. The value of his work is, therefore, not merely in the life of the objects he created, but also in the life that lies beyond them. His last building of all, the Corbusier Centre in Zurich, completed in 1968 after he had died, may well prove to be the most significant of the 20th century. Designed on his modular scale of human proportions, its plan and form are derived from the square. It could belong to no time except our century, yet its outline suggests a Greek temple. A large canopy covers the roof which is no more than $4\frac{1}{2}$ metres from the ground, and its facades blaze with colour. It is made of steel, the most suitable material available. This building, I believe, maps out quite clearly the direction architecture may one day take, in the distant future.

# 10

# Artists

## LUKE HERRMANN

Art is created by individuals, but the artist himself is the creation of his environment and of his time. Europe – and the same is true of all other civilizations – has never, as far as we know, been without art. Since his beginnings European man has made two- or three-dimensional representations of himself and of the animals and objects among which he lives. On the other hand, there have been only two quite brief periods in European history when the artist as we think of him today – a highly individual, independent and often unconventional person – has had a place in our society. The first of these periods was that of Classical antiquity from 4th-century BC Greece to 4th-century AD Rome. Then there was a gap of some 1,000 years before the Renaissance brought the artist back to Europe. In modern times it is not until the 15th century that one can truly begin to differentiate the artist from the much broader category of the craftsman. It is only since the later 18th century that the current concept of the artist as a highly independent "Bohemian" has become commonplace.

Very little is known in detail about the artists of Classical antiquity, though we should remember that these men and their works served as models for the "new" artists of the Renaissance. These artists were still very far from being their own masters, and those that were not attached to ecclesiastical foundations could only exist if they were employed or patronized by a ruler, a great aristocrat, or an ecclesiastic. In the period between the fall of the Roman Empire and the early Renaissance it was largely the Church and its royal patrons that had enabled artists to exist and to develop their skills and techniques. From the 7th century onwards churches were decorated with wall paintings and sculpture, largely designed to enhance the piety, worship and understanding of illiterate congregations. These traditions blossomed with the advent of the Gothic style in the 12th and 13th centuries, which added the medium of stained glass to the artists' repertory, while the growing demand for decorated (illuminated) prayer books and the like also provided employment for many artists. Gradually individual masters of painting and sculpture begin to emerge, but it is not until the 15th century that we can start to think of art as an identifiable "profession".

Some 500 years ago Leonardo da Vinci wrote in one of his Notebooks: "The painter strives and competes with nature . . . The painter ought to be a solitary and consider what he sees, discussing it with himself in order to select the most excellent parts of whatever he sees. He should act as a mirror which transmutes itself into as many colours as are those of the objects that are placed before it. Thus he will seem to be a second nature." At this time it was the ambition of all artists to paint as realistically as possible – to "hold a mirror up to nature". The most renowned example of success in this vein is probably Jan van Eyck's *The Arnolfini Marriage*, painted in 1434 and signed to indicate that the artist was himself present as a witness at the wedding of the Italian merchant. One of the figures reflected in the circular mirror at the back of the room may well represent the artist, and his actual "presence" within such a composition emphasizes the secure position which a painter such as van Eyck could hold in Netherlandish society by this time. One reason for this was certainly admiration for Jan van Eyck's practical skills, for he did much to perfect the use of the relatively new medium of oil colours, with which he was able to achieve the most telling rendering of detail and the most subtle effects of light.

Such skills had long been taken for granted when some 50 years ago Pablo Picasso said in an interview: "They speak of naturalism in opposition to modern painting. I would like to know if anyone has ever seen a natural work of art. Nature and art, being two different things, cannot be the same thing. Through art we express our conception of what nature is not." Picasso, one of the pioneers of truly modern art, came to express himself in a highly personal manner, which ranged from relative realism to almost total distortion and abstraction. In *The Three Musicians*, which was painted in 1921, there are just enough signposts of reality to make the work understandable to the majority of viewers. Yet the style and technique are so unrealistic that such a canvas would certainly not give any artistic satisfaction to a connoisseur who had not already experienced the preceding changes in painting and sculpture of the early 20th century. Today *The Three Musicians* is considered as a "classic" and a masterpiece, but there will still be many who do not appreciate it because of its relative lack of realism. For the majority art is only acceptable when it reproduces nature; those who agree with Picasso that "nature and art . . . cannot be the same thing" are in the minority. In the 1970s we have an enormous variety of painting ranging from the total abstraction of a bare white canvas to *trompe-l'oeil* even more realistic than the work of van Eyck. However different in appearance, all these art forms have one thing in common – for their creators (the artists) they each have individual and unique qualities; what differs so greatly is how much these qualities are recognized by those other than the artist himself.

Things were, however, very different 500 years ago, for then the painter, who was invariably trained as an apprentice or assistant in an older artist's workshop, did not work for his own satisfaction but for that of his patron or employer, who in the 15th century was likely to provide him with very precise instructions ranging from subject-matter to the materials to be used. Thus when Pietro Perugino was commissioned in 1495 to paint the main altar-piece for the church of S. Pietro at Perugia the contract stipulated: "the picture must be painted in the following way: In the rectangular panel, the Ascension of our Lord, Jesus Christ, with the figure of the glorious Virgin Mary, the Twelve Apostles and some angels and other ornaments, as may seem suitable to the painter . . . The predella below is to be painted and adorned with stories according to the desire of the present Abbot. The columns, however, and the mouldings and all other ornamentation of the panel should be embellished with fine gold and with other fine colours, as will be most fitting, so that the panel will be beautifully and diligently painted, embellished and painted from top to bottom as stated above and as it befits a good, experienced, honourable and accomplished master. It will be executed within the space of the coming two and a half years . . ." Perugino was a popular and successful artist with a large studio, in which Raphael worked for a time, rapidly adopting and then adapting the very harmonious and personal style of his master, as, for example, in the beautiful *Ansidei Madonna*, an altar-piece painted for the church of S. Fiorenzo in Perugia in about 1505.

Soon after this Raphael moved to Florence, where his Peruginesque manner must have seemed very provincial and old-fashioned. Here he was strongly influenced by Leonardo and Michelangelo and developed rapidly to his own personal style, which came to full fruition in Rome in the last ten years of his all-too-brief life. In Rome he created some of the greatest masterpieces of the Renaissance, working for the two popes, Julius II and Leo X. It was for the former that he decorated the Stanza della Segnatura, the first of a series of small rooms in the Vatican, with two large frescoes representing Philosophy and Theology, and known respectively as the *School of Athens* and the *Disputa*. These works represent the apogee of Renaissance achievement in their combination of perfect harmony and balance with stimulating individuality and diversity. In the *School of Athens* every figure and feature has a vital role to play in fulfilling the very complex "programme" of the composition – a programme that would have been readily understood by the educated man of the day – yet the composition also stands as a unique and highly personal work of art which only the mature Raphael could have created. He has included a portrait of himself, standing beside and behind his master Perugino, in the extreme right foreground – a fair indication that at this supreme moment in European painting the artist could place himself on a par with the greatest intellectual figures.

Raphael was already a leading personality in Vatican circles, at the head of a large studio of assistants and pupils and living in almost princely splendour, when he died in 1520 at the early age of 37. His Venetian contemporary Titian, whose exact year of birth is unknown, was in his nineties when he died in 1576. He was so highly regarded that he had for years been literally courted by some of the most powerful rulers in Europe, including the king of France, François I, the Habsburg emperor, Charles V (who ennobled him), and his successor as king of Spain, Philip II. An artist of genius in the painting of religious and mythological subjects, he also contributed greatly to the development of portrait painting, which had been a major occupation for Italian and northern artists since the later years of the 15th century. Titian's portrait of Jacopo Strada admirably displays the artist's painterly qualities and powers of composition – it also tells us a great deal about the remarkably many-sided sitter, who was at once artist, scholar, collector, antiquarian and dealer. This portrait serves to remind us that by the mid-16th century the successful artist had achieved an independent position in society and was no longer forced to live and work as part of the entourage of a patron. Titian himself was a man of property and wealth, recognized as one of the leading citizens of Venice. Jacopo Strada, born in Italy of Netherlandish stock, was something of a wandering artist and scholar, who spent the last 30 years of his life working for the Habsburg emperors, becoming Imperial Antiquarian, and buying for them books, paintings and works of art of all kinds. Thus he became a middleman between the artist and the collector, and can be designated as an art dealer. From now on the dealer played an increasingly important role in the buying and selling of works of art. By the 19th century artists throughout Europe had come to rely very largely on dealers for the sale of their work, and in our own day direct contact between painter and collector is rare – in a sense the dealer has now become the most important patron of the artist.

Another sign of the growing independence of artists was their breaking away from the medieval craftsmen's guilds, to which they had had to belong. In many centres they formed their own academies to enhance their professional standing, to cater for the training of young artists, and, at a later stage, to aid the dissemination and sale of their work through regular public exhibitions. The first such academy was founded in Florence in 1563 by Giorgio Vasari, with the aged Michelangelo, who had done even more than Titian to raise the status of the artist, as its nominal head. Similar institutions were soon formed in Rome and elsewhere in Italy, but none of these achieved the all-powerful position of the French Academy of Painting and Sculpture, first founded in 1648. The heyday of such academies, most of which were under royal patronage, was reached in the late 18th and 19th centuries when, as in the case of the Royal Academy in London (inaugurated in 1768), these bodies held almost complete sway over the well-being of artists within their area of authority. However, the innate conservatism of most of these institutions meant that the more independent and advanced artists rarely found membership or involvement acceptable. Throughout the 19th century artists broke away from the established academies to found rival exhibiting societies of their own, for by then the public exhibition had become a recognized means of bringing their work to the attention of potential buyers. During the same period there was also a great proliferation of art schools, some run by individual artists, some by groups of artists, and some by public educational authorities. All these developments came as a result of a great explosion in the demand for the work of artists caused by the social consequences of industrialization and colonization. This growth of demand meant that there was potential employment for more and more artists, but it is comforting from the point of view of the integrity of art that few of these artists rose above a status of obscurity. More than training and opportunity is needed to make a true artist.

In the two centuries that separated the foundation of the Roman Academy and the Royal Academy in London there were few artists who achieved the extraordinarily powerful position of a Titian or a Michelangelo, though many attained independence and a livelihood on a humbler level. Of the former, Sir Peter Paul Rubens is outstanding, both for the quality, quantity and influence of his painting and drawing, and for the importance of his contribution to the social and political life of the Europe of his day. A native of Antwerp, he studied under various artists in that city and became a master of the Antwerp Guild of St Luke in 1598, at the early age of 21. The medieval apprenticeship and guild systems survived in Antwerp and most of the Netherlands until well after Rubens's death in 1640, but Rubens himself was so successful that he was not seriously affected by this situation. In 1600 he set out for Italy where he stayed for eight years, studying and working in several cities, notably Mantua and Rome. Soon after his return to Antwerp he established his pre-eminent reputation by two great altarpieces, commissioned for the church of St Walburga and for the cathedral, in which he fully demonstrated the triumphant melding of his northern training with his Italian studies. Rubens had already been appointed court painter to the governors of the Netherlands, the Archduke Albert and the Archduchess Isabella, for whom he also carried out diplomatic missions. The demand for his paintings was such that he was forced to develop a large studio with numerous assistants, and though he usually supervised the design and composition of the works that left the studio, they were frequently only barely touched by his own brush.

Today connoisseurs and art-historians are constantly exercised trying to establish which "Rubenses" are from, or mainly from, the hand of the master; in his own day some of the more percipient patrons tried to ensure that what they bought from Rubens was not the work of assistants. Nevertheless the prestige of Rubens was so great that there was ample scope for the sale of studio work, and also for paintings in which Rubens and his studio had collaborated with independent specialists, such as Frans Snyders, the animal painter. An example of the latter practice is the huge _Prometheus Bound_, which was included in a list of available pictures that Rubens compiled for an English patron in 1618 as "Original, by my hand, the eagle done by Snyders". Painted at about the same time as the _Descent from the Cross_, this powerful mythological piece demonstrates the strength and range of Rubens's art, which have hardly ever been rivalled in the annals of European painting. Religious, historical, mythological, allegorical, genre, portrait and landscape subjects were all within the scope of Rubens and his assistants, and in each field he added new inspiration and life to European painting in the age of the Baroque.

At present the reputation of Rembrandt is probably higher than that of Rubens, but this was not the case in his own day. Some 30 years younger than Rubens, Rembrandt, who was born in Leyden in 1606, spent the greater part of his career in Amsterdam, alternating periods of considerable success and prosperity with times of failure and hardship. The bulk of his commissioned work was devoted to portraiture, but though in our own time his portraits are considered among the greatest paintings of the 17th century, contemporaries regularly thought more highly of such painters as Bartholomeus van der Helst, who is almost unknown today. Rubens's work was totally acceptable to, and indeed helped forge, the taste of his time; Rembrandt's was too advanced for the contemporary Dutch public, though it had a profound effect on many of his more adventurous fellow artists, and there is a larger recognized school of Rembrandt pupils and followers than there is of those of Rubens. The portrait of _An Old Man in an Armchair_, which is signed and dated 1652, shows Rembrandt's superlative handling of paint and his instinctive understanding of colour and light. These radical qualities in the master's work were what other artists were moved to emulate, but they failed to impress their more conservative fellow citizens who preferred more conventional portraits of themselves and their families. This situation of the artist and his work being ahead of the taste of the contemporary patron has remained a commonplace in Europe in the last three centuries – the most notorious example is that of another Dutch painter, Vincent van Gogh (1853–90), who failed to sell a single painting in his lifetime, though they now change hands for enormous sums of money.

Rembrandt and Rubens stand at the head of the hundreds of painters practising in northern Europe in the 17th century. Here rapidly developing merchant and middle classes provided a wide range of sales, while in Italy, France and Spain patronage still remained essentially aristocratic and ecclesiastic. In all these countries the painting of portraits had become the most common means for an artist to make a living – and it has remained so ever since – but in the north there were also steady sales for landscape, marine, still-life, and genre subjects suitable for hanging in prosperous but not palatial middle-class homes. The demand for much more modest works led to the great proliferation of painters on the level of "little masters", whose well-being was also assisted by a growing fashion for illustrated books for which they provided the drawings to be engraved. This development of more "private" classes of painting in the Netherlands was the beginning of a major shift of emphasis in what was required from painters by subsequent generations. The days of religious and state art were on the wane throughout Europe, and more and more artists worked with private patronage in mind. Perhaps the most significant of the new "classes" of painting was that of landscape, to which a large number of Dutch and Flemish artists devoted their skills in the 17th century. One such was Jan Wijnants, a native of Haarlem, who was especially successful in creating telling compositions of ordinary Dutch landscape scenes. These were in distinct contrast to the "classical" and idealized Italianate landscape paintings of the same period by artists such as Claude Lorraine, a Frenchman who spent most of his working life in Rome.

These two very different modes of landscape art held sway for over a century with numerous practitioners in many parts of Europe. They came together in the later 18th century in Britain, hitherto only on the fringes of European painting, where landscape painting was established by Richard Wilson and Thomas Gainsborough and was to rise to new heights in the 19th century in the work of John Constable and J. M. W. Turner. All these four artists were largely self-taught in their landscape art but had undertaken comprehensive studies of their 17th-century and, in the case of the last two, 18th-century predecessors. Thus Constable's vivid view of *Dedham Vale*, exhibited in 1828, combines a Claudian classical composition with a very naturalistic Netherlandish technique. Constable did not live long enough to develop greatly beyond this level of achievement; Turner was to work on for another 20 years or more during which he surpassed all traditions to create such highly personal masterpieces as *Norham Castle: Sunrise*, which was painted in about 1840. From a minor genre, landscape painting had by now risen to being among the most fashionable in Britain, but there were no artists in the decades after Constable and Turner who were sufficiently gifted to continue the notable progress that these two had made. However, their work became known across the channel through the activities of dealers in the case of Constable and through the medium of steel engraving in that of Turner.

In France there were a considerable number of landscape painters at work or in training, whose knowledge of the art of Constable and Turner helped them in their resolve to break away from the shackles of academic art-school courses and standards which dominated the rising artist's life. These men emerged gradually until by the 1870s some of them were ready to make their first collective declaration by organizing an independent exhibition in Paris in 1874. Among the canvases shown by Claude Monet was *Impression; soleil levant*, which to critics and public alike appeared one of the most "outrageous" works in an exhibition full of such; from its title one critic dubbed the group as "The Impressionists". Painted at Le Havre in 1872 this is a study of colour and light, which eschews all attempts at realism in the academic sense of the word. On the other hand, Monet and his fellow Impressionist exhibitors – who included Degas, Pissarro and Renoir – were reacting against the artificiality of super-realism imposed by the official *salon*, and were trying to create paintings closer to nature, as Constable and Turner had done. The Impressionist "revolt" of the 1870s, as it was considered then, stands at the watershed of modern art. Post-Impressionism, the Fauves, Cubism, abstract art and other advanced movements, all followed in quick succession. Since the 1870s the majority of artists have grown more and more individualistic and independent and have ignored the controls of popular fashion and taste.

As a result artists have become increasingly cut off from society, living and working in isolation either on their own or in groups. Since the early 19th century there have been relatively far more of them than in previous periods, for the demand and outlets for their work have greatly increased with the continued expansion of the middle and commercial classes. However for the majority of artists it is difficult to make a living, and one way of eking out the meagre income brought by sales of their work is employment as a teacher in one of the hundreds of art-schools that are spread throughout the cities and towns of Europe. Thus ever more young men and women train as artists, though there is now no significant increase in the patronage of which they can hope for a share. In all countries of Europe contemporary art has always been and still is supported by a tiny minority – on the other hand the dramatic developments in the media, in book production and in travel, mean that more and more people are exposed to works of art. The time is still far off when art will again be as much an essential element of life as church building and decoration made it for the citizens of 15th-century Europe, but there is every sign that the enjoyment of works of art is on the increase. What still has to be overcome is the barrier that exists between the living artist and the general public, caused by the inevitable clash of the former's instinctive radicalism with the latter's innate conservatism.

Gradually, but in less than a century, the more advanced artists have broken away dramatically from the norms of art accepted since the Renaissance. Yet today whatever an artist says is art is immediately accepted as such by a significant minority. In the 1970s, especially in the United States, where New York has ousted Paris as the "capital" of contemporary western art, the artist is the initiator of taste. Critics, dealers, collectors and gallery officials are determined not to be caught out again as their predecessors were a century ago when they dismissed the advances of the Impressionists as "non-art". Today museums and collectors vie with each other to acquire works which have only just been created, often in materials not previously associated with works of art. These can be as contrasted as a canvas painted uniformly black and a strikingly realistic life-size sculpture of a dishevelled housewife pushing an actual supermarket trolley full of real goods. In 1977 both Leonardo and Picasso can be considered correct – on the one hand a black canvas expresses "our conception of what nature is not"; on the other the artist "strives and competes with nature". However it is unlikely that Leonardo, and perhaps even Picasso, would have recognized either the black canvas or the housewife sculpture as works of art.

# 11

# *Musicians*

## DENIS STEVENS

The musician in Europe is everywhere, and yet he is nowhere. It has ever been thus, for musicians – amateur and professional, young and old, men and women – have travelled far and wide across the breadth of the continent, out to the islands, back again, singing and playing instruments, inventing new melodies, fresh harmonies and colours. Eight centuries ago, the troubadours flooded Provence with their songs of enchanted passion, while a lonely voice in northern France bewailed the murder of Thomas à Becket in a solemn threnody. Nowadays, leading tenors and highly paid divas fly from Covent Garden to La Scala by way of the Salzburg Festival, while the chaplain's quiet invocation "O Lord, make speed to save us" echoes through the dim interior of a near-empty cathedral. In the past, the jongleur would display his skills, drawing forth from his vielle an evocative prelude to his master's voice-patterns; now, the pianist clad in formal evening dress attacks the colour-matching keyboard of his concert grand, setting the atmosphere for the *Lied* with which the baritone is about to enchant his expectant audience. In 17th-century Venice, the male orchestral musician would find his employment aloft in the galleries of St Mark's or below in the pit of San Cassiano where the latest opera was being given, while his distaff counterpart, an orphan or a nun perhaps, would fiddle away behind the grilles that supposedly separated the sacred from the profane. In 20th-century London, both men and women play together on the concert platform, in opera houses, in radio, television and recording studios, often more remote from their listeners than ever the Venetian girls were.

If it is impossible to decide whose contribution to music is the more important – that of the amateur, or that of the professional – one must admit that the amateur musician is the one who most easily and naturally transcends the boundaries of class. Those who choose, for love of their art, to cultivate what has aptly been called "the chamber-music life" can enjoy within the seclusion and comfort of their own homes the entire range of masterpieces written for two, three, four, five or more instruments; and the time-span is no less generous than the variety of resources. The musician of the evening, by day an office worker, derives as much pleasure from tackling a Haydn quartet as does the millionaire collector of violins by Amati, Stradivari or Guarneri del Gesù; yet, interestingly enough, some collectors are also good players.

Their distant predecessors, witnessing the dawn of chamber music in the early 16th century, were no less able as executants. Kings of England, counts of the Palatinate, dauphins of France, and the whole range of princes and dukes from the Italian courts did not disdain to take their part in a consort, joining in a lively masque-tune or a solemn fantasia. In earlier times one finds not only royal chamber music players but royal composers. Richard Coeur-de-Lion was a trouvère in the very best northern French tradition; Henry IV and Henry VIII of England left compositions of considerable interest; the Habsburg emperors Ferdinand III, Leopold I and

Joseph I wrote with agreeable fluency in both sacred and secular styles; Maximilian Josef III of Bavaria was a very able amateur musician, and Frederick the Great of Prussia excelled in sonatas and concertos for the flute.

No account of Europe's amateur musicians would be complete without mention of the vocal and choral bodies which flourish now as never before. In villages, towns and cities they bring a zestful enthusiasm to whatever portions of the repertory are given them to learn, whether oratorio or opera, madrigal or modern, catch, glee or part-song. Many choirs are of such high quality that they overlap into the professional world, providing the choral parts when leading orchestras and conductors perform outstanding works from the time of Bach and Handel up to the most complex of present-day scores.

If the amateur musician of Europe, rich or poor, noble or humble, plays an important part in musical life as a whole, it is the professional who fills the role of the star, either as a strong but lonely light, or as a member of a galaxy. The professional, whatever his speciality, often works to a timetable that an amateur would find outrageously demanding – a succession of events whose built-in problems and tensions might be considered more likely to blight music than nurture it, and more apt to kill the musician than keep him alive. Problems, of course, ensure that the mind is constantly at work; and tension heightens that peculiar kind of awareness that every artist is at pains to develop. But the opera singer who is in demand, the conductor whose multiple appointments span several continents, and the busy orchestral musician share with the constantly travelling virtuoso a feeling of pursuit: the pursuit of music as a means to various ends, artistic, financial and personal.

These different goals are not new; nor are they restricted to the musical profession. Taken as a trinity, however, they exert a powerful fascination over all who choose to become involved in Europe's musical life, whether as creators or interpreters. The composer is sometimes thought of as a distant and lonely figure, intent on his exacting task of drawing music out of the air and setting it down on paper, oblivious to the pressures and practicalities of the raging world outside his studio. Although a handful of composers undoubtedly do fit this picture, by far the greater number lead the kind of existence that is not far removed from that of their colleagues the interpreters. Pianist-composers constitute a case in point; and if one glances only at the greatest among them – Mozart, Schubert, Chopin, Liszt, Brahms, Rachmaninoff, Prokofiev, Britten – it soon becomes perfectly clear that fame and fortune can be acquired without too much help from publishers, however powerful they may be.

Europe has been unusually well supplied with conductor-composers, but these (unlike the pianists who are bound to give an audible account of themselves) tend to vary in the quality of their technical accomplishments and range in consequence from the brilliant to the pathetic. On the rostrum, Beethoven, Brahms, Tchaikovsky, Wagner, Debussy were not perhaps their own best interpreters, if one puts faith in the published remarks of those who saw and heard them. On the other hand, Berlioz, Richard Strauss, Elgar, Enesco, Britten and Boulez – to mention only the most outstanding – belong to a group of composers who have been known to excel in conducting the music of others as well as their own.

Nevertheless, the greatest power and wealth undoubtedly belong to those conductors who, by avoiding the demands made by the art of composition, are free to devote their lives to one principal pursuit – the interpretation of music within a framework of artistic and technical perfection. Although it may seem that such ideals can only be realized in a great city wealthy enough to support a permanent orchestra of the highest quality and a conductor of equal stature under contract, much excellent work has been done in a less rigid occupational context, where a pool of talent supplies ensembles whose actual personnel tends to vary from concert to concert.

Generally speaking the conductor of today rarely has to contend with the problem of fluctuating personnel for the simple reason that almost everybody concerned with the efficient running of an orchestra realizes that stability ranks as a desirable ingredient in the building up of a great reputation. Yet this stability, like the conductor in pursuit of perfection, does not belong exclusively to our own age. It began at least as early as the 15th century, when the city-courts of Europe set out to provide themselves with professional ensembles both instrumental and vocal; and by the 16th century the level of artistry had risen so high as to overflow its predominantly secular banks and seep into the very soil that had given birth to it in bygone

days. Hercole Bottrigari's account of the concerts given by the nuns of San Vito in Ferrara
proves not only that discipline led to fine ensemble, but that conductors used batons four centuries ago. Last but not least it shows that women conductors, who have so successfully come to the fore in our own time, were neither unknown nor unappreciated in the age of humanism:

> They are indubitably women; and when you watch them come in (for I will say "come" rather than "go", since I seem to be present there now) to the place where a long table has been prepared, at one end of which there is a large clavicembalo, you would see them enter one by one, quietly bringing their instruments, either string or wind. They all enter quietly and approach the table without making the least noise, settling themselves in their proper place; for some sit, who must do so in order to use their instruments, while others remain standing. Finally the Maestra of the concert sits down at one end of the table, and when all the other sisters are clearly ready, she gives them – with a long, slender and well-polished wand (which was placed there ready for her, because I saw it) – several signs to begin, and then continues by beating the measure of the time which they must obey in singing and playing.

The Maestra to whose concert Bottrigari listened with such rapt attention led a comparatively simple life, musically speaking, for her main tasks were those of rehearsal and performance. Nowadays the pattern takes on a much greater degree of complexity, for the conductor has more and more avenues open to him – or to her. True enough, the ancient ritual of rehearsals and concerts continues, but to this are added new concepts of communication born of the viability – at first gradual and tentative, now rapid and vigorous – of the electronic scene. The conductor is able to place on record his interpretations of the symphonic and operatic repertory, available in mono, stereo or quad; and on disc, tape, cassette or cartridge. These are the brain-children of the 20th century, and they have helped to place the conductor on a pinnacle he had never previously reached. Through the royalties they bring in, they have made him a rich man.

But this is not all. In the 1930s conductors began to be seen on film, though with a sound-track that frequently left much to be desired in the way of synchronization and sound-quality. In recent years, however, technical advances have brought both the visual and the audio aspect to a high degree of excellence, with the result that films made either for general distribution to cinemas or to television stations have come to offer a new view of the conductor's art and a new projection of his personality. Herbert von Karajan's series on "The Art of Conducting", so ably directed by Clouzot, demonstrated the need for a creative eye in photographing an orchestra. It is not enough to mix distant shots with occasional close-ups: the complexity and beauty of the medium demand a more subtle approach. Since then, the marked improvement in camera techniques has led to satisfying results even in the diffusion of live concerts; and if the operatic equivalent poses more serious problems they are slowly being solved, often with remarkable success. In fact, the repertory of opera films made in 15 or more European countries becomes larger and more varied every year.

Even more widespread than recording and television is the radio, which enjoys a greater degree of perfection and independence in Europe than in any other part of the world. The maintenance of orchestras and choruses enables the conductor to rehearse without worrying too much about the financial considerations attendant upon comparable ventures in the concert world, while he can perform either for an exclusive radio audience by means of studio broadcasts, or for a combined concert and radio audience by tolerating the presence of microphones in a large hall.

Circumstances affecting the careers of conductors frequently apply to those of the great virtuosi, whether instrumentalists or singers, the main difference being that the virtuosi do not enjoy the security of a firm appointment. Their careers are consequently more fluid, they travel much, and they may spend a fair amount of time in teaching privately, or perhaps at a conservatory in one of the major European cities. Of their number, the pianists are still the most sought-after by reason of their remarkable self-sufficiency. While a violinist, cellist, oboist or trumpeter will usually need (as do *Lieder* singers) an expert accompanist, the piano virtuoso – thanks to his instrument and the splendid array of composers who wrote for it – provides ready-made harmony and counterpoint as a matter of course.

It has always been so, ever since the days of the keyboard composers whose names resounded beyond the national barriers of Renaissance Europe. Germany had Paumann, Schlick, Froberger, Buxtehude, Bach and Handel; in Spain there were Cabezon, Correa de Arauxo and Soler; in Italy, Frescobaldi and Domenico Scarlatti; in England Tallis, Bull, Orlando Gibbons and Purcell; in France, de Grigny, Clérambault, Couperin and Rameau; in the Netherlands Sweelinck and Luython. They were masters of the organ or harpsichord, sometimes of both; and by the end of the 18th century their successors wielded the same kind of power with the aid of the pianoforte.

Some years were to elapse before the pianist became sufficiently well established to command the kind of audiences that would make his efforts really worthwhile. Mozart as a mere boy toured Europe extensively with his father and sister, but fame and fortune on a large scale eluded them, and it was not long before the composer was obliged to give lessons to stay alive. The writer Melchior Grimm, in a letter to Mozart's father, attempted to express some of the perennial problems that beset and bother a youthful genius: "He is too good-natured, not active enough, too easily taken in, too little concerned with the means that may lead him to good fortune. Here [in Paris], in order to break into the world, one must be crafty, enterprising, bold. To get ahead, I could wish that he had only half as much talent and twice as much ability to handle people; and then I would not worry about him."

Spurred on by the fantastic technique of the violinist Paganini, Franz Liszt determined to show the world that he could handle a piano, as well as people, in a way that Mozart could never have dreamed of. Combining the elegance of a courtier with the *souplesse* of a diplomat, this arch-pianist of the Romantic era soon had the whole of musical Europe in the palm of his hand. Travelling on board ship, he was rarely bothered by customs officials. Travelling on a boat train from Dover to London, he was able to alight at a small station near the house of a friend, even though the train was supposed not to stop until it reached the terminus. Exceptions were made everywhere and by everyone for the man who claimed to be the first ever to give a solo recital.

Liszt opened the door through which every subsequent virtuoso pianist has passed, some of them so famous and so particular as to have their favourite piano sent around with them on tour. Even at the most sombre recital, there is always a feeling that something extraordinary is going on: one executant attempting – and often perfectly able – to control the emotions of a large and heterogeneous crowd. Claude Debussy once wrote of the virtuoso: "The fascination he exerts over the public is very similar to the kind that draws crowds to the circus. People always hope that something dangerous is going to happen – Mr X may play the violin with Mr Y on his shoulders, or perhaps Mr Z will finish his piece by lifting the piano with his teeth."

Virtuosity entered the realm of chamber music at a somewhat earlier stage, when Beethoven in his late quartets began to challenge the competence of even the finest players of his day. But the Schuppanzig Quartet took up the challenge, as did the Joachim Quartet with the music of Brahms; and in more recent years the Lener, Hungarian, Italian, Pro Arte, Busch, Amadeus and Budapest quartets have contributed mightily to the world reputation of European chamber groups.

Perhaps the greatest adulation is reserved for singers whose natural talent and industry have placed them on the pinnacle of international fame. Although at times they may cultivate *Lieder* and oratorio, their principal place of activity is the operatic stage, where they must act as well as sing, learn many roles in four or more languages, work hard at rehearsals, give of their utmost in performances that may last for three, four or five hours, and snatch what rest they can on days when there are no studio broadcasts or recording sessions. Fortunately for them, opera flourishes in state-supported houses throughout Europe (and especially in Germany), so that a busy season may see them in Stockholm, Geneva, London, Berlin, Milan, Paris, Brussels, Rome, Zurich, Munich, Vienna and many other cities. Activity on this scale is not possible in any other part of the world, because the compactness of Europe allows – and indeed encourages – a tighter schedule than would be possible anywhere else.

Virtuoso singers have always been in demand. Long before the birth of commercial opera, masques and intermezzi called for the finest vocal talent, and earlier still the private chapel of a duke, a prince or a cardinal would pride itself on the number and quality of its musical members. Scouts were sent off to discover new talent, and when they found it they were authorized to make offers of fees and living conditions in order to ensure that the best men were engaged on a permanent basis. Choirboys too were sought after, many being brought from villages and small towns to the great cities of Europe whose musical life has flourished with such vigour and for so many centuries. A royal warrant or a purse full of gold was usually quite efficacious in persuading reluctant parents to part with their progeny; but when these methods failed, recourse would be had to outright abduction. Orlando di Lasso, whose music ranked as one of the greater glories of the Bavarian court in the 16th century, possessed a voice of such extraordinary beauty that he was twice spirited away from home before he was out of his teens.

Italian singers enjoyed remarkable prestige and fame even before the firm arrival of solo song and opera. In his *Discorso sopra la musica*, written about 1628, Vincenzo Giustiniani tells us that "in the Holy Year of 1575, or shortly thereafter, a style of singing appeared that was very different from that preceding. It continued for some years, chiefly in the manner of one voice singing with accompaniment, and was exemplified by Giovanni Andrea of Naples, Signor Giulio Cesare Brancaccio and Alessandro Merlo the Roman. These all sang bass with a range of 22 notes and with a variety of passage-work new and pleasing to every ear." Others were not slow to follow their example, and in due course these splendid bass soloists were followed by outstanding tenors such as Giulio Caccini, Jacopo Peri, Francesco Rasi; by male sopranos including Giovanni Luca Conforto and Ottavio Durante; by sopranos to whose musical gifts were joined beauty and charm of personality – Ippolita Marotta, Adriana Basile, Vittoria Archilei.

Travelling outside the bounds of their native country, their successors brought the art of *bel canto* to the whole of Europe. Those who reached the highest peaks of brilliance and vocal power were the castrati whose slow migration from the papal chapel to the opera revolutionized singing technique and drew from even the most critical pen such praise as has rarely been heard since. When Dr Charles Burney heard the Italian castrato Carlo Broschi, known as Farinelli, he wrote:

> In the famous air *Son qual nave*, which was composed by his brother, the first note he sang was taken with such delicacy, swelled by minute degrees to such an amazing volume, and afterwards diminished in the same manner, that it was applauded for a full five minutes. He afterward set off with such brilliancy and rapidity of execution, that it was difficult for the violins of those days to keep pace with him . . . He possessed such powers as never met before, or since, in any one human being; powers that were irresistible, and which must subdue every hearer; the learned and the ignorant, the friend and the foe.

The cult of the castrato slowly died out, but the role of the star singer in European musical society became more important as the number of opera houses, concert organizations, studios and festivals increased. Competitions and festivals, of course, flourish throughout Europe and attract the finest artists, judges and audiences. They have a long history and a distinguished one, yet its chronicles have never been the subject of a major study covering all aspects of time and climate. France in the Middle Ages knew the excitement and emulation of a kind of festival competition sponsored by literary and musical guilds – the *puy*, which lasted in that form until the early 17th century. Wales has its Eisteddfod: a bardic festival originating at least as early as the 7th century, and still active today in two branches. The National Eisteddfod retains as much as possible of the old bardic ceremonies and traditions, while the International Eisteddfod at Llangollen encourages choral singing and folk-dancing, with ballet and orchestral concerts to provide contrasting repertoire. In Ireland the annual gathering of traditional musicians is called Fleadh Ceoil na hEireann, and takes place in varying centres at Whitsun.

International festivals are generally speaking of more recent origin, although local ones tend to have deep roots in the culture of their peoples. The Pythian games of 6th-century BC Greece were essentially musical festivals, and a festival element soon began to adorn the concerts of choral and orchestral music given in the cathedrals of Gloucester, Hereford and Worcester from 1724 onwards. The Three Choirs Festival, as it came to be known, has maintained a continuous tradition of music-making which – though local in essence – gave rise to far-reaching results. Many works heard for the first time within the framework of this festival have subsequently been performed again in London and other cities. In Germany, the Lower Rhine Festival,

especially from 1817 onwards, concentrated on choral and orchestral classics; while from 1859 a
similar function was performed by the Tonkünstler-Versammlung of the Allgemeine Deutsche Musikverein. Holland, beginning in 1834, developed a great series of festivals under the aegis of the Maatschappij tot bevordering der Toonkunst.

Certain festivals offer mainly the music of one composer. Ansbach, Leipzig and Schaffhausen have had Bach festivals, Beethoven can be heard in Bonn, Handel in Halle (with worthy predecessors in Westminster Abbey, London), Mozart in Salzburg, and Sibelius in Helsinki, to name only the most outstanding. Donaueschingen is famed for its espousal of the cause of contemporary music. The Wagner festivals at Bayreuth, which date from 1876, are unique in concentrating on the music of a single composer in a theatre that he himself designed for his operas. More general in their appeal are the festivals at Salzburg, Florence, Lucerne, Lisbon, Berlin, Edinburgh, Vienna and Amsterdam. There are many more, and their number increases yearly. As focal points for artists and audiences, their place in the European scene is well established and fruitful. They have done much to promote new music, and have also retained a healthy respect for the classics besides catering for recent interests in early music.

The existence of a music industry – for that is the only way to describe all the various activities ranging over concerts and opera, radio and television, film and recording, teaching and learning – presupposes the existence of composers who provide the necessary raw materials for performers. Fortunately they have existed (and still do) in vast numbers, as even the most rapid glance at a musical dictionary or a record catalogue will confirm. But their lot has not always been a happy one, and some of the most productive among them have been the least successful financially, as in the case of Bach, Mozart and Schubert. The problem is really a sociological issue, in some ways related to the vastly varying situations of writers and artists.

The dawn of European civilization saw the Church as the main employer of musical talent, and within this affluent society there flourished such men as Perotin, Machaut, Dunstable, Dufay, Josquin, Palestrina, Byrd and their peers. Ecclesiastical benefices gave the composer a guaranteed income and not infrequently a house to live in. The most sought-after lived comfortable, even luxurious lives, and could better themselves by moving from one part of Europe to another, and from court chapel to collegiate chapel to cathedral as opportunity arose. Their duties were seldom heavy, for they often enjoyed the services of skilled assistants. Monteverdi made this point when his former employers, the Gonzagas, tried to tempt him back to Mantua from his assured position as director of music at St Mark's, Venice. He told them that in Venice he enjoyed freedom of movement, security in his appointment and help from a paid assistant. The same was true, by and large, of all those composers who were fortunate enough to have found a responsible and well-paid directorship.

As the centuries passed and the power of the churches waned, their organists and choirmasters were less well rewarded and harder pressed to do so much work in little time. The age of music printing, coupled with the rise of instrumental music, witnessed considerable changes in the lives of composers, many of whom found that there was just as much to be achieved in secular and ceremonial works as in church music. Newly acquired tastes for opera and ballet led royal patrons into patterns of monopoly, typified by the reign of Louis XIV and his favourite composer Lully, or into complexes of rivalry, as in the smaller German and Italian courts. Composers who could afford to concentrate their efforts almost exclusively on the liturgy became few and far between, while those able to move easily from sacred to secular spheres enjoyed an entirely new kind of fame and wealth.

Opera and oratorio became two facets of the same musical talent, with the result that Charpentier, Berlioz and Debussy in France, Purcell, Handel and Britten in England, Mozart, Beethoven and Henze in Germany – indeed composers from every part of Europe – found it both possible and desirable to reach the widest audience with the most catholic tastes. The emerging concept of grand rights, whereby composer and author were entitled to a share in the proceeds of ticket sales, helped to make a firmer foundation for the creative aspect of the performing arts. In the symphonic sphere, composers had to work harder for recognition. It was not until well into our own century that societies were formed to collect performing and mechanical rights, thus guaranteeing composers a suitable financial reward for their labours. They are less able to find university appointments than American composers, though some welcome changes are being made in this direction, as in the increasing incidence of their employment in conservatoires and colleges.

Nevertheless the European composer has usually been able to hear his music played by orchestras ranging from the competent to the superlatively fine. In every large city one finds at least one orchestra, while some cities boast several. Outstanding by reason of their past tradition and continuing excellence are the Berlin Philharmonic Orchestra, the Vienna Philharmonic and (of more recent origin) the Royal Philharmonic of London. The Berlin orchestral tradition goes back to the time of Frederick the Great, whose private chamber orchestra was conducted by the composer Graun. Founded in 1882, the Berlin Philharmonic has been tonally and artistically moulded by such conductors as Nikisch, Furtwängler, Celibidache and von Karajan; and if its programmes lean towards the conservative (unlike those of RIAS, the Berlin Radio Orchestra), its performances exude a quality difficult to equal, let alone surpass, throughout the entire world of music.

The most venerable however is the Vienna Philharmonic, whose earliest concerts were given in 1842, so that by 1942 it could claim to have performed 2,319 works by 532 different composers. The Sunday morning subscription concerts still rank among the most important of musical and social events in the city, while repeats of those concerts and admission to final rehearsals enable a wide audience to enjoy the varied repertory presented by resident and visiting conductors. Among other long-established orchestras are the Concertgebouw of Amsterdam (1883) and the London Symphony (1904). In recent years London has also witnessed the creation of two orchestras by one man – the London Philharmonic (1932) and the Royal Philharmonic (1940), both of which were brought into being by the magic wand of Sir Thomas Beecham.

The truly great orchestras and opera houses of Europe must be counted among her greatest gifts to civilization. Over and above their consistently high standards of performance, they each possess and cherish a distinct and recognizable personality – for they are indeed the musical faces of Europe.

# 12

# *Actors*

## MARTIN ESSLIN

Actors have always been – and still are to some degree – looked down upon, despised, outcasts of society; yet they also have always been – and still are – admired, adored, objects of almost religious adulation. This ambivalence, this dual aspect of a single activity, its position at the two extreme ends of the social spectrum gives the occupation, the craft, the art of acting (whichever of these descriptions it might deserve) its very special flavour and significance; for such a high degree of ambivalence is always indicative of emotions which emerge from very deep strata of the individual and collective subconscious of the human mind.

Why are actors despised? Because in some sense their calling is akin to prostitution: actors are people who exhibit themselves, their bodies and their emotions, for material gain. This seems the principal reason why actors have so long been treated as rogues and vagabonds. To the early Christian Church in Imperial Rome the theatre, closely allied as it was to gladiatorial contests and public spectacles of great lewdness and cruelty, seemed to embody the very essence of a depraved and crudely materialistic civilization. Hence, with the triumph of the Christian religion, they were cast out of society; and yet, as there was still a craving for worldly entertainment among the people, strolling players, jugglers, acrobats, clowns, ballad-singers and jesters continued to roam the Europe of the Middle Ages, performing feats of physical prowess, cracking jokes, acting out crude farcical scenes. They had no fixed position in society and were classed with gipsies and tinkers and denied the ministrations of the Church.

But there are deeper sources for the irrational dread and unease which actors arouse: all human society is based, and was so more than ever in the Middle Ages, on a fixed, hierarchic order by which each individual is assigned his position in the social structure and thereby assured of his own identity and self-image. An actor, by definition, is a human being who can assume any such image at will, can be a beggar one day and a king the next; and, being potentially everything, he is ultimately nothing and thus outside the social order altogether. The court jesters of the Middle Ages, whose calling was closely related to that of the "joculatores", the strolling jugglers and jesters of the time, could tell kings and princes the truth about themselves and be as rude to them as they wanted, precisely because they themselves were *nothing* and thus their opinion had no impact on their targets' honour or self-respect. For if, as Hamlet says, the players are a mirror held up to nature, the mirror itself is just a blank surface; it is the absence of a picture in its frame that allows it to contain the image of the world within it. Thomas Gainsborough, who found it hard to paint Garrick's portrait, is said to have remarked: "He has everybody's face but his own."

Having no social identity, on the other hand, the actor also becomes – and that is no less disturbing – an image for man in general, without any of the trappings of social position, of a fixed, socially based identity. The actor can play any role, the average man in society just has a

few; but underneath their costume all men are, like actors, reduced to their essential humanity.
*Totus mundus agit histrionem* is said to have been the motto above the stage of Shakespeare's Globe
Theatre; and, in Shakespeare's own words:

> All the world's a stage,
> And all the men and women merely players;
> They have their exits and their entrances,
> And one man in his time plays many parts,
> His acts being seven ages.

The very same image is the basis of Calderón's great *auto sacramental, El gran teatro del mundo*, in
which God, the divine stage manager, makes the as yet undefined human beings pick their
costumes at random, to become beggar or king, lets them play their parts, until, in the hour of
death, they hand their roles back to the master of the great theatre which is the world.

The actor thus is outside the social structure and a constant reminder of the illusoriness of
each individual's supposedly firm and assured place in the order of society, the transience of the
social role he may be playing at any given moment: that the admired beauty of today may be
playing the part of a toothless hag in a few years' time, the prosperous courtier that of a haggard
beggar. And that is why the actor was – and still is – held in awe and feared. But, on the other
hand, the actor also is at the very centre of the individual's innermost ultimate sphere, his
fantasy life. If all the world is a stage, the stage also is all the world – and an embodiment of all
the world's dreams, more substantial, more concrete than any other form of fantasy. On the
stage everyone's fantasies come to life: those who dream of being great lovers or mighty kings
can identify with the gorgeous figures, larger and far more glamorous than life, they see in the
theatre. When Nicholas Nickleby and his protégé Smike join the company of strolling players
headed by Mr Vincent Crummles in Dickens's novel, the theatre appears dismally sordid:

> . . . bare walls, dusty scenes, mildewed clouds, heavily daubed draperies and dirty floors. He
> looked about him; ceiling, pit, boxes, gallery, orchestra, fittings and decorations of every kind, –
> all looked coarse, gloomy and wretched.
> "Is this a theatre?" whispered Smike, in amazement, "I thought it was a blaze of light and
> finery."
> "Why, so it is," replied Nicholas, hardly less surprised, "But not by day, Smike – not by
> day."

By daylight the actor may be the outcast of society and a source of uneasiness, by night he
stands in a blaze of light and finery and becomes the embodiment of the individual's fantasy
world. And the glamour of that world may, in turn, reflect back on the actual personality of the
actor or actress. Having appeared more beautiful than any real human being, an actress may be
more ardently desired, even by members of the highest society, than any woman in everyday
mundane surroundings – and so actresses (including, of course, opera singers and ballet dancers
who are part of the same fantasy world) have become the mistresses of aristocrats and rulers;
having seemed more heroic, more pure in spirit and more ideal, actors may become a more
potent focus for the aspirations of young men of ambition than the real holders of political or
military power with all their faults and compromises.

Acting as a full-time occupation, a trade, craft or profession, is a relatively recent growth in
European society. Neither the performers of the great Athenian theatre festivals nor those of
medieval mystery and morality plays were professionals. There were professional actors in
Imperial Rome; and their descendants, miserable gipsy bands of jugglers and mountebanks,
continued to live, precariously, by their trade, but this could hardly have been called acting; it
was more akin to the work of circus artistes of today.

It is only with the rise of a money economy, the growth of larger centres of population
which could provide a more stable public, and the rediscovery of Classical drama in the
Renaissance that acting as a professional activity in its present-day sense could develop at the
point in time and in those places where the modern form of a "capitalist" money economy
arose, in France, Italy, England and Spain.

In France the medieval societies that had originally provided the organizational framework
for religious spectacles gradually turned into commercial enterprises; in Italy the descendants of

the jugglers and mountebanks began to improvise sharp, witty topical comedies and thus created the Commedia dell'arte. It must be emphasized that the term simply means a theatre of *craft*, theatre as a professional activity, as skilled work. By the end of the 16th century the various Commedia dell'arte troupes had acquired a reputation throughout Europe and rivalled French performers of farces and tragedies in the licensed theatres of Paris. In England, which looked to Italy as a source of high culture in the 16th century, similar troupes had arisen; to secure some sort of standing in society they were technically deemed to be servants in the pay and under the protection of powerful noblemen and called themselves accordingly the Lord Chamberlain's Men, the Lord High Admiral's Men etc., although they also performed, for money, in the public theatres of London and elsewhere. And although these players had to compete with other attractions, such as bear-baiting and troupes of child actors, some of these early actor-manager-entrepreneurs made their fortune – among them Edward Alleyn (who used some of his wealth to found Dulwich College), Richard Burbage and William Shakespeare.

An analogous development in France led to Molière's troupe becoming the king's preferred company and the fountainhead of the Comédie Française.

Strolling Italian Commedia dell'arte players who went north to Austria and southern Germany, and English troupes who toured Europe as early as the end of the 16th century, and in greater numbers after the closure of all theatres in England by the Puritans (1642), carried the professional theatre into central Europe, notably Germany. In Spain a vigorous popular theatre had also developed at about the same time through the emergence of troupes of itinerant players who performed at first in public squares or the courtyards of inns; they laid the foundation for the flowering of the great Spanish classical drama of the Golden Age of Spain in the 17th century.

The actors of this period stood, characteristically, on the borderline between outlawry and acceptance by the highest orders of society, between illiteracy and refined learning. While, on the one hand, they became the companions of princes to whose courts they lent the lustre of their prestige, they might still, on the other, be refused the right to be buried in consecrated ground by the Church. The fact that women were not allowed to appear on the stage in Shakespeare's time emphasizes the suspicion with which the profession was still regarded at a time when, in fact, actors not only had become highly respectable householders and capitalists but had also established intimate personal relations with the highest in the land. Yet so morally tainted appeared the theatre to the English Puritans that it was prohibited altogether when their revolution triumphed.

In the 18th century the French pattern of troupes of actors attached to a court became dominant all over Europe. No prince who wanted to hold his own among his peers could afford to be without his company of Italian singers, his troupe of actors on the pattern of the Comédie Française. The late 18th-century court theatre, miraculously preserved intact in the grounds of Drottningholm Castle outside Stockholm, and the Empress Maria Theresa's court theatre at Schönbrunn outside Vienna, give us a vivid glimpse of the actors' world in that period, or at least of one end of the spectrum of that world. For at the other end the strolling players of the countryside were still eking out a miserable existence. While the actors in the courtly theatre aimed at sublimity and refinement of emotion, the itinerant practitioners of popular entertainment presented rough and bawdy comedies in which comic stereotype figures like Harlequin or Hans Wurst mingled obscene jokes with even more obscene or scatological gestures. And yet the actors themselves might well have made the transition from the low world of folk theatre to the high atmosphere of courtly culture; and back again, in periods of decline of their faculties, from the higher to the lower world.

For the individual actors involved, this amounted to a constant struggle for respectability, acceptance by the ever more important and dominant stable society created by a rising bourgeoisie. Not many were completely successful in this endeavour, yet some achieved their aim. Of David Garrick, the greatest English actor of the 18th century, Dr Samuel Johnson, his fellow countryman from Lichfield and the schoolmaster of his youth, said: "Garrick has made a player a higher character." And in 1777 when, during a debate in the House of Commons, the Speaker had decided to clear the public gallery and it was discovered that in fact David Garrick was present, the great Edmund Burke moved that he be excepted from the ban, considering that he was the greatest master of eloquence in the land and had taught many of the members all they knew of the art of oratory. Whereupon Charles James Fox also rose and seconded the motion and the whole House voted that Garrick should remain to listen to the debate. But Garrick had proved himself not only an actor of outstanding genius; he had also been an outstanding manager of the Theatre Royal, Drury Lane, whose estate, when he died, amounted to some £100,000.

In France François Joseph Talma (1763–1826) played an important part in the Revolution and became an intimate of Napoleon. In Germany, where the struggle for a national identity as a precondition for national unity and political independence centred, during the 18th century, around efforts by the intellectuals to raise German culture to a point where it could become comparable to that of the great established European nation states, France, England and Spain, the actors were wooed by literary figures like Gottsched and Lessing. For only if the actors abandoned the vulgarity of the popular stage could Germany aspire to a dramatic literature that might compete with the works of Shakespeare, Molière or Racine.

In 1737 the Professor of Poetry at the University of Leipzig, Johann Christoph Gottsched (1700–66), actually persuaded the principal of one of Germany's leading companies of players, an energetic woman called Frederike Caroline Neuber (1697–1760), to banish Harlequin from the stage in a solemn public ceremony. The emergence of a strong national consciousness in Germany is intimately linked with the rise of a national tradition of drama, created by great playwrights like Lessing, Goethe and Schiller, but equally by the development of a school of highly intelligent and respectable actors like Konrad Ekhof (1720–78) who collaborated with Lessing in the creation of a national theatre at Hamburg (1767–69); Friedrich Ludwig Schroeder (1744–1816), the first to abandon the declamatory tradition for naturalness; and August Wilhelm Iffland (1759–1814), the great master of sentimental prose drama. Goethe, himself a passionate amateur actor, directed the court theatre at Weimar and made it the centre of a refined and highly respectable style of acting.

The development of a national consciousness, a national identity and a national literature in the younger nations of central and eastern Europe followed the German pattern; here too the creation of a national theatre occupied a central position in the struggle for nationhood and playwrights and actors played a decisive role in it.

No wonder then that in many of the cities of modern Europe the national or municipal theatre occupies pride of place as a veritable shrine of the secular cult of the new religion of nationalism. The most venerable of these, and the model for most other national theatres, is the Comédie Française, constituted by Louis XIV on 18 August 1680 by the fusion of the two rival companies of the Hôtel de Bourgogne and the Théâtre Guénégaud and in opposition to the Italian troupe, the Comédie Italienne. The Comédie Française, housed since 1791 in the Salle Richelieu, is governed by an ancient statute by which the "sociétaires" form a self-governing body with special privileges of tenure. No other theatre in the world can present the sense of tradition and continuity which the Comédie Française exudes: here on the programme brochures for the great French classical drama to this day each performance is counted from the first so that *Phèdre* or *Le Malade imaginaire* appears to have had an unbroken run of many thousands of performances. The Odéon, constructed in 1783, which housed the Comédie Française briefly before it moved into the Salle Richelieu, is another venerable temple of the dramatic muse, and so is the palatial Paris Opéra, which was opened in 1875 and dominates the Paris boulevards.

Among the great opera houses of Europe only the Teatro della Scala in Milan (opened in 1788) and the Vienna Opera House, badly damaged in World War II but reopened with due pomp and as a symbol of the liberation and rebirth of Austria after it, can rival the majestic splendour of the Paris Opéra. The Royal Opera House, Covent Garden, in London which houses Britain's premier opera company has through most of its existence been one of the two licensed London theatres, the other being the venerable Theatre Royal, Drury Lane.

The Vienna Burgtheater, founded as a German national theatre by the Emperor Joseph II in 1776 and now housed in a sumptuous 19th-century building on the Ringstrasse, is another national symbol of the first importance. These great representative buildings (and hardly one of Europe's nations is without at least one of similar significance) are repositories of tradition and national pride. Not all of them have, at all times, been of equal artistic excellence. They have often tended to become staid, bureaucratic and traditional in the worst sense of the words.

Movements for a renewal of the artistic vitality of the theatre have often sprung up in opposition to these upholders of ancient values. Max Reinhardt's company at the Deutsches Theater in Berlin, from which much of the contemporary concept of the artistic unity of production sprang, operated in defiance of the classical ideals of the old-fashioned Prussian State Theatre; Stanislavsky's company which became the nucleus of the Moscow Arts Theatre was an equally revolutionary *avant-garde* force, before it in turn became the repository of a tradition which by now is markedly old-fashioned and conservative. In France the companies of great pioneers like Antoine (at the Théâtre Libre), Lugné-Poë (at the Théâtre de l'Oeuvre), Jacques Copeau (at the Vieux Colombier), Charles Dullin (at the Théâtre de l'Atelier), Louis Jouvet (at the Athenée) and Jean-Louis Barrault (at the Théâtre Marigny and later in the converted Gare d'Orsay) all started in opposition to the style of the Comédie Française, although many of the actors and directors concerned in the end took their place on those hallowed boards. It is from this dialectic between the established tradition and the revolutionary *avant-garde*, which in turn becomes the new tradition, that the art of the theatre moves forward.

Companies of actors grow around major personalities, the actor-managers of the 18th and 19th centuries, the great directors of the 20th; and occasionally around a great playwright like Bertolt Brecht's influential Berliner Ensemble, established in 1949 and housed in the old Theater am Schiffbauerdamm in East Berlin, where Brecht had achieved his greatest popular success with the *Threepenny Opera* 21 years earlier.

As national and municipal theatres sprang up all around continental Europe in the second part of the 19th century and as the decline of religious faith led to an increasing secularization of life, the actor, outwardly at least, became increasingly integrated into bourgeois society. The elevation to the order of knighthood of the great English actor Henry Irving by Queen Victoria in 1895 was the outward symbol of that process.

And yet, integrated into respectable society as he may be, the actor still stands for a different and freer life-style. By turning into a different personality at will, he escapes the foremost hall-mark of the bourgeois mode of existence which is based on order, regularity, routine, habit. Even outwardly actors have remained far more mobile than ordinary citizens. Even if they have long-term contracts in established theatres like the municipal muses' temples of Germany or Scandinavia, they still change their places of operation more often, they tour and travel. Having to act out the most intense emotions they tend to be more fickle in their own lives, freer in their sexuality. And so the old suspicion still lingers around them. Goethe's great autobiographical novel, *Wilhelm Meister*, which describes the development of the son of a merchant family into an artist and thinker, starts with his escape from the world of bourgeois routine into the company of actors; he joins a troupe of strolling players among whom he finds mystery and high emotion and deep love. He outgrows this stage but it marks his first steps on to the higher plane of a life outside the narrow confines of respectability.

So the world of the actor provides an escape for individuals from the routines of daily life, while the world the actor puts before society allows society itself an escape route from its daily life into a world of fantasy. That circumscribes one of the most important functions of the actor in society. To achieve this objective requires great skill and not a little sublime art. Acting is a hard and dangerous pursuit – and not only because its economic foundations have always been precarious in the extreme. From the time of the jugglers and tumblers a great deal of physical prowess has been required, much control of the body and the voice, much discipline in the learning of complex parts, much wit and presence of mind in meeting unforeseen circumstances.

In the 18th and 19th centuries actors had to be able to fit themselves instantly into a large traditional repertoire with a minimum of rehearsal. They had to know dozens, even hundreds of parts by heart. To facilitate instant casting each actor knew into which of the traditional basic categories of role he belonged – stereotypes like leading man, *père noble*, heavy character actor, comic etc. Before the introduction of gas, and later electric, lighting the auditorium was as evenly lit as the stage and the audiences were far less concentrated; people chatted with each other during the performance, came and went or made loud remarks to the actors. And not infrequently dissatisfaction with the acting manifested itself in the throwing of raw eggs and tomatoes at the offending performers, not to mention the violent riots which occasionally shook the theatrical world of cities like London and Paris right into the 19th century.

It took great courage to face these crowds; no wonder that some of the greatest actors looked upon the audience as a kind of adversary who had to be tamed and subdued like the bull in the Spanish *corrida*, subdued by the sheer force of the most violent emotion or by the coldest and most calculated skill.

These have always been the two basic approaches to the theory of acting. There were those who wanted an actor to *live* his part to the full, to *feel* every emotion; and there were those who argued, as Diderot does in his dialogue *Le Paradoxe du comédien*, that only the coolest and most rational control could produce the illusion of true emotion. In our own day this debate takes the form of a conflict between the school of Stanislavsky (or in its American version "the method") and that of Bertolt Brecht, the advocate of the *Verfremdungseffekt* – that is to say the actor's detachment and critical evaluation of his character as against the great Russian director's demand for a total identification between the actor and his character.

The truth of course is that there are more than two; there are innumerable approaches to the art of acting, as indeed there are numerous different types of actors: there are the instinctive and the cerebral performers, the protean artists who can change their personality at will, and there are those whose personality is so strong that they are content merely to exhibit that personality itself. It is the latter who do not essentially search for ever new and changing characters in a large variety of plays, but tend to go for a character which reappears in play after play. The former type is the one who requires great plays by playwrights of genius, the latter is content with vehicles hack-written to fit the stereotyped part he has chosen. For there is drama in which the playwright is dominant just as there is actor-dominated drama. Nor is that by any means necessarily the worse. It may not read as well as literature but it may be more vital as drama. Some of the greatest actors of all time, like Frederick Lemaître, the idol of mid-19th-century Paris who revelled in the part of Robert Macaire, the arch-criminal, or the great mime Jean-Gaspard Debureau who invented the melancholy clown Pierrot, belonged in that category. And so did some of the greatest 20th-century actors, the heroes of the great age of cinema like Chaplin, Buster Keaton or the Marx Brothers.

The actor who makes his own personality into a type which becomes a living part of folk myth continues the tradition of the old "improvised" Commedia dell'arte (which incidentally was not totally spontaneous as each actor knew hundreds of prerehearsed verbal or physical gags by heart, so that once the first cue was given, he could instantly respond with the correct reaction), a tradition which extends from Harlequin and Brighella to the recurring characters of personality actors like Humphrey Bogart, Mae West, W. C. Fields or Marilyn Monroe. Joe Grimaldi, the creator of the immortal Harlequin of British early 19th-century pantomime, belongs to this tradition, as do the famous comic figures of the Viennese folk theatre of the 18th century, Stranitzky and Prehauser, or the no less great lean and melancholy philosopher-clown of the Munich beer halls of this century, Karl Valentin, who exercised such an influence on the young Bertolt Brecht.

For make no mistake about it, the actor is the central, the essential element in all drama. There can be drama without a writer or a written, prerehearsed text, but there can be no drama without actors. The improvising actor, the actor who uses his own personality as the raw material for his role, is his own playwright, while actors like Garrick and Henry Irving who excelled in plays without literary value furnished the decisive creative element to these texts through their performances.

Garrick wrote and adapted many texts for himself. He may not have been a major playwright, but he knew the secrets of stage effect, the mechanics of the actor's craft. In this he had the advantage over the poet who pens his play in his garret. No wonder then that many of the finest playwrights were in fact actors: Shakespeare, Molière, Ben Jonson; or the masters of Viennese folk comedy who continued the tradition of Hans Wurst and lifted it to sublime heights, Ferdinand Raimund and Johann Nestroy, not to mention Emmanuel Schikaneder who wrote the libretto of Mozart's *Magic Flute* and sang the part of Papageno; and, in our own time, Noel Coward, Sacha Guitry, Harold Pinter, John Osborne, Roger Planchon. Other actors have made their essential contribution to great drama by providing the inspiration for playwrights

who wrote parts to suit their personalities: Racine created his masterpiece *Phèdre* for Mlle
Champmeslé, his mistress, to mention only the most famous instance among many.

If the 19th century was the age of the actor-manager, the 20th century is that of the director. As technological progress increased the complexity and the possibilities of stagecraft, as the tradition of conventional staging faded, the need for a coordinating mind, a total concept behind the staging of each production, created a vacuum which was filled by the director who could blend all the various strands which now make up a dramatic whole into harmonious clarity. Many of the greatest directors were actors: Stanislavsky, Reinhardt, Dullin, Jouvet, Pitoëff, Jean-Louis Barrault, Roger Blin, Meyerhold, Otomar Krejča, Laurence Olivier. Nevertheless, the present age is the age of the director in the theatre and even more so in the dramatic media which are even more technological: the cinema and television. More and more the modern actor tends to become the *Übermarionette* of which that prophetic genius Gordon Craig dreamed more than half a century ago.

And so today the actor no longer, as in the time of Henry Irving, Iffland, Beerbohm Tree or Sir George Alexander, presides over his tightly knit company which he rules as its patriarchal manager; he has become a pawn moved across the board by the director. And yet, more than ever, he is the central element, the main point of attraction, in all dramatic forms: the television serial has elevated a whole gamut of actors into the heroes of folk myth not only for one city or country, but worldwide: there is no corner of the globe where Perry Mason or Kojak or Lucille Ball's Lucy is unknown, where they do not take their place among the modern *lares et penates* in innumerable households. Television is at present eclipsing even the cinema in its mass appeal and worldwide penetration. Yet the cinema with its grander sweep and more-than-lifesize canvas has contributed major figures to the secularized pantheon of our days: Chaplin, Garbo, Dietrich, James Dean, Humphrey Bogart, Marilyn Monroe have become major cult figures of our time.

The rise of the mass media, one of the most important revolutionary developments in human history, has propelled the actor into the very centre of human consciousness. At a time when the decline of religious certainties has reduced the power of all sacred mythic structures which used to provide a stable framework to the psychological needs of the large masses of the population, a time when the glamour of kings and queens has declined and even in the most rigidly controlled totalitarian societies the personality cult devoted to political leaders is received with cynical scepticism, in such a thoroughly secularized world the folk heroes of the mass media are bound to fill the vacuum. For mankind needs models, heroes and heroines to emulate and imitate. Some heroes of world sport fulfil that need, but even more so the actors and actresses whose exploits on the small television or immense cinemascope screen provide exemplars of how to look and to behave.

For the individual actor who rises to such prominence this situation creates its own stresses and problems. The glare of publicity, the intoxication of public adulation of an image which frequently departs far from the real personality of such public idols, set up tensions which in not a few cases go beyond breaking point. Under totalitarian regimes prominent actors are wooed by governments (Hitler's and Goebbels's use of actors is notorious, as is the privileged position of actors in the Soviet-controlled world) for the support of such folk heroes seems essential to the dictators who have to establish the myth that they are loved by everyone. In the *laissez-faire* societies of the West actors who rise to the level of figures of folk myths reap enormous financial benefits. And these too often prove destructive by offering an endless succession of temptations to dissipation while forcing the individual to live his private life in the glare of merciless publicity (the tribulations of that Welsh miner's son raised to the status of a cult figure, Richard Burton, provide a good example of these problems). A very strong character and a very solidly based personality are needed to withstand these pressures.

At the other end of the spectrum the actor's world in the West is still, to some extent, tainted by the age-old suspicion of rogues and vagabonds. This is particularly the case in countries without a strongly institutionalized and subsidized theatre: there the struggling beginner, the exceptionally talented maverick, is still forced into the fringe theatres located in cellars or carried from town to town in a truck. The world of the *avant-garde* is the present-day equivalent of the medieval actor's life on the margin of society. In countries with a strongly institutionalized theatre, like Germany, where the commercial theatre has become a marginal phenomenon, the beginner's life is easier. But here too the lesser-known actors in the smaller cities are badly paid and, while not outlaws, certainly lead an existence without much social prestige. There can be hardly an occupation in today's world where the span between the earnings of the lowest- and the highest-paid practitioners is so immense as in the world of the actor. The lowest-paid are far below the poverty line while the highest-paid are among the richest in the world. This explains the attraction of the actor's craft in the western world today, but it also accounts for the high percentage of total failures and shipwrecked lives among those who have embarked on such a career. Noel Coward, an actor from earliest childhood, knew what he was talking about when he wrote his song "Don't send your daughter on the stage, Mrs Worthington."

In the totalitarian societies of the Soviet world the actor's life is far more secure. Once an aspiring artist has passed the final examinations at his conservatoire his career is secure till he retires. If he is successful he will move up from small provincial to major metropolitan theatres and into the cinema and television on a well-regulated ladder of promotion. But with increased security there is far less adventure. And there is no room for the wildly unconventional outsider. And yet it is with the unconventional outsider, the wild experimenter, that the future always lies. There are signs today that the era of the director's dominance in the theatre is fading, that the actor is moving back into the central, controlling position. Today's most advanced *avant-garde* efforts in drama are preoccupied with breaking out from the confinements of the conventional theatrical space, with re-establishing spontaneity through involvement of the audience. Improvisation, spontaneous, on-the-spot, extemporizing invention is the watchword of all these efforts. And this requires a new type of actor, a truly creative individual who can be the poet evolving his story-line and words at the same time as he is enacting and embodying them. Peter Brook's expedition with his group of experimental actors from Paris across the Sahara into Nigeria and Dahomey to test out an improvisational theatre which does not rely on verbal communication may have been a quixotic enterprise but it provides a foretaste of developments to come, developments which may well close the circle and establish a link with ancient beginnings. For such developments would bring us back to bands of strolling players improvising their shows and relying on their physical prowess, the expressive powers of their bodies, their skill as musicians, rather than literary texts or even mere words. And that is what the medieval jugglers and tumblers were doing.

What happens and what succeeds in the experimental theatre inevitably affects the mass media in the end. The spread of the mass media which now effectively covers the entire population of the world thus acts as an immense amplifier for events which originally take place in small café theatres or cellars among tiny bands of actors and spectators. Never in the whole of human history have performing artists had such influence, such an important function in society, as today. Man does not live by bread alone: he lives a large and often determining part of his life in his imagination, his fantasies, among his ideal models for imitation and emulation. Performing artists – actors and their peers, dancers, singers, pop-stars – play a decisive part in the formation of the imagination of the world's masses. They thus form a vital element in the social fabric of our present-day world and in the creation of its future.

# PART FOUR

*Believers and Worshippers*

*Philosophers and Intellectuals*

*Scribes, Scholars and Students*

*Scientists*

*Doctors and Nurses*

# 13

# Believers and Worshippers

## JOHN McMANNERS

Europe, unlike other civilizations, has tried to explain – or even, to explain away – its religion. Some writers of the Italian Renaissance used the comparative method in studying the religious observances of Classical antiquity, and in the late 17th century the critique of curious divergences of creeds and practices became an obsession of the republic of letters as information from geographical discoveries circulated. Thereafter it was a story of "noble savages" and Chinese mandarins, together with Egyptian sages, Stoic philosophers and deistic pontiffs of imagined Utopias – for the magic novelties of new continents were mingled with the fragments of Classical learning which were still the basis of higher education, the old legends of a Golden Age joining with new dreams of continual progress. Faiths other than Christian were publicized by Jesuits seeking supporters for their missionary activities and accomplices in the syncretistic compromises by which they hoped to make themselves the spiritual directors of the Chinese Empire, and also by sceptics and deists who wished to challenge the uniqueness of Christianity – or to demonstrate how all religions are sacerdotal inventions. This crude accusation of "imposture" became a staple of anti-clerical journalism during the French Revolution, and thereafter gave way to more sophisticated arguments for explaining religion: it was a consoling myth generated among the oppressed proletariat, a sublimated expression of the sexual drive, a totemistic symbol of the binding forces of the social order, a survival in the minds of civilized men of primitive, magical thought patterns. These theories, whether of Marx, Freud, Durkheim or Frazer, have been welcomed by a generation which has lost its old certainties without finding new ones. We are insecure, but at least we have "come of age".

In fact, the day of reductionist analyses is passing. Though religion has linkages with the "hierophanies" of nature and with the "collective unconscious" (or whatever other terms we use to describe the mysterious affinities which haunt us), and though it will always borrow the language of dreamers, lovers, moralists and spell-binders, it seems more reasonable today to accept it as a fundamental inclination of the mind, something which cannot be omitted from any complete picture of human nature. Men seek – whether justifiably or not is a question that cannot be handled in terms of intellectual proof – an ultimate reality, transcendent, but not unapproachable, knowing that if they find what they are seeking, their response must be total and, for good or ill, have a transforming effect on their lives.

The search may be conducted at various levels. The spectacle of nature awakens the poet's intuitions:

> And I have felt
> A presence that disturbs me with the joy
> Of elevated thoughts; a sense sublime
> Of something far more deeply interfused,

Whose dwelling is the light of setting suns,
And the round ocean and the living air,
And the blue sky, and in the mind of man:
A motion and a spirit, that impels
All thinking things, all objects of all thought,
And rolls through all things.

The "presence" Wordsworth speaks of moves us, but our response, though unfathomable, is passive and instinctive. In 1799, the year after these lines were published,[1] Schleiermacher brought Romanticism nearer to religion by defining the godward inspiration as the feeling of "absolute dependence". Viewing this formulation as dangerously subjective, Rudolf Otto in *Das Heilige* (1917) concentrated on the "wholly other" which both repels and fascinates us, the "numinous". Before it, our essential reaction is "awe". Dependence imprisons us within the sense of our own frailty: awe marks the psychological point at which — albeit in fear and trembling — we can break out of our prison. "Das Schaudern ist der Menschheit bestes Teil."[2]

There is, however, another starting-point for the journey towards the transcendental: we may start from conscience, and seek an objective sanction for moral obligation. This was the preoccupation of the deism of the Enlightenment, with Kant summing up the process, drily eliminating Rousseau's sensibility from the argument. For long in the European mind the moral imperative as discerned by reason was overlaid by a brooding sense of judgement, enforced by the certainty of death and by the uncertainty of what comes after it. This has been the theme of centuries of preaching, often hectoring and lurid, but sometimes refined to the surgical precision that touches the nerve of unease in the sermons of John Donne — to awake at midnight and hear the question, "Is there a God? and if thou darest, say No."[3] In the 17th century, even as Donne was preaching, Hell was declining, its flames being quenched, not so much by science and scepticism as by a growing conviction that the New Testament was, above all, a message about a God of love. Even so, the deists of the Enlightenment and the liberal theologians of the Victorian era after them did not quarrel with the punishment: what they repudiated was its useless, eternal duration. A life after death directed by a God who rewards and punishes was, for them, the surest sanction for moral conduct. The idea remains in the European consciousness even when God has been forgotten or rejected. If morality has eternal significance, to ignore it is to accept one's own existence as ephemeral and futile. The oath, "I'll be damned if I do" is, ambiguously, a faint recognition of a spiritual dimension. A sociological essay could be written about the phrase as a vestigial credal formula preserving the decencies among multitudes lost in a post-Christian urban and technological society.

Dependence, awe and fear of judgement — if we speak in terms of these emotions, are we referring to the impact on our minds of vast mysterious forces, or are we referring to "someone"? Here is the decisive issue where the higher religions diverge. A believer can feel uplifted, inspired, "saved" even, by turning to a transcendental reality, but can he know that reality as personal, and can he face it without fear of annihilation or absorption? The Judaic-Christian idea of God is of a being at once totally rational and personal, awareness of his presence involving the intensification of individuality in the believer, not its loss. The meeting of man with his maker is, in Martin Buber's famous phrase, an "I-Thou relationship".[4] We are near here to the explanation of the dynamic role which Christianity has played in European history, whether in its own right, or indirectly through innumerable wayward and paradoxical inspirations. It is a religion of rationality and individual choice, of responsibility and decision, an affirmation of human personality before a personal God.

No doubt the unique character of European civilization is connected with the influence of the Christian ideas of God, man and the universe working pervasively over the centuries. Did the concept of a God with "the energy of a Jehovah and the rationality of a Greek philosopher" lie at the origin of the scientific outlook?[5] And did a reverence for human personality provide the spur for elementary labour-saving technological innovation? Certainly, the insistence on an individual and personal religion forced on the development of cultural self-awareness and self-criticism, which culminated in the analysis of religion itself as a subject for literary, sociological and scientific criticism. Culture and religion were bound to diverge in Europe; it was a necessity arising from the very nature of the religion in question. From the former "Christian" west has arisen an autonomous culture which is conquering the planet, cramming the folkways and glimpses of eternity of other civilizations into the framework of technological necessities, and fusing – sometimes degrading – old ideas into novel forms in the white heat of alien passions – nationalistic, materialistic, egalitarian. If a new barbarian tide sweeps over us, what equivalent would there be of a "universal religion" (to use Toynbee's concept) to soften the harshness of the postdiluvian world?

For most men in the past, we have no evidence concerning their religious experience beyond the records of outward ceremonies; indeed, for most of them existence was so precarious and opportunities for abstract thinking so few, that we should ask ourselves what higher insights of personal religion were available to them beyond the call to self-sacrifice which keeps families and communities in being – though this is, maybe, the highest insight of all if we were permitted to see it *sub specie aeternitatis*. The religious festivities of ancient Greece were bound up with the pattern of the agricultural year, with the human cycle of birth, marriage and death, and with the intense political life of the city-state; but we know little of what was in the minds of the Athenians who celebrated the broaching of the new wine in February, whose children carried branches of olive or laurel hung with cakes and figs as the summer thanksgiving for harvest, who poured oil, honey and water into the graves of their dead, and observed the cult of their tutelary goddess Athena as the citizens of Cyrene honoured Apollo and those of Ephesus served Artemis. One kind of observance shaded into another. The Eleusinian mysteries, a prelude to the autumn sowing, claimed to provide initiates with preferential treatment in the life to come, and dedications to Athena of the 6th and 5th centuries BC show how the goddess of the city could also be the object of individual piety. Sometimes ordinary people following formal ceremonies would break through to some new quality of generous conduct and, more rarely, to some new, reflective awareness. This, certainly, was the astonishing achievement of the Greek intellectuals, whose religious quest and fulfilment are documented with a splendour unsurpassed in other literatures. "The God of inner devotion," writes Festugière, "the God of Hesiod, of the tragedies and the philosophers, was never the object of public worship in Greece"[6] – this God was the discovery of thinkers of genius. It is Plato rather than any Christian philosopher who is the origin of the great mystical tradition of western devotion – teaching a life of detachment from the world to enable the soul to rise above the flux of becoming and participate in the higher world of Ideas or Forms – and these, completed at their highest by the Form of the Good, are the very thoughts of God. Plato also remains the most influential and serene of those who have imagined an existence beyond the grave where rewards and punishments are given. "A man of sense will not insist that these things are exactly as I have described them. But I think that he will believe that something of the kind is true of the soul and her habitations, seeing that she is shown to be immortal, and that it is worth his while to stake everything on this belief."[7] Though a man might yearn for immortality and union with the ineffable deity, there could not be love between man and God: as Aristotle said, the distance is too great. Yet Greek tragedy is full of the mystery of suffering, and the gods are not immune to pity: "if gods could weep", Artemis would mourn for the dying Hippolytus.[8] If gods, even legendary gods, could weep: the unique force of Christianity was to lie in the audacious claim, to the Jews a stumbling block and to the Greeks foolishness, that suffering enters into the final transcendental meaning of the universe.

The higher thought of Greece continued to illuminate lofty minds in the glittering and dangerous days of Imperial Rome. Platonism and Stoicism (the latter contrary in philosophical outlook to the former, being pantheistic and monistic against Platonic idealism, but identical in implications for moral conduct) were the private consolations of an élite. Seneca the patrician (4 BC–65 AD) and Epictetus the slave (c. 50–130 AD) taught the fatherhood of God and the brotherhood of man – but Seneca was the minister of Nero, and when it came to a religion for the people he advocated the worship of political fictions to bind the masses to the regime. There were two standards of morality, one for aristocrats of the spirit and one for the generality of mankind; to believe thus is to surrender to a noble despair. The Stoic Emperor Marcus Aurelius (ruled 161–180 AD), immersed in the Herculean task of saving society, regarded himself as a puppet, an actor in a play, a shadow lost in infinite space and time.[9] Yet, we must do our duty. The legacy of Stoicism to Europe was the glorification of the courage to go on without hope, and to accept death rather than bow the knee to tyranny. Epictetus tells of the reply of Helvidius to the Emperor Vespasian who threatened to execute him if he attended the Senate. "Did I say I was immortal? You will do your duty and I will do mine. You put me to death: my part to die."[10] For 15 centuries the rhetoricians (and the schoolboys) of the continent were to set the death of Cato (who killed himself as a gesture against tyranny) alongside the death of Socrates and Jesus as supreme examples of public-spirited heroism, and in the French Revolution, when the pagan spirit revived, it was Cato who was present in the minds of Girondins and Montagnards as they mounted the steps of the guillotine, repudiating the faction in power, while remaining loyal to the revolution which had been their creation.

Apart from the honours paid to deified emperors, Imperial Rome had no official religion. A man could seek his peace in one of the schools of Greek philosophy or, more picturesquely, in one of the mystery cults – with Isis from Egypt, Mithras from Persia or, if he liked grim ceremonies and flagellant priests, with Attis and Cybele from Anatolia. There were observances to promote good luck in this life and to ensure immortality, whether in the Elysian Fields or, for great heroes, among the shining spheres of heaven. Rome tolerated most religious enterprises, though there was a committee, the *quindecim viri*, to exercise censorship of a utilitarian kind. But there was no qualitative discrimination in the Imperial *pax deorum*, and the devotees of different mysteries were little troubled by the passions of exclusivity. There was one religion in the Empire, however, which repudiated all syncretism. The Jews, God's chosen people, bound together by the practice of the Synagogue and the observance of the Law, worshipped the one true God who had delivered them from bondage to Pharaoh, established them in their own land, brought them back again from exile, and in the fullness of time would restore them to greatness, whether material or spiritual, in a messianic kingdom. To the rest of the Mediterranean world, history was an endless cycle: to the Jews it was the onward march of providence. Most synagogues (there was at least one in every major city of the Empire) had an outer circle of Gentile sympathizers, and the philosophical background of Jewish theology was becoming Hellenized – in the writings of Philo of Alexandria (c. 20 BC–c. 50 AD), for example, whose allegorical exegesis of Scripture found many a theme of Greek speculation there, and who saw the *logos* of Greek thought as the agency of creation and the voice that spoke to Moses out of the burning bush. Yet the central core of Jewish monotheistic belief was not modified. The Hellenistic Judaism of the Diaspora may have wished to approach God by Greek modes of thought, but the God was the God of Israel.

Christianity was an exclusive creed like the Judaism from which it sprang. In Paul (a missionary of the first generation, coopted to membership of the original apostolate by the blinding revelation of the Damascus road), it had a leader who thought in Imperial terms worthy of the Empire whose free citizenship he proudly claimed. He looked away from the parochialism of Jerusalem (a city soon to be destroyed) and westwards to Rome and Spain; he brought the Gentiles into the inheritance of the Resurrection directly, in defiance of the traditional understanding of the Jewish Law; he reordered the Gospel to make it intelligible to the Hellenistic world, insisting on Christ as the "Wisdom" of God, active in creation and redemption and present in his Church. Yet Paul did not compromise. Those who were "in Christ Jesus" belonged to a "new creation", where there was "neither Jew nor Greek, . . . bond nor free"; one of the reasons why Christianity conquered the Mediterranean world was its insistence on total commitment and its offer of total salvation. Renan once asked what would have happened if Mithraism had prevailed. It was an unhistorical speculation. "A man used Mithraism," says a modern writer; "he did not belong to it body and soul."[11] Pagans distrusted the Gospel for its demand for "faith" and the severity of its moral discipline, and they despised it because it proclaimed a God incarnate in human form who suffered. In Rome a graffito of the 3rd century shows an adoring figure at the foot of a cross, and on the cross the body of a man with an ass's head; below, in Greek, "Alexamenos worships his God".[12] The cross, a punishment for slaves, was at first avoided by Christian iconography – the fish, the phoenix, the peacock, the shepherd, the anchor were preferred. But in the long run, to suffering humanity the suffering of God incarnate and the sublimation of his and all other suffering into victory constituted a message of salvation which had no parallel in the cults of paganism. The Christian martyrs died with a different sort of courage from that of the Stoic philosophers,

*44. The Geographer.* Painting by Jan Vermeer, 1668.

*45. Overleaf: The Anatomy Lesson of Dr Tulp.* Painting by Rembrandt van Rijn, 1632.

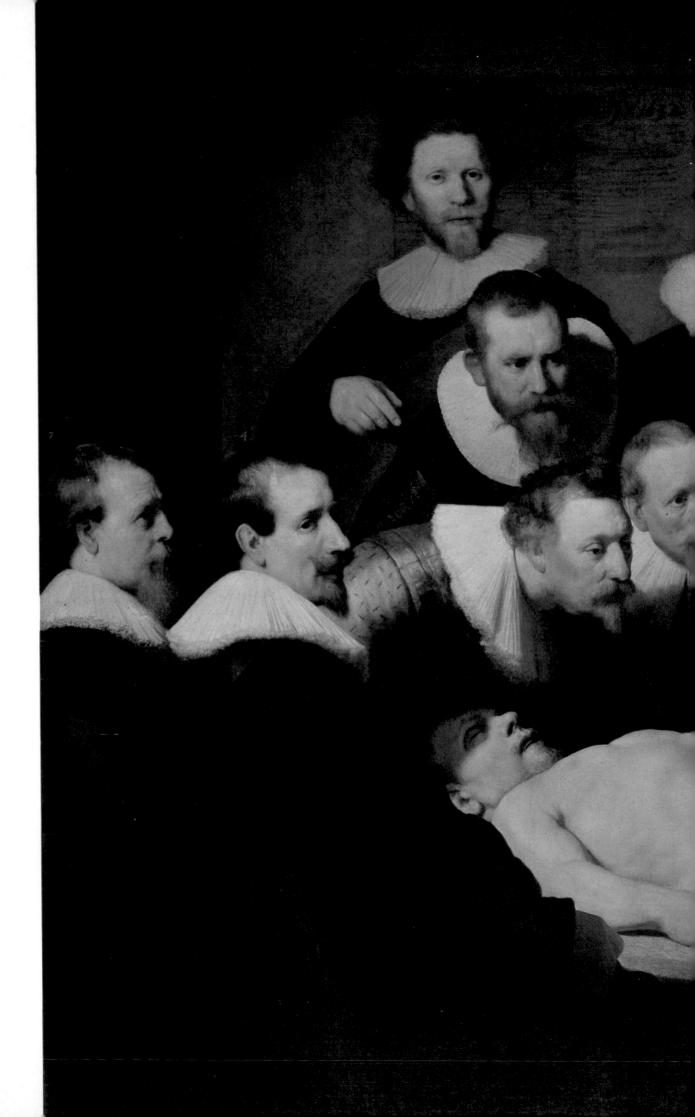

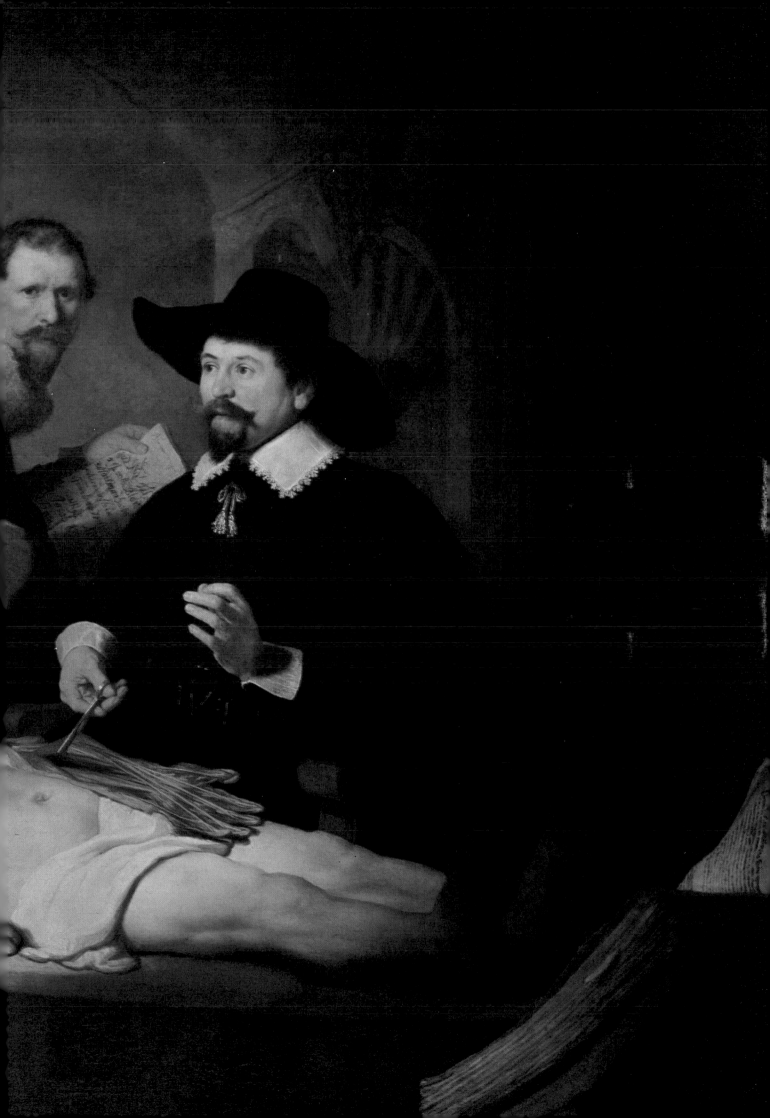

46. The ratification of the Dutch-Spanish Treaty of Munster. Painting by Gerard ter Borch, 1643.

*47. The Maids of Honour.* Painting by Diego Velazquez of the Spanish Infanta Margarita-Teresa, c. 1656.

48. *Tending the Orphans*. Painting by Jan de Bray, commissioned for the Orphanage of the Poor, Haarlem, 1663.

49. An artisan and his family. Painting by Gerard ter Borch, c. 1650.

50. A family making music. Painting by Jan Miense Molenaer, c. 1650.

51. *Auto da fé*, Madrid. Painting by Francisco Ricci, 1681.

Reinando Carlos Segundo
Rey Catolico de las Españas
y Emperador del Nuevo Mundo
y siendo Inquisidor General
D. Diego Valladares Sarmiento
Obispo de Oviedo y Plasencia
del Consejo de Estado de su Mag.
Año de 1680.
a 30. de junio

52. Louis XIV's minister of finance Jean-Baptiste Colbert. Portrait by Claude Lefebvre, c. 1670.

53. Tsar Peter the Great. Portrait by Godfrey Kneller, 1698.

60

54. *Overleaf*: The Four Days' Sea Battle (1666). Painting by Abraham Storck, 1700.

55. Scene from an Italian comedy. Painting by Nicolas Lancret, c. 1730.

conscious, however obscurely, of being witness to something new in history, "the power of his resurrection and the fellowship of his sufferings".

Though Christians were accused of subversive activities, they did not teach revolt against the established order. They paid taxes ("tribute to whom tribute is due"); they worked conscientiously ("if any will not work, neither shall he eat"); they did not reject slavery, though a slave was to be treated as "a brother beloved". Their faith did not spread as "a proletarian mass movement", but rather as "clusters of more or less intense groups largely middle class in origin".[13] In their communities a quality of mutual aid and friendship was found which the teeming warrens of the cities had not known; they looked after their widows, orphans, sick and aged, treated women generously, upheld the sanctity of marriage; they transcended the barriers of class and of self-righteousness (as the pagan Celsus complained, they welcomed sinners and fools into the kingdom of God). When a man became a Christian, he "belonged" – a phenomenon which sociologists today take as the cause of the success of some of the sects coming into Europe from America and the east. "Christians", writes E. R. Dodds, "were in more than a formal sense 'members one of another'. I think that was a major cause, perhaps the strongest single cause, of the spread of Christianity."[14]

After ten generations of expansion, with the conversion of Constantine (sole emperor 324–337), Christianity became the official cult, allied with that of *Sol invictus*. By the edict of 380, Theodosius outlawed paganism. "Vicisti, Galilæe", the pagan Emperor Julian is (unreliably) supposed to have cried, fatally stricken by an arrow in his Persian campaign of 363. A victory, true – but was it for the man of Galilee? An expanding religion is subject to inexorable mutations: mass recruitment dilutes enthusiasm, the spirit of charity and community becomes formalized, a hierarchy becomes necessary and heresies inevitable. And about half the population of the Empire was still pagan at the time of Theodosius. As Rome ground down to destruction, its rulers turned to the one vital religious force available as a device of social consolidation. Conversion and political loyalty became synonymous (though not always blatantly: the senatorial aristocracy at Rome was drawn in by "the commonplace workings of culture and marriage" rather than by the threats of power).[15] Men had always had gods for the agricultural seasons, for the human life cycle and for the tribal complex. Christianity, the religion of inner devotion, for the first time offered to every man, had achieved a parody of its own democratic universalism. Imperial Rome was dying, but the cultural heritage of the ancient world was to be passed on through a wilderness of barbarism by the followers of the crucified Galilean.

In the winter of 406 the Vandals and Suevi poured over the frozen Rhine into Gaul, and in 410 the Goths sacked Rome. For almost six centuries the history of Europe was to be the story of the conversion of successive waves of barbarians. At first, the frontier itself was the converting agency: the tribes who settled within the Imperial boundaries adopted the Roman religion as one of the amenities. Kings, converted often for political or superstitious reasons, brought their followers with them *en masse* into the Church. War spread the faith – and preserved it: what would have happened if the Eastern Empire had fallen to the Saracens in 717, or Charles Martel had lost to them at the battle of Poitiers 15 years later? (Gibbon liked to think of the pulpits of Oxford resounding to the Koran,[16] the Enlightenment being willing to ascribe the sway of great religions to accident.) Charlemagne converted the Saxons with the sword, and the German drive eastwards dragged in Slavs, Magyars and Hungarians. But there were also charismatic and courageous missionaries. Some were sent out by popes; others turned inwards from the fringes of the continent, like Columba who came from Ireland to Iona and Aidan from Iona to Lindisfarne, haloed by the asceticism and insight into natural creation which distinguishes Celtic Christianity, or Winfrith, who went from England to Germany and was adopted by Rome under the name of Boniface. Everywhere, culture accompanied religion, though the west had no example so spectacular as that of Cyril and Methodius, who went from the Eastern Empire to the Slavs in the 9th century, and created for them a literary language, Old Church Slavonic, through which they gained access, not only to the Scriptures, but also to Greek patristic speculation and Byzantine learning. The religion of Rome, allied with its culture, cast a tenuous, though comprehensive, web of civilization over the barbarian kingdoms. As a "conversion" it was inevitably superficial – though we cannot tell how many glimpsed (as in the 8th-century *Dream of the Rood*) the young hero who had died for them.[17]

The Church which converted the barbarians had perfected its structure – credal, administrative and liturgical – during the first four centuries. The councils, from Nicaea (325) to Chalcedon (451), had defined the doctrine of the person of Christ – one person in two natures, perfect God and perfect man – thus providing safeguards against interpretations which would have made the suffering of the crucifixion irrelevant to human yearnings, whether unreal in some condescending theophany, or hopeless in a purely human representative. The system of government by bishops, independent in their dioceses but linked in universal confraternity validated by the apostolic succession, was well suited for survival in difficult times and for expansion as opportunity arose. The fanatical austerity of desert anchorites had been curbed by rules for a monastic life of prayer and work in community. For 600 years the chief instruments of the Church for the education of barbarian society were to be the Benedictine monasteries, oases of prayer and literacy scattered over a rude and violent society, autonomous institutions with their roots in their own locality, but enjoying membership of a wider community. The Rule of the Benedictine houses, compiled in the middle of the 6th century by Benedict of Nursia, was a serene and humane document emerging from the chaos of a disintegrating society; it prescribed a life of poverty and obedience, with the day divided into three equal parts – liturgical prayer in the form of the night office and the seven day offices, sacred reading and physical labour. Designed to save souls, its place in history must be judged by different criteria. Living within its inspiration, Bede, concluding his *Historia Ecclesiastica Gentis Anglorum* (731) with the shadow of the Viking invaders dark over Northumbria, is a symbol of the alliance between monasticism and scholarship which saved the intellectual heritage of Europe.

The message which the Church took to the new peoples was enshrined in its liturgy. Here a warrior could see enacted the heroism and regal dignity of the Lord to whom he gave his fealty, and by his own actions could demonstrate his loyalty. There was a liturgical calendar (this had grown up by a slow process); there were the 40 days of Lent, Christmas at the winter solstice (thus the birthdays of Mithras and *Sol invictus* had been annexed), Epiphany brought in from the east and tardily assigned to the Magi, and the anniversaries of martyrs. Baptism, the Jewish rite for receiving Gentiles, was the ceremony of initiation, with a declaration of Trinitarian faith. The heart of worship, marking especially the day of the Lord's resurrection, was the Eucharist, the primitive "breaking of bread", rehearsing the fellowship meal Christ had shared with his disciples the night he was betrayed, with the recitation of his mysterious words. It was an observance rich in potential meaning – expressive of the fellowship of believers, their self-offering, their sharing in the passion of their master and in his resurrection, "the antidote against death", as an early 2nd-century writer had said, "which gives eternal life in Christ Jesus".[18] With this gift of immortality the greatest of kings rewarded his faithful warriors. During the four centuries after the fall of the Roman Empire, the liturgy developed in Rome itself in sacramentaries notable for borrowings from the Greek Church (more especially the *Kyrie*) and collects of pure and concise language, in Spain with the Mozarabic rite and in France with the Gallican, dramatic and sombre in its echoes of Celtic penitentials. From all these a new synthesis was made, at the court of Charlemagne, who presided over a brief and brilliant cultural renaissance at the end of the 8th and the beginning of the 9th centuries. The missal produced by his scholars, under Alcuin of York, was adopted by Rome and became the foundation of the many local rites used during the Middle Ages. Treasures from east and west, from the Roman and the barbarian worlds, were combined to form the great western rite. It was a liturgy for a new civilization. Charlemagne, the Frankish war lord, was crowned by Pope Leo III on Christmas Day 800. In a ruder and more vital world than Rome, there was once again a Christian emperor.

When the old Rome had fallen four centuries before, there were Christians who had mourned the end of a providential institution. Augustine, ruling his diocese in North Africa and awaiting the coming of the Vandals, had spoken in different terms. States and kingdoms are but bands of robbers. Rome has sought glory, and has received her reward; now she has come to judgement. The Christians within her frontiers are *peregrini*, resident aliens. They do their duty, but their citizenship is elsewhere, in the heavenly Jerusalem. The importance of Augustine lies, not in his predestinarian theology, but in his broad assessment of the place of the

Church and its members in the world. Against the Manicheans he affirmed the goodness of all creation; against the Donatists he established the Church as the home for sinners, not the closed corporation of the righteous; against Pelagius, he proclaimed the omnipotence of God, though in a fashion elevating man rather than annihilating him – predestinarian theology since has been notable for the fierce spirit of independence which it has inspired in its adherents, men knowing they stand or fall to God alone. In his *Confessions* Augustine explored the detours of the mind's response to God; to the Neoplatonic and Christian quest, mystical and moral, he added the intensity of his own volcanic nature. "Give me a man in love, he knows what I mean. Give me one who yearns, give me one who is hungry."[19] To him Christianity was the realization of the higher religion of the individual which only the loftiest minds of Greece and Rome had dreamed of; it belonged to "the City of God", and only by accident had it become the formal cultus of the social complex. In spite of all the temptations of power and Caesaro-papism, Augustine's view of the Church was to prevail. The converted barbarian kings did not become deified as leaders of a social cult; they joined a church which was universal, greater even than the fallen Empire whose grandeur lingered in the shattered columns and broken aqueducts, a church which served ends beyond the accidents of time. And, in an age when it was almost unthinkable to resist custom and the collective will, the spiritual hierarchy claimed its own peculiar right of resistance. Athanasius defying one emperor and Ambrose excommunicating another were exemplars for Hildebrand keeping Henry IV waiting in the snow at Canossa (1077), Anselm defying William Rufus and Henry I, and Becket courting martyrdom. On the practical issues at stake, a reasonable man would sympathize with the secular power, except for the fact that in western Europe there has been a noble tradition of valuing freedom more highly than efficiency.

Look at the west about 1173, the year of Becket's canonization, three years after his murder. Already pilgrims were flocking to his shrine as they flocked to St James of Compostela or the tombs of the Magi at Cologne. Crusaders still held the Holy Sepulchre, though the Muslims were planning their final deadly blow. All relationships with the eastern Church were severed, and in 1204 a misbegotten crusade was to sack Constantinople. The papacy in Rome enjoyed immense prestige, more from its network of impartial justice than from its enterprises against secular rulers. The Church was the keeper of all consciences, and the Fourth Lateran Council of 1215 was to make annual confession obligatory. The bishops were secular magnates, and the clergy performed innumerable secular duties. These were the early years of the Gothic style of architecture, aspiring to heaven with thrust of spire and pinnacle, rich with pictorial glass and statuary amid its lofty play of light and shade. In the last 75 years the new Cistercian reform of the Benedictine Order had built over 500 abbeys, mostly in desolate places, creating new wealth by the labours of their numerous lay brethren. Early in the next century the friars – Franciscans and Dominicans – were to arise to evangelize the towns and, ultimately, to lead in theological scholarship in the universities.

It was a Christian civilization in that all learning, imagination and aspiration were expressed in Christian forms. There were rigorists who feared for the purity of the Gospel. Peter Damien would reject even Euclid: "Christi me simplicitas doceat." What use, asked Bernard of Clairvaux, are carvings of centaurs, and tigers with stripes and spots? – "will they melt a sinner's heart?"[20] Yet these complaints were exceptional. There were 12th-century writers who "knew just as much about the Latin epic as the pundits of the High Renaissance",[21] who accepted the Roman poets as "animae naturaliter Christianae", and cheerfully included the goddesses of paganism in their allegories. There was a general exuberance to adapt and improve on Classical antiquity – not just shaving the head of the slave woman before marrying her (in Jerome's ungenerous old metaphor) – but "spoiling the Egyptians" comprehensively. Abbot Suger replied to his friend Bernard's puritanical question: "we should do homage to the rite of the Holy Sacrifice . . . in all inward purity, and all outward magnificence." True, beneath this splendour and edification, life was brutal. Though in theory all were equal before God (as Francis of Assisi was to demonstrate by going to the lepers and beggars as the friends of Jesus), one may wonder what the men-at-arms, artisans and serfs knew of the religion they automatically professed. The grim confusions of history had left the Church with the role of preserving culture and renewing it; by unique accident a "Christian civilization" had arisen far ahead of all possible processes of individual conversion. Indeed, as conversions to a dynamic personal religion multiply, the monolithic unity of ecclesiastical institutions is likely to fragment and revolutionary fissures begin in secular ones. A precondition for the existence of Christendom was that the vast majority of its members should not break through to the inner Christian consciousness.

For the intellectual and spiritual élite, the 12th century has been described as the age of "the discovery of the individual".[22] Theology made its contribution. The idea of the early Fathers, that the dead sleep to the Resurrection, was abandoned in favour of an individual judgement immediately after death, with most ordinary Christians sent to purgatory. This was a logical development now all men, without personal choice, were within the Church, but it was forgetting the strong current of Christian teaching in favour of the corporate nature of salvation; it was a sinister affirmation of the responsibility of the individual. Up to now the traditional explanation of the efficacy of the death of Christ had been the theme of a victory over the powers of evil; now Abelard advocated the exemplarist view – "our redemption is the great love awoken in us by the Passion of Christ."[23] We are moved, we are active in our own salvation. And Christ is an individual, who yearns for our love as we yearn for his. The Cistercian cult of friendship owed something to Cicero, but at its heart was the conviction that we all meet "in Christ", giving our relationship a spiritual and eternal quality. The mystical tradition which had been handed down through St Augustine and, more especially, through Dionysius "the pseudo-Areopagite" (c. 500) had been derived from the Neoplatonic speculations of Plotinus; Dionysius had replaced the impersonal "One" with the Christian God, but had retained the "negative" contemplative way of darkness, with reason and the senses left behind. In the 12th-century spiritual writers, the way is illuminated by love. Love kills the pride of life: Bernard, the first great mystical writer of the west, familiar of popes and kings, was pre-eminent in the monastic virtue of humility. Through love, the intellect comes to its own: "amor ipse intellectus est." Sometimes, the bridal imagery of the Song of Songs is used, but in the *Dulcis Jesu memoria* a voice of love is heard on a different plane from the eroticism of Solomon, the pagan poets or the troubadours, the voice of an ecstasy that is endless yearning.

In religion nothing fails like success. In a church with worldly power the flock is sure to find shepherds who know the price of wool. A reformation was inevitable. Yet when it came it was not just a matter of indulgences, immoral popes and monastic idleness; it was also a movement to fulfil the original aim of the Gospel and to bring thinking religion and personal commitment to all men. Two centuries before Luther this movement began, with the mystics of the 14th century, who took up the cause for which some heretics had died and Francis had lived. Boast not of your inner light, said Eckhart; union with God is for all: "whoever seeks God in some special way, will gain the way and lose God."[24] The mystical path, said Tauber, is precious solely because it increases our charity and strengthens our will to suffer. In the Netherlands and Rhineland, communities like the Brethren of the Common Life arose, taking no formal vows, and regarding ordinary labour as sacred. The inspiration of these movements and of the mystics was the life and death of Christ. In 1224 Francis had received the Stigmata. This was a symbol of the highest goal of the Christian life, to suffer with Jesus. "Love Jesus, keep him for thy friend", said Thomas à Kempis in the *Imitation* (first circulated in 1418), the most influential spiritual treatise ever written: "Jesus hath many lovers of his heavenly kingdom, but few bearers of his cross."[25] Religious art began to mirror the anguish of the crucifixion, first in the faces of the bystanders, then in the holy face itself, livid and blood-stained – until at the end of the 15th century the Italian Renaissance forgot the man of sorrows and turned to the antique hero with the muscled torso, attended by Raphael's serene angels, or splendid in death against Tintoretto's forest of spears in the darkening sky.

To Burckhardt the Italian Renaissance was "the discovery of man". A modern art historian adds, "but it is man conscious of his individual role in the great plan of redemption"[26] – man playing his part in the cosmic myths of creation and judgement in Michelangelo, or drawn into the supernatural glory of Botticelli's *Nativity*. Music, for long nurtured in the Church (evolving through Gregorian chant and polyphonic experiment to the complexities of the Cathedral School of Cambrai in the 15th century), with Palestrina burst into a new world of devotional expression, seraphic yet passionate. Humanistic scholarship, which in Italy had a sharp edge of secularity, north of the Alps was religious in tone, concentrating on the Bible, with Erasmus as

its exponent. Dante had loved Virgil, but kept him for his guide only until he met Beatrice in
the earthly Paradise; by contrast, the Renaissance combined every inspiration, Christian and Classical, spiritual and earthly, in a new zest for living. The discovery of the individual, as in the 12th century, was a religious phenomenon as much as a humanistic one. The recognition of God's majesty and the individual's lonely duty before him coincides with the discovery of the immensity and beauty of the universe and of man's vast potentialities. The culminating glory of this breakthrough came in the second half of the 17th century, not the least of its achievements being the rise of modern science. In this age of the Baroque, the secret glimpsed by Pascal on the night of fire of 1654 – the God of Abraham, of Isaac and of Jacob, and not the God of the philosophers – was embodied in poetry by Milton and Racine, in painting by Rembrandt and in sculpture by Bernini. The Middle Ages had found the inwardness of religious experience in miracle: the Baroque found it in ecstasy, and those who seek the secret of love, whether erotic or divine, will always look with wonder at Bernini's cloud-cradled Saint Theresa, and the ambiguously smiling angel wielding the cruel dart, and ask, not without fear, whether men do well to claim the dangerous gifts of God.

Theologians today, redefining the ecumenical ideal as federal and cooperative, no longer see the disruption of the unity of the Church at the Reformation as unrelieved tragedy. Indeed, it is difficult to imagine how the Church could have been reformed on a centralized pattern in a politically divided Europe, and how Christian individualism could have been rediscovered without breaking the doctrinal structure of Catholicism. Disunity hastened the victory of the idea of toleration; after bitter strife, Christians recognized that the only true converting force is love – an aspect of the teaching of Christ almost forgotten in the Middle Ages. Going beyond Augustine and breaking the Aristotelian structure of rationality systematized by Aquinas in the 13th century (a structure already weakened by late medieval logic and epistemology), Luther spoke of justification by faith alone as instantaneous, "not in pieces but in an heap"; Calvin's predestination was the sombre side of his reliance on God's universal providence. In their eyes, all that mattered was a man's standing before God, and the Christian who lived in the fear of God achieved a vertiginous independence – in Luther's words, "we are free from all things." There was a priesthood of all believers; all men must read the Bible, join in reciting the liturgy in the vernacular, listen to sermons. Catholicism evolved in the same direction – parish life revived, seminaries were invented, new religious orders and confraternities proliferated. Music, with congregational participation, became a part of Christian worship as never before. "Next after theology," said Luther, "I give music the highest place."[27] His invention of the chorale led to the perfection of art in Bach; by contrast, the counter-Reformation style was the oratorio, until Handel adopted it into Protestantism. The printing press made the Bible and devotional literature universally available, and in both Protestantism and Catholicism a widely diffused lay piety sprang up, intensely Christocentric in nature, meditating on the Gospel story, the teaching of Christ, his example, his sufferings.

Above all, the Reformation brought vocation to the laity in the ordinary duties of life. "Set Christ before you as the only goal of your whole life", said Erasmus, "and direct all your efforts, all your activities, all your leisure, all your business in His direction."[28] Catholic moralists concurred, sometimes with the agreeable inclusion of innocent pleasures of the world – as Francis de Sales said, an adventurer from Peru, laden with silver, might add curious monkeys and parrots to his cargo. Thereafter, Christianity was to show a more intense concern with the unwavering fulfilment of all the obligations of ordinary life, and with strict moral conduct as the rule for all men, a preoccupation more evident in Puritanism, Jansenism, Pietism and Methodism, but rarely neglected in any church or sect. And it was a morality independent of the monastic ideal, a morality centred on the family. Luther playing with his children and Calvin urging married couples to use the "remedy against concupiscence joyously"[29] are indications of the beginning of a new attitude to women, children, love and marriage which improving economic circumstances and the advance of civilization were to generalize in Europe and North America, and which has become incorporated in secular idealism even after the directive social force of religion has faded.

The decline in religious practice since the French Revolution was not caused by Voltairean ironies or historical criticism of the Bible, so much as by the breaking of the old cadres of society by industrial change, the population explosion and great migrations. There arose a non-thinking absence from formal religious observances in place of non-thinking attendance. But in any case, culture and religion were bound to part company in Europe, and a religion which has returned to its original role of a faith of intense personal choice and commitment cannot remain a communal symbol backed by massive practice. By contrast with the statistical decline, there were the explosive overseas missionary ventures of Europe which brought in more converts in the 19th century than in all the previous 18. The cause of true interior religion is not necessarily identified with either the internal contraction or the external expansion – it does not lose or win so easily. The history of religion as technically written today tends to be a statistical-sociological analysis of institutional progress or decline.[30] The history of religion, from a religious point of view, should consider each man as equidistant from eternity, with only a superficial and limited part of his experience of worship available to the researcher to be woven into an ongoing story. The main structural theme of such a history would be secular – what religious men and religious institutions have contributed to the happiness, enlightenment and elevation of mankind. In this respect, what was significant in the 19th century was the war on slavery, misery, exploitation, disease – the story of Wilberforce, Shaftesbury, Kingsley, Maurice and William Booth in England, of Lamennais, Albert de Mun, Léon Harmel and the Abbé Lemire in France. If there is a statistical record of their contribution to humanity, it is kept in registers which are not accessible to the terrestrial historian.

An institutional church is a necessity. "Can Jesus be proclaimed in the whole world without ecclesiasticism?" wrote an exponent of charismatic religion in the early years of this century. "Can molten gold be carried from place to place in anything but crucibles of iron and steel?"[31] Necessary the institution may be, but its success involves the dilution of enthusiasm. The Christian tradition accepts this sort of failure. Augustine did not mean that the Church itself was his "City of God", his heavenly Jerusalem, nor have theologians after him so considered it. Always the Church has been a home for repentant sinners. Christian thought at its best has considered salvation as corporate, the intense emphasis on individual conversion and responsibility being balanced by the idea of the community of saints, in which those who are "saved" turn back to rescue those that falter. More than this, the thousand years during which the Church preserved and evolved the culture of Europe have left, as a residual legacy, a strong conviction of the duty of religious men to the whole community within which their lot is cast. Unlike the odd fundamentalist or mystical sects of modern invention, which offer comfort to their devotees but nothing to society, the ideal of a church is of a community which serves the world, if necessary at the risk of losing its own soul. Failure is the true destiny of the great historic churches. Maybe, as they have declined, they have succeeded in passing on the socially necessary part of their moral teaching; perhaps western society has absorbed enough of Christian principles, whether directly or by way of Rousseauistic deism and socialistic ideas, to continue to have a formal established morality (whether still connected with a church or churches or not), and to carry on like the Greek city-states, sustained by the cohesive force of their civic spirit and some helpful myths and formulae of a religious nature. To this social religion, Christians have a duty to contribute; there is no warrant in their charter for satisfaction at the approaching fall of a godless civilization.

The history of the religious life of Europe is like a vast unfinished tapestry of infinitely varied interlocking patterns. Each observer must make his own assessment of what constitutes its significant and dominating theme, an assessment which involves a study of the past and also a guess at the future. The search for God in Europe has taken an infinity of detours – if Huysmans and Péguy arrived, Baudelaire and Rimbaud were for ever on the journey. The ways of interior piety are multifarious and unpredictable; a place must be found in our conclusion for George Herbert and Oliver Cromwell, John Wesley and Père de Caussade, Dostoevsky and Mr Gladstone, Paul Claudel and Charles de Foucauld, William Temple and Albert Schweitzer. But the essence of the religious experience of Europe can be more easily defined today than it could be in ages of rigidly structured belief and general conformity. There is a moral demand upon the individual, accepted in loneliness, but fulfilled in the service of men: in Friedrich von Hügel's analogy, the cloth of gold of prayer has the threads of the woof running from God to man and man to God, and the threads of the warp joining men to each other. Then there is the meeting with the person of Jesus, whether as a man, or more than a man, a figure in history or a figure in the accumulated tradition and in living experience. This meeting involves the acceptance of suffering and, paradoxically, is the source of inner peace – it is joining "the fellowship of his sufferings". Dietrich Bonhoeffer, theologian and conspirator, described his own experience in letters from prison – shortly before he was executed – in words that may serve to summarize the spiritual legacy of Europe. "All that we may rightly expect from God, and ask him for, is to be found in Jesus Christ . . . If we are to learn what God promises . . . we must persevere in quiet meditation on the life, sayings, deeds, sufferings and death of Jesus . . . it is certain that our joy is hidden in suffering, and our life in death; it is certain that in all this we are in a fellowship that sustains us . . . Please don't ever feel anxious or worried about me, but don't forget to pray for me . . . You must never doubt that I'm travelling in gratitude and cheerfulness along the road where I am being led."[32] To the definition of religion in terms of "presence", "dependence", "awe" and "moral imperative", the European experience of worship would add, companionship.

## REFERENCES

1 W. Wordsworth, "Tintern Abbey" in *Lyrical Ballads* (1798); F. D. Schleiermacher, *Reden über die Religion* (1799).

2 Goethe, *Faust*, Part 2, Act I, Sc. v. The motto on Otto's title-page.

3 Sermon, "They changed their minds", 25 Jan. 1628–29 in *Sermons of John Donne*, ed. G. R. Potter (10 vols., 1956), VIII, p. 333.

4 Martin Buber, *Ich und Du* (1923; English trans. 1937).

5 Whitehead, cit. Arend Th. Van Leeuwen, *Christianity in World History: The Meeting of the Faiths of East and West* (English trans. 1964), p. 327. See also for the rest of this para.

6 A. J. Festugière, *Personal Religion among the Greeks* (English trans. 1934), p. 5.

7 *Phaedo* 63.

8 Euripides, *Hippolytus*, 1436–40. The goddess is forbidden to look on the deaths of mortals.

9 Marcus Aurelius, *Meditations*, II. 14, VII. 3, XII. 32, 36.

10 Cit. A. D. Nock, *Conversion: The Old and the New in Religion from Alexander the Great to Augustine of Hippo* (1933), p. 195.

11 Nock, op. cit., p. 14.

12 P. Thoby, *Le Crucifix des origines au concile de Trente* (1939), p. 19.

13 Robert M. Grant, *Early Christianity and Society* (1977), p. 11.

14 E. R. Dodds, *Pagan and Christian in an Age of Anxiety* (1965), p. 138.

15 Peter Brown, "The Christianization of the Roman Aristocracy" in *Religion and Society in the Age of St Augustine* (1972), p. 181.

16 E. Gibbon, *The Decline and Fall of the Roman Empire* (ed. J. B. Bury, 7 vols., 1912), VI, p. 16.

17 "The young Hero stripped himself (He was God Almighty), strong and stout-hearted. He ascended the high gallows manful in the sight of many, being minded to loose mankind" (*The Dream of the Rood*, trans. H. F. Brooks (1942), 38–40).

18 Ignatius, *Ad. Eph.* XX. 2, in H. Bettenson, *Documents of the Christian Church* (1963), p. 105.

19 Peter Brown, *Augustine of Hippo* (1967), p. 375.

20 For Bernard, and Suger's reply, D. Knowles and D. Obolensky, *The Christian Centuries*, II (1969), pp. 277–78.

21 R. R. Bolgar, *The Classical Heritage and its Beneficiaries* (1954), p. 193.

22 Colin Morris, *The Discovery of the Individual, 1050–1200* (1972).

23 P. Abelard, *Commentariorum super S. Pauli Epistolam ad Romanos* in *Opera*, ed. V. Cousin (2 vols., Paris, 1859), II, p. 207.

24 Cit. R. W. Southern, *Western Society and the Church in the Middle Ages* (1970), p. 301.

25 *De Imitatione Christi*, Bk. II, Caps. VII and XI.

26 R. Wittkower in *New Cambridge Modern History*, I, *The Renaissance, 1493–1520* (1957), p. 135.

27 A. G. Dickens, *Martin Luther and the Reformation* (1967), p. 111.

28 Erasmus, *Enchiridion Militis Christiani* (Basle, 1519), "The Fourth Rule" (trans. R. Himelick, 1963, p. 94). For St Francis de Sales, see *Introduction à la vie dévote* (1609), Pt. III, Cap. 4 (English trans. by M. Day, 1956, p. 102).

29 A. Bréler, *L'Homme et la femme dans la morale calviniste* (1963), p. 61.

30 For a revision of our assumptions about the field of religious history see Ch. Langlois, "Des Études d'histoire locale à la sociologie religieuse historique", *Revue d'Histoire de l'Église de France*, LXII (1976), pp. 329–47. See also his *Le Diocèse de Vannes au XIX^e siècle, 1800–1830* (1974).

31 Friedrich Naumann, cit. Kurt Leese, "The Church and the Future . . . the Vision of F.N.", in *Religion and Culture: Essays in Honour of Paul Tillich*, ed. W. Leibrecht (1959), p. 262.

32 D. Bonhoeffer, *Letters and Papers from Prison*, ed. E. Bethge (1971), pp. 391, 393 (21 and 23 Aug. 1944).

# 14

# Philosophers and Intellectuals

## ANTHONY QUINTON

The technological transformation of the world in the last two and a half centuries, begun in Europe and spread out from it by the commercial and military energy of Europeans, had its original intellectual ancestor in the naturalistic cosmology of the Ionian philosophers. If the natural world is seen as a machine, rather than a divine manifestation, there is encouragement for the idea of influencing it by purposive manipulation rather than prayer. More generally, rationally premeditated action comes to be more attractive than resigned acquiescence in the workings of fate.

Greek speculations about the nature of the world, after the first, Ionian beginnings, were not always as potentially fruitful as the atomism of Democritus turned out to be. In Magna Graecia (southern Italy) Pythagoras was led by his mathematical discoveries into number-mysticism and the leadership of a religious cult. Parmenides argued against the reality of change and motion, phenomena that the celebrated paradoxes of Zeno, like that of Achilles and the tortoise, were devised to undermine. Both of these thinkers contributed substantially to the philosophy of Plato a century and a half later. Closer to the secular, naturalistic spirit of Thales and his followers was the moral and social thinking of the Sophists. The first of them, Protagoras, came, like Democritus, from Abdera, being born there 20 years earlier, but was mainly active in Athens.

A special peculiarity of the Sophists was that they were professional teachers, indeed of a vocational sort, who earned a living by giving instruction in public speaking to intending lawyers and politicians, in what must have been an unprecedentedly oratorical age. At the time they were unfavourably regarded on that account, specifically for taking money for what should be done in a gentlemanly fashion for its own sake. A solider ground for complaint is the fact that they aimed to equip their pupils for argumentative victory rather than the discovery of truth. The disapproval they met with survives in the disparaging sense today of the words *sophistry* and *sophistical*.

On a larger view, however, it may be that they deserve respect as, inadvertently, the discoverers of reason. The formulation of fallacies led to self-consciousness about reasoning and the deliberate search for the conditions of its validity. That side of Sophism was very much in evidence in the thinking of Socrates, who is, indeed, represented by Plato as a frequently unscrupulous arguer. Discussions of a logical and near-logical kind abound in Plato's dialogues and that line of interest culminated in the great works that make up Aristotle's *Organon*, an intellectual achievement of such systematic and final-seeming magnificence as to dominate European thought on the subject, in an ever-increasingly stifling way, for two millennia.

Plato and Aristotle are the first thinkers whose works have survived in bulk. Plato's are of a literary quality to which none of his predecessors, and few of his successors, seem to have aspired. Between the two of them they cover the whole range of human intellectual interests, not only the central philosophical disciplines of theory of knowledge, metaphysics and ethics, but also politics, aesthetics, psychology, physics and, in the case of Aristotle, biology and, of course, logic. No other writings, apart from the Bible, can compare in regard to the depth and breadth of the influence they have exercised on the European mind.

The moral ascetism Plato learnt from Socrates was the point of departure for a dualistic view of the world in general, austerely and impersonally religious, in which reality is a supernatural order of timeless essences, accessible to reason, while the world of natural objects in space and time is only appearance. Fortified with substantial infusions of Oriental mystery and magic this body of ideas became, by way of the Neoplatonism of Plotinus, the philosophy of the Fathers of the Church and, in particular, St Augustine, to be partially, but never wholly, displaced from the time of the recovery of Aristotle by Europe from the 12th century onward.

Aristotle put together what Plato had so unequivocally sundered. Everything is made both of form, grasped by the intellect, and matter, by which it is made concrete in space and time, from God, who is pure form, at one extreme limit to bare matter, the raw potentiality of existence, at the other. Between the extremes everything is ranged in a continuous hierarchy. Man, too, is a compound of matter and form; his mind and body are not conceived in Plato's way as two quite distinct and self-subsistent things. A similar moderation inspires Aristotle's ethics, an endorsement of worldly good sense which takes theoretical contemplation to be the highest form of life, and his politics, in which he prefers a constitutional republic, governed by laws rather than men, to Plato's totalitarian project of rule by an intellectual élite.

Until the Emperor Justinian closed the philosophical schools 800 years later, Athens remained the philosophical capital of the world, the natural place of intellectual pilgrimage for a cultivated Roman like Cicero. Herodotus passed through Athens to settle in southern Italy, and write his great history of the Persian Wars there, having begun life in Asia Minor. Thucydides, historian of the war against Sparta, about 20 years younger, was an Athenian. They were, respectively, a little older and a little younger than Socrates. Xenophon, the third great historian of Classical Greece, was Socrates' pupil and biographer.

After the Socratic age the centre of the intellectual life of the world moves outside Europe to Alexandria, founded ten years before his death by Alexander the Great and soon after the battle which ended the division of Greece into endlessly conflicting but creatively vigorous city-states. Within a century it had overtaken Carthage as the chief city of the Mediterranean and it remained important well into the Christian era as the greatest of the provincial capitals of the Roman Empire. It was always of more scholarly and intellectual significance than Rome and kept its place until the depredations of the Christian Emperor Theodosius at the end of the 5th century AD. In particular, it was the seat of the world's greatest library, the centre of mathematical and scientific study and, most influentially of all, it was the point at which Oriental religion made contact with Greek philosophy in a way that determined the elaboration of Christian doctrine by the Fathers of the Church.

The great constructive age of Greek thought, ending with the deaths of Alexander and Aristotle, was less than 300 years long. The impetus it developed was sufficient to impose a measure of unity on the thought of the next nine centuries. The more direct line of Greek influence was through the philosophies of life which prevailed at Athens after the death of Socrates and then, in a popularized, boneless form, came to be the spiritual nourishment of cultivated Romans until the fall of the Roman Empire in the west.

The best-known of these philosophies, Stoicism and Epicureanism, were connected with doctrines developed by contemporaries of Plato. The Stoicism of Zeno, a Cypriot who taught in Athens, derives from the world-renouncing Cynicism of Antisthenes and Diogenes, and the philosophy of Epicurus, a native of Samos in Asia Minor, is in some respects a milder version of the Cyrenaicism of Aristippus. In their original, Greek versions Stoicism and Epicureanism were comprehensive philosophical systems in which as much attention was given to logic and the philosophy of nature as to ethics. But in the Roman world they were reduced to rules for the conduct of life, promising to secure peace of mind for their adherents by techniques of resolute self-control and indifference to fate in the case of Stoicism and of the detached pursuit of mild, spiritual pleasure in that of Epicureanism. So diluted, Stoicism was the favourite philosophy of Romans of the ruling class: Cicero, Seneca and Marcus Aurelius, but also of the freed slave Epictetus. Epicureanism in the Roman world had the good fortune to be expressed in the world's greatest philosophical poem, the *De Rerum Natura* of Lucretius, which seeks to dispel the fears inspired by supernatural religion.

The third of the main post-Aristotelian philosophies of Greece, that of the sceptics, is the most intellectual in emphasis. Yet it too was governed by the practical aim of securing peace of mind in a world where the well-being of the individual was beyond his power to influence directly. The ideas of the sceptics, preserved encyclopedically in the compilation of Sextus Empiricus, were to come to the surface again in another time of religious confusion and political turbulence: the 17th century. The arguments of Descartes and, to some extent, the attitude of Montaigne were anticipated by the ingenious members of the 500-year tradition of Greek scepticism.

The conquests of Alexander, and the imperial expansion of Rome which in some measure repeated them, brought Oriental ideas into the Mediterranean world. On the religious level this led to wide and enthusiastic popular attachment to various mystery cults, exciting in their promises of salvation. The most important of these were Christianity, which saw everything as the creation of an omnipotent God, and Mithraism, a Persian dualism which conceived the world to be the battlefield for the strife of two opposed principles, one good, the other evil. In philosophy there was a comparable division between Neoplatonists and Gnostics.

There were many copious writers after Plato and Aristotle but none with anything like their scope, let alone their genius. Alexandrian science degenerated into mere compilation after the Roman conquest of Egypt, apart from occasional flashes of genius with the algebraist Diophantus and the trigonometer Ptolemy (best known for his long-lived astronomical system). Rome itself produced some great historians – Caesar, Sallust, Livy and, above all, Tacitus – but in the sciences only compilers such as Varro and Pliny. Literary criticism was sustained by the great Roman poet Horace and, in a more sophisticated way, by Longinus, the unknown Greek, of, it seems, the 1st century AD, who wrote *On the Sublime*.

Alaric the Goth sacked Rome in 410, inspiring Augustine to compose *The City of God*. The Roman Empire in the west formally ended in 476. In 529 the Emperor Justinian, the great codifier of Roman law, closed the philosophical schools of Athens. Some of the expelled philosophers took refuge with Chosroes, king of Persia, but before long they seem to have been allowed back to Athens. That city, however, did not recover its position. Soon afterwards the incursions of the Lombards into Italy destroyed the conditions for thought and learning.

But while the Anglo-Saxons were displacing the Celts in England, Ireland preserved the freedom from interference it had enjoyed while the Romans occupied Britain. Christianized in the 5th century, Ireland was the most vigorous cultural centre of the early Dark Ages. In the westernmost part of Europe learning soon came to flourish in the new monastic centres.

The first distinguished intellectual product of newly Christianized Britain and Ireland was Bede's *Ecclesiastical History*. Bede's Jarrow was in the kingdom of Northumbria, at that stage the most settled of the early English kingdoms. At another of its towns, York, a pupil of Bede's set up a school where Alcuin studied, gaining the scholarly qualifications that led Charlemagne to engage him as founder of his palace school. Charlemagne's grandson, Charles the Bald, recruited the most impressive intellect of this epoch, the Irish Neoplatonist philosopher John Scotus Erigena. If the Golden Age of Irish learning in the centuries after St Patrick seems shadowy and even fabulous, the extremely learned and dialectically sophisticated rationalism of Erigena proves that the Irish culture of the Dark Ages was not a myth.

Britain and Ireland were soon inundated with Norse invaders. In Britain they were checked by King Alfred who was himself both a learned man and an energetic patron of learning, translating Bede's *History* and Boethius' *Consolation*, among other things, into English. Whatever the political disorders of the age, the Church survived with its organization intact and the Church was the essential bearer of literacy and culture. The crucial institutions were the schools attached to cathedrals like Notre Dame or Chartres, anticipating, and in some cases directly giving rise to, the universities of the high Middle Ages.

After Charlemagne had imposed a measure of order on the mainland of western Europe and,
a little later, the Normans had settled down to enjoy their varied conquests, the reasonably
peaceful conditions required for steady intellectual development were satisfied. Learned men
could congregate in cities and communicate easily, while in the Dark Ages they had had to lurk
in monastic houses whose chief security was their remoteness. Until the 15th century the two
great centres were Paris and Oxford, each housing several thousand students, disposed to
endow their more admired teachers with a kind of heroic status. The very oldest, Italian
universities were overshadowed by the two great 12th-century foundations, partly because of
their confinement to a single subject, but mainly because they were governed by their students
and not their masters.

From the point of view of society as a whole the universities were the educators of the
priesthood. That, in effect, meant that they were the educators of the literate minority of the
population and, in particular, of the administrators who ruled the community at first under,
but soon alongside, the more conspicuous military leaders of royal or noble blood. Intellectually
the universities monopolized the thought of the age and they managed to exercise the
monopoly in an invigorating way because, while their ecclesiastical status protected them from
outside interference, they were still highly autonomous within the whole church system as
independent corporations, not under the immediate control of pope or bishop.

The initial arts course covered grammar, rhetoric and, above all, logic and also some rather
sketchy mathematics and music for liturgical purposes. Beyond that lay theology, law and some
quaintly bookish medicine. Logic for the most part was a traditional drill; intellectual energy
and originality were focused on theology, in particular on the rational interpretation and
articulation of the truths revealed in the scriptures.

Anselm, the Italian who was an abbot in France before becoming archbishop of Canterbury
soon after the death of William the Conqueror, was the first great philosopher of the high
Middle Ages. In the directness with which he approached and answered such central issues as
the existence of God and the nature of the atonement he is unrepresentatively unencumbered
by tradition. The more persisting style of medieval thought was given it by Abelard. In his *Sic et
Non* he brought together apparently incompatible statements from the Bible and the writings of
the Fathers. His pupil, Peter the Lombard, applied the same method in a less provocative way
in his *Sentences*, taking his exemplary texts only from the Fathers, in particular Augustine. This
was the standard manual of theological instruction and the received form for a theological
treatise was a commentary on the *Sentences*.

Anselm had given a brilliantly uncompromising example of how pure reason could be used
to defend the articles of faith. At first in the 11th and early 12th centuries the main problem on
which reason was exercised was the insubstantial looking issue of the existence of universals:
does the species *man* exist as well as the individual men that are members of the species? The
problem had some theological interest through its connection with various mysteries of the
faith, such as explaining the innate sinfulness of the newly created soul without blaming God for
its defect. But it was the recovery of the main encyclopedic mass of Aristotle's works that gave
the dialectical vigour of the new scholastic thinkers something to work on.

While Europe was labouring under the ravages, first of the Lombards, and then of various
Scandinavian peoples, the Arab world had been united and revived by Muhammadanism. The
first major Arab philosopher, Al Kindi, was a contemporary of Erigena, two centuries after
Muhammad's death in 632. His two most influential successors were Avicenna, who died
around the time of Anselm's birth in the early 11th century, and Averroës of Cordoba in Spain,
who died in 1198. In the century following 1120 the whole of Aristotle was translated from
Arabic into Latin and became available to European thinkers together with the great Arabic
commentaries. These last were naturally not concerned to harmonize Aristotle with Christianity. But Averroës, concerned to reconcile his thought with the doctrine of Islam, had
introduced a sharp distinction between natural and theological knowledge, which he took to be
quite independent of one another, that was to be influential.

The main intellectual preoccupation of the high Middle Ages was the harmonious
integration of the great recovered mass of pre-Christian but irresistibly authoritative-looking
knowledge in the works of Aristotle with the Christian faith. Albert the Great, a German,

assembled the materials for the task which was carried out with grand comprehensiveness by Thomas Aquinas, an Italian of noble descent who taught at Paris. His system sought to use philosophic reason to supply convincing proofs of all but the most mysterious elements of Christian belief, expressing the greatest possible optimism about the compatibility of reason and faith. This was a considerable achievement given that Aristotle's God is not a person (and even less three persons), Aristotle's world is eternal and uncreated and in Aristotle's view the soul is not immortal.

Aquinas' most influential critic Duns Scotus, an Oxford Franciscan where Aquinas was a Paris Dominican, emphasizes the limits of man's reason in the interests of magnifying the autonomy of God's will. An extreme academic professional, Duns Scotus was noted for the thoroughness and technical refinement of his destructive criticisms of rational theology. His fellow Briton, William of Ockham, agreed with him about the limits of reason in the supernatural domain, but went beyond him in arguing for the possibility of natural knowledge derived from the senses. In this he is the chief precursor of British empiricism.

Ockham and quite a number of other philosophers died in 1349, of the Black Death. His own endorsement of the mind's power to secure knowledge of nature initiated a line of physical inquiry, not tied down to the ideas and methods of Aristotle, that leads on to the scientific interests of the Renaissance. Another tendency was the emergence of a purely mystical attitude to religion, especially in Germany, an intelligible outcome of the depreciation of reason in the domain of faith. If that point of view anticipates the doctrinal side of Protestantism, with its emphasis on the remote and mysterious majesty of God, the ecclesiastical objections of the Reformers to the claims of the priesthood are to be found in the philosophically backward-looking John Wycliffe. A further link between him and Luther is that both aimed to make priests unnecessary by making the Bible available in the vernacular language of the ordinary believer.

The thinkers of the high Middle Ages were priests, for much the most part members of religious orders. By no means all the thinkers of the Renaissance were laymen but even when, as with Erasmus, they were not they were no more institutionally than intellectually confined within orthodox church limits. The movement began, of course, as a rediscovery, above all of the wealth of Classical imaginative literature. The first name here is that of Petrarch, in the 14th century. A more perfectly representative figure is Lorenzo Valla in the century that followed. Valla established, by the techniques that for the next 500 years a Classical education fitted its ablest recipients to apply, that the Donation of Constantine, assigning great temporal powers in the west to the pope, was a forgery put together half a millennium after the alleged donor's death. He wrote some dialogues in defence of pleasure against medieval asceticism. He wrote with great power of the superiority of Classical to medieval Latin. All aspects of humanism are to be found here: the rejection of pious lumber, the enjoyment of natural pleasure and the beauty of the natural world, the idealization of Classical culture.

Gemistus Pletho, coming to Florence from Byzantium with a profound devotion to Plato, led Cosimo de' Medici to found the Florentine Academy. In it a somewhat mystical and aesthetic version of Platonism was developed by Marsilio Ficino and Pico della Mirandola. More substantial was the work of the Italian philosophers of nature of whom Giordano Bruno was the last and most important. He stands between the backward-facing reaction which used Plato, usually in mystical Neoplatonic form, against Aristotelian scholasticism and the truly scientific study of the natural world brought to maturity by his younger contemporary Galileo.

Italy, until it fell under Spanish domination in the mid-16th century, corresponded to Classical Greece in its most creative period before Alexander: in both a linguistic and cultural unity was politically divided into lively, prosperous and variously competitive city-states. If philosophy was still largely concerned with the high metaphysical themes of the Middle Ages, it was not carried on in the old manner of dialectical manipulation of authorities.

As non-ecclesiastical men were taking to thought, so minds were being exercised on non-religious topics. Machiavelli's secular political studies of the technique of statecraft and of an idealized Roman Republic were defiantly secular. Although his close contemporary Thomas More was orthodox enough in religion, to his own disadvantage, his *Utopia* considered social problems from a wholly earthly point of view. In the Middle Ages history had degenerated into chronicles, typically polluted with fabulous elements. With Machiavelli and Guiccardini it returned to the world of knowledge from the realm of the imagination. Literary criticism was revived by the very late translation of the otherwise repudiated Aristotle's *Poetics*, into Latin at the end of the 15th century, into Italian 50 years later. The combative scholar Scaliger managed to extract from it the doctrine of the "unities" that was to have an influence on imaginative writing that was at once restricting and stimulating.

The Protestant Reformers were copious writers but their interests were not theoretical. Luther, in particular, was an intellectual barbarian, abusing universities which he saw as temples to the harlot Reason. Generally Protestants fought the life of the mind by their insistence on the devoutly unreflective acceptance of the Bible as literally the word of God. With this Bibliolatrous addition, the Protestants revived the gloomier aspects of the doctrines of St Augustine, in particular his pessimism about the capacity of men to achieve knowledge or virtue without the agency of divine grace. Only in bringing about sectarian divisions within Christianity, which have proved, even in eras of religious indifference, to be incurable, has Protestantism, quite unintentionally, contributed to the intellectual well-being of man.

The most attractive side of humanism is shown in the life and work of three men who were propelled by the flagrant religious frenzies of their time towards a tolerant reasonableness: Erasmus of Rotterdam and the Frenchmen Jean Bodin and Michel de Montaigne. Erasmus was and remained a Catholic priest, despite his criticisms of the Church, but led the life of a man of letters and scholar. Bodin, a lawyer, wrote a large treatise on political theory and was led by the savageries of the French wars of religion to endorsement of a very comprehensive measure of religious tolerance. Montaigne raised the question posed by the violent collision of opposite certainties: do those who are prepared to kill for what they believe really know what they think they do?

By 1600 the map of Europe had not quite settled into the divisions between Catholic and Protestant nations and regions that have persisted to the present day, but by then the variously enthusiastic and exploratory period of the Renaissance was about to give way to an epoch in the history of thought whose newly introduced assumptions make it much more intelligible to us than any earlier thinking. The crucial innovators are Francis Bacon and, 30 years later, Descartes. Bacon's importance is really negative. In marvellous prose he ridiculed intellectually sterile traditions: scholasticism, the delicate but merely ornamental learning of the humanists and the superstitious nonsense believed in by the exponents of various forms of magic. Following Averroës and William of Ockham in the sharpness with which he distinguished natural from supernatural inquiries, he implied, in effect, that only in the former could progress be made that was worth making. As he said, knowledge is power, something to be accumulated in a methodical, inductive way by cooperative research and to be put to the relief of man's estate.

The type of natural science Bacon described did not really come into existence for another two centuries: Darwin's account of evolution is perhaps its most glorious exemplification. In the 17th century it was the mathematical aspect of the new science of nature that seemed, rightly, to be the explanation of its extraordinary successes, not the patient accumulation of masses of observed detail. Descartes's revolutionary approach to philosophy by way of a critical inquiry into the nature of knowledge turned the unsystematic scepticism of Montaigne, with the aid of arguments drawn from the Greek sceptics, into a radical elimination of old habits of belief.

It was not the content of the conviction at which Descartes's doubt was compelled to stop that mattered, but the example it gave. The indubitability of "I think therefore I am" he took to warrant every belief that was logically or introspectively self-evident. He confidently inferred that he was in essence a substantial soul, not a perishable body, and that God existed. The physical world remained problematic and has continued to be so for theorists of knowledge until very recent times.

Two lines of influence run from Descartes. On one are to be found the great metaphysical constructions of Spinoza and Leibniz, baroque fulfilments of the promise of Descartes's method. In both the senses are disparaged as confused surrogates of thought. Pure reason is invoked to produce on the one hand Spinoza's logically unified natural order, on the other Leibniz's notion of an infinity of souls arranged by God in a systematic correspondence with one another. It was a watered-down version of Leibniz's philosophy that became the object of Kant's criticism.

The other philosophical descendants of Descartes are also the descendants of Bacon and even Ockham. They are the British empiricists, in particular Locke, the slightly unwilling initiator of the Enlightenment, and Hume, a sane and capable historian and a far-seeing economist as well as a major philosopher. The thinking of the English-speaking world has on the whole been governed by their main assumptions ever since, allowing for occasional wanderings from the orthodox path. For these thinkers all substantial knowledge is derived, a bit precariously, from the senses. Value is this-worldly: pleasure or happiness. The state is a human contraption, designed to serve the ends of human individuals and to be judged by results.

The philosophy of Locke was the main inspiration of the unoriginal but brilliantly expressed and historically influential thinking of the French Enlightenment. For Voltaire, Montesquieu and the Encyclopedists that philosophy was associated with the great world-system of Newton's physics (Locke said that he was Newton's underlabourer) and with British liberty, hammered out in the confused aftermath of the Civil War.

Two other 17th-century thinkers had grimmer things to say that did not come to the centre of attention until our own age. Pascal, a mathematician of almost Descartes's capacity, oppressed by the desolate condition of man on earth, revived St Augustine's stress on man's dependence on divine grace. Hobbes, the most systematic materialist since Lucretius, was most notable for his defence, on purely secular, self-interested grounds, of an authoritarian sovereign, limited only by his power to secure obedience.

One of Locke's lesser works, totally opposed to Pascal's way of thinking, is *The Reasonableness of Christianity*. To most thinkers of the 18th century Christianity was not acceptable unless it was reasonable and to many of them it was not. A typical view of the age was Deism, which sees God not as a person, let alone as an anxious and concerned father, but as a rational principle, a pure intelligence capable of setting up the great world-machine whose workings Newton described. Voltaire and Bolingbroke were distinguished adherents of a movement set going by a host of lesser men. Hume argued for atheism without quite drawing the conclusion explicitly. Like other religious sceptics of the period he owed much to the ironic deployment of conflicting dogmatisms which Bayle produced in the interests of religious toleration. Along with other imperfectly orthodox thinkers of his time, Bayle found it wise to take refuge in Holland. Spinoza, who lived there already, was outlawed by his own religious community but managed to live and work without serious molestation. Descartes and Locke both prudently spent some time there.

The leading places occupied by Thomas More, Montaigne, Bacon, Descartes and Locke in the thinking of Europe in the 16th and 17th centuries enforce the point made at the beginning of the previous section: that laymen came at this time to play an increasingly important part in thought (even in thought about religion, as it turns out). For the 300 years between the middle of the 15th and the middle of the 18th centuries, what is more, these lay thinkers were private individuals, in no way enclosed within or dependent upon institutions. Some were men of inherited property and position, like Montaigne; some made their own way in the world, like Bacon; some depended on individual patrons, like Locke.

In these three "early modern" centuries the universities still remained a field of ecclesiastical monopoly. Because of sectarian strife and the large extent to which the absolute rulers of the epoch came to dominate the churches in their countries, purely clerical universities ceased to be centres of original and independent thought. The leading English thinkers of the period – Bacon, Hobbes and Locke – all showed scorn for the universities in which they had been educated, condemning them for the timidly pedantic Aristotelianism they stuck to, as if nothing had happened in the world of ideas.

But in the 18th century, in some places at least, universities began to revive, particularly where, as in Germany, laymen were admitted to the professoriate. The first German university of the new kind was Halle, founded in 1694; Göttingen, founded in 1737, in due course supplanted it in the leading position. In the middle of the 18th century the universities of Scotland, already in existence for some centuries, shared interestingly and fruitfully in the remarkable reanimation of Scottish culture, one which brought it to a leading place in Europe it had never held before, following full political union with England.

The two ancient universities of England in the 18th century were in a very torpid condition. Cambridge at least had the late 17th-century glories of Newton and Bentley to look back on. Oxford had achieved little after the restoration of the royal house for which it had undergone so much. In France, too, the universities remained barren under obvious royal and ecclesiastical pressure.

In these two countries, therefore, a concern for general ideas came to be the business of independent writers and thinkers. Some of them made a living wholly from their writings: Voltaire gloriously in France, Samuel Johnson more precariously in England. In these independent thinkers of the 18th century may be seen the first tentative approaches to the emergence of that characteristic modern type, the intellectual. Several obvious, but not altogether superficial, features of an intelligentsia proper are to be found in the *philosophes* of 18th-century France or in the literary circle which had Johnson as its centre: metropolitan residence; an affable, sociable style of life, turning on salons and cafés; an easy, unpedantic mode of expression, using literary forms very different from the standard treatise – the essay, the dialogue, the letter, the fable.

In mid-18th-century Germany, then, there first emerges the modern secular university, closely bound to the state and its purposes, indeed, but comparatively free from ecclesiastical interference (it was the state, not the Church, that chastised Kant for the radical character of his religious speculations and also Bolzano a few decades afterwards). In France and England, with the universities in unimproved decrepitude, the chief intellectual energies of the community found their expression outside them in informal sociable circles of intelligent men. Scotland, somehow, managed to achieve both, perhaps because of the practice of vesting the appointment of professors in town councils, rather than, as in Germany, the agencies of the central government.

The largest figure in the Scottish Enlightenment, David Hume, is now seen as a technical philosopher in the strictest sense of the word. His own ruling ambition, he tells us, was literary fame. If much of his writing is technically philosophical, a great deal is not: his essays on subjects ranging from currency to suicide, his best-selling history. What is more he exerted himself to write in a polished, agreeable way. Hume failed to secure a university chair; his religious unreliability was too great. But his friend, Adam Smith, the first to codify the principles of economics in a scientific system, was a professor, as was Adam Ferguson, whose *Essay on Civil Society* is reasonably considered to be the first genuine treatise on sociology. An Edinburgh that included such men as these in its intellectual society fully merited its claim to be the Athens of the north, a position retained for it by lively and distinguished exponents of the human and social sciences until early in the 19th century.

The greatest professorial figure of the French Revolutionary period immediately preceding our own historical epoch is unquestionably Immanuel Kant, the finest product of the new German university system. His whole career as a teacher of a surprisingly large array of subjects was spent at the remote university of Königsberg in east Prussia. As a theoretical philosopher he was led by his study of Hume to reject the claim of the Leibnizian orthodoxy in which he had been brought up, that reason is able to establish on its own what the true nature of the world is, hidden behind the veil of sensible appearances. Kant contended that we can know, in advance of sense-experience, what the general structure of the knowable world is, but that is only because that world bears the inescapable marks of our own minds' innate and constitutional manner of working an order into the experiences they receive. The only world we can know is a joint product of what the senses give us and our own, order-producing intellects.

Kant's German successors soon gave up the substantial element of empiricism in his thought. Although they did not resurrect Leibniz, they did reinstate, in a more sophisticated and flexible form, his idea that reason alone can establish the true nature of things. The greatest of these successors was Hegel. With absurd but magnificent ambition, he set out all possible objects of thought in what he took to be a rationally necessary order. He saw the dialectic process of philosophical reason, in which an idea suggests its opposite and that, in turn, a further thought that can reconcile the two, as exemplified in history, this being the part of his doctrine that was particularly taken up by Marx.

The other side of Kant is his ethics of absolute obligation, in which religion is made to depend on morality and not the other way round and the complete detachment of morality from pleasure is austerely insisted on. Kant acknowledged that he got much of the inspiration for these ideas from Rousseau, the most uncharacteristic of the *philosophes*. The intensity of Rousseau's demand for the self-directing autonomy of the individual led him, paradoxically, into being the most influential ancestor of the theory of modern totalitarianism. As an educational theorist he inspired an ideal of natural, unconstrained self-development. But politically, through the dangerous notion of a general will that can force its individual participants to be free, his thought points in exactly the opposite direction.

Rousseau is more of an intellectual in the modern sense than the Parisian *philosophes* of his age with whom he fitfully and uneasily associated, in contributing, for example, to Diderot's *Encyclopédie*. His thought has a marginal, irresponsible character that theirs did not. they were not all excluded from positions of power; Rousseau could not have been given power without a revolution. There is an extravagance about his opinions that has marked much of the independent thought of modern Europe and beside which the liberal, rather paternalistically philanthropic tradition that descends from the *philosophes* seems tame and conformist. With Rousseau old religious passions are revived in new secular forms after a merciful interval of civilized moderation.

The political ideas of Hegel can be seen as a compound of the metaphysical idea of the general will devised by Rousseau and the sense of men as formed by the historically evolved customs and institutions of their societies sonorously propounded by Edmund Burke, an admired figure on the periphery of Dr Johnson's circle. In them, as much as in his ideas about religion, the individual is somehow absorbed into the totality, whether it is the state or spirit, a kind of impersonal world-soul.

Much of the technical philosophy of continental Europe from the moment of Hegel's death took the form of more or less vehement polemic against some large part of his body of ideas from a position in agreement with others of them. Schopenhauer attacked Hegel's slippery optimism from the standpoint of the Kantian orthodoxy Hegel had started from. Marx accepted the dialectic but took it to be crucially expressed in history in the material, economic activities of men, not in the spiritual domain of ideas and beliefs which, for Marx, are a mere super-structural by-product of those activities. Kierkegaard attacked the complacent, cosily functional view of man's place in the world given by Hegel and asserted against it a view of man's isolation and of God's remoteness and mystery something like the doctrines of Augustine and Pascal.

None of these major critics of Hegel was really a professor: Schopenhauer tried academic life briefly and soon gave it up, Marx thought of it, but was doubly unacceptable, as a Jew and a radical. The leading thinkers of Britain for the greater part of the 19th century would not have seriously considered immuring themselves in such stagnant places as Oxford and Cambridge. Broadly to the left, socially reforming and anti-religious, were the Philosophical Radicals who developed and spread the ideas of Bentham, most notably the lucid and scrupulous John Stuart Mill. Mill himself invoked the name of Coleridge as a necessary corrective to a certain mechanical and desiccated quality in the thought of Bentham, while preserving his primary allegiance to the latter. The great energy-releasing reforms of Victorian England, the first of modern mass industrial societies, were inspired and guided by the utilitarianism of the Philosophical Radicals. The opposition of Coleridge to them and the urban and industrial order they worked for was not merely backward-looking. In more strident form it reappears in the thoroughly unacademic Thomas Carlyle and John Ruskin, the former contemptuous of a Benthamite age's deification of happiness at the expense of self-perfection, the latter revolted by the material coarsening of the world and of the work done in it.

The only influential thinking to come from the English universities until the last decades of the century was self-consciously retrospective, the Oxford Movement in which Newman and a gifted generation sought to respiritualize the Church after its long, secularizing subservience to

the state. With Newman's conversion to Catholicism in 1845 the new impetus faltered,
although it left its marks on the Church, even if little on society at large.

Much the same state of affairs prevailed in France. It was not until well on in the century, in the 1860s, towards the end of the Second Empire, that any notable thinkers were attached to universities, when Renan intermittently held a chair of Hebrew and Taine had a post at the Collège des Beaux-Arts. Taine and, to a lesser extent, Renan were part of the aftermath of Comte's positivism. Taine brought scientific determinism to the study of literature; Renan a scholarly scepticism to the study of Christianity. Auguste Comte broadly corresponds to Mill in England, but was less restrained by doubt and more given to grand constructive enterprises of thought. But in one respect, a very basic one, he and Mill were in close agreement: all true knowledge is to be acquired by the methods of inductive science, in particular the social and moral knowledge which man needs if he is to improve his relations with other men to the extent that technology has improved his mastery over nature.

In Mill quietly, and with reservations, in Comte loudly and precipitately, the tide of confidence in the emancipating possibilities of the scientific way of thinking reaches its greatest height. Two years after Comte's death in 1857 the most important event in 19th-century science took place: the publication of Darwin's *Origin of Species*. Tracing the emergence of man from the lower animals as the outcome of chance, it contained, as well as its obvious rebuttal of the religious conception of man as both a unique and an intended creation, melancholy implications for the kind of scientific optimism that might have seemed the natural replacement for supernatural religion in the mind of Europe.

During the lest 100 years in Europe philosophers strictly so called, professorial exponents of an academic discipline, have come to have less and less influence as sources of general ideas and beliefs. Of the three most influential figures – Darwin, Marx and Freud – only Marx had a philosophical training and its main gifts to him were a vocabulary and a polemical technique.

The *philosophes* of the 18th century saw man optimistically, as qualified in both intellect and virtue to fend for himself in a world in which God, if not expelled from it altogether, had been driven to its remoter limits. In the revolutionary era after 1789 and its Napoleonic aftermath, a widespread return to the religious view of the world, together with a romantic reversal of the Enlightenment's disdain for the historical past, took place: in Britain with Burke, Coleridge and Newman; in France with Chateaubriand and de Maistre. In the thinking of the late 19th century secularism returned, but in a new, pessimistic form.

Darwin represented mankind as simply the most developed of the primate species. Man's distinctness as a species, all the achievements which he had taken to mark him off from all other living things, were for Darwin the outcome of a competitive struggle for survival in which victory went to those creatures endowed with accidental variations that were competitively advantageous. Man was not Hamlet's beauty of the world and paragon of animals, but only the temporary victor in an unending struggle.

Marx too, working on a narrower historical scale, saw the history of man as a struggle, this time between economic classes. Ideals are only ideologies, weapons in the battle which reflect the material interests of those who wield them in confident ignorance of their true nature. Nietzsche based a comprehensive scepticism about the objectivity of all beliefs on a generally Darwinian conception of men as impelled into activity, including the activity of thinking, by a primal, inarticulate urge – the will to power. Freud, finally, saw the human mind as a field of strife between the self-preservative impulses of the conscious self and the erotic and destructive tendencies of the unconscious layers of the personality, in his conception by far the greater part of the mind as a whole.

All these currents of thought conspired to undermine the older secular view of man as a naturally rational and virtuous being, prevented from reaching perfection in thought and conduct only by the evil machinations of kings and priests. On that view the death of God announced the emancipation and maturity of man. After Darwin and Nietzsche men came increasingly to see their place in the world as a forlorn one, the powers of mind on which they must rely to improve their condition being the slaves of destructive and irrational impulses beyond their control.

This sense of alienation from what a century before had been seen as a glorious inheritance expressed itself most unmistakably in the gloom and rage of the most powerful and interesting imaginative literature of the period: the poetry of Baudelaire, the novels of Dostoevsky. More sedately it was encouraged by the new social sciences. After the primitive sociological systems of Comte, the naive scientific optimist, and Herbert Spencer, who saw evolution as leading from military to industrial forms of social order, came the more melancholy Weber with his conception of advanced societies as entering a phase of bureaucratic rationalization in which disenchantment extinguished the traditional sources of hope and confidence.

Spengler's *Decline of the West*, in its colourful, over-heated way, gave this mood of despair about the historical situation and prospects of mankind memorable expression at the moment, that of Germany's defeat in 1918, most obviously appropriate to it. The stance he recommended, one of heroic resolution, together with the social form he expected to prevail, what he called "Caesarism", were close to the theory of Fascism that was soon to exist in practice, first in comparatively innocuous form in Italy, later, with unpredictable disgustingness, in Spengler's own Germany. He lived long enough to be honoured by, and to repudiate, the Nazism he had foreshadowed.

Spengler was an intellectual of the same general type as Marx and even, in a way, Hitler; the rather solitary, fitfully educated constructor of a personal system. The Russian Revolution of 1917 was the work of intellectuals, Lenin and Trotsky above all, of a familiar 19th-century kind; haunters of cafés, disseminators of ill-printed manifestos. Trotsky, with his dramatic presence, his fluency, his broad literary culture, is more representative of the order than Lenin, a bureaucrat in intellectual's clothing who prepared the way in his short reign for the bureaucratic terrorist, his pupil Stalin.

Socialism, in effect a product of the French Revolution, came, from the last quarter of the 19th century, to be more and more Marxian. Skill and resolve in organization and the theological elaborations of the doctrine helped Marxism to overcome other milder variants of socialism, except where these were embodied in a large reformist political party with a special concern for the welfare of the industrial working class. In the trade unions of continental Europe and among left-wing intellectuals everywhere Marxism prevailed. Its influence was intensified by the economic disasters of the early 1930s.

Many of its adherents outside Russia loyally strove to serve the interests of Stalin's regime, vigorously peddling its lies and even supplying spies for it. Other, more thoughtful Marxists resisted the rigidly deterministic form in which Engels had, with perfectly honourable dim-wittedness, presented it after the master's death. Lenin took over this cruder version of Marxism. Lukács was the first, and most important, of those who found in Marx's earlier writings (not yet published when Lukács first wrote) an antidote to the anti-intellectualism of the gospel according to Engels and Lenin.

In Germany the Critical Theorists of the Frankfurt School developed the comparatively libertarian version of Marxism that the authority of the Communist Party soon forced Lukács to recant. With the approach of war the leading members of this group made their way to the United States. In the late 1960s one of their number, Herbert Marcuse, was to be the most revered theorist of the widespread outburst of protest, physical and intellectual, to the Vietnam War and, by a natural development, to the late capitalist society that was waging it.

Britain and France, unlike the other three large nations of western Europe, were only superficially touched by Fascism in the 1930s. It has often been observed how many of the leading imaginative writers of the inter-war years were more or less sympathetic to Fascism, most conspicuously the three greatest poets writing in English at the time – Yeats, Eliot and Pound – but also distinguished French writers such as Montherlant and Céline. On the whole Fascism had little to offer on a more theoretical plane than Yeats's dreams of an aristocratic society.

Nevertheless the existentialism of Heidegger which dominated continental European thought was originally combined in him with a leaning towards Fascism. Like many of the right-wing poets and novelists of the period Heidegger detested the latest developments of industry and technology. Capitalists and communists alike embraced these developments with enthusiasm, so anyone opposed to them both was his natural ally. In fact, however, there is nothing intrinsically primitivist about existentialism. Sartre is as much an existentialist as Heidegger, but neither an exponent nor a practitioner of the simple virtues of country life. The core of existentialism is a conception of man as utterly different in fundamental nature from everything else in the world. In this metaphysical defiance of Darwinism man is seen as having a special kind of existence that is described in varying ways, all amounting in the end to man's being a self-creator, not a thing whose nature is imposed on it from the outside.

Heidegger arrived at this position by developing the conception of man as an irreducibly individual entity, found in Kierkegaard's passionate critique of Hegel, in the technically philosophical idiom of phenomenology. That involvement with academic subtlety brought intellectual excitement to the universities of the nations where existentialism prospered. In the English-speaking world philosophy was lively but less engrossing to the educated public.

Two small but significant things happened in the middle of the 19th century. Two English mathematicians took up the study of formal logic pretty much where Aristotle had left it and started the enormous enlargement and sophistication of the discipline that broke through to a measure of general notice with the work of Frege and Russell and has since had effects far outside philosophy. In philosophy the effect was the emergence of a doctrine in which the defence of science as the highest kind of knowledge was carried on with the sort of thoroughness and rigour of science itself. The logical positivism of the Vienna Circle, generally notorious for the extremity of its scepticism about religion and morality, was only one, even if the most stable and persistent, form of this tendency. A great generation of philosopher-scientists around the turn of the century prepared the way: Clifford and Karl Pearson in Britain, Poincaré and Duhem in France, Mach in Austria, C. S. Peirce in the United States. The present state of the development is the various but still cognate analytic and linguistic philosophies of the English-speaking world which it is so hard to see as engaged in anything like the same activity as the existentialists of continental Europe.

The other significant event was the rather late discovery by English-speaking philosophers of Hegel. For a time, the last quarter of the century, the fairly high-minded, socially responsible version of the ideas of Hegel they presented, one that called men firmly to the duties of their station, carried all before it. Russell and G. E. Moore, the inspirer of Bloomsbury, routed it between 1900 and 1914. In the last decade or so, however, Hegel has returned to be a stimulus to thinkers hostile to the intellectualistic detachment of the philosophical *status quo*. But the Hegel that interests radical philosophers is not the inspirer of conscientious citizenship revered by the British idealists of the 1870s and 1880s. He is, rather, the more freely imaginative and less system-bound Hegel of the *Phenomenology*, the object of criticism by, but even more the source of influence upon, the young Marx.

If the analytic philosophy of the English-speaking world has little contact with existentialism, it has more in common with the broadly structuralist current of thought which has largely replaced existentialism in continental Europe. Language is a central, perhaps the primary, concern of both movements of thought. Chomsky, who has made the most dramatic contributions to a structuralist conception of language, trained as an analytic philosopher. Wittgenstein, the unclassifiably vagrant genius who set up such violent turbulences in the smooth surface of British academic philosophy, saw language as permeating all human activities and institutions, arriving at a conception of human conduct not unlike that of Lévi-Strauss, even if from a very different direction.

The nature of man, the problem of how he can achieve an understanding of himself, is the commanding issue of nearly all lively schools of thought at the present age. In one way or another human nature has always been a central philosophical problem, but often in a disguised way. Now seen as central by all parties, it supplies a unity of interest, although not, of course, of opinion.

The intellectual is, in his origins, essentially a European phenomenon. But in the last century and a half his significance as a bearer of new ideas has been world-wide. Ideas first entertained in Europe, in 19th-century Paris or Vienna or the Jewish Pale of eastern Europe, among them the idea of the intellectual and of his role in society, have spread across the world, from Latin America to the Far East, with a transforming effect upon the history of the 20th century.

# 15

# Scribes, Scholars and Students

## LUCY SUTHERLAND

The intellectual world with which this somewhat heterodox collection of categories presents us, shows as much as any of the other "worlds" included in this volume the nature and scale of the debt which modern western civilization owes to the linked cultures of Greece and Rome, yet also how far their successors have travelled from them.

The background is a great territorial empire, at the height of its strength in the two centuries after the birth of Christ, whose centre lay on the middle and eastern shores of the Mediterranean, but whose powers spread over the then known world. This empire was itself the culmination of a period of dominance, territorial and cultural, over what were then the most advanced civilizations of Europe and the Middle East, including the city-states of Greece and their Hellenistic successors. Its decline was slow, gradual and traumatic. In part the decline took the form of the breaking up of its great centralized administrative and military machine. Thus from 364 AD the Empire of the east was permanently separated from that of the west, and a whole section of their joint culture became for centuries a closed book to the developing peoples of Europe, a book only to be opened when the Eastern Empire was about to fall. This Eastern Empire, with its centre in Constantinople, survived in a defensive form, only disappearing in 1453 when overrun by the Ottoman Turks.

The end of the Western Empire, including the great Mediterranean provinces of North Africa, southern Gaul and Spain, was earlier and more dramatic, and its results affected a larger area. It fell by attrition before the attacks of migrant, warlike and uncivilized peoples, who were part of the waves of what the Romans called collectively "barbarians" who had at this time swept over the interior of Europe (from their eastern and northern homelands) under pressures still very imperfectly traced by us. The fall of the Empire left a power vacuum of the most formidable kind. It also left a cultural vacuum and (when once sufficient peace and security had become established) a series of peoples able and anxious to learn from their predecessors how they could fill it. It is not the purpose of this chapter to examine the content of the literature, learning and institutions which the Empire handed on. It is enough to say that, thanks largely to its Greek elements, but also to the more slowly developing but remarkable capacities of the Romans, and reinforced by influences from various Middle Eastern civilizations, it made up a unique body of imaginative literature in poetry and prose, a corpus of philosophy, of which Plato and Aristotle were the greatest exponents, a body of thought on abstract mathematics and science, including medicine, and the works of historians, rhetoricians and geographers. The purpose of this chapter is to indicate first how this superlative but intangible heritage came to be transmitted (at least in part) to posterity through more than 2,000 years of war and neglect, interspersed by occasional outbursts of destructive religious fanaticism. It is also to show that this survival was achieved, partly as a result of the sheer delight in the exercise of the mind and appreciation of beauty among a small number of men throughout the ages, and partly by the tenacity of institutions set up for more practical ends. It also serves to illustrate how, through the tendency of man-made institutions to follow lines of internal self-development, they ended by transmuting what at first they thought merely to transmit.

The instrument by which this cultural heritage was transmitted can be summed up in one word, the book, though the survival and spread of books was assisted by another type of survival, that of certain institutions from among the ruins of Roman might. No more fragile instrument of survival is imaginable in the years of chaos and destruction than the manuscript record of a man's thoughts – this was true whether the book took the most frail of all literary forms, the ancient papyrus scroll (none of which survives today except in the fragments mostly rescued by 19th- and 20th-century papyrologists from ancient tombs) or the somewhat more solid "codices" written on parchment introduced under the Christian influence after the 2nd century AD. In the course of some 2,000 years there have no doubt been grievous losses, and there have been centuries when the survival of precious texts hung by a thread, but the fact that so much has been preserved, and preserved in a reasonably uncorrupt form, is due to several factors in antiquity as well as to developments in post-Classical times. It is due in the first place to the fact that the Greek and Roman peoples were literate (and that to a degree almost inconceivable to those accustomed to most periods of modern history) and a high proportion of them bilingual in Greek and Latin. It was also due to the fact that they had evolved a standardized, though informal education system, that they early developed a sophisticated trade in the production and sale of books, and that they greatly encouraged the building of public libraries. Hence there existed, when bad times came, numerous manuscript copies of good editions of at least those books which were in high demand, and an educated public which ensured that these demands too were numerous.

In Athens, where, as in so many societies, literature preceded literacy, it was believed in antiquity that the first Greek book to be written was one containing Homer's poems, ordered in the 6th century BC by its ruler Pisistratus. If so, it was no doubt intended as an official record of the poems recited at the Panathenaean religious festivals. As early as the 5th century BC books could be bought in the open Athenian market, though they were rare, and in the next century private book collections (though as yet no public ones) existed. But the credit for the real breakthrough in the production of books and their provision to a learned public must go to Ptolemy Philadelphus, ruler of the city of Alexandria about 280 BC. Here Ptolemy built a Mouseion or shrine for the Muses where he maintained at royal expense a number of scholars whose main functions were concerned with the foundation and upkeep of what became the most famous library of the ancient world, and the centre of scholarly work on books as well as their collection. All types of Greek learning were encouraged by it, including those in science and medicine, and the most ambitious of their literary enterprises was the attempt to collect, collate and evaluate all known texts of Homer.

The days of Alexandria and other Hellenistic libraries founded in emulation of it were not long, though the widely held belief that the great library itself went up in flames during Caesar's Egyptian campaign in 49 BC seems to be exaggerated. It should be noted, however, that its operations were concentrated on Greek language and literature, and that what was to affect the Middle Ages was either Latin literature or Greek thought mediated through it. But the mantle of the Hellenistic pioneers fell on the broad shoulders of Rome, and it was with all the material resources of its greatest days that it carried on the work of disseminating the book. In the last years of the Roman Republic educated Romans such as Cicero and Lucullus had entirely absorbed Greek culture and taken full advantage of Hellenistic advances in its transmission. Large private libraries were collected, skilled Greek scribes employed, and well-recognized methods of publication developed. When the Republic gave way to the Empire, public libraries founded by emperors or powerful subjects sprang up everywhere, and patronage of literature and the arts, Roman as well as Greek, became a commonplace. As late as the 4th century AD, when Rome was in full decline, it was calculated that there were 28 public libraries in the city. Even in the 5th century at least one had survived the sack of the city and the ensuing centuries of chaos.

If the materials for the revival of culture survived in the collapsing Empire, so too did an organization set up for very different purposes, that of the Christian Church. The poverty and simplicity of the early Christians had given no indication of the astonishing rapidity with which they were to overrun the existing pagan cults, nor the dominant part they were to play in the Empire even before they could claim the status of an official religion. For the good Christian their conquest was essentially the triumph of the true over the false gods. Eusebius of Caesarea (d. 339) quoted with delight the story recorded by Plutarch of some travellers in the reign of the Emperor Tiberius, in whose reign Christ was born, who suddenly heard a loud cry in the waste places "the Great Pan is dead". But the organization of their congregations into bishoprics had political as well as spiritual significance. In the last days of the falling Empire the bishops were often the only officials left to organize and defend their flocks and the signs of a wider organization with the bishop of Rome at its head were beginning to take shape, using many of the forms though as yet enjoying little of the power of the former emperors. The days were still far off when Thomas Hobbes in the 17th century could call the papacy "no other than the Ghost of the deceased Romane Empire, sitting crowned upon the grave thereof", but they were foreseeable. Moreover, the leaders of this Church, themselves educated with their pagan contemporaries, used the philosophical weapons of these opponents in their own controversies, and some (though not all) of them shared in the love of the secular pagan literature. How interlocked were the old and the new can be illustrated from the two writers of these twilight years who were most deeply to affect their successors in the earlier Middle Ages. The first was St Augustine (354–430), bishop of Hippo in North Africa, whose most famous book, the *City of God*, was inspired by the shock of the collapse of Rome, and who describes in his *Confessions* how much he owed in his intellectual Odyssey towards his final faith to reading in Platonic and Neoplatonic sources. The other was Boethius (c. 480–c. 524) of a Roman senatorial family to whose Latin translations the west owed all it knew of the works of Aristotle until the Judeo-Arabic sources flowed in in the 13th century, and to whom it even owed the structure of its scholarly curriculum. He had apparently been at one time a Christian but his famous work on the *Consolation of Philosophy*, written while he awaited death in prison, was purely pagan in inspiration.

But if the survival of the culture owed much to institutional developments and the attitude of mind of distinguished churchmen, it owed at least as much to a spontaneous explosion within the Church, the rise from the end of the 3rd century AD of monasticism. Originating within the eastern Church, it was at first an expression of passionately individualist devotion to God and a complete revulsion from the world. From the hermits who sought their God in the deserts of Lower Egypt, society had little to hope, but particularly as the movement spread to the west, retreat into communities of like-minded persons became the normal pattern, and it was such communities which spread along the trade routes of the Mediterranean and into northwest Europe. Such communities were not only centres of Christian devotion but islands of literacy, providing in their libraries comparatively safe havens for books, and preserving the Latin language for the purposes of their liturgy. Also it became customary among the Benedictines in particular for the monks to take on as part of their monastic duties copying (and sometimes beautifully illuminating) the manuscripts which had come into their possession.

The medieval intellectual movements which called upon this inherited wealth were episodic and irregular, the outcome of varying needs and circumstances. The first which put to the test the institutions which preserved the past was that of the late 8th and early 9th centuries which has been called the Carolingian Renaissance after Charlemagne, ruler of the Franks and the first western ruler to claim to be the spiritual successor of the Western Emperor of Rome. With the aid of his former tutor, Alcuin (a product of the monasticism of northern England), he brought together a brilliant court of scholars over which he presided, and he collected about him learned churchmen (for at that time none but churchmen could be learned) to administer his empire. Under the influence of Alcuin he ordered the establishment of schools attached to cathedrals and monasteries, and (of the greatest value to the future) he had the monastic libraries ransacked for copies of Classical texts. His empire crumbled on his death, though it left a tradition in which later rulers were to follow him, and his educational schemes were only imperfectly carried out, but he left two important legacies. In the first place the

scribes in their monasteries, writing in the new, practical and elegant Carolingian minuscule
script they had invented, transcribed to such effect that, as has been said, "if one were to take
stock at the end of the ninth century of the classical books available, it would be clear that some
authors were so well entrenched in the literary and educational tradition, and so thick on the
shelves of the libraries that their survival was no longer in question" and the standing of many
others was greatly improved. It was not the fault of the monastic scribes that Latin translations
of but few of Aristotle's works (and even fewer of those of Plato) were among them, but if they
had been they would not have had the impact on western learning that they were to have three
centuries later, for the Carolingian Renaissance was essentially a literary one.

The second legacy which was left was in the field of educational organization. Charlemagne's educational system was not implemented, and the years which followed were dis-
tracted by Viking invasion and other disorders. When tolerable conditions, however, were
re-established, some of the successors of the cathedral schools he had established proved to have
remarkable intellectual resilience and led to greater things. This was not true of the monastic
schools, though they continued to educate the members of their own orders, and the great
abbeys whose superb buildings added glory to the European scene continued to be centres of
civilization and of a fine Classical tradition. Their scribes still produced magnificent copies of
texts, but as demand grew they gave place in the production of the books required by scholars
to commercial scribes, whose work soon began to be produced on a capitalistic basis. On the
other hand two religious orders, the Preaching Friars or Dominicans and the Priors Minor or
Franciscans, rose to take a prominent place in the new intellectual movement. Indeed the work
of two members of the Dominican Order, Albertus Magnus (c. 1193–1280) and St Thomas
Aquinas (c. 1225–74), was to set the crown on medieval learning.

Charlemagne could not have affected his renaissance had there not been men ready to play
their part in it. But nor is it likely that it would have taken place when it did had not a powerful
ruler given it a lead. This was not so of the intellectual movements which began in the 11th
century and culminated in the 13th. No doubt external conditions gave them some encouragement. Some of what were to be eventually the sovereign independent states of the modern
world were beginning to take shape; the papacy, despite many setbacks and its struggles with
the descendants of Charlemagne's Roman Empire, was exercising increasing control over many
aspects of a still united Christendom; the city-states, particularly those of northern Italy, were
developing their self-governing institutions and brilliant civic civilizations. But no independent
ruler, lay or clerical, brought together the young scholars coming from far and wide to hear
Peter Abelard (1079–1142) lecture in the 12th century on logic and theology at the schools of
Ste Geneviève and the cathedral of Paris, or the more mature scholars to come from even further
afield to listen to the great jurist Irnerius and other doctors of Bologna as they expounded
systematically for the first time the whole *Corpus Iuris Civilis* of Justinian's codification which
exposed to western Europe the full scope of the Roman legal system and eventually made
possible the reception of Roman law throughout most of the continent. In the case of
philosophical and scientific studies, including that of medicine, it is true that the movement,
once started, was given an immense stimulus when the completion of the reconquest of Spain
from the Moors gave access to Latin translations of Arab versions of Greek texts produced in
Toledo and other Spanish centres (including the entire works of Aristotle) and to a great mass
of philosophical, scientific and medical material, the fruits of Judeo-Arabic contact with Greek
learning in the past. But the movement was well advanced before their Classical sources were so
greatly reinforced, and, in the case of legal studies, the material which was worked on had been
available for study for some time.

But perhaps as important in the long run was the emergence of an institution to preserve
the past and coordinate new scholarship, that of the university. The Middle Ages were fruitful
in the creation of institutions which were effective for their own needs and capable of adaptation
to future ones. One of these was a type of community which may be called the guild or union, an
association of individuals coming together to achieve a defined object, with regard to which
they enjoyed full self-determination. The university (a word which originally meant no more
than any such association) was the application of this institutional form to the needs of
education and learning.

The institutions which today enjoy the right to the name of university have become so varied in size, reputation and curriculum, and are scattered so widely throughout the world, that it is well-nigh impossible to contain them within one definition. In July 1974 members of the International Association of Universities were drawn from no fewer than 108 countries. Almost the only thing they have in common is their past — the medieval institution with its claims of self-determination and freedom of expression — and behind this again the heritage of the ancient world. How far individual universities are able to take advantage of this dual heritage depends not only on them but on the societies in which they exist, but of its continuing existence there can be no doubt.

What we call the university was at first known as a "studium generale" — a place of study which was widely frequented. It soon became accepted that it applied only to institutions which provided a preliminary course in arts and further courses in at least one of the three higher faculties, Theology, Law and Medicine. Whatever the differences in their constitutions and customs, each of these "studia" consisted of a body of men of learning who made their living by imparting to students (all thought of as adults even though many of them might be no more than 12 or 14 years old) the learning they had acquired and which they sustained and sought to amplify by disputations, lectures and the meticulous reading of sources. Equally part of the community were the students whose university training was a preparation for positions in Church and state, in some cases for university teaching itself, and for what are still called the learned professions. The great majority of both teachers and taught were churchmen; most of them were poor, as were the institutions to which they belonged; all the instruction was in Latin.

The two earliest and most famous of these "studia" were Paris and Bologna. Both of them, as also Oxford (the earliest and most famous offshoot of Paris), came into existence without legal recognition, though they later sought it. "Studia" coming into existence later were normally founded (though not always) by papal bull, and all found it necessary to have their liberties recognized by the appropriate local ecclesiastical and secular authorities. The much-prized right for their graduates to "teach everywhere" was conveyed by papal bull alone. By 1400 there were 65 such institutions in existence, and in the 15th century 34 more were added.

Paris and Bologna, though associations for similar purposes, differed greatly in their constitutions. Paris was what was called a university of Masters. In this the supreme authority lay in the congregation of all teaching Masters of Arts under their elected Rector, a system still in force with only minor amendments in Oxford and Cambridge today, and one which has provided the background (though usually greatly modified) of all modern universities. Bologna on the other hand was a "students' university" in which supreme authority lay with congregations of students and their Rectors, and did this so exclusively that their teachers were altogether excluded from these bodies, and the association or College of Doctors or teachers was subordinate to them. The organization was a curious one which originated partly from the fact that the law students coming to study in Bologna tended to be older and more influential than those attending the universities north of the Alps, but more from the fact that few of these students were citizens of Bologna and (as was customary among foreigners coming for trade or other purposes to Italian city-states) they found it desirable to associate themselves to protect their legal interests. The teachers, on the other hand, were all Bolognese citizens, held a position of great respect in the city, but were in consequence ineligible for membership of congregations which gained the predominance in the university. Though this organization led to a good deal of friction, it did not detract from the fame and achievements of Bologna University, and a number of Italian universities followed its example. It did not prove as stable as the rival system, but its instability seems to have been due rather to a growing oligarchy in the students' congregations and a retreat into formalism among their officers than to clashes between students and teachers, common though these were.

The student bodies of all universities were from the beginning of their history notoriously disorderly, as was inevitable when numbers of young men were crowded together without links of family or locality and under the slightest possible control. They fought among themselves, they engaged in bloody contests with the local citizens; the dissensions of their seniors were sometimes the occasion of their clashes. Most (though not all) universities made some attempt to control the excesses, the most effective means being the licensing of their lodgings and the formation of resident colleges, once common among continental universities, but now hardly surviving outside Oxford and Cambridge. But in the main the chief interest of the university authorities was less the control of their junior members than the establishment of special courts to protect them against the hostility of the citizens among whom they lived.

It may be claimed that the university reached the climax of its corporate reputation in the high Middle Ages. It had as yet no rival institutions in the world of letters. Until printing was invented in the mid-15th century it was responsible for supervising the work of the booksellers whose scribes copied out the books in which the learning of the past was preserved and for checking the accuracy of the texts provided for their students. When printing was invented this part of their duty to the past was almost at an end. By 1500 more than 35,000 separate editions of books had been produced and the numbers were rapidly growing.

Thanks to the great scholars they produced, the universities had achieved a body of learning uniting pagan philosophy and Christian theology, the principles of which, though constantly under review, were generally acceptable. It was admitted by all that these institutions existed for the furtherance of the faith but that the faith could best be served by the furtherance of learning, and the concentration of learning into stable communities enabled a freedom of speculation to grow up which would otherwise have been impossible. It would, of course, be idle to pretend that this freedom was absolute. The issues involved were often those deeply concerning the rulers of the Church (with their fear of heresy) and of the Empire and the increasingly powerful territorial monarchs, among whom religion and nationalistic issues merged with those of power politics. But on the great matters of the day the universities could speak, as they did at the Council of Constance which ended the Great Schism in the papacy in 1415, as repositories of the conscience of Europe.

It could not be expected that the universities should retain this eminence. The world was moving and institutions are ill adapted to rapid change. Moreover the changes afoot were major ones. The Reformation destroyed the religious unity of Europe of which these scholars were a part. The principle of "cujus regio, ejus religio" – "who rules the state determines its religion" – took the place of this unity in the midst of war and civil contest. Even in those countries which escaped the Wars of Religion and the Thirty Years' War freedom of thought in the universities was drastically curtailed and scholarship set back. But before this major blow had been suffered the universities had already had to face, in what was for them an acute form, the result of an increasing laicization of society which was to erode their intellectual monopoly. This was the sudden rise of the 14th- and 15th-century humanist Renaissance in Italy, the last movement which arose in what had been the centre of the ancient Roman world; it also brought to the west the last great accession of Classical manuscripts. Its occasion was the final collapse of the Greek Empire before the Turks in 1453, and before and after the catastrophe the coming of Greek scholars and their collections of Greek manuscripts to the west. Here in Italy they found eager and brilliant scholars and men of letters to receive them. Already small and enthusiastic bodies of Italian scholars were seeking out the books which their forbears throughout Europe had so sedulously collected and had begun using them for a new purpose, a study of the ancient world, not as the precursor of Christianity, but (as the earlier scholars could do only uncertainly and as a secondary interest) in its own right. These scholars and the subjects of their study were taken up by the brilliant courts of Italy at its highest point of wealth and culture. Lorenzo de' Medici of Florence, the popes and other rulers saw in themselves successors to the Roman emperors as patrons of the arts and learning. It is to them that we owe some of the greatest of European libraries and museums, and the collections made by monarchs of succeeding centuries only followed in their footsteps. In so far as the scholars of these glittering days came together in any organization it was in small academies set up by their munificent patrons.

Beside this splendid outburst of literature and learning, as well as the visual arts, the studies of the scholars of the existing universities of the north seemed limited and pedantic enough. It is to their credit, however, that the best at least of the northern universities were in the end able to absorb the scholarship of this splendid movement while evading its paganism. That they did so is due, above all, to the influence of a great man and scholar, Erasmus of

Rotterdam (c. 1469–1536). By 1600 all prominent universities had absorbed much of the Greek learning and they (and the schools leading up to them) were teaching the Greek language. It was fortunate for the intellectual history of Europe that they had done so, for the glorious Italian episode ended abruptly in war, invasion and the appalling sack of Rome in 1527. The "liberal education" which was the aim of educationists from the 17th to the 19th century was largely a humanist creation.

In other ways, when the religious turmoils were over, the universities continued to make their contribution, in the study of theology, of Oriental languages in so far as they subserved theology, and (a new development) in the antiquarian study of their own national past. Several universities gained an international reputation especially in their graduate studies, for example Leyden (the university founded by William the Silent in 1574) in law and medicine, and the universities of Montpellier and Padua in medicine. It is also in this period that university libraries began to become prominent – for instance the Bodleian at Oxford, refounding an earlier venture, began the course which was to make it one of the greatest libraries of the world. University presses (usually it would seem, originating from the traditional duty of the university to ensure the purity of texts used by their members) began to be founded, some of which were to have a great future.

But all the universities, Protestant and Catholic, suffered from one fundamental defect; they were by their ecclesiastical basis excluded from the rising philosophical movements of their time, and their attitude in the face of change was inevitably defensive. When new intellectual interests arose such as that in natural science, these found their centre outside, not in the universities. It was not till the 19th and 20th centuries that the universities were able to take their lead in research into the natural sciences which since the 17th century had increasingly absorbed the most active minds of western Europe.

By the 18th century their reputation was at its lowest ebb and a powerful propagandist machine, that of the French *philosophes* which had captured the world of letters, provided bitter assailants of the Church and its related institutions. They not only attacked the universities for their weaknesses (which were often obvious) but even despised the learning for which they existed. At no period was the institution so near to destruction, for their enemies not only began to demand their abolition but suggested an alternative system of education and learning to replace them. Their undergraduate students, it was suggested, should be kept for instruction in improved grammar schools, those studying for the higher faculties should be trained for their professions by professional organizations, and men of outstanding learning and love of study should become members of academies, patronized by or even presided over by the benevolent kings or other rulers of the states in which they resided. Nor were these proposals merely academic. Enlightened despots had already begun to experiment with them when the universities of France disappeared overnight with the rest of the institutions of the *ancien régime*, and in the years of Napoleonic conquest ahead many in other countries, which Bonaparte considered otiose, followed them.

It is one of the strange reversals of history, but also evidence of the inherent strength of the universities as institutions, that not only did they escape this fate but entered into a period of rapid revival. The reasons are complex. It is improbable that the schemes propounded by the *philosophes* would in any case have been universally accepted. Neither England nor its recently emancipated colonies, now the United States of America (and a new country that took educational matters seriously from the beginning), would have been attracted by the idea of focusing the patronage of learning in a king or other ruler, nor was the condition of existing universities as parlous as was suggested. Some of them, including the Scottish ones, were showing that it was possible to serve the needs of their Church and at the same time to develop an educational system on new lines without irreconcilable disagreement. Still further, at Göttingen (later to be one of the glories of the German Empire but then in the Electorate of Hanover) Baron K. F. von Münchhausen, minister of George II, succeeded in the mid-18th century in building up a very successful university containing many of the features which were to characterize the German universities of the next age. But most of all the universities themselves suddenly found a voice and a philosophy which restored the vitality they had long lost. In 1770 at the University of Königsberg a hitherto obscure professor, Immanuel Kant

(1724–1804), began the lectures which were published in 1781 as the *Critique of Pure Reason*, and
in this and in his later works he became the founder of the first great metaphysical school of the modern age. What is more he was immediately surrounded by enthusiastic disciples, was received with adulation in all quarters, and not only saved the future of the university as an institution, but he and his successors for generations ahead gave it a moral and intellectual centre such as it had not possessed since the Middle Ages.

For the 19th century was to prove the second Golden Age of the university, and the universities of Germany were to be its centre. When von Humboldt came to reorganize the education of Prussia after its disastrous defeat by Napoleon there was no question but that the university would provide the pinnacle of the hierarchical system he set up, and the prestige of its philosophers, and their claims for the freedom of their speculation, gave the university a unique position in an otherwise regimented regime.

The German universities of the 19th century exercised a preponderant influence far outside their country's borders not merely because of the remarkable advances they made in research, scholarship and organization but because, thanks to worldwide increases in population and wealth and general developments in education, many new universities were being founded and old ones reformed and enlarged. The United States of America in particular added to their unparalleled growth in wealth and population an intense interest in all matters concerning education, and the German universities exercised a great influence over their scholars and administrators. But the influence of the reformed British universities was also important in ensuring that the expansion of Europe brought with it the further spread of the heritage to which they all paid tribute.

The great days of the German universities did not, however, long outlive the 19th century. Their inability to stand up to the militancy which was leading their country (and in consequence the rest of the civilized world) into the disasters of World War I deeply disillusioned their foreign admirers, and the miseries of defeat undermined their own confidence; but much worse was to come when the horrors of Nazi anti-Semitic fanaticism not only wrecked the universities themselves but provided a shattering reminder to the rest of the world of the frailty of the civilization built up over 2,000 years of effort and aspiration.

In the 20th century the growth of the number and size of universities has continued, and the institution has found its way into parts of the world which have hitherto had little direct contact with the traditions universities have sought to foster. In the United States in particular the ideal that the university should be open to all citizens of average ability who wish to enter it has led to the founding of a great number of universities of a size never before envisaged. Past patterns have been able to give little guidance to these vast institutions, or to the curriculum fitted for a student population so different in outlook and often in interests. There has thus been a great deal of experimentation in both curriculum and organization and at no time has it been harder to define the nature of the university as an institution, or to foresee its future development.

There is one grave problem, however, which faces in particular the best and most successful of modern universities, which critics of the university first raised as early as the 18th century and which with the growth of modern research became apparent before the end of the 19th, the fact that the link between the undergraduate teaching carried out by university teachers and the research activities which they engage in (particularly those in the field of the natural sciences) is becoming so tenuous as to threaten the unity of the institution as a whole. It has been held to be of the essence of the idea of the university that these activities coexist in it but it cannot be denied that conflicts of interest arise and this over an increasingly wide field of study. Whether or not this conflict of interests is standing in the way of the free development of fundamental research is not clear. On the other hand it has certainly been a factor in the growth of a malaise among the undergraduate body which has developed of recent years and which reached a crisis in the violence of the 1960s.

As has already been pointed out, university students have always had a reputation for sudden outbursts of disorder and violence. Until modern times, however, such disorders had been local in origin and expression and readily explicable. It was not till the 19th century in the years leading up to the 1848 Revolution that a new type of widespread and organized student unrest began to appear, and though it remained endemic in some countries thereafter, it was not till the present century, after the two Great Wars, that it assumed a really disruptive form. No doubt in both these periods the discontent was fostered by a particularly rapid increase in the number of students and by a sense of alienation between students and those controlling their teaching and organization. It should be noted, however, that in both these periods other powerful influences were at work, and that these were of an ideological nature.

In the 19th century the years following the defeat of Napoleon's world power left reactionary governments, often in reconstructed states, and an undercurrent of frustrated nationalism among intellectuals which was indissolubly connected with the French Revolutionary ideas of liberty and equality. The years following the two World Wars of the 20th century were affected by even more combustible ideologies. In both these periods, in short, an intellectual climate had been built up to which ardent-minded students were inevitably attracted, and in both of them student bodies proved capable of mounting an organization which overrode local boundaries and which, temporarily at least, enabled them to play their part in a wider movement with explosive effect.

In the years leading up to the 1848 Revolution it is not surprising that it was among the German students that the first associations of this kind were formed, for the Germans were noted for their autonomous organizations, and though these, the so-called "Students' Corps", were aristocratic social clubs in no way attracted by liberal causes, it was in reaction against them that a new type of organization grew up. In the 20th century such organizations were not hard to form (though no easier to keep in being than in the past) and they obtained support from outside their own resources. The causes for which student organizations went into action were much the same in most countries – anti-Nazism, anti-colonialism, the defence of minority rights – but the situations in different countries led to a different emphasis in their campaigns. Thus in the United States, for instance, questions of Negro rights and the Vietnam War provided the focus; in France, it was support of the General Strike by which the country was crippled in May 1968. In Great Britain the ideological basis of the movement was less powerful than in most leading countries.

The complaints of the dissatisfied students against their own universities inevitably varied – those attending large universities complained that they were "anonymous", those at small ones that their private affairs were interfered with, but all of them demanded less academic discipline and most of them a curriculum more immediately related to the interests of the average man or woman. There were only two things they had in common. They all at some stage broke into physical "direct action" or violence and this came to an end almost as rapidly as it arose.

It is too early to assess the results of these curious outbursts. It cannot be claimed that the ideological causes they supported have in most cases gained much from these brief incursions. As a French trade union leader remarked of the Paris week on the barricades, "May 68 was certainly not a revolution. A revolution cannot in any circumstances be a fête." Paradoxically the effects on the universities themselves have been more striking and some of them will certainly be permanent, but even these do not amount to a major break in the long history of this most flexible and adaptable of institutions.

Science may be considered one of Europe's greatest cultural inventions. But of equal importance in her heritage is the transmission of knowledge, combined as it is with the extension of knowledge through research and new thinking. Nowhere else in the world have these two activities been combined with the education of students as they have been in the European institution of the university. It may be that this triple combination – transmission of knowledge, research and teaching – cannot be held together for much longer, but as long as it lasts it is one of Europe's great contributions to the world.

# 16

# *Scientists*

## YEHUDA ELKANA

Organized knowledge grows by an ongoing critical dialogue between competing ways of viewing the worlds of nature, of society, and of man as a biological entity and as a psychological individual. The components of the world-view are both intellectual and social, both conscious and not conscious. On the purely conscious level, i.e. disregarding the mysterious world of subconscious motivations, world-views consist of bodies of knowledge with their pertinent scientific metaphysics, of images of knowledge and of social and political ideologies. Images of knowledge are those all-important views about knowledge which tell the professional as well as the layman what are the legitimate and trustworthy sources of his knowledge, what are the socially acceptable and morally preferential aims of gaining knowledge, the kind of methodology which is sure to bring about the best results, and in addition to many other considerations, what are the criteria according to which problems on which to concentrate should be selected from among the great number of possibilities. It is the images of knowledge which tell us today to rely on our senses rather than on revelation in the laboratory, just as they tell us that one of the main sources of religious knowledge is revelation. In every culture, in every society, some kind of knowledge gains preponderance. The kind of knowledge which we try to subsume under the name "scientific knowledge" emerged only in Europe and, though today it is the hall-mark of the whole industrial world, it is still European, not only in origin but in character. Yet it is difficult, if not impossible, to pinpoint exactly where the difference lies. Every single characteristic which was thought at one time to typify science (writ large) turned out to be unsatisfactory: technology, utilitarianism, scientific rationality, fundamental principles, separation of knower from the known, secularization, all these were tried and found not to define European science unambiguously. Perhaps the main fallacy of the search is rooted in the presupposition that science had to develop the way it did because there is an absolute "if" which is outside us and which is being discovered and described by science and its laws. If we drop this presupposition we are left with the much more elusive, pluralistic claim that, though there may be an "if" to be discovered, there are many ways of doing it; the typically European creation which we call western science is that very specific blend which developed in Europe, had some roots in antiquity, but flourished mainly from 1600 onward; and its mode of growth is that dialectical process involving the body of knowledge, images of knowledge and socio-political ideologies which took place only in the framework of European history.

Science is both a world of ideas and an activity – or a way of life. Science (unlike *Wissenschaft*) is that body of ideas whose subject is the material world, be it the physical world or that of living beings.

Science became a full-fledged profession in Europe in the second half of the 19th century and it is then, typically for that age of Victorian clarity and certainty, that its boundaries are best

defined. Both before and after that time the boundaries are blurred. While the 16th century was
still mainly a culture of religion in Europe, the 17th century saw the beginning of the process by which European culture became predominantly a culture of science. This can be best seen perhaps if we understand that until the 17th century mainly religious ideas were being manipulated for political purposes. The very process of manipulation of ideas for political purposes is rooted in ancient Greece and it is typically European. It is only after Newton that ideas about the physical world are systematically invoked for or against a political-religious ideology. It is enough to remember how the Boyle lectures in the 1690s used the Newtonian world-view to re-establish order and the Low-Church Anglican ideology in a shattered and unstable England; or how Leibniz used his ideas in mechanics to promote his chief political aim of reuniting the divided churches of Europe. For the Scholastic philosophers or even for the 17th-century Cambridge Platonists the discussions about the nature of space were still in the realm of theology. By the time Newton and Leibniz were debating whether space could be viewed as the sense organ of God in 1717 they were actually subsuming theology to a discussion of natural philosophy. The 19th century saw the emergence of modern biology with its cell theory, functional physiology, nervous electricity and finally evolutionary theory. By the 1870s, 20 years after Darwin, biology and the unsolved problem of the origin of life and its vital forces became scientific issues. As mentioned above, the limits of science were as fuzzy in the 17th century as they are today. It would be difficult to justify why Paracelsian medicine, with its curious mixture of popular lore, pseudo-chemistry, anatomy, genuine botanical knowledge and a vague spiritual principle, was accepted as knowledge (even if attacked by the established physicians) while Rosicrucianism, with its similar blend of half-baked ideas and reliable knowledge, was considered illegitimate and outside the accepted "science". Similarly today, although methodologically indefensible and medically debatable, psychoanalysis is "in", while the equally dubious astrology is "out". Moreover today, under the general title of the world of science, one would have to include the activities of science teaching, science policy, history and philosophy of science, and – I think – even science fiction. It is only in the late 19th and early 20th centuries that it seemed to men that the boundaries of science in European culture were well defined.

How do we judge important epochs in the history of a culture? From the vantage point of the age from which they are viewed. Since in our everyday metaphysics we tend to conceive the physical as well as the biological world in terms of discrete particles between which forces are acting through media or void, the age which has given birth to this conception is called by us the age of the scientific revolution, namely the 17th century. This metaphysical view is behind our view of the solar system, the universe, the atom or the cell. It is metaphysical because the statement that the world consists of discrete particles and forces acting between them is neither testable nor provable. Indeed it was Newton's scientific metaphysics that the world consisted of such particles and that all forces acted radially along the axes between each two particles. It was the contrary and new world-view of Faraday, Ørsted, Ampère, Helmholtz and Maxwell that not all forces were central forces (i.e. not all forces acted along the axis between two particles, but that some acted like electro-magnetic lines of force in circles around the charges) and that the universe was actually a plenum of forces.

If and when our world-view shifts and we conceive of the world in terms of elementary processes and not particles and forces, the 19th century with its evolutionary biology will become the age of the scientific revolution. Whether we shall ever be able to abolish in our common-sense thinking the distinction between matter and space – one of the metaphysical lessons which could be interpreted to follow from Einstein's general theory of relativity – is an open question.

How far can we go back in time in order to trace the origins of the present state of science? By some stretch of imagination and a continuum theory of history we could go back to ancient Babylon, or at least to the Greeks, the cradles of European civilization. But this would not be very reasonable. Such claims are debatable and partially biased, but questions like "Why had the Greeks no technology but only abstract science?" or "Why were there no scientific developments in Christian Europe in the Middle Ages?" or "Why did Arab science collapse after its period of glory in the 10th and 11th centuries?" do call for an answer, just as does the

question recently posed about the phenomenon of rich Chinese technology yet no science. The
fact is that no one has ever denied that there was science from 1600 onward, and therefore it is
justifiable to look at European science from the 17th century on.

With the advent of the Renaissance new social and intellectual trends came to replace the
closed world of the Middle Ages. Europe sent out seafarers and explorers, produced astron-
omers and philosophers, economic innovators and religious dissenters; internal strife between
Christian and infidel sent the monks and scribes from Constantinople to Italy; they all helped to
break down the confines of a finite, hierarchically ordered world. Vasco da Gama, Columbus
and Magellan opened up the seas and broke the limits of Europe and the Mediterranean.
Copernicus and Kepler, Bruno and Galileo removed the conceptual and technical obstacles from
viewing the universe as infinite. The closed world of tiny Europe became the infinite universe.
The sun became the centre of the planetary system, the earth just like every other planet
moved regularly around it; not only the earth had its satellite(s): so had the sun, Jupiter, and
possibly millions of other stars in the now understood Milky Way, and possibly even beyond.
And perhaps life existed elsewhere too. This new, open-ended universe was held together by
ordering forces of an unknown nature, perhaps magnetic as Kepler had thought, or perhaps
gravitational as was assumed vaguely by Galileo and Descartes and Huygens and as it was to be
presupposed and mathematically formulated by Newton. But before that, the new solar model
inspired Harvey to view the heart as the centre of circulation of the blood, just as the sun was of
the planetary system, or as the king was in the new view of society where the rigid hierarchical
ladder from labourer up to king and pope and God was no more. Since the astronomical
revolution had removed the earth, i.e. man, from its central position, it also gave man a new
individuality as against the universe. His place no more rigidly fixed, he had to claim it by his
own individual exertions; yet this new man was European still – his world was quite different
from that of the Chinese, the Japanese or the African. Now came the Reformation and the
downfall of the infallibility of the Catholic Church which established a search for a new kind of
relationship between man and God. The clergy as intermediary was rejected and each
individual sought a direct link with Providence. The individual in sculpture, painting, music
and literature was now the centre of interest.

These developments gave rise to at least two new intellectual movements: a search for
regularity and laws in the world as created by God and a deep crisis of faith, an age of
scepticism. As to the first, the search for laws has now replaced the admiration for the wondrous
and irregular. Medieval herbalia and bestiaria exhibiting the unique and irreproducible (uni-
corns and two-headed calves) gave way to what has been called the geometrization of space or
mathematization of nature: both ideas, Greek in origin, were on the margins of consciousness
until now European. In descriptions of the phenomena of life an orderly survey of what there
was, like Vesalius's magnificent book on the human body, now became possible. In accordance
with the belief that God had given man two books of equal importance – the Bible written in
words, and the Book of Nature written in mathematical characters – Kepler formulated three
laws of planetary motion; Galileo expressed mathematically the law of free fall and tried to unite
all motions of all bodies (celestial and terrestrial) into one theoretical model; Descartes
discovered the law of inertia and Huygens the law governing the motion of the pendulum of
clocks. All this culminated in the first vast synthesis of the behaviour of the physical world in
Sir Isaac Newton's *Mathematical Principles of Natural Philosophy*, published in Latin in 1687. By
three laws of motion and the law of universal attraction the world was regulated. By the time
the Newtonians were debating with their opponents whether light was mainly corpuscular (as
had been initially claimed by Newton) or whether it was primarily wave-like (as Huygens and
his followers in the 18th century had claimed), or when the Newtonians and Leibnizians
disagreed on the nature of space and its relation to God, the fundamental, well-regulated,
mathematically expressible nature of the universe had long been accepted.

But, before Newton, the crisis of faith had to be resolved, because without it there would
not have been – could not have been – a Newton; or at least Newton would have made no
impact.

During the bitter fight between Reformation and counter-Reformation a crisis of scepticism arose, challenging the basic principles of theology, humanistic studies, moral studies and

the sciences. Man's confidence in discovering truth by the use of human reason – a confidence so typical of both Scholastic and Renaissance naturalists – was undermined by a devastating attack from the philosopher-essayist de Montaigne. But total scepticism could not last long. The "pyrrhonics", as they were called, dwindled, and the generation after Montaigne emerged optimistic. It gave three different answers to its teacher's scathing criticism. One was the religious answer of Father Charron, for whom any scientific theory is actually blasphemy because every theory presumes to limit God's power and ability to that which man can understand. Thus the very foundation of science – the presupposition of nature's comprehensibility – is anathema, for certain knowledge can be gained only by revelation.

Secondly, Francis Bacon offered experience as a remedy. Bacon's programme failed scientifically but succeeded socially: his remedy became part of the ethos of science. From the 17th century till today, our image of certain knowledge has relied mainly on experience.

The third response, reason, came from Descartes. Going beyond common sense and classification he followed the order of ideas, not of things.

Common to all three answers – faith, reason, experience – is their exclusiveness, in itself an aspect of European analyticity. This analyticity seems to be the cause of certainty: the image of knowledge is that the only possible knowledge is certain knowledge. The opposite of this is the vague, metaphysical synthesis, based on the belief in the comprehensibility of nature, the dialectical complement of analyticity in the mentality which is uniquely European. It is broad, tolerant and much less certain than revelation, or clear and distinct ideas, or induction. The greatest representatives of this other tradition are Leibniz, Euler, Faraday, Helmholtz, Boltzmann and Einstein: all conservation ideas stem from it. Their contributions to the body of knowledge are well known; however, their images of knowledge are often forgotten. From the 17th century onward, scientific knowledge claimed certainty, and it claimed to have found it in either reason or experience – mostly, in experience. The polar reactions to the 16th-century scepticism can be characterized as *constructive scepticism*, which became the hall-mark of science, first in the 17th century and then again more forcefully in the 19th century. The great natural philosophers of the 17th century, e.g. Galileo, Descartes, Gassendi, Newton and Boyle, were all constructive sceptics.

The Newtonian synthesis came at a time when Europe was settling down to a relatively long peaceful development, reorganization, industrialization and agricultural as well as social revolution. The men of knowledge in England after the English rebellion, the Interregnum, and even more after the Glorious Revolution, and on the continent after the Thirty Years' War and its aftermath, were seeking to unite in groups of their kind, acknowledged by their equals and betters as pursuing a legitimate activity, forgetting the acrimony of religious quarrels and trying to concentrate on issues on which all could agree and where the results were general. In the Royal Society of London, in the Académie Royale des Sciences in Paris, and somewhat later in the various academies in the other European capitals, the seeds of consensus were sown: consensus as an aim of science, consensus as a style of doing science, consensus as a new hall-mark of a slowly emerging profession, which was meant to produce a united front and to cover up personal ambitions and personal and national rivalries. (A case could be made that the idea of consensus as a tool of social and scientific progress is another product of the European cultural milieu and could not have grown on other ground.) In these academies knowledge about the material world was collected, sorted out, stored or diffused, through the growing number of their publications and journals. The life-style of the natural philosophers changed accordingly: they had to think, communicate, write, promote, travel, teach and often preach. It was slowly becoming a full-time activity, however deeply involved in social life. In order to legitimize their knowledge, they had to strike a delicate balance between seeing to it that the broad society in which they lived had an idea of what it was all about, and ensuring that enough of it remained their personal knowledge to justify the mystique of their separatism. All these aspects of science are with us still today, but the foundations were laid by those early academicians and Fellows of the Royal Society in the late 17th and early 18th centuries. Many of the practitioners filled dual roles in the government and diplomatic service. Thus doing "science" and serving the state became mutually reinforcing activities. This was not yet the time for "ivory-tower" science. That was to be the creation of the 19th-century balance struck between the totalitarian state

56. *Le Cabinet physique de M. Bonnier de la Mosson*: the collection of a scientific dilettante. Painting by Jacques de Lajoue, c. 1730.

57. *Overleaf*: A view of London. Detail of a painting by Giovanni Antonio Canaletto, c. 1750.

59. Wolfgang Amadeus Mozart. Painting by Joseph-Siffrède Duplessis (1725–1802).

58. *John Cuff, Master of Spectacles*. Painting by Johann Zoffany, c. 1770.

60. *Overleaf*: *Cognoscenti in the Uffizi*. Detail of a painting by Johann Zoffany, 1780.

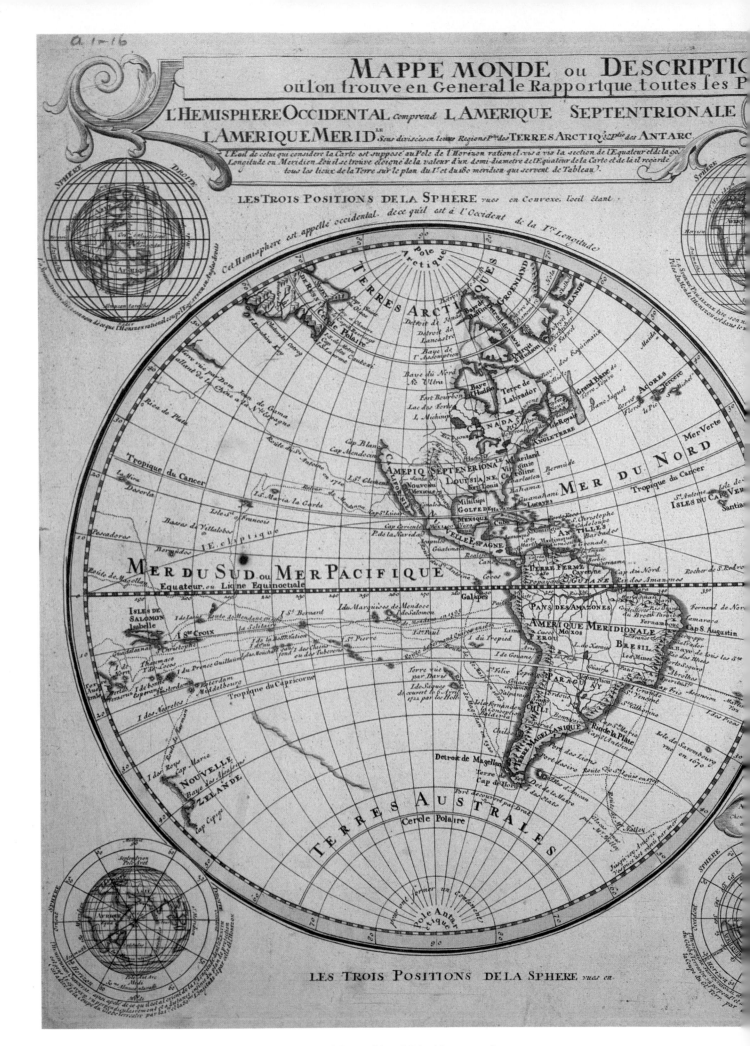

61. A map of the world, published in Amsterdam, c. 1750.

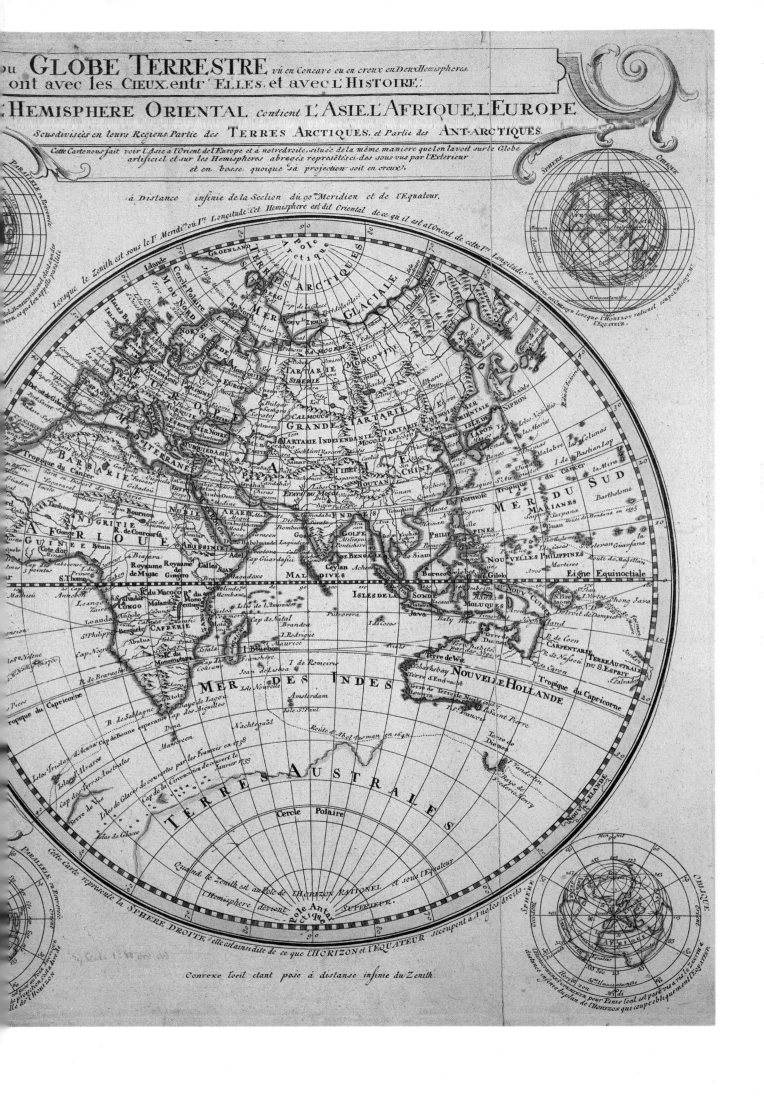

63. William Penn concludes a treaty with the Red Indians. Painting by Benjamin West, 1771.

62. Europe beyond Europe: George Washington at Princeton, 1779. Painting by Charles Wilson Peale.

64. *Overleaf: The Orrery.* Painting by Joseph Wright, 1766.

65. The French admiral and explorer La Perousse receiving instructions from Louis XVI. Painting by Nicolas-André Monsiau, c. 1780.

66. Catherine the Great, empress of Russia. Detail of a painting by Giovanni-Battista Lampi I, 1793.

67. The attack on the Tuilleries during the French Revolution (10 August 1792). Painting by Jacques Bertaux, 1792.

and the concept of academic freedom emerging then, mainly in Germany. Until the mid- or late 18th century science was socially involved, albeit not connected with the universities: the universities remained more or less the wardens of Classical humanistic education and only the early 19th-century reforms in Germany and the late 19th-century reforms in Cambridge and Oxford succeeded in bringing science in tune with, and making it part of, liberal education.

The 18th century was dominated by the social career of the Newtonian and anti-Newtonian ideas. The French philosophers' outlook on religion and their social philosophy too were, according to them, based on Newton. So were the new theories of life and the emerging theories of chemistry. In Germany, on the other hand, 18th-century historical philosophy and theories of medicine and biology were all rooted in the Leibnizian world-view as developed by Wolff and Euler and then brought to a new systematization by Kant.

There were at least three great traditions or scientific research programmes competing for primacy in 18th-century science. These were the Cartesian, Newtonian and Leibnizian. The critical dialogue between these three was conducted in pairs: Newtonianism v. Leibnizianism, Newtonianism v. Cartesianism, and again separately Leibnizianism v. Cartesianism. The main argument between the matter-theorist Cartesians and the Newtonians centred on the primacy of the concept of force. This concept is one of specifically European character and is deeply interwoven with the other uniquely European concept, namely progress.

The mind-body dichotomy was part of the Cartesian tradition but played only a very minor role in the controversy with the Newtonians. This problem was, however, the core of the Cartesian-Leibnizian critical dialogue. The Cartesians separated mind from body, and also scientific metaphysics from theology. Both the Newtonians and the Leibnizians, on the other hand, attempted to justify their scientific metaphysics by their theology. This justification became one of the focuses of the Newtonian-Leibnizian critical dialogue, as exemplified in the Leibniz-Clarke correspondence and as continued by Euler in the *Letters to a German Princess* written in the 1770s.

The central Newtonian conception is that of force, whether acting at a distance or at short range by contact. Newtonian physics, astronomy, chemistry and physiology all involve forces. Whether the forces are inherent in matter or reducible to their relational properties is another focus of the dialogue between Newtonians and Leibnizians. On the other hand, the concept of force is as foreign to the Cartesian as it is inseparable from both the Newtonian and the Leibnizian research programmes. Another deep-seated difference between these two European intellectual traditions is in the role of conservation principles. These are alien to the former but fundamental to the latter. But even if alien to Newtonianism, they hearken back to Stoic philosophy — that uniquely European characteristic which makes a continuous attempt to combine progress and morality with tradition.

The conclusion drawn from Newton's unprecedented success was that certainty of non-revealed knowledge is possible. The need for certainty is absent in most non-European thought-worlds just as it was new in Europe in the 16th and 17th centuries. This new quest for certainty, however, has typified our science, philosophy, literature and politics ever since the 17th century; since Freud, the quest for certainty has been described as an innate human need (i.e. non-cognitive and non-environment-influenced) shared by all human beings (if not indeed by all live creatures). Yet comparative studies seem to confirm this claim mainly, if not exclusively, for the western, i.e. European, tradition. Because of the Baconian influence this certainly centred around the concept of "fact" in England; in France (because of Descartes?) it looked to mathematics. Germany, after Leibniz, sought certainty in a metaphysical synthesis that would harmonize the differing schools and discover underlying unitary principles (conservation laws in nature) that apply to everything.

These views on the role of science and metaphysics combined with the strongly Puritan view of German pietism, which stressed the habit of self-renouncing labour, of singleness of purpose. This was a *sine qua non* of developing for scientific metaphysics the unshakeable foundations needed to build a whole system of science, ethics and social theory and an anthropology.

The central concepts in the physics of Newton were space, time, mass and force. By the end of the 19th century the central concepts in physics were space, time, mass and energy. The general concept of energy became meaningful only through the establishment of the principle of conservation of energy in all its generality; thus the story of the emergence of the energy concept and the story of the establishment of the conservation law are difficult to disentangle. The man who first formulated the principle mathematically, in all its generality, was Helmholtz in the 1840s. His was a towering scientific personality, and his life's work has left its mark on all branches of 19th-century science, from theoretical mechanics to applied physiology. The concept of energy as we know it today ("today" meaning classical, pre-relativity physics) has emerged from Helmholtz's work. Until that time no one had a clearly defined concept of energy.

But the problem is not a purely scientific one. In view of the prerequisites for the establishment of the principle of conservation of energy, this final step had to take place in 19th-century Germany; it could not possibly have happened in England or France. In German universities the student, whatever he studied, could not have avoided facing sooner or later the great metaphysical problems posed by the various *Weltanschauungen*; although in England "science" was pursued, or in the traditional spirit "natural philosophy" was taught, German *Philosophie* covered the whole of the human intellectual enterprise. Speculation was encouraged. In Germany the "schools" or "laboratories" of the great scientists represented a complete philosophical system, and every student was required to take a stand. One could not work in Weber's physical laboratory or in Liebig's laboratory without forming a considered philosophical approach to Kant's epistemology or to the mechanistic-vitalistic controversy. In that atmosphere, then, one could not readily separate experimental data from highly speculative hypotheses.

This intellectual climate which was detrimental to many other scientific problems (e.g. to the first formulations of electrodynamics -- where all German theories failed, while the English, French and the isolated Ørsted achieved positive results) was indispensable for the establishment of the conservation-of-energy principle, i.e. the emergence of the concept of energy. In those German universities the "schools" of Liebig, Woehler, J. Mueller, Weber and Magnus were founded. And there the further prerequisite – namely, the cross-fertilization between physical and physiological thought – was made possible. Moreover, it was there that biology was born. Men like Virchow, Bruecke, Du Bois-Reymond and Helmholtz matured in these universities.

The confusion between "force" and "energy" (as we use these terms) in the works of Helmholtz, Faraday, Mayer and some of their contemporaries was not merely a verbal one, but a necessary prerequisite for the final clarification of the concepts. Only an undefined entity could have been the subject of a general belief in principles of conservation in nature; and only in the romantic *Naturphilosophie* of the early 19th century could such a vague concept be rooted. It is this dialectic between the competing European traditions of sharply defined mathematical clarity and the vague, unifying principles that ensured progress in science. Both the dialectic and the progress to which it led are typically European and understandable in terms of the socio-political development of Europe. German *Naturphilosophie*, with its search for underlying unitary principles and mystically potent conservation laws, was the complete antithesis of the English matter-of-fact, common-sense, inductivist philosophy of nature. The former was speculative, idealistic, broad and very often vague; the latter was empirical, materialistic, narrow and often too precise.

The two competing images of knowledge thus described dominated the 19th century. Both had great influence on choice of scientific problems in their cultural environments: all over Europe there were representatives of both conceptions. The influence of the German *Naturphilosophie* – an influence that combined the Hegel-Fichte-Schelling romanticism with Kantian metaphysics and the search for underlying unitary principles – spread to England through the works of Coleridge and T. Young. It introduced the acceptability of the Eulerian wave theory as a legitimate area of research, and in the hands of Young and Fresnel it triumphed. Though Young tried to appear Newtonian, his was the first direct proof that Newton had been wrong in the critical dialogue between the Newtonian and the Leibniz-Euler-Kant scientific research programmes.

At the same time the German scientists, physicists and biologists alike, who turned away from *Naturphilosophie* with disgust, instituted what amounted to a reign of terror on behalf of empiricism. Scientific papers that contained even the slightest attempt at a theory not yet proved by hard experiment were rejected (Helmholtz's famous paper of 1847 was turned down by Poggendorff; and in 1905 Einstein's relativity paper was nearly rejected).

The Victorian image of knowledge was a vulgarized Baconianism of great power. The image is of knowledge triumphant – certain, inductively collected, down-to-earth knowledge. And the Victorians, in their thoroughness, documented their view of knowledge by rewriting the history of the accumulation of scientific knowledge. This huge undertaking was then supplemented by creating a tradition in typical 19th-century biographies of great scientists, all of whom had been ardent experimentalists and hard workers from early childhood.

The 19th-century Victorian image of knowledge also created the myth of the Protestant ethic as a cause of the development of modern science. The self-image of the 17th century, as we have seen, was of the theologically non-partisan, latitudinarian gentleman of leisure as the source of all new ideas. This image was now systematically replaced by the hard-working, preferably lower-middle-class boy, who lived up to God's expectations for the genius with which he had been endowed.

The Victorian image of science was sustained by another new tradition, the writing of textbooks – no longer treatises written from the personal point of view of the author, but impersonal reports of the organized and well-ordered progress of scientific success. The need for textbooks arose from teaching science on a vast scale in the newly institutionalized scientific profession. But its result was the final establishment of the Victorian image of knowledge.

In this comparison between Germany and England in the 19th century the whole spectrum of science in Europe is encapsulated. In addition to two major competing images of knowledge two widely different social distributions of knowledge took place. In England the universities neglected science, while the practitioners became more and more professionalized and organized in hundreds of societies, institutions, academies etc. where all the different disciplines became legitimized as they emerged. In order to justify their social roles most of these scientists were educational reformers and took an active part in providing the channels of diffusion so that broad layers of the population – the lower middle classes and the working classes – received an elementary scientific education: a minimal but widespread scientific literacy. As a complementary phenomenon, the cultivation of science became an open avenue for a successful entrepreneur to became a gentleman. In the final account this supplied England with a far from negligible layer of technically educated workers and foremen who showed some internal understanding of their growing industrial economy. On the continent – at least up to the 1860s – there was a scientifically much better-educated intellectual class but no widespread basic scientific literacy. By the 1860s this began to change. The minimal scientific literacy in England was no longer satisfactory for the sophisticated, new, technology-based industry, and there was no proper educational system to replace the various extra-curricular, extra-mural channels of adult education. In Germany and France, on the other hand, a well-organized educational system, now including science in its curriculum, provided all the population with the necessary technical know-how for it to fulfil the needs of the growing industrial society of Europe. By 1900 England was fast being overtaken by Europe – while previously it had built up an empire and sustained it, now it was kept afloat by its empire.

While these social and educational changes were going on in Europe, in the body of knowledge two opposite trends were taking place, for the first time since the 17th century separating the physical sciences and the life sciences into quite different camps as far as scientific metaphysics went and also with regard to their sources of knowledge, aims of knowledge and kinds of legitimate knowledge.

In the physical sciences Maxwell's electrodynamics, with its prediction of the discovery that light was one of the phenomena of the electro-magnetic field, and the succeeding discovery of electro-magnetic waves by Hertz, had put the crown on the Newtonian programme. The physical world seemed to be simple, obeying two fundamental law systems of the gravitational and the electro-magnetic fields; the language of its description was mathematical, its fundamental truths were eternal; and the task was for the scientists to fill the remaining gaps. The open questions of the physical world were seen as "not yet known" (*ignoramus*) and not as "cannot be known" (*ignorabimus*). The Einsteinian revolution, when its meaning became understood, was indeed as much an upheaval of a social ethos as it was a scientific shock.

The biological sciences were developing differently. Into the reductionist, physics-oriented cell physiology, as it grew from the original theories of Schleyden and Schwann, into the newly emerging organic chemistry of Liebig and Woehler, and into the neuro-electrical psycho-physics of Du Bois-Reymond and Weber and Fechner (Freud's psycho-analysis was an outgrowth of the theories of conservation of energy which Freud generalized to include mental energy and a reductionist psychology) burst Darwinian evolutionary theory. It introduced a different time-scale into biology; it had to be viewed as science, yet it was not predictive; it touched directly on the very basis of human nature, the social institutions and religion. Science was talked about, in terms of natural selection and the origin of man, in the 1860s and 1870s in every newspaper and every pub and coffee house of Europe, and it was very controversial. The ideal of the Royal Society to do science in action (*nullius in verba*) and to escape civil strife by so doing was all gone now. The concentration on evolutionary biology and the related geological and anthropological sciences (this last deeply entangled with the colonial policy of Europe) took the limelight off the physical sciences. Their classical structure continued to be built undisturbed. Some occasional technical developments like the telegraph, the electric light or the underwater cable were the exceptions.

The great new ideas in the physical sciences were the theory of special and general relativity of Einstein (1905 and 1916) and the new quantum theory as developed by Einstein, Bohr, Heisenberg, Schrödinger, De Broglie, Dirac and Pauli, to name only a few of its founders. Relativity theory became vulgarized into the fallacious "everything is relative" (actually it is a theory of the absolute) and quantum theory froze into the accepted interpretation of Heisenberg's uncertainty principle according to which the world is predictable only in terms of statistical averages and not fully deterministic in terms of single particles – an interpretation which some of the founders like Einstein or Schrödinger never fully accepted. The claim in terms of the ultimate source of knowledge in 20th-century physical science, namely that there exists a mathematical proof by von Neumann, according to which the "accepted" interpretation of that principle is the last and final word on the subject, is not a proof at all but a removal of the interpretation to a more distant plateau.

In the biological sciences a new reductionist metaphysics which sought to reduce all phenomena of life to physics and chemistry, started by European physicists like Delbrück and Schrödinger, has paid off in the revolutionary discovery of double helix and the genetic code as formulated by Crick and Watson. This view too became embedded in what the biologists themselves call the "central dogma"; but biology is much more vulnerable to criticism today – and thus more open to new basic ideas – than is physics.

The world of the scientist today is one of great variety. There is pure, abstract (mostly mathematical) science and there is experimental, applied and industrial science. There is small science of the individual thinker or the laboratory of a small group at a university, and there is big science of the multi-million-dollar projects of CERN at Geneva, or SLAC and Brookhaven and the CLA in the USA. These are huge machines with crews of hundreds of mathematicians, theoretical physicists, engineers, technicians and administrators all aiming at creating artificial situations of enormous speeds and energies which are not otherwise encountered in our human environment (even if extended to the dimension of our nebula) and which allow men a probe into cosmic distances and long-past ages as measured in terms of light years. The very size of big science may have introduced the first genuine non-European element into science – though it is still typically western. The often-met polarization of pure science as against technology, the one being the prototype of original thought or first principles, the other that of mere clever application, is a fallacy. There is as much originality and need to rethink first principles in abstract problems (i.e. not "useful" science) as there is in technical problems, just as there is a purely mechanical repetitive end both to science and to technology.

The world of science has its own tensions. The scientific ethos is still characterized by the norms of sharing knowledge and its speedy communication, the norm of disinterested pursuit of truth, the norm of the internationality of science. But at the same time there is fierce competition, fighting for priority (because only first discoverers are rewarded), striving to get hold of resources at a time of decreasing support, serious moral dilemmas like national survival which counteract the other norms. On the one hand, it is true that results are being published in an internationally valid form and language and there is an international scientific community which to some extent is supernational and even above the big-powers rivalry. On the other hand, since problem-choice and methodology and relative importance are all decided upon in terms of images of knowledge, there are national styles and culturally delimited features of science. Again, a European science in the 19th century (including the then only marginally developed America) is better defined than today's, even though it was the 19th century which pointed out in great detail the specifics of German chemistry, or English model-oriented mechanical science, or French mathematics and theoretical physics. The reward system of science – academic positions, lucrative advisory jobs, industrial applications which lead to financial gains, the non-teaching research institutes, and the award of the Nobel prize – in some areas all these interfere with the process of scientific activity and mould its features not only by emphasizing excellence but even more by shaping the images of knowledge which bring about the choice of problems.

One of the most dynamic features of the scientific world is its continuous division into new disciplines. Such redistribution is caused both by intellectual developments in the body of knowledge and by growing social pressures on resources and positions. Often the new disciplines emerge at the interfaces of two or more old ones: biology and chemistry into biochemistry for example. What accompanies such occurrences is the establishment of new journals, new professional societies and new university chairs. This again creates new groups of people who now share a common language and common interest and form their own ideas about the sources, aims and legitimization of knowledge which then influence their choice of problems.

Nineteenth-century models of professionalization and the old-fashioned structure of the universities clearly do not cope with the size of science today, nor with its predicaments. The number of scientists in the world is in the order of magnitude of millions. The number of scientific journals is in tens of thousands. The need is for highly competent, highly trained technicians, engineers, experimental and theoretical scientists. Such a training presupposes dedication, single-mindedness and a feeling of consensus in an ever growing international community. Yet the problems they are tackling are not easily subject to consensus. The risks and rewards are such that most practitioners succumb to the pressures diverting them from dedication and single-mindedness. The great national and big-power rivalries steer them away from internationalism. And finally the moral issues which are connected with science – nuclear weapons, education of the poor and the underdeveloped, recombinant DNA problems of genetic engineering – are such that if anything at all can prepare the individual for taking a responsible stand on them it is a liberal, humanistic, broad education and not the kind of single-mindedness which scientific competence seems to presuppose.

Where will the solution lie? Well, here ancient Europe may have the answer. Luckily most of the pressures as described above are on the shoulders of the rich, powerful, competing blocs of the USA, the Soviet Union and possibly China. Europe is to some extent left out and left alone. Perhaps in the more thoughtful, less pressurized and less competitive atmosphere of the European scholarly community some new social ideas will emerge which will help reorganize the institutions of science, enabling them to cope with the problems of the present age as well as opening up its rigorously defined areas of research to new and bold ideas.

# 17

# Doctors and Nurses

## F. F. CARTWRIGHT

The patient who enters a hospital or attends a doctor's surgery at once senses a distinctive atmosphere. He knows that he is surrendering his most intimate possession, his body, to the care and perhaps to the assaults of a comparative stranger, a step from which he would almost certainly recoil in everyday life. The circumstances are unusual, for the patient is not in his ordinary state of health. He suspects that he is ill and demands either to be reassured or that the cause of his illness shall be determined. But although the doctor will diagnose the cause and institute the proper treatment, he will not allow his patient to follow the steps which have led him to his diagnosis. The doctor's notes are confidential, only to be revealed to a colleague called into consultation or for a well-defined purpose. The atmosphere is one of mystery. The mystery does not depend upon the intricacy, however baffling to the layman, of modern machinery or skills. The complex apparatus of operating theatre, radiotherapy room or intensive-care ward is no more involved than that of a scientific laboratory. The techniques employed by doctor or nurse demand no greater ability or knowledge than is possessed by a competent craftsman. The surgeon and his team performing an operation on the heart may indeed hold their patient's life in their hands but to an extent no greater than does the pilot of an aeroplane. The mystery stems from the concept of the doctor as a privileged member of a closed caste, virtually a priesthood, who is not expected to divulge the secrets of his lore. This concept stretches back into antiquity. The Hippocratic Oath of about 400 BC, although often cited as an ethical code, is essentially a promise to maintain the art of medicine as a secret within the closed group. Orthodox medicine has been practised by specially trained communities for over 2,000 years. The group has at various times depended upon transmission of acquired knowledge from father to son, from master to apprentice, from teacher to pupil.

Just as this code of conduct derives from ancient Greece, so do the theory and practice of European medicine. Hellenic teaching that disease is of natural origin and that cure is not necessarily miraculous reached western Europe through the writings of the Greco-Roman physician Galen in the 1st century AD. Monastic medicine, practised in the scattered Christian settlements of Europe during the Dark Ages, retained debased fragments of Hellenic knowledge but owed more to pagan magic and the Christian belief that cure can be effected only by supernatural means. Medicine passed into the hands of the Church to become part of the mystery of priestcraft. Church dominance, although encouraging learning and the tender care of the sick, stifled experimental thought. Churchmen recognized Galen as the sole medical authority. Since Europe possessed only mutilated and incomplete texts, erroneous ideas were perpetuated. Both theory and practice stagnated until contact was made with the more virile and liberal medicine of Islam.

The first limited encounter took place at Salerno in southern Italy. Here gathered in the 9th century a company of physicians, a *civitas Hippocratica*, which developed into the first European medical school. The legend of foundation by four masters, Christian, Greek, Jew and Arab, cannot be accepted but Salerno is remarkable for its international and pantheistic character. Constantinus Africanus, who came to the school from Tunisia in the 11th century, achieved fame as a teacher of Arabian theory and methods. His teaching was widely spread by European pupils. In 1224 the school imposed regulations which may be regarded as the first medical curriculum. The student must undergo a five-year course with an additional year of practice under supervision. After examination by masters, he graduated as either *doctor* or *magister*. It is commonly believed that the courtesy title of "doctor", applied to a medical practitioner who does not necessarily hold a university degree, derives from Salerno.

A second and closer contact with Arabian medicine followed the fall of the Western Caliphate in 1266. Libraries in the south of Spain, notably the important manuscripts housed at Cordova, became available to Christian scholars. These Arabian texts of Galen were the most complete and least corrupt of those available in the west and were eagerly translated from Arabic into Latin. The bulk of the European pharmacopoeia, overburdened with useless remedies prescribed as late as the 19th century, derives from the writings of Hispano-Arabian physicians.

The town of Salerno was sacked in 1194 and the school started upon a long decline ending with its suppression by Napoleon on 29 November 1811. Teaching of medicine passed to multi-faculty universities such as Paris, Bologna, Oxford, Padua and Cambridge. Montpellier in France developed into the main centre of European medical teaching. Founded in 1180, it was declared a "free school of medicine" in the following year by William, Count of Montpellier. Regulations introduced in 1230 imposed a curriculum similar to that of Salerno. During the next six centuries the medical calling was more respected in France than elsewhere and, until the Revolution, ambitious doctors of all countries aimed to visit one of the French centres. Clinical instruction assumed an importance in French teaching not to be found in other lands. In 1517 Montpellier framed a statute authorizing students to accompany doctors in their private practice and in 1698 students were required to visit patients in hospitals and in the city as part of their training. Bedside teaching in France was generally assured after 1544 when all ecclesiastical hospitals became public or municipal charities by edict of François I and were declared to be "free schools of medicine". Medieval France even conferred a limited prestige upon the despised surgeon. The Collège de St Côme, Paris, founded by Jean Pitard in 1210, created a privileged caste of surgical graduates, known as "of the long robe". University instruction in other European countries tended to be academic, divorced from the bedside, and entirely confined to a class of medical practitioners who called themselves "physicians". Surgeons and apothecaries, despised by the physician, learnt their trade by apprenticeship to a master. John Kymer, Chancellor of Oxford University, tried to mend the rift between physician and surgeon by establishing a conjoined faculty in 1423 but his endeavour failed.

Until the 16th century all physicians were clerks under episcopal jurisdiction. Although sometimes priests, the majority belonged to the third grade of minor orders, the exorcist. Such is the origin of the bishop's licence to practise medicine which, at discretion, might be granted to a person who did not possess a university degree. Loss of power and prestige during the long years of plague following the Black Death of 1346–50 weakened Church control and cast doubt upon her usurped ability to heal. Rediscovery of older and purer Greek texts in the 15th century revealed the blunders of Arabian and Christian commentators. The invention of printing in 1440–50 ended the monopoly of the monastic copyist, ensuring a higher standard of accuracy and a wider dissemination. In the fields of science and medicine, more widely circulated knowledge and release from the bonds imposed by Church discipline rapidly induced destructive and constructive criticism. Hardly had the less distorted manuscripts of Byzantium been examined than scholars began to question the truth of ancient learning. For instance, critical examination revealed the errors perpetuated by Galen and his followers who had based human anatomy on that of the ape and the pig. Renaissance artists required precise knowledge. Raphael, Michelangelo, Dürer and Leonardo da Vinci all studied human anatomy and showed the mistaken ideas of Galen. Their findings culminated in the first "modern" textbook, *De*

*Humani Corporis Fabrica*, by Andreas Vesalius of Padua, published in 1543. A realistic approach to anatomy stimulated advance in surgery, exemplified by the achievements of the mid-16th-century surgeon Ambroise Paré. Jean Fernel of Clermont corrected many of Galen's medical errors and in 1554 published a book which sought to relate disease to physical causes. A more rational approach to both diagnosis and treatment is to be found in the methods of Paracelsus of Basel (1493–1541) who is credited with the introduction of chemotherapy.

Weakening of ecclesiastical control forced doctors to form their own organizations. The 15th century is the Golden Age of the quack. Some were mere charlatans who imposed upon the credulous by trickery. Others relied upon folk-medicine, selling herbs which were usually harmless and sometimes beneficial. Many had gained a knowledge of astrology, one of the pseudo-sciences which contaminated the good sense of Arabian medicine. But it is interesting that even astrology could be turned to good account in the hands of an observant physician. The astrologist's pretended ability to "water-cast" the sex of an unborn child by the position of the planets and the state of the mother's urine developed into the art of "uroscopy", diagnosis and prognosis by examination of the urine, which is the first parent of modern biochemistry. Proliferation of quacks impelled government action, as a rule on the petition of orthodox practitioners. The English Medical Act of 1511–12 imposed fines upon those who did not possess a university degree or bishop's licence and was followed by chartering of the medical corporations, the Royal College of Physicians of London in 1518 and the United Company of Barber-Surgeons in 1540. In Scotland the Royal College of Physicians of Edinburgh received its charter in 1505 and the Royal College of Physicians and Surgeons, Glasgow, in 1599. Inauguration of the Escola Medico-cirurgica at Madrid in 1536, the Board of Barber-Surgeons controlling practice from Stockholm after 1571, and the institution of a Collegium Medicum at Augsburg in 1582 are other examples.

An improvement in medical training followed the foundation of the University of Leyden by William of Orange in 1575. Like Salerno, Leyden was non-sectarian and international in character. The university attracted students who were unacceptable in their own countries because of religious intolerance. Protestants from Roman Catholic lands, Catholics and non-conformists from Britain and the American colonies, flocked to Leyden. The teaching of medicine at first was entirely, or almost entirely, academic. In 1709 Professor Hermann Boerhaave introduced bedside teaching, having been allotted ten beds in the town hospital for that purpose. Boerhaave is often credited as the first tenant of a university chair to merge clinical instruction with an academic syllabus. The renown of his many pupils bears witness to his success. Edinburgh University is closely linked with the history of Leyden and was founded on similar liberal principles. The medical department, associated with the Edinburgh Royal Infirmary since 1736, became famed for the excellence of its clinical teaching. Leyden and Edinburgh developed into prominent centres during the 18th century and their importance was greatly enhanced by the closure of the French medical schools in 1792.

Meanwhile discoveries in allied sciences had begun to exert an effect upon medicine. Inductive reasoning, advocated as the road to learning by Francis Bacon in England and the Frenchman René Descartes in Holland, led to a surge of objective thought exemplified by the work of William Harvey who disproved the ebb-and-flow theory of Galen and described the circulation of the blood in 1628. Experimental proof rather than speculation underlay the findings of four young Oxford scientists who, while studying chemistry and physics in the decade 1660–70, almost casually discovered the true purpose of breathing. Thus, between the years 1628 and 1670, the basic elements of circulatory and respiratory physiology were established and the art of medicine was in process of being changed to a science. Natural classification, introduced by Isaac Newton and Carl Linné, suggested its application to diseases, signs and symptoms taking the place of petals or leaves. But the doctor had as yet insufficient knowledge of disease processes to make effective use of the new science. The result was a welter of theorizing which perhaps reached ultimate absurdity in the Brunonian System, accepted by many European physicians of the late 18th century. Devised by John Brown of Glasgow and Edinburgh in the 1770s, the system aimed at simplification by forcing all diseases into two categories, sthenic and asthenic, and by classifying all remedies as depressants or stimulants.

The trouble was that scientific medicine must necessarily depend upon exact diagnosis of a disease and identification of the cause. Eighteenth-century physicians did not know why the majority of diseases occurred. Having few aids to diagnosis, they could depend only upon the five senses. Even the pulse could not be accurately timed until John Floyer introduced a special watch, running for one minute, in 1707. The clinical thermometer, although used in unwieldy forms by enthusiasts, was not a practical instrument until 1866. The signs elicited by a modern physician remained unknown until Leopold Auenbrugger, an innkeeper's son who had tapped barrels to determine the fluid level, described the method of percussion in 1761, but this simple way of differentiating areas of relative dullness and resonance was not taught until 1808 when Jean Corvisart of Paris demonstrated its usefulness as a clinical aid. Corvisart's pupil, René Laennec, tried to amplify the sounds heard on percussion by means of paper tubes and so was led to the complementary method of auscultation, producing the first stethoscope in 1819. Laennec gave names to many of the sounds of normal and abnormal respiration which are still in use.

The 19th-century physician still depended largely upon his unaided senses. He prided himself on his acute observation and intelligent experience. Many physicians sought to impress colleagues, students and patients by the lightning or "snap" diagnosis, a habit frowned upon in modern times. Ferdinand von Hebra of Brünn and Joseph Bell of Edinburgh are two outstanding exponents of this technique. Hyperacute senses and a retentive memory enabled them to detect, often at a glance, not only the disease from which the patient suffered but also his occupation, place of work, and town or village of residence. Bell is the genesis of one of the best-known characters in British fiction. Arthur Conan Doyle, who learned surgery under Bell at Edinburgh, acknowledged that he modelled Sherlock Holmes upon his teacher.

Diagnostic aids multiplied during the 19th century, concluding with the discovery of X-rays by Wilhelm Röntgen of Würzburg in 1895. The century witnessed discoveries which profoundly affected the concept of disease. In 1803 Marie François Bichat of Paris published his theory of membranes or tissues which ended the old idea of an organ as an indivisible entity and led, through the discovery of the cell nucleus by Matthias Schleider and Theodor Schwann in 1831, to the momentous work of Rudolf Virchow. Virchow's postulate of 1858 that the body is "a cell-state in which every cell is a citizen" forms the keystone of modern pathology. No less fundamental is the germ theory, first propounded by Louis Pasteur of Lille in 1864, although it remained only a theory until 1881 when Pasteur and Robert Koch of Breslau independently proved that "germs" or pathogenic organisms are the causative agents of infections. Initially Pasteur's germ theory, as yet unproved, exerted its greatest influence upon the practice of surgery. Constructive surgery was made possible by another 19th-century advance, the introduction of anaesthesia in 1846, but it carried a high mortality. Joseph Lister, then professor at Glasgow, first used his "antiseptic" method in 1865. Antisepsis, by lessening the danger of wound infection, made open operation reasonably safe and so widened the scope of surgery.

Organization of medical training is another feature of the 19th century. In France the decree of 12 August 1792 abolished the privileged medical caste and ended formal teaching. In 1803 Napoleon revived the Montpellier faculty and instituted new schools of medicine. These were in conjunction with the ancient hospitals, some of which had been used as prisons during the terror and were now restored to their former service. Here the tradition of bedside instruction remained. England lost the great majority of its hospitals with the suppression of religious houses and charities under Henry VIII and Edward VI. The plight of poor people instigated the 18th-century foundation of voluntary hospitals by rich men, a unique British contribution to care of the sick. The College of Physicians required its fellows and licentiates to attend the poor free of charge. Many subscribed to this rule by accepting an unpaid appointment at a hospital. They found that the wealth of clinical material attracted apprentices willing to pay indenture fees. Hospital managers discovered that young men, eager to gain practical experience, would undertake routine work in the wards as unpaid "house pupils".

British teaching developed as "the firm", a band of apprentices headed by a member of the honorary staff and assisted by a senior house pupil, who in later years became known as the house physician or house surgeon. The system, already fairly prevalent in the late 18th century, was adopted throughout Britain after the Apothecaries' Act of 1815. The Act, the foundation of present-day medical education in Britain, is a curiosity. Apothecaries were regarded as inferiors, yet the Act gave virtually the whole control of medical practice into the hands of the Society of Apothecaries. The Society's new regulations for licensing included a term of apprenticeship, set courses in anatomy and theory, and six months' compulsory attendance in the wards of a recognized hospital. "Walking the wards" became an essential part of student training. Members of the honorary staff started to offer courses in anatomy, physiology and the theory of medicine. Thus medical schools developed in conjunction with the hospitals. Several British provincial universities have their origin in these rudimentary medical schools.

Teaching in Britain and France tended to be practical, bedside instruction taking precedence over formal lecturing. Although many teachers held professorial status they remained practising doctors. A different system obtained in Germany and in those parts of central and northern Europe dominated by Teutonic culture. Here the university with its incorporated medical faculty was the prominent feature. Teaching of medicine remained principally academic and, when conducted at the bedside, the patient filled the role of pathological specimen rather than of suffering human. The clinical laboratory, a German contribution to medical science, played an increasingly important part in both training and practice throughout the second half of the 19th century. In 1800 the microscope was an instrument almost unknown and practically valueless in medicine. By 1900 Pasteur's germ theory and Virchow's cell theory had made the microscope a necessary instrument of diagnosis and the clinical laboratory an essential of practice.

Nineteenth-century discoveries not only transformed medicine from an empiric art into an applied science but effected a change in the practitioner. Better training and broader education produced the doctor-scientist. Physicians, but physicians only, had usually been university graduates with some pretence to gentility. But physicians were few in number; the larger majority of practitioners were surgeons and apothecaries, regarded as tradesmen. They had learnt their trade by apprenticeship. Now the complexities of their subject could no longer be taught by one semi-educated master. Apprenticeship first assumed a secondary place in training and then disappeared. Ending of the apprenticeship system removed much of the stigma of trade. Apothecary and surgeon now underwent a training similar to that of the physician. All three groups merged into the "physician and surgeon", the fully qualified general practitioner or family doctor. A specialist physician or surgeon took the same primary course as did the general practitioner but achieved his distinctive status by postgraduate study and, in most European countries, by a higher degree or diploma. Doctors inevitably rose in the social scale. This is particularly true of the surgeon. Eighteenth-century surgeons were no better than semi-skilled technicians, employed by the physician, having little prospect of advancement. Surgeons of the 19th century acquired honours higher than any awarded to physicians of previous centuries. Joseph Lister was not only the first medical man to be created a peer but was also one of the first recipients of the new Order of Merit. An outstanding example of this change is the German military surgeon Friedrich von Esmarch whose social standing enabled him to wed a royal princess and so to become uncle by marriage of Kaiser Wilhelm II. All doctors were regarded as members of a learned profession before the end of the 19th century.

Although the doctor now knew something of the causes of disease, he could only rarely effect a cure. It has been truly said that, had the medical profession been faced with an epidemic of bubonic plague in 1930, they might have done something to prevent it becoming widespread but would have been just as powerless to cure it as were their predecessors in the Black Death. Surgery, rendered tolerable by anaesthesia and relatively safe by antisepsis or asepsis, had some claim to be curative. The main usefulness of physician and general practitioner lay in alleviation of symptoms and in stimulation of the natural defence mechanisms by which the patient combated his own illness. Twentieth-century discoveries put effective weapons into the hands of the doctor for the first time, permitting him to attack the organisms of disease directly and so to cure the patient. Examples are salvarsan and the "sulfa" group of drugs. These have in turn been replaced by the successful antibiotics. The idea of antibiosis as applied to pathogenic organisms originated in 1877 when Louis Pasteur and Jules Joubert observed the destruction of large anthrax bacilli by smaller bacteria and proposed that micro-organism should deliberately be set to make war upon micro-organism. The antibacterial action of certain penicillium moulds had been noticed by Professor John Tyndall as early as 1876 and was later described by Joseph Lister among others. In 1928 Alexander Fleming of St Mary's Hospital, London, prepared a filtrate of penicillium-infected broth to which he gave the name "penicillin", drawing attention to its potential value. Fleming's suggestion that penicillin might prove "an efficient antiseptic" was pursued by Ernst Chain and Howard Florey at Oxford in 1939–41, leading first to the introduction of a practical preparation and thence to a number of antibiotic drugs antagonistic to a wide range of organisms.

Besides the many advances in diagnostic aids and in treatment, the 19th and 20th centuries are remarkable for the extension of social medicine and an increasing tendency for doctors to be employed by the state or municipal authority. The trend originated in Germany, where both doctors and professors derived part of their emoluments from the state and accepted ranks and precedence similar to those of the civil service. State employment increased after Otto von Bismarck introduced a system of insurance against illness in 1881. The British Insurance Act dates from 1911. The Act changed the so-called "sixpenny doctor", who provided the poorer class with advice and a bottle of medicine, into the "panel doctor", committed to attend the insured worker freely in return for a state-paid capitation fee. National insurance against sickness led naturally to the concept of free treatment for everybody, that is a health service financed by compulsory insurance but with all medical facilities available to the insured without additional payment. The earliest National Health Service is the Russian, dating from 1862. Medical attention was free, without insurance premiums, but poor in quality, depending too much upon the unqualified assistant or *feldscher*. The tsarist government found it economical of manpower to form small centres, staffed by a doctor superintending lay helpers, practising all branches of medicine. These are the forerunners of the polyclinics upon which the present Soviet medical service is based. Norway and Sweden are other countries which adopted health service at an early date. The British National Health Service, implemented in 1948, now employs the great majority of practising doctors.

Diagnosis and treatment are the province of the doctor but day-to-day care of the patient is the province of the nurse. The tradition that the nurse is always female and the doctor male has no long history. Although the first woman doctor is usually stated to be Elizabeth Blackwell who qualified in 1849, female graduates of Salerno are known by name, and women physicians practised in London in the 14th century. Medieval hospitals probably depended for their nursing upon less ill patients and relatives, a method still obtaining in some medically underdeveloped countries. The first regular nurses were male, belonging to orders established in the Crusades, an early and notable example being the Lazarists who cared especially for lepers from the 12th to the 14th century. The first known female nurses are the Beguines who originated in the Netherlands during the medieval period and spread widely in Europe. The Augustinians and the Tertiaries of St Francis, employing both men and women, are other examples. Monastic records of their attendance on sick inmates suggest no strict differentiation between doctor and nurse or between male and female. The most famous of all nursing orders, the Sisters of Charity of St Vincent de Paul, was founded in Paris at the end of the 17th century.

Nursing remains part of the Church organization in Roman Catholic countries and survived the Revolution in France, although the initial revolt of the mob was not at the capture of the Bastille on 14 July 1789 but at the sacking of the headquarters of St Vincent de Paul on the previous day. The Reformation ended religious orders in Protestant lands, where nursing rapidly declined to reach the status of lower domestic service before the end of the 18th century. Robert Gooch, a London physician, and the poet Robert Southey advocated the formation of Protestant nursing orders in the 1820s but failed to attract support.

In 1833 Pastor Theodor Fliedner of Kaiserswerth, Prussia, began to care for discharged female prisoners at his home and in 1836 started a school of Lutheran deaconesses as part of his rehabilitation scheme. His school rapidly developed into a large order interested in nursing among other activities. Ten years later there were over 90 deaconesses at Kaiserswerth, not bound by vows but living under religious discipline, who mainly devoted themselves to nursing the sick poor. The order spread throughout Germany, resulting in the foundation of 36 subhouses, their members primarily engaged in the nursing of hospitals.

The first Anglican nursing sisterhood, the community of St John the Evangelist or St John's House, started work in 1848. The sisters, not bound by vows, recruited nurses, brought them under discipline and sent them to hospitals for practical experience. In 1856 St John's House undertook the nursing of King's College Hospital, London, and in the following year Sister Mary Jones, Lady Superintendent, founded the first British nurses' training school. The experiment proved from the start to be successful. A number of similar sisterhoods were founded and took charge of English hospitals.

In 1854 Miss Florence Nightingale, having already gained some experience at Kaiserswerth, headed a party of 20 sisters and nurses to Scutari where they cared for sick and wounded of the Crimean War. The venture, although not wholly successful, received public acclaim and served to stimulate interest in nursing. Miss Nightingale founded a school at St Thomas's Hospital, London, in 1860. She and Sister Mary Jones worked closely together for the next eight years. This collaboration determined the future of British nursing. Although the Nightingale school had no Church affiliation, the influence of the sisterhoods persisted. British nursing developed as a "vocation" rather than as a profession or trade, members submitting themselves to strict discipline, long hours and poor living conditions with inadequate pay. This semi-religious concept of nursing remained long after Low-Church agitation had virtually destroyed the sisterhoods and hospital managers had started their own lay schools on lines similar to that of Miss Nightingale.

The doctrine that those who care for the sick are privileged found expression in the international Red Cross organization. The battle of Solferino, fought in 1859, resulted in more than 40,000 casualties. Henri Dunant, a young Swiss, visited the battlefield to find dead, dying and wounded lying together without succour. He devoted the next four years to a European campaign for better treatment of wounded in war and in 1862 published *Un Souvenir de Solferino* which stimulated formation of a committee at Geneva "to turn Durant's inspiration into fact". An international meeting led to a diplomatic conference attended by representatives of 12 governments on 8 August 1864 which drew up a treaty establishing the obligation to care for wounded, whether friend or enemy. There followed the first Geneva Convention declaring the principle that wounded, their attendants and medical supplies are immune and must be protected from hostile action. The Red Cross organization worked through voluntary aid detachments which, at the start, were recruited by the generosity of private individuals. These detachments first proved their worth in the Franco-Prussian War of 1870 when nurses and doctors from the combatant countries and from Britain, Russia, Italy and Switzerland cared for the wounded under the Red Cross symbol.

Doctors and nurses retain their privileged position. Mystery still surrounds the healing art. But the image is fading. Medicine depends, far more than in the past, upon extraneous experts; the physicist and electrician are examples. There is a recent trend among doctors, particularly when employed by local or national governments, to seek higher emoluments and to threaten industrial action if their demands are not met. The same is true of nurses. A question for the future is whether doctor and nurse can claim rights similar to those of a trade unionist and still preserve the respect hitherto accorded them as members of a closed but devoted profession.

# PART FIVE

*Women, Half of Europe's
Population*

# 18

# Women, Half of Europe's Population

## NAOMI GRIFFITHS

What comes to mind for the image of Woman? the wife of the hunter, sower of seed and home-maker? the mate of Socrates, eternally distracting genius with earth-bound triviality? Calpur-nia, her cruel suicide dictated by her vision of Caesar's needs, or the woman of Proverbs, her price above rubies as she tends her household, runs the estate and loves her spouse? Eve, whose transgression brought the world its sorrow, or Mary, whose sorrows brought the world its salvation in Christ? There is no lack of exemplars, for it is the paradox of European attitudes towards women that, at one and the same time, they are given more than enough attention and far too little consideration. It is a moot point whether woman as erotic partner or woman as child-bearer has been more commented upon by poets, artists, moralists and law-makers. The result, however, has been ever the same: the dominance of Woman, goddess or devil, brood-mare or earth mother, and the overshadowing of women. Somehow or other in the organization of European life the infinite variety of human beings who are women have been bundled into tidy packages, rendered down into stereotypes.

In one way, of course, the existence of stereotypic images of women is only to be expected and, indeed, is paralleled by like imagery for men. The biological differences between men and women, the sexual identity of the individual, have always been a matter for cultural comment in European civilization. From the earliest times of literary records one can trace ideas of proper behaviour for men and women, beliefs about what actions will reveal the core of manliness, the essence of womanliness. From earliest times too, the images for women have been less varied than those relating to men. Hesiod, for example, writing in the 8th century BC, presented a complex enough description of the strong and noble character of the gods, summing up masculinity in Zeus, father originator of the moral order, creator of life. The poet included in his work the goddesses, Athena, Aphrodite and Hera. None of these had the multi-faceted abilities of Zeus. While gods lived a variety of experiences, overlapping in powers and escapades, the goddesses became identified with particular, specific powers. Apollo, athlete, aesthete, lover, for counterpart needs both Athena, warrior, intellect and ever-virgin, as well as Aphrodite, sexuality without issue.

Further, no matter how strong male stereotypes are, no matter how clearly they indicate particular modes of action, they are always shadowed and given perspective by being accompanied by details of a more varied reality. The ideal is set amid ordinary experience. Classical heroes move among the sulks of Hector and the brutality of Achilles, Socrates instructs not only the quick-witted but also the dull. The "verray parfit gentil knight" seeks out salvation and honour but Piers Plowman tills the fields and remarks upon

Rich and poor    al manner of men
Working and wandering    as in the world we must.

256
*Women*

The extent and scope of male experience, the perception of the lives of individual men as variable quantities, have always been so lengthily reported and so continuously observed that there has always been a human context for male ideals. Hero, teacher and saint have been able to serve as beckoning lights because representations of "al manner of men" have constantly softened the tyranny of any one model. The disciples of Christ in fact, saints without question, come with all callings and all qualities: fishermen, politicians, mystics, tax-collectors, people prey to ambition, struggling with cowardice. Women, however, are made invisible in the light of Mary, Mother of God: all manner of women are darkened in one glory.

It is worthwhile remarking here that women are very definitely present in both the Old and the New Testaments, as human beings worthy of understanding. The love borne to a life-long companion is the love between Sara and Abraham; Jacob's enduring desire for Rachel is the strength of love an individual woman can arouse, not to be sated by another human. The love of human friendship is underlined in the story of Ruth and Naomi. In the New Testament there is Mary Magdalene, her sins forgiven because she loved much, Mary and Martha running a household, the woman of Canaan, with desperate self-confidence importuning for the life of her child. What is lacking, however, is the representation of women as partners, helping in small businesses, the sisters of the women spoken of at the close of Proverbs. Even the strength and abilities of Mary, her courage in journeying alone to find her cousin, her ability to look after guests at a wedding feast, are there as minor attributes to her fundamental role as mother. In the Gospels, as elsewhere, for most of European history, the literary record of women's experience is slight and the imagined vision of women's role very great. More than almost any other factor it is this lack of statement of reality, of what truly occurred, combined with the proliferation of theory, that has led to images of motherhood dominating the reality of the experience itself. This is not an argument against the primacy of motherhood in the lives of women. It is obvious enough that the vast majority of females who live beyond puberty bear children. What is being suggested, however, is that the reality of motherhood has been little understood in Europe and, as a result, since it has been so little understood it has not been properly valued; nor have those, whose action it is, been properly considered.

The most confining representations of the impact of motherhood are based upon the premise that to bear and rear children is a task, by definition, both so exhausting and so fulfilling, physically, mentally and emotionally, that there can be nothing else to the individual so engaged. Women who are mothers are allowed no experience not encompassed in and focused upon child-bearing and child-rearing. Further, bearing children is not only seen as an experience which will subsume all other activities, but it is also depicted as the sole experience which completes women, making them adult human beings. Rilke, poet, humanist, a man who valued women, wrote, on the birth of his daughter: "For the woman – according to my conviction – a child is a completion and a liberation from all strangeness and insecurity; it is spiritually, too, the mark of maturity." Women may not be considered fully people unless they are mothers. The childless are, inevitably, barred from the achievement of true human stature. If brutal to the barren, and denying the stature of total human to the young woman not yet mother, Rilke at least accorded women the "capacity of reaching all the artistic heights the man can reach" when the child has been born.

From a vision of motherhood as the sole path for women's completion one turns to a vision that is both more free and more confining. It has been expressed well enough by a 4th-century BC Athenian, and since then endorsed by many another writer, male and female. Demosthenes took up Hesiod's belief about goddesses and adapted it for mortal women: females, unlike men, are capable of only one function at a time. Thus he wrote: "Mistresses we keep for pleasure, concubines for daily attendance upon our person, wives to bear us legitimate children and be our faithful housekeepers." The evidence that there were women who combined some or all of these roles without much difficulty was not something Demosthenes, and later supporters of his ideas, found worth considering. There was something too appealing about the categorization for reality to be allowed to intrude. It is from this root that beliefs grow which deny the possibility of sexual pleasure to "good women" and insist that women whose lives are spent in the pursuance of ambitions outside the family must eschew motherhood. In this attitude towards women, there is at least the possibility of varying capacities for the individual female of the species, even if each capacity can be indulged in only at the expense of all others.

The most brutal vision of motherhood has been most clearly asserted by a 20th-century gynaecologist, Edmund Overstreet, in 1963: he wrote, "when you come right down to it, perhaps women just live too long. Maybe when they get through having babies they have outlived their usefulness – especially now that they outlive men by so many years." Aeschylus had put it a different way for Apollo, when in the *Oresteia* the latter declares that "the mother is no parent of that which is called her child, but only the nurse of the new-planted seed that grows. The parent is he who mounts." Both statements make children products, their disposal a matter for authority, and that authority outside the bounds of women's influence. European civilization has seen a multitude of variations on this theme. In one of its most frequent forms it is made as an appeal to women as the providers of sons for war. Victor Hugo remarked in his diary in 1848 that war with England was now possible, for the mothers of France had done their duty and made good the losses of the Napoleonic Wars, and provided enough men for battle. Very often, mixed in with this image of motherhood is the related notion that it was sons alone that should be born. Female infanticide hovers on the edges of this nightmare and makes of woman a cross between a baby machine and a prophylactic device. While not subscribing to it himself, Plutarch has this view stated brilliantly by one of his characters, Protogenes, in his *Dialogue on Love*: "[the union of a man and a woman] is necessary for the propagation of mankind . . . [but] I certainly do not give the name 'love' to the feeling one has for women and girls any more than we would say flies are in love with milk, bees with honey, or breeders with the calves and fowl they fatten in the dark."

If lack of literary record of the actual experiences of motherhood has handicapped women in their fight to balance the ideal with the real, another great handicap has been the grain of truth about the experience itself contained in each of the major images of the role that Europeans have developed. Rilke has something right: the experience of motherhood in the best of circumstances, economic and emotional security, the physical health of the woman, can be a magnificence. Unfortunately, far too frequently pregnancy has been accompanied by sickness, by a heavy burden of chores to be fulfilled, and has concluded with physical distress, a conclusion so common that childbirth pains have become an expected accompaniment to the labour. Further, even the first pregnancy of many women has been, and is, a time when business-as-usual is a necessity. So often the economy of the family means and has meant that women must work as late as possible in the pregnancy. In the urban, industrial context of recent centuries this may mean factory work until close to term, and a return to the assembly line within a month or so of the birth. In some situations, the position of women on farms, as fishermen's wives, as partners in small businesses, the burden of pregnancy has had to be carried through a continuing share of the necessities of the family occupation. In the vast majority of cases, child-bearing has been against the background of household management, cooking and serving meals, washing, ironing, mending clothes, cleaning the house, taking care of the garden, organizing the storing of future food supplies. The ideal of motherhood, set in leisure, in physical health, and in the conventionally approved circumstances of marriage, with the help of servants, has to be balanced by much more complex realities. Further, if the woman already has one or more children, then the situation is liable to be even less idyllic. As one Acadian woman, mother of 12, was heard to remark when the Virgin Mary was held up as a model: "Huh! Some Model! She only had one and she couldn't keep her eye on Him during the holidays."

Very often related to ideas of motherhood as a spiritual fulfilment for women is the idea that women are instinctively good mothers, knowing how to cope with all the demands that will be made by the new infant and the young child. It is this blind belief that has so often led a terrified girl to abuse her baby, when the infant will not stop crying and she as mother does not know what to do. It is an idea, too, that has supported the exclusion of men from parenting, depriving women of much-needed aid and men of a wide area of human experience. After all, the argument goes, if women are by nature endowed with a special capacity for nurturing, with an instinctive knowledge of the care and upbringing of children, it is the height of foolishness for the incompetent male to interfere with child care. As Sweden has discovered, however, in the public approval bestowed upon the recent provisions of that country for paternity leave, men are not only capable of a much greater role in child-rearing than has hitherto been granted them by explicit European traditions, they also find considerable enjoyment in the duties of parenthood.

If the views summed up by Rilke's image of motherhood err in the estimation of its unmitigated joys, those expressed by Demosthenes err equally by overemphasizing the practical difficulties of mothering. Basic to the proposition that each man requires three or more women to satisfy his varying requirements is the image of motherhood as exhaustion, mental, emotional, intellectual and physical. While for some women this is undoubtedly true, there have always been others capable, at one and the same time, of bearing and rearing children, cherishing their husbands and pursuing other activities as well. The evidence here is both more extensive and narrower in application than that available to challenge other images. One has considerable literary records of the multi-faceted lives of women who were part of the ruling structure throughout European history but much less about the majority of women. Nevertheless the evidence mounts, century by century, to show that women, as a sex, are capable enough, given the right circumstances, of undertaking more than one function. Aristophanes had sufficient confidence in the common acceptance of intelligent women among the Greeks to create Lysistrata, mother, lover and political activist. Roman women can stand to a funeral oration which celebrates a woman capable of pursuing her parents' murderers, defending her inheritance, helping her husband in his political affairs: while not mother, Turia was wife and lover. A slow parade walks down the centuries: Boadicea; Cleopatra; Eleanor of Aquitaine; Eleanor, Countess of Montfort, a 13th-century wife and mother, quite capable of managing her children, her husband, her estates and lodging for 300 men at a moment's notice. But the cumulative weight of such evidence has not altered the image of women as incapable of performing differing activities, at one and the same time.

In fact, it is the lack of consideration of available evidence rather than the lack of evidence itself which is most striking when one comes to consider the image of woman based upon her definition as a walking womb, needed seed-bed of humanity, herself not, to quote St Augustine and a recent work of feminism, made in God's image. This image of women makes the reproductive function, motherhood itself, not merely a role that consumes all the capacities of women but also the very be-all and end-all of their existence. It is an odd form of recognition that without motherhood humanity ends. What is peculiar about it is that it is very much less a statement concerning women than a statement about human beings. It implies an image of humanity that links sexual activity exclusively with procreation, denying entirely the possibility of sexual relationship as human communication. It is an image that ignores any possibility of life-long affection between men and women. In its crude ugliness it is the reduction of human beings to the level of a strange cattle, men as sperm banks, women as ovaries.

In many ways the basis of this line of reasoning has nothing to do with the role of motherhood in the lives of women. It is, instead, an equation of women with child-production and it proposes motherhood as a service for men alone instead of motherhood as a result of human cooperation between two sexes for the continuance of them both. Such a belief might have been taken less seriously if there had not been other factors in European civilization to circumscribe women. The acceptance, from very early times, of the predominant right of the male issue to inherit property and status obviously worked to women's disadvantage. Aristotle's will, for example, while providing for his daughter, left the administration of his estate to men. The impact of Germanic custom upon Greek and Roman tradition did ameliorate to a certain extent the lot of women in the matter of inheritance. The Visigothic code, for example, gave women the right of guardianship. Nevertheless, in general terms, European traditions gave pre-eminent inheritance rights to males, even if an elder sister lived.

With this tradition of property right was linked the tradition of noting descent by the male line. One of the most obvious results of this tradition has been the perception of the chastity of women as a matter of property. Adultery could mean the inheritance of estates and titles by someone who had no blood right to such properties. France, in the 17th century, saw at least one woman, persuaded to enter a convent rather than marry, compound her mother's sin of adultery by passing her mother's husband's property into hands that had, in the eyes of

contemporaries, no moral right to inherit. Coupled with the necessity for a secure base for
child-bearing, this concern over the morality of wives was a powerful factor in the development
of the home not merely as the centre of women's work but as the sole, permissible sphere for
women's activities.

Pressure towards general observance of such a convention, the restriction of women to the
domestic sphere, was also exerted by the precarious access of women to direct political power
during most of the centuries of European development. Neither Greece nor Rome gave women
legitimate stature in the political arena. The Greek city-state, in fact, has been referred to, with
some accuracy, as "a men's club". Rome, too, excluded women from direct political power, and
emphasized the position of husband and father with laws that gave the man almost the rights of
a slave-owner over his wife and family. With the collapse of Rome, however, came monarchies,
queens as well as kings. Nevertheless, the exclusion of women from direct participation in the
political process was so generally part of European attitudes that, as parliamentary democracy
developed, the rights of women to be considered full citizens, and to vote, had to be argued,
fought for and won. The earnestness of the struggle can be gauged by the fact that Switzerland
gave women suffrage rights only in 1971.

To these handicaps must be added the attitude of some of the religious leaders of European
civilization. As has already been suggested, St Augustine, preaching in the 4th century, had
considerable doubts as to the equality of women, coming finally to the conclusion that women
were in the image of God only when completed by being joined to men. "Man alone," the saint
wrote, "he is the image of God as fully and completely as when the woman too is joined with
him." The ascetic strain within Christianity very often also worked to the disadvantage of
women, making sexuality a question of sin, and transferring all responsibility for the sexual
appetite to women. St John Chrysostom and many other Christian preachers, Catholic and
Protestant, believed that the weakness of the human race was exemplified by Eve tempting
Adam, not by Adam choosing to accept the apple. "The sex", St John explained, "is weak and
fickle . . . The whole female race transgressed." One particularly eloquent misogynist managed
to sum up the general disapproval. In a diatribe delivered probably at the close of the 13th
century, he declared: "What is woman? Woman is the confusion of man, an insatiable beast, a
continual worry, a never-ending battle, a daily injury, a house of fury, an impediment to
chastity, the shipwreck of incontinent men." In later centuries there would be strong
Protestant echoes of such sentiments, and Milton, with his famous line, "He for God only, she
for God in him", would provide a logical conclusion for the beliefs of St Augustine.

It is extraordinary, given the multiplicity of pressures, that women managed to continue
their statement of their own human nature. They were enormously aided in this struggle,
however, by the constant presence of men, at all stages of European development, who
considered women partners, not slaves, human beings, not lesser animals. In the 6th century BC
an anonymous Greek poet sang of the delights of a wife who was both a friend and a fellow
worker, someone to be joined with as a companion. The *Digest* of Roman law saw marriage as
"the union of a man and woman forming an association during their entire lives and involving
the common enjoyment of divine and human privileges". Within Christianity, while there is
material for the denigration of women, there is an extremely strong tradition for the acceptance
of women as human. Christ had friendships with a number of women. The doctrine that there is
neither marriage nor giving in marriage in Heaven questioned the need of women always to be
considered in relation to men. St Paul, frequently accused of being anti-feminist, nevertheless
declared a doctrine of complete sexual equality in the text of his Epistle to the Galatians:
"There is neither Jew nor Greek, there is neither bond nor free, there is neither male nor female:
for ye are all one in Christ Jesus."

Even with the traditions of Christianity that suggested the equation of women, sexuality
and sin, there was the possibility of women attaining sainthood by the paths of consecrated
virginity. The single life for women, led through the cloisters of medieval Europe, led also to
considerable influence and power: Hilda of Whitby in the 8th century, controlling a monastery
as well as a convent, according to one source "saw to the education of five bishops, encouraged
the scholar and historian Bede and even aided the cowherd Caedmon whose moment of vision
flowered into the first English poetry". The role of such women, advisers to the popes, such as

Catherine of Siena in the 14th century, doctors of the Church, such as Teresa of Avila in the 16th century, educators and dispensers of medicine, was socially acceptable and is of fundamental importance in considering European traditions and women.

Further, while many of the Protestant divines would agree whole-heartedly with certain Catholic traditions concerning the generally weak nature of women, the emphasis of the Reformation upon the rightness of marriage gave to the role of women in those European countries which followed this interpretation of Christianity a dignity which it had rarely had before. The extent to which this support for the assumption of the real humanity of women affected their status within European civilization has yet to be assessed. This is partly because from the early 17th to the mid-20th century, as Europe reached out to the rest of the world, sometimes with honour and sometimes with greed alone, sometimes with laudable curiosity and outstanding bravery, sometimes with exploitation in mind, bigotry in action and cruelty for method, the internal organization of the continent became a matter of the enforcement of control and conventions, institutional, economic and social. During these years of rigidity there was never a time when the human nature of women was without champions but the building of the political process into the modern state, the erection of categories for the citizenry, the solidifying of local custom into national tradition, all worked to exclude woman from public consideration, to make her natural habitat seem somehow apart from the ordinary environment of men.

The widespread acceptance of this belief, that the lives of women were centred upon some sphere other than the normal world of men, was due to a combination of factors: perhaps the most important single factor being the development of an urban, industrial way of life for the majority of Europeans, whose manners and beliefs then became to a very large extent for a considerable number of years something presided over by a thrusting middle class. It is in the pride of men whose circumstances permitted them to dispense with the labour of the women of the family that the vision of wives and daughters as decorative sideboard ornaments is rooted. The paradox of 19th-century Europe, the time when women were explicitly barred from so many avenues of action but yet so obviously influencing prison reform, medical professions and the development of social policies by political institutions, is that men – part of whose fortunes depended upon women working ten hours a day in mines for a pittance, or in factories for the same length of time, moving looms and tending other sorts of heavy machinery; and whose homes were comfortable because of skivvies hauling coal six flights of stairs to keep the warmth in the room, of laundry maids scrubbing, boiling and ironing wools, linens and cottons, of cooks roasting, basting, stewing over coal stoves with implements that were not only not labour-saving but quite definitely work-demanding, copper and iron pans whose preparation and washing was unpleasant work – these men could blithely talk of the fragile nature of womanhood, of the need to cherish and protect the weaker sex.

The ability to indulge in such a delusion sprang in the first place from the psychological torment of many men caught up with a notion of human sexuality current in much of urban Europe during the 19th century, when sexual morality, for a considerable and powerful sector of Europe's population, came to be centred upon an idealized vision of marriage which considered sexual feelings as something which the well-bred woman did not have and which the well-bred man should control. The most obvious and immediate result of this attitude was the recourse of the middle-class male to women whom he could consider in some way his inferior, but who could respond to sexual demands. Quickly enough the picture of women emerged, the angels of the home, builders of a sanctuary to which men could return from the rigours of organizing the world, women capable of bringing up children, boys with manly virtues of courage, honesty, valour, self-abnegation and restraint, and girls with the comparable qualities of innocence, compassion, amiability, knowledge of aesthetic delights. Then there were the women not of the family, people who must deserve the fates of poverty and hard labour, dominated by animal passion, unrestrained by good breeding and right morality, women who were the final cause of male sin, for men would be models of continence were women not available, beckoning to "the expense of spirit in a waste of shame".

Even without the problems caused by some of the contemporary European conventions of sexual morality, it was easy enough to consider women less capable than men: after all, where

were they? Not in universities, not in the professions, not in the political institutions, not
recognizably in the military, not behind the music of the concert halls, the pictures in the art
galleries, not visibly names as authors. At this precise moment in the development of European
civilization, when women were more explicitly controlled by laws barring them from higher
education in many disciplines and in most universities, hampered by other laws controlling
their rights to property far more severely than was the case for most men, with models of
behaviour making them Good or Bad but never ordinary humans, the emergence of history as a
university discipline merely added to their difficulties.

As the circumstances of everyday life in Europe altered with startling rapidity in the 19th
century, as the towns spread their streets across the landscape and the railways and steamships
moved goods and people with a speed not previously envisaged, as telecommunications linked
staff with line officers in battle, imperial governments with outlying colonies, head offices with
local salesmen, the search for mechanisms to control such a development led to a search for the
past. What had the human experience been? What were the old traditions of life? Historical
tradition and perspective were seen as clinching arguments for present issues. Social philosophers framed their beliefs in historical terms, theologians turned to history for evidence for
particular interpretations, and the enormous impact of theories of evolution, codified and
publicized by Darwin in the *Origin of Species*, published in 1859, brought the phrase "history
teaches . . ." an immense force. Given the circumstances of 19th-century Europe, as the
legitimacy of historical study was recognized, in Cambridge with the appointment in 1869 of
Sir John Seeley to the Regius chair and in Oxford in 1890 with the appointment of Thomas
Frederick Tout, it was a discipline established by people whose vision of the world was that of
an economically secure gentleman. The thrust of historical study came to be the discovery of
the nature, organization, growth and development of political institutions, the analysis of legal
structure of communities, of the theories of property rights, lightened by the occasional
biography and complicated by philosophical considerations of the historical evolution of
ideologies. A much-quoted statement of Sir George Clark, appointed Regius Professor at
Cambridge University in 1944, sums up the logical base of this perception of the work of
historians. In his inaugural address at Cambridge he said:

> It is in public institutions that men express their will to control events, and therefore it seems to
> me that historians will go wrong if they try to resolve political and constitutional history into
> other elements, just as our practical men will go wrong if they follow the current fashion of
> treating "cultural" interests and activities as if they could be altogether separated from the affairs
> of states. The history of institutions must in some sense be central.

Twenty-two years later, as Arthur Marwick has pointed out in his work *The Nature of
History* (1974), Denys Hays, editing a new series on the history of Europe, expressed virtually
the same opinion: "The desire for political power", Hays wrote, "is the motor which drives
men to public action . . . It is . . . the politically dominant, a small fraction of the total
population at most times . . . who are largely responsible for the cultural qualities of the age."

With this perception of the historical discipline, the contribution of women would never be
seen as something which, of itself, could merit serious historical investigation. After all, the
argument went, and still too often goes, women are human, and important human affairs are the
province of men, public and political. Women's history, therefore, has already been told: it will
have been expatiated upon as and when it has had an influence upon important matters.
Anything that has been overlooked can only be peripheral, marginal, trivial and idiosyncratic.

While this general view of what history should be about is still current, the discipline itself
has gradually developed. In particular the French historians Marc Bloch and Lucien Febvre,
who launched the journal *Annales d'Histoire Économique et Sociale* in January 1929, brought
questions of economics, sociology and psychology to the historian's notice. Joined by others,
and in particular Fernand Braudel, who added an interest in geography to the consideration of
the disciplines surveyed by Bloch and Febvre, the vision of these French historians led to the
establishment of what has generally become known as the *Annales* school. By the mid-1970s
the essential methodology of this school, the investigation of the past by the collection
and analysis of every possible record relating to the particular question being asked, had led

to a proliferation of lengthy monographs, many of them demographic in nature, attempting to portray the reality of the historical experience of a geographic region, or a strictly limited sector of the population, in a particular period.

Written with enormous attention to detail, using quantitative methods, looking above all at patterns of birth and death, at the incidence of disease, and trying to see how the economic structure of life was linked with political activities and the reception of new ideas, the studies produced by scholars concerned with this perception of the historical discipline inevitably give greater place to the contributions of women than do those studies linked with the particular emphasis upon a definition of politics narrowed to the consideration of direct, official, recorded action in public matters. Any close analysis of demographic change quickly involves the researcher in an investigation of marriage patterns, dowries, contracts and wills. Almost without effort, one aspect of the contribution of woman is revealed: her role as the necessary economic partner in the family unit. From Armengaud's work, *La Famille et l'enfant en France et en Angleterre du XVI<sup>e</sup> au XVIII<sup>e</sup> siècle* (1975), on French 17th-century women – the Breton wife capable of organizing the oyster beds and the vegetable gardening and the wife of the shepherd in the Pyrenees, carding wool and looking after the house while the husband takes the flocks to market – to contemporary reports, such as those of James Howell, *Epistolae Ho-Elianae*, and Sir Josiah Child's survey of trade possibilities, both of which examine women in 17th-century Holland, educated in writing and ciphering to manage the books of their husband's trade, and Laslett's description in *The World We Have Lost* (1971) of the baker's wife in 17th-century England organizing husband, apprentices, children and ovens, the picture is the same: women as an essential part of the family enterprise, not merely the source of the next generation but of continuing necessity for the present.

The restoration of women to history, however, will only be partially complete even when the economic nature of the family in European history has been fully understood. For the essence of the proper depiction of the position and status of women in European history lies in the acceptance of women as being, in all matters of human action, half the story: one of the two parents, both equally necessary for each human being. Final acceptance of this proposition could lead to the perception of the task of history as something that must value the organization of private life of men and women as much as the institutional structure of public activities. It would also inevitably lead to investigations of the border between the two spheres of activities, and commentary upon the social heritage which has given many men, but not all, facility in public affairs but ineptitude in private life, and many women, but not all, capabilities for personal relationships and no confidence at all for public action. From this standpoint, of course, the development of women's history becomes part and parcel of the continuing struggle against discrimination against women.

The historical continuity of this struggle, a struggle that in some sense can be seen in the fight for the vote, but which in reality is as ancient as the first act of discrimination itself, has been overshadowed in the 20th century by the immense disruptions of the two great wars. The inhumanity of these wars produced as an immediate aftermath a dream of fair women in peaceful homes, holding the loveliness of life in their hands, by instinct and natural abilities returning the world to sanity. Women as munition workers, as combatants in almost all roles, even including that of killers (for example as gunners with anti-aircraft emplacements), were swept away in a vision as false and as welcome as the marsh-lights to weary travellers, promising warmth and comfort, delivering death. Its most lethal result is the production of men like Hoess, commandant of Auschwitz, good father and husband at weekends and in the evenings, efficient administrator of gas ovens and extermination procedures during working hours. The idea of home as sanctuary, as repository of virtue, leads quickly enough to codes of public and private morality, to beliefs that the action taken under orders is something for which the individual has no moral responsibility, and to assumptions of two codes of morality, one for private life, one for public action.

It is, however, upon the more immediate plane of daily existence, the concerns of the economics of the home, the need for social support for the right to work, that the struggle for women's rights has been built. The ideal of women as attending solely to the house and home is something of little relevance to the working classes of Europe, urban and rural, in the 20th century. The world wars saw the entrance of women into the labour force, into the arena of paid work, on an unprecedented scale and neither cessation of hostilities turned back this tide. As a result, questions of equal pay for equal work, of pension rights, of career rights assumed an importance hitherto unknown. By 1971, according to Juliet Mitchell, who published on the matter that year, all European countries except for Austria, Iceland and Switzerland had an active, organized revolutionary movement in being, a movement dedicated to changing the whole structure of society to bring to an end any possible suppression of women as women.

As is to be expected, there is an immense variation in the character of this movement within Europe. A very few broad generalizations are possible: nowhere is the status and equality of women as fully human a matter of such general acceptance as to exclude public debate on the issue; not even in Sweden, the country held up as most advanced in the establishment of equal rights for women. The question of some work-related matters still remains to be settled. In most of Europe the question of abortion laws is a matter of emotional argument, with the rights of the father, the rights of the mother and the rights of the child all being debated. As in other ways, Europe as a civilization shows a bewildering local variation. It is still accepted in part of Sicily, for example, that a raped woman should marry her aggressor, thus wiping out the crime. Yet in some ways the position of professional women in Italy seems to be a matter of less comment than it is in the United Kingdom, a country where a recent verdict on a rape case seems to deny the possibility of such a crime if the man believes that the woman has, in fact, consented. It is almost impossible to assess the extent of support for the organization of feminists in the mid-20th century, as one moves from a consideration of the numbers of women in the various political institutions of Europe to the reality of the limited presence of women in so many aspects of European life.

Perhaps the best estimation of the present situation would be the recognition that, in general, Europeans see sexual prejudice and discrimination against women as one aspect of the wider problem of human prejudices that civilized countries have to control. The changing demographic picture, the need in most countries to think in terms of population control rather than unexamined expansion, has added a totally new dimension to the conception of the role of women. This demand for reconsideration has been underlined by the medical advances which make child-bearing and -rearing something of much less risk to mother and infant than it has ever been. It is becoming more and more apparent that, whatever past circumstances might have required, present circumstances do not bind motherhood necessarily to exhaustion and the extenuation of the individual concerned.

Perhaps, in the mid-20th century, women have a greater possibility of being recognized as human than ever before. It would be a pity, however, if, as Europe adjusts to a different population pressure, to a reorganization of family life and to a new level of participation by women in public life, the social heritage of European gender ideals was disowned without examination. The need is not for women to reject virtues of gentleness, kindness, love of beauty, care of detail, sensitivity towards emotional wants of others. It is, surely, to make certain that these characteristics are displayed by both men and women, valued by both men and women, the responsibility of both. The acquisition of supposedly exclusive "male" characteristics of organized work habits, public responsibility, economic sense should not demand the surrender of traits which have been nurtured to make the private life of individuals something supportive. Charles Fourier has asserted that it is in the treatment of women that the true nature of a society is displayed: "The extension of privileges to women", he has written, "is the general principle of all social progress." In a sense, Europe has less to extend privileges to women than to decide to develop those aspects of its traditions that support the equality of women. The ending of legal disabilities for women, the restructuring of marriage laws, of property rights, the final granting of equal pay for equal work, are all immediate, necessary, vital goals for women, in some European countries of greater urgency than in others. But the real estimation of half Europe's population must go beyond such structures, and must result in the recognition of the value for both sexes of virtues previously ascribed as the exclusive properties of the gender pattern of either one. What is the image of women? As complex as Medea and as simple as Chloe, as wicked as Catherine the Great, as saintly as Mary, as urgent as Joan of Arc, as organized as Florence Nightingale, as human as Edith Cavell and as warped as the moors murderer . . . and as human as Kristin Lavransdatter, daughter, lover, mother, wife and woman of her particular mark, the soul bought at the exchanging price of Christ.

# PART SIX

*Soldiers*

*Rogues and Villains*

*Travellers and Explorers*

*Craftsmen and Guilds*

*Engineers and Technologists*

*Merchants and Bankers*

# 19

# *Soldiers*

## JOHN KEEGAN

The image of the warrior, the outline of his form, the print of his foot, the press of his palm, the trace of his tools on the stones of his strong places, the touch, sight, almost sound, smell and taste of him, await rediscovery by the time-traveller at every level and turning-point of the journey into Europe's past. He trails his spear across the shards of amphorae from 7th-century Greece. He climbs the slow spiral of Trajan's column in Rome, armoured and ranked for battle, stripped to build a bridge, naked and bleeding under the surgeon's knife, garlanded to celebrate an emperor's triumph. His coat of mail is stitched into the fabric of the Bayeux tapestry and stamped into the coinage of the crusading kingdoms. He kneels at prayer before the easel of Piero della Francesca, takes his marmoreal rest under Donatello's chisel, prances above the heads of the passing world in bronze cast by Verrocchio. He is Rembrandt's corpulent and complacent civic pikeman, Wouwerman's picaresque and hideously grimacing soldier of fortune, Delacroix's doomed votary of Romantic death by battle. His silhouette flickers comically, even in the moment of extinction in no-man's-land, across the first newsreels of war, and his dumpy representation, muddied and puttied and clumsily accoutred, commemorates his modern martyrdom at the corner of village churchyards from Pomerania to Brittany, from the Tyrol to Inverness.

Who is he, this universal man of Europe, as widespread in his wandering and settlement as the tiller of the soil and, from age to age, almost as commonplace? As warrior, he is Everyman, builder and destroyer, trader and pirate, citizen and slave, sheriff and outlaw, explorer and stay-at-home. He is hoplite, legionary, Frank, Visigoth, Viking, knight, crusader, condottiere, Landsknecht, streltsi, pandour, stradiot, grenadier, hussar, guerrillero, zouave, marsouin, Frontkämpfer, poilu, Tommy, para. He is the ever-present man of war, war of city-state against city-state, civil war and war of empire, war of religion and war of ideas, feudal war and war of nations, war of kings and war of peoples. But as a soldier – a paid, trained and disciplined bearer of arms, servant of a permanent master, fed and housed at his expense and subject to his command, come peace, come war, or an uneasy truce between the two – he is a more isolated and occasional figure. But by no means less important; indeed, very much the contrary. For war, as a universal condition, is the enemy of civilization, and a Europe of warriors therefore a world of barbarism and disorder. The story of Europe's rise is also then that of the transformation – erratic, patchy, much resisted and sometimes completely reversed – of warrior into soldier.

When did that transformation begin? It is impossible to date. Everyone's, perhaps even the professional historian's, imagination is furnished with the folk memory of a heroic age in which men carried weapons as generally and naturally as they herded animals or raised crops. It is this folk memory which invests the barbarian invasions of the Roman – the first pan-European –

world with their peculiar fascination and menace, taunting us as it does with the image of a
society of warriors equal and free because all strong and armed. But the very little we know of "Free Germany" tells us that this democracy of arms probably never existed. Even there it seems likely that, as in Odyssean Greece, the war chiefs were surrounded by bands of picked men to whom the weaker deferred as much in peace as in war. In the earliest European societies of which we have detailed knowledge, the city-states of antiquity, arms were always the prerogative of an élite, the property-owning minority who could afford to arm themselves and to whom political power in consequence belonged. Within that élite, military obligation was carefully adjusted to wealth. "In fifth century Athens", as Yves Garlan has written, "the members of the first *census* (property) class were responsible for manning the fleet. For service in the cavalry one had to belong at least to the second *census* class (*hippeis*); for the hoplite phalanx to the third class (*zeugites*); while the lowest class, the *thetes*, were restricted to the light infantry." The propertyless played no military role, except in direst emergency, when even slaves might be pressed into service – though the enlistment of slaves was always unusual enough to be recorded. It happened, for example, in Athens on the eve of the battle of Marathon. That it was not more general was not simply precautionary: it was rather that the role of the warrior was too honourable to be compromised in such a way. When it was so of necessity the slaves were customarily manumitted after, but sometimes before, the battle for which they were enrolled.

In Rome, where a version of this sytem later took root, the archaic constitution similarly divided the citizens (the *populus*, originally a word of specifically military meaning) along property lines. It was nevertheless based on male citizen suffrage in which all alike possessed the same weight and enjoyed the same rights, whether they belonged to the first or fifth class. In the 2nd century BC, however, as Livy tells us, "Servius introduced a graduation, so that while no one was ostensibly deprived of his vote, all the voting power was in the hands of the principal men of the state. The knights were first summoned to record their vote, then the eighty centuries of the infantry of the First Class; if their votes were divided, which seldom happened, it was arranged for the Second Class to be summoned; very seldom did it happen that the voting extended to the lowest class." This "Servian reform" marked the beginning of a trend, through which the Greek city-states had by then already passed, towards the separation of civil power from military service. In both societies the movement was the consequence of increased military activity, which took soldiers away from home for longer and longer periods and greater and greater distances, making participation in political life increasingly difficult, if not impossible. The upper classes in both cases found means, however, to abdicate their military duties without forfeiting their political rights, and yet to provide for the defence of the state: the Greeks by the recruitment of foreign mercenaries, the Romans by the voluntary enlistment of their poorest citizens as regulars.

Some mercenary specialists – archers from Crete, slingers from the Balearic Islands – seem to have been, in small numbers, frequently embodied in ancient armies. But the transformation of the citizen militias of the Greek states into mercenary armies in the 4th century BC was a new and much more important, because eventually emasculating, development. For, as employers of mercenaries always discover, military skills and qualities cannot ever be safely bought. Sooner or later the seller is made aware of the political power inherent in his possession of arms and uses them to take it for himself. Hence the rise of the tyrannies and empires which ultimately overthrew the democracies of the Greek world. In Rome the eventual emasculation of the state was very much longer delayed. Militia service was still theoretically an obligation on all citizens as late as the 2nd century AD, but it fell in practice only on the poorest and, even in that class, the unwilling were always able to find substitutes to volunteer in their place. With the extension of citizenship to most free men in the Empire, by the edict of Caracalla in 212 AD, the legions came to be recruited largely from these new citizens whose Romanization was incomplete, and latterly, when the taste for legionary service had palled even there, from non-citizens, either barbarians domiciled by treaty within the Empire or those brought into its service from beyond the frontiers by agreement with their tribal leaders. At that stage, when the guardians of the Empire and its enemies had come so closely to resemble each other, its dismemberment was close at hand.

Of the five military types which the history of antiquity reveals to us — the warrior chief and his close companions, the citizen militiaman, the mercenary, the regular and the slave soldier — all but the first were to disappear from western Europe for the 1,000 years following the fall of Rome. The Merovingian, Carolingian and feudal kingdoms were warrior societies, in which military duty devolved on a very limited class, attached either to the person of the ruler — as were the Frankish warbands to Clovis, and 500 years later the housecarls to Harold — or to land held from him in return for service. Land and arms had been intimately connected in the ancient world: it was in part because of the qualities of endurance and effort (*ponos*) learnt by husbandmen in the fields that the city-state looked to them, rather than to its housebound artisans, for its defence; it was the promise of a grant of land, still the surest source of livelihood, which in the later Roman Empire chiefly attracted men into the legions; and it was in return for military service that the Ptolemaic rulers of Egypt granted tracts of frontier territory to their Greek mercenaries. But the high feudal system, in which all land, even that of the Church, was by the 11th century held from the ruler in exchange for military service – 40 days a year was the statutory period – was something new. It was new too that the military class should have adopted a single and uniform mode of fighting – in armour, on horseback. In the ancient world serious fighting had been done on foot. But the particular threat which the post-Roman world had to face, that of constant marauding across its frontiers, by Muslims from the south, Magyars from the east, shipborne Vikings from the north, required that its defenders be able to move quickly between battlefields and, on the battlefield itself, to ride down and crush opponents who, if not annihilated on the spot, would simply scatter to plunder, burn and kill again. It was the technique of the armoured charge, made possible by the adoption of the stirrup in the 9th century, and perfected in the settlement of incessant territorial quarrels, which made the western knight, and particularly the superbellicose Normans, the most recently domesticated of Christian Europe's invaders, so successful on the battlefield when it took the war to the Muslim world in the opening Crusades of the 11th and 12th centuries.

The Crusades were, at one level, the expression in military form of an intense religious faith, an armed pilgrimage to the Holy Land, the religious character of which was reinforced by the foundation of knightly religious orders – the Templars and Hospitallers – to garrison the conquests of Tancred and Bohemond, and which themselves served in turn to foster among many of the late medieval military class a sense of spiritual vocation and code of elaborate manners which came to be called chivalry. But at another level the Crusades were a function of a major demographic change, the sudden appearance of a surplus of warriors, among a population proportionately swollen, in a continent where standards of public order, thanks partly to the efforts of the Church, were beginning to improve after 600 years of right is might. The reason for the sudden growth of population in the 11th century is not known; the results of the growth of the knightly class are. Temporarily absorbed by the Crusades, which came to include the wars against the Spanish Moors, the pagan Slavs, local heretics like the Albigensians and even, inexcusably and disastrously, the rump of the Roman Empire in Byzantium, the free lances – men of knightly status but without the property necessary to sustain them in knightly style – came eventually to constitute a loose, masterless, international army, available for hire to those with money – now circulating again with the return of order – to spend and wars to fight.

These new mercenaries, who were to dominate European warfare until the 17th century, operated first as individuals but, like those of the Hellenistic world, were by the 14th century organized in permanent bands or companies (*con pane* – "with bread", a term of their employment), centred on well-defined market areas. Cape Taenarum, in the southern Peloponnese, where out-of-work soldiers congregrated, had been such a market in antiquity. In the 14th century northern Italy, where the Wars of Investiture had destroyed the structure of feudal allegiance, increased the power and wealth of the larger city-states, and attracted warriors from as far afield as south Germany and Catalonia, became another. The city-states had a tradition of communal militia service, not dissimilar to the Greek. But with the growth in prosperity of the cities' military classes in the 14th century, they too found it convenient to hire mercenaries, of whom the intermittent character of local warfare made a surplus always available. The market was dominated between 1338 and 1354 by the Great Company, described by Michael Howard

as "a band nearly ten thousand strong and totally international in membership which . . . ran
what would now be called a protection racket on a very large scale". Ten years later its place was taken by the White Company, a mass of *routiers* left unemployed by the ending of the Hundred Years' War, who rode southward under the standard of the Englishman, Sir John Hawkwood. He was to become one of the most famous of the *condottieri* (*condotta* – "contract") and to die honoured by the city of his adoption, Florence; others were later to make themselves masters of the cities they had originally contracted to serve and to set up, like the Sforza of Milan, as dynastic rulers.

But the era of the *condottieri* was comparatively short. In the 15th century the appearance of firearms brought an end to the tactical dominance of the mounted warrior, whose place was taken in the mercenary market-place by better-organized and more businesslike infantrymen, military "enterprisers" from south Germany, commanding disciplined, hierarchical companies of *Landsknechte* and, best known of all, the Swiss, who were recruited on a cantonal basis by direct contract between their cantonal authorities and the employer. The latter's frugal and hardy style of life in their unproductive mountains made them excellent soldiers, and they were to find ready employment with European paymasters until the mid-19th century – indeed until today, if allowance is made for the Swiss Guard of the popes, a vestigial remnant of a much larger force in continuous employment of the Vatican since the days of its temporal power. In time other nationalities would become prominent in the trade. English companies took service in the 1570s with the Dutch in the wars against the Spaniards, who were themselves large-scale employers of Germans and Burgundians. Scots, who displayed some of the same highland virtues as the Swiss, appeared in many armies, and one regiment, Sir John Hepburn's, served both Sweden and France before returning to its Stuart sovereign in 1685 to become the senior unit of modern British infantry, the Royal Scots. Even as the armies of the emergent nation states began in the 17th century to become regular, mercenary units continued to supplement the new domestic regiments, with which they served side by side. German and Italian regiments (Saxe, Royal Bavière, Royal Italien) appeared in the French army list until 1789, hired contingents from the small German states in the British army during the American War of Independence, and specialized units of light infantry and cavalry from the Russian and Austrian frontier with the Ottoman lands – hussars, pandours, Croats, stradiots, Polish uhlans – in several European armies until the Napoleonic Wars.

Nor did the stricter definition of frontiers on linguistic and religious lines put an end, as might have been expected, to mercenary emigration. Failing effective control of movement across frontiers, the enforcement of ideologies within them encouraged it. Irish Catholic soldiers formed an important element in the French army during the 18th century: the regiments of Dillon, Berwick and Walsh are indeed generally accorded credit for the victory over the British at Fontenoy. Catholic Irish and Scottish Jacobite officers turn up in the army lists of all the Catholic states during the 18th and 19th centuries, including the newly independent republics of South America, and Protestant Huguenots and Scottish Covenanters in those of the Protestant states and Russia. With the extension of European power and influence beyond the continent, French, Dutch, German, Swiss, Italian, English, Scots and Irish soldiers were to take service in the armies of the decaying empire of the Moguls (there had always been room for Europeans who would acknowledge the Prophet in the Ottoman armies) and some were to rise to great position, notably Benoit de Boigne, an Italian who had served in an Irish regiment of the French army, a Greek regiment of the Russian army and a British East India Company regiment before joining the Mahrattas; he died a Marshal of France and a Sardinian count. Some French engineers found their way in the 18th century as far eastward as Vietnam where they built fortifications for the emperors of Annam, so continuing a trend begun in the 15th century when the secrets of the *trace italienne*, which was to make fortifications the key element in warfare until Napoleon, were brought into France by local experts, whose wandering pupils were later to disseminate their teachings all over the military world. And eventually during the 19th and 20th centuries, the European empires were to yield a flow of mercenaries in the reverse direction, so that French officers would lead *goumiers* from Morocco against the German defenders of Italy and, against the Japanese, British officers Gurkhas from the mountains of Nepal.

But persistent and indeed probably inextinguishable though mercenarism is, it had already by the 18th century begun to acquire within Europe itself a taint of disrepute, as the nation states fielded armies which were increasingly national in character and nationalistic in temperament. The first of these regular armies had appeared in Spain at the end of the 15th century, where the newly victorious monarchy actually succeeded in recruiting an army by conscription: the Ordinance of Valladolid of 1494 made one man in every 12 liable for military service either at home or abroad. Conscription fairly quickly gave place there to voluntary enlistment, but the national principle had been established. So too had that of the permanent instead of temporary employment of soldiers, a development desirable in itself because ridding the countryside between wars of unemployed soldiers looking for work or, failing that, trouble. Few states were rich enough until the following century to imitate the Spanish *tercios*, though the French began to take mercenary bands into regular service in the 1470s (thus allowing the modern *1er Regiment d'infanterie* to claim descent, spuriously, from the *Bandes de Picardie*). And in the 17th century states were selfishly ready to employ mercenaries *en masse* in wars fought outside their own territories: hence the veritable no-man's-land which south Germany became in the later, bankrupt stages of the Thirty Years' War.

Gradually, however, and everywhere by the beginning of the 18th century, national states, and those with pretensions to the title, got themselves regular armies. The process by which they did so varied from place to place. In Britain the crown raised regiments by voluntary enlistment, with the grudging approval of parliament, but continued to officer them by the sale of commissions until 1870, a practice which kept alive both the mercenary principle and the warrior spirit in the propertied class. In France the crown began after 1660, when it had at last established control over its turbulent provinces, to raise regiments in the same way, though it subordinated the officers more closely to state control. In Sweden Charles XII inherited from Gustavus Adolphus a form of conscription which he regularized as the *indelta* system; under it the country was divided into military districts, where soldiers were allotted parcels of land which their neighbours were obliged to farm for them when they were called up to form the local regiment. Primitive, even tenuously feudal, though the system appears, it provided the Vasas with one of the cheapest and most efficient armies in Europe and influenced military organization in many adjacent states. The Habsburgs instituted something similar along their military frontier with the Ottomans, the Prussians after 1739 a *Kantonsystem* which attached the peasant to a territorial unit officered by the local Junkers, while in Russia the tsars transferred the duty of finding recruits to the landowners, who selected the required quota from their serfs. For those chosen, the village priest would say a requiem mass, since service was for life, the soldier boys illiterate and their anguished farewells to their families therefore a final separation.

But the regularization of armies in the 18th century meant everywhere a growing separation of the lives of soldiers and civilians, as it had done with the regularization of the legions in the later Roman Empire. For though soldiers were regularly billeted on civilians, regiments were deliberately garrisoned far from their centres of recruitment; and the practice, bitterly disliked by householders, diminished as fortifications multiplied and barracks were built in the major towns. The result was that each army tended as the century wore on to become, in Clausewitz's words, "a state within a state in which the element of violence gradually faded away". And desirable though the trend was for the sake of internal peace, the social and political consequences of the separation were to be literally revolutionary. The French middle class, which shunned service in the ranks, and was excluded from the officer corps – ever more jealous of its aristocratic status as its real feudal role diminished – came to see the stability and prosperity it enjoyed not as an achievement of the royal autocracy which had tamed the wild military men of the 17th century but as the manifestation of a new spirit of human rationality with which they were in tune and the king and his uniformed supporters were not. But the triumph of reason in 1789 quickly revealed to its devotees that peace is not self-defending. Internal revolt and external attack impelled the men of the revolution to a frantic search for soldiers, in which they could afford neither to despise the service of the *ancien régime*'s whitecoats nor too scrupulously to respect their own proclamation of universal liberty. Citizens, they found, had to be compelled, as they had not as subjects, to bear arms in defence of the state. Out of the *levée en masse*, proclaimed by the Committee of Public Safety in 1793, was thus reborn a sort of army which, so the classicists in the National Assembly were delighted to recognize, Europe had not seen since the overthrow of Athenian democracy, a militia of the political nation.

A strict examination, however, of the military histories of European countries would reveal that this renaissance was not as absolute as was claimed. Traces of a universal military obligation could be found in the medieval *arrière-ban*, the assemblies of the inhabitants of town and countryside which were occasionally called out in France and the imperial lands during the Wars of Religion and which were extensively revived for internal defence during the 17th century. In the towns, moreover, the right to form a militia had become one of the most cherished seals of civil independence during the revival of urban life in the later Middle Ages, and these burgher militias played an important municipal role, above all in the mercantile countries, Britain and Holland, during the 16th and 17th centuries: the *Night Watch*, painted by Rembrandt, was one such militia, though they were even then losing their military significance, and would gradually decline during the 18th century into purely symbolic status or become town constabularies.

Militias of a more serious sort were widely founded or refounded during the 18th century in Britain (the County Militia), in France (*milice royale*), Spain, Bavaria (*Landfahnen*), Denmark (*Vaern*) and Piedmont, usually in response to some sudden external or internal threat – the War of the Spanish Succession in France, the '45 in Britain. But all were intended either for local defence or as a reserve for the regular army. The *levée en masse* was, in two respects, a new departure: not only did it embrace, in theory at least, the whole population of military age but it imposed on the population the duty of defending the national frontiers, not because the law declared them to be soldiers but because they were citizens. "From this day", decreed the law of 23 August 1793, "until that when our enemies have been chased off the territories of the Republic, all Frenchmen are on permanent requisition for military service." And Carnot, the organizer of the new army, defined the way it would fight: "no more manoeuvres, no more military art, but fire, steel and patriotism."

In a vital respect, however, the new citizen armies were different from the city-state militias of antiquity. There the army and the political nation had been one because the former was simply the latter with weapons in its hands, weapons which were the personal property of the militiamen, an expression of their individual wealth and indeed their title to citizenship. The French Republic had declared all men citizens but the arms which they were to bear were the property of the Republic, an abstract authority superimposed on those whom it called to its defence. There was, therefore, from the inception of the modern citizen army an element of authoritarianism in its character alien to the spirit of the ancient militias. And it was to grow more marked throughout the 19th century as France's neighbours, in deference to the effort they had taken to defeat her in the long wars of 1792–1815, themselves adopted universal conscription. It achieved its most perfect and extended form in Prussia after 1859, when not only did every youth become liable for full-time military service of three years at the age of 20 but for part-time service thereafter until 40, first in the reserve and then in the *Landwehr*, a body which had begun as a civilian militia and a guarantor of bourgeois liberties, but had been captured by a jealous army and incorporated into its structure. By these means France and Germany were provided by 1914 with standing armies three-quarters of a million strong and were able on mobilization in August to raise their strength to four million each. Austria and Russia, by different methods, raised armies respectively rather weaker and rather stronger. As the war progressed and the machinery of conscription ground forward, new annual contingents of youths, and of men previously judged insufficiently robust for military service, further swelled the ranks, so that by 1918 Russia had mobilized 12 million men, Germany 11 million, France eight million, Austria seven million, Italy four million, and Britain and America, latecomers to conscription, eight and four million each; countries as small as Romania and Serbia each found 700,000. "La Gare de l'Est [the Paris station for the battle front] a mangé nos fils", mourning Frenchmen would say in the disillusioned 1920s, and the casualty figures lent substance to the cannibalistic analogy: 1,700,000 German dead, 1,700,000 Russian, 1,300,000 French, 1,200,000 Austro-Hungarian, 900,000 British, 600,000 Italian. War had eaten the children of nations before. No one who had seen the debris of Borodino or Waterloo could have thought battle laudable or glorious. But none had consumed soldiers' flesh on so Lucullan a scale as World War I; not even was World War II to do so, though the machinery of conscription was to stock the larder as plentifully as it had done 20 years before.

In the aftermath of its self-destruction, Europe took stock. The conscript armies, the most complete expression of the power of modern states, had succeeded in turning their members into something like slaves – often, and especially at the beginning of the two great wars, willing slaves, whose officers were flattered to think themselves the descendants, as many still were by blood, of feudal warriors. But the fact of bondage could not be hidden or ignored. During the 19th century it had been represented as the bondage of the classroom, where the nation's youth learnt "the republican virtues", "the imperial idea", "love of the fatherland" – the name of the lesson varied from country to country. But the real lesson which Europe had learnt through its military experience of the 20th century was that to make soldiers of all its citizens was to inflict on the majority a monstrous cruelty and on its own ideals of public liberty and justice a nearly fatal wound. There had been slave armies in Europe before, the serf hosts of the tsars, the kidnapped Christian boys of the Ottoman janissaries, the helot contingents of Sparta, but each served a system deeply hostile to the European creed. It was with something akin to relief, therefore, that late 20th-century Europe, accepting the terrifying consequences of its own and its American siblings' scientific genius, recognized that nuclear power had finally dissolved its military dilemma. It could not of course ultimately do without some soldiers. But increasingly it saw that those it needed could be chosen from that minority, apparently present in all societies, temperamentally drawn to the military life or at least not conscience-stricken by its implications. What it has yet to discover is whether the military virtues – of self-sacrifice, courage, obedience, abnegation, *ponos* – can safely be left to wither away with the armies in which they were nurtured.

# 20

# Rogues and Villains

## C. H. ROLPH

Considered as a whole, the developed rules of conduct in Europe, as indeed elsewhere, can hardly be said to have a history. There is no such sequence of connected changes and adaptations as the word history implies. But there have been changes in each component part of the criminal law of European countries; and it is in the criminal law of any country that you may read the history of its rogues and villains. Homicide, violence, robbery, kidnapping, cheating, stealing, perjury and sexual crime – each has a lineage going back nearly 4,000 years to the famous code laid down by the Emperor Hammurabi of Babylon *circa* 1760 BC; and it is the mildness or the ferocity of the punishments attached to each proscription that has always reflected the temporary needs and superstitions of society, the fear of some metaphysical wrath from on high, and the morality which accepts that (so long as the wrath can be dodged) "rules are made to be broken."

But there is absolutely no way of discovering whether in the past century Europeans in the mass have become less or more conformable to their laws. European countries have become vastly more efficient, some of them even punctilious, in reporting and recording the deeds of their rogues and villains, in publishing annual statements about them, in comparing one year's figures with another's, one decade's with another's. Looking back so far as a century, as distinct from the more recent comparisons now producing widespread anxiety and even fear, social historians remain on the whole sceptical as to the extent of *absolute* increases in the percentage of crime, especially of theft, fraud and violence. Fewer than a dozen countries, most of them small, keep any reliable crime statistics; but recent comparisons show that in those few countries recorded crime has increased enormously in the past 50 years. Even in the past 10 it has gone up by 54 per cent in the Netherlands, 44 in Sweden, 40 in Italy, 27 in Denmark, 26 in Germany, 25 in Austria. These figures represent only the known cases, taking no account of the great volume of crime (probably outnumbering them by ten to one) that never comes to the notice of the police. This "dark figure" hovers over all criminological theories, invalidating almost every conclusion; its presence is acknowledged by criminologists of all countries – and it is the subject of a valuable Dutch monograph by G. N. Peijster, *De Onbekende Misdaad* (1958). The communist countries are of course in a dilemma. Communism is bound to destroy the roots of crime, yet crime continues to flourish as if roots were superfluous. Why? Because it is still having to compete with capitalism on every side, and it all takes time. It is in these countries that fraud, and especially fraud upon the public, is held to be a crime of supreme gravity, and the British press occasionally reproduces from somewhere like Romania the story of a shopkeeper put to death by firing squad for overcharging his customers (in Britain he would have got a rebuke from the Office for Fair Trading).

Many thousands of potted histories could parade Europe's rogues and villains against that backdrop, and for present purposes a stringent selection must be made. Selection of course involves subjective preferences, and the crimes of many persons eminent in the popular demonology are really of small importance (Crippen, Gilles de Rais, Oscar Wilde, Dominici). It should also be noticed here that totally innocent people like Dreyfus, because their innocence involves the indictment of a whole system of national justice and becomes of intense interest to the entire world, are often wrongly included in such selections of "rogues and villains"; and they are many. Moreover, it is in the nature of public interest in the criminous that every decade adds a fresh layer of romance to a prominent offender's crime, and every century (if his name lasts so long) a new gloss of heroism to his memory. We have to recognize also that there is an indeterminate period, lasting for some centuries after the Roman Empire, during which the punishment of crime slipped away from sovereign power, even from that of barons and prelates, and lay at the pleasure of wronged individuals. Because of this, there is little record of individual crimes until the 13th century; and if we begin then, in the reign of Richard I of England and the days of Robin Hood, we are beginning with the horrifying story of a merciless predator whose name today is revered by children above those of all the saints. In those days, the process of romanticizing rapists and thieves was slower, and in 1606, more than two centuries after Robin Hood's supposed death, Sir Edward Coke, English Chief Justice of the Common Pleas, was writing in his *Third Institute* that Robin Hood, so far from being the debonair and swashbuckling outlaw of Sherwood Forest, was "nothing more than a brigand who lived, in woods and deserts, by robbery, burning of houses, felony, waste and spoil, principally by and with vagabonds, idle wanderers, night walkers and draw-latches". The story that he robbed the rich and gave to the poor probably cloaks his appearance as the first recorded English exponent of the protection racket. But Maid Marion, Friar Tuck, Little John *et al.* had been added in the 1370s by such fanciers as Langland and Stowe, and the first published collection of ballads about them was the *Lytel Geste of Robin Hood*, printed by Wynkyn de Worde in 1490. The legend that Robin Hood was the disguised and outlawed Earl of Huntingdon (Robin Fitzooth) had inspired an epitaph in 1247:

> Hear, underneath his latil stean,
> Laiz Robert earl of Huntingdon;
> Nea arcir ver az hie sae geud,
> An pipl kauld him Robin Heud.
> Sich utlaz az he an hiz men
> Vll England nivr si agen.

In England by the time of Charles II a very profitable protection racket was being operated in his native Yorkshire by the highwayman William Nevison, who was hanged at York on 15 March 1684. He began his life of theft as a small boy, ran away from home, and for three years worked for a brewer who then detected him in the act of embezzlement. He fled to Holland, married a burgher's daughter, joined the English army and fought in Flanders against the Spaniards; he then deserted, came home to York and went into business as a highwayman. He too earned a Robin Hood reputation, mainly by reason of the histrionic courtesy with which he robbed his victims. He exacted a quarterly "tribute" from cattle farmers and drovers, and it bought them genuine protection not only against his own gang of about 20 thieves but against any lesser gangs inclined to dispute his sovereignty. In 1676 he was convicted, but secured a reprieve by promising to turn king's evidence against his companions. There is no record that he ever fulfilled this promise, but the pretence that he would brought him a breathing space and, eventually, commutation of the death sentence to military service. He soon deserted again from the army and returned to highway robbery for five more years, at the end of which he was trapped by an innkeeper named Darcy Fletcher, who drugged his beer in the hope of handing him over for reward. Nevison must have been difficult to drug, for he fought his way out of the inn and got away; and in shooting the innkeeper dead he committed the only known murder of his career. Soon afterwards he was captured, and again escaped from prison, to resume his life of crime for three more years. Once more it was at an inn that he was run to earth, this time asleep in bed. And this time he was hanged.

A few years later there was born the legend of William Kidd, the most celebrated of all the British pirates – and the scourge of Europe. It was the heyday of the "privateer", the armed seagoing vessel owned and officered by private individuals but acting under a commission ("letters of marque") from the state, which allowed the owners to keep the prizes they seized, and gave them £5 for every man of the enemy killed or captured. The skipper and crew of such a vessel were not called pirates or treated as such, though that is what they were. And in 1695 William Kidd, a respectable Scottish sea captain, was invited at the age of 50 to lead a privateering "expedition" financed by leading members of the British government who included the Lord Chancellor, the First Lord of the Admiralty and the Secretary of State. The king himself (William III) had rather wanted a share in what was going, but he was unable to raise the money. Kidd was to seize a number of pirates who were operating in the Red Sea, to the annoyance of the seafaring countries of Europe; but since England and France happened to be at war he could also take French prizes if they presented themselves. After many months of seemingly unrewarded cruising he captured two Armenian ships operating under licence from the French. The Armenian owners, virtuously denying any French connection, complained to the British government; and when Captain Kidd put in at New York harbour to recruit more men he found that, because of his failure as a dividend-earning privateersman, his own government had proclaimed him a pirate. While bargaining for his freedom he hid some of the plunder which could have shown him to be more successful than his traducers believed, and eventually he was tricked into going ashore. He then produced the French licences to show that the Armenian ships were legitimate prizes – and he was never to see those documents again. He was arrested and sent home in chains. At his trial for piracy two years later, the French licences had disappeared and the court decided that they did not exist. He was convicted and hanged on 23 May 1701. More than 200 years later the French licences were found in the Public Record Office in London by an American researcher, Ralph D. Paine. They proved beyond the smallest doubt that Captain Kidd was innocent of the charge on which he was put to death. But their rediscovery came too late to destroy the legend that Captain Kidd was Britain's most spectacular pirate, or to stem the flood of books about his homicidal career along the tortuous boundary between legitimate war and private crime.

At about the same time there flourished an English criminal who has long been regarded, even in other European countries, as the most skilful and impudent exponent of the art of selling stolen property back to its rightful owner. This was Jonathan Wild, who was hanged on 24 May 1725. He was born at Wolverhampton in 1682, went to London when he was 25, and soon qualified there for imprisonment as a debtor. In prison he met a prostitute named Mary Milliner, and on his discharge she introduced him to the eminent thieves with whom he was to establish a successful relationship as a receiver. So successful was this, indeed, that it brought him into contact with Mr Charles Hitchin, the City of London Marshal, a thoroughly corrupt official whose speciality was the combination of thief-catching, receiving and the resale of stolen property to its original losers. A Hitchin-Wild partnership actually lasted two years, and two years is a long time in a criminal partnership. When they quarrelled and Wild had set up on his own, he opened an office as a private detective, where robbers called at the back door to sell the property that was being reported as stolen at the front. In a few years he was organizing a small army of thieves and planning their expeditions. He allocated gangs to separate divisions of London and the surrounding countryside. If a thief disputed Wild's leadership he was denounced, convicted and hanged on evidence which Wild could always, with impunity, supply. On the other hand, if anyone threatened to expose him, Wild the thief-taker could bring against him a capital charge on fabricated evidence which, with the same result, was always believed.

Except in the demi-monde where his way of life was known, he was widely esteemed as a public benefactor. He announced himself in the newspapers as Thief-Taker General of Great Britain and Ireland, opened an office near the Old Bailey, set up a branch office under a manager and acquired a country residence with a butler and a footman. He rented a warehouse in Flushing and purchased a ship, in which he took stolen property from England to Holland and smuggled dutiable goods from Holland to England. He paid good money to men who worked well for him, and hanged at sea those who did not. In 1723, by which time he had been 10 years leader of the underworld, he petitioned the Lord Mayor of London to make him a Freeman of the City. The petition mentioned that he had sent over 60 criminals to the gallows. The Recorder of London, Sir William Thompson, who was a judge at the Old Bailey, knew quite a lot about Jonathan Wild and was able to advise the Lord Mayor on the merits of the petition. It did not succeed. A year later (1724) Wild was giving false evidence against one of his victims, a highwayman named Blueskin who had fallen foul of the Wild organization, when the enraged man leapt at him in court and cut his throat. In anticipation of his death Jonathan Swift the Irish satirist wrote an elegy called *Blueskin's Ballad*; but Wild recovered and Blueskin was hanged. The following year Wild was at last arrested and convicted for receiving and trading in stolen lace – and Sir William Thompson was the judge who tried him. When he was asked if he had anything to say before sentence of death was passed, he pleaded that his services to the country had sent 76 criminals to the gallows. But he became inexorably the 77th.

Dick Turpin (1705–39) is an English highwayman whose career is less attractive than the legends which have clustered around it, to say nothing of the cinematic exploits of his horse Black Bess. He is famed for a desperate "ride to York" which never took place. After apprenticeship to an Essex butcher he established a shop of his own which he stocked by stealing sheep. He then took to housebreaking with the ill-famed Essex gang; and his reputation as a courteous highwayman may not have begun at the time when he told a helpless widow, on her refusal to show him where her money was kept, "God damn your blood, you old bitch, if you won't tell us I'll set your arse on the grate." When she still refused, Turpin and his four merry men did indeed hold her on the fire until she spoke. A week later the same five men beat a farmer unconscious, emptied a kettle of boiling water over him, and then took it in turns to rape his serving maid. As a highwayman he operated from a cave in Epping Forest, and more than one forest keeper was murdered upon discovering its whereabouts. In 1738 he was arrested in York under the assumed name of John Palmer for armed poaching, and as he awaited trial in York Castle he was further accused of stealing horses and cattle. He sent a letter to his brother asking for intercession with the authorities; but the letter was unstamped and its recipient, failing to recognize his brother's handwriting, refused to pay the postage due. By coincidence the letter was seen by the village schoolmaster who knew Turpin's writing, and who promptly went to York to reveal that John Palmer was really Dick Turpin and to claim the £200 reward being offered for news of him. (This may well have been the famous "ride to York".) Before his execution, which was watched by a huge crowd on the Knavesmire at York on 7 April 1739, Turpin had hired five mourners for his funeral. Even if one resists the pseudo-historical nonsense about such characters adding to the gaiety of nations one can accept that, when they and all their victims are long dead, they can be seen to have slightly diminished the solemnity.

This, at all events, was the achievement of Count Cagliostro, father of all modern confidence tricksters, money-making quacks and religious cults charging enrolment fees. Giuseppe Balsamo, born into poverty at Palermo in Sicily in 1743, grew up into a world of charlatans and sorcerers who more than half-believed in their own quackery, defying the Voltairean age of reason itself. He took the title of Count Cagliostro by way of importing credibility into pretensions that should never have been credible under any name. He had fled from Sicily when a series of ingenious frauds was rightly traced to him; and he then travelled through Greece, Egypt, Arabia, Persia, Rhodes (where the Greek scientists taught him alchemy and other fertile superstitions) and Malta. And it was in Malta that, by way of securing presentation as a fellow alchemist to the Grand Master of the Malta Order, he appointed himself Count Cagliostro. Taking it from there, he obtained introductions to all the nobility of Rome and Naples, moving in 1771 to London, where he professed to be the founder of a new system of freemasonry. He was back in Paris in 1785, one of his besotted devotees and victims being Cardinal Archbishop de Rohan, whose story, no less than Cagliostro's, might well have inspired a whole series of 18th-century comic operas. It involved Cagliostro in "the affair of the queen's necklace", which landed him in the Bastille, to be released after six months and hounded out of France.

He went to England again, this time to meet with a hostile reception. Almost as the conventional criminal is said to return to the scene of his crime, he went back to Rome, the one city where his neo-freemasonry (or freemasonry of any kind) would surely get him into trouble. The Inquisition arrested him and he was condemned to death for heresy. The pope commuted this sentence to one of imprisonment for life, and Cagliostro died six years later (1795) in the Castle of San Leo, a papal fortress. As an all-round charlatan of consummate impudence he has never been surpassed. But public gullibility, which seems to have changed little, should ensure that he will always have hopeful imitators.

The Franco-British war that broke out in 1778 put an end to the 30-year smuggling career of John Carter and his seven brothers. This famous octet of rascals plied their trade between Cornwall and Roscoff in Brittany. John Carter was known as "the king of Prussia" for no better reason than that he acquired that nickname in childhood by playing soldiers and always casting himself as Frederick the Great. (The beach near Helston in south Cornwall where he and his brothers had played came to be called, and is still called, Prussia Cove; it is tucked under an overhanging cliff and hidden by an island from the open sea, a perfect base for maritime smugglers.) The Carter brothers were interested mainly in brandy and gin. And although of course they acquired, as the worst of rogues seem eventually to acquire, a reputation for generosity and charity, in their case its foundation may be quite easily seen: either they came to benefit from the public indulgence extended to smugglers as experts in what so many of us would do if we dared; or it was true. They fought a continuous war with French privateersmen as well as with British and French customs men. John Carter and his brother Henry were captured when they put in at St Malo one day for repairs. They were in the same French gaol for two years. Henry was captured again by the French during the Revolution and narrowly escaped the guillotine. But he lived to write his memoirs, *The Autobiography of a Cornish Smuggler*, in which John Carter is the leading figure.

In the early 19th century Eugène-François Vidocq (1775–1857) established new standards as a "reformed" thief turned detective, a poacher turned gamekeeper. During the Napoleonic era Vidocq's knowledge of the underworld, coupled with the underworld's knowledge of Vidocq, made it desirable that he should work more and more closely with the police. It is not too much to say that he became a great criminal investigator, equipped with criminal and prison experience (though no French prison had been able to hold him for long), with reckless courage, with great technical skill and with a unique mastery of disguise. In the end the Prefecture of Police allotted him his own detective squad, many of whom were ex-prisoners; and the success of this little group against the post-war crime wave, from 1811 until 1827 when he left it, could provide lessons for the police of the western world today. The Vidocq squad indeed became the first Paris Sûreté (now the Police Judiciaire). In 1832 Vidocq set up in business as the first of all the "private eyes", with a fraud squad and a number of counter-espionage cells. This gradually earned him the resentment of his one-time colleagues at the Prefecture, who eventually took him to court on a trumped-up charge of conspiracy. He won his acquittal, but the costs of the case temporarily ruined him. He then wrote a number of long novels, valuable today for the verisimilitude with which they portray the criminal scene of his time; and he did *not* write the famous and much-translated *Vidocq Memoirs*, which is the work of hacks and of which he profoundly disapproved. Inevitably he was "taken up" by a number of eminent writers, including Honoré de Balzac, who put him in the *Comédie humaine* as Vautrin. He died peacefully at the age of 82, by this time a true if belated son of the Church.

A contemporary of Vidocq's, and almost as popular as he with the literati of Europe, was Pierre-François Lacenaire (1800–36). Gautier called him "the Manfred of the gutter", Dostoevsky is said to have drawn upon him for the character of Raskolnikov in *Crime and Punishment*, and in modern times he has figured in the classic film *Les Enfants du paradis*. Lacenaire was a thief, forger and murderer; an educated man with a literary bent which found expression in poems and published essays about crime. Because in some of his published work he had attacked the policies and the character of King Louis Philippe he became popular for a time with the Opposition; but his crimes were not as spectacular as he himself seems to have thought them. His principal claim to our attention is that, when he was on trial for murder jointly with the illiterate accomplices over whom he had arrogantly ruled for years and who had now betrayed him, he virtually took over the prosecution by way of ensuring that, whatever happened to him, none of them should escape. None of them did: they all preceded him to the guillotine. His swaggering career is epitomized in the remark he made when, arrested at last in the provinces, he learned that he was to be tried in Paris. "It would be most disagreeable", he said, "to be guillotined by a provincial executioner."

But the aristocrat among crooks is seldom that falsely glamorized figure, the highborn rogue. More likely, he is a man of lowly birth whose crimes are made interesting by the sort of ingenuity that so many of us like to think of as low cunning. Such a man was Charles Peace (1832–79), a highly skilful "cat burglar" who was born in Sheffield and started his adult life as a mill hand. In those days the nearest approach to a cat burglar was what had been known as a "portico thief", but the agility of Charles Peace took him above portico level. Although he was permanently lame, he shinned up rainpipes by means of specially adhesive pads on the inside of his trouser legs; and he climbed up to third-floor window-sills by means of a hooked folding ladder made of pivoted wood slats just thick enough to afford toehold (the complete gadget, folded, fitted exactly into an attaché case, and you can still see it in the Black Museum at New Scotland Yard). He could so distort his monkeylike features for long periods as to be completely unrecognizable. He had fitted a false left forearm with a hook on it, to compensate for a useless hand maimed in an early accident. He committed a number of murders, usually when cornered and evading arrest, and at least one innocent man was sentenced for a murder committed by Peace in another name. (He confessed to this just before his execution on 25 February 1879.) He has been romantically described as a brilliant violinist, but in fact he was a fairly reliable "scraper" to whom a period of street fiddling provided a useful interlude for watching the houses he proposed to rob, and just good enough for the occasional job in a theatre orchestra which could be turned into an alibi.

Almost every country has its "Jack the Ripper", a multiple murderer who strikes terror throughout a town, a state, a canton, an entire country. The identity of England's Jack the Ripper (1888), unlike that of the Boston Strangler (1963/4) or New York's "Son of Sam" (1977), was never established. He probably killed five or six women, all of whom were prostitutes and drunkards, all within a square mile on the eastern boundaries of the City of London, and all of them at night. The victims' bodies were mutilated in a manner that was accepted as showing expert anatomical knowledge and experience of surgery. The Ripper's success in eluding capture, and the public anger resulting from it, led to the resignation of the London Commissioner of Police (Sir Charles Warren) and to the formation of numerous vigilante committees to provide the protection which the police were "unable to supply". An anonymous writer sent semi-literate letters, allegedly written in the victims' blood, to the police and to news agencies, sometimes giving accurate warning as to the date and place of the next killing. Inevitably a number of fantastic theories concerning the Ripper's identity have formed the subject of mutually contradictory books; but the most likely man still seems to be the Russian émigré Vassily Konovalov, known to the police in London as Mikhael Ostrog, a barber-surgeon who had worked at a clinic in Camberwell, south London.

Germany, a little later, had an identified mass murderer in Peter Kurten (1833–1931), "the Düsseldorf Vampire". He was one of 13 children born in Cologne-Mülheim to a man who committed drunken assaults on wife and family and who in 1897 went to prison for incest. From the age of 14 Peter Kurten was committing sexual assaults on young girls, and after a term of imprisonment he went to live with a woman who had a 16-year-old daughter. This woman was a sexual deviant, who got him into prison on a false charge of having threatened her with the violence she had unsuccessfully invited him to commit. He was 17 when he came out, to live on burglaries and thefts which earned him further imprisonments. He began to satisfy his sexual appetites by setting fire to buildings and watching them burn. His first murder victim was an eight-year-old girl, and of that charge he was unaccountably acquitted. He married in 1923 at the age of 40, but continued his attacks on women and girls, none of them fatal until February 1929, when he stabbed to death a nine-year-old Düsseldorf child and burnt her body in a churchyard with the aid of paraffin. When he was finally arrested he had committed nine murders and attempted another seven. He was executed on 2 July 1931 at Klingeplütz Prison, Cologne. It is difficult to believe that in modern Germany, free from the political obsessions and excitements of Kurten's time, and equipped with some of the best scientific methods of criminal investigation in the world, Kurten would evade capture for a month after his first murder;

instead of being put to death, he would then be studied as a valuable source of psychiatric information.

Contemporary with Kurten in Germany was the French Henri Landru (1869–1922), of whom the French police maintained – almost, it seemed elsewhere, as a matter of national prestige – that he had murdered 300 women. He was a confidence trickster and swindler, who satisfied his sexual needs by advertising for women friends "with a view to matrimony", gaining control of their money and then killing them. He burnt their bodies in his domestic stove at the Villa Ermitage in Gambais, a village whose population must have been strangely incurious about the kind and the quantity of smoke issuing from each other's chimneys. All that the police found, when they took up the Landru floorboards and dug up his garden, were the bodies of two pet dogs which had belonged to one of the murdered women. And there was nothing wrong, he pointed out, in giving them a proper burial. More difficult to explain was the presence of women's clothing and property (all subsequently claimed by relatives), and his anthropometric identity with a much-wanted criminal under many aliases. Landru protested his innocence to the last. And Mr Charles Chaplin, fully entered now upon what may be called his ham-sociological period, made a thoroughly distasteful film about him under the title *Monsieur Verdoux*.

While all this was going on, Sweden captured the headlines with the crimes of Ivar Kreuger (1880–1932), the "Match King". Having made a large fortune in America as a constructional engineer, of which it can only be said that legitimate fortunes are thus to be made, he went home to Sweden and established the firm of Kreuger and Toll, ferroconcrete construction specialists. Kreuger's father was a match manufacturer, and when he died, the son reconstructed the business as the Swedish Match Company. He then set out to capture the entire match-making industry of Europe, buying up foreign match monopolies in eight different countries at a cost of £100 million in ten years. He appears not to have foreseen the economic blizzard of the late 1920s: the entire Kreuger empire was faced with ruin, and he resorted to gigantic forgeries of which the counterfeiting of Italian bonds worth £28 million was typical. However vast the sums of money he was losing or winning, they were by this time mere figures to him, divorced from reality. Finally in 1932 a frightened Kreuger board meeting assembled in Paris to discuss the future of the group and especially of Kreuger himself. The latter issue, it was learnt, had been settled the night before. Kreuger had shot himself in his Paris hotel. And at that time the forgeries had not even been discovered.

Russia's main contribution to modern European crime was the career of Alexandre Serge Stavisky (1888–1933), a Ukrainian jeweller who changed course, another product of the depression and the currency chaos between the wars. In Paris, having charmed the necessary money out of a rich woman, he ran a profitable night club frequented by theatrical and society celebrities. At the same time he became involved in drug, gambling and prostitution rackets. Over a long criminal period he bought his immunity from prosecution by spectacular bribery among police and magistrates; and came finally to grief over a £2 million swindle on the French national pawnbroking system. Like Kreuger, he shot himself before he could be arrested (though there has always been a rumour, firmly credited in France, that Police Inspector Charpentier, who had gone to Chamonix to arrest him, killed him on orders from those in high places who feared the revelations that would have come out at Stavisky's trial). He ruined countless small investors, damaged – perhaps irremediably – the confidence of the French in their police and courts, caused rioting in the streets of Paris and brought down the government of Edouard Daladier.

Less unattractive than any of the foregoing was Han van Meegeren (1889–1947), a Dutch artist who first used his outstanding skill to deceive and expose the critics he had come to despise, and then decided that, instead of exposing them, he would continue as a commercial enterprise the art forgeries that were making him rich. In 1916 he had held a highly successful one-man exhibition at Delft and seemed launched on a career. Then the critics dropped him and, determined to prove that he was a great painter, in 1932 he decided to fake a painting in the style of Vermeer – knowing by this time that the critics would certainly be deceived. He worked five years on a picture he called *Christ at Emmaus*. He told everyone that he had acquired the painting when an old French family secretly sold some heirlooms. Experts pronounced it a genuine Vermeer, and the Boymans Museum in Rotterdam bought it for £58,000. Van Meegeren then painted forgeries to which he gave the names *The Last Supper*, *Christ and the Adulteress*, *The Washing of Christ's Feet*, and *Isaac Blessing Jacob*. *Christ and the Adulteress* was bought by none other than Hermann Goering, the Nazi field marshal, for £165,000; and in all, the paintings earned van Meegeren £750,000. After the war, when Goering's property was being examined for loot from the occupied countries, the discovery of the van Meegeren picture led to his being accused of collaborating with the enemy during the German occupation of Holland. The only way to refute that charge was to reveal the truth about the faked "masters". While he was in prison awaiting trial he was asked to paint "a Vermeer", and produced one he called *Jesus in the Temple*, which the critics hailed as a masterpiece. And although a committee of distinguished critics had watched him paint it, they were disbelieved by equally distinguished ones who declared it a genuine Vermeer. But van Meegeren died before completing a 12-month prison sentence; still rather a hero with the masses, who had enjoyed seeing the critics fooled and their own scepticism vindicated, he was nevertheless survived by art criticism itself, an imperishable industry.

I conclude with an English example, the so-called Great Train Robbery of 1963, because it is likely to be the supreme example in this century of the process by which a gang of armed robbers can be transformed by cliché-ridden publicity into something like national – or even European – heroes. This process was possible partly because the victim of their crime was not a frail white-haired widow or last year's Miss Universe, but a number of banks deprived of used bank-notes to the value of £2,500,000. If you rob or defraud a very large and impersonal victim, and you display daring, courage or ingenuity in the process, the public of almost any country will push aside its moral teaching when it comes to judge what you have done.

Seventeen men and three women took part in the crime. The principals were William Boal, aged 50, a small-time manufacturer of precision instruments; Charles Wilson, aged 31, a bookmaker; Thomas Wisbey, aged 34, owner of a betting shop; James Hussey, aged 31, a painter and decorator; Leonard Field, aged 31, a florist; Douglas Goody, aged 34, a hairdresser; John Wheater, aged 42, a lawyer; Brian Field, aged 29, a solicitor's clerk (Wheater was his employer); Robert Welch, aged 35, a club proprietor; Roy James, aged 28, a silversmith; Ronald Biggs, aged 34, a carpenter; Ronald Edwards, a club owner; James White, an unemployed ex-paratrooper; and Bruce Reynolds, aged 32, the acknowledged leader of the gang. The last three evaded capture for some years, but were finally brought to trial and sentenced. Ronald Biggs, who escaped from prison in 1969, was still at large at the time this chapter was being written. What astonished the British public, at a time when the efficacy of long prison sentences was coming seriously into question, was that seven of the men were sent to prison for 30 years and three of them for 24 years. Since they would have been much less severely punished on conviction for murder, this was widely regarded as a reversion to the early Roman, Gothic and Anglo-Saxon principle under which murder was a matter for private redress between families while theft was officially visited with ferocious punishment. More probably it was a decision to promote the needs of "deterrent" sentencing above those of individual deserts and of "tariff" comparisons.

The robbers, whose strategy and planning have been extravagantly praised, had studied the assembling, loading, scheduling and manning of the night mail train from Glasgow to London, which sometimes carried bank-notes on their way from the Bank of Scotland to its various branches in the south of England. On the night of 8 August 1963 it was carrying 128 mail bags containing £5 and £1 notes to the value of £2,500,000. At Leighton Buzzard, Bedfordshire (half an hour from London), there is a "distant" signal, which in emergencies shows an amber light requiring the driver to be ready for a stop at Sears Crossing, three quarters of a mile further on. The Glasgow mail train was stopped here, and the driver saw no apparent reason. At his suggestion the fireman jumped down to use the signal-box telephone and find out. Its wires were cut. He was then overpowered by two men, who threatened to kill him if he shouted. They took him back to the train, where he found that the driver had been struck on the head and was bleeding profusely, and that the cab was full of men in boiler suits with Balaclava helmets masking their faces. The postal workers on the train were then overpowered and made to lie on the floor of the mail coach, while all but eight of the mail bags were loaded on to a van. The gang then left for Leatherslade Farm, a hide-out previously rented for the occasion. Patient police inquiry, prolonged but perfectly straightforward – and greatly aided by the incredible stupidity of the robbers in the leaving of fingerprints and other clues – led to a series of arrests and (not always connected) discoveries of stolen bank-notes, sometimes in hidden or abandoned lots of £100,000 or more at a time. More than £2,000,000 has never been recovered, and the "Great Train Robbers" are now, at their appropriate intervals, coming out of prison on parole. The stringency of supervision on parole can vary greatly, but stringency seldom has the incentive supplied by official curiosity as to the whereabouts of a stolen fortune of £2,000,000. Even when these men have completed the many years of supervised parole that lie before them, their lives – and their "life-style" – will be conspicuous in a way that the average man's is not; and the money may elude them for ever, or until it becomes obsolete through currency changes and is no longer legal tender.

Behind all these stories of infamy and treachery and contempt for the rights and lives of others, there stands an assembly of human beings who, however execrable, have contributed their share to the story of Europe. The non-criminal areas of their lives are not known because they are not interesting: they were too busy becoming interesting as predators and parasites and outcasts. They were nonconformists; and the laws to which they would not conform, in parts of Europe otherwise at variance, are now becoming in effect European laws, enforced by systems of policing and jurisprudence growing constantly closer in pattern. The continuing existence of such offenders, their steady emergence through the generations, has sustained a huge and ever more expensive apparatus whose purpose is to punish those whom it cannot deter, and to "rehabilitate" those whom it has punished. A decade ago it was the belief of European lawyers and criminologists that "treatment" of various experimental kinds should now take the place of punishment, which was doing no good. Punishment has been condemned by many of Europe's philosophers from Seneca to Jeremy Bentham. "Crime will never go unpunished," wrote Seneca, "since the punishment of crime lies in the crime itself." And "All punishment is mischief", said Bentham; "all punishment in itself is evil."

But in the past ten years the principle of "retribution" has suddenly become respectable again, retribution in the sense of a re-tribute, a paying-back by the offender, both to society and (where appropriate) to his victim. Among the general public this may well be a simple reaction to the widespread increase in recorded crime. Among scholars it is more likely to reflect a turning-away from utilitarianism and the growth of an intellectual respect for the "natural rights" of victims. What no one seems to foresee, whatever new systems may be evolved, is any significant reduction in the supply of rogues and villains. They seem likely to be always with us.

# 21

# Travellers and Explorers

## CHARLES VERLINDEN

The great discoveries, contrary to the all too common misconception, do not start with Columbus and the discovery of America. Far earlier, at the height of the Middle Ages, the inhabitants of Europe were anxious to know what allies they might hope to find, or enemies they might have to fear, in Asia and Africa: what wealth they might be able to gain or products they might ultimately sell there. As Christians, they were always on the lookout during their travels for allies against Islam. The disciples of Muhammad, whose homeland was the desert sand of Arabia, not yet a source of oil, had burst like an irresistible flood upon the Christian world of western Asia and the Mediterranean seaboard of Africa. The tomb of Christ in Jerusalem fell into the hands of the caliphs, successors of the Prophet, a bare few decades after the latter's death in 632 AD. The threat to the Byzantine Empire reached the foot of the walls of its capital, Constantinople, and thereafter the advance swept along the whole length of the coast of North Africa, from Egypt to Morocco. Even the sea did not halt the Muslim advance, though the only ship they had previously known was the ship of the desert, the camel, both transport for, and indeed to some extent instrument of, their first victories. Islam was on the crest of the wave: she occupied Crete and Sicily and crossed the Strait of Gibraltar. By 711 AD Spain was a Muslim country. Then the tide swept over the Pyrenees and was only halted at Poitiers in central France when it encountered, and ebbed before, a barrier of heavily armed horsemen stationed there by the Frankish mayor of the palace, Charles Martel.

Europe, having given up all hope, had not the strength to launch a counter attack; none was destined to come until the Crusades to recover Jerusalem. She turned instead to dreams of the mysterious Prester John, monarch and religious leader, who was believed to be able to help her in her struggle against Islam. Prester John's kingdom was as mythical as its ruler. Originally it was placed in east Asia, which was completely unknown, and then further west in the same continent. Eventually Prester John was identified with the Negus or sovereign of Abyssinia in the Horn of Africa. It took two centuries for the gradual movement of this fabled kingdom from east to west to win full acceptance in the contemporary European mind. Nothing, of course, came of the anti-Islamic alliance for which kings and popes alike hoped, though many journeys were undertaken in the search for the undiscoverable.

For a period the Tartars, nomadic tribes who had left eastern Asia and who were moving inexorably westward, were believed to be destined as the allies sent by providence. Pope Innocent IV commissioned the Franciscan Giovanni di Piano Carpino to make his way to Mongolia to meet the Great Khan there. He was received by him in 1245 AD at Sira near Karakorum, traditionally the seat of the great Tartar chiefs; but he secured nothing except a summons to the pope and the Christian princes to acknowledge the "Supreme Ruler of the human race", namely the Great Khan, Kujuk. We have the account of the Franciscan's journey, which contains the first detailed and, on the whole, fairly accurate description of central Asia.

Louis IX of France, the "Saint Louis" of the last Crusades, dispatched the Flemish monk Guillaume de Rubroek to the same area. His account also has survived. On leaving the Crimea he soon met the first Tartars, an experience which he describes as giving him the impression of living in a different century. The truth is that this hard-headed Fleming had a keener sense of being in a foreign country than Giovanni di Piano Carpino. He was also a more accurate observer, for he understood that the Volga ran into the landlocked Caspian, whereas the papal envoy's account merely contained a mass of errors on the subject. At Karakorum Guillaume found a considerable number of Frenchmen and Germans. They had originally been brought there, as prisoners, by the Mongols; but they had stayed and become prosperous either through trade or by acting as what would nowadays be called technical advisers. Nevertheless, the Mongols, who had conquered half the then known world, regarded the countries of the west as the underdeveloped; and they had promised themselves sooner or later to sally forth to subdue them, as they had already subjugated so many other nations from the Pacific to the Black Sea.

The greatest Asian explorer and traveller of the age was Marco Polo, a native of Venice. In him we have passed the era of the cleric, half-missionary and half-diplomat, and are dealing with a merchant. He was 17 when he set out with his father and uncle, who both had first-hand knowledge of Mongolian Asia. His account of his travels was a huge success and exercised great influence, particularly on Columbus, who was fired with the desire to make the same journey by sea and rediscover those wonderful countries which the Venetian had described so admirably. For Marco Polo had not, like his precursors, been only in Mongolia but he had stayed and travelled for 26 years in China and the Indies and had spent 17 years in the service of the Emperor Kublai Khan, on whose behalf he had executed various commissions. On his homeward journey he had made an enormous round voyage all along the coasts of the China Sea and the Indian Ocean, returning to Venice by way of the Persian Gulf, Iran, Asia Minor, the Black Sea and the Mediterranean. He was the man who made Europe aware of the Orient and its riches. His account, *The Book of Marvels*, is for the most part remarkably accurate; but he was so dazzled by the wealth of the Khan and his capital, Cambaluc or Peking, that wherever he looked he saw gold and untold wealth, so much so that his fellow Venetians dubbed him "Ser Marco Millioni". These were the gold and the millions which Columbus and the other explorers of the age of the great discoveries were ambitious to rediscover by sailing westwards.

Columbus, the son of a Genoese craftsman, had made his way to Portugal and subsequently to Spain as a business intermediary, but his real interests lay in geography and cosmography. He was widely read and perfectly prepared, either himself or through others, to cross-question the most distinguished scholars of his day; and this was how, in Lisbon, he managed to get from the Florentine doctor and humanist Paolo Toscanelli the information which was to set the pattern for the remainder of his life. Toscanelli was keenly interested in the dimensions of the earth and more especially in the distance between the east coast of Asia and the western coasts of Europe. Unlike most scholars he attached great weight to the evidence of Marco Polo, who had given such a good description of Cathay (China) and Cipangu (Japan), even though he had never seen the latter. Indeed, he thought more highly of him than of even Ptolemy, the Alexandrian geographer, who was generally regarded as the ultimate authority by the learned world. When he was consulted by Columbus, he replied that it would be both easier and shorter to reach China, Japan and the Indies by sailing west rather than by following the African coastline, as the Portuguese had done hitherto without yet knowing whether one day they might reach Asia. Toscanelli, using the longitudes of Marco Polo in preference to those of Ptolemy, calculated the position of the east coast of Asia as 30 degrees further east than the Alexandrian scholar had done. Japan, on this assumption, would be found to be about 1,500 miles away in the ocean, the total distance between the Iberian coast and China would be roughly 5,000 nautical miles and the non-existent island of Antillia would form a convenient stopping-point on the journey. Columbus himself regarded these estimates, actually far too low, as still much too high, and thought that the distance from the Canary Islands, which had long been known, and Japan was no more than 2,400 miles. In fact this figure represents the distance between the Canaries and the Virgin Islands archipelago in the Caribbean – i.e. in

America, of whose existence Columbus had of course no idea. It was a mistake of incalculable consequences, for it changed the face of the world.

Columbus's four voyages, and especially the first, were the most remarkable feats of exploration in recorded history, combining mistakes and good luck, two invariable elements in every such successful enterprise, to an astonishing degree. His plan was simple: first he would sail to the Canaries, following a course well known for at least 150 years, where he would, according to the conventional geography of his day, be on the same latitude as Japan, the Cipangu about which he had ceaselessly dreamed in consequence of Marco Polo's exploits. From there he would sail before the east winds . . .

On leaving Gomera, one of the western Canary Islands, he set sail in search of the unknown at 3 a.m. on 8 September 1492; according to his log he found an easterly wind and by the evening of the 9th he was out of sight of land.

From this moment onwards life for the crew settled into a routine of watches and spells of look-out duty. During the voyage Columbus took his bearings with a quadrant, which was simply a quarter-circle of wood. The navigator looked along one of its straight sides beside which two sighting holes enabled him to get a steady view of the star which he was using as his guiding mark, while a plumb line hanging from the apex of the quadrant marked the latitude on the 90° arc. That was all the navigator had; moreover on a moving ship the plumb line was bound to be very unreliable. The methods of determining longitude were even worse, and remained so long after Columbus's day: they were only remedied by the invention of the chronometer in the 18th century. At the date of Columbus's discovery of America, the only way of calculating longitude on board ship was to read the compass, estimate the distance covered in a given time as measured by an hour-glass and plot the resulting point on the map. The differences between magnetic and geographical north clearly affected the resulting answer but, luckily for Columbus, his voyages were carried out in areas of slight or no variation. Magnetic deviation was negligible since his ships, besides being very small, were wooden and had little metal on board. The calculation of longitude depended on knowing precisely the ship's speed, but the log and its knots were not invented until the 16th century, and in Columbus's time the speed had to be estimated by ocular observation.

Columbus plotted his position every day at dawn, which was not especially difficult since he was travelling steadily in the same direction, though it was a very different story on his homeward journey, for bad weather forced him to change course repeatedly, with the result that he made his landfall in Portugal and not in Spain, which had been his objective. This illustrates the unpredictable hazards of navigation by dead reckoning. But Columbus was one of the few men who knew how to reduce these unknown factors to a minimum. Keenly alive to all the signs that a sailor can read in sky and sea, he was a man of unceasing watchfulness, great physical endurance and incomparable determination.

Throughout Columbus's first voyage navigation presented no problems. The luck, which makes great successes possible, was on his side. He encountered neither gales nor dead calm, but only a few gusts of wind of varying strength. The blue sea sparkled in the sunshine, the majestic clouds of the trade winds sailed high overhead, while the canvas billowed in the mild air. On 16 September Columbus recorded that the morning felt delightfully fresh, like April in Andalusia: only the nightingale's song was missing. The same day they entered the Sargasso Sea, thick with floating seaweed. On the 21st and 22nd they felt they were sailing in a vast greenish-yellow field; but familiarity dispelled their sense of anxiety. There followed a spell of light winds; but in the first week of October the ship was travelling considerably faster and making about 140 miles a day. At the time the course was more southwesterly, owing partly to compass variation, but it was nevertheless a stroke of luck, for otherwise America would not have been reached as early as 12 October. On the 7th they sighted great flocks of birds which at that time of year migrate from North America to the Bermudas, and Columbus, one eye always on the sky, decided to follow them. It was a crucial decision for otherwise the tiny convoy of three caravels would have been swept on to the Florida coast by the Gulf Stream and pounded to pieces there. Even if it had escaped the violent whirlpools, the currents would have driven the ships parallel with the coastline of the United States whence, with luck, they might have made the passage back to Europe, sometimes drifting and sometimes sailing, having perhaps had occasional glimpses of the coastline but without making any discovery. It was the flocks of birds that lifted the curtain which hid the New World from Europe.

On 11 October there was a strong wind and the ships were moving fast. Evidence of land – a green branch with a small pink flower, a plank, a little worked stick – was accumulating. Human beings could not be far away. That night clear moonlight illuminated everything on the ships' course, yet everyone was keyed up for fear of reefs. At 2 a.m. Juan Rodriguez Bermejo, traditionally known as Rodrigo de Triana, who was look-out on the forecastle of the *Pinta*, saw a sandy beach glistening on the western horizon and shouted "land ahead, land ahead!" America was six miles away.

It is not my intention to say more about the European explorers and their discoveries. Columbus can stand as an example and pattern for all who have followed in his footsteps, from Magellan who was the first to circumnavigate the globe to Cook who, in Australia and New Zealand, revealed to Europe a world destined to develop as a distant reflection of Europe or a new America, and to the later explorers of the North and South Poles in the 19th and 20th centuries. To make this possible we must attempt some mental analysis of the man with whom the modern world began, and we must seek to discover the characteristics and reasons which give Columbus the right to be called a man of genius.

From an early age he showed a remarkable capacity not merely for adaptation but for a fundamental change in his personality. Starting as a craftsman and small trader like his father, he became a sailor and gained a grasp of large-scale business without using his own capital to engage in it: indeed, he did not possess any. Then he taught himself geography and actually became a cartographer. He passed through all these different phases with a distinguished ease of manner which caught the attention of those who were, by birth, his social and cultural superiors, while he steadily narrowed the gap between himself and them. Nor did his acquisition of new capacities lead to any loss of the abilities and knowledge which he already possessed. As soon as he took up navigation he very rapidly became expert not merely in commanding a ship but, long before the end of his career as Admiral of the Ocean, an entire fleet. He was a man of constantly widening comprehension and he had no difficulty in adapting his behaviour in society with the same degree of natural grace. All this may not amount to genius, but it does bespeak a nature of exceptional endowments, always alert and underpinned by a strong and ambitious willpower; and this is the principal characteristic to be found in all the explorers and discoverers who have widened European man's knowledge of the world.

Where Columbus did display his genius was in the special fields of discovery and navigation, a quality discernible also in varying degrees among his main followers in the field. It lay primarily in his ability to conceive his tremendous enterprise, though it sprang from no precise or scientifically corroborated ideas – rather, indeed, the contrary. Nor did this quality resemble the genius of the scholar in search of abstract truth. Within the realm of ideas, it was an expression of the unshakeable strength of his conviction derived from applying all the information at his command, whatever in other respects its objective value. It was the power and not the precision of his thinking which was so exceptional.

In the realm of pure navigation Columbus's sensitivity to all the natural phenomena which can serve to help the sailor was astonishing, and here too his ability for deduction and his resourcefulness were extraordinary. He was beyond question one of the greatest navigators by dead reckoning who ever lived and, from that point of view, we see him as the perfect craftsman in a still unperfected craft which he gradually brought to perfection in more than one respect, a characteristic which he shared with all the great European explorers by sea or land.

His moral and physical courage were indescribable; but they were not aspects of genius in the personal and intellectual sense, but of sheer willpower. Over and over again Columbus gave countless instances of an unrivalled determination no less during the extremely taxing years which led up to his departure than during his four actual voyages. This is yet another characteristic which can be observed in those who followed him and it explains the success which crowned the efforts of the European explorers.

Nor should we overlook a typical feature which is to be found at a lower pitch among the entire population of Europe: namely, their unique determination and wish to travel. Chinese or Hindus, African Bantu or American Indians have travelled incomparably less than Europeans or, since the beginning of the 20th century, than the Americans. But these last are after all only Europeans who have left their homeland and for whom the Atlantic crossing was simply a continuation of the great westward migration.

All the various nations which were formed in Europe after the age of the migrations numbered among them travellers, whether single or in groups. Among the Greeks, who created more than one of the traditional foundations and dominating ideas of western civilization, Jason and his fellow Argonauts went in search of the Golden Fleece on the shores of the Black Sea. Only after wandering over the whole of the Mediterranean did Ulysses return to the island of Ithaca, his native land, and his faithful wife Penelope. Ever since, a long and circuitous voyage or *periplous* has been known as an Odyssey, after the epic poem written by Homer and dedicated to the hero to commemorate the adventurous traveller of unfailing guile, which delivered him from the cave of Polyphemus or Circe's den where men were turned by magic into pigs: at once a simple and brutal proof that, ever since, travellers have been prone to yield to obvious temptations. Homer implies that Ulysses too succumbed, but that his cunning saved him. Moreover, his adventures were an incessant temptation to him. Did he not keep his ears open to hear the Sirens' song while ordering his crew to block theirs with wax? But once again he kept his head, and had himself bound tightly to the mast.

Countless other Greeks followed in Ulysses' wake over the Mediterranean, bearing with them the message of Greece from Athens or Corinth to Marseilles, itself a Greek foundation like Syracuse, Odessa, Cyrene and Cadiz. Others again made their way past the Pillars of Hercules, later known by its Arab name of "the Mountain of Tarik", and finally as Gibraltar. Pytheas, a Massiliot Greek, travelled as far as the Cassiterides, perhaps the modern Isles of Scilly where Cornish tin was exchanged, and up to the Baltic, with its wealth of amber. He was in fact an explorer much concerned with promoting commerce and industry for, despite Plato and Aristotle, the Greeks were also merchants keenly interested not merely in the resources which offered them the certain prospect of profit but in their relations with the distant countries from which they came. It was a Greek who first observed the monsoon on his passage to India, with which there was constant Greek intercourse after Alexander had widened the bounds of their world as far as the River Indus and given his name to Alexandria, the great Egyptian capital and starting-point of the Greek merchants and seafarers who set their course for the Malabar coast; though it was not a Greek but a Carthaginian, Hanno, who can reasonably be regarded as the first man to sail right around Africa.

Rome, the capital of the Empire and soon to be that of the Church, has always exercised a magnetic charm. In antiquity men travelled there from the furthest extremities of Gaul or Asia Minor to carve out careers in politics, the armed forces, administration or business. From being the pagan capital of an empire which stretched from the Euphrates to the Atlantic and from the Rhine and Danube to the Sahara, Rome became the focal point of a religion which aimed at universality and the seat of a pope who proclaimed himself Vicar of Christ. From the Middle Ages onwards the city was called eternal, as much for its antiquity as because thenceforward it opened the gates of eternity to those who came to pay their homage to the saints and to the representative of God on earth. Every 25 years the jubilee was celebrated, which attracted even more pilgrims than usual. So dense were the crowds that epidemics broke out, but all believers, whose faith increased in proportion to their wretchedness, hoped for indulgences which could be expected to deliver them from the torments of hell. They sought first to obtain them by self-imposed deprivation and mortification. They rubbed their knees raw on the steps of the "Scala Santa" near St John Lateran, they scourged themselves, they wore coarse habits over their bruised flesh.

But Italy was not the only country in which pilgrimages were the earliest form of large-scale tourism. The same phenomenon occurred in Spain. Long before the summer influx from almost every country in Europe and from a good many further afield had started to make, in their hundreds of thousands or even millions, for the miles of concrete which line the Costa Brava or the Costa del Sol, a far smaller number of pilgrims, the staff of St James bearing the emblem of the cockle-shell in hand, were making their pious way to worship at the saint's tomb at Santiago de Compostela in Galicia. A road known to archaeologists as the *Camino Francés*, or "French Road", and marked by fine Romanesque churches, several of which have been admirably restored in the last few years, led from the French Pyrenees across northern Spain to Compostela. It is an interesting fact that close on the heels of the pilgrims came the merchants, and that markets owing their existence to this international traffic sprang up all along the "French Road". In the heyday of Spanish political power in the 16th and 17th centuries, these markets were also important centres of banking, and capital wealth, as it travelled on the ancient *Camino Francés*, took priority over piety and repentance. If the *fondas*, frequently more picturesque than sophisticated, were still patronized by the pilgrims, they would find businessmen also mingling there with *picaros*, who had every intention of taking the first opportunity of robbing both impartially.

Fairs generally developed simply from trading but they acted as a magnet for a variegated clientele of merchants and rogues. This was certainly true of those held in Troyes, Provins, Lagny and Bar-sur-Aube in the districts of Champagne and Brie, where the merchants of a wide range of commodities, though mainly textiles, from northern France and Flanders met their Italian counterparts travelling north after crossing the Alpine passes. Such fairs were the pattern for many others which sprang up in England, Germany, Switzerland, Italy and Spain. They began, grew bigger and embraced the very areas in which city life and its consequent industry and long-distance trade developed, and gradually established themselves in central and eastern Europe, even as far away as Novgorod in Russia. Groups of merchants, known in certain countries as *hanses*, combined to travel together to the fairs and trade there, since the roads were unsafe and travellers on them had to be able to protect themselves, not merely against the brigands who infested the main highways but also the robber-knights who exacted ransom from any passer-by they happened to meet. But the kings and great princes were fully aware that it was not the knights, be they brigands or soldiers, but the merchants who held the sinews of war, and consequently they extended their protection to the fairs and made great efforts there to establish "the king's peace" – or indeed the peace of any duke or other prince who exercised sufficient power to give any would-be aggressor second thoughts.

The Jews were the first itinerant merchants to travel widely in Europe: indeed it would be true to say that this was how they became Europeans. After their expulsion from Palestine by the Muslims they turned to selling goods, which they brought from areas where they were plentiful, to places where they were scarce, and in the process they covered enormous distances. Our knowledge of this derives from the great quantity of surviving Arab travel literature. This was how the "Rhadanite" Jews, starting from the Slavonic countries east of the Elbe, travelled right across France along the valleys of the Moselle, Meuse, Saône and Rhône as far as the Mediterranean coast. From there they made their way to Spain, which was still a Muslim country and thence, by sea and land, to Egypt and so to the shores of the Red Sea. Some Jews went to India and others actually reached China. Unquestionably the travels of similar bands of Jewish merchants were a contributory factor to the origin in Christian Europe of the legend of Ahasuerus, the wandering Jew who could find no resting place since his ancestors had delivered Jesus to the might of Rome and so condemned him to suffer on the Cross. But the Rhadanites and the rest of the Jewish merchants whose caravans quartered Europe were far from being wandering Jews. Their routes were extremely well chosen and at one time they were almost the only reliable commercial link between Europe and the Muslim worlds of Asia and Africa, re-enacting the role which the Byzantine capital Constantinople, as the Roman Empire's successor, had claimed to continue or even replace.

The large-scale international business conducted personally by the Jewish merchants throughout Europe had come to an end shortly before the Crusades had degenerated into little more than a cause of pogroms and persecution. The commercial relations with the Muslim world which the merchants had secured simultaneously became much harder to maintain, while Byzantium herself began to decline. The great itinerant Jewish merchants became pawnbrokers, which all too often led to their suffering not merely hatred but actual physical violence.

Henceforth the economic role which they had played was assumed by Christians who, like them, travelled in groups of merchants which, as I have already said, were frequently known as *hanses*. They, like their predecessors, would travel to the fairs; but, unlike them, when their members had acquired enough capital, they preferred to give up travel and live a quiet life in the towns, where they formed the ruling class, leaving it to their employees to travel with goods for sale, to set themselves up as agents in some foreign country or move on constantly from one trading centre to the next. Business trips, so common a feature of the 20th century, had in fact begun, though this did not prevent the wealthy merchants, who had become men of property and bankers, from continuing to form partnerships, the best-known being the Teutonic *hanse* or league whose membership included the aristocracy of many towns in Germany and some neighbouring countries. Their members were for many years the dominant power in seaborne trade from the Baltic to the Bay of Biscay. Their branches in London, Bergen, Novgorod and Bruges were kept regularly in touch with each other, not merely by normal sea traffic but also by the constant changes of post of the league's agents and officials. Establishments like the Steelyard in London or the Deutsche Brücke in Bergen occupied whole areas of cities, where the houses were used indiscriminately as inns, warehouses, offices and banks. There were moreover comparable trading districts in other large business centres. Thus in Venice the German traders were concentrated in the Fondaco dei Tedeschi – a name which shows that in Italy they were based on the pattern of the *fondouks* or merchants' bazaars of Muslim countries – occupied by both employees of the group and itinerant foreign business representatives; and the same was true of the great depots kept for the sole use of defined groups of merchants, such as the English Merchant Venturers at Calais, or of specific wares, such as those for wool or woollen goods, which frequently moved from one area to another in response to economic or political changes. Travellers on their journeys wove a network of links whose density could not fail to grow proportionately with the general rise of living standards in Europe and the accumulation of capital wealth and technical and human potential which for centuries made Europe the economic hub of the world.

But it was by no means only businessmen who travelled. Those who were in different countries variously called Bohemians, Tsiganes, Gitanes or gipsies passed along the highways with their horse-drawn carts which were also their homes. They had come at some unknown date from India; they mended metal objects which some Europeans, endowed with more learning than charity, took as evidence for their descent from Tubal or Cain. They are sometimes described as nomads, but inaccurately, for real nomads own herds which they follow or lead over enormous distances but still within boundaries fixed by agreement. The Bohemians by contrast are perpetual wanderers, for ever on the move, even if nowadays they have changed their horse and cart for a car, always mistrusted and feared by people of regular habits who stay in the same place.

Another category of wanderer, though in a much more restricted area, were the tramps – now an almost vanished race – who would move from town to town picking up odd jobs. Once upon a time many workmen or fellow craftsmen used to make what was known as the Tour de France. The Companions of the Tour de France used to travel, often on foot, from town to town in search of work which they were competent to do. It was a respectable and well-run organization; and if there were occasional disputes between its members and the "Masters" who ran the guilds, they were settled between men who were alive to their duties as well as to their rights.

The 19th century was destined to witness fundamental changes in modes of travel as in everything else. Almost simultaneously the stage-coach was replaced by the railway, and the sailing ship by the steamer. The coach itself had a long line of predecessors, starting with the two- or four-wheeled chariots of the Roman *cursus publicus* – vehicles actually drawn by two or four horses where speed of travel was required – and ending with the post chaise of the *ancien régime*. Since the roads, where they existed at all, were ill paved, the traveller on them was not merely cramped but badly shaken as well as often being liable to unpleasant surprises. There was nothing legendary about the highwaymen who infested the main roads and who would not hesitate to level their blunderbusses at the postilion or even knock him down off his high seat if he did not halt at the first summons. The travellers for their part could count themselves lucky if they could get away without luggage, money and jewellery, but managed to keep their clothes. If the journeys took any length of time – and they easily could, for the stage-coach moved slowly – the inns were far from all being as well appointed as the many *Alte Post* of southern Germany. The innkeepers, for their part, were often enough working hand in glove with thieves and robbers to strip the rash or inexperienced traveller driven by storm, flood or some other natural disaster to seek shelter beneath their roof.

The disappearance of these particular forms of unpleasantness corresponded exactly with the substitution of the train for the stage-coach, but they were replaced by other kinds of discomfort. Not only were the earliest railway lines, like that from Stockton to Darlington in England, or Malines to Brussels in Belgium, extremely short, but the trains themselves comprised only a few carriages, very few of which were covered and fewer still enclosed. The engines, which developed little power, belched clouds of smoke and live sparks, and sometimes even fire. Yet the first steps or, to choose an apter metaphor, the first revolutions of the wheels, had been taken on what might be called a way which was destined to expand on a vast scale and to cover Europe with a great network of rails which in due course carried hundreds of thousands, then millions, and finally hundreds of millions of travellers in a degree of comfort which varied according to classes − a concept introduced to define different categories of coaches and compartments. There were luxury expresses with their sleeping cars and restaurant cars, which before World War I (and in some countries until World War II) were commonly thought to represent the quintessence of luxurious refinement. Trains did, and still do, cross the Alps through a large number of tunnels, the earliest of which, at Semmering in Austria, now seems hardly more than a children's toy.

Meanwhile the steamship replaced the sailing vessel which was inevitably at the mercy of wind and waves. Travel became quicker and more comfortable, and great luxury liners crossed every ocean. This was the age of the formation of as many great steamship lines as there were already railway companies; and in this field, where the state did not own the network, it was set up under private administration. Harbours and stations were reconstructed to be able to cope with an ever-increasing number of trains and size of ships. Transport of both passengers and freight became a huge industry. Travel agencies, the first and best-known of which is still known as Cook's, undertook to organize travelling arrangements for individuals, to arrange their transport by sea and land and their accommodation in hotels which steadily increased in size and comfort and were indeed soon to form part of what are now known as "chains".

But side by side with this growth of comfort, the miserable discomfort of other so-called "travellers" stood out as a blemish. As factories multiplied and consequently became more unhealthy, the railways conveyed an ever-increasing number of men and women from the country to work in them. Many of them huddled together in squalid suburbs at the very foot of factory chimneys belching smoke and soot. By sea, countless penniless Europeans crammed themselves in utter confusion on to ships lacking the rudiments of comfort, bound for North or South America where they hoped to find wealth or at least the bare means of subsistence. Many of them initially found only the very poverty they had been trying to escape, though others made their fortune, and the luck of the few was sufficient to maintain the exodus. The birthrate, accelerated in Europe by both advances in medical science and better nutrition, had its repercussions on the populations of the United States, Canada, Argentina, Brazil and Chile, which grew at a rate inexplicable by reference simply to natural conditions and local economic circumstances. Some Europeans also used steamship lines like the P. & O. or the Messageries Maritimes, or the major international railways, such as the trans-Siberian railway, to reach either their national possessions or areas where their countries could exercise the influence which the more advanced European technology had enabled them to secure in Africa, Asia or Australia. No matter whether they were personally wealthy, members of the public service or employees of the great industrial or commercial companies, they had no need even of a passport in a world where European prestige commanded world respect. But those days, which lasted until the first of the suicidal great wars in 1914, which marked the beginning of the self-destruction of the western Atlantic powers, are long since past and we shall not see them again.

Not very long before that crucial date two new forms of transport had appeared upon the scene − the car and the aeroplane; and they were destined once again completely to revolutionize the world of travel and those who engaged in it. We can occasionally see vintage cars moving in convoy on our roads. These were the engagingly primitive origins of what became, especially after World War II, a society in which every family aspired to own a car. For many people it was simply the natural successor of the bicycle on which their fathers, workmen and employers alike, had made their way to work, and they used the car not for travelling in any real sense but simply as a means to an end. But there were others for whom the car became the best way of getting to know Europe well and appreciating the beauties it could offer in greater variety, but also on a more human scale, than could be found in any other continent. If he wants to travel a long distance, the modern European driver has autostradas or motorways at his disposal, while he has no need to work out the stages of his journey beforehand, for he need not stay in a town but can eat, drink and sleep in motels.

Europe has regrettably not as yet got special roads for the use of lorries, and the enormous growth in the transport of goods by road in recent decades means that all too often car drivers in the role of "travellers" eventually find themselves doing the same kind of hard work as lorry drivers. They make great efforts to find relief by getting off the motorways or their equivalents and taking to the country roads which are less crowded, often prettier and sometimes quicker. But large-scale tourism, a strongly marked feature of the present day, generally sticks to the motorway in buses or luxury coaches which convey the passengers cheaply and so swell the number of heavy and cumbersome vehicles, thus causing the traffic blocks which are the curse of travel today. Another present-day habit which plays no less a part in causing overcrowding on the roads is that of going away for the weekend, which no one can give up without losing some degree of social standing. As early as Friday afternoon onwards, every vehicle of every size sets out, including luxury coaches with their parties of weekenders. There is a lull on Saturday afternoons and Sunday mornings, for the travellers have reached their destinations, but by Sunday afternoon the overcrowding and the queues have begun again, which means that the fatigue caused by this habit is added to that of the five working weekdays. Ours is indeed an odd world, in which comfort so often degenerates into discomfort.

The aeroplane appeared on the scene very soon after the motorcar. These strange bird-like objects rose into the air and quite often crashed to the ground within a few yards. The pioneer fliers were men of extraordinary boldness or perhaps even heroism. But the aeroplane had hardly begun to fly when it became a weapon in World War I, scarcely used for bombing since its load-carrying capacity was tiny, but for hunting the enemy. Aerial warfare took the form of a succession of duels of no true strategic importance. A few survived to become national heroes or to start the first airlines. These were the fathers of the modern air traffic which covers vast distances and flies over the highest mountains. Lindbergh, with his heroic trans-Atlantic flight, marked the end of the great pioneers, and from that moment on, air traffic became worldwide. Aircraft design was constantly improved and the aeroplanes themselves became bigger and more powerful, and acquired a heavier load capacity as they flashed across the skies, at first of Europe and soon of every continent. Airports became huge aeroplane depots and air companies grew quickly in number. A new field of capitalism, first of all in air transport and consequently in travel, came into being.

By the outbreak of World War II the load-carrying capacity of the aeroplane had reached the point where the bombing of towns, factories and civilians was a decisive factor in the outcome. The war also led directly to the different forms of nuclear energy which once again was destined to revolutionize methods of transport. During the 1960s jet propulsion came into almost universal use and the concept of distance was drastically curtailed. Moreover Douglas and Boeing aircraft carried hundreds of passengers on a single flight.

What might be called the "jet revolution" could not have taken place without the almost universal use of the air charter system. This means of mass air travel has revolutionized the lives of the lower-middle and working classes to an extraordinary degree. Hundreds of thousands of German and Scandinavian workers are decanted annually on to the beaches of the Canary Islands, after a flight of a few hours. And this is equally true of the Tunisian coast, the Spanish Mediterranean and much of Italy and Greece. Moreover, the Iron Curtain countries are plainly anxious to share in this uncovenanted bonus from tourism and here too charter flights guarantee full houses for hotels in Mamaïa in Romania and in Soukhoum and Sochi in the USSR, as well as Dubrovnik and San Stefano in Yugoslavia. We live in an age when charwomen and hall porters are heard discussing their holiday travels to Turkey or Rhodes and the European middle classes can, by group charter flight, be in Machu Picchu or be standing in front of the Pyramid of Cheops in a matter of hours.

# 22

# Craftsmen and Guilds

## HAROLD OSBORNE

Whereas most species of animals have evolved by adapting themselves to their environment, man is distinguished from his fellow creatures by his exceptional ability to adapt the environment to his own comfort and needs. Animals which live in conditions of cold grow layers of blubber or thick fur, moulting in summer. Men make garments for warmth from the skins and fur of animals, build shelters, light fires, invent central heating and – eventually – air conditioning. The chief agents of mankind's material progress have been craftsmanship and technology.

Tools have been fashioned for the manipulation of the environment for at least a million years, from the time when the human race lived by hunting, fishing and food-gathering without settled communities. Our knowledge of the earliest archaeological periods is restricted because except for a very few fortunate freaks only the more durable materials have survived, so that there is a temptation to exaggerate the importance of stone as the original tool-making material, and because it may be difficult to recognize a stone tool as such until a tradition of tool-making has been established.

The invention of the potter's wheel, probably about the end of the fourth millennium BC, may have converted the making of pottery from a household task of the women into a specialized craft. The need to win agricultural land from virgin forest stimulated the development of woodworking tools from the stone axe and adze to the two-man saw. The period saw enormous advances in the production of carts, ships and furniture and all the more common carpenter's joints known today came into use at this time. Many of the older utensils and tools were developed for new purposes, such as the quern for grinding grain and the stone-bladed sickle. Basketry, leatherwork and the spinning and weaving of woollen textiles also originated or were substantially advanced in this period.

The gradual urbanization which took place from about 3000 BC onwards had repercussions on the social position of craftsmen. With the increasing demand for consumer goods, the rapid growth of trade and the specialization of social function attendant on larger human agglomerations, craftsmen themselves became a valuable asset. Certain cities or localities became renowned for particular crafts. Craftsmen were transferred over large distances as captives or by other inducements. Late Bronze Age smiths travelled Europe, visiting local fairs with their cases of tools and samples. In the Neolithic Age, if not before, craftsmanship came to be regarded as a jealously guarded tradition handed down from generation to generation within a family or closed society. The hard-won skills and know-how were treasured as an arcanum or "mystery" sometimes protected by religious sanctions. It goes without saying that, at all times before large-scale factory production in the modern sense, human society was dependent on its craftsmen for the comforts of life as well as the prestige paraphernalia of the wealthy and powerful. But do-it-yourself versatility was taken for granted and flourished to an extent which is hard to credit today, while then as later the small artisans were competent for most practical needs.

The social stigma attaching to the artisan and to handwork as an occupation was firmly established in Classical antiquity. In the typical Greek city-state craftsmanship, workshop industry and retail trade were the province of the metics, resident aliens without full citizen rights. The word "banausic", regularly linked with "handicraft", was a term of contempt. Plato – and Aristotle after him – was expressing a deeply rooted Greek prejudice when in the *Laws* he said: "As to the arts and crafts we should proceed as follows. In the first place, no native, and no servant of a native, is to practise a craft as his calling." Even the fine arts of painting and sculpture were not admitted to equality with poetry as "liberal arts" until the Renaissance. This prejudice against handwork was rationalized on moral grounds clearly set forth, among many other places, in a speech attributed to Demosthenes: "Our character depends on our avocations, and a man's mind takes its colour from the nature of his pursuits. He who consumes his days in paltry occupations or vulgar toil can no more feel lofty aspirations and manly courage rising within his bosom than can pusillanimity and a grovelling habit of thought find a place in the soul of him whose pursuits are noble and honourable."

The contribution of the Romans consisted of organization rather than innovation. Their efficient administration of the Empire brought into being conditions which favoured the migration of craftsmen and the dissemination of their products over an area extending to Scotland in the north and including the Near East as far as Parthia. Raw materials – timber, iron, copper, silver, tin etc. – were transported from their places of origin to centres of manufacture on a hitherto unprecedented scale. Craftsmen set up new centres of production, carrying their traditions and know-how with them. Inscriptions throughout the Empire testify to the ubiquity of the *collegia fabrorum*, the guilds of smiths. Metalworking became more specialized and localized. Bronze vessels made in a factory at Capua have been found as far afield as Scotland, Germany and Scandinavia. Loosely organized guilds of timber workers were set up at Rome and elsewhere, such as the *lignarii* of Bordeaux.

This wide dissemination of workshop industry with new techniques and know-how was encouraged by the flourishing trade in consumer goods but still more by the migration of craftsmen. Although the social stigma attaching to craftsmen and artisans did not disappear in Roman times – skilled workers might well be slaves or freedmen – the Romans seem to have had a more practical understanding of their function and importance in maintaining the life of the community. In Rome craftsmen worked alongside the Via Sacra, where the Emperor Nero allocated shops to them. Tombstones at Aquileia and Ostia show blacksmiths at work with their tools and wares, and a well-known grave relief, now in the Vatican, shows a cutler's shop with rows of specialized knives. Woodworking was more essential to the daily conduct of life then than now and both tombstones and wall paintings show carpenters at work with their tools. Partly because of its importance for the manufacture of military equipment, the leather industry was carefully fostered. Hides formed part of the tax imposed on Spain, Gaul, Britain, Illyria and the Alpine provinces. The remains of tanneries have been found as widely dispersed as Pompeii and Lullingstone, Kent. At first the Romans carried on existing traditions in furniture but from the 2nd century AD a type of couch with high back and sides spread through the Empire. The Romans also developed cupboard and shelf furniture. The steel saw with teeth projecting alternately to left and right seems to have been introduced during the Roman period. There is a tradition that the plane was a Greek invention but the earliest known examples come from Pompeii. Panelled doors which survive show that by about the 1st century AD woodworkers must have had at their disposal some five or six different types of plane.

The disintegration of the Roman Empire was the signal for a massive deterioration throughout western Europe over a wide range of skilled crafts which the Romans had fostered. From the time of Charlemagne the great abbeys of northern France and Germany did much to preserve practical skills in building and agriculture. But throughout the Middle Ages western Europe was heavily dependent on the east for craftsmanship. It was in Byzantium, and later the Islamic world, that traditions of fine craftsmanship were kept alive and they were also the channels by which the more inventive craftsmanship of China and the Far East penetrated to the west. When recovery got under way in the later Middle Ages the trend was not towards the highest reaches of craftsmanship but was manifested rather in the exploitation of windpower and waterpower to a hitherto unprecedented range of practical uses and in the more efficient application of heat to such activities as smelting metals and firing ceramics. This is the distinguishing feature of European culture. In craftsmanship it did not rival ancient China or pre-Inca Peru except in some few isolated cases. But in the rapid extension of proto-technology to almost all areas of industrial production western Europe knew no rival. And this particular characteristic of the culture made its appearance long before the Industrial Revolution. In the medieval period also the distinction between artisan and craftsman, never very firm in antiquity, was sharpened and formalized by the craftsmen's guilds. Whether working with the new technology or independently, it was the artisans who were responsible for meeting the day-to-day requirements of the mass of population. Increasingly the craftsmen catered for the refinements and luxuries of life. The general outline of this picture can be filled in by reference to particular crafts that were typical of much else.

In ceramics the potter's wheel fell into abeyance over large parts of western Europe on the collapse of the Empire, pots being built up clumsily by coiling strips of clay. It was not until the 10th and 11th centuries that the technologically more advanced kick-wheel came into general use. Lead glazes, which had been known to the Romans, and to the Chinese from the 3rd century BC, also fell into disuse, coming back from Byzantium during the 11th century. The ancient craft of stoneware seems to have developed independently in the Rhineland as a result of the special clays available there, and with it the use of salt glazes, towards the end of the 14th century. But the red stoneware which became popular in the 18th century was developed under the direct inspiration of the so-called Boccaro ware in which Chinese tea was imported to Europe. Tin glazes had first appeared in Mesopotamia during the 9th century and were exploited by the Baghdad potters in an attempt to reproduce the qualities of Chinese porcelain. The technique penetrated to western Europe by way of Moorish Spain and in the 14th century formed the main inspiration of what was variously called majolica, faience and delftware. The techniques of hard-paste porcelain remained a closely guarded secret until a formula was discovered at Dresden early in the 18th century, but even so European production could not equal the thinness, translucency and resonance so much admired in the finest petuntse porcelain.

The craft of fine glassware too was perpetuated mainly by Byzantium and Islam. The technique of soda glass was lost in the west after the break-up of the Roman Empire and the centralized glass industry of northern Europe was fragmented into a scattering of glass-houses isolated in the forests which supplied them with fuel and with the wood ash they needed for the manufacture of green *Waldglas*. The arts of glass blowing and of decolourizing the glass by the use of manganese dioxide, which had been lost to western Europe during the Dark Ages, were revived in Venice during the 15th century and a colourless metal was produced which was named *cristallo* because of its likeness to rock crystal. The art of colouring glass was also brought back, the shapes were influenced by contemporary silverware, and by the end of the century Venetian glass was beginning to reflect all the magnificence of the Renaissance. Early in the 16th century the Islamic art of decorating with enamel on glass was introduced and the colourless *cristallo* was decorated with threads of opaque white glass (*latticino*) until by the middle of the century the glass of Murano had become a highly sought-after luxury product. This was craftsmanship at its best. The industry was organized in an elaborate guild system. The craftsmen were granted extraordinary privileges, but their techniques and skills were a jealously guarded state secret, the workmen were virtually state prisoners, and for a glass master to flee the republic carried the penalty of death. Nevertheless the skills and know-how did spread, particularly to the Netherlands around Liège and Antwerp, and by the 17th century knowledge of how to make glass in the Venetian style, *façon de Venise*, led to a decline in the dominance of Venice. The art of cut-glass decoration was practised mainly in England about the middle of the 18th century, while glass engraving was taken to its highest perfection in the Low Countries.

In textile manufacture flax was the most important vegetable fibre of western Europe until well into the 18th century and European fine linens acquired a widespread prestige. Hardly less important were improvements in the technology of wool processing, which included the spinning wheel and the application of waterpower to new methods of fulling. Manufacturing techniques of cotton textiles spread from Moorish Spain during the 12th to the 15th centuries and silk making, which had long been a Chinese secret, was established in Italy during the 12th century. Except in certain techniques of bookbinding, tooling of missal cases, budgets etc., pursued under the auspices of the monasteries, leatherwork reached no great heights of craftsmanship. Despite the name *cuir boulli*, medieval leather was incapable of being boiled but was moulded after being rendered plastic by thorough soaking in water. The famous Spanish cordovan, which gave a name to the cordwainers, was originally made by the Moors from the skin of the moufflon and was subsequently copied elsewhere in goatskin. But the use of the welt and the heel in shoemaking did not come in until late in the 15th century.

After the breakup of the Roman Empire joinery virtually disappeared except in certain districts of Italy and over most of western Europe all woodwork, including furniture, was in the hands of the carpenters or constructional workers. The ancient techniques of veneering and inlaying, intarsia and marquetry, and the use of tenon and mortice joints, were revived in Italy, then in the Netherlands, and were introduced into France during the first half of the 17th century. The more elaborate types of "seaweed" marquetry and tortoiseshell and metal marquetry, as practised by Boulle in France and Gerreit Jensen in London, were made possible by the invention in the 16th century of the fine metal-framed fretsaw. It was from the time of Louis XIV in France that the techniques of luxury furniture were carried to a level of elaboration which for sheer craftsmanship has seldom been equalled. The traditions of the Boulle workshops were perpetuated in Germany by Oeben and Riesener and by David Roentgen, who established a centre at Neuwied in Westphalia. Craftsmen from Neuwied took their skills as far afield as Poland and London. Despite the traditions established by Robert Adam and Thomas Sheraton, however, marquetry never became so popular in England as on the continent. The height of technical virtuosity was achieved by the French cabinet makers of the 18th century. But after the invention in 1780 of the marquetry cutter's donkey, by which a dozen or more copies of the same design could be sawn together, the tendency towards repetition and mass production swamped originality.

Apart from luxury furniture, the fields in which European craftsmanship chiefly went ahead of all others were the manufacture of musical instruments, particularly instruments of the violin and woodwind families, and the making of timekeepers and other precision instruments.

The great period of violin making extended from the middle of the 16th to the early decades of the 18th century and was centred on Cremona. The musical excellence of instruments made by the Amati, Guarneri and Stradivari families, which has not elsewhere been equalled, depended upon superb functional craftsmanship. Functional rather than decorative craftsmanship was also responsible for the notable evolution achieved by instruments of the flute, oboe and clarinet families in the period before factory manufacture. Although flutes and reed instruments have been made and blown in virtually every region of the world, nowhere else have they achieved such accuracy of pitch or beauty of tone. The early keyboard instruments were regarded not only as musical instruments but also as fine furniture and provided occasion for the display of elaborate decorative craftsmanship. It was nevertheless the very high quality of their precision craftsmanship that made possible their astonishing evolution up to the modern factory-made pianoforte.

Timekeepers also provide an example of a particularly close combination of decorative with precision craftsmanship. Clocks were regarded as articles of fine furniture and watches as articles of personal jewellery, so that both afforded opportunities for the display of artistic craftsmanship and decorative ornament. But it was the high quality of their functional craftsmanship and the skill and ingenuity of craftsmen in inventing devices for enhancing accuracy of timekeeping within the compass of practical convenience that made possible the evolution of modern factory-made clocks and watches. Spring-driven clocks originated in the second half of the 15th century and after the introduction of the pendulum in about 1660 cased spring-driven clocks became standard form — the English "bracket" clocks and the "mantel" clocks of France and Switzerland. From Louis XIV to Louis XVI in France the cases became ever more elaborate and developed almost into an independent art form with the clock dial merely one not particularly prominent element in the overall design. Clocks as purely precision instruments made corresponding progress and whereas in the early 18th century an accurate case-clock might be expected to run an error of some two or three seconds a day, the Dent clock made for Greenwich Observatory in 1872, the most accurate all-mechanical clock before the advent of modern electrical time-keeping instruments, varied by only about a hundredth of a second a day.

Measuring instruments were common in Roman times. Bronze dividers and folding rules have survived and they, together with set-squares, levels etc., were favourite subjects for the tombstones of carpenters and other artisans. But the modern development of the instrument makers' craft was an outcome of increased skill in the accurate working of metals. The modern tradition of instrument making goes back to the craftsmen of Nürnberg and Augsburg in the second half of the 15th century. From Germany the craft spread to Louvain. But as a result of the Thirty Years' War and disturbances in the Netherlands in the 16th and 17th centuries London became the world's most important centre of instrument making. Besides time-keeping devices, this work included astronomical, navigational and surveying instruments, balances, telescopes, microscopes and other optical instruments. The late 17th and 18th centuries saw a notable advance in the techniques of lens grinding and polishing. In the course of the 18th century also the exquisite decorative workmanship which had been the pride of earlier craftsmen was subordinated to functional efficiency, and the severely practical appearance which heralded the modern scientific instrument became standard. It was the skill of these generations of instrument makers and the functional exactness of their workmanship which led up to and made possible the precision instruments and machines which from the time of the Industrial Revolution have been the mainstay of modern technology.

As has been indicated, under one name or another, craftsmen's guilds go back to the dawn of history, the special skills and know-how of each craft being regarded as trade secrets, sometimes protected by religious or political sanctions. From the later Middle Ages most crafts in Europe were in the hands of trade guilds. Although their modes of operation, the recognition accorded to them and the strictness of the control they exercised varied greatly from country to country and from craft to craft, their objects were by and large the same: they were, primarily, to obtain social privileges for their members and to maintain the quality of workmanship by securing a monopoly and imposing a high standard of efficiency as the price of membership. The title of master locksmith, for example, was first conferred in Germany in 1411 and from the early 15th century professional locksmiths began to enjoy a unique position. A master locksmith was a craftsman of great technical virtuosity and a master of decorative ornament. Famous locksmiths travelled from court to court making locks and keys for the nobility and wealthy merchants. The French were acknowledged to be the best, after them the Germans, and after them the Italians. In order to maintain this prestige a strict system of apprenticeship was instituted and before he could obtain admission to guild membership an apprentice had to submit a sample of his best work. The standard imposed for admission was very high and these "apprentice locks" from the 17th and 18th centuries are among the finest examples of virtuoso steel working which have survived. Similar conditions applied in other crafts.

In this way the guilds protected both their own members and the general public from the pretensions of inferior workmen. As a rough and ready parallel in the modern world one might point to the privileges accorded to and the restraints imposed by the societies of accountants, auctioneers, valuers, medical practitioners etc. Yet one of the most important social consequences of these activities of the guilds has too often been overlooked. By imposing severe conditions of membership they widened and made more rigid the distinction between craftsman and artisan. More and more it was the regional artisans who supplied the everyday needs of the population; more and more the recognized craftsmen catered for the luxury trade and the wealthy. The guilds imposed their control only slowly and very partially. But in so far as they did succeed, the inevitable result was to set their members in a category apart. In France, for example, furniture and constructional woodwork alike were originally the province of the *charpentiers* or carpenters, and it was not until the middle of the 15th century that the *menuisiers* or joiners obtained exclusive rights to furniture and other portable wooden wares. The craftsmen specializing in ebony veneering were originally members of the guild of *menuisiers* but were known as *menuisiers en ébène* or *menuisiers-ébénistes*. With the growing popularity of this kind of furniture the shortened term *ébénistes* became current, but it was not until 1743 that it was accorded official recognition when the name of the association was changed to Corporation de Menuisiers-Ebénistes and it was laid down in the statutes that specialists in marquetry and veneering should be so named. In England, although the history of the carpenters' guild can be traced back to 1388, they did not receive a charter until 1570. It was not until 1632 that the guild of joiners, an offshoot of the carpenters' guild, obtained the exclusive right to all but the roughest kinds of furniture. It was only after the Restoration that craftsmen in the new techniques of veneering and marquetry began to call themselves "cabinet makers" and gradually broke away from the joiners. But in France, as in England, and indeed in other countries too, whatever rights and monopolies were granted to the guilds, the great bulk of furniture and woodwork for ordinary people continued to be done by regional artisans without guild membership, and this includes much that is now highly prized in the antique trade.

The medieval craft guilds flourished most strongly from the 11th to the 16th centuries. Whether they arose independently on the analogy of religious and other associations or whether there was a direct link between any of them and the 4th-century Roman *collegia* is a moot question. Subject to many variations, they were typically three-layered hierarchical bodies consisting of masters, journeymen and apprentices. Some guilds included suppliers and wholesalers. The masters constituted a privileged élite in control of guild policy and distinguished both by technical competence – admission to the grade required submission of a "masterpiece" of craftsmanship – and by social eligibility or wealth since they functioned as employers. There was often friction between masters and journeymen, and occasionally associations of journeymen were set up in opposition. But the importance of these has been exaggerated and, except sometimes in 15th-century Germany, they were rarely a serious threat to the guilds. While differing in detail, the aim of most of the guilds was to secure as complete a monopoly of production as possible and control of trading conditions in favour of the masters. Their weakness lay in the impracticability of imposing the authority postulated by their regulations. Outside the large towns their control over jobbing artisans was restricted, and within the towns municipal or even governmental interference in matters of trading and craft policy was frequent. For instance by statute of Elizabeth I the period of seven years for apprenticeship was established in theory for all trades throughout England. The authority of the guilds, never as strong in practice as in theory, was seriously eroded long before they were abolished by statute – in 1840 in Spain, 1860 in Germany, 1864 in Italy, 1871 in France. Perhaps the most important and the most lasting contribution made by the guilds was to create and sustain a class of *professional* craftsmen distinct from the artisans and to identify them, in theory at any rate, with the employers until the growing power of factory technology brought about the emergence of a class of entrepreneurs who were not necessarily themselves competent either in craftsmanship or in the technologies of production.

Despite the prestige of high craftsmanship, it was in other fields that we must look for the most remarkable advances in Europe during the Middle Ages until the recession caused by the outbreak of the Black Death in 1348. These advances were in what may be called proto-industrial techniques and in those areas where craftsmanship and rudimentary technology were most intimately linked to revolutionize traditional crafts by new applications of ancient but hitherto unexploited technological principles. It was here rather than in pure craftsmanship that western Europe made its most important contributions, without which modern technological civilization could hardly have emerged. One might point to the revival of brick making, which had been a state monopoly after the fire of Rome in Nero's time. With the exception of minor activity in Byzantium, northern Italy and Moorish Spain, brick making became virtually a lost art on the fall of Rome until between the 11th and 13th centuries it spread northwards from southern France and became the main basis of building in the eastern counties of Britain and from the Low Countries to the Baltic. Bricks were made cheaply and in quantity by the use of unskilled labour. Herring and cod fishing – important because of fast days and Lent – was industrialized on an altogether new scale by techniques of salting and packing in barrels. It remained a monopoly of the Hanseatic League until the early 15th century when the Dutch introduced drift nets and replaced the open coastal vessels by decked "busses". For merchant shipping the Hanseatic cog was improved by two innovations of eastern origin, the lateen sail and the stern-post rudder, until in the latter part of the 15th century it was replaced by the carvel-built carrack. Horse traction – the most generally available source of power in that age – was made some five or six times more efficient when the iron horseshoe, shafts and the padded horse collar became general in the 12th and 13th centuries.

Still more revolutionary in their effects were new developments in the industrial application of waterpower and the windmill. An enormous expansion in the practical applications of the millwright's craft was one of the most significant features of the age. Watermills were not only widely used for grinding cereals but were adapted to a great variety of other purposes. The use of waterpower for fulling profoundly influenced the organization of the English wool industry in the 12th and 13th centuries and in the 13th century it was introduced in silk-throwing mills of Italy. It was used to power sawmills and the stamping mills operated in the manufacture of paper. Perhaps its most important applications were in the metallurgical industries. Water-powered stamping mills facilitated the crushing of ores and water-driven hammers were used in forging iron. It was the application of waterpower to large bellows which made possible the conversion of the old *Stückofen* to the modern style of blast furnace. In the 14th century waterpower was utilized for the drawing of iron wire in the manufacture of nails and in the 18th century for the boring of gun barrels. From the 16th century until well into the 19th waterwheels were the most important source of industrial power in Europe and the harnessing of waterpower to so wide a variety of operations provided an impetus for the elaboration of machinery and gearing without which the Industrial Revolution would have been hampered and retarded.

The European windmill with horizontal axle was more efficient than the eastern type which came into use in Persia during the 7th century AD and is thought to have been derived from the Vitruvian waterwheel. The post-mill, in which the whole superstructure turns about a vertical post, was well established by the end of the 13th century. The improved tower-mill, in which only the top section carrying the sails is turned, was in common use by the end of the 14th century. Windmills were applied not only to grinding corn but to a large variety of other uses as well, such as pumping water, hoisting, driving saws etc. Though less important industrially than the waterwheel, they shared with it the privilege of being one of the precursors of the Industrial Revolution.

In most respects modern factory production is not a continuation but the antithesis of traditional European craftsmanship. The use of machines is not foreign to craftsmanship. There is indeed no clear-cut distinction between a machine and a tool, and the potter's wheel is a stock example of an elementary machine. But as machines become more sophisticated, so they become more automatic, gaining in accuracy and precision at the expense of versatility. And as the machine becomes more specialized, so the demand for human skill in the process of production diminishes, or at any rate changes direction. In modern machine industry judgement, experience, ingenuity, dexterity, artistry and skill are largely concentrated on the planning of the product and programming the machine before actual production begins. In traditional craftsmanship they are necessary from beginning to end and the craftsman exercises a continuous control throughout the process of production which the modern machine operator lacks. The sophisticated technology of the modern world has divided the functions of the craftsman between the engineer who plans the machine and the industrial designer who plans the product and draws up a blueprint for programming the machine. As was made very apparent in an exhibition "Enterprise and Innovation" staged by the British Design Council on the occasion of the Silver Jubilee in 1977, in a profit-and-loss economy the chief pressures on the industrial designer tend in the direction of economy and cheapness in production and effectiveness rather than durability or appearance in the product. The other aspect of factory production which contrasts most prominently with traditional craftsmanship is its uniformity. As machines have become more sophisticated, they have not only achieved a degree of precision and accuracy which in previous generations was no more than an unrealizable ideal, their products have become stereotyped to an extent beyond all previous imagination. Once a modern machine has been built and programmed, it can turn out the same thing over and over again with a minimum of variation. Machine products are standardized and so become impersonal. The small irregularities and imperfections which are the marks of handwork, causing each article to differ slightly from every other, are eliminated. It is this standardization and impersonality which seem to be the inevitable concomitants of mass production. It is this which makes us restive, and it is reaction against this which has led to a false and sentimental value being ascribed to handwork as such.

Before briefly discussing the place of craftsmanship in contemporary European society, however, a word should be said about a new conception of craftsmanship which has arisen in the machine age. Besides the engineer and the industrial designer a factory requires, of course, the men to operate the machines. In much factory production, particularly where automation is advanced, their work is stereotyped and mechanical. But it is not always so. And it is not uncommon nowadays to hear talk of a new type of craftsmanship in the sense of skill resulting from practical experience in the efficient manipulation of a sophisticated machine. The importance of craftsmanship in this sense is most obvious in the two new crafts which have come to birth in historical times in western Europe, namely printing and photography.

Although printing from carved blocks and movable type had long been practised in the Far East, while playing cards and religious pictures were being printed from wood blocks in Venice and southern Germany before the beginning of the 15th century, the printing of books from movable type seems to have arisen independently in Europe about the middle of that century, its origin being usually attributed to a goldsmith of Strasbourg, Johann Gutenberg. The impact of the invention was tremendous and the effect of a rapidly increasing output of printed books made itself felt over the whole range of learning and the practical crafts. Although the production of printed books may sometimes be a purely mechanical process, it has lent itself from the start to the exercise of a very high level of craftsmanship. Craftsmanship has been manifested both in typography, the designing and cutting of types, and in the design and layout of the book page. In modern times craftsmanship in these fields was cultivated most self-consciously and deliberately within the Private Press Movement, whose pioneer was William Morris. Since the discovery of lithography early in the 19th century this too has become not merely a technique of mechanical reproduction but both an independent art form and a field for the exercise of fine craftsmanship. Photography is in a similar case. Since its invention in the 1830s photography has undergone enormous technical improvements and complications, while also being simplified for the amateur. Yet besides being an industrial recording and reproduction technique and a popular hobby, it too has become both an independent branch of fine art and pre-eminently a field offering scope for fine craftsmanship with its own skills and expertise.

The survival of craftsmanship in our technologically dominated age bears testimony to the depth of its roots in human nature. Two contrasting attitudes are taken towards it. There are those who indignantly proclaim that for the technological world of today craftsmanship in the traditional sense is no more than an anachronism, the artificial perpetuation of primitive technology as a time-wasting hobby into an age which has advanced beyond it. There are others who with an almost mystical fervour ascribe a spiritual value to craftsmanship as an antidote to the soulless standardization imposed upon modern man by the encroachment of mass production. Arguments are advanced for both views.

In the Preface to the *Oxford Companion to the Decorative Arts* I pointed out that from the remotest periods of prehistory "a genuine pride in the process of production itself, a pride which drives a man to make whatever things he makes as well as they can be made, even beyond economic considerations of reward" has been integral to the long traditions of European craftsmanship. Anthropologists now recognize that both this and an aesthetic impulse go back as far as human tool making can be traced. Graham Clark and Stuart Piggott, for example, in *Prehistoric Societies* (1965) find evidence in the Lower Paleolithic Age of what they call the "cult of excellence, the determination to make things as perfect as they could be made, even if at a purely utilitarian level perfection might seem excessive..." The motivations of an industrialized society, and the reduced responsibility of the machine operator for the factory-made product, leave little room for this cult of perfection and this is why, apart from a few isolated pockets, it is rapidly disappearing from contemporary life. Yet it is one of the most ancient and deeply rooted of human drives. It has been largely responsible for progress from primitive barbarism to civilized comfort and it is probably still a necessity for a fully integrated personality, so that its excision causes a sense of unexplained loss and a bewildered feeling of spiritual emptiness. Closely allied to this is the sense of *quality* and the respect for quality. This too is an attitude of mind which is integral to craftsmanship but foreign to factory industry where economic considerations override the valuation of quality for its own sake. The feeling for quality also is disappearing among producers and consumers alike. Yet it is a precious thing as every craftsman knows, and if the craftsmen who are still active in the world can do something to maintain the cult of excellence, the pride in a good job well done, and the respect for quality, then they are no anachronism but one of the few forces remaining to stem the deterioration and dehumanization of contemporary society.

The spontaneously surviving fields of European craftsmanship are mostly to be found in the luxury sectors of production. Most notable among them are, of course, *haute cuisine* and *haute couture*. Although factory-made clothes are worn by the vast majority of people in Europe today, the leading couturiers, whose "creations" are not made for duplication, are still professional craftsmen in the old sense. There are also still the "artisans" of the trade – tailors and dressmakers who work by hand from a pattern, adapting it to the individual client. Food, again, has never been so stereotyped as it is today (the contents of each brand can taste the same as those of every other), yet the varieties of available choice have never been so great. Outside the area of mass production, however, it is fair to say that never in the past did the preparation of food become an art or involve craftsmanship of the same level as the finest luxury food of Europe today. In certain other crafts, which have virtually surrendered to mass production, a small area is retained by the craftsmen at the most expensive end of production both because their work is finer and because it is more individual than that which is turned out by the factories. Examples of such crafts are bookbinding and jewellery. In addition to the mass-produced jewellery and "costume jewellery" on the one hand and the amateur handmade jewellery on the other, there are still craftsmen jewellers whose work has a fine excellence and is not mass produced.

In addition to this the dissatisfaction of a significant minority of people with the uniformity of factory-made goods in daily life has provided the incentive for attempts to revive handicraft industries in Europe. This has occurred chiefly but not exclusively in textiles (hand weaving etc.) and ceramics. Sometimes local folk-art traditions have been organized to cater for the needs of a more sophisticated urban market. More often attempts have been made to revive ancient traditions of craftsmanship on an amateur basis. But a tradition which has lapsed cannot be "revived" at will, particularly in a culture where handwork is no longer economically viable. Very rarely it has been possible to inaugurate a new hybrid tradition, as when Bernard Leach in the 1920s founded a new tradition of artist pottery based on a conflation of the English slipware tradition with Japanese traditions of stoneware ornamented with brushwork and wax-resist decoration. More often such movements have been related to artistic and stylistic novelties rather than to traditions of craftsmanship – as was the case with the Nancy school founded about 1890 by the glass maker and furniture designer Émile Gallé. The old craftsman possessed a hard-won skill derived from life-long immersion in a centuries-old tradition involving inarticulate knowledge of materials and tools, inherited skills and dexterities, principles of design and beyond all a pride in excellence of workmanship. This cannot be quickly or easily recovered and the modern glorification of handwork for its own sake, however inexpert or inept it may be, has little to recommend it.

Revolt from the impersonal sameness of the factory product can lead to a romantic exaltation of handwork for its own sake and something of this acts as a ferment in the philosophies of the many societies which exist for the encouragement of amateur handicrafts. But it is just here that false values creep in and caution is necessary. In the past men valued accuracy, precision, regularity and fine workmanship because these were the symbols of care and skill, dexterity and experience. These were the qualities which could not be faked, the marks of the best craftsmanship reserved for prestige products made for princes, the Church or in honour of the dead. In reaction from the mechanical regularity of the machine we nowadays tend in contrast to set a higher value on the irregularities and imperfections which proclaim that a thing is handmade. But this is a false value opposed to the age-long ideal of craftsmanship.

In a technological age it is no doubt good for us, a source of spiritual refreshment, to use our own hands from time to time and make something for ourselves. But we must beware of supposing that the product of handwork has a merit or an added beauty *simply* because it was made by hand. There is no merit, no increment of aesthetic quality, merely in the fact that a thing was made by hand, nor even in the fact that it bears the evident signs of having been made by hand. The benefit is to the worker, not to the consumer. Being made by hand does not guarantee the excellence of the product. What is needed is the pride of the professional in superior workmanship and skill.

# 23

# Engineers and Technologists

## SIDNEY POLLARD

Today's engineers and technologists belong to the world of science and, in the eyes of some, they are rather inferior denizens of that world, being responsible for the practical application of the ideas of others. Such a view, where it exists, contains an element of travesty even today, a reflection of the power of those who create words as against those who create things. For the engineer, even if he were unfairly to be considered to be merely an imitative scientist, still has to function at two other levels as well: his work must satisfy a social purpose, and it must be aesthetically pleasing.

The symbol of the social purpose is the necessity of finding someone able to pay for every project: a rich individual, a society of private citizens, a ruler or a government, and behind them, there must be some real social need to be satisfied. The social purpose is also defined by the significance of the element of cost, which means a nice sense of judgement between alternatives, balancing technical perfection against the power to raise resources, and the best possible methods in theory against the technical ability to carry them out without undue delay and experimentation in practice. The technologist, further, has to bring into play his skill in dealing with human beings: the sponsors, the workers, the suppliers of materials, public authorities.

There can be no dispute as to the aesthetic element in the case of bridges, roads or other constructs of civil engineering. But even a crane, a car or a turbine will be judged, however unconsciously, by its looks, and there are few engineering drawings of former centuries in which embellishments are not depicted with at least equal care as the moving and working parts.

These two additional elements are by no means subordinate to the scientific. On the contrary, in the European past they have as a rule predominated in the work of the engineer and technologist. Science, indeed, was as often as not the product rather than the foundation of his work, although it is probably true to say that technical progress tended to be most rapid in those periods and places where science and technology were most closely intertwined.

There is a sense in which the engineer and technologist is a product of the late Middle Ages, of the Renaissance even, and that there is no precedent for him in earlier stages of human history. Yet when the man of 1500 AD looked at the magnificent bridges and aqueducts surviving from the Roman period, at the enormous lighthouses from still earlier ages or at buildings such as the Pantheon in Rome, he must have wondered about those who designed them and put them up, and he would have wondered with some justice.

The view that Classical civilization rigidly kept apart the philosopher, with his abstract scientific insights, and the craftsman, who built machines and erected public works, and that therefore there was no room for the engineer to occupy a place in between, derives from the works of these philosophers and literati, like Plato, Plutarch and Seneca themselves. It tells us something about the status of the engineer, as well as about the preoccupations of the well-bred author, but it is plainly untrue. Vitruvius, who helped Augustus to rebuild Rome, was quite certain that even the humble builder of siege engines, let alone the constructor of temples and aqueducts, had to know the principles of science as then established, and his handbook remained standard for centuries; conversely, Frontinus, placed in charge of Rome's nine aqueducts of 400 kilometres' length (ultimately there were to be 13), true marvels of engineering, failed to get beyond the levels of contemporary science, and thus left out of account the speed of flow of water when charging consumers.

Nor were engineers entirely without status and prestige. While the Egyptians built tombs to their greatest irrigation engineers, and Xerxes similarly honoured his military engineer Artachaies, the early Greeks invested the engineers of some of the more spectacular achievements, like Eupalinos of Megara who built the aqueduct at Samos (probably in the reign of Polycrates, 533–522 BC), with something of the same epic qualities as their early architects or philosophers. Such engineering feats as the Colossus of Rhodes and the Pharos of Alexandria were counted among the seven wonders of the ancient world. Among the Romans, Frontinus, ex-consul and former provincial governor, did not deem it to be beneath his dignity to study engineering theory and practice when he became water commissioner in 97 AD. The names of engineers like Apollodorus of Damascus, who built Trajan's bridge over the Danube, as well as some monuments in Rome have come down to us as those whom the Romans wished to honour.

There was indeed a gap in Classical civilization inhibiting the development of engineering, but it was a gap in social demand. On the one hand, there were the massive public works, the 80,000 kilometres of Roman roads with their splendid bridges and tunnels, the hundreds of kilometres of aqueducts, and thousands of kilometres of defensive walls. These were certainly great achievements, but mostly in stone, using a few simple techniques, repetitive and with little potential for development. At the other extreme, machinery with moving parts was limited to small domestic size mostly, and therefore remained at the handicraft stage. Such objects of larger mechanical engineering, like siege engines, or the remarkable set of eight waterwheels driving 16 grain mills at Barbegal near Arles, built c. 308–316 AD for the southern army in Gaul and another one for the northern army in Tournus, remained exceptional and therefore limited in development.

The Dark Ages following the collapse of the Roman Empire in the west were particularly dark in the field of engineering. Abstract learning might survive, if only in Arabic translations, but the decline of the kind of settled urban communities which could maintain great public works meant that not only was there no scope for the civil engineer, but even the surviving works were allowed to fall into sad decay; they were robbed of their building materials, sometimes even their purposes forgotten.

Handicraft skills and traditions, as always, survived. Thus 5,624 watermills have been counted in the English *Domesday Book* of 1086, or one for every 50 households: these were the improved vertical wheel type, superior to the Roman or "Norse" horizontal wheels. Windmills began to spread about the same time, probably from the Near East, and by the 14th century the superior tower-mill had begun to replace the post-mill. While both these more concentrated forms of power supply were originally used mainly for grinding corn, they were soon also applied to other purposes, such as powering fulling mills, hammers or bellows. More spectacularly, they were also adapted to raise water in the continuous battle of the inhabitants of the Low Countries to stop the encroachment of river and tide on their sinking lands, and indeed win back dry land from marshes and the sea.

Monasteries, as the largest functioning economic units, were among the leaders of current technology. Thus the water supply and drainage system of Canterbury Cathedral and priory, completed in c. 1153 by Prior Wilbert, was drawn in detail in a remarkable plan, probably by its engineer soon after. Clairvaux Abbey, by 1140, had tamed a complex network of streams to drive watermills as well as provide water for domestic use. The famous bridge at Avignon, begun in 1177, had a monastic designer, and some of the most advanced grinding and pressing machinery as well as clocks were to be found in religious houses. However, the hydraulic works in the northwest of Europe, with their dikes and drainage channels, their power-driven pumps, their boat canals and ultimately ship canals, were probably the most extensive engineering works in Europe in the first few centuries of the second Christian millennium, yet they too were extensions of traditional methods, locally applied, apparently without professional engineers. The same can also be said about the builders of Europe's magnificent cathedrals, who must still be characterized as itinerant master craftsmen, carrying practical experience with them.

By contrast, what is significant about the Renaissance designers whose written work has come down to us and who, at first sight, may dazzle us with their percipient or wayward brilliance, from the sail-driven battle wagon and crank-driven paddle boat of Guido de Vigevano, an Italian physician (1335), to the designs of the greatest of them all, Leonardo da Vinci, is that whenever they were innovating rather than describing current practice, they were impracticable, given the engineering knowledge of their time, no matter how ingenious they might have been in principle. They thus represented no real advance on the flights of fancy of Roger Bacon, or that presumably English genius of c. 1326 who proposed to use a wind-driven post-mill to fling beehives into a besieged town. They lacked the essence of true engineering: the power to turn ideas into workable "engines" on the ground. The spate of books on technology which began to appear about the same time, like Vannocio Biringuccio, *De la pirotechnia* (1540), Georgius Agricola, *De re metallica* (1556), Jacques Besson, *Théâtres des instruments et des machines* (1569), A. Ramelli, *La diverse et artificiose machine* (1588), described practice or indulged in fantasy rather than advanced their subject.

Thus the gap of the Classical civilizations, the gap between the abstract thinker and the practical tinkerer, transmitted now into the gap between the designer of military and public works, and the builder of workshop machinery, remained even at the beginning of the modern era. The engineer and technologist as we know him is a creation of the modern world, as much as he is a creator of it. He personifies the change of social purpose from a mere demand for instruments to make war and to fortify the dominion of king or priest, to a demand to satisfy the economic needs of the population at large, which is the true distinction between modern European civilization and all others that have preceded it.

At the risk of oversimplification, his rise may be described as the process of closing the gap from both directions. Those engaged in public and above all military engineering, who were often men equipped with formal scientific education, were gradually driven towards a greater use, as well as greater understanding, of the needs and capabilities of the actual construction, and those who built for private and often competitive markets were similarly obliged increasingly to absorb the systematic scientific knowledge, as well as the control over large resources and the harnessing of politics which had been the hall-mark of the other. Although the rapprochement began with the Renaissance, full integration did not occur until after the Industrial Revolution, in the 19th century.

Inevitably, it was military engineering, in its widest sense, that first made the running. The Italian city-states formed its ideal forcing ground. For ever embattled in running warfare conducted by mercenary armies, they also provided work for the designer of defensive walls, siege engines and guns. They represented a world small enough for innovations to spread rapidly and stimulate further advances, and for the engineer to move from one employer to another: the restless mobility of the engineer has, from the start, been one of the driving forces of modern society. Between contracts for war purposes, such engineers as Francesco di Giorgio Martini (1439–1502) and Leonardo da Vinci (1452–1519) designed palaces, engineered theatricals and water fountains, and built canals and locks. Their practice and their surviving sketchbooks bear witness, on the one hand, to a wide interest in the scientific basis of their work, and on the other they allow us to trace the mutual fertilization of ideas about such devices as hoists, hydraulic and pneumatic machinery, new forms of gearing, as well as other contraptions of varying realism and practicability. Filippo Brunelleschi (1377–1446) had designed the magnificent dome of Florence Cathedral, the largest in the world, at the beginning of this movement (built 1420–61); at its end, in 1566–69, Bartolomeo Ammanati (1511–92), another architect, designed in the city's Ponte Santa Trinita what is possibly the finest example of another engineering innovation, the segmental arch bridge.

It has been asserted that Renaissance engineering science reached its peak with the Dutchman, Simon Stevin (1548–1620), designer of great dikes among many other things, and

*68. Previous page*: Napoleon I as emperor. Painting by Jean Auguste Dominique Ingres, 1810.

70. Franz Liszt playing in the company of (from left to right) the elder Alexandre Dumas, Victor Hugo, George Sand, Niccolò Paganini and Gioacchino Rossini. Painting by Josef Danhauser, 1840.

69. The French writer Émile Zola. Painting by Édouard Manet, 1868.

71. A comment on the incidence of fraud associated with early banking ventures in France. Lithograph by Honoré Daumier, 1831.

72. A scene in the mule-spinning room. Engraving from *The Life and Adventures of Michael Armstrong, the Factory Boy*, London, 1840.

73. *The Steel Mill*. Painting by Adolf von Menzel, 1875.

75. Brunel photographed by Robert Howlett, 1857.

74. *The Great Eastern*, designed by Isambard Kingdom Brunel, photographed during construction at Millwall, 1857.

*76. The Sower.* Painting by Jean François Millet, c. 1850.

77. The artist in his studio. Detail of a painting by Gustave Courbet, 1854–55.

78. *The Departure of the Diligence*. Painting by Abraham Solomon, c. 1862.

79. *The Emigrants*. Painting by Erskine Nicol, 1864.

*80. The Races at Longchamps.* Painting by Édouard Manet, 1864.

_ On dit que les Parisiens sont difficiles à satisfaire, sur ces quatre banquettes pas un mécon=
_tent _ il est vrai que tous ces Français sont des Romains .

*81. They say the Parisians are hard to please.* Lithograph by Honoré Daumier, 1864.

*82.* A café concert at Les Ambassadeurs. Pastel by Edgar Degas, 1877.

*83. Overleaf: Newgate: Committed for Trial. Painting by Frank Holl, 1878.*

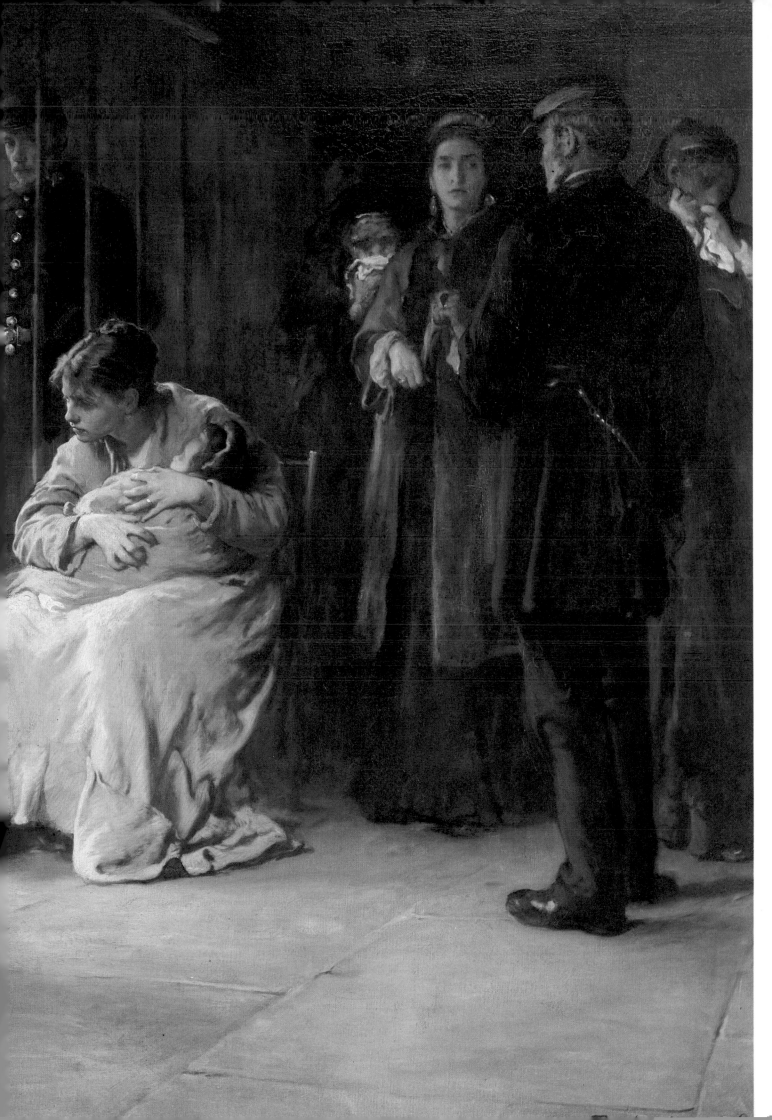

*84.* The proclamation of the German Empire at Versailles on 18 January 1871. Painting by Anton von Werner, 1871.

# THE "DAILY MAIL" COMMERCIAL MAP OF AFRICA.

# THE CAPE-TOWN TO CAIRO ROUTE.

The Cape Town to Cairo Route is shown by a thicker red line than the other railways. The total length of the route is about 5,664 miles, and of this length 2,334 miles are already open, with trains running between Cape Town and Bulawayo (1,373 miles), Cairo and Aswan (583 miles); and Wady Halfa and the Atbara (378 miles). The railway line between Aswan and Wady Halfa (200 miles) has still to be constructed, the 150 miles between the Atbara and Khartum is under construction, and a further extension of 480 miles to the Sobat River is sanctioned. The section of 900 miles between Bulawayo and Lake Tanganyika is to be proceeded with as rapidly as possible. This leaves 1,570 miles between the Sobat and the southern end of Lake Tanganyika, which has not yet been sanctioned. Between Uganda and Rhodesia the line must either pass through the Congo State or German Territory, but the navigation of Lake Tanganyika is free, and on this section a steamer may form the connecting link between the railway lines at the north and south ends of the lake.

*85. Imperial Europe in Africa, 1889.*

*86.  The Potato Eaters.* Painting by Vincent van Gogh, 1885.

87. *The Strike*. Painting by Jules Adler, 1899.

*88. Aristide Bruant on a Bicycle.* Pastel by Henri de Toulouse-Lautrec, 1896.

Jan Adriaanzoon Leeghwater (1575–1650), "millwright and engineer". Even before their time, however, the basis of military engineering had begun to be transformed. Just as the cannon, first used c. 1325, had by 1450 ended the military capability of private feudal armies, so in turn the new, complex, geometric designs of defensive works, that ensured that every wall could be enfiladed, ended the military credibility of small princes, who could no longer afford them. The first such fortress construction was that of Michele San Michele (1484–1559) for Verona in 1527–44, and the first bastioned citadel was that built by Francesco Paciotto (1521–91) for Antwerp in 1568, but the focus of further engineering advance now inevitably shifts to the great nation state, to France.

François I, king of France in 1515–47, invited Italian engineers to build his fortifications as well as other works like the towers at Toulon and Le Havre, and the Château d'If. Before long they were replaced by French engineers, and France, without a doubt, became the centre of the world's formal engineering science, the model and inspiration of the rest of Europe. She held this place until the middle of the 19th century.

Among military engineers it was Sebastian le Prestre de Vauban (1633–1707) who did most to confirm the technical superiority of the armies of Louis XIV. The sheer quantity of his work, made possible by the vast resources available to the French king, was overwhelming. He constructed, modified or repaired more than 160 fortified places, and although he shares with the Marquis de Montalembert (1714–1800) the reputation as leading engineer of defensive works, he was, in fact, more successful as a destroyer of defences. He led attacks, as chief engineer, on no fewer than 40 places, each one with success. Ending his days as a marshal of France, his career exemplified the need of the engineer of public works to be an organizer as well as a technologist, a master of men as well as of metal. It was he who, as early as 1672, had proposed a Corps des Ingénieurs de Génie Militaire, to give the military engineer status and self-respect as well as a framework within which to learn and to propagate his technology.

Still more important was the creation, in 1716, of the Corps des Ponts et Chaussées, the first great professional body of civil engineers, and this was followed, in 1747, by the foundation of the École des Ponts et Chaussées, their official college. The French Academy of Science had been founded in 1666, and of Architecture in 1671. By the end of the century, there were five provincial academies, and in the following century, almost another 40. Their membership often overlapped, and both scientists and engineers belonged to them.

French organized technology may be seen as but one aspect of the energy of the French state carried along by the buoyancy of its economy in that period. In its forward surge this technology made its mark on Europe in at least four different directions: actual constructions; the discovery of appropriate scientific laws; the description and the codification of existing practice; and the spread of these achievements abroad, by means of literature, visits and the settlement of French technologists in other countries.

Among the actual constructions, it was the great public works in which France was beginning to lead Europe. First there was the great network of roads and bridges itself built by such engineers as Jean Rodolphe Perronet (1708–94), first head of the new Engineering College. Then there were the canals, beginning with the 65-kilometre-long Canal de Craponne of 1560, named after its engineer, the Canal de Briare, built 1604–42, 65 kilometres long with 41 locks to link the Seine with the Loire, largely built by Hughes Cosnier (d. 1629), and the Canal d'Orléans, of 120 kilometres, 1682–92, engineered by Sebastien Truchet (1657–1729). The greatest of them all was the Canal du Midi or Canal des Deux Mers, linking the Atlantic with the Mediterranean by a water route of which the man-made section was 238 kilometres long, rising to a summit height of 189 metres above sea level by means of 120 locks (having a length of 35 metres between the gates), built in 1666–81.

This latter canal, a stupendous feat of engineering even by modern standards, was the work of Pierre-Paul Riquet de Bonrepos (1604–80). Once more, although the canal was a technical marvel, and included important innovations, particularly relating to its locks and the complex water supply to the summit, at least as much effort had to go into the organization of the 10,000 men who were employed to build it, and into the raising of the necessary funds for such a venture. Some of the money came from the central government, and some from the provincial authorities, both of which had to be bullied and cajoled incessantly against the advice of those who thought the project impracticable or who had other plans for the sums involved. A considerable part of the building costs, however, had to be provided by Riquet himself, who was given some tax farms in order to raise his share of the huge contribution. Riquet was neither the first nor the last French engineer associated with a work which might well be presented as contributing to human welfare or to national glory, but in fact needed strength of purpose amounting to an obsession to ensure its successful completion. He died before the canal was fully open, his death hastened by his exertions, and the canal was completed by his son. Apart from his political skill, Riquet also exemplified another aspect of the new engineer: since he began as a relatively minor excise officer, his career showed that the profession was open even to men of the lower middle classes without means, and that it had become one of the ladders by which the bourgeoisie made its way into the centres of power in Europe.

Two other works belonging to the two centuries before the French Revolution deserve to be picked out. One was the supply of water to the palace and fountains of Versailles. Requiring 14 waterwheels to pump the water up some 160 metres, it involved some path-breaking engineering calculations by Edmé Mariotte (1620–84) and a budget larger than that of many European states at the time. It was later calculated to have developed 75 horsepower. The other was the school of naval design, opened in 1739, and the experimental models for hull design tested in 1763–67 and 1776. The resultant superiority of French ships continued until the Revolutionary and Napoleonic Wars, when British ship builders copied the lines of captured French vessels, although by that time the British output of ships was several times as large as the French.

Among the innovators in the field of engineering science and technology were J. R. Perronet (1708–94), the first head of the École des Ponts et Chaussées, who devised a testing machine for the strength of stones, his assistant Antoine de Chézy (1718–98), who developed the hydraulic formula which still bears his name, and Pierre Trésaguet (1716–96), who devised a new base for road building, later adapted in Britain by Telford. Daniel Bernouilli (1700–82), a member of a most gifted family of French exiles, advanced the theoretical foundations for hydro-dynamics and the elastic properties of materials, and other fundamental advances on the theory of stresses and equilibrium of forces were made by Charles-Augustin de Coulomb (1736–1806). Finally, in this group, Gaspard Monge (1746–1818) should be mentioned, the founder of the École Polytechnique in 1795, and deviser of the modern method of engineering drawing, considered so important by the French authorities that they kept it a military secret for a quarter of a century.

Significantly, the British managed to develop their own and in some respects superior system without that help, and what is as striking as the French achievements in the field of civil and military engineering is their failure in the kind of mechanical engineering and industrial chemistry which depended for its sponsorship on individual enterprise and market forces. Thus the early atmospheric pump of Denis Papin (1647–1714) was neglected, and so was the demonstration of a practicable steam wagon in 1770 by Nicolas Cugnot (1725–1804). Similarly, chlorine bleaching, discovered by C. L. Berthollet (1749–1822), and the soda process, developed by Nicolas Leblanc (1742?–1806), benefited the British textile industry rather than the French. Even when, characteristically, French engineers like Gabriel Jars (1729–1808) were dispatched to Britain to spy out and observe the new technologies for Frenchmen to imitate, and English technologists like John Holker and the Wilkinson brothers were encouraged to set up works in France, they had little success.

In the third sphere, the description and systematization of existing practice, we have such contributions as those of Hubert Gautier (1660–1737), who published a treatise on road building in 1715 and on bridge building in 1716 and Bernard Forest de Belidor (1693–1761) whose *La Science des ingénieurs* appeared in 1729 and *Architecture hydraulique* in 1737. A survey of existing technology was prepared by one of the most original scientists of the day, Remy Antoine de Réaumur (1683–1757), and published by the Academy of Sciences in 1761–89, while Diderot and d'Alembert published their encyclopedia in 28 volumes in the period 1751–72, which plagiarized some of it, but also contained some of the best descriptions of technology and engineering practice extant. Finally, French engineers contributed to the advancement of Europe by inspiration and personal visits and migration. Many new universities derived from French examples and so did most academies of science, which became true international centres of knowledge, experimentation and practice. By 1790 there were around 220 of them in Europe, over 20 of them having Benjamin Franklin as one of their members in 1785. The German states, the Habsburg lands, Italy and Russia had Frenchmen among their engineers and engineering instructors; even Britain still found use for French engineering talent, as in the case of Charles Labelye (1705–81), the engineer of the Westminster Bridge opened in 1750, then the largest of its kind.

Side by side with the engineers of the grand public enterprises, the manipulators of governments and generals, the collectors of titles and medals, there also grew up a second type of engineer, more humble often in origin and ambition though not necessarily less affluent at the end of his career, basically more concerned with reducing costs than with gaining glory, a problem solver rather than an extender of known methods to a grander scale, often remaining in obscurity, one of a crowd, unaware even perhaps of the wider implications of his contribution. On the margin these two types overlapped, and in the later days of the British Industrial Revolution, by the time of the building of the railways, the two streams had come to mingle completely.

The leading country in this type of engineering in the two centuries from c. 1650 was Great Britain, but its roots were to be found in other regions of Europe. Many of the improvers and innovating designers of waterwheels, pumps, ploughs or metal furnaces remained anonymous, links in a long chain of modest gains which went back right across the Dark Ages. Their practices easily crossed such frontiers as existed, and in the days of the Renaissance, if not earlier, what is most striking is the rapid movement both of men and of ideas across the whole of the continent, wherever opportunity beckoned.

Thus printing, involving a fairly complex technology for which there was, however, a growing market in the European Renaissance, built on the earlier practice of pictorial printing, which had become quite widespread in the 1440s; and even the key innovation of movable type has been claimed, with some justification, by two centres, Mainz, where Johann Gutenberg (c. 1400–c. 1467) operated, and Haarlem, the city of Laurens Coster (fl. 1440). Within 30 years there were at least 382 presses in existence, of which 236 were in Italy, Venice being the main centre, but 100 years later the best printing had migrated from Venice, Basle and southern Germany to the Netherlands, to such families as the Plantins of Antwerp and the Elzevirs of Leyden.

In England and Scotland, most of the early printers and papermakers were German. It was also Germans who were largely responsible for that vital technological breakthrough, Elizabethan mining of tin, copper, lead and silver, and the making of brass. For Britain, then relatively backward, the practices introduced by such as Daniel Hochstetter of Augsburg (d. 1581) and Burchard Kranich (1515–78), mining entrepreneur and engineer, who introduced water-powered ore-crushing machines to Cornwall, represented a huge step forward. German mining engineering had made rapid strides from about 1450, when the rising monetary demands for silver for the expansion of commerce, as well as copper and tin for bronze gunmaking, called forth a great investment in central European, Italian and Spanish mining. German mining technologists swarmed over the mineral riches of many countries. With them they brought a whole range of innovations, such as horse whims with gearing, fan and bellow ventilation, rag and chain as well as suction pumps, a varied use of waterpower, and rail transport, as well as their language. Sometimes, indeed, linguistic borrowing went back even further: thus the ubiquitous "hund", or miners' railed waggon, though it sounds as though it is the German word for "dog", is likely to have its origin in the old Czech and Magyar languages, where it stood for a coach or a carriage. Hungary, Bohemia and Slovakia were the location of some of the most prolific mines and mineral works of the age.

A century later, the influx of the precious metals from the Americas, and the substitution of iron for bronze cannon, removed the basis of that central European prosperity, but the technology was not lost. Some of the more critical advances, particularly of a theoretical nature, continued to be made by Germans: thus Otto von Guericke (1602–86) demonstrated the power of a vacuum, or rather of atmospheric pressure, by first exhausting the air from two bronze hemispheres fitted together, and then proving that 16 horses could not pull them apart, until he opened the air valve. It may have astonished the members of the Imperial Diet, who came to watch, but more significantly, it laid the foundation for the atmospheric, and ultimately the steam engine. Other Germans invented and improved the watch, designed scientific instruments and advanced metallurgy, but the mantle of engineering leadership passed to Holland and ultimately to Britain.

Seventeenth-century Britain owed much to Dutch technology, in agriculture, for example, in pottery, in shipbuilding. It was Cornelius Vermuyden (?1590–1677) who undertook the first modern drainage scheme of the Fens. Before long, however, native engineers took over such schemes as drainage, river improvement and canals. They were often of humble origin. It was typical that biographical details even of such a leading engineer as George Sorocold (*fl.* 1690s) are missing, while James Brindley (1716–72), engineer of some of the main canal works which accompanied the British Industrial Revolution, had none of that polite learning which characterized the French, little or no formal science, and indeed little knowledge of technology, being obliged to "reinvent" innovations well known elsewhere. It was not long, however, before the British outdistanced their continental rivals. This is even more true of the local engineers.

Probably the most versatile British engineer of the mid-18th century was John Smeaton (1724–92), designer, inventor and inveterate improver. He conducted systematic experiments to improve the performance of windmills, water mills and atmospheric engines, designed cylindrical bellows for iron furnaces, built bridges, canals, dams and harbours, and found a way of building a safe Eddystone lighthouse after two earlier ones had been destroyed. His versatility was a response to the manifold opportunities opened to engineers and technologists in Britain: it has been said that a continental contemporary, like J. K. Hell (1718–85) of the great Schemnitz mines in Hungary, might have similar talents, but there was nowhere for him to exercise them outside the mine complex. With Smeaton, engineering edged forward to professional status in Britain, and the first group of engineers to organize regular meetings was called the Smeatonian Society.

As an innovator, Smeaton was overshadowed by possibly the most original engineering genius of the 18th century, James Watt (1736–1819). Trained as an instrument maker and employed at making and repairing instruments, laying out canals and the like, his interest in a model of the Newcomen engine, used at Glasgow University in 1763–65, led him first to improve its performance and economy by a separate condenser, and ultimately to change it into a true steam engine. Thus while the atmospheric engine designed by Thomas Newcomen (1663–1729) was limited in power by the pressure of the atmosphere, Watt's engine held the promise of almost unlimited power with ever greater steam pressure and ever greater thermal efficiency. For the next 100 years or so, he had solved one of the central problems of engineering, the problem of power.

Watt's basic idea rested on a scientific, calculable foundation, and throughout his lifetime he took an active interest in several pure sciences as he continued also to invent all kinds of other practical devices. His engine, however, was more than an abstract idea. He had to develop a whole range of subsidiary innovations, to create a whole new sub-branch of engineering, in order to make it work in practice; he had, in common with his partner Matthew Boulton (1728–1809), to devise new ways of marketing his engines, of fitting them for new uses, of reorganizing workshops to produce them. He had also to train a whole generation of engineers, many of whom in turn went out to set up businesses of their own, which further developed the practice of engineering, and became in turn practical academies to train fresh generations. The family tree of these builders and innovators can be traced for over a century, spreading its branches ever further in Britain and abroad, until replaced by more formal means of training.

Suddenly it seemed as though the whole country was teeming with engineering talent. The opportunities to build, to get rich, were there, and there were no vested interests, no guilds, no professional bodies to stop the innovators. The names of many of them are well known. Abraham Darby (1677–1717), discoverer of the coke-smelting process for iron making, for example, and Henry Cort (1740–1800) and Peter Onions (*fl.* 1780s) who developed the puddling process to make bar iron; or, in the cotton industry, Samuel Crompton (1753–1827), designer of the spinning mule, building on the earlier inventions of James Hargreaves (d. 1778) and Richard Arkwright (1732–92). But beyond them, there was a whole world of tinkerers, builders, improvers and projectors, many of humble origins, many of them untutored and even unlettered, who drove forward the practices of a hundred industries. Since almost everyone built his own machines – it was only in the 1820s, for example, that the first large cotton machinery makers set up in Manchester – everyone had an opportunity of adding his own small improvements.

In this fertile soil of provincial Britain probably the most portentous changes which occurred were those of the northeastern coalfield around Newcastle. There the need to work at ever greater depth to meet a growing market for coal in London and the east coast had created a closely knit group of managers and engineers known as coal "viewers" who proved remarkably inventive in accounting and management practice, in three-dimensional underground surveying and, above all, in mining engineering. Their pioneering work ranged over ventilation, geology, power and transport, among other fields, and it was by developing first the iron railway, and then the locomotive, that the northern engineers changed the world. George Stephenson (1781–1848), a humble engine tenter who rose to be the pioneer and builder of many early railways, was only one of many. A whole school of his associates and disciples, of whom Joseph Locke (1805–60) was perhaps the most talented, together with some others, like Isambard Kingdom Brunel (1806–59), began to cover Britain, and before long Europe and other continents, with railways developed directly from the pioneer coal-conveying lines of the Tyne, Wear and Tees.

The railways were not only by far the largest engineering works ever undertaken by man, they were themselves also the most powerful agents for change. In railway building two mainstreams of engineering, characterized here as the French and the British, met briefly, before the advance of technology split the profession into an ever larger number of specialisms with their own societies, examinations and training schemes. Railway engineers were not only technicians and designers: they were organizers of men, negotiators with governments and leading finance houses, they were instrumental in changing property laws relating to land, and ultimately they had a hand in changing social systems.

George Stephenson recorded once, in his early days of railway engineering, his amazement at the rapid changes of fortune in the course of one survey: one day getting wet through out on the line, sleeping rough in some poor cottage en route; the next, being feasted in a city-centre hotel; then back again among earthworks and tunnels. He personified the multi-faceted aspects of the new engineering. The engineers who fanned out from Britain to France, to Italy and Spain, and then soon after the Frenchmen who built railways in Italy, Austria or Russia, and ultimately the Italians, Germans and Austrians who came for the same purpose to the Balkans and Turkey, brought with them not only engineering workshops, ironworks and timetables. Many formed the first real contacts of sleepy towns and isolated countryside, of whole provinces often ruled autocratically and ignorantly, with the progressive capitalism of the west. In Britain railways were built to fulfil a need; in other parts of Europe, they were often built, or sanctioned by ambitious governments, to create a need, and to stir hidebound societies to catch up with the 19th century.

It is no accident that many of the revolutionaries in Russia, in the Austrian Empire, had science and engineering training, since technology itself was based on the notions of progress and on questioning tradition, including traditional privileges unjustified by utility. This marriage of ideas was best expressed in France by the St Simonians, a group usually characterized as socialist forerunners, but more aptly thought of as exalting the technocrat and his public works as a means of rationalizing the organization of society. St Simonians became railway pioneers, financiers and engineers, carrying the idea of public works as stimuli to economic advance across France as well as other parts of Europe. Perhaps the most famous result of their influence, the Suez Canal, built in 1859–69 by Ferdinand de Lesseps (1805–94) largely to the plans of A. von Negrellis (1799–1858), itself marked the achievement of the next stage in man's control over his environment.

From the early 19th century onwards, the work of engineers and technologists became too many-sided and advanced too fast to be adequately covered in a brief review without doing grave injustice to one or another aspect of it. Here only a few main trends and individual highlights can be picked out.

One was the gradual decline of the role of the gifted amateur, as the science grew and the mechanisms became more complex. The practical man still had a role to play for a more or less extensive period. Thus shipbuilding and marine engineering, after the change-over to iron and steel hulls, after the introduction of compound and even triple and quadruple expansion engines, and innumerable other technical innovations allowing greater speed, lower costs and larger size, might have been expected to be an early field for science-based constructions, but in the leading country, Great Britain, practical training in a goods yard or engine works appeared sufficient to the end of the century and beyond, except for those building naval vessels in royal dockyards. Other countries, it is true, linked ship and engine design to scientific principles earlier than Britain. Charles Parsons (1854–1931), designer of the steam turbine to be used in ships and power stations, was, however, a man of the new, formally trained school.

Again, much mechanical engineering, road building and even railway construction in Britain and elsewhere continued to rely for long on practical rules rather than fundamental understanding. Yet the signs of the times were there, and their symbol was the German *Technische Hochschule*, the technological university inaugurated with Darmstadt (1822), Karlsruhe (1825) and Munich (1827), to acquire by the 1890s, with its associated *Realschule* instead of the classically based *Gymnasium*, the prestige of the traditional seat of learning in Germany, and countries taking their lead from her. Behind its success also lay state-run laboratories, a high level of training for subordinate engineers, and a long-standing interest of the traditional universities in the natural sciences.

Germany took a leading role early on in electrical engineering and the chemical industry, both requiring a systematic science-based training. Werner von Siemens (1816–92), brother of William (1823–83), the inventor of the regenerative furnace, was an early experimenter in such problems as the conversion of mechanical into electrical energy and cable insulation, and became the head of one of the two giant electrical engineering companies which dominated Germany and Europe before 1914. Emil Rathenau (1838–1915) founded the other, partly based on early American patents. It was only within the framework of such giant concerns, with their enormous resources, their extensive research departments and their control over the market, that electrical and other engineers could find the facilities to operate and drive forward their subject within an increasing range of specialisms. Engineering increasingly became a matter of teamwork and of large-scale operations.

The development of chemical technology was not dissimilar. On the basis of the work of such chemists as R. W. von Bunsen (1811–99), who first used the spectrum for analysis purposes, studied the properties of gases and invented the carbon-zinc electric cell, and Justus von Liebig (1803–73), pioneer of agricultural chemistry, German chemical and pharmaceutical technology became dominant in Europe, based on a small number of giant firms. Their vast laboratories, manned by battalions of university-trained chemists and other scientists, represented a new departure in the pursuit of knowledge.

Possibly the most characteristic engineering product of the 20th century, the motor car, was the result of a number of innovations made in several countries by different engineers. Being a product of the assembly of numerous components, its design itself was an assembly of ideas.

One group of ideas was derived from the bicycle, converted from the pedal-less hobbyhorse, and developed rapidly in the 1870s and 1880s on a mass-production basis by such engineers as James Stanley (1801–81) of Coventry. These included wire-spoked wheels, pneumatic tyres, chain drives and ball bearings. The second innovation was that of the internal combustion engine. In 1859 Étienne Lenoir (1822–1900) designed an engine powered by an explosive mixture of gas and air, fired by an electric spark. Another Frenchman, Alphonse Beau de Rochas (1815–91), patented the four-stroke cycle for a gas engine, and this idea was incorporated in a more practical way by a German engineer, N. A. Otto (1832–91), in 1878, and became the prototype of numerous mass-produced stationary engines. These were developed in various ways by the end of the 19th century, but were unsuitable for vehicles which could not be expected to carry a supply of gas with them.

The third idea was to use liquid hydro-carbon fuel. One type of engine using oil as fuel, and compression as ignition, was the engine appropriately patented in England in 1892 by a German engineer born in Paris, Rudolf Diesel (1858–1913). Another German engineer, Gottlieb Daimler (1834–1900), who had developed a light-weight, high-speed motor ignited by hot-tube, designed a surface carburettor, converting petrol and air into an explosive mixture, in 1885. His patent engine of 1889, having two cylinders working on a common crank, was practical enough to be used in motor cars and motor boats as well as for stationary purposes.

Yet another German, Karl Benz (1844–1929), put this type of engine on a vehicle in 1885, adding further innovations, such as an induction coil and accumulator to provide the electric ignition. His first vehicle was a three-wheeler, but by 1893 he had designed a four-wheeled vehicle: the motor car had arrived. It was left to an English engineer, F. W. Lanchester (1868–1946), to reconsider the total design, not merely as a horseless carriage with adaptations, but as a means of transport of a different and novel character. His first vehicle of 1895–96 had a steel-tube frame and many features still found on motor cars, such as an epicyclic gearbox and differential, and Dunlop pneumatic tyres. Soon after, much-improved Lanchester types were on the road. The next stage of development belonged to the production engineer, finding his apotheosis in the USA where Henry Ford had got the first large-scale conveyor-belt assembly line going by 1912. Motor-car technology fundamentally affected the manufacture of numerous components, and led to innovations in such things as electrical equipment, safety glass, cellulose paint and rubber tyres, as well as to new technologies in road building and oil refining.

In the realm of civil engineering, new materials and new technology have in the last 100 years allowed the engineer to put up ever larger, ever more magnificent and breath-taking structures, while working to finer safety tolerances. At the beginning of that period, Gustave Eiffel (1832–1923), builder of bridges and expert on aerodynamics, constructed a 300-metre tower as an attraction for the 1889 Exhibition and a triumph of engineering, though at the time of little practical use: it became one of the few constructs ever which bore, for all the world, the name of its engineer. Tunnels like those across the Alps became longer and circumvented ever greater difficulties. Some roads, such as the Italian Autostrada del Sole, seemed to overcome the most daunting obstacles of nature with ease and a sense of beauty. The hydro-electric barrage at Kuibyshev, built in 1950–58, involved more moving of earth than the building of the Panama Canal, to yield 11·3 milliard kilowatt hours a year. The ability to reduce scantlings and weight without loss of strength was shown by such suspension bridges, built in the last 30 years, as those over the Seine, the Severn and (as yet incomplete) over the Humber. In Germany a complete Rhine bridge was moved sideways by several metres.

Some of the newest and most spectacular technologies are no longer pioneered in Europe, but are accepted from North American engineers and scientists. The telephone and gramophone were essentially American inventions. Radio, it is true, was based on the discoveries of European scientists and the technical genius of Gugliemo Marconi (1874–1937), but the main breakthroughs in television technology were due to the Americans, H. E. Ives (1882–1953) and V. K. Zworykin (1889–). Electric computers are largely built in the USA and, lately, in Japan. Powered flight, despite many early experiments in Europe, was first achieved by Americans, though some important later developments, like the jet engine designed by Frank Whittle (1907–) and supersonic commercial flight embodied in the Anglo-French Concorde and a Russian equivalent, were European. Rocketry became largely a German science, but its most startling results, the launching of satellites, of manned flights to the moon and unmanned flights to other planets, have so far been left to Americans and Russians to carry through.

Today's engineer or technologist has little in common with the lone geniuses who people the pages of history. He is an organizer of men, of materials, a manipulator of governments or of international consortia. He has the support of specialists, of instruments, calculators and electronic aids to design, undreamt of even by the most optimistic of his predecessors. A scientific literature and an up-to-date information retrieval system allow him to tap the latest ideas and discoveries from anywhere around the world. It has been calculated that the present generation of technologists, alive today, is larger than that of the whole past of humanity since history began, and they have a better formal training, grander universities and colleges, more specialized professional examining bodies, a safer career than ever before.

Will this swamping of the individual also stifle genius and originality? There is no sign of it yet. On the contrary, we are tapping ever new reserves of talent left fallow before. Equipment and technology take the tedium out of the engineer's work rather than blanketing his initiative. The variety of approach which characterizes European engineering derives from the rich and varied tradition of a crowded continent in which nations are sufficiently separate to compete, yet sufficiently close to learn from each other. Other regions of the world, such as North America or Japan, have now joined Europe in the van of technical progress, but the role of Europeans in this field remains as productive as ever before.

# 24

# Merchants and Bankers

## JOHAN DE VRIES

Long before merchants and bankers had taken the fate of the European economy into their own hands, determining both the political and the cultural look to a great extent, some continuity had already become apparent in trade and banking. This continuity is too characteristic to be left unmentioned as all essentials are rooted in the beginnings of history and what appears later can only be seen in perspective against this background.

Trade originated in primitive forms of bartering in kind during the Neolithic period. This was a transitional period between the stage at which man foraged and hunted for food and the time when agriculture and husbandry became widespread. The period is sometimes known as the Neolithic Revolution, referring to the marked growth in population which has taken place since then, the new types of production which began – including the manufacture of pottery and the building of mud huts – and the change-over from barter to organized trade. The urban revolution followed and it was during this period that the agrarian society started to form the economic and cultural foundation of the earliest class-structured society. The old Oriental civilizations evolved with population concentrations that we could call towns, where a wealth of productivity made building on a monumental scale possible (such as the temples) and where there was a clearly defined power and authority structure which also laid down the rules for economy and trade. Gradually the primitive collectivism surrounding the family hierarchy as a close-knit institution made way for a differentiated collectivism which led to a progressive formation of states, seen from a political viewpoint, and a permanent differentiation in the social and economic spheres.

One is no less important than the other and both are characterized by a division of labour, the social differentiation created by professions leading to social groups which descend from kings and similar charismatic figures, priests and other servants of deities (the magic and religious spheres) down to the nobility, the military, slave owners, free merchants and traders and finally the slaves. Economic differentiation is the other side of this: the diversification of production, the refinements in consuming, and above all, the development of distribution, which is our main concern here. This is reflected in the change from providing one's own needs (of the family, clan or community) to bartering in kind, and finally to the creation of markets and use of money, backed by the growth of the function of capital and many forms of loans and interest.

During the Neolithic period the formation of capital actually functioned as a form of economic differentiation, the most important factor in the progress of society. This concept of capital underwent some refinements as a result of the use of metal money in the ancient lands of the east. The combination of growth – however slight – and the refinement of the function of the economic system are the essential factors for the formation of an element of continuity in trading and banking. Trading and banking are part of an enriched life in two senses. They are also an expression of permanence. This is why there was no trade, let alone banking, during the Paleolithic and Mesolithic periods. There was some bartering of ornaments such as shells, pearls and amber, often as part of a dowry for a bride at her wedding, as other ritual gifts or possibly in exchange for tools. However, at this stage it was still too intermittent and unconnected with particular people as the instigators of the economic function, i.e. with merchants and bankers. However primitive the forms of trading may seem to our eyes, real trade started during the Neolithic Age and was characteristic of the growth and refinement of the economic system. For a long time it was connected with elements of robbery (such as piracy) and bound to primitive forms of money such as shells, pearls, salt and stones, and a little later also certain tools such as axes and metal rings known as "tool money" until metal money was first used. After this, trading and banking became functions which might still be repressed in certain societies but no longer permanently. They changed form depending on the state of economic development. There were no limits to their growth – another typical characteristic of continuity, totally in keeping with the nature of their dynamic character. It is an obvious and not very striking fact that different areas were linked together by trade at the start of the second millennium BC. Amber was taken south from the Baltic area, shells went to central Europe from the Aegean. Naturally this was only a trickle of goods. It is a modern trend to think in terms of expansion; it is the persistence which counts.

Up to now, these things say more about trading and banking than about merchants and bankers, let alone about Europe. But it is quite clear that trade is based on economic needs, i.e. on purchasing power and on the spatial distribution of goods in the expectation of profit. Trading will start within a very simple and institutional framework of politics, economics and law. Banking, as trade in money, is a direct consequence. The border between the two remained obscure for a considerable length of time.

Beginning in the Neolithic Age, there are many things to consider before we can arrive in Europe, as it were, and look at merchants and bankers in more meaningful detail. The elements of continuity indicated above form the common line which can be summed up as the link between the development of trading and banking, merchants and bankers, and the growth and refinement of the economic system. The road is certainly not a straight one, seen through time. For this we have only to look at the centrally administered river-bank economies in Egypt and Mesopotamia and the centrally governed economies of the east, China and India, during the Neolithic Age. For all their historical and cultural differences, these were all despotic economies founded on a religious basis which effected a redistribution of wealth upwards from the productive population to the ruling class by means of a large state administration. They formed a basis for the development determined by agriculture and public works in which trading and banking play only a marginal role. The dead weight of a despotic state with its centralized economy and insecurity for the individual and for property is a serious handicap to general economic progress. People do not go into production on a grand scale if they are immediately robbed of their rewards by the powers above. As it was, the authorities levied heavy taxes on trade and slowed it down with numerous tolls when they did not control foreign trade themselves; this was the case with Egypt. Nevertheless, trade can never be totally repressed even though it may go underground in the form of smuggling. Trading caravans were organized to cover long distances and overcome certain dangers. In some cases there were even trading colonies, like those of the Assyrian merchants in the 19th century BC, over 1,000 kilometres from their mother city of Assur.

At this point banking also became a well-defined activity. In the beginning it took the form of private individuals, merchants, the palace (i.e. the government and especially the temples) giving loans from their own means, usually for agricultural purposes. This is how things were in both the Old and the New Babylonian periods (from about 2000 to the 5th century BC). During this period banking was refined to the point where loans were also given to trading companies; a few received deposits and so avoided the necessity of borrowing money at the same time. Some economists consider that it is only at this stage that we can start to use the term "bank" but this is merely a question of definition; a bank could just as easily be defined as a creator of money. The fact that to receive a deposit in the Babylonian period was exceptional as a banking activity with a payment of interest, while it was common practice in Greece in the 5th century BC, is connected with the arrival of the coin. In Babylon payments were still made in kind or in quantities of silver. In this respect banking was enriched in Greece so that it became possible to receive deposits on the basis of an easier method of payment, the coin. In fact it is irrelevant whether the Greek bank was founded on precursors in the Near East or not.

The small states, often no larger than cities, which arose in the last millennium BC, proved very fertile for the development of banking. It was there that for the first time in history the individual could maintain his independence and become a foundation stone of the economic system. Think of Phoenicia, the Aramaic cities such as Harran and Damascus, and, above all, the Greek city-states. The social or unambiguous acceptance of private property and the resulting concepts of law are an extension of the *political* philosophy, as of the *economic*. Economics is not only a political affair but also a private matter. The slave system was the only primitive aspect of this society.

Against this background merchants and bankers appear in a far more distinct light. Greece and Phoenicia were infertile regions and therefore led to expansion and colonization. Individualism, the lust for adventure and the love of action became enriched with the love of freedom and the spirit of scientific investigation when freed from the obsessions of the old belief, the fear of the supernatural and the constriction of life after death. In this period of dynamic economy and a more refined differentiation, new sorts of traders evolved during the 7th century BC. These were the *naukleres*, merchants who traded from their own ships; the *emporos* who, as a passenger, ferried his wares to distant markets; the *kapelos*, the professional established trader and wholesaler. Gradually wholesalers emerged as specialists concentrating on particular goods, in addition to those who traded on commissions, and brokers. Banking activities, which we have already looked at, were becoming refined and were carried out on a greater scale, independently or as a subsidiary activity of shipowners, merchants and landlords, receiving deposits, loaning money against security, and with the precursor of an exchange. This was also true of maritime insurance. However, they were not big business and there was little productive credit in trade and industry.

This was a line of development which is reminiscent of recent European history, but was in fact collapsing continuously in the Western Roman Empire. There is no need to outline the course of this dramatic downfall, but it is worth remembering that parallel to this course of events the vigorous, more or less free-enterprise, economy of the 5th century AD made way for the decentralized manorial system which was the dominant characteristic of the Middle Ages in Europe. In addition, the Mediterranean Sea became a virtually Arabian inland sea a few centuries later in about 750 AD as a result of Arab opportunism. The economic life of Europe may not have disappeared altogether, but trade was certainly pushed back to an insignificant component compared with the all-powerful agrarian branch of the economy which determined everything, a consequence of the trading connections through the Mediterranean Sea being cut off. Once this page was turned, a new chapter began.

The history of real European trade and, following in its footsteps, banking, is the story of its struggle to escape from the feudal system characterized by the manorial economy. Trade never quite stopped completely and the bond with the east was not entirely broken. For example, between the 5th and the 11th centuries changes in the ratio of value between gold and silver in the Arabian world became noticeable almost immediately in the west. In addition, the Arabs by no means prevented European seas other than the Mediterranean from being used. In northern Germany and Scandinavia there were traders bringing eastern goods to the west through Russia. Haithabu was an example of one of these settlements, and the Dutch Dorestad was also part of the picture of north Germanic trade. Frisian trade certainly continued to flourish until the 11th century. Today even the Vikings are thought to have stimulated trade because their raids put a lot of precious metals into circulation; these had previously been used as vessels in religious ceremonies. It was not a very nice thing to do; nor were the activities of the slave traders who were especially common in Verdun. They had a good, captive market for slaves in Muslim Spain. In general the traders did not operate outside society, though the Church had little sympathy for the many bandits and plunderers among them. It is not indicative of great development that the ruling groups in the early Middle Ages gave each other many gifts, but by the 11th century there were definitely regular groups of traders. These included many Jews who were often at an advantage because of their relations with fellow believers in the Muslim world. There were also numerous Christian *mercatores* who were often in the service of the Church or an abbey, or of rulers or other influential people. It was always possible for the religious and secular domains to sell off surplus land to make up a deficit. Of course these traders dealt in luxury goods, but above all in grain, wine and fish.

Nevertheless this was all marginal to the agrarian system founded on autarchy and it cannot merely be attributed to the fact that transport was poor during the Middle Ages that it remained marginal for so long. In fact the opposite is the case: transport, particularly overland, continued to be bad because trade was relatively unimportant, and consequently the trader was socially inferior and had no power to effect improvements. His significance lay in his very presence and it was this that ensured continuity in trade, few in number and undefined though traders were. This was the connection with the new era that came with the 11th century.

It was only then that the dynamic development of trading and banking and their offshoots of transport, traffic and insurance became the determining factors for economic growth. (The causes for this are indicated below.) This phase of commercial, financial capitalism was not to merge into the industrial era before the Industrial Revolution at the end of the 18th century. At this stage merchants and bankers did not disappear but they did get rather lost in the accelerating development; between the 11th and the 18th centuries they had still been ahead of all this. The expanding proportions of population, affairs and business mean that we can look more closely at the business and transactions of individuals; their area of activity was expanded because of the possibility of, and the numerous demands made by, the population explosion, the growth of a consumer society and the expansion of economic space. The economic aspect of the *integrated* developmental process of Europe, together with its political, social and cultural aspects, was personified by the merchants and bankers of the time. It is less interesting to know to what extent they relied on the old traditions than to know what new and unique practices they added to their sphere. For it is, above all, these things that determined their typically *European* character. Obviously it was all part of a continuity, but the continuity expanded and took a new direction. It had never happened before that merchants and bankers had taken the economic fate of an entire continent into their own hands and determined the political and cultural situation; it is unique, seen against what happened before – which is why we have to accept it – and against what will happen – which is why we shall have to accept it: a mutation which can never be repeated because of its very nature.

It seems to be an enigma how things could go so far, even though anyone thinking in evolutionary terms will have no difficulty detecting some hints of it in the economic system of antiquity with its accent on greater individualism and legal security. At that time political affairs were given more serious consideration than economic affairs. The latter were left to freedmen and slaves as an inferior activity; it was therefore a handicap to economic development which could not be overcome in one phase of civilization. It required a change of outlook to end the rejection of business and all its mundane aspects. It was not until the Middle Ages that a world existed where business could be seen in another light.

After the 11th century the line of European economic development was geared to a world with increasingly earthly values and it flourished because of the demographic growth which had occurred, the colonization of eastern Europe, the Crusades and repulsion of the Arabs who lost Sardinia, Corsica and Sicily in the 11th century. It was during this century, and especially in the next, that renewed contact was made with the east and began to have an effect. Focal points of economic activity evolved in Italy and the Netherlands. Italian cities like Venice, Genoa, Florence and Pisa had commercial contacts in the Near East, and from the 12th century with countries north of the Alps; over the Brenner Pass with southern Germany and over the St Bernard with France, where their merchants visited the annual markets of the Champagne district. These Italians met merchants from the Netherlands who were responsible for maintaining trade between south, west and northern Europe.

After this, economic development did not proceed at such a fast rate, slowed down by overpopulation, failed harvests, endemic warfare and the Black Death. These overwhelmed

Europe in the middle of the 14th century and it was not until the second half of the 15th century that it was to recover. This all happened on the eve of the great voyages of discovery, *the European adventure before space travel*, which extended the boundaries of the market-based society all over the world, to America and India. With their muddled motives of curiosity, missionary zeal and greed, they encapsulated the essence of the daring economic pioneer in his impetuosity. It is not necessary here to describe the complications and foresee the typical details which actually resulted from these. The economic expansion which was a consequence was admittedly divided unequally throughout Europe, but nevertheless produced all the typical characteristics of pre-industrial society which was preceded by the formation of nations, urbanization and the beginnings of a refinement in economic institutions and techniques and which resulted in the expansion of political and economic dimensions as well as the continued development of institutions and techniques – whether political or economic – which were necessitated by this. As far as economic affairs were concerned, the merchants and bankers were the builders of this new European world. Agriculture still formed the fundamental basis of the economy; the industrialists, if they may be called such so soon, reached for their best stones in order to build. Frequently one person fulfilled both a mercantile and an industrial function. In any case, merchants and bankers dominated the economic scene at this time just as industrialists were to during the next phase of history. They enable us to build up a portrait from a few characteristics and their multiple activities add colour and shade.

All differences of time and place (the time: from the 11th to the 18th century; the place: Europe) conjure up not one but many images, not a static but a moving portrait; nor do they eradicate the fact that the social aspects can be enclosed like the four sides of a picture frame by the phenomena of progress, specialization, creation and penetration. They show us the merchant and the banker as daring but not reckless, laying a network of economic affairs throughout the world for seven centuries. The stream of goods, money and capital was pumped through these channels while the functions of wholesaling and retailing, transport, insurance and financing became more and more specialized through various individuals; i.e. several functions were no longer carried out by one person. For this the necessary techniques and institutions were created and there was a breath of new life stimulating a very different economic spirit, finally also penetrating the social, political and cultural spheres with shades of influence which ended in a complete assumption of power. Both small and great, magnates and hagglers, fit into this picture, depending on the way our historical telescope is focused.

With regard to the stimulation of trade noted above, it is not only important that increasing quantities and an expanding range of old and new products were involved, but also that it brought about a transition from travelling to established merchants. From the 11th to the 13th century merchants travelled with their goods in the hope of finding a market. In later times this kind of merchant reappeared, reduced to an insignificant pedlar in terms of the total economic picture. During the late Middle Ages there was a development towards merchants becoming established in trading centres managing their affairs overland and overseas through small and large trading companies. To do this they would exchange letters with factors in other trading towns in the Netherlands and abroad giving them knowledge of the possibilities of buying and selling as well as telling them about the necessary channels to accomplish their business. This change from travelling to established merchants spread throughout Europe from the Italian commercial centres on and near the Mediterranean coast. It spread so far that the Venetian merchant, Guglielmo Querini (1400–68), never actually set foot outside Venice. The development continued as a result of the improvements in shipbuilding and navigation techniques; it then evolved further in the Hanseatic north and western Europe with the numerous trading towns that were members of this league during the 13th and 14th centuries; the great trading companies of the 17th century are an especially good example of the development.

Is this really so different from Classical antiquity with its comparable commercial phenomena and practices? In themselves the periods were not very different, though the development was, and more particularly, so was the way it continued. We must remember that one of the innovations was the progressive movement towards an increasingly defined differentiation. This occurred in all practices which were old, borrowed or copied to form the specifically new European trading system.

This is also true of the second element noted above: specialization. Essentially the transition from travelling to established merchants is an example of this because it presupposes a division between people who stayed at home and those who took care of transportation. But a similar transition can also be seen in the economic subjects themselves. Previously the merchant had done a variety of different jobs. In the past the important things had been *looking at* and *seeing* people and objects, but then came Willem Servat. This man from the south of France who had established himself in London from the 1270s was an exporter of wool and an importer of silk, spices, sugar and wine, as well as lending money to King Edward I among others. Apart from these activities he became a marriage broker, for he was sent to Norway with a great deal of money by King Edward to bring about the marriage of his son to the daughter of the Norwegian King Eric. The latter in his turn also used Servat's services by having him collect taxes for commission. Good relations with the courts were profitable in yet another way when Servat only received a light sentence for committing the common crime of counterfeiting. Two centuries later, things were not very different for Jacob Fugger der Reiche, who controlled the well-known trading company of Augsburg from 1510 to his death in 1525. He was a merchant and industrialist with interests in silver and copper mines in the Tyrol and Hungary, and he acted as a banker for the pope and the Habsburgs among others. Without Fugger, Charles V could not have become emperor in 1519, and this is the step that takes us from specialization to penetration. It was a deliberate step and shows us how interrelated all these activities were.

Specialization, which comes down to a splitting up of functions, only happened gradually. Examples are the split between wholesalers and retailers and the separation of secondary functions such as insurance and freighting; something of this can be seen in the 16th century when professional representatives and brokers dealing in goods first appeared. By the 17th century *cargadores* were also dealing in space in the holds of ships. The most striking development, though, was the interaction of commercial functions with banking activities; even as early as the second half of the 18th century there was a close connection between trade and banking in the distinguished Amsterdam house, Hope & Co. The most impressive aspect was the specialization of regions and products which gradually developed as trade expanded with the opening up of the world through the voyages of discovery.

The whole of Europe, from the extreme north to the south and from the west to the furthest east, participated in these developments and felt the effects. The Italian cities of the late Middle Ages had acted as the centres of gravity in relation to the Mediterranean Sea; the centres of gravity now moved to Bruges and Antwerp in Flanders during the 15th and 16th centuries because of the movement towards the Atlantic Ocean which was a consequence of the voyages of discovery. Finally London and Amsterdam became the centres during the 17th and 18th centuries for political and competitive economic reasons. They were like the peaks of a mountain range in which smaller trading concentrations also contributed to the whole and were in fact essential to it. During this period the European character of the merchant banker and the banker was formed. The nuances of Goethe's poem catch the essence:

> War, trade and piracy,
> Three in one, indivisible.

However, creative, opportunist organization and disposal of risk also became hall-marks of traders and bankers, not very different from – and therefore comparable with – the demands made by warfare and piracy, as the diversity of a new management under the common denominator of the risk factor.

Neither of these things is new: neither the requirement of conquering from a distance, nor the necessity to cover risks. It is the combination of great distances, geographical and practical, and the increased scope of trading and banking activities which created the original dimensions and were probably responsible for the way in which both problems were overcome, although we should not imagine that this was an easy process in the sense that it was not without defects;

old stones were used to build the new edifice – as happened in many European activities and ways of thinking – incorporating their own original aspects. It is an odd European contrast that national boundaries were given more significance at the same time that the economic culture in institutions, instruments and life-styles grew together to form a more closely knit unit. Outside Europe, the European merchant or banker could be recognized at a glance, but only when he spoke would people recognize his nationality: Italian, Portuguese, Spanish, German, French, Flemish, Dutch or English. He was greeted as a conqueror, a saviour, barbarian, intermediary from a more advanced civilization, or something of each, depending on the time and place in this specific mixture of power and superpower experienced by nations outside our continent. If the economics and politics of Europe were characterized in any way, it must have been by the mercantilism of the young European nations which varied considerably from each other but outwardly kept solidly to the *pacte colonial*. This meant that the sole purpose of the colonies was to serve the fatherland, providing its staple market of raw materials, buying industrial products and leaving the transport between the colony and the fatherland entirely to the latter. In all this there was a spirit which could be described as an attempt to limit risks in the economic sphere, not to mention the political aspects. It was more apparent in the one than in the other and at the same time it permeated the institutions, instruments and life-styles of the European merchants and bankers – the attempt to limit risks which, as we all know, conceals the need for security.

The history of the institutions and instruments of trading and banking during the commercial, financial capitalist era is at the same time the history of risk taking, and the way in which risks were covered for the money and goods which were being pumped into circulation. Ways of doing this were learnt and practised. An empirical edifice arose, built on this foundation, as impressive as any other cultural phenomenon, though less unanimously appreciated by later generations because they no longer had an understanding of the economic aspect of risk taking and the realization of its less savoury aspects had disappeared – aspects that can be discarded in playing with risks. It was this speculation that tested the new instruments and institutions as a sort of piracy in playing and gambling, often resulting in economic aberrations as a consequence of an unbridled passion for gambling. However, reputable merchants and bankers of any standing were not so reckless, for in this respect as in others their activities were risky enough, even when the risks were limited.

The evolution that began in the 11th century led by the Italian cities was transferred to the Netherlands and England in the second half of the 16th century. There was a curve in the trade of goods which assured their presence at annual fairs, staple markets and trading fairs. Goods were traded at the fairs in a context that was legally and judicially protected and regulated; mass goods determined by type and quality from samples passed from hand to hand. This kind of market arose in Bruges and became important in Antwerp during the 15th and 16th centuries. In 1611 an exchange was established in a building in Amsterdam. Here merchants met to make deals, shipping factors arranged voyages and cargoes, insurance policies were taken out, and there were also exchanges, speculations and gambling. By the 16th century business in advance (i.e. sales with a condition of delivery at a later date) had become accepted in Antwerp. The unpredictable price of pepper or grain was a good enough reason for speculation on a large scale. In 17th-century Amsterdam there were complaints about "cornering the market"; i.e. buying up supplies in order to create a monopoly, for example in the sugar, copper or saltpetre trade.

The enlargement of scale created the possibility of mobilizing capital and spreading risk. This can be seen in the *contratto di commenda* which started in the 10th century and subsequently spread elsewhere to become very common. This system involved two partners: one providing the capital and one travelling. It originated in Byzantium and initially the arrangement was only valid for one sea voyage, but by the 13th century it covered longer periods of time and had become more common. Small and large providers of capital could participate in the system and for this reason the *commenda* has been compared to the stock exchange. Similar combinations also occurred in other places like the *Sendeve* or *Gegensteitige Ferngesellschaft* in the Hanseatic towns, but these differed considerably from the great trading and banking houses of Lucca, Piacenza, Siena and Florence which conjure up the names Alberti, Frescobaldi, Peruzzi and Medici. These were family companies with unlimited liability for the capital taken up from partners and third parties. There was a strong element of continuity in the family connection and such a striking element of risk-spreading that no further explanation is needed. In 1408 legislation in Florence put an end to this unlimited liability of the passive partners, i.e. those who only provided the capital. Obviously this meant that they increased in numbers, and it is also clear that it led to the exploration of a form of organization which resulted in the great trading companies of the 17th century after centuries of experimentation in combining people and capital. One of the first of these companies was the Nederlandse Verenigde Oost-Indische Compagnie; it was founded in 1602 and was the precursor of the limited company. This was widely copied in England in the same period and during the 18th century. Here the possibility of spreading out risks reached a temporary high point, though at the same time the danger of abuse had not yet been curbed by legislation. This became apparent in 1720 with the foundation of a number of "bubble" companies.

Historical presuppositions can be justified if they throw light on other topics; for example, if the Industrial Revolution with its need for capital combination among industrial companies had not prospered in the 19th century, the need for the limited company would also have been less acute. Admittedly the great trading companies were precursors of limited companies and pointed to an expectation of something better, but at this time they were all too often economically "top heavy", incompletely organized, supplied with government patents and the resulting protection from above which made possible many trading ventures but also made them more complicated. The international houses were far better organized up to the 19th century and even in our own time. They originated in the Italian merchant cities, as we saw above, and became well known later thanks to Fugger. They developed fully in harness with the economic expansion and the persecution of religious minorities during the 17th and 18th centuries. The contacts between the mother company in a particular commercial centre and the establishments controlled by it abroad were facilitated by existing family ties. This can be seen in the Dutch Jews who came to London when it succeeded Amsterdam as the international centre of trade in the 18th century. After this they played a major part in the London banking and insurance world and as investors in the government debt. No less famous are the activities of the Huguenots in the same era; they connected centres like Geneva, Berne, Paris and Frankfurt with London through their family relations, virtually monopolizing the financial relations between England and France. During the 1830s and 1840s large numbers of Turks came to London, mostly originating from the Greek Orthodox minority. There are numerous examples of this sort of thing, also in countries across the Atlantic Ocean. But even leaving these aside, the intolerance – though not always present in the spread of international houses but so common from the time of heterodoxy that we could call it an institutionalizing element of continuity – had a strangely beneficial effect.

These international houses conducted not only trade in goods but also financial transactions, some of them exclusively. This was long after the time that western business techniques could not compare with those of the east, for even during the 13th century Venetian merchants had advanced further than Byzantines in this respect, and by the beginning of the 11th century Europe was the most developed area of the world as far as business was concerned. This was true of both money and banking, in institutions and instruments. One thing is clear above all others: when economic activity started to increase in the late Middle Ages, bringing with it the regular use of money, there was a growing need for a reliable form of exchange to fulfil this monetary function. It was obviously a general need, but it was particularly evident in the expanding world of trade which needed a coin – one might say the *ideal* coin – which was not subject to the risk of devaluation by monarchs or private individuals, especially when paper money had become established, albeit at the mercy of the whims of a press which was controlled by human beings. The attempt to achieve this ideal followed a long course and much of the last lap was run in our own time; in any case it opened the way to a great deal of creativity both in those people who used it to build and in those who used it to destroy. There is no need to dwell on all the particulars and it is easy to imagine that there must have been a certain amount of well-ordered national and international payment before trading and financial transactions increased.

The path followed in this respect led from concrete – hard cash – to abstract – paper money – with an increased control over it through the regulation of the national states. New coins were minted in many places in the late Middle Ages which made it difficult to disregard the shortage of metal money. For many systems it was a reason for money changers to become important again, and this in fact happened in the 11th century. In the meantime trade continued to flourish but the quantities of metal could not keep pace. It was only at the end of the 15th century that the production of silver from central European mines increased because of technical improvements, and it was only in the 16th century that the voyages of discovery led to a constant flow of metal from the Americas. Before this the lack of metal had been the biggest problem, especially as much gold and silver had flowed eastwards in payment for luxury articles imported into Europe. Once more, inventiveness provided a solution and the exchange came into use in the 12th century, probably based on Arab examples; by "exchange" we mean an order for payment based on a trading transaction. Initially this took a very simple form, but soon it developed into the promissory note and by the 15th century endorsements were introduced as a real form of paper money in addition to the form of cheque used at that time. This paper money not only had the advantage of supplementing the shortage of other money but gradually made the need for carrying cash or coins superfluous. This also limited the element of risk involved, e.g. of robbery. It does, however, presuppose the presence of a flexible intermediary to hasten and execute the process. During the same period this practice spread worldwide, starting with the banks in the Italian cities of Florence, Venice, Genoa and Pisa with their branches in all the important European centres like those of the Medicis, and then, in the centuries that followed, it spread to the banks of the successive world trading centres: Bruges, Antwerp, Amsterdam and London.

A pattern emerged in all this, such as in the similarity of the books of the Lomellini in Genoa and of Collard de Marke and Guillaume de Ruyelle in Bruges during the 14th century. It is obvious that new banking functions were added to the old. Credit was given not only for productive but also for consumptive purposes by the Lombards in their numerous money-lending houses, not to mention the creation of a bank transfer system. It is well known that the Amsterdamse Wisselbank gave some order to the chaotic coin problem by providing merchants with a stable currency, the so-called "trade coins" which squared debts with countries when there was a passive trade balance. The creation and growth of the transfer bank were promoted and controlled because the authorities decreed that payments of bills of exchange over 600 guilders should be paid through a bank. The bank's reserves made available in this way formed a stable element in financial transactions. These bills of exchange became increasingly common; in 1634 there were 12 rates of exchange in Amsterdam. In addition to advancing goods on security, giving a discount on exchange was a common practice and a way of giving merchants credit. Drawing credit made it possible for Holland to finance a considerable part of world trade during the 18th century; as the Amsterdam bankers gave extremely reasonable terms, foreign merchants made great use of this form of credit. During the same period the issuing activities of the Amsterdam merchants and bankers – of which Hope & Co was the greatest – gained an international reputation for placing loans from foreign powers in Dutch colonies.

It is not a big step from the bill of exchange to the bank note, which after all is "real" money to us. In 1661 the Bank of Stockholm became the first bank to issue bank notes, but the development was particularly striking in England during the 17th century where merchants gave their stores of coins to goldsmiths for safekeeping in return for the so-called "goldsmiths' notes". Soon the merchants realized that they could spend more notes than they had coins in safe-keeping, obviously a sign of their credit standing. This was essentially the start of the issuing bank. The first was the Bank of England, founded in 1694 by the government and therefore official. It was granted permission to issue bank notes; England was ahead of other countries in this respect, and even more significantly the bank notes of the Bank of England had the general confidence of society by the beginning of the 18th century. This is characteristic and praiseworthy considering the risk, for the worth of what after all was only paper still had to be proved.

The Bank of England and its bank notes weathered the storm of 1720 particularly well, and this is as typical of the advances in financial capitalism as it is of the dangers threatening it. The roots of this go back to the 17th century when stocks and shares started in Holland, especially shares in the East India Company and the West Indies Company which were known as "parts" or "parties" at the time, soon to be called "actions" (or shares). After this, government bonds came on to the market and were dealt with in a separate corner of the stock exchange. Speculation or gambling on the stock exchange sprang up alongside real trade; this was described by De la Vega in *Confusions de confusiones* which appeared in 1688. It was the first important book about the stock exchange, describing all the traders' twists and tricks, their habit of selling short and speculating for a rise. Great merchants took up a reserved position as far as the stock exchange was concerned; they preferred to leave it to traders of lesser importance, though this did not lead to total impartiality. The members of the Trip family invested heavily in government bonds but were not averse to gambling in large sums. Playing the stock exchange became a permanent pursuit for all levels of society.

This appetite for speculation was something new, a continuation of the already present and primitive gambling instinct. It had surfaced before in the commodities trade; the tulip boom of the 1630s in Holland is a celebrated example. In the 18th century this speculation fever was associated with the year 1720 and the name of John Law. This Scot founded an issuing bank in France in 1716 modelled on the Bank of England, but he circulated too many bank notes and gave over-large loans to the state and the Mississippi Company which he had himself founded in 1717. Neither the bank nor the company could withstand the fever of speculation in the company shares and the well-founded distrust of Law's management. In 1720 the Mississippi bubble burst. In the same year speculation in England brought about the collapse of the South Sea Company which had been founded in 1711. It is striking that the consequences of these excesses of speculation were felt not only in England, Holland and France, but in all the important trading centres in Europe. The development of the limited company was held back and there was general suspicion of the big banks which issued paper money, though the Bank of England survived it all very well. The issuing banks were to become a product of the 19th century after all, as was the improved coin standard, whether as the gold or the double standard. Both the issuing bank and the coin standard were the result of centuries of development, and as long as governments managed to control their love of splendour and warfare, they were also an example of the equilibrium between controlled government operations and private activities. In this the government ensures that the rules of the game are followed by private individuals who are responsible for these institutions flourishing for the sake of the economy, national and international. Human failings have seen to it that this system never became more than an aspiration which disappeared entirely in the wake of World War I, but this does not detract from the fact that even in their temporary character both institutions formed an eternal monument to the European spirit of inventiveness. At the same time they were a keystone for what was to follow – as is usually the case with this sort of monument.

Everything that has been said here about the instruments and institutions – showing their creative possibilities as clearly as the difficulty of determining the boundary between the two allows – contains an undercurrent of notation, registration and calculation which endeavoured to diminish the risks in the fields of communication and accountancy or even eliminate risks altogether. For the first – communication – it can be formulated briefly as follows: the European world of merchants and bankers had become a world of correspondence in which letters were the primary vehicle of communication until the invention of the telegraph and the telephone. The government postal services had literal "forerunners" in the sense that much of the post was taken by foot. These forerunners were the private messengers and messengers for special occasions for merchants and for particular towns. The significance of receiving news in connection with market situations is clear, and this is why the Dutch trading towns demanded daily postal deliveries from the government postal service though it was not considered necessary for the other parts of Holland: a rather free interpretation of public interests determined by the merchants' interests.

Accountancy requires more careful scrutiny; it could be described as the application and use of a written system of calculation, made by and for the use of private individuals, companies or the government. An image of musty book-keeping by dusty book-keepers is what springs readily to a layman's mind. This image is not completely without truth, though it reveals only one side of the picture, indeed not much more than the surface. Accountancy as it has developed since the 11th century is a major part of the new management required by dispatching goods over greater distances in larger amounts. It is the foundation, and far more than the mere technique, of book-keeping, however important this might be, an integral part of management, directorship and policy formulation. There was no comparable system for observation and notation during the Classical period and the Middle Ages. At those times economic life was not permeated by a rational pursuit of profit which required strictly defined placing and calculation of costs, for example in the sense that Cipolla means when he says that "the Dutch of the 17th century had a genius – if not an obsession – for reducing costs." There was no world-embracing market structure to aid the placing and registration of long distances. Only when trading and banking acquired any status did accountancy become more refined, though it had not yet reached the refinement of double-entry book-keeping. This was only introduced at the beginning of the 13th century in the Italian merchant towns as part of what is known as the commercial revolution. In the second half of the 15th century Benedetto Cotrugli and Luca Pacioli laid down what was to form both a codification and a manual for this new type of accountancy. Their system was followed by a long series of similar instructive guides with increasingly advanced techniques which have been published ever since in all the world's trading centres. This development culminated in the 19th century in a complete form of accountancy with the typical figure of the accountant who leaned towards an independent function.

Inevitably the merchants and bankers of Europe who had moved to the forefront became specialists and creators from the 11th to the 18th century, and they were also penetrators of society; this is the fourth side of the picture frame of their portrait. There are various levels and gradations of penetration. During a time of little specialization merchants and bankers represented more than just their trading and banking functions; for example, during Florence's Golden Age they extended them to embrace industrial functions acquiring the characteristic appellation of "entrepreneurs", i.e. organizers of a domestic industrial production – in Florence's case the product was lawn, but there are numerous other examples. At this stage they still stayed close to home; this was also the case when banking became more concerned with lending to smaller and greater rulers. A gradation of lending on credit in general, one might say, but this step is one that leads easily to another level, that of politics. Whether a ruler sent a merchant who happened to be available on a diplomatic mission – as in the case of Servat described above – or whether he was dependent on a moneylender for financing his wars – as Charles V was dependent on Fugger – is a very different matter. No merchant has ever had to encourage a ruler to wage war, but the term "trade warfare" would never have arisen if this sort of web of interests had not been spun. There are countless more examples of points of contact than those described here and a web of interests characterized the Renaissance and later the reciprocal support of politics and economics. Economics served power politics and power politics served economics; this is most obvious in the merchant republics of Venice and the Netherlands, though at this level it can be considered no more than a step on the way.

Nevertheless the multiformity in this respect is just as typical as, and not unconnected with, the growth of national boundaries; the face of Europe is full of wrinkles. This also strikes us when we look at the differences of social penetration. Obviously the merchants and bankers of the Italian trading towns and of the Republic of the Netherlands were at the top of the social hierarchy. In 18th-century Amsterdam it was rumoured that the town hall was to be affiliated to the stock exchange, as it had been in the Netherlands' Golden Age. In France and Spain, on the other hand, merchants were thought to be little better than swindlers or smugglers, except in the big trading centres. All this is naturally connected with the success or lack of success of trading and banking in England; there merchants and bankers did not, however, reach the very top; this was reserved for landowners and the aristocracy. This does not mean to say that, as everywhere else, there were not merchants and bankers who gave up their jobs to live on the interest on their land and capital; and vice versa, that there were not young aristocrats who entered the world of trading and banking. On the whole, looking back over these centuries, there was considerable social penetration, and merchants and bankers were allowed to assume an essentially different status, a specifically European one.

Finally, the most striking aspect is their cultural penetration, especially where it created large differences in status in people's opinions and thinking about economic life. This is the spirit of earth-bound matter which permeated every aspect of life and which, as the capitalist spirit, grew into an admired, envied, pitied and abused category in every case, without exception, and started to lead a virtually independent existence. We are not concerned here with its origins and its interrelation with religion, the Church, philosophy and politics. It is enough to remember how the static Middle Ages and the dynamic new era are marked, and the world of trading and banking, represented by merchants and bankers, perfected the motor functions of European economic growth through the struggle with the Church's opinions on prices, usury and finally the work ethic, serving the transition to the industrial era, a new cultural phase. For what was created before as a market society with worldwide consumer preferences and a parallel coordinated system of prices became a vehicle for the new industrial society from which merchants and bankers did not disappear – on the contrary they found many new areas of activity with regard to industrialization – but where they were more in the background, in the shadow first of all of the industrialist and later of the pure manager, a less European type than that of the most industrialized new society, American society.

European culture – and this is essential for its artistic expression – is no longer contained in the terms of the world of banking and trade with their stringent reaction, positive and negative, to the value of money and capital and to the ethos involved with this. It is now brought into relation with what is much more essential for its industrialism than the elements noted above: speed and dimensions, such as the permanent productive capacities of large industries which require people and things to maintain continuity. Obviously merchants and bankers are no longer typically European and Europe is no longer typical of them. Banking is now a worldwide affair, but its European origins have left a permanent impression, an impression which forms an integral part of the legacy of Europe.

# PART SEVEN

*Rulers and Politicians*

*Civil Servants and Bureaucrats*

*Lawyers*

*Rebels, Heretics and Revolutionaries*

*Europe beyond Europe*

# 25

# *Rulers and Politicians*

## DOUGLAS JOHNSON

It is impossible to consider government, rulers or politicians, without considering the state. The origins of political rule are confused with the origins of the state. Sometimes this is understood in a legendary sense. According to legend, the unorganized people of Athens were organized by a politician, Theseus, who brought about the concentration of government. Again, according to story, the people came together in the city of Rome, consciously to create a state. Aristotle believed that the Cyclopes were the earliest type of political society. There each man was a ruler, since he made laws for his wives and children, whilst living without fixed institutions. Perhaps they represented the "state of nature" which many thinkers have considered to be important as a hypothetical concept.

At all events political rule, in its origins, is associated with the family, with religion and with political consciousness. So far as the first named is concerned, what counts in the concept of "rulership" is not so much whether the somewhat simplistic theories which describe the family as the essential unit of primitive society are true or not, as the fact that it has invariably been assumed that some sort of patriarchal system is at the origins of the state, that the eldest male parent is naturally supreme in his household, and that this unit forms an essential part of the political community. Although it is now universally recognized that "primitive" is very different from "simple", and that any patriarchal theory of authority may easily be contradicted by others such as a matriarchal theory, for example, the idea persists that the nature of civil authority is imbrued with the notion of the organization of the family, with the authority of the father over his children, and with the idea that within the framework of this authority there was a bond of blood or kinship. In Europe it was common for rulers to see themselves, in some way, as the fathers of their people.

The importance of religion in the political organizations of early societies has never been contested. Common worship, common devotion to ancestors, common acceptance of laws, sanctions and ceremonies, formed the basis of states and therefore of their rulers' authority. The nature of command and obedience was established by religion, and by the dreaded apprehension of the punishment which would be afflicted on anyone who broke the laws of religion. It was natural that rulers often combined the functions of a religious figure with the functions of secular rule. A priest-king could be expected to perform the duties of ceremonial observances and to direct magical rites and incantations for the benefit of the community. Even when these functions diminished with the progress of time, the king could still retain the function of conducting religious ceremonies. The ruler was thus something of a magician, someone who was divinely inspired, or who was in a privileged position *vis-à-vis* the gods. It could therefore be that it was the cleverest, most knowledgeable or most unscrupulous men of the community who were able to win the position of ruler and maintain themselves in this position.

The development of political consciousness was obviously a gradual process. But it is difficult to imagine any society which is not conscious of the need to protect itself from the dangers of aggressive neighbours or from the upheavals consequent upon populations which were frequently in movement and migration. Thus it was that the problems of war, whether defensive or aggressive, created kings and the ablest in war became the ruler. But primitive societies also needed security, whether it was the security of wealth, property or person. Thus is was that laws were evolved, which consisted either of an organized form of customary law or of a series of particular judgements. As population increased it became necessary to have institutions, or agencies, which would control the many activities and relations of individuals, and organize them within a system of order. Thus the ruler could become he who was renowned for his wisdom, or he who, because of his age and experience, was versed in the tradition of his community, or who could explain its history and evolution.

Thus, the history of governments and rulers in Europe must begin with mention of these three elements. It is certainly the case that there existed the greatest variety and complexity in governmental forms, and in this the primitive societies of Europe are no different from those of other continents. It is with the emergence of the Hellenic city-states in the region of the Aegean Sea that more particularly European forms of political organization became established. This represents the beginning of the Classical epoch. It was during the period from 800 to 500 BC that a series of local kingships were replaced by forms of tribal aristocracy which founded and organized many hundreds of cities. This coincided with an expansion of trade, and the cities were dominated by a privileged and hereditary nobility, usually taking the form of an aristocratic council. But as trade grew, as Hellenic wine and olive cultivation prospered, as the increasing use of coined money changed the nature of the economy, and as the population increased, so certain individuals grew richer, and the poorest classes found themselves threatened in their positions as small landholders. The result was the era of the "tyrants", from the middle of the 7th century BC. These "tyrants", often representative of the new rich, joined with those who were experiencing hardship and who were menaced in their welfare to overthrow the aristocratic monopoly of power. At the same time relations between the cities led to the development of a self-armed citizen infantry, dependent upon the support of the small-farmer class in the cities.

Although the history of one part of Greece could differ considerably from another – that of Athens, for example, from that of Sparta – a pattern emerges whereby an individual (whether classified officially as a "tyrant" or not) imposes a solution upon his region, and secures personal power as a result of reforms granted to popular classes. Solon, in Athens, put an end to the growth of noble estates and broke the nobles' monopoly of political office. Pisistratus, some years later, organized supplies of public credit which enabled the medium and small farmers to survive and even to prosper. In Sparta the semi-mythical figure of Lycurgus divided the land into equal portions which were inalienable. The result of this division, and the importance of the Spartan citizens' army, led to the constitution of a full city assembly and of an elected body of magistrates which possessed considerable powers. Although Sparta was in no way a model for the other city-states of Greece, nevertheless they also adopted systems of government where the citizens met and deliberated together in order to make laws. In Athens the assembly of the citizenry debated and took decisions on all political matters. There was little or no bureaucracy, and there were no specialized officials. Athens and other states are usually given as examples of direct democracy.

The history of Greece affords examples of types of rulers which are often to be found in the subsequent history of Europe. The position and the destiny of rulers were affected by economic change, and the nature of politics was often an expression of the tensions that existed within the social community. So the aristocracy attempted to maintain and extend its power and privilege at the expense of the small and medium farmers, and the "tyrants", often themselves the products of a buoyant economy, intervened in order to maintain a balance. Although the "tyrants" had limitless power, their survival depended upon their not using that power other than in the interests of the poorer sections of the community. In the Classical Greek state the citizens were able to exercise their political rights because the economy was worked by slaves (who were excluded from the deliberations of the assemblies). Government was a matter of privilege and leisure, and in the absence of a bureaucratic machinery it was characterized by a certain amateurishness, except where the constitutions were manipulated by skilful politicians, usually belonging to families where there was a tradition of political experience and privilege. In this sense a form of aristocratic privilege persisted, although it was never institutionalized.

The Roman experience was not dissimilar, although several important differences have to be noticed. For one, the hereditary nobility preserved its power and influence. For another, Roman expansion took place on a gigantic scale and was sustained because it was based on a system of economic inequality. The importance of the armies was reflected in the careers of certain army commanders, who started civil wars, played their role in factional politics, and were at times able to appeal to the ordinary soldiery and to the urban proletariat. But the most striking characteristic of the Roman state was its system of civil laws, which had evolved under the Republic and which was to continue to evolve under the Empire. It was the first time in history that such an organized body of jurisprudence had emerged, and although successive emperors were able to legislate by edicts, according to their own policies and judgements and according, for example, to their response to petitions, the main body of civil law remained intact. The emperor could enjoy the right of being arbitrary and oppressive, but he could not change the essence of the law which enshrined the privileges of the possessing classes and which ensured their continued predominance. It was this legal reality which was the great contrast to the Hellenistic state and which constituted the real heritage of the Roman state.

The decline and fall of the Roman Empire, in itself an "event" that covered several centuries, produced a state of political confusion which defies description. The fragile tribal democracies of the invading Germanic tribes, the uncertain nature of developing Christianity, the need for migrating peoples to find some system of land and property law, and the growing contrast between the Western and Eastern empires (in the former the authority, both political and religious, of government was always more consistently maintained) were important elements in the final resolution of the political system into one of feudalism. In this the political arrangements were largely the outcome of a form of rural settlement, where village communities and peasant property were presided over by a legally defined, and usually hereditary, aristocracy. Within this system are to be found characteristics both of the Empire and of the Germanic tribes. From the latter there probably came the tradition of a formal reciprocal obligation existing between the rulers and the ruled, so that a form of contract system prevailed. From the former came the codified and written law. The monarchs who came to rule, often uneasily, over the feudal complex had something both of the Roman imperial ruler, who was sacred and autocratic, and of the Germanic war leader, who was responsible to, and sometimes elected by, the tribe and who was expected to perform certain specific secular functions.

This feudal system was complex and it evolved over the centuries. Under Charlemagne, a group of magnates, chosen by the emperor and close to him in family and personal terms, was designated to govern the outlying provinces and to ensure the integration of a vast imperial ensemble. The authority of the emperor was clearly revocable, and his agents were rewarded with landed endowments and revenue taken from the regions where they served. But gradually the magnates began to assume greater authority on their own behalf, and vassals owed fealty to them as they owed fealty to the emperor. Hereditary benefices undermined the central authority, and as western Europe became the prey of various invaders (Saracens, Magyars, Vikings and others), so local magnates constructed their castles, arranged for their own defence by themselves creating their own particular chains of tenure and defence.

Authority was split. Imperial unity gave way to a system which, in theory, formed a great chain of dependency, from noble to peasant. At the highest level was the sovereign or monarch. Economic exploitation and political power were closely linked to all levels, since the monarch's economic resources lay in his personal domains like those of any other lord. Political power became dependent upon success in war, in diplomacy, in marriage and inheritance and in the administration of justice. The Church became an independent force. Towns grew and developed their own forms of influence and power. The feudal ruler had to be active, well acquainted with members of his family and with other feudal seigneurs, well versed in traditional law, and somehow able to win the support of his equals and dependants.

The feudal system saw a perpetual oscillation in the nature of power. The nobility realized that their privileges would be threatened, were there any rise in central power. But at the same time the feudal system itself could not withstand anarchy. This oscillation was finally ended in the 14th and 15th centuries, when a complicated series of catastrophes (the Black Death, famine, decline of population and therefore decline in demand and in labour services, a monetary crisis, peasant revolts) hit seigneurial revenues. The nobility tried to remedy this by warfare, and throughout western Europe there were both civil and international wars and important modifications of the feudal system. Out of this long period of crisis emerged the modern state. Rulers asserted their power over their over-mighty subjects and extended their authority so as to unify their kingdoms in such countries as England, France, Spain, Portugal, Sweden. In the smaller states too this pattern of monarchical authority was often to be followed. Although the destiny of feudalism was to be different in eastern Europe, serfdom becoming more important there as it declined in the west, the authority of the ruler in central Europe or in Russia was also to increase and the nature of the state to become firmer.

The form of government which characterized the beginnings of the modern world is usually described by the word "absolutist", meaning that the government possessed absolute power over its subjects and territory. This was hardly new, since it had always been possible for rulers to rule as despots or tyrants, paying no respect to the laws, obligations, conventions or traditions which had been accepted by their contemporaries. Nor was absolutism ever complete. If serfdom was declining in the west, it was not abolished; if there were strong monarchs who succeeded in taming the aristocracies of their countries, there were also weak monarchs who allowed anarchy to gain control of their states; and everywhere the nobility continued to exist as a privileged, powerful and wealthy élite, uniquely capable of taking advantage of any situation that might arise. But the tendency towards absolutism was irreversible. The political landscape of Europe moved from being a criss-cross of feudal dependencies into a patchwork of national states, and even where the principle of nationalism was slow to develop, as in Germany or Italy or the Habsburg Empire, the principle of absolutist rule was well exemplified in individual German, or Italian or Habsburg states, such as Prussia, Savoy or Austria. Although it is fashionable to say that such changes in the political and national organization of government did not affect the lives of ordinary people, who remained immersed in their poverty and their struggle to exist, it is also likely that the tendency of the times was to make people aware of the existence of a power and authority that lay beyond the local seigneur and the local church. Many observers have seen this period of "absolutism" as a transitional stage between the period of feudalism and that of capitalism. The absolutist ruler held the balance between the landowning aristocracy and the new middle classes, created by changing methods of production and exchange.

Strictly speaking, the absolute ruler had no obligation to share his power. Most states were monarchies and it was accepted that the interests of the state were identical with the interests and aspirations of the ruler and the royal family. Treaties were signed between states, alliances forged and wars fought because of dynastic interests, or because of the manner in which a ruler interpreted an increase of territory, a marriage agreement or a commercial advantage. Monarchs could use ministers who rivalled them in their fame, as Henry VIII appointed Cardinal Wolsey or successive French kings turned to Cardinals Richelieu and Mazarin, or monarchs could appoint ministers who were outstanding as reformers or innovators, as Henry VIII employed Thomas Cromwell or Louis XVI Turgot. But it was always the monarch who made the decision. The ruler could be weak and indecisive, and it could happen that a king was unfit to rule, either because he was a child or because he was mentally backward. But the legend persisted that it was in this one person that the sovereign authority of the state was concentrated. Strictly speaking, the power of the monarch began nowhere and ended nowhere; it was all-pervasive and usually there were no legal arrangements for defining or delimiting this authority. More than this, whether the national principle prevailed or not, the identity of the nation was focused around the person of the monarch. It was through his person that the inhabitants of a state were united.

This meant that a particular form of ruler was required: industrious and serious, intelligent and well informed, able to converse with diplomats and to give instructions to bureaucrats, capable of judging whose advice or which policy to follow. But although many monarchs worked long hours at their desks (Philip II for example) and were the chief animators of the machinery of government, a monarch was essentially different from a bureaucrat. The king, or queen, or prince, was a continuation of a dynasty, he was the head of a family, and the leader of a nobility. However hard he worked in order to inform himself about diplomatic, military or financial reality, he was expected to hold a court and in that court to show himself to be grander and more magnificent than other mortals. The court was a means of displaying the quality and wealth of a country; it also demonstrated the hierarchies which existed within the state, and sometimes those that existed between different states. The ritual of court life, the ceremony surrounding royal births, marriages and deaths, the pageantry of receptions and royal pastimes (such as hunting and dancing), were all designed to show the magical and mystical attributes of monarchy. A monarch was also supposed to be the leader of his people in war, and was expected to play his part in battles. But most important of all was the belief that kings should be obeyed because it was by divine will that they were there at all. French kings went to Rheims in order to be crowned and anointed with sacred oil, thus spectacularly demonstrating that they were in a line of kings which stretched back beyond Clovis to David's anointment by Samuel; it was usual for all monarchies to be supported by the forces of organized religion, a support which affected everyone in the state, whether they belonged to the court or to the great mass of ordinary people. The court was also a centre of national culture. The most celebrated artists, architects, dramatists and musicians of Europe owed their fame to the patronage of their court, and it was often taken for granted that the royal family should play the role of promoting the arts and culture of the state. The Renaissance in Europe is inconceivable without the assistance and initiative of the rulers of Europe and their followers.

It was the monarch who was the promoter of change within a state, and it would be rare to find a bureaucracy, or a king's minister, capable of effecting reforms or innovations without the personal decisions of the ruler. Whilst no one believes that the Reformation took place in England simply because Henry VIII wished to divorce his wife, and historians have for long pointed to the social, political and theological developments which preceded the break with Rome, nevertheless the course and the nature of the English Reformation were heavily marked by Henry's personality and ideas. Similarly, it could be argued that whilst there were many bureaucrats who were able to supply Louis XIV with legal arguments to bolster his diplomatic aspirations, and whilst the king was subject to various influences in his religious ideas, the two great acts of his reign, the claiming of the Spanish succession and the revocation of the Edict of Nantes which had given toleration to Protestants, essentially belong to the king himself.

In the 18th century the initiatives of royal personages were all the more remarkable because there was a consciousness of crisis and a realization of the need to remedy this. The so-called "enlightened despots" sometimes showed an enthusiasm for the advanced ideas of contemporary thinkers who were prominent as leaders of the Enlightenment. Frederick the Great of Prussia cultivated a celebrated friendship with Voltaire; Catherine the Great of Russia regarded herself as a collaborator of Diderot; and Louis XVI employed as a minister Turgot, who was in favour of the enlightened traditions. But these relationships were a form of public relations, in keeping with the tradition that rulers had a cultural role to play. What really counted was the realization of each of the rulers that his state was undergoing some sort of crisis and that there was no alternative to the ruler as the force which would introduce reforms. Usually the remedy took the form of centralization and a greater rationalization of government, and often the ruler showed little respect for either historic rights or institutions. Frederick the Great of Prussia, for example, realized that he was the ruler of a state which, geographically divided and weak, could easily become the victim of more powerful neighbours. His policy was to increase the number of inhabitants, to augment and improve his army, to stimulate the economy, whilst, all the while, extending his domains so as to make them less vulnerable. His reforms introduced religious toleration, reduced the number of serfs on the royal estates and turned the economic resources of the state towards greater economic activity. Frederick, sometimes called the sergeant-major king, was a fierce and determined monarch, for whom the business of government and war formed the sole basis of his existence.

The Empress Maria Theresa was a conservative monarch, whose life was devoted to piety and to the upbringing of her many children. But the fact that, shortly after her accession to the throne in Vienna, her domains were attacked by Frederick the Great, led even her to a survey of the privileges of the landowning nobility, since her state required greater revenues thereby the better to organize its defence. Her son Joseph II was prepared to adopt even more drastic measures. He attacked the Church because its corporate privileges stood in the way of general reforms, in such areas as the law and education, and of important particular reforms, such as increasing the revenue from taxation. The emperor also attacked the beliefs of ordinary people, which he regarded as superstitious, reducing the numbers of convents and seminaries, as well as wayside chapels and crosses. Joseph is a good example of the absolute ruler who tried to force his ideas and principles on to his subjects.

Catherine II of Russia endeavoured to do many of the same things as Joseph. She tried to create a real and effective state in an area which had no natural frontiers and where the geographical size of her territory made any form of administration particularly difficult. As she expanded the Russian frontiers and incorporated more and more people who were not Russian within her state, these problems increased rather than diminished. Nevertheless she reformed the legal and administrative systems and asserted her military authority, whilst preserving the facade of an enlightened and cultured monarch who was striving to force Russian society forward, out of its barbarism.

The rulers appeared to represent, in themselves, the art of government. Yet however great the personality of a Catherine, however determined and devoted a Frederick the Great, or however resolutely convinced that he was in the right, as Joseph II was, there were inevitable limitations on the power which these sovereigns wielded. Society consisted of a series of groups which fitted into a system of privileges. There was the nobility, which enjoyed special conditions of economic and social life, and which could usually not be replaced in the service of the state by bureaucrats, because there was neither the personnel nor the machinery with which to install an effective bureaucracy. There were the corporations which existed for the furtherance of various professional, economic or social purposes. There was the whole weight of tradition, whether it took the form of legal formalism, superstition or inertia. And there were the indelible realities of regionalism, where knowledge, understanding, recruitment of personnel and economic activity were all organized on a local plane which could not easily be overridden by the central state. Individuals, like groups, like towns or regions, could point to their legal status and could defend a particular form of existence as a result.

Thus it was that even supposedly absolute rulers were unable to do exactly what they wanted. It was not simply that their laws had to be written on human skin, as Catherine put it. It was rather that they had neither the technical nor the personal means of doing everything that they wanted to do. Such rulers tended to be more sensitive to opposition than their constitutional obligations forced them to be. Whilst rational and despotic in theory, they had to be realistic and supple in practice. They form an impressive collection of political realists.

There were two important exceptions to this general conformity of government. One was England, where the move towards absolutism under Charles I had been thwarted by the Civil War and where the attempts to revive absolutism under Charles II and James II failed. Instead, England, which had always found a parliamentary system to be a convenient method of raising taxation or of pursuing religious reformation, established the principle that it was the sovereign in Parliament who was supreme, with the corollary that it was necessary to manage Parliament if one was to be an effective ruler. More important perhaps was the fact that in England social status was associated with the peerage and was limited to the peer's eldest son. More important certainly was the fact that the English system allowed the government to dispose of the country's natural wealth without having the powers of despotism. England possessed a form of government which reformers wished to extend rather than to transform. It was therefore stable. It gave countless examples of compromise and ambiguity, so that when George III, who might have had some hankering after being an enlightened despot, insisted upon appointing the younger Pitt as his prime minister, his policy prevailed, but only because it was approved in a general election. The importance of the king of England was never questioned. But in order to maintain that position he had to become the first of the electioneering gentlemen of England.

The rulers of England were not only distinctive because of their deep-seated concern with economic and commercial affairs, but also because of their concern with elections and patronage. The British aristocracy were less exclusive than their continental equivalents, and the British bourgeoisie were less determinedly devoted to their immediate class interests.

The other important exception was France. At first sight this is astonishing, because the French monarchy, as portrayed by Louis XIV, was the very epitome of absolutism, and Louis XIV, whether or not he said "l'État c'est moi", was the model of a ruler completely and utterly identified with the state over which he ruled, a sovereign whose private and public lives were completely absorbed the one in the other. But, in fact, the facade of absolutism, personified by the magnificence of Versailles and the ritual of the Sun King's daily life, concealed the limits of this absolutism. The bureaucracy surrounding the intendants, an institution which is usually seen as incorporating the essential elements of centralism, was typically inadequate. In practice, an intendant, sometimes a foreigner to a region, often absent, usually badly seconded by his aides, necessarily in difficulty because of bad communications, was of little real help in making royal rule a going concern. The king's need for money and for soldiers made him all the more ready to compromise with the privileges of towns or the rights of regions. It could be that the complex history of France is sufficient to explain its complicated version of absolutism. It could be that the complicated geography of France rendered its development unlike that of other countries. Perhaps if France had consisted of a maritime province, with its capital at Rouen, then it might well have developed in a manner comparable to that of England. But the existence of the vast, and totally different, regions of the interior, in the centre and in the south, made this impossible. For France an absolutism was necessary in order to keep the state together. But for this very reason this absolutism was always contested and always imperfect.

It was England and France which launched the revolutions that ended the system of absolutism. After the English revolutions of the 17th century and the French Revolution of 1789, the ideal system of government was seen as parliamentary, and the rulers of Europe have ever since been dominated by this ideal, except for those who indulged in dictatorship, or those who since the Russian Revolution of 1917 and World War II, have established forms of communist regimes.

The parliamentary principle of government is necessarily more complicated than the absolutist, even in theory. It presupposes that there should be a constitution, however rudimentary, and however limited. In England the Bill of Rights was concerned with procedure rather than with principles. In France successive constitutions, such as those of 1791, 1814 and 1830, were more explicit and were taken as models by other countries. It also supposes a system of election, but whether elections are direct or indirect, whether the right to vote is given to all the inhabitants, or is restricted to those who are male, or to those who enjoy a certain degree of wealth, or who have some other qualification, is by no means self-evident. Equally, relations between the different powers of the state are uncertain. For some, the parliamentary system necessarily means a separation between the legislative, the executive and the judiciary, and this is sometimes specifically stated in the constitution. But it has not been the characteristic of all parliamentary systems. Other observers believe that it is only with a monarchy that a balance of power can be established which can confer a degree of stability on the system. Thus a new form of ruler emerged, the constitutional monarch. Sometimes the importance of his activity was obvious and evident to everyone at the time. Louis Philippe was almost indistinguishable from other contemporary politicians. There were some monarchs whose importance in political affairs was only appreciated after their death. A good British example of this is George V.

Thus it is difficult to define the type of ruler who predominates in the parliamentary system. It is often said that parliamentary government is coincidental with the rise of the middle classes and with the predominance of the bourgeoisie, and it is certain that the 19th century, and the early part of the 20th century, saw economic and social developments which brought the middle classes into positions of power and influence. But the progress and the success of parliamentary institutions were not limited to those states in Europe where industrialization was important. And in such a state as Great Britain, where industrialization was most successful, the importance of the landowning aristocracy within the parliamentary system was remarkable. Even after the appointment of a Liberal prime minister of humble origins (Lloyd George) and a Socialist prime minister with a background of poverty (Ramsay MacDonald) and of a number of wealthy business men (Bonar Law, Stanley Baldwin, Neville Chamberlain), it was still possible to have British prime ministers who were aristocrats or who had aristocratic connections (Winston Churchill, Harold Macmillan, Sir Alec Douglas-Home). It was rare to find plutocrats playing an important role in British politics: Joseph Chamberlain amassed a large fortune and established a great reputation as the Mayor of Birmingham before entering the House of Commons, but his career was exceptional, and in any case he never reached the highest office. Lord Randolph Churchill had nothing but contempt for a business man, such as W. H. Smith, when he entered politics.

In Germany, during the parliamentary period from 1870 to 1914, when the two emperors were still dominant in politics, the political class remained essentially traditional. At its head was the Chancellor, Prince von Bismarck until 1890, then successively General Caprivi, Prince von Hohenlohe-Schillingfurst, von Bülow and von Bethmann-Hollweg. The electoral system was weighted, so that a deputy in the Reichstag, elected in Berlin, usually represented some 125,000 electors, but a deputy from the agricultural strongholds of eastern Prussia represented, on average, a mere 28,000 voters.

In such countries as Belgium and Holland, where the monarch remained highly influential and where the parliamentary system was bicameral, a similar traditional political class persisted. In France the evolution was less clear. Under the parliamentary monarchy (1815–48) the aristocracy, whether "legitimate" or "Bonapartist", was still important, and certain famous aristocratic names were to appear under the Third Republic, such as de Broglie (and a descendant was to be a minister during the period of the Fifth Republic), but the French parliamentary system was always to show a penchant for political leaders who were, in origin, academics from the teaching profession. During the July Monarchy, there was Guizot; the Third Republic was known for a time as La République des Professeurs, and such figures as Edouard Herriot and Edouard Daladier were distinguished representatives of this profession; the longest government of the Fourth Republic was headed by a former schoolmaster, Guy Mollet, and one of the ministers who held office most frequently was another, Georges Bidault; a president (and prime minister) of the Fifth Republic, Georges Pompidou, began his career as a schoolmaster at Marseilles. In 1976 the tradition was renewed when Professor Raymond Barre became prime minister.

The situation in Italy was again different because, in the constitution of united Italy after 1870, there was a Catholic boycott of the parliamentary elections, and a consequential predominance of the small bourgeoisie. By the end of the 19th century it was estimated that two out of five Italian deputies were barristers by profession.

The general reason why the development of parliamentary systems in most European countries proceeded steadily and without dramatic upsets or changes was because the access to parliament tended to be reserved to such political élites. A certain solidarity was thus easily established between the aristocracy and the bourgeoisie. Socially and politically they were agreed on the necessity of preserving the regime and of avoiding revolution; ideologically they tended to agree on a broad basis of liberalism and moderation. When, in the course of the 19th and 20th centuries, the political oligarchy thus created was extended, as the vote was given to more and more people and as the conditions for eligibility to parliament were extended, the balance of power in parliamentary states was not immediately or drastically upset. The enlargement of the suffrage was gradual. In Great Britain a succession of parliamentary acts was passed between 1832 and 1918; in Italy, after 1870 and the reform of 1882, universal suffrage was introduced in 1912; in France the suffrage was slightly increased between 1815 and 1848, then the sudden introduction of universal adult male suffrage in 1848 was short-lived; after the experiments of the last days of the liberal empire in 1869, universal adult male suffrage was introduced in 1870, but the vote was not given to women until 1946. In other countries universal suffrage was introduced around the time of World War I (1909 in Sweden, 1919 in Belgium). The result of the gradualness of these developments was that there was no change in the traditional nature of the rulers. For a time at least the new electors chose the same social authorities. Only gradually did new socialist parties grow up to challenge the aristocratic-bourgeois predominance, and again, because this change too was gradual, the new parties soon adopted many of the traditional qualities of moderate conservatives and liberals.

Most parliamentary systems depend upon a limited number of considerations. There is, for example, the nature of political parties. Although the two-party system was never established either as firmly or as simply in Britain as legend would have it, nevertheless the British political party system has always assumed the existence of important party organizations. This has meant that there has always been a type of political leader whose main preoccupation was to control the working of his party and to ensure that the normal areas of party support in the country would not be lost. Thus such leaders as Disraeli, Salisbury, Bonar Law, Stanley Baldwin and Harold Macmillan arose in the Conservative party, because (by different methods) they could claim to be successful in Parliament and in the constituencies where people voted. A Liberal leader such as Asquith and a Labour leader such as Attlee could make similar claims for their leadership of their respective parties. But the contrary is perhaps inevitable. A leader who has a strong personality and a number of determined convictions, who is faced with particular problems and situations, may well split his party. Thus Sir Robert Peel split the Conservative party which he had created over the Corn Laws, Gladstone split the Liberals over Ireland, Lloyd George divided (and perhaps destroyed) the Liberals over his ideas of post-war government and tactics, Ramsay MacDonald divided the Labour party over the international economic crisis of 1931. In addition, within the British system, there were always personalities who found it difficult to adapt themselves to the restrictions of party discipline. They have depended upon their national reputation as men of integrity, who tended to see their political party as it should have been rather than as it was, such as John Bright (a Liberal) in the 19th century, or Enoch Powell (a Conservative) in the 20th; or they have depended upon the security of a local organization, such as Joseph Chamberlain; or they have called upon a mixture of a national and a parliamentary reputation, such as Lord Randolph Churchill (a Conservative) in the 19th century, or Aneurin Bevan (of the Labour party) in the 20th century. It was the circumstances of war and national emergency which catapulted Winston Churchill, a former Liberal and difficult rebel amongst Conservatives, to a position of supreme power. But it must be noticed that in normal times it is the political managers who are the most successful. No one who has attempted to come to power outside the traditional organization of political parties has ever been successful in Britain: Sir Oswald Mosley and his Fascists, Sir Richard Acland and his Commonwealth party, several leaders of the Communist party of Great Britain form an eloquent testimony of a particular type of failure.

In France political parties did not always grow beyond the status of groups; it was rare to find a political party which could establish any dominant position; the very existence of parliamentary government was sometimes interrupted (by the Second Empire, by the government of Vichy) or threatened by particular crises (by the movement led by General Boulanger in the 1880s, by the riots of 1934, or the threat of an army coup in the late 1950s and early 1960s); there was also the tendency for important new parties to be formed, which sometimes were opposed to the parliamentary system itself, such as the Communist party after 1920, or the parties led by General de Gaulle after 1946. In these circumstances the typical French political leaders of the parliamentary monarchies, of the Third or Fourth Republic, were men who were skilful at keeping coalitions of parties together, at avoiding clashes, and at giving an impression of momentum to a political system which was necessarily motionless. The leaders of the left, such as the socialists Jaurès and Léon Blum, because they were usually excluded from power, were able to appear more positive, but it was the leaders who appealed beyond the parties to nationalist sentiment who were most able to challenge the system. The two most obvious examples were associated with the two World Wars, Clemenceau and General de Gaulle, with the crisis of the war in Indo-China, Mendès-France, or with the crisis over the Algerian war, General de Gaulle again.

In parliamentary Germany, whether under the emperors or under the Weimar Republic, there was a similar failure of any political party, which was willing to work the parliamentary system, to establish any lasting supremacy. The political leaders were either temporary appointments, endeavouring to postpone a crisis, or representatives of particular interests. It was not until the ending of World War II and the establishment of the Federal Republic of Western Germany that any solid implantation of parliamentary institutions became possible. Even then, with the presence of the army of occupation and the absence of viable political parties and traditions, such a party as the Christian Democrats could become little more than a collection of various ideas and interests, whilst the Socialists necessarily became a party of compromise and conciliation, very distant from any socialist orthodoxy. In these circumstances the political leadership became highly personalized, and political issues took on the appearance of struggles within the interior of the party. Thus Chancellor Adenauer dominated West German politics until the elections of 1961 and turned political issues into personal issues. The decline of the Christian Democrats after that date, and the divisions amongst their ministers, led to the resignation of Adenauer and his replacement by men who were forced to adapt themselves more to party politics. But the principle remained that German politicians, even when they did not have the age, reputation and skill of Dr Adenauer, were forced to fight within their parties as well as lead their parties against various opponents in an unstable situation.

Other countries where parliamentary systems existed, such as Italy, Holland and Belgium, have been characterized by multi-party systems, where the political leaders (even the communists in Italy) have had to show qualities of tact, persuasion and dexterity. But in all parliamentary states two issues have recently become apparent. One is the relationship between the political leaders, who are elected, and the bureaucracy, which is not elected, as the task of government becomes more complex and technical. The bureaucrats can claim that it is they who, in effect, govern. But the parliamentary leader can reply that he is skilled in decision, and he can explain, negotiate and manoeuvre in a way which few bureaucratic officials would or could choose to do. The whole issue of public relations is one where the parliamentary leaders can predominate. But the second issue involves a decline of parliamentary power and influence. Other institutions in the state, such as the trade unions, the organizations of employers, the public-opinion pollsters, or certain international organizations, such as the European Economic Community or the World Bank, have acquired power of their own. In these circumstances the political leader in a parliamentary state no longer looks only to his parliamentary majority and to the conditions of his political party. The constitution of the Fifth Republic in France, since 1958, has deliberately reduced the power of the French Parliament. The experience of Britain between 1974 and 1979, where governments existed with tenuous majorities and were not always able to command support in the Houses of Parliament, is another example of the way in which contemporary parliamentary leaders may have to negotiate in areas which are well beyond their parliaments and to seek for support in their nations as a whole.

Not all the states of Europe adopted parliamentary systems of government. There have been various forms of rule which have been described in general terms as "dictatorships". One of these which is easily identified, because it was situated in the same country and occurred on two specific occasions, was the Bonapartist dictatorship. Both in 1799 and in 1851 the dictatorships established by Napoleon Bonaparte and by his nephew Louis Bonaparte were means of getting out of a situation where democracy was not working properly. In 1799 there was fear of anarchy and of many types of conspiracy, both revolutionary and counter-revolutionary, whether inspired from abroad or home-grown; in 1851 there was fear of social revolution. Both the Bonapartes sought to give stability at home and to play an important role on the world stage. They sought to incarnate in their individual persons the national identity, and they claimed to have the support of the mass of the population, as demonstrated by the use of referenda. These could be manipulated and the Bonapartists used control of the press and a secret police in order to repress criticism. But the essence of Bonapartism was economic progress. It was as if these emperors had taken over the political aspects of French national life in order to establish a framework within which the French bourgeoisie could become prosperous. Napoleon I established the Bank of France, Napoleon III presided over the most important phase of the French Industrial Revolution. Although they were very different as men, Napoleon I being talkative, energetic, authoritarian and brisk, as if he knew that he was destined to rule for only a short period, whilst Napoleon III was silent, lazy, inscrutable and sensitive, always striving to anticipate changes in the political scene, they both exercised their rule by administrative means. Their weapon was neither a political party nor the army; it was rather the bureaucracy which they sought to control and direct, and which was a long-standing part of French society.

Purely military dictatorships have occurred in a number of European countries from time to time. That is to say, forms of government were established, in 19th-century Spain for example, or in Greece and Turkey in the 20th century, where there was no form of political organization which had any effective or direct form, other than the army. But, in Europe, unlike underdeveloped territories outside Europe, this form of military dictatorship has usually been a temporary affair in which the army has intervened in order to break a political deadlock or in order to overcome a particular political danger, such as communism.

A dictatorship based upon Fascist ideology has often been associated with military rule, but is a more complex and lasting phenomenon. It became a characteristic of a number of European countries in the period which followed the ending of World War I, and should probably be seen as a phenomenon of that period. The most famous examples of a Fascist dictatorship were Italy under Mussolini and Germany under Hitler. Many of the characteristics of Fascism were common to both states. There was the cult of the leader; there was persecution of political opponents; new methods of communication, such as the radio, were fully exploited in a continuous effort of propaganda; there was a Fascist party which was never fully amalgamated with the apparatus of the state, but which sought to permeate every organization of society; within a framework of strident nationalism, Fascist governments presented themselves as highly successful and vastly superior to the decadent democracies which were their neighbours. It was also true that in both countries Fascism became powerful once both parliamentary democracy and capitalism seemed to be failing. Fascism claimed to be a half-way house between unbridled capitalism and socialism, and the basis of its support usually came from the small bourgeoisie. In fact, whilst both Hitler and Mussolini were supreme and above any concept of law, their rule was tempered more than is usually thought by respect for the privileges and position of the wealthy classes. The Nazi policy of Anti-Semitism was an exception to this tendency, but the German version of Fascism was much more intense than the Italian, and was based essentially on the concept of governing in a continuous emergency. Fascist rulers, such as Mussolini and Hitler, had to make themselves the idols of the masses and to do so by means of continuous performances demonstrating their strength and vigour, but they also had to be resourceful politicians, controlling their parties and exploiting every opportunity of success.

This form of Fascism was more extreme than the versions which developed in Spain and Portugal, and which survived World War II, or the type of Fascism which existed briefly in France between 1940 and 1944 and which is usually described as the government of Vichy. In Franco's Spain, Salazar's Portugal or Pétain's Vichy, although there was the cult of the leader, it was the cult of a leader who was bringing peace and tranquillity, rather than of a leader who was urging his people to live dangerously. The leader incarnated traditional values rather than claiming to inaugurate a new age, and the aristocracy, the Church and agricultural interests were of considerable importance in the ideology of these regimes. Whilst these regimes were associated closely with the army, and although the army, like the secret police, was a vital element in their survival, they were in no way assimilated to any military organization. Nor were the political parties (in Spain the Falange, in Portugal the National Union) at the centre of power. This type of Fascism sought to establish a working equilibrium within the societies where they operated. They most resembled the regimes of Hitler and Mussolini in so far as they were unable to arrange for their continued existence once their founders died or were removed from power.

Another form of authoritarian government is associated with the communist government that was installed in Russia after the 1917 Revolution, one which has been extended to most eastern European countries since World War II (Albania, Bulgaria, Poland, East Germany, Hungary, Romania, Czechoslovakia and Yugoslavia). Although there are differences between these countries, essentially communist countries are ruled by the Communist Party, which thereby establishes a form of party dictatorship. Theoretically only one party can exist because political parties are thought to represent social classes and, since the communist regimes have supposedly abolished antagonistic social classes, there is therefore no place for a multi-party or bi-party system. Thus the supreme authority within the state is the Communist Party and the effective authority is the small group of men who control the party. The party is highly disciplined and structured; it is organized around Marxist theory and around programmes of economic planning; it is secretive and it is difficult to know how it works. But it is clear that a one-party system, which is closed and permanent, is one where the members are obliged to move in whatever direction the leaders choose to go, and one where the appearance of unity is carefully preserved. In fact, within the party there can be considerable discussion about the nature of policies and about their success or failure. This discussion, because it is secret, can easily become intrigue, or can lead to the elimination by force of individuals or groups who are becoming troublesome. The existence of a one-party system over a long period of time can result in corruption and inefficiency. It also means that there can be a difficulty of succession, as was experienced in Soviet Russia after the death of Stalin, or as is expected in Yugoslavia after the long rule of Tito. The one-party system can become a court system, with ambitious men seeking to gain the confidence of the leader, and with the leaders trying to build up the support of a solid body of party members. The communist state is a bureaucratic state where, because it is impossible for any opinion to be expressed other than official opinion, the bureaucracy can make important mistakes, and can come into conflict with sections of the public. But these conflicts usually take place within a closed and particular area and the position of the rulers is to maintain the limits of this conflict as far as possible.

The communist system reduces the role of the rulers to that of bureaucrats. It is true that, since the death of Stalin, Soviet and other eastern European rulers have become accustomed to travelling in foreign countries and have therefore had to meet democratic politicians and audiences. It is also true that the spread of television has brought government out more into the open, and has brought pressure on communist leaders which are not dissimilar from those encountered by the rulers of democratic countries. Soviet rulers, such as Khruschev and Brezhnev, have many of the characteristics of American or western European politicians. It is also true that, for technical reasons, it is everywhere the case that the bureaucracy is becoming more competent and more highly organized. When faced with decisions it is therefore less likely to be blindly obedient to orders from those who are in command. The need to maintain contact between those who govern and those who are governed cannot be denied. But, except in some countries such as Yugoslavia, this has not been met by modifying the nature of institutions and establishing (as has been done tentatively in Yugoslavia) any form of open elections. It has usually been by introducing an element of liberty of expression, which can be withdrawn if it is thought necessary. Thus the communist rulers, totally caught up as they are in the machinery of their communist parties and the apparatus of their bureaucracies, must be amongst the most calculating and amongst the most desk-bound in the world.

All rulers today find themselves in a paradoxical situation. There are those who are expected to grant greater liberty to their subjects and there are those who are expected to allow greater opportunities for their subjects, sometimes in a particular region, to contribute to decisions which affect their lives. At the same time, all those who rule are held responsible for the general welfare of society and for the general level of economic prosperity. Rulers are subject to pressures in every conceivable way; they can come from particular economic interests or ideological groups; they can come from their rivals; they can come from international organizations or from foreign countries. Rulers are expected to master and control the techniques of bureaucratic organizations and of technological processes. The problem of decision making has never been so difficult.

There have always been rulers who have approached their task in different ways. Some have been conservative and have sought to preserve the minimum benefits of established order. Some have been liberal and have exercised the arts of tolerance. Some have been radical, and have sought to promote social change whereby all groups in their states have had an equitable interest in the prosperity and survival of their communities. It is the achievement of European rulers that they have illustrated all of these tendencies, and that the history of Europe, and of western Europe in particular, presents all the elements of the art of ruling. If, as Aristotle said, politics is the master science, it is the rulers who are the scientists.

# 26

# Civil Servants and Bureaucrats

## SAMUEL FINER

The bureaucracy is the armature of the modern state; and the modern state has, everywhere, been modelled on the European state. This armature is (supposedly at least) powered by the ruler. It is also to a greater or less extent (sometimes not at all) checked and balanced by organs of popular control. Between the three elements – rulers, bureaucrats and popular organs – there is a perpetual tension. A shift in the balance is tantamount to a shift in the regime. Where the organs of popular control over the ruler and his bureaucracy are strong enough to make them answerable to the public, this is the necessary though not the sufficient condition for a democracy. Where these organs are feeble or absent, and the ruler effectively leads and commands his bureaucracy, the regime is authoritarian, possibly absolutist. Where however the ruler is lazy or inept and the organs of popular control equally weak, there we find bureaucracy in its original pejorative sense: the impersonal rule of anonymous and faceless officials.

It may be that the officials who head such a bureaucracy are themselves men of genius and imagination, far different from their juniors who are the more circumscribed and routine-ridden the lower their rank. The top bureaucrats may, in these circumstances, innovate in ways which their skill and dedication put beyond the capacity of the nominal rulers, and in directions unhindered by the harrying of representative assemblies or the courts of law. Such an ideal – founded at present on an enthusiasm for what supposedly passes in France – is clearly desired by a number of present-day students of politics. Their view leads straight into the inescapable central dilemma of bureaucratized polities: the more the bureaucrats enjoy discretion, the less are they accountable, and the more accountable, the less they enjoy discretion. In a word – the bureaucrat can be either creative or formalistic, but never both at once. This inner tension in the bureaucratic role is an ever-recurrent theme in its long march through European history.

A thousand years ago it was "difficult to find anything like a state anywhere on the continent of Europe".[1] In the rubble of the Roman Empire only a rudimentary arrangement for maintaining public order had emerged. It was no longer based on the subjection of each individual to impersonal rule and to an abstract entity called state or republic, but was a reticulation of dyadic ties between lords and lesser lords; lords and serfs. This was the so-called feudal system – a coalescence of two tendencies, each traceable before it emerged and distinct from it: a lordship-and-tenant tie prevailing over the relationship of the citizen to the community and, secondly, the determination of political role and status by the individual's relationship to the land. Consequently the distinction between what was private and what public was everywhere effaced, whether this related to dispensing justice, to levying taxation or to maintaining defence. Private rights were the obverse of public duties and vice versa.

In this feudal system there resided, however, a contradictory, even an alien, element. This was the kingship. In respect to his feudal vassals the king was *dominus*, the lord of lords, the apex of a pyramid of subordinations which, in such a work as the *Customs of Beaumanoir* (1280–83), are supposedly of an ordered completeness. The king's rights *vis-à-vis* his vassals are contractual and reciprocal, though not necessarily symmetrical. But not only in respect to these vassals but to every person in his domain, the king is also *rex*. Consecrated by Holy Church he possesses the *regalia*: the supreme right and duty to dispense justice and to keep the peace. His justice allowed minor vassals and freemen to appeal to him past their immediate overlords, allowed him to enter his vassals' courts to enforce his own rights and claims and permitted him to adjudicate the rival claims of litigious magnates. By reserving certain pleas to the Crown (as in England) or allowing appeals to the Crown (as in France) the king effectively restricted and controlled the activities of the local magnates, and since administration was carried out in judicial form (as it was up to the end of the 19th century in England, by way of the quarter sessions), this was tantamount to expanding the scope of the central administration. Furthermore public order is bound up with the dispensing of justice; it is the king's peace that must be preserved and as the pleas of the Crown increased, so did its responsibility and capacity to enforce court orders, repress riots and rebellion, and put down rogues and vagabonds. And all these functions merged into defence. As *dominus* the king was bound to aid a vassal who had been unjustly invaded and dispossessed. As *rex* and heir to the old Germanic tradition of kingship, the king was nothing if he was not a war leader. The rise of the modern state is first of all the history of the expansion and the ever stricter enforcement of the *regalia*, and the consequent concentration in the king's hand alone of the powers of war and peace, justice and mercy, order and protection. It is next his confrontation with the great lion in his path – the Estates of the Realm, the Parliament, the Cortes, the Courts and such like – i.e. the assembly which represents the political forces in being at the time and seeks to limit and control the use of his *regalia*. To the prince there comes to correspond an anti-prince.

Every extension of the *regalia*, each additional effort to exercise them, generated more royal officials: more specialized, more skilled, more permanent, more numerous. The growth of the royal power is not merely coeval with the growth of the royal bureaucracy: it is its reflection.

For since it is the kingly power that in the end absorbs into itself all those private rights/public duties scattered vicariously through the feudality, it is natural that the germ of the modern bureaucracy should lie in the royal household and that it should be officers like the Chamberlain or the Constable or the Seneschal who first assume general administrative duties or that the first generation of the Crown's officers in the localities should, like the *prévôts* in France or the sheriffs in England or the Ministerials in Germany, be at the beginning concerned with administering the royal lands. By the 13th century three basic sets of institutions had emerged almost everywhere in Europe: for judicial business, there were the courts of law; for finance and revenue, offices like the English Exchequer and (later) the French *Cour des Aides*; and finally a general documentation and administrative centre, viz. the Chancery. At this stage these institutions were not highly specialized and most of their personnel were household retainers. But it did not take long for one of the great perennial tendencies in bureaucracy to manifest itself: the routinization, impersonalization and consequent autonomy of a department, over time, as it developed its own special skills, outlook and *esprit de corps*. For example, by the 14th century the routine of the ordinary law courts had become so tradition-bound in England that a new more flexible court, Chancery, had to be established. Likewise in France the Parlement differentiated itself as a sovereign law court from the personal *curia regis*, and then threw off a *Chambre des Requêtes* and a *Cour des Aides*. By the beginning of the 14th century the feudal kingship had reached its perfection in England and France; feudalism had indeed become a system, controlled and balanced by a set of royal officers working to set routines in specialized departments and insulated from the personal intervention of the king. If the monarch desired new initiatives and new procedures – as Edward III required more rapid and flexible financial arrangements for his wars with France – then he had only one resource: to bypass the bureaucracy by creating a new officer or finding new uses for some obsolete one; in Edward's case by utilizing such an office as the Royal Wardrobe.

But the king was not alone in developing a bureaucracy. In the provinces his great vassals, with their vast estates, began to administer them in a similar way and they too developed their exchequers and treasuries, their chanceries and their system of courts. So equipped they were better able to resist the constant encroachment of the Crown. Always set on a collision course over their respective rights and duties, Crown and magnates began to clash, in the late 13th and early 14th centuries, over a matter vital to the independence of either, but novel in form, and contributing more in substance to the growth of bureaucracy than all the developments so far mentioned. This matter is *taxation*. So central is it that Joseph Schumpeter, in a famous essay on "The Tax State", affirmed that "without financial need the immediate cause for the creation of the modern state would have been absent".[2] That need arose, I would say, exclusively from one cause: warfare. As *domini*, kings were entitled only to service in kind or its cash equivalent from their vassals. That and the revenues from their own private estates were all that they had for fighting their campaigns. Since it was everywhere held that a tax was an extraordinary device to be used only in emergency, and always by the consent of the freeman, so, as kings required more and more liquid cash to fight their wars, they were compelled to convene representative assemblies of taxpayers to consent to giving it. Thus as the 14th century ushered in the entrenchment and routinization of administrative institutions, in brief of the royal bureaucracies, so it also ushered in the representative assemblies to check and control them: parliament, estates, *cortés, corts, landtag, rigsdag, Snem, Sejm* — all over Europe in numbers which run into hundreds.[3] As the prince had institutionalized his power in the bureaucracy, so did the anti-prince in these assemblies.

So began three centuries of swaying battle. The stake was crucial: absolute control of financial resources was the key to absolute control of the population. The more money a prince took from his subjects the more soldiers he could hire to take still more money from his subjects and the less they had left to pay taxes to their own immediate overlords. The struggle for the right to tax was a zero-sum game: what one gained the other lost. Furthermore the issue was momentous not only on the constitutional plane, but for the future of bureaucracy as such. For a tax required collectors; and it is significant that if we leap forward from the 14th century to the eve of the French Revolution we shall find that throughout Europe between two-thirds and four-fifths of bureaucratic personnel are involved in collecting and controlling the expenditure of taxes and in activities related to these.

Sometimes the assembly, sometimes the prince was uppermost. In both France and Prussia the last decades of the 17th century saw the rulers perfecting a bureaucracy on the one hand and destroying the organs of popular control, not just the central estates but the local ones and the municipal councils, on the other. Absolutism triumphed. The only issue was whether this was the personal absolutism of the prince or the impersonal despotism of the bureaucracy, but in either event the permanent core of the state was by now the bureaucracy. Of France, the financier John Law is recorded as having said in 1720: "Sir, I could never have believed what I saw while I was administering the finances. Understand that this kingdom of France is governed by 30 *intendants*. You have neither *parlements*, nor *comités*, nor estates, nor *gouverneurs* — I am inclined to add, almost no king nor ministers either. It is upon 30 *maîtres des requêtes*, commissioned to the provinces, that their happiness or misfortune, their fertility or sterility, depend."[4] Frederick the Great (1740–86), who ruled Prussia in person, nevertheless described his status as "the first servant of the state", dedicated the Hohenzollern family estates as public property, and regarded himself and his dynasty as being as subject to private law as any other citizen. The state had become an impersonal regime of a far-reaching and numerous bureaucracy, hard-working, abstemious and correct, but which stultified all individual initiatives. When Frederick died, his energy and motivation died with him. Thenceforth Prussia was ruled by an impersonal and anonymous apparatus, insulated from the public and left directionless by its ruler: it was this routine-ridden bureaucratic absolutism that led to the disasters of Jena and Auerstadt.

With the exceptions of the Swiss Confederation and the United Netherlands (both republics), of three or four of the German principalities (notably Württemberg), of Poland (the *reductio ad absurdum* of the estates' supremacy) and a temporary lapse (1720–72) in Sweden, the power of the estates in continental Europe was everywhere neutered or extinguished during the 17th and 18th centuries, leaving the princes and their increasingly numerous and sophisticated bureaucracies supreme. The change occurred in Denmark in 1660, was completed in Spain within 20 years of the accession of the Bourbons in 1713, was accomplished in Austria under the Emperor Joseph II (1765–69), while Russia, which had always been a despotism, developed some administrative apparatus modern enough to count as a bureaucracy between the reign of Peter the Great (1682–1725) and the Empress Catherine (1762–96). Indeed, among the major nations, there was one notable exception only. That was England.

In that country also the kingship had strengthened itself by developing conciliar organs and asserting itself over the local magnates. By the accession of Charles I (1625) there existed some 1,400–2,000 officials including a few hundred customs officers, crown-land administrators and clerks to the J.P.s. On varying assumptions the number of full-time senior officials might be put between 350 and 650. This is not dissimilar from the numbers of senior central officers in contemporary France which has been estimated at some 650 or in Castile, where the guess stands at 530. The great difference lies in the number of local officers of the Crown. For readily understandable reasons the Crown in England had never desired or been wealthy enough to establish its own personal agents in the localities. Instead, local regulation and police had been devolved since the 14th century upon the gentry in the capacity of judicial officers commissioned by the Crown, i.e. as J.P.s administering in judicial form. There existed almost no equivalents of the paid permanent field officers of France or Prussia – only a few customs officers and the like. In the 17th century it is estimated that the number of royal officials in Normandy alone stood at 3,000–4,000 and for the whole kingdom of France the figure could be about 20,000.[5]

As on the continent, so in England Charles I also strove to overcome his "estates" and become financially absolute. But the outcome was profoundly different. Parliament won and abolished the entire prerogative machinery of the Crown. The bureaucracy remained tiny and was concerned with defence, foreign affairs and the collection and expenditure of revenue – the last, be it noted, along lines determined by Parliament. Central administrative control over the local J.P.s other than by the judicial control of the high courts was abolished. These arrangements were completed by the Revolution Settlement, between 1689 and 1714. Thenceforth local police, sanitation, public assistance, labour regulation and the like were carried out either by private bodies under the authority of a Private Act of Parliament or by bodies of unpaid citizens who were elected, coopted or appointed by rota, under the supervision and control of the local J.P.s. This is the "local self-government" which the German historian Gneist was to "discover" in his *History of the English Constitution* (1882).

Thus on the eve of the French Revolution two wholly diverse traditions had matured. England had carried her tradition into Scotland and Ireland and beyond the ocean to the 13 American colonies where after independence the ordinary courts of law and the popularly elected organs were all-important, the rulers' authority was minutely circumscribed by them, and the paid permanent bureaucracy was tiny. On the continent of Europe, with the exceptions already noticed, it was exactly the other way around. The prince was absolute: the organs of popular control had either lost their powers or disappeared; and the bureaucracy was numerous, ubiquitous and all-powerful. In 1797 there were in Britain only 16,267 public officials of whom 12,584 (77 per cent) were Customs and Excise; 2,026 (12·5 per cent) in the post office, and the stamp, taxes, lottery offices, and in the treasury. Thus almost nine out of every ten officials were concerned with finance. In France on the eve of the Revolution, however, the total number of central and local officials is estimated at 300,000, including – to point the contrast – gaugers of hay, salt salesmen, coal controllers, sealing-wax warmers, administrators and engineers of the roads and bridges administration, and so on, all the way up to the personnel of the sovereign Parlements. For Prussia the best figures we have exclude local officials except for the police. Even in 1800 there were some 23,000 officials outside these categories in a population of about nine millions, as contrasted to the 16,267 British officials for a population of 16 millions. Comparatively speaking, then, there were five Prussian officials for every three British ones – and unnumbered local officials besides.

Napoleon perfected the closed bureaucratic state. The symmetrical hierarchical order he imposed on France, the mayors responding to the prefects who in turn responded to the minister of the interior who himself was the servant of the emperor, was to be widely copied elsewhere on the continent of Europe and in France itself has survived to this day the defeat of the imperial regime. But at the very moment of its perfection, reaction set in against it. Throughout Europe (until by 1905 even the Russian autocracy began to bend) there came the revival of organs of popular control. In Britain, on the other hand, where Parliament was never stronger or more admired, there commenced the slow accretion of a more sizeable and also a professionally qualified bureaucracy. In this fashion the two traditions of Europe began to converge. In Europe the legislature was the innovation and was grafted, at first very clumsily and often half-heartedly, on to the traditional organ of government, that is, on to the bureaucracy. In Britain, it was the other way around: here (as in the USA) the bureaucrats were the detested innovation, grafted piecemeal on to the traditional organ of authority, the legislature. In the last 30 years of the 20th century, the assimilation between the two traditions has become rapid but the original difference still shows. In general – certainly in the larger states of western Europe – the European societies are more regulated, more tolerant of red tape, more deferential to the public official than in Britain and the USA; at the same time, the tradition of ministerial responsibility to the legislature is less salient, the anonymity, self-effacingness and political neutrality of the top bureaucracy less of a requisite and the participation of the senior officials in policy-making more overt. Nor does the difference stop there. As we shall see, the 19th-century legislatures of Europe were relatively ineffectual compared with the British Parliament. Hence these countries came to rely on a remedy for maladministration other than the political challenge by the legislature. This remedy was the auto-limitation of the bureaucracy, by its acceptance of fixed canons on public law – as for instance in the German concept of the *Rechtstaat*. Administrative courts had been established in which, effectively, officers of the bureaucracy sat in judgement on cases affecting it. But with the onset of 19th-century liberalism and, later, of democracy, these self-regulating courts tardily began to acquire their own autonomy *vis-à-vis* the active administrators, and developed their own case-law in causes where the citizen claimed his rights against them. Hence what at first was an internal self-regulation of the bureaucracy by the bureaucracy became at the end of the century an external limitation. The prime example is the French *Conseil d'État*, but this has its parallels throughout Europe. In Britain, with its tradition of independent and powerful courts and sovereign legislature, confidence continued to be placed in these organs and the administrative law system of the continent took no root.

We have described the development of the bureaucracy so far in terms of the rise of the prince, then (with the medieval assemblies) his limitation by the anti-prince, and then – on the continent – the renewed triumph of the prince at the head of his bureaucracy. The revival of the elected legislatures in continental Europe after 1815 did no more, at first, than revive his old antithesis: the ruler and his bureaucracy on the one side checked and balanced by the new legislature on the other. Until the very end of the century with the solitary exception of France after 1870 (and, it is possible to argue, perhaps Italy after 1878) parliaments were not sovereign policy-making organs, but were no more than control organs facing a self-confident, powerful and irremovable royal bureaucracy. The 19th century was liberal, not democratic. The crowned heads of the new "constitutional" monarchies of Scandinavia, Belgium and Holland, France and Savoy, let alone Germany and Austria-Hungary, did not follow the self-effacement of the British monarchy but played an active political role. And the bureaucracy and armed forces were theirs, not Parliament's. This held true whatever the constitution might or might not say; but in significant cases the constitution did specifically confer this independence on the executive branches of government: the most obvious and most important example is the constitution of the German Empire (1876–1918).

Not until the collapse of the central powers in 1918 did the royal control over the bureaucracy disappear, as the new democratic constitutions of Europe proclaimed the right of the legislature to control ministers who were fully answerable to it for all the acts of omission and commission of their servants, the bureaucracy. In this way, and according to the British tradition, the bureaucracy was made vicariously responsible to the public. But this intention was frustrated, not just for the banal reason that in states such as Italy, Poland, the Baltic States and the like, the democratic constitutions were quickly subverted, but for another and fundamental one. To revert to our princely metaphor: World War I had indeed destroyed the prince, apparently leaving the field to the anti-prince, the legislature. But at the same instant that this occurred, the anti-prince was taken over by a new prince, of a wholly different type from ever before: a collective prince, a popular prince. In Gramsci's words: "The prince of today, the metaphoric prince, cannot be a natural person, a concrete individual: only an organization, a complex element of society in which a recognized collective will has already begun to embody itself and, in part, to affirm itself in action. This organization is already a datum of historical development and *it is the political party* . . ."[6] Just at the very moment that the legislature became sovereign and not a mere counterbalance to the sovereign, so the political party took it over. Nowadays, with a possible qualification made for the Fifth Republic of France, the legislature in modern Europe is both sovereign and subject, policy-maker and critic – in a word both anti-prince and prince. It is debatable whether the executive today is the extension of the legislature (as the theory would have it) or whether, on the contrary, the legislature is not the extension of the executive (as in practice it usually is). This self-contradiction and the corresponding retreat of legislatures from their historic mission of supervising and controlling the bureaucracy have become all the more alarming because of developments in the bureaucracy itself: its size has become unprecedentedly enormous, and it has become a self-contained and self-regulating corporation.

Within the last half-century what were often untidy and unsystematized aggregates of public servants have become self-governing, self-regulating professional organizations largely insulated from outside interference whether popular or partisan. Recruitment had previously been made by patronage, often by party patronage, and while this still holds good for the upper echelons in some countries (Belgium, for instance), the overwhelming bulk of civil servants have for as much as a century past in certain countries (in Britain, for example) been recruited only if they possessed publicly defined qualifications. Thus in Britain, France, Belgium and Italy today the upper civil servant is recruited by competitive examinations; and in Scandinavia, Holland, Switzerland and Germany on the basis of specified paper qualifications. In France the recruit receives a special training if he is to be retained; in Germany he will proceed to in-service training and must then pass a state examination; elsewhere recruits become probationers and are set to "learn on the job". But in all cases, qualifications are needed and an impartial board, insulated from party and personal pressures, is the body that recruits the candidates. By the same token the civil servant everywhere today enjoys an almost perfect security of tenure. This was true of most countries even in the 19th century, where only Spain, Italy and Belgium provided exceptions. Today there are no exceptions: if dismissal is to take place, it must be decided by a special and highly circumscribed disciplinary procedure. True the security is not absolute; but whatever the reason for a dismissal – national security, impropriety or rank incompetence – it will require in some form or another the active participation and acquiescence of other members of the civil service.

In short the bureaucracy has become a professionally qualified meritocracy recruited by impersonal standards and guaranteed tenure: this insulates it from political, personal and public pressures and so do arrangements for pay and promotion. It is true that the regulations governing these can be fiddled somewhat for party advantages, but the general conditions of pay and service are usually established by a central department or council: the Civil Service Department in Britain, the *Direction de la fonction publique* in France, the *Secrétariat permanent de recrutement* in Belgium, the *Consiglio superiore della pubblica amministrazione* in Italy. Additionally, in many European states the rights and duties of the civil servant are formulated in a document like the *Statut des fonctionnaires* in France with similar codes in Germany, Belgium or Italy. Furthermore in most west European countries – Britain and the Irish Republic being the major exceptions, since they are common-law countries – such statutes or codes are adjudicated by the administrative courts.

The obverse of such insulation is the political neutrality of the civil servant. Since he is appointed and removed on the basis of his technical capacity to serve the state, he is expected to serve it without regard to persons or to the party complexion of the government of the day. Consequently all states impose some kinds of restrictions on the political activities of civil servants. Little difficulty arises in assimilating the rights of the junior civil servants to those of the general electorate, for these are concerned in routine functions. The problem only arises for the upper 2,000 or 3,000 "higher" civil servants who occupy that sensitive hinge area where policy and administration merge. Britain perhaps imposes the severest limitations on the rights of the civil servant to campaign for a political party or to stand for election to Parliament, and Germany perhaps the least. In similar ways higher civil servants are usually debarred for a certain time from taking posts in private business after they have resigned or retired from the service. The degree of insulation from active politics or private business varies, as one would expect, from country to country but the general tenor is plain enough: the career is to be self-sufficient and full-time and dedicated to the impersonal "state". In practice the general rule is breached in individual cases, particularly in the sensitive highest echelon: in most of the states of the continent, some posts are regarded as "posts of confidence" where the political leanings of a civil servant are held to be relevant, as will be seen later. But, except for a few such posts at the very top, the bureaucracy in contemporary Europe is not only intended to be but is a non-partisan corps expected to serve all and any ruling parties.

The industrialization of Europe and World Wars I and II generated consequences which together pushed for a vast bureaucratic explosion after 1918. Industrialism engendered a new self-conscious, industrial, working class, soon canalized into socialist parties demanding universal suffrage. The economic system was liable to massive boom and slump, prone to occupational and health hazards: all of these invited government attention. All such consequences pressed the aristocratic and upper-middle-class governments of Europe into "preventive modernization"; that is to say into measures of social amelioration self-consciously taken from on high to ward off threats of socialism, unrest, perhaps even revolution. Bismarck's social insurance laws of the 1880s are only a blatant example of this tendency. The influence of the wars pressed in the same direction. They were qualitatively quite different from all previous wars in involving entire civil populations. The sacrifices demanded were made by everyone out of nationalistic fervour. But it is in the logic of nationalism that, if all members of the nation offer equal and perhaps fatal sacrifices for the sake of the nation, then they are likewise entitled to equal rewards and opportunities inside it. The taxation, the direction of labour, the conscription of materials and property that were imposed to win a war, could, it was plausibly argued, continue to be imposed in order to equalize social benefits and opportunities. This is why in all the belligerent countries the level of non-military spending makes a quantum jump immediately after the close of hostilities, and stays at or above that level thereafter.

All the elements mentioned so far were absorbed into a third, namely the emergence of mass parties. Nowadays every parliamentary democracy in Europe is powered by the competitive outbidding of parties, and in this the all-out collectivizers – the Communist and Socialist parties – naturally set the pace.

The effect of these factors is to be found in the scope, the scale and the direction taken by every bureaucracy in Europe. As to scope, in 1849 the main expenditures of states went on *sine qua non* activities (defence and foreign affairs, justice and public order, taxation and post office to service all these) and the distribution is not markedly different in 1914. The new departments and agencies that have been added since then relate to the control or even the direction of industries and to social and educational provision. An admittedly crude estimate of the division between defence and public order expenditure on the one hand and social service expenditure on the other, expressed as a proportion of the national budgets, gives the following figures for 1973:

| | UK | SWEDEN | GERMANY (Fed. only) | HOLLAND |
|---|---|---|---|---|
| Defence, public order | 12·6 | 18 | 21 | 10·7 |
| Social services | 46·3 | 34 | 31 | 27 |

The scale of government has expanded accordingly, perhaps more than accordingly even. Realistic comparison between the various states is impossible because each country classifies its civil servants in a different way. The best figure for France (1970) is some 1,317,913 officials in the central services, and some 650,000 in the municipalities: a ratio of 1:25 for the population as a whole. In Germany a somewhat comparable count, including the federal, land and municipal officers, yields 2,108,124 persons or 1:29 for the total population. For Italy, in 1970, the number of centrally employed officials (this omits the overstaffed provincial administrations and the local authorities) stood at 1,697,020, which is 1:31 to the total population. The figures become more significant if they are expressed as ratios of the total *working* population, however, in which case they stand at France 1:10·7, Germany 1:11, Italy 1:11. A better indicator, because it is strictly comparable in the countries concerned, is the total employed in "the public sector" in all capacities, excepting only the armed services. These figures can be estimated at:

FRANCE    (1968):  22 per cent of the labour force
GERMANY (1968):  12 per cent of the labour force
BRITAIN    (1975):  27·8 per cent of the labour force.

The public sector in Britain employs just under seven million persons of whom 1,197,000 are in central employ, 3,024,000 in local employ, and 2,008,000 in the nationalized industries. Had we taken the comparable figure for 1961, however, the figures would have been much lower; only 5,369,000 or 22·3 per cent of the labour force.

Finally, it is important to notice the directions into which this new bureaucratic activity has flowed. This complicates the problem of ensuring public control and accountability. Briefly it has moved into three new areas – that of the previously voluntary agency, that formerly occupied by the private firm, and that formerly occupied by the elected local authority. In so doing the advantages of large scale and universality may well be gained; but it is possible and indeed likely that there will be corresponding losses. This will be discussed later.

For the moment, however, we may sum up the position thus: in the last half-century there has occurred throughout Europe a bureaucratic expansion of enormous proportions. In every state the administration has become a self-contained and self-regulated profession, organized in a pyramid of authority, with a dominant tendency to universalize and centralize.

At the apex of the bureaucratic pyramid the civil servant comes into direct contact with his masters, the politicians, and therefore the top 2,000 or 3,000 bureaucrats in any country demand special attention. All western European political systems, with a quirky qualification for the Fifth French Republic, have proceeded along English lines in relating the bureaucracy to the legislature, which is purportedly the repository of the national will and purpose, and therefore the ultimate directing and controlling authority over the bureaucracy. It would be possible to arrange for the bureaucracy-legislature relationship along the pattern of a British local authority: that is to say by establishing committees of the legislature to which senior civil servants would work and from whom they would take direction. Instead all the states of Europe have adopted the British practice of heading the departments by a politician – a minister – of the ruling political party, and making this minister accountable to the legislature for all acts of omission and commission by the civil servants of his department: these being deemed to be his servants and assistants, under his direction and control. This formula of "the individual responsibility of the minister for his department" is carried to greater lengths in Britain than on the continent where legislative committees have greater contact with individual civil servants who play a more open role in policy formulation. For all that modal relationship is that the minister is the conduit between the legislature and the bureaucracy.

The top bureaucrats who come into immediate and personal contact with ministers – and with legislative committees – are wholly unrepresentative of the social make-up of their countries, even more so than the legislatures which are themselves far from being a representative cross-section. The "administrative élites in Britain, Germany and Italy are", we are told,[7] "mostly middle-aged, mostly long-time civil servants, mostly university-educated, mostly from middle- and upper-class backgrounds, and mostly male". As for France, they "all belong to the *bourgeoisie* or to those social groups which hope to enter the *bourgeoisie* . . . they come almost entirely from urban backgrounds . . ."[8] The introduction of the *École Nationale d'Administration* has in no wise democratized the social base; indeed the most recent inquiry suggests that it has narrowed it.

The academic training of these administrative élites differs from country to country. The British have studied in mostly literary fields – history, classics and so forth. On the continent the largest proportion of higher civil servants will have graduated in law, and a high proportion of the remainder in economics. This is to leave out also the higher technical staffs, particularly influential in France where they represent the Napoleonic tradition of the *Polytechnique*, the *École des Mines* and the *Ponts et Chaussées*.

A cross-national survey of their attitude towards their political masters shows that in Germany, Britain and Holland (Italy is a strong exception) only a minority considered that technical considerations should be given more weight than political ones, and even smaller minorities thought that the so-called interference of politicians with what was "properly the affair of civil servants" was "disturbing". Even the inter-party struggle was regarded benignly by half the British and some two-thirds of the German respondents. Only the Italian higher bureaucracy displayed, on the whole, technocratic and anti-politician bias. The reason is idiosyncratic to Italy; for one thing the polarization and fractionalization of the political parties there are such as to make an anti-politician stance justifiable. More significantly, however, the bulk of the higher civil service were first appointed under the Fascist regime and, it would seem, reflect some of its values.[9]

In Britain the doctrine of individual ministerial responsibility for the department operates nowadays as a highly impenetrable screen between the legislature and the civil service. At the same time, it is in Britain that movement between the top positions in the bureaucracy and Parliament is less, apparently, than in any other country except Denmark. Certainly in France and Germany and Norway there is a good deal of movement between the two. In the Fifth French Republic, for instance, over half the cabinet members have been selected from the higher bureaucracy and no fewer than six presidents or prime ministers have been ex-bureaucrats also. In Germany, too, the movement is easy: in the 1961–65 Bundestag no less than 22·3 per cent of the deputies had previously been officials and state employees.

Furthermore the top bureaucratic posts are more highly politicized in continental Europe than in Britain. The role and influence of the senior administrator are more overt: in France for instance it is not uncommon for such men to write highly polemical books about their policies. Correspondingly some of these countries have developed usages for making the top echelon of the bureaucracy more politically sympathetic to the ministers. In Germany, for instance, the head of the chancellor's office is such a key figure that it has become the practice to move him to another place in the service, replacing him by a more politically compatible bureaucrat, when a change of government makes this seem desirable. France has developed the ministerial *cabinet*, which nowadays is mostly composed of career civil servants (and is no longer merely the personal entourage of the minister as it once was), but they are personally selected by the minister himself. (This device, sadly misunderstood, is advocated by members of the Labour Party in Britain but got no further when Labour was in power than provision for the appointment of two dozen "personal advisers" among the various ministries.)

Such politicization is not a mere matter of "jobs for the boys" as cynics might affirm. It is a mechanism for making the bureaucracy follow the lead of the ruling political parties. For, it is argued, if the political party is the expression of public opinion and if the bureaucracy is responsive to the political party, the end result will be a bureaucracy that is responsive and accountable to public opinion. And how to achieve this precise result is, today, the central dilemma of big government and big bureaucracy.

The large-scale bureaucratization of western societies has created a set of problems concerning public accountability and control which are inherent and, it would seem, intractable. These problems stem from three root causes: the nature of the bureaucracy, the mutual incompatibility of the qualities popularly sought for in government, and the nature of the social losses incurred by substituting the bureaucratic order for its predecessors. To begin with, the politician and the bureaucrat are very dissimilar animals: they have different outlooks, timescales and constituencies. As an elected representative the politician is partisan, passionate, responsive: as an officer appointed on merit, the civil servant is critical, remote and neutral. The first serves a cause, the second pursues a career. The time perspectives of the politicians tend to be short – M.P.s and, nowadays, ministers move in and out of office and, more markedly still, in and out of any particular department; the civil servant, however, looks forward to perhaps half a century in the service, and perhaps in the same department. Furthermore, in entering the service he is made to feel that he is part of a permanent and continuing corporation which will be left to pick up the pieces long after the politicians have moved out of office. Irrespective of their technical and intellectual qualifications (which are nowadays often considerable) the sufficient condition for politicians being selected is popularity. In contrast the civil servant is chosen on the basis of publicly established criteria of intellectual or technical skill.

The bureaucracy therefore is regarded as the "ballast" of the democratic state, counterpoising the volatility of politicians and electorates. The combination of these two elements via the parliament-cum-cabinet system is regarded as the supreme achievement of the modern democratic state, blending the organ of popular direction and control with the organs of permanency and impersonality embodied in the bureaucracy.

Unfortunately this view is too bland. There is a basic inconsistency in the qualities which the public expect in their government. The most canvassed requirement is that it shall give the public what the public say they want – the *representative* principle. But citizens, at the same time, do not like their governments to be always chopping and changing. They demand a measure of consistency, predictability and stability in policies: this is the *stability* principle. Finally they will not pardon a government which, it turns out, has lacked elementary foresight and failed to provide, in the past, for needs that have become pressing in the present; this is the *futurity* principle. The last two principles clash with the first. For the representative principle demands that as soon as public opinion alters, the policy should alter also, whereas the stability principle requires that it stays the same. Representativeness requires a turnover of rulers; order and stability require their permanence. Representativeness demands that these rulers respond to expressed preferences: care for the common welfare and especially for the future welfare may well require the opposite. Between the three attributes of representativeness, stability and futurity, any number of mixes is possible, but it is unlikely that any single one will satisfy all the public all the time.

Finally, the bureaucracy's product is qualitatively quite different from most others. It offers a service that is *public*, and therefore inherently wholesale, unpriced and (usually) monopolistic. It is impersonal and universalized, treating all in the same category with a scrupulous impartiality. It is precisely to afford this kind of service in contrast to one that differs from locality to locality, or from one purse to another, that its provision is taken over by the state – in short, bureaucratized. But when this happens losses are made as well as gains and these stem from those three salient dimensions of the bureaucratic breakthrough which we mentioned earlier: increased scope, increased scale and diverse direction.

In widening its *scope*, government finds itself in the area of techniques, science and technology; for instance nuclear policy, underwater technology, managerial techniques and the like. The decisions in these fields are no longer made by corporations competing for private gain, whose profit is presumably bound up with getting the right answers. They have to be made by ministers, who have to rely on the second-hand opinions of their expert officials, and manifestly are no more likely to get the right answers than private consortia. Hence the introduction into modern bureaucratization of substitutes for these losses in knowledge: public inquiries like the Windscale inquiry into uranium reprocessing, or tolerated and often publicly financed "counter-information" units like the American Brookings Institute or the British NIESR, or a host of advisory committees consisting of civil servants, trade unionists and interested business men who, in France and in Britain, are brought in to assist the ministries.

The second new dimension – large scale – creates at least three separate kinds of losses which again must be made good as well as possible by some kind of substitutes. The first loss stems from the increasing differentiation of an organization as it grows larger, and with it the widening spans of control and the lengthening of the hierarchical chain of authority. These consequences will occur in any organization as its size increases, whether private or public; but the public organization, in this case the modern bureaucracy, is, as we have seen, very large indeed. As spans of control grow wider and the chains of command longer, the spatial and the time distance between the citizen and the official who will finally decide on his case both become bigger and bigger. Hence a dilemma: if special consideration is to be given to the case it will take a long time to decide it; if on the other hand it is to be decided quickly, then the decision will have to be a routine one.

A second loss from the increased differentiation of the organization is the tendency for the specialized subunits to pursue their own narrow goals, losing sight of those of the organization as a whole. The efforts of the Crown Agents' Office in Britain to give itself an independent financial base, ignoring the cautions, queries and complaints of its controlling bodies (the Treasury, the Bank of England, the Comptroller and Auditor General's Department), provide a grotesque illustration of this point.

Finally, large-scale bureaucracy has made the traditional control mechanism – viz. ministerial responsibility to Parliament – more and more nugatory. Whereas the numbers of M.P.s and ministers have increased very slowly over the last 75 years, those of the bureaucracy have exploded. The much-cited figure for Britain taken from the Royal Commission on the Constitution (Kilbrandon) illustrates a general west European trend: in 1900 29 ministers and 31 junior ministers controlled some 50,000 civil servants, whereas in 1969 48 ministers and 58 junior ministers were supposed to control over half a million civil servants. In short, the number of all ministers doubled, but those of the bureaucracy increased tenfold. In no country in western Europe can ministers, or for that matter committees of the legislature, supervise their officers on anything other than a "spot check" basis.

An immediate consequence is to throw a heavier burden on the other traditional organ of public control, the courts of law. Here the civil-law countries of the continent, which possessed administrative courts, were better off than the common-law countries, Britain and Ireland. In these the courts have had difficulty in grappling with many classes of cases involving the citizens' complaints against the civil service; in particular in reviewing the *substantive* merits of rules, orders and regulations made by the bureaucracy under the authority of parliamentary statute, and for that matter the adjudications made by a civil servant in pursuance of one of his innumerable new powers of intervention entailed by the ever-expanding scope of governmental activity. But even the administrative law courts of the continent of Europe are in many respects inadequate for the task of public control. For one thing they can ensure strict conformity with the law – but cannot offer relief from the official's insensitivity or unfairness. Again, they are formalized and very slow. Furthermore some governments set aside unwelcome rulings by enacting new legislation. The French government habitually does so in respect to income tax appeals which its servants have lost in the administrative courts.[10]

As legislatures and courts cannot offer sufficient remedy, substitutes and ancillaries have had to be invented. For instance, to allow appeal against the flood of bureaucratic decisions in such matters as social security payments, fair rents, planning decisions, value-added tax and the like, more or less informal tribunals have been established where the citizen enjoys the right to a hearing and the right to appeal upwards; often indeed the right to appeal to the ordinary courts of law, if a matter of law is involved. The bureaucracy has, in short, "judicialized" a number of its processes. Another substitute is the *ombudsman*. For well over a century this institution was active in Sweden alone. In little more than a decade it has been seen as an answer to the complaints, not of illegality on the part of the bureaucracy, which is a matter the traditional courts can look into, but to unfairness and sheer bad administration. Hence a rash of adaptations including the Parliamentary Commissioner in Britain and the *médiateur* in France.

Such devices do indeed mitigate or, if one wishes, palliate the impersonality, inflexibility and remoteness of large-scale government with greater or less (on the whole considerably less) success. For none of them can excise the root problem of all bureaucracy, large or small, which is this: the more effective is public control, the greater are bureaucratic routine, legalism and inertia. For, if such devices keep the civil servant up to the mark, in the same process they keep him down to the mark also.

Finally come the social losses that can be put down to the new directions of this bureaucratic activity – the take-over of the voluntary society, or the local authority services, or those of private firms and enterprises. These had each possessed certain qualities – local or technical knowledge, incentives or dedication, proximity to the consumer, and, above all, flexibility. The voluntary society could and did tailor its service to the individual need; the private economic enterprise was subject, to some extent at least, to the pressures of the market. Once again governments have tried to provide substitutes. For what previously was local self-government they offer devolution or regionalism. For the competitive discipline of the market they offer consumer councils. For the intimacy of voluntary service they provide advisory councils in the social security services. Unfortunately such devices are among the very least successful of the entire catalogue we have outlined.

All such mechanisms are designed to achieve what may be styled the "objective control" of the bureaucracy. By this term it is implied that the bureaucracy is, or at least may be, dissimilar to the public in its attitudes, methods and goals, and that it can only be made to conform to these by devices which in various ways make it accountable to the public. All that need be added is, to the extent that this strategy is successful, farewell creativity, innovation and even flexibility on the part of the administrators.

There is, however, another strategy for making the bureaucracy accountable, and it is claimed that it is superior to the former in that it will also permit of bureaucratic creativity. This arrangement may be described as "subjective control". It means that the bureaucracy is to be made so similar to the general public that their attitudes, methods and goals will coincide. If this were achieved, a bureaucracy could be allowed to innovate to its heart's content, since, by definition, its innovations would all be what the public desired. To bring this happy state of affairs into being requires that the bureaucracy be made *representative* – either socially representative or politically representative, or both. As to the first alternative, the higher bureaucracy are, as we have seen, wholly unrepresentative of the societies which they conduct and it is for this reason that radicals of all persuasions seek to extend the narrow basis of recruitment.

The second alternative is to politicize the higher civil service until it reflects the specific policy commitment of the elected parliamentary majority. We have already seen how in some countries, like Germany and France and Belgium, certain key positions in the higher bureaucracy are regarded as politically sensitive and are treated accordingly. In Britain such politicization has not occurred, and it is not surprising that it is in this country that elements in the Labour movement have called over the years for politicization of the higher civil service, which, they continuously reiterate, is socially and politically inimical to their goals. The Sedgemoor Report (a minority report attached to the Report of the House of Commons Expenditure Committee on the Civil Service, 1977) is an admirable illustration of the entire rationale of "subjective control". The basis of recruitment is to be widened, much larger numbers of ministerial advisers are to be introduced at the top of each departmental hierarchy, and the permanent officers of that echelon are to be subordinated to the minister much more strictly than at present. Then the minister, now (it is supposed) in full control of his department, will in turn be subject to the supervision and control of select committees of the Commons – which in plain language means the backbenchers, and indeed, in still plainer language, means the ruling party's backbenchers. In this way the ruling parliamentary party will control and direct the minister who in his turn will direct and control the bureaucracy. Thus the political programme of the party will be transmitted via the electoral process into the higher reaches of the administration.

Unfortunately all such plans for establishing "subjective control" of the bureaucracy suffer the same fatal drawback: the more socially and politically "representative" the bureaucracy becomes, the less will be its skills, its professionalism and its objectivity. Moreover in those countries where major parties rotate in and out of office, such as Germany, Britain and potentially France, such political representativeness would require a large-scale reshuffling or replacement of senior civil servants each time the government changed hands.

Yet all public opinion polls attest that the peoples of western Europe all feel they are overgoverned and incapable of controlling what is being done in their name. Nowhere is the mix between representativeness, stability and futurity thought to be right. The truth is that there is no ideal "mix". Some problems, for instance those arising from the sheer size of the bureaucracy, can be solved only by reducing its size, or not at all. Others flow from the now ambiguous nature of the chief organ of public control – the legislature. Beginning, as we have seen, as an anti-prince to control the prince and his bureaucracy, it has in the last 50 years absorbed the prince's sovereignty by making the cabinet dependent on itself – while continuing none the less to pretend to itself that it is still the anti-prince. The reason is, as already stated, that both it and the prince are nowadays dependants of the true prince of modern times, the political party. This party will go to extreme lengths to perpetuate the rule of "its" cabinet; and so it will and it does, at the end of the day, abandon its critical role. This is the mechanism that has turned anti-prince into the prince's poodle. And this is the reason why the efforts to control the bureaucracy are being made outside the parliamentary arena, in such things as entrenched bills of rights or institutionalized critics like the Ombudsman, or on a drastic decentralization that would multiply the number and variety of elected critics and at the same time reduce the workload of the central legislature.

But the one impossible expectation is that the bureaucracy shall at one and the same time be both creative and controlled. If the French higher civil service is to be admired for its creativity – as in many quarters it is – then it must also be remembered that this is only possible because the countervailing forces of trade unions, employers' organizations and political parties themselves are much weaker than they are in Britain, while the principal organ of popular control – the French Parliament – has been lopped of most of its former powers of criticism and control to the benefit of a vastly strengthened executive branch. Such creativity is not possible in Britain where there still exists the widespread, even if naive, belief that creativity is the job of the elected politicians, not the appointed bureaucracy. In this country there still survives from the 17th century the tradition that the bureaucracy must be subject to popular control, just as in France there survives the 17th-century tradition of Louvois, Le Tellier and Colbert and the authoritarian state. That the bureaucracy has been not just coeval with the formation of the modern state but is its essential core has been the burden of this essay. Whoever says state, says bureaucracy. The benefits it has brought to populations are incalculable. To paraphrase William James, it is "the enormous flywheel of the state, its most precious conservative agent".[11] But for every gain it brings, there are attendant and inescapable losses. To permit it to create freely, entails that one must forgo control. To impose tight control entails that it may not innovate freely. One is the obverse of the other. As the late Levi Eshkol said, though on a different matter: "You've got the dowry – the trouble is you've got the bride as well."

REFERENCES

1   J. R. Thayer, *On the Mediaeval Origins of the Modern State* (Princeton, N.J., 1970), p. 15.
2   J. Schumpeter, "The Crisis of the Tax State" in A. T. Peacock *et al.* (eds.), *International Economic Papers* (New York, 1954).
3   R. H. Lord, "Common Features of Parliament throughout Europe" (1929) in P. Spuffard (ed.), *Origins of the English Parliament* (London, 1967), p. 22.
4   Marquis d'Argenson, *Journal et mémoires de 1679–1757*, ed. E. J. B. Rathery (Paris, 1859–1967), Vol. I, p. 43, n. 2.
5   G. E. Aylmer, *The King's Servants: the Civil Service of Charles I, 1625–1642* (London, 1974), p. 440.
6   A. Gramsci, *Opere* (Rome, 1955), Vol. V, p. 5.
7   R. D. Putnam, "The Political Attitudes of Senior Civil Servants in Britain, Germany and Italy" in M. Dogan (ed.), *The Mandarins of Western Europe* (London, 1976), ch. 3.
8   B. Gournay, "Higher Civil Servants in France" in M. Dogan and R. Rose (eds.), *European Politics: a Reader* (London, 1971).
9   R. D. Putnam, op. cit.
10  J. Hayward, *The One and Indivisible French Republic* (London, 1973), pp. 127–28.
11  William H. James, *Selected Papers on Philosophy* (London, 1969), p. 59.

# 27

# Lawyers

## RONALD GRAVESON

"If there were no bad people," wrote Charles Dickens, "there would be no good lawyers." With this comforting, if unconvincing, assurance from *The Old Curiosity Shop*, let us first look at law: law as a concept, law as a vital organ of society or an obsolescent survival, law as a major unifying factor in European civilization, law as a creative achievement of the human intellect, law through the eyes of the men who made it.

Sir William Blackstone, the first professor of English law, defined the subject of his Oxford lectures in 1758 as "A rule of civil conduct prescribed by the supreme power in a state, commanding what is right and prohibiting what is wrong" – a bland description for "a good gentleman's law book, clear but not deep", to recall Horne Tooke's observation on the Vinerian Professor's *Commentaries on the Laws of England*. Such a great civilization as the Chinese has regarded law as a secondary and inferior form of social control. One's duty is respect for one's fellow human being, a respect ensured by ritual and a concern for the saving of face and compromise of differences. For the Chinese a legal attack was little better than a physical or moral one, and this traditional view has merely moved into the legal subconscious with the introduction of modern codes of law in a communist society. Again Marxist-Leninist theory, to which we shall have to refer later, looks to the obsolescence and eventual disappearance of law with the ending of conflict through the ending of social classes.

In the face of such diversity and contradiction, how can we hope to find a common factor for a definition, even in respect of Europe? Have these diverse systems anything in common? First, we may agree, they all deal with human beings. In this broad sense law would include any obligatory rules of behaviour, formal or informal, written or unwritten, that ensured that two or more human beings could associate together. In this sense law is an essential element in the existence of society at every level – domestic, local, national or international, just as oxygen is an indispensable constituent of water – indeed of life itself. Yet law so broadly described, which would include the code of the Mafia or the unspoken agreement of a man and a woman to share a common home, must be circumscribed to fit the pattern of that political society we call the state. As such, it is one of the several forms of control and organization, alongside morals, religion, conventions, honours, rewards and other mechanisms by which society ensures its existence, its survival and its progress. Law is the body of rules enforceable by the state. The proportion of law in this mixture of social devices varies from place to place and from time to time in the same place, as well as in the matters regarded as susceptible to legal control. Roman law, for example, made gratitude a legal obligation in an emancipated slave. Should our law compel a capable swimmer to rescue a drowning child? A comparative appreciation of the limits of legal control is a necessary approach to an understanding of the place of law in European society.

In such an approach how can we regard the laws of Europe? Do they possess such common features as should justify a general statement? The modern movements towards common political institutions such as the Council of Europe and the European Economic Community presuppose a community of interests and values among the many participating states. Beyond politics (in theory at least), the European University Institute established by the European Economic Community at Florence is dedicated to the study of common European culture in the fields of history, politics, economics and law, a refreshing extension of the narrow economic purpose of the Community. This recognition of law as a major factor in European life deserves examination, and we propose to consider the three main legal systems of Europe, namely Roman law, Soviet law and the English common law, a trilogy that in some respects confirms and in others contradicts the broad cultural unity of our continent.

Her legal system and her language were Rome's greatest gifts to the world. In both language and law the Roman was empirical, systematic and elegant. The 2,000 years of Roman rule between the philosophy and artistic achievement of ancient Greece and the cultural explosion of the European Renaissance represent a period of practical consolidation of gains through military, religious and legal control of a society in triumph and decline. We cannot sum up a civilization in a sentence or describe its legal system in the traditional Twelve Tables. Yet we may find a convenient focal point for retrospect and prospect in the dominant central figure of the Emperor Justinian, for the work he inspired summarized the past and directed the future of Roman law in Europe and much of the world.

Justinian came to the throne in 527 AD. By the time of his death in 565 AD he had built his own memorial in a great compilation of the law, a task for which his renowned minister, the jurist Tribonian, must take much of the substantial, as distinct from purely formal, credit. The early law had consisted of customary law and elementary legislation culminating in the 5th century BC in the important republican enactment of the Twelve Tables. According to Cicero this body of law was even taught at school. It constitutes an early historic marker akin to the legislation of Edward I in England, the Code Napoléon of 1804 and the writings of Lenin in Russia. In the course of time it was supplemented by magisterial edicts, resolutions of the plebeians in their council, quasi-legislative resolutions of the Senate and eventually imperial decrees. The judicial administration of the law by magistrates and especially by the praetors ensured that legislation made in the Senate was effective in the Forum, and that non-Romans were not excluded from the system. But probably the most important group of persons concerned with law in Rome to the end of the Classical period, about 250 AD, were not the plebeians, not the senators, not the praetors, not even the emperors, but the jurists.

Originally members of the priesthood and of patrician families (for early law always seeks added strength in divine association), their important monopoly of interpretation and exposition of the law ended in the 3rd century BC when plebeians began to share in giving legal opinions in public. Thus developed a group of legal scholars, eventually men of distinction in the service of Rome, who assumed the public function of interpreting the law for the benefit of magistrates no less than litigants and even for the praetor on the contents of his edict. Their tasks were as specific as advising clients on particular problems, especially in litigation, and as general as the production of treatises on the law. Yet they were not practising lawyers in a modern European sense of a professionally organized body. Advocacy they left to the orators. Their task was more that of consultant.

The first important treatise they produced was the 18-book account of the civil law by Quintus Mucius Scaevola 600 years before the death of Justinian. In the centuries between, jurists of greater or less distinction systematized, rationalized and filled many of the gaps in the civil law by their invention of new forms of action.

The Golden Age of Classical jurists ended with the death of Modestinus in 244 AD. It had been enriched by the extensive and comprehensive writings of many jurists, of whom perhaps the most distinguished and influential were Gaius and Ulpian. One aspect of their importance was that through their writings and opinions custom became law, a tradition that is still found in the work of jurists of the civil law. Justinian perceived the need to preserve for the future the best of the past and instructed Tribonian to make an up-to-date digest of the most important

and useful of earlier juristic writings. The result was a *Digest* reduced to a twentieth of the size
(according to Justinian) of the 2,000 titles considered. One scholarly consequence of this distillation of juristic thought was the intense early medieval study of interpolations and omissions.

Although one purpose of the *Digest* was legal education, it was realized that a much simpler introduction to the legal system was necessary. This need was the inspiration for Justinian's *Institutes*, an elementary work in four books, principally on the civil law of Rome, which for the time being displaced the distinguished earlier work of Gaius.

The third element in Justinian's compilation related to the codification of the law, or its authoritative restatement in systematic form. His great Code had both its prologue and its epilogue. The former was his early code, an updated version of the work of Theodosius, together with a series of imperial decisions for the solution of major problems, the so-called Fifty Decisions. The epilogue was the emperor's post-code legislation, an important body of enactments known as the *Novellae*. The major part of the *Corpus Juris Civilis*, namely the second code, consisted of a collection of imperial legislation in force at the date of publication of the Code (534 AD), arranged systematically in 12 books.

Justinian's retrieval of Classical Roman law was an act of the greatest importance for European civilization. Of the many values he preserved and transmitted, those of system and order in a society then still largely barbaric are outstanding. But less obviously he asserted the value of human intellect as applied to legal problems and the general importance of the jurist in civilized society. These values, protected in the Eastern Empire until the fall of Constantinople, transcended the Dark Ages of the west and found root again in the 12th century in the universities of northern Italy. In the Byzantine Empire itself the momentum of Justinian's work ensured a continuation of juristic effort, but that effort had largely exchanged its initiative and originality for the task of commenting on the overpowering work of the late emperor. Beyond the useful Greek code of the 7th century, the Byzantine influence had passed its creative zenith and was thereafter largely confined to southeastern Europe and Russia.

Thus we return to Italy, where a brilliant new age of Roman law begins. And of great significance for the future of the system as an element of European culture, its study begins in the universities, where it has continued without interruption to our day. Bologna, a city that still enjoys a contemporary reputation for uniqueness, was the most renowned centre for the study of Roman law from the 12th century onwards. The fame of its professors spread far beyond the frontiers of Italy, of whom none should be remembered with greater gratitude and affection than Azo and Bartolus of Saxoferrato. Students of the law faculties of the north Italian universities were numbered in thousands and drawn from as far away as Scandinavia. Some returned and introduced the teaching of Roman law in the newly founded universities of Paris and Oxford.

Why did they come to Bologna, to Pavia, to Florence and the other great Italian law schools? The countries from which they came – France, Spain, Germany, England – all had their native systems, often embodied in codes such as the Breviary of Alaric, the *Fuero Juzgo*, the *Sachsenspiegel* or the Laws of Alfred. Various reasons may be suggested: the opportunity of scholarly study in an academic community; the more systematic and highly developed character of Roman law; even a consciousness of the underlying similarities of the needs of various national groups; perhaps an awareness that much of Europe had once formed part of the political Roman Empire and was again largely within the spiritual Roman Empire. Medieval communities of learning, religion and commerce were international, and a sense of unity within each group transcending national frontiers must have been normal. Whatever the reasons, the result was a second Roman conquest of Europe. But whereas the Roman military empire lasted for three centuries, the Roman legal empire has already lasted three times as long and spread to provinces undreamed of by the Caesars.

The European lawyers-to-be who studied in the law schools of Italy returned to their homelands to practise the law they had learnt. For them its quality greatly surpassed that of their local, native law. Two consequences ensued. A contemporary form of Roman law was generally applied, except where conflict arose between native law and Roman law in any particular case. In such conflicts of applicable law the native law was in principle held to prevail.

Secondly, the existence of a scholarly profession tended to ensure wherever possible the development of national law, whether by legislation or judicial decision, and particularly by means of juristic opinion, on the principles and concepts of Roman law. Roman law thus became the common law of Europe, not simply side by side with local law, but also at a level of principle rather than detail which permitted local variation within the broad framework of the system.

Responding to this need to adapt Roman law to new times and new places, the universities developed a *usus modernus Pandectarum* which flourished particularly in Germany in the 18th and 19th centuries. In this movement Karl von Savigny (1779–1861) was an inspired historical scholar, and despite his opposition to codification, the movement was crowned by the publication of the German Civil Code. The century which began with the Code Civil des Français in 1804 and ended with the Bürgerliches Gesetzbuch in 1896 saw the complete revival of Roman law in modern dress. First the Code Civil followed Napoleon's armies through Europe, and indeed continued throughout the century to advance to other continents, notably South America and Africa, in its wide rational appeal of a comprehensive system of written law. The influence of the German Civil Code may be seen in parts of Europe as disparate as Austria, Greece, Turkey and Sweden. Thus we may properly speak of contemporary Roman law as Romano-French and Romano-German. The common factor is manifest.

Although it is tempting to consider the English common law as the second great and contrasting legal system of Europe, it is to those of the socialist countries that we shall first turn. All these systems share a common ancestor in Roman law, though one of their more immediate parents may have been Romano-French or Romano-German, with an intermediate ancestor in Byzantium. For this reason, it is convenient to consider them as an extrapolation of Roman law into a seemingly incongruous and anachronistic world of economic and political theory. Secondly, these systems are territorially of greater European significance than the English common law, whose external mission historically has been limited to the other four continents. The systems of the socialist countries differ among themselves, just as do the systems of non-socialist civil-law countries. Their distinguishing common factor is, of course, the economic doctrine that dominates to a greater or less degree the law of all socialist countries, and this feature is so pervasive as to justify a distinction in kind between themselves and others of Roman derivation.

Socialist law is founded on the 19th-century German philosophy of Karl Marx and Friedrich Engels, as expounded politically in the 20th-century writings of Lenin. Their scientific socialism, deriving from philosophical bases of materialism and evolution, regarded law as a superstructure on the economic foundations of society. Its use is to enforce the will of the economically dominant, and law is in essence accordingly unjust. Capitalism is considered as the exploitation of one man by another, whereas, as a distinguished Polish communist friend drily observed, communism is just the reverse. As a system, law is appropriate to a class-organized society, a society considered to connote conflict between the classes. This conflict arises through the private ownership of property and should cease, as would classes themselves, with the extinction of private property. Law would then become unnecessary, for society would be united in a single purpose. The semantic question here lies obviously in the meaning given to the word "law". In our use of the term law would be a precondition for the existence of any society, classless or otherwise.

For the soviet lawyer belief in the truth of Marxist-Leninist philosophy is a matter of faith as well as necessity. Its merits may be extolled but never questioned. Herein lies the intellectual dilemma of jurists of the system. Dissidents must be properly educated. Delinquents must be brought to accept willingly the efforts made by society to convict, punish and reform them. The ruthless logic of this system, far more thoroughly founded on abstract philosophy than either Roman law or the common law, may be thought naive or fatalistic, but must be accepted as a substantial fact of European life. Although it would be inappropriate here to argue the merits of an important philosophy, we may perhaps observe that Marxism-Leninism appears less vulnerable in its logical consequences than in its premises. Even in its operation, however, it has retained a class-organized society, in which the privileged minority of Communist

Party members in some countries dominate the remaining large majority of the population.

It is helpful to an understanding of the acceptance of this system to recall the lack of any strong legal tradition in Russia. The law was largely customary, recorded as early as the 15th century in the *Russkaia Pravda*. Various attempts at codification or consolidation were made between 1649 and 1855, which introduced elements of Byzantine and Romano-German law. The customary law was supplemented, particularly for the towns, by autocratic legislation. Moscow University, the first in Russia, was established only in 1755, and until the latter part of the 19th century there was little evidence of juristic thought. The concept of legally protected rights played a minor part in the expectations of the masses. Thus, the historic association of law and morality and popular confidence in the system in western societies was much weaker in countries of the Soviet Union (as distinct from the majority of other socialist states, notably Hungary and Czechoslovakia). The Bolshevik Revolution of 1917 changed many things, but did not uplift this popular view of law.

The characteristic of socialist law today is its function as an instrument of state power for the ultimate achievement of a communist society, a long-term aim to be reached necessarily in stages. The period of the New Economic Policy (1921–28), for example, saw the promulgation of extensive codes and the establishment of the principle of socialist legality. To ensure the application of this principle the Prokuratura was founded in 1922. Instead of a withering away of the law and the state, the law became more complex, the state more powerful. The realization came that even the USSR had to live in the world. It had to deal with capitalist economies, by which it felt itself surrounded, and preserve an adequate system of private international law. If it were to try to achieve the disappearance of law and state in a communist society by 1980 (as declared at the 22nd Congress of the Communist Party) difficulties such as that of the international recognition of a self-declared non-state might arise. Not surprisingly (to the common lawyer, at least), abstract philosophy had failed to take account of specific reality.

Soviet courts are educational institutions in which the reasons and justice of law are made manifest to all citizens, including the defendant. The principle of socialist legality means that all must conform to the legal order of the socialist state. The Supreme Soviet alone is immune from this principle, which otherwise is strict and imperative. It is the duty of all citizens both to obey and to ensure its observance by others. Socialist legality is protected by the Prokuratura, an independent office uniting the functions of several institutions of non-socialist systems, such as aspects of the Conseil d'État and the Law Officers of the Crown. The principle of legality means also that a member of the bar, the Advokatura, must act in conformity with the principle as an officer of the court, even to the possible detriment of his client.

The hierarchy of soviet courts is unremarkable, but the attributes of judges reflect the subordination of substantive law to the principle of socialist legality. For judges at each level are elected for five years and need have no legal or other professional qualification. At first instance the judge sits with two assessors, themselves chosen from an elected list. The strong lay element in the judicial process is both an aspect of the educational function of the courts and a step towards eventual administration without law (in the Soviet sense).

In pursuance of this same principle socialist systems have greatly developed the technique of deciding disputes by arbitration. The attractiveness of this device is enhanced by the economic structure of the state, in which all the industrial and commercial enterprises are publicly owned. Their disputes accord better with awards made by technically qualified arbitrators in compliance with the principle of socialist legality than with normal litigation. All such disputes must be submitted to arbitration.

On the other hand, private arbitration is voluntary and chiefly employed in disputes arising from international commercial contracts. This form of arbitration is much encouraged and the USSR has provided a facility for hearings in establishing the Arbitration Court of the USSR Chamber of Foreign Commerce. Private arbitration between Soviet citizens, however, is not favoured. They should not try to evade the educational benefits of a normal judicial proceeding.

If one sought a specific cause for the revival of the study of Roman law in Italy in the 12th century one could point with much justification to the inspiring discovery at Amalfi in the late 11th century of a comprehensive manuscript copy of the *Digest*. If one sought similarly for a cause for the creation of a common law in England one could fairly adduce the Norman invasion of 1066 and the political need for centralized control of the country. What is the link (or its absence) between these events which pointed the two legal systems in different directions? It may be suggested that the answer lies partly in their coincidence in time and partly in the urgency of political action in the wake of conquest. The non-reception of Roman law in England was thus not initially deliberate, but a necessary and unintended (in the sense of never consciously considered) consequence of the political centralization of the administration of justice through royal judges on assize throughout England. In terms of political expediency the law they had to apply must be native; in terms of centralized control it must be common to the country. The legitimacy that William I claimed for his succession was thus substantiated by his support of this important English institution. His safeguard lay in putting the legal system under the control of his own judges. From the very outset, accordingly, English law came to be regarded less from the point of view of its substance and content than from that of its judicial administration. An accident of history robbed England of a comprehensive and well-developed legal system. In exchange it gave her a system of creative administration of justice which many regard as unequalled elsewhere.

Into this world was born Henry Bracton, a Devonshire man whom Holdsworth was to describe as one of the most important makers of English law. From 1248 to 1257 he was a judge of the King's Bench and a member of the Curia Regis. In his professional practice and judicial appointments he compiled notes of some 2,000 cases of the first 24 years of the reign of Henry III. This great body of decisions formed an essential basis for Bracton's treatise, *De Legibus et Consuetudinibus Angliae*. The *leges* were the sparse statutes, provisions and charters, the *consuetudines* the rules of customary law for the most part enshrined in judicial decisions. It was all splendid English stuff as far as it went. But what of the gaps in the law? And how did Bracton achieve his systematic presentation of this disparate and empirical body of material represented by the title of his work? To both questions there would seem to be a single answer: Roman law. The century and a half since the Norman conquest had given time not only for a judicial approval of much customary English law; it had witnessed the spread of the influence of academic teaching of Roman law soon to begin in the new university of Oxford. The structure of Bracton's treatise indicates the influence of Azo of Bologna and Justinian himself.

So far as concerns substance, Bracton discussed many matters from Roman law that were not covered by common-law decisions, and provided possible solutions to native problems. The result was not a reception of Roman law in the sense of its wholesale acceptance on the European continent, but a selective enrichment of English law by suitable rules taken from or inspired by the more sophisticated system.

Of greater significance for the future of the common law was Bracton's exposition of the system both in procedural terms of available writs and empirical terms of judicial decisions. Despite his death in 1268 with his great work incomplete, his treatise was nothing less than the blueprint of the English legal system.

In the administration of royal justice the possibility of a legal remedy for a wrong or injury depended on the existence of the appropriate writ, or royal command to the defendant to answer a complaint before the king's judges. In this period of expansion new forms of writ were readily obtainable to meet new forms of damage. But in this procedural formalism the system contained the germ of its own limitations. Substance was in danger of being submerged in technicality, a complaint about the law that is by no means new. While the strictness of the writ system was mitigated by the invention of actions by analogy to existing writs, the common law nevertheless remained defective in its range of remedies.

It fell to the early chancellors, ecclesiastics until the removal of Cardinal Wolsey in 1529, to provide relief to the petitioner on the ground of their concern for the defendant's conscience. This ecclesiastical intervention, at first informal, developed into a court with a jurisdiction parallel to that of the common law. It dealt with matters neglected by the common law, such as its great invention of the trust; and it provided remedies against the person of the defendant, such as ordering the specific performance of an undertaking, where the only available remedy under the other system was the payment of damages. The new court of the chancellor took the title of the Court of Chancery and the body of law it developed came to be known as Equity.

Following the death of Ellesmere, Francis Bacon became Lord Chancellor in 1618 and gave himself the task of consolidating the work of his predecessor. He had a reforming zeal that led him to improve and systematize the procedure of the Court of Chancery. Among his more general proposals may be mentioned a revision of statutes, a digest of law, and several texts, such as an introductory book of institutes, of obviously Byzantine inspiration. His decisions manifested a wise restraint where they touched the frontiers of the common law. Yet he fell victim, almost unaccountably for a man of his sensibility, to the moral corruption of the age. The House of Commons investigated complaints of bribery and corruption among judges and officials of the Court of Chancery, including Bacon himself. He was impeached, convicted on his confession and sentenced, though that was remitted. Four years later, in 1626, he died.

Little of Bacon's remarkable quality appears from this brief reference. As an advocate, whether in court or in Parliament, he was considered superb. Ben Jonson's moving testimony is worth recalling: "The fear of every man that heard him was that he should make an end." He set an example of forensic advocacy that is part of the long tradition of the English bar.

Bacon's life-long association with Gray's Inn was notable for his service to that honourable society both as Treasurer and as Reader. In the former capacity during the long years 1608–17 he added lustre by his personal distinction and greatly strengthened its corporate life by his encouragement of moots and social occasions. While in fact he was the first, in his *De Augmentis*, to subject English law to criticism on a level of jurisprudential thought, a wider philosophical renown rests on his plan of human control of the forces of nature. This rationalist philosophy, based on an experimental inductive method in the natural sciences, manifested the high qualities of Bacon's original and independent mind. But apparently he never realized that his own doctor, whose name was Harvey, was benefiting mankind no less in investigating the circulation of his blood.

The four Inns of Court – Gray's Inn, Inner Temple, Lincoln's Inn and Middle Temple – developed from around the 14th century as centres of training and professional life in English law. The training of students was by readings in their Inns, by pupil-type association with practitioners, and by constant attendance at the courts. From roughly the same date Roman law was taught in English universities, though its students were not intending practitioners in the ordinary courts, but in the ecclesiastical and prize courts.

Not until the middle of the 18th century was English law taught in the universities. The consequences are important. In the first place an academic qualification in law has only become essential in the last few years for practice: indeed, until the 20th century a lawyer's university qualification (and most were graduates) was unlikely to be in law. Secondly, there is no professional career as judge, as in civil-law systems. Judges are appointed from members of the bar (though recently solicitors also may be appointed) on the basis of their standing and reputation as practitioners. Thus there is a close and continuous association within the various Inns of Court from the newest student to the most senior judge, and the strength of the bar lies in this link of personal confidence. A further important consequence of this situation is the authority of the judge, who has law-making powers in the English system, which he exercises by his decisions. It is the judge in England who largely fulfils the functions of the jurist in the civil law as the authoritative source of interpretation of the law. The medieval quality of royal representative attached to Justices on Assize still gives to Her Majesty's judges a very high status in English society.

In contrast to the position of the judge we must add a word about the legislator. At the public level he is the Member of Parliament, elected to the House of Commons, or a hereditary or life member of the House of Lords. At the private level a great deal of legislation is made by civil servants under powers delegated by Parliament to ministers. Many of these legislators, both M.P.s and civil servants, are lawyers. Yet when one speaks of law in England one does not primarily think of legislation, but rather of the entire system of law in which statute traditionally takes a lower place than case-law. The struggles of the 17th century between Parliament and the judges of the common law, and notably Sir Edward Coke, resulted in a healthy constitutional respect for the common law.

Partly because of the constitutional situation mentioned above and partly because no general reception of Roman law ever took place, English law has never been codified in the sense of civil-law systems. It is a difference of form of law that greatly affects the lawyer's approach to problems. In a codified system, with the long tradition of Justinian's Code, the judge regards his function as merely applying the law to the case before him, and for this purpose the law is the relevant article of the Code. This relatively modest function is often established in written constitutions prescribing the separation of powers between (*inter alia*) the legislator and the judge. Codification accordingly involves much more than the outward form of law. It puts in issue the law-creative function of the judge.

The academic perception of the need for broader legal horizons reflects the growth in our time of international institutions of a regional or functional character, most of which carry legal implications. Lawyers of civil-law systems have in the past been more conscious of these developments than those in the common law, partly because their environment was continental rather than insular and partly because of their common ancestry in Roman law. Nevertheless the now venerable international bodies, the Institute of International Law and the International Law Association, were founded jointly by men of both systems over a century ago. The theme of cooperation that inspired and motivated the League of Nations, the United Nations Organization, the Council of Europe and the European Economic Community led to the establishment of important organs of legal character, in all of which lawyers of both civil- and common-law systems, and in some cases those of socialist systems, collaborated.

Most recently the European Economic Community has become the instrument, under the Treaty of Rome, for enacting uniform legislation directly applicable in the countries of its member states and for exercising a supreme unifying jurisdiction over a wide range of economic life of the Community through the Court of Justice of the European Communities at Luxemburg. Again by way of example we may note the work throughout the 20th century, but most conspicuously in the past 20 years, of the Hague Conference of Private International Law. Beginning as a group of continental European nations united by their civil-law origin, the Conference expanded in the 1950s to take account of both the common law and the English language, factors which resulted in an expanded non-European membership including the United States of America, Canada and Australia. Membership nevertheless remains predominantly European, and it is gratifying to note that it includes one or two states, notably Czechoslovakia and Yugoslavia, with socialist legal systems. The international factor involved in the operation unites all systems in the common and necessary purpose of legal coexistence.

Perhaps it is the perversity of human nature to unify the diverse and to diversify the unified. The complex reasons of politics, religion and the vicissitudes of power in the past millennium of European history would go far to account for the cycle of legal unity and legal change that one may discern. The military conquests of Rome, like those of Napoleon, brought in their train the widespread adoption of their legal systems. The Code Civil des Français in its original edition of 1804 fitted as easily into the knapsack of every soldier as into the pocket of every citizen. To add that it also fitted the European spirit of the age explains its retention after the military sanction had been withdrawn. The post-1945 communist political conquest of eastern Europe carried with it the socialist legal system. Following such events each state jealously guards its newly acquired law. It is politically necessary to acclaim its virtues, real or imagined. But in time the truth of reality prevails and compromise becomes attractive. Thus in a political sense we find developing in west European countries the compromise of so-called Euro-communism.

When we look back to the Holy Roman Empire, the claims to world spiritual supremacy of the medieval pope and the reception of Roman law in continental Europe, we may perceive a variety of dissociated reasons for the broad unity of law in Europe at the time of the Renaissance. If this result is less than a coincidence, it is more than an accident of history. However historians may analyse or try to explain it, the broad unity of law in 1500 was a substantial reality, the common law in its secular aspects being a notable exception. Such unity of law was an aspect of the European concept of a common culture and a common faith, strengthened by the revival of Greek natural-law concepts as propounded in Christian form in the *Summa Totius Theologiae* of St Thomas Aquinas. Universalism was in the air. The educated élite proclaimed it, though the common man, conscious only of the struggle for existence under his local customary law, probably never noticed it.

The disintegration of unified Europe into the individual jealous sovereignties and principalities of the 17th century, while diminishing the concept of a unified law, led to the development of means of coordinating the variety of individual systems into a viable international legal community. This movement took two main lines. The more important was impetus towards a more rational and humane body of public international law (then called the law of nations or *jus gentium*) led by the great Dutch jurist and diplomat, Hugo Grotius. He too employed the argument of natural law, but in this new Age of Reason one devoid of the theological factor, as in its exposition by St Thomas Aquinas. The second path towards a new unity was also made largely in the Netherlands, although the French jurists, Dumoulin and d'Argentré, had earlier contributed to it. It lay in the development of a new theory of private international law, notably by Ulrich Huber and John Voet, on the basis of respect for territorial sovereignty, with exceptions to the application of national law on the principle of reciprocity.

The interest of both these new developments (for neither was a complete innovation) lay in the attempt to achieve an over-all unity while preserving the individual diversity of national systems. It was a realistic compromise which has retained its basic importance into our own times, when we are once more witnessing a return to uniformity or harmonization of law. The ground is suitable for this type of growth: by and large Europe has a common history, culture, religion and level of civilization. It is not easy to unify on different planes of thought. Secondly, there exists a modern version of the ancient motives in military or economic unity, and a will to unify is necessary. Thirdly, the increasing internationalism of our times in industry and mass destruction renders traditional legal frontiers, for these purposes at least, irrelevant. The scale of international life, regarded positively as commerce or negatively as crime, calls for a degree of coordination, and logically of unification, in the relevant branches of law. Unification of law, as the example of the European Economic Community shows, depends on a coincidence of national self-interest and collective needs. The strength of the movement towards collectivity and incidentally the unification of law lies in a growing awareness that this is the safest way to national survival in an economic, political or military sense.

In these respects, however, is Europe returning to one law or two? Will the Iron Curtain (the phrase already has an obsolescent sound) continue to divide Europe legally, as it does politically and economically? The answer, we would submit, lies in necessity. Is it necessary to the life of Europe as a whole that law should be uniform in those areas (notably commercial law) where uniformity is most useful? The fundamental differences in the political and economic bases of society in the east and the west will prevent the unification of all law relevant to those differences, whether it concerns the ownership of property, the freedom of contract, the rights of succession or any other affected topic. On the other hand, jurists of socialist systems are actively involved in United Nations bodies concerned with international law, comparative law and the unification of private law. It is reasonable to suggest that at this international level of unification all Europe is involved. To be able to indicate that degree of unity of law is gratifying, for an international path, when local methods fail, may lead in due course to internal results. In a different context such were the means by which a much-criticized century-old English statute, the Wills Act 1861, came to be repealed in 1963.

The task of unifying or harmonizing European law also becomes less frightening if we recall our basic philosophical concept of law as an essential element in society. Between this basic conceptual level and that of international law, private or public, lies the grey area of national law. It is an area for discussion and negotiation in the interest of making a better life for the peoples of Europe in our time.

But law does not end with Europe – not even law of European origin. All three systems we have discussed are worldwide in their representation. An introspective view, however, would accurately reflect the complacency and sense of patronizing superiority of Europe's lawyers at least until the end of the 19th century. This is an ancient tradition. Could any barbarian law compare with that of Rome, however much the unenlightened Gaul or Saxon might prefer it? This attitude has persisted in two particular respects: in the colonial territories (or former territories) of Europe's civil-law countries the imported civil law has generally been placed above native law in the legal hierarchy: such was not the case with the common law.

Secondly, in the operation of the system of private international law the courts are faced with two principal questions: which law shall apply, or which court shall have jurisdiction? The English courts, for example, in these situations have in the past looked only to what Dicey in 1896 described as the law of civilized societies. At various times courts have regarded this description as excluding the law and jurisdiction of such systems as those of China and Turkey, quite apart from that of a native African tribe. It seems that civilized society in the application of private international law was synonymous with European society, or if one considered the application of non-European law, for example the law of New York, it had to satisfy the unspoken premise of being the law of a Christian community.

There may have been some explanation, but scarcely justification, for this European conceit. It should now form part of our history, for Europe has much to learn, in law as in other things, from the rest of this shrinking world.

# *28*

# *Rebels, Heretics and Revolutionaries*

## FRIEDRICH HEER

Europe is a process which owes its vigour, its mobility and its motive power to the collaboration of its rebels, heretics and revolutionaries with the Establishment. This collaboration is shown up in a variety of forms. It is shown in the rise and fall of the master group (of class, caste, the master race, be it Romans, Franks, Normans, Spaniards, English, Russians), in mutations of the "rebels" and in mutations of the master caste. The opponents, even the deadliest enemies, change reciprocally in dialectical processes which often neither side comprehends (this is the only way to understand European "conservatism" and "right-wing" reaction in the 19th and 20th centuries). So it is in revolutions and in counter-revolutions, and it is not seldom that the collaboration assumes tragic forms.

"Crucify them!" There follow crucifixions, burning, life imprisonment. Expulsions and "voluntary" emigrations have very fruitful results, the exodus from Europe and the exodus within Europe. Clerics flee from the Carolingian Empire to a Spain dominated by Islam, there to convert to Judaism. Anglo-Saxon nobles, faced by the harsh Norman domination after 1066, flee to Novgorod and Constantinople, the first to emigrate from west to east. In the 14th century, radical Italian Franciscans and Joachimites flee by way of Sarai on the Volga deep into Asia, to the court of the Great Khan of the Mongols.

The two great sons of Europe, the USA and the USSR, are inconceivable without the exodus of nonconformists, mostly religious, from the continent and England to America from the 16th to the 20th century, without the exodus of political and ethnic refugees in the 19th and 20th centuries, and without the exodus to the land of the tsars which occurred from the 17th century onwards, a journey which was made, often at express invitation, by a variety of German fanatics, pietists and sects. Lenin's German mother, Maria Blank, came from this environment.

Old European society is largely a *polis*, an *urbs diis hominibusque communis*, a religio-political community with a common law, cult and life-style. The *polis* sees its rebel as a traitor, as a heretic and a revolutionary rolled into one. He is accused of wanting to ruin the whole religious, political, moral, legal framework of the *polis*. This was the accusation levelled at Socrates, at the young man from Galilee, at the young German terrorists of 1977.

The European RHR (my abbreviation for the rebels-heretics-revolutionaries complex) has illustrious forbears. Prometheus was recognized by the young Goethe, by Shelley, by Polish, Russian, Spanish and Italian poet-rebels of the youth movement in the early 19th century, as their supreme father in his rebellion against Zeus, and was finally proclaimed by Karl Marx as the great ancestor of the spiritual, religious and political revolution. In the light of the history known to us, in the glare from their fire, the prophets of the Bible come to us; they proclaim salvation out of destruction. Israel, the bride of Yahweh, has become a whore, she will be struck down, the people will be scattered. The kings will fall, and the temple in Jerusalem will be destroyed. The Last Judgement is the threshold of the "new age", of the *New Age* – the title of communist magazines in the 19th and 20th centuries. The leader of the German student uprising of 1968, Rudi Dutschke, gives his son the name Amos. Religio-political rebels are particularly fond of hailing the prophet Amos as their greatest forbear.

The prophets of the Old Testament, known to us by name, known to us by the writings ascribed to them, are only the tip of an iceberg, or rather, of a volcano. Before them, beside them, against them (as false prophets, their competitors) and after them appear, not for the last time, prophetesses, women, Cassandra figures who proclaim the fall, the great destruction of the whole religio-political order as a disorder inimical to Yahweh, who proclaim this destruction as a prerequisite of salvation, of the great transformation, of the birth of the "New Age", of the "New Man", of the "New Israel", of the "New Humanity".

There are some pinnacles, written masterpieces still surviving, remarkable *chefs-d'oeuvre*, which rear up out of the anonymous mass of this volcano's fire and slime. These are the numerous "heathen" and Jewish apocalypses of the centuries surrounding the birth of the young man from Galilee, among which the Henoch Apocalypse stands out supreme. These apocalypses bring to life and accentuate the deep unrest among the Jewish people under the harsh oppression of its Jewish masters and their oligarchic hangers-on, under the oppression of the hierocracy, the cliques around the high priest, under the terrible oppression of Rome.

From the bloody sea of these apocalypses rises the Apocalypse of John. Since the high Middle Ages this has been adopted particularly by Christian religio-political rebels as their Bible of Revolution. One may examine Albrecht Dürer's "Apocalypse" prints and the accompanying "Illustrations" to the contemporary Peasants' War.

The Johannine Apocalypse presents us with an extraordinarily meaningful psychological profile of those "children of light" who take up stations for their battle – a battle which has lasted 2,000 years so far – against the children of darkness, as black and red puritans. There is a little flock, a little group of elect, a sworn brotherhood, which knows itself to be signed with the "sign of the lamb" – a symbol of salvation on its banner – and which knows itself to be engaged in a murderous life-and-death battle. This battle will end with the extermination of the enemy.

C. G. Jung, the melancholy parson's son, looks in horror on the orgy of hatred, on the fury of annihilation, on the psycho-terror, on the monstrous aggressiveness, on the spiritual requirement to hate, to kill, to annihilate, which are compressed here in the Johannine Apocalypse (see his *Reply to Job*). This *agnus dei*, this Lamb of God, is, in this apocalypse, a raging murderous ram.

We look the annihilating power, the terror which emanates from this God, in the face. We confront it in the terrible Christ, God of Vengeance, in the Last Judgement on the 12th-century tympanum of Vézelay in Burgundy, we confront it in the Christ of Michelangelo's *Last Judgement* in the Sistine Chapel in Rome. Here the young man from Galilee has turned into the "sommo Giove", Jupiter in the Highest – the name Dante has already given to Christ in Judgement.

In the psychological profile of the young man from Galilee himself, which indeed to a large extent is a profile of the faithful in the first generations after his death (we know Jesus only through the pictures drawn by the wishes and fears of early Christian congregations, through their visions of hope – and in so far as Europeans are existential Christians, by the radioactive rays which stream out from this man), two essential elements can be pin-pointed, which are significant for the psychological profile of all RHRs, above all in Europe. These elements are a difficult, complex relationship with the father and a very strong, but at the deepest levels no less difficult, relationship with the mother. I personally believe that the great recipe for a healthy, whole, normal human life, which the Bible proclaims in the famous watchword, "honour thy father and thy mother", was formulated with an eye to the many restless sons and daughters of Israel, who found it far from easy to accept their father as he came to meet them, in the fullness of his strength, in the fullness of his weaknesses.

The psychological profile of Mao Tse-tung, of daughters of the Russian nobility, of sons of orthodox priests, of Jewish Polish Marxists in the 19th century, confronts us in the psychological profile of the young Martin Luther. The same profile confronts us in the monks, priests and parsons' sons who, before and after Luther, each in their own great church, resist the Holy Father in Rome, resist the bishop of the Danish established Church (the case of Kierkegaard). The same profile confronts us in the 1,000-year struggle between father and son, son and father, which we see in the permanent crown-prince complex of the epoch of Charlemagne and Louis the Pious, and which we see in the centuries which Shakespeare calls to memory, right up to the decline of the old Europe with the collapse of the Austro-Hungarian Empire, in Emperor Franz Joseph's conflict with his son Rudolf and his nephew Franz Ferdinand. In that instance, this father-complex "above" in the ruling castes and families repeats itself "below"; the young assassins of Sarajevo 1914 fight their fight against their own "corrupt" fathers, who show themselves loyal to the supreme father, the emperor in Vienna, as a fight against the emperor and his representatives/successors.

In the psychological profile of the young man from Galilee, there appears a cross, a crux, a coordinates system. The vertical is formed by the difficult father relationship. The place of the father on earth, of Joseph, of the Holy Father, of the high priest in the Temple, is taken by the Father in Heaven. The horizontal is merely hinted at, the mother relationship, remarkably uncertainly, opaquely – as in the Gospels. "Woman, what have I to do with thee?"

All the more clearly does the mother bond step into the light, into the fire, into the front line against the terribly strong father (with crown princes and theological rebels), against the alarmingly weak father (as seen by revolutionary leftists in the 19th/20th century in the shape of their exploited proletarian fathers, perhaps also in the shape of a peasant bondsman, of a poor Jewish devil in a little town in the land of the tsars). RHRs very often have a passionate mother relationship, which can develop to a religio-political mother complex, in the form of a bond with "the pure maid", the Mother Church, who must be freed from the violations of the corrupt father in Rome-Babylon. This holy Great Mother, salvation in her womb, working in the collective, appears there present as the pure congregation, the new people, the nation, the bosom of the party – philosophically expressed, as "substance", as the "masses" (as collective source of redemption, as first mover of the history of the world, instead of as the *massa damnata*, the "damned mass" of Augustine), as "Nature". Nature is the deistic mother-godhead, the *magna mater* of the English, then of the French, early Enlightenment in the 17th to the 19th century. Nature is always an embodiment of the old Mother of God, of the *magna mater*; from the biographies of the 17th to the 20th century it is easy to read the mother bonds of non-conformist RHRs.

It is the passionately existential, erotic and neurotic bond with a land, a people, which stamps Europe's RHR. Under the spell of this bond his own land is elevated to the Holy Land, his own people to the Chosen People. This results in certain difficulties when the religious and political Establishment itself already has at its disposal a pronounced cult of the nation. So it was in the days of the young man from Galilee.

His name, the course of his life (scarcely known to us), his fate indicate moreover how the borders between rebels, heretics and revolutionaries become blurred. Jesus was brought before Pilate as a rebel against the emperor, and as such put to death, as "King of the Jews". Jesus was seen as a heretic by some religio-political factions of the Jewish Establishment surrounding the high priests. To the present day, Jesus is honoured by religio-political revolutionaries and idealists of the "theology of revolution" as a first-class revolutionary, indeed as *the* great revolutionary of the first hour of European civilization. The young man from Galilee understood himself neither as rebel, nor as heretic, nor as revolutionary. He wanted only to do the will of his Father in Heaven.

"Nation" was a prosaic corporation, at medieval universities. A "nation" united there as an administrative unit often very diverse "nations"; so it was in Paris, in Bologna, in the early Prague. At the 15th-century reform councils in Constance and in Pisa, already "nation" is no more a harmless thing, but a "national" thing. The fires which burn Jan Hus in Constance point back and point ahead to the fires of the spirit, to the fires, the religious movements, which bring the new nations to birth, then weld them together in wars; the nation as spiritual nation, as chosen people, as nation of salvation, as the "New Israel".

Joan, does God hate the English? Joan of Arc, devalued by Shakespeare, burnt by the Church as a backsliding heretic, wanted to lead a crusade against the Hussites. But primarily she is a midwife to French nationalism, which owes its first birth to the first Crusades. "Gesta Dei per Francos." God does his deeds on earth supremely through his beloved Franks. Right up to Napoleon as Charlemagne reborn, French royalist theologians above all understand the French people as "people of the *true* Franks", as people of Charlemagne. The Germans are a perverted variety of the Franks. The very question referred to is a question in the trial – an élite of French theologians sits in judgement on Joan. The girl rejects this questioning; she knows herself to be commissioned only by God to drive the English from the fair kingdom of France.

Long and winding are the ways from Wycliffe and his early adherents, past the Lollards to Scottish and English radical puritans, to the Scottish revolution, to the English revolution of 1640–60. (The Glorious Revolution should to a large extent be understood as a counter-revolution, as a great restoration.) "To your tents, O Israel!" The first Cromwell, a magnificent and terrible and at least at the end tragic figure (does Churchill's portrait of Cromwell bear features of a self-portrait?), is just as convinced about his vocation – to forge England into a people of God, chosen nation, on the battlefield – as are some of his bitterest enemies in radical nonconformist movements, and on the "right", if one may put it like that just now. Then this: the great Milton, who sings the swan-song of the frustrated revolution.

The puritan revolution, the terror which emanates not least from its purges (Committee for Scandalous Ministers), the fanaticism of a Pym, who proclaims a belief in radical destruction as the foundation of salvation (as in his speech at the opening of Parliament in 1640, "We have one chance now to make the country happy, in that we remedy all grievances and tear out the cause of all evils by the root"), all these have to this very day instilled an inextinguishable fear in English politicians, in men of the ecclesiastical-political Establishment. Without these radicals, who began as rebels against the Stuarts, who as heretics against the Church of the royal bishops (who with Laud defend "the beauty of the saints") and as true revolutionaries wanted to establish the Kingdom of God in England and Scotland, without them it is impossible to understand two imposing institutions, or better, dispositions of mind of the English body politic. There is the will not only to suppress radical movements from the religio-political underground, but also to intercept them, through reforms – in fact to bridge the divide between the "two nations" (Disraeli, before Engels), a divide which indeed still endures today. And then there is the understatement, the underplaying of very great opposites, of ultimately insoluble conflicts, which openly proclaimed tear the nation apart, or at least put it to a severe test.

Radicals, true revolutionaries, before and after 1640–60, find it difficult to win any recognition in England's religious or political spheres; so it was for the adherents of English Jacobism, for the men around Erasmus Darwin, then around the young Tom Paine, then around Shelley, and finally for the rebellious women of the early suffragette movement.

Jan Hus is well known to be the ideological descendant of Wycliffe. Bohemian students bring "the English poison" to Prague. Hus does *not* hate the Germans, declares emphatically that he prefers a good German Christian to a bad Czech Christian. "The Kingdom of God in Bohemia": radical left-wing Hussites, "Taborites", understand it as cell, as stronghold, as the nation in arms for the cleansing of Europe from the lechery of the Babylonian Church of Rome. Moderate Hussites are the fathers of religious, political, and not least educational reform movements, which stretch past Jan Comenius-Komensky to Thomas Garrigue Masaryk. Hus and the Hussitism which early detaches itself are in the 19th/20th century (here I always see the 19th and 20th centuries as a unit) understood by Czech nationalists, by "Rome-free" Catholics, by "liberals", socialists, communists, as patriarchs of the Czech national consciousness, as true founders of the Czech (*not* the Slovak!) nation.

Jan Hus, the forest peasant's lad, quiet, long turned in on himself, introverted, did not understand himself as rebel – he wanted to be the loyal servant of the king in Bohemia and of the Holy Roman Emperor. He did not understand himself as heretic – he wanted to serve the "true" Church. And in no way did he understand himself as a revolutionary – a man of conservative mentality, shy, long uncertain, a man of bourgeois life-style, trapped until his death in a monastically restrained sexuality. Great, epoch-making rebels, heretics and revolutionaries understand themselves not uncommonly as restorers of an old holy order which has been "corrupted", corrupted by diseased fathers, by degenerate mothers (churches, parties).

The German monk, who was seen by Thomas Carlyle as "a Christian Odin", openly acknowledges that he is a pupil of Jan Hus – Dr Martin Luther. Luther battles against "rebels"; he was furious with the German peasants who dared to rise up against the divinely ordained rule of the nobility. Luther battles against "heretics", above all against his left-wing sons, from whom is descended even the radical young "New Left", the rebellious student generation of 1968–78. Luther rages against the fanatics, against the Baptists, against Thomas Müntzer, but he also rages against those who refuse to join in controversy, who withdraw from *his* Establishment, the Lutheran established Church; so it was in the case of Schwenkfeld, in the case of Sebastian Franck. Luther battles, ever more angry, furious, raging against revolutionaries in Heaven and on earth; battles against the Devil, who is for him increasingly embodied in the Jews (in the Nürnberg Trial of 1946 Julius Streicher, the editor of *Der Sturmer*, invoked his teacher Luther); battles against the Devil who is embodied in the papacy and in *every* revolution on earth.

The great German conservative Martin Luther, who embraces a petit-bourgeois life-style, like many German professors after him, who enjoys his tipple and eats plenty, is honoured to this very day by German conservative princes, politicians, officers, by citizens and country folk, by men of the Church and theologians – and also by American Lutherans – as the cornerstone of a religious and political conservatism. As honourable shield of a cult of obedience, in the service of "throne and altar", of law and order, he made a particular impression in Prussia.

The young Luther is one of the greatest European revolutionaries; although he lacks political genius, he inspires Europe's two greatest political geniuses, Calvin and Lenin (conservative traits are not infrequently present in quite great revolutionary thinkers, as with Hegel, with Marx, with Sigmund Freud). "Radically", literally indeed grasping at the roots, Luther to the very end calls old Europe's 1,000-year religio-political order in question, puts an end to it, not only in the papacy but in the entire tradition of the theologians and intellectuals. This is what excites the horror of an Erasmus and of a Melanchthon.

Martin Luther is a creator, a patriarch of the German nation, even of a German nationalism. As creator of a new German language in his translation of the Bible, a language without which a Goethe and a Bertolt Brecht are unthinkable, he achieves the salvation of the nation by the salvation of the language of salvation. Through him the German language becomes the language of salvation, of the nation's discovery of itself. Luther's hymn, his song, "A safe stronghold our God is still", is *the* German "Marseillaise", the national anthem of evangelical Germany right up to the height of the 19th century.

The great religious rebels, heretics, revolutionaries deprived the Latin of the Holy Father and of the Latin-speaking Roman Mother Church of its power; they created *the* national language; in such a way they form the nation into a "nation of salvation". Here too Czechs set the example on the continent. Before Hus, the reformer Thomas Stitny asks, "Does God love Czech less then Latin?" Europe's revolutions are from the 16th to the 20th century made in Heaven, reproduced on earth.

When looking back on the 1,000 years of old Europe's rebels, heretics and revolutionaries, these "practical" questions pose themselves with regard to the positions and situations of today's rebels, heretics and revolutionaries. The questions are, where, in what place (locality), in what society (organization etc.) does the rebel, heretic, revolutionary find his foothold? Where can he put down his roots? The "radical", who would like to uproot a state, a society, a party, who would like to destroy and/or modify right to the "roots of the evil", himself requires a place, a permanent location, in which he can put down his roots.

Whoever is a great mover and takes over the role of the first mover (as Aristotle, Aquinas, Dante and also the great mystic and seeker Isaac Newton conceive of the Godhead) must himself possess a place and a station, on which he stands "unmoved". Whoever makes others uncertain, whoever would invalidate old deeply rooted certainties, must himself be certain, so that he is not picked up this same night by the security police.

A first look at the customs, the rich experiences and the practices of persecutors, secret agents, security police in the European 19th/20th century – from the implementation of the Karlsbad Resolutions against German radicals of the Metternich era via Metternich's own agents to Bismarck's police, the Okhrana, Cheka, GPU, to the Gestapo and its European sisters in socialist and Fascist regimes today – convinces us that in the 1,000 years of old Europe it was often easier for rebels, heretics and revolutionaries to find places of refuge than today.

A second look at old Europe's inquisitions, at Roman inquisitions, at royal Spanish inquisitors, at the inquisitors of Calvin (who pursued and tracked his presumptive enemies throughout Europe, far towards Poland and Siebenburger and of course also to England, as "satellites of Satan" – the origin of the "communist satellites" in John Foster Dulles's religio-political language) warns us to be cautious.

In the relatively open Europe of the 12th century a theologian who had been persecuted as an arch-heretic in Spain could soon afterwards become Rector of the University of Paris. First cells in which they develop their "heretical" thoughts, and which then also became first refuges for heretics, are cloisters, isolated abbeys, subterranean chambers, rooms in the city underground (Bernard of Clairvaux sets his sights directly on these in his struggle against heretics in the rich city of Cologne).

Bishops and cardinals and abbots receive heretics. Thus there are followers of Arnold of Brescia and Abelard in Rome as early as the 12th century, and then in the following centuries until the Jansenism of the 18th century; so it is in their Roman palazzi, where also a political opposition to the ruling pope and his relatives plays a role in this resistance, not always, but not seldom.

Noble seats, fortresses, castles, manors, parsonages (in which the nobleman is patron of the church, as his own church), noble connections protect much-persecuted nonconformists, among them Wycliffe, Hus, Luther, English deistic nonconformists in the 17th century and French radical atheists of the Enlightenment in the 18th century.

Whoever wants to understand the gigantic phenomenon of the rebel-heretic-revolutionary complex in Europe should never ignore the fact that 1,000 years of domination by the nobility, a noble world in old Europe, means also a 1,500-year resistance. Right up to Russian revolutionaries and heretics of the 19th century (surrounding the excommunicated Leo Tolstoy) it is sons, often younger sons, from the 18th to the 20th century often noble daughters, who became rebels against their own fathers, against the king and emperor, the tsar, against the primate of the established Church etc.

The pure rebel is often a being without a history; rebels are like the sands of the sea. Rebels fall like leaves from the trees in autumn; they often go into the wood, like Robin Hood figures. The wood, *bois, bosco,* is the place of the noble robbers, pure rebels without any political and religious background. The wood becomes then a favourite environment of the political resistance, as in the 18th century in the transition from the old pure rebel, who has set his business on nothing, to the political rebel. In this world of transition is set Friedrich Schiller's drama *The Robbers,* the first German drama of a rebellious youth movement. In the 20th century men and women go into the wood, into the *macchia* in Provence. Albert Camus fights here as Hypnos. In the woods of the Balkans Tito's partisans fight, the grandsons and great-grandsons of the Serbians, Croatians, Greeks who fought the Turks. *Wald und Wiederstand* (wood and resistance), the two words are often synonymous – a pity that the German expression has no English equivalent.

Beside and instead of the wood, the hamlet, the remote farmstead, the village in the Alps (refuges for Waldensians and Albigensians, Austrian Protestants etc.), other sparsely populated areas (as in the south of France for the much-persecuted Huguenots' Église du Désert), highlands (the rebellion in the Cevennes mountains) and again the cloister, the secluded abbey (in Calabria and Spain cloisters belonging to the Joachimites, the radical adherents of Joachim of Fiore, then to the left-wing Franciscans) in Italy, southern France, south Germany (cloisters as places of asylum for much-persecuted mystics) and again fortresses (medieval Germany had far in excess of 10,000 fortresses) all become refuges.

Beside and instead of the places of refuge belonging to the agrarian-feudal and monastic world of old Europe appears the city. In the early Middle Ages the city was already called, and thus attacked as, refuge of heretics and political rebels, Lyons, Paris, Toulouse, the cities of Provence, of Flanders and of the Rhineland. Amsterdam and other cities of the Netherlands and London become excellent places of refuge in the Europe of the "New Age". London is an old stronghold first of English religious and political nonconformists; from the late 16th to the early

20th century it is a place of refuge for a profusion of European communities of non-conformist groups, beside which there then appear the cells of political refugees, party cells of continental "democrats", nationalists, atheists, liberals, socialists, communists. In the course of all this the political cells struggling with each other and against each other in the great city take over the legacy of the rivalries and animosities of the religious communities in the 16th- and 17th-century underground.

The religious cells of the religious continental-European underground which is based there in London leave a legacy which continues today. This legacy is the inner conflicts between political sects, between majorities and minorities within them, between "Bolsheviks" and "Mensheviks" (here understood in the figurative sense of the words as adherents of the majority and of the minority), and the inner self-understanding of each one political cell, of a movement in the underground which sees itself as the incarnation of the truth and fights for its "pure" Marxism against "spies", "traitors", dissidents. In the 16th/17th century in London there are Baptists (Calvinist ones and mild right-wing ones from the Netherlands), Mennonites, Anti-Trinitarians, fanatics of very different denominations, all settled next to each other. London is a capital of Europe's religious, then political underground long before Karl Marx took up residence here in Dean Street, Soho, and – to give an opposite extreme – the great Alexander Herzen settled here. The men are gathering in London who are going to shatter old Europe's 1,000-year-old sovereign order before 1914.

Paris only became a centre for political rebels, revolutionaries, in the 19th century, much later than London, after the fall of the last Bourbon king. But it was not a centre of the religious underground – it first becomes this to a small extent after the October Revolution of 1917 when thinkers of religious Russia grouped round Berdyaev settle here. In Italy, Venice and particularly the university of Padua provide a refuge for religio-political dissidents from the 12th to the 18th century; in German-speaking states at different times Hamburg ("the London of Germany" in the 18th century), Frankfurt and Nürnberg (with its Altdorf University) are refuges; in Poland there is Cracow.

The city guerrillas, present as they are today in political tracts, in ideologies and in revolutionary actions in South America, but also in the Federal Republic of Germany, in Italy, in France, can appeal to urban traditions.

Let us return to the sociological basis, to the social origin of our RHR complex, and remember first, the transitions from the rebel to the "revolutionary" are fluid. It seems often to depend on an accident whether a historical action, the founding of a new dynasty, comes out of the rebellion of a noble gentleman against his sovereign, or whether this permanent struggle of fathers, sons, brothers, uncles, daughters (Lear's daughters as models), of mothers and other ambitious ladies (Queen Eleanor of Aquitaine, consort of Louis VII of France, then of Henry II of England) and some Lady Macbeth figures, particularly in Russia, forms a "game" of rebellions which resolve and dissolve into each other like South American *pronunciamentos*.

Very briefly it can be said that the rebel has the chance to become a revolutionary when he himself and/or a caste, class, clique united with him which strives to assume power, unites with political and religious movements, ideologies etc., with the cause of the "pure Gospel" (practically it is a matter of the secularization of the rich church properties), of the Reformation, with the cause of the Enlightenment, with the cause of the people (as in the case of the Narodniki in Russia), with the cause of the proletariat.

The relationships of the historically mighty revolutionary, the revolutionary achieving historical significance (and the relationships of his older brother, the heretic) to himself, to his own person, to his cell/group/community/church/party, are often at least as difficult as his relationships to the men of the ruling order, whom he would unmask and overthrow as a total disorder.

Our RHRs live indeed in the 1,500 years of our Europe (permit me the continental slip of including England here occasionally in Europe, even though it has from the early Middle Ages considered itself to be an *alter orbis*, a world of its own which measures man with its own yardsticks), not simply in a counter-culture like the one the American hippies dreamt of (their successors, the yippies, already had clearer political-social insight); they do not live in a counter-culture which wanted to build a sort of island for new Swiss Family Robinsons, a

*89.* A portrait of the French artdealer and publisher Ambroise Vollard, painted in 1910 by Pablo Picasso.

*90. Overleaf:* European monarchs meeting for the funeral of Edward VII of England in 1910. From left to right (standing) Haakon VII of Norway, Ferdinand of Bulgaria, Manuel of Portugal, Kaiser Wilhelm II, George I of Greece, Albert of the Belgians, and (sitting) Alfonso XIII of Spain, George V of England and Frederick VIII of Denmark.

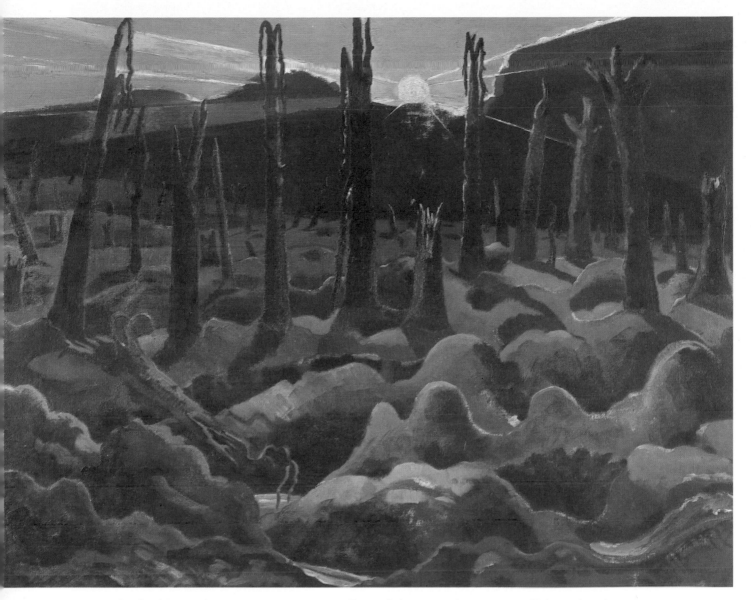

*92.* A battlefield in northern France. Painting, ironically entitled *We are making a New World,* by Paul Nash, 1918.

*91.* The arrest of the suffragette leader Mrs Pankhurst outside Buckingham Palace, London, in May 1914.

94. Cardinal Pacelli (later Pope Pius XII) visiting Paris in 1938. Photograph by Henri Cartier-Bresson.

93. The German dramatist and poet Bertolt Brecht. Painting by Rudolf Schlichter, c. 1925.

95. *Overleaf*: The destruction of Warsaw in 1943: Jews being marched away under guard by German troops.

*96.* The London blitz: *Tube Shelter Perspective*. Drawing by Henry Moore, 1941.

*97.* The "Liberation Window" in St John's Church, Gouda, Holland, by Charles Eyck, 1947.

*98.* The French existentialist philosopher Jean-Paul Sartre, photographed in 1946 on the Pont des Arts, Paris, by Henri Cartier-Bresson.

*99.* A Dutch poster of 1948 calling for a united Europe.

*100.* Albert Einstein, photographed in his Princeton study in 1950 by Ernst Haas.

*101. The Mechanic.* Painting by Fernand Léger, 1950.

102. Suburban conformity reflected in *Golconde*, a painting by René Magritte, 1953.

103. Interior of the chapel Notre-Dame-du-Haut at Rondchamp (1950–55) designed by Le Corbusier.

*105.* The theatre at Epidaurus in use today.

*104.* The May-Day Parade, Moscow, 1969.

*106. Overleaf:* Incident in the goal mouth during a game of soccer.

*107*. The opening session of the elected Assembly of the European Economic Community, Strasbourg, July 1979.

*108. Family Group.* Sculpture by Henry Moore, 1945.

Utopia – at which clever minds of the American youth rebellion early called on the Founding Fathers of the USA as precedents, on the old American dream, life, a blessed life on the land, close to nature (long before Emerson and Thoreau). Our European rebels, heretics and revolutionaries grow up in the middle of the society they are fighting against. Fringe figures which come out of the wood, fanatics, prophets in the Middle Ages, then early Rasputin figures never achieve historical power. Our RHRs live in the middle of the old Church, in her cloisters, cathedrals, universities, in the middle of the noble society, in the middle of the bourgeois society, in the middle of the cultural world of their age – as in the case of Wycliffe, Hus, Luther, Calvin, Robespierre, Marx, Trotsky, Lenin etc.

The significant European revolutionaries and their older brothers and fathers, the religious heretics, have peculiar intimate connections, intimate erotic, not only neurotic, relationships to the Great Mother, to the society, to the religio-political traditions which they want to "break up", liquidate, and that means literally make liquid. Karl Marx has produced the most imposing assessment of the achievement of European capitalism in world history. Karl Marx, who knows Heraclitus and the Attic tragedians, Dante (whom he quotes from memory), the west European belles-lettres from Cervantes to Balzac, the English political economists and the French political thinkers so familiarly, like his mentor Hegel who owns that Plato is as familiar to him "as her uncle is to the farmer's wife".

In a Berlin prison the great Karl Liebknecht writes to his son in 1917, "Herodotus, Xenophon, Thucydides, Demosthenes and the divine Plato, Homer, Virgil, Catullus, Horace . . . take in your hand a history of culture, of science, of art – these names shine in it. They have been shining for thousands of years and for thousands of years they will continue to shine . . . If you do not learn to know them you will lose something infinite for your whole life."

A look at Mao shows how this man who calls on heroes of the old Chinese epic, emperors, figures from romance from 3,000 years, knows himself to be secure in the same tradition.

To Russia's significant radical socialist and communist revolutionaries, the arch-priest Avvakum, head of the Raskol, of the "Old Believers", who describes in his autobiography his martyrdom at the hands of the tsar's Church, is just as familiar as the great European literary tradition. That applies to Lenin and Trotsky and the great classical Russian old Bolsheviks, the patriarchs of Russian socialism and communism. Far from this European tradition stands the Georgian Stalin; in opposition to the West he tries to root himself in *his* Russia, turns into the patron of pan-Russian nationalist reaction.

At first glance this appears almost comic, or at least tragi-comic. Our RHRs have their greatest difficulties not with the future, with their society of the future, with their Utopia, with their communist society which will unfold itself in long ages in many transitions from 1917 to today, then on to the third millennium, as it were in a permanent revolution. Our men of dissent have great difficulties not with their "heavenly Jerusalem", which they want to force down on the earth; it is rather that they want to force this immediately – like the radical Baptists in Münster, like Jacobins in Paris in great fear of a victory of the counter-revolution in France, in fear of conspiracies in their own camp, in fear of the Prusso-Austrian invasion, in fear of the peasant revolts in France, in fear of their own noble generals and officers. Revolutionaries who want to use their *Putsch*, their *coup d'état* to create, or at least proclaim, a new order fall overnight back into the old disorder. Right up to their downfall, this fear animated leading national socialists who were conscious that their national revolution had the character of a *Putsch*. Revolutions of such a broken-winded sort that make their appearance during the day, and during the night appear as counter-revolution, already carry the embryo of this in themselves.

Here we should not overlook or underplay the great disillusion, the early disillusion, which heretics, reformers, revolutionaries experience after their precarious seizure of power, in their Establishment. The disillusion of Luther, and Trotsky's great fear of the victory of the Bolshevik bourgeoisie. But this already points to the greatest difficulties of all which significant heretics and revolutionaries encounter as builders of a new society, of a new state, of a new church. These are not so much the old powers which they have just destroyed or at least suppressed. It is "the old Adam" who in his own cell, community, party, army, church raises his head as a many-headed Hydra.

Sorrowfully the great prophet Muhammad already complains in a saying later attributed to him, "My congregation will split itself in 73 *firaq* [heresies] and only one of them will be saved!"

Great Islamic heretics invigorate old Europe's intellectual, mystic and poetic underground, coming from Spain. Great Jewish heretics invigorate old Europe first between Maimonides and Spinoza. The explosive, creative European spiritual life of the 19th century to 1933 is unintelligible without the east Jewish and west Jewish heretics who break out from the bosom of their orthodoxy, where the greatest creative force is released when east Judaism and west Judaism collide in the breast of one man.

Sorrowfully the twin-faced Saul-Paul (he bears two names side by side: as Jew he is called Saul, as Roman citizen he is called Paul. The German saying "how a Saul is turning into a Paul there" does not make sense!) sees how in Corinth and other Christian communities there is developing a wealth of contrasts, conflicts, hostile factions from early counter-churches. In the 3rd century there are already several hundred sects and special churches which are overthrown in hard struggles by the great Church, during which this Church itself splits – as later does the communist great Church – into two opposing churches which to this very day form the basis of the European East-West conflict, in that they create two different mental hemispheres, the Greek, Orthodox-stamped east European and the Latin hemisphere of western Europe, with Poland as its extreme spearpoint against Moscow.

Luther, Calvin, Karl Marx, Karl Liebknecht and Rosa Luxemburg, Trotsky and the radicals of today, who splinter on the revolutionary left into at least half a dozen hostile groups, have the greatest difficulties to fight against internally. These difficulties come from intimate enemies in their own party, in their own central committee, in their own land; and as well the inside opponent is at times accused of collaboration with the class enemy, with right- and left-wing deviationists, treachery in a thousand forms, Trotskyism, Titoism, appeasement, Euro-communism, revisionism, "anarchy as an infantile disorder of communism".

Here, in this internal political struggle occur the great decisions. Not the guillotine, not the hangman, not the firing squad, not the garotte in Spain, not the incarceration in the St Peter and Paul Fortress in St Petersburg, not the banishment to Siberia, not the burning by *autos-da-fé* in Portugal and Spain, not the excommunication and damnation by Rome (by a party tribunal, a central committee), these do not make the great historical decisions. How ineffectual such tribunals are, tribunals which are always proclaimed triumphantly by the ruling class-church-party as a Last Judgement, as a final annihilation, extermination of the heretics-rebels-revolutionaries, is shown by the utter failure of the long-famous maxim, "Roma locuta est, causa finita." When Rome has given judgement, the case is settled. Thus popes up to 1945 triumphantly pronounce the extermination of the Albigensians, Waldensians, Wycliffites, Hussites, Lutherans "and the other sons of Belial". These sons of Satan are sitting fresh, happy and free together – in the symposium in Rome in the era of John XXIII. The reception of the greatest living European heretic as guest in the Kremlin, Tito in the Kremlin-church, is an example which will find, already has found, many followers. Stalin's excommunications and executions have not been able to shift these leftists out of the world, out of world history. It is only a question of time before the greatest of all heretics, the "red Origen" as I call him, that is Trotsky, moves into the Kremlin: perhaps just on the threshold of the third millennium. In the Soviet underground already today he has a very strong influence.

Certainly, we know, reprisals, acts of terror, inquisitions, banishments etc. can kill rebels, heretics, revolutionaries as individual people; but not simply destroy their work.

Europe lives, like a volcano, on its religious, political undergrounds. These very old undergrounds endure in sometimes narrowly locally defined areas through many centuries up to today, where a religious movement when it is driven into the underground often secularizes, politicizes, radicalizes itself in the underground. From the successors of Protestant noncon-formists come "reds" in the French south and in middle and lower Italy. From crypto-Protestants in Austria come national socialists. It is no accident that our 20th century explodes for the first time in the area around Sarajevo, in the Balkans. There in the struggle against the Byzantine emperor and his Church, against Turkish pashas, against the Roman-Latin Church, which wants to reconquer the Balkans, against the house of Habsburg, which is seen as the sword of Rome, so many religious, political, tribal, national motives are concentrated; the underground movements of a millennium, since the Bogomils in the 12th century working as missionaries also in the Latin west. The time-bomb of these centuries explodes in the hands of boys who are between 16 and 22 years old. This time-bomb kills first the Archduke heir to the throne Franz Ferdinand and his wife, then in the civil war tears apart Croats and Serbs and unfolds itself, with the European civil war from 1914 to 1944, into a world civil war.

We live in the middle of this civil war (in Europe, not in England!), which feeds on these fires from the religious, political underground.

Back then to this problem circle. The great decisions occur in the person of the rebel who can turn into the revolutionary, of the heretic who can turn into the church stormer, into the great destroyer of a church and the builder of a new church, a new creed (analogue in thought, in philosophy – as a dissenter, atheist, materialist or positivist can turn into the builder of a new closed system), in an inner struggle which is simultaneously the decisive argument with his own revolutionary cell in the underground, with his own party, with his brothers and comrades, with the comrades in arms of the first hour.

Our model number one again provides an exemplary omen. The Gospels do not hide the exceptional difficulties which the young man from Galilee has with his disciples, "brothers", comrades; at least one is named who betrays him to the enemy; "Judas", a symbolic figure, indeed already in the Gospels a secret code for heretic, majority, of the first hour. Peter betrays Jesus – again a model case for many other "betrayals" on the part of his disciples with the Word. Others lapse, become unbelieving; others struggle bitterly even in his lifetime for the primacy, for their rights of succession.

It would be simplistic to see here only personal petty jealousies, animosities, mean and trivial rivalries, such as we find in every family, every clan, every tribe, party etc., in every village. Crudely and curtly expressed, surrounding the person of a leading rebel, heretic, revolutionary are to be found at least three factions – a certain left wing, which radically urges the destruction of the existing order and total assumption of power; a certain right wing, which is not disinclined to collaborate with the ruling Establishment at least for the time being, if not in the long term; and a more or less broad centre which waits to see how the wind changes, which way it may blow from tomorrow (so Stalin listened to the wind for a long time before he spoke clearly). That is a centre which waits, waits for the victory of the "master", of the wonder-rabbi, of the revolutionary, in order to fit itself in to the new order as soon as possible, or in the case of his defeat, to tear him in pieces (Hosanna and Crucifige are one process!).

This inert mass, this often silent majority bears the future in its broad lap, the counter-revolution, the freezing in a new ecclesiastical, political, social establishment. This inert mass (did Augustine think of himself, in his subconscious, when he addressed the enormous majority of all mankind as *massa damnata*?) inclines naturally to the right. Against these "conservatives" prophetic women stand up in protest in the early Church, and then male heretics, and the first storm of monks rises up first in the 4th century.

It is with these three factions, which stand here as model for often very complicated combinations and cross-connections, that Hus, Luther, Calvin, Marx, Lenin and today's leaders in the left underground and in the right underground have to reckon. More and more Marx dedicates the main part of his political battle to his many "internal" political opponents, in the German social democracy around Lassalle, in the "romantic" French socialism, in the course of which occasionally personalities of extraordinary weight come to meet him, such as Bakunin (who has a great, hidden, silent influence on Lenin).

Trotsky's first early rebellion against Lenin is famous. Trotsky sees in Lenin the new Robespierre, under whose guillotine even Marx's lion's head would fall (Trotsky, *Our Political Task*, Geneva, 1904).

"For a long time now you have been carrying the heavy cross of the revolutionary Marxist" (Rabowski to Trotsky confined in Alma Ata in Mongolia, 1928). The *passio*, the passion narrative, this way of the cross of the heretic and revolutionary is created primarily by his brothers, his comrades, who want to force him on to their track, on to their path.

What determines the historical potency of significant RHRs is the fact that they go between the fires to the right and the fires to the left – in the furnaces of their own communities – right through the middle of the mire, the central morass, they go to their goal. They never reach it. The "red Moses", Mao, knows that. His 10,000-mile march to Yenan is early compared to the journey of the first Moses through the wilderness. The great RHR dies on the threshold, at the border, in the border. He himself does not set foot in the Promised Land. That is the Moses-fate of many significant RHRs.

Cynics and cool observers who see themselves as audience, as spectators in the great world theatre (as Calderón and Spanish-French and German baroque see and fashion it), like to say "that is their good fortune." What would have become of them, had they lived to see the victory of their "movements"? Jesus – in the Rome of the papal Church? Here he would truly have been burnt as a heretic. Marx in Moscow in 1936, in the year of the great purge? Marx in East Berlin, in Prague today? Sigmund Freud, one of the few great dissenters in the realm of the spirit in his epoch; how could he have lived in the giant ghetto of the American orthodox Freudians, in the discord of half a dozen psycho-analytic churches, he who already in his lifetime suffered so severely from the rebellion of his sons, from the defection of G.C. Jung and half a dozen other highly gifted spiritual sons? He, the patriarch of a world revolution which, in his understanding of himself, was betrayed by his children?

The fact that many RHRs die so young also creates the historical power, the colossal effect on the future. They die as an "unfinished symphony", as young seers, visionaries, revolutionaries. Their early death, their very defeat, their failure (as the 1,000-year epoch testifies, the people love the failed heroes more than the victors: Hector and Achilles, Siegfried, the Serbian princes dying on the battlefield and the falling Russian rebels) opens the future to them, sets free from their downfall their mortal wound which is experienced as source (as "seed of the martyrs"); gigantic radioactive elements, from this uranium, from the stuff from which they are formed, formed first as transient characters only as a figure of a time, clay from the potter's hand.

In the end is the beginning. In their downfall are released the powers of faith, of love, of hope, of great yearning; the great tension which produces an effect; the hope for the return of the master who then in the Last Judgement recognizes those true to him, rejects the deserters, and then brings about the "end of the ages", the New Age. After the burning of the old age, after the overthrow of the evil middle age, of the Middle Ages, seen since Tertullian as the *tempus medium* of sin, of corruption, after the destruction follows the advent of the New Age.

It is precisely the extreme brevity, the failure, the collapse into the ashes in which the sparks remain, that open the future, that unbind and bind very strong powers of belief. The death of the master, heretic, revolutionary impedes a bad happy end, the denial, the disenchantment, the demythologization, the great disillusionment; the great disappointment. The cross, the grave, the death in the dungeon, the burning are the places at which the resurrection of the Crucified begins (Cardinal Beran makes his confession at the second Vatican Council; the fires of Jan Hus are burning today, in Bohemia).

In my little book *Werthers Weg in den Underground – die Geschichte der Jugendbewegung* (1972) I have demonstrated this continuity which unfolds from first about 1770 to 1970. From the conclusion I quote:

> A rapid, public failure. That goes for the young Germans of the "Sturm und Drang" around the young Goethe, goes for the young Americans around Mario Savio, goes for young Japanese around the Zengakuren leader Kenichi Koyama. An ever recurrent failure, answered by sparks leaping from the ashes. The phoenix, as bird of passage of the future, the future which for many members of youth movements does not come, which they themselves do not live to see (not all that seldom their good fortune not to live to see), young people swarm out; they are seeking Prometheus, Prometheus, the father of the human man. They are seeking the fire which has slipped through the weakened hands of their own fathers.
>
> They choose for themselves "artifical fathers" as leaders through the wilderness of history, on the "long march" to the Promised Land. The secret religion of all youth movements worships a wandering God, a God of the wandering peoples who moves on before them, a wandering volcano. Secret and openly proclaiming itself in manifestos, the belief of these youth movements is that this volcano burns up all old pictures of God, all pictures of man and institutions. In creative destruction of all old Pompeii cities, this volcano with its glowing lava masses creates new, fertile landscapes on which grow vines, wheat, rice, myrtle and laurel. The dream of Shelley and Byron and Blake. On this New Land will a cradle stand, the cradle of the new man.
>
> A thousand years of disappointment have not been able to kill this great dream of the youth movements which have created all our civilizations.

A thousand years of disappointment mobilize, activate Christendom which is indeed to be understood only as a permanent struggle of all against all. Precisely the great churches live on their heretics (Paul: "there must be heretics"), who are often disqualified by their establishment as rebels, as criminals, particularly in times when the word "heretic" has already become a sort of title of honour, as in the 19th and 20th centuries. The mistake of the young man from Galilee and the mistake of Saul prove to be enormously fruitful – Jesus as well as Saul-Paul, who is psychically and mentally infinitely alien to him and who for his part has no interest at all in the historical Jesus, in the "Jesus in the flesh" – both believe this, that the Kingdom of God, the Reign of God stands before the door, stands at the gate. They live in immediate expectation, they derive from it their revolutionary elan, their courage, their dynamism, their ethic. This ethic can only be understood as inspired by this breath (whence the failure of all Christian morality) – the Kingdom of Heaven is quite close. It can be there early tomorrow, perhaps it is coming this evening during supper. So do not think of courting a wife, buying a field, going in for everyday politics.

The collapse of this immediate expectation has not only produced – as in the 19th/20th century – mountains of paper, a wealth of controversial theological writings, but also has a straight dynamic effect on "heretics" who want to bring the Kingdom of God here by force, on this earth, into this land, in England and Scotland and Germany and Russia. Against this revolutionary renewal of the immediate expectation of Jesus, of Paul and of enthusiastic early Christian congregations, against the fanatics, the men of the ecclesiastical Establishment immure themselves in their strongholds of God, cathedrals, dogmatic systems, with their ecclesiastical police and inquisitions: again and again very successful and very futile.

What is a rebel today in Europe? That is a very difficult question, difficult also for this reason, that both political and ecclesiastical establishments as well as the high priests of the Church of the European university, orthodox "pure science" (which today excommunicates its heretics no less harshly than other closed ruling systems did before), deny the heretic and revolutionary these honourable titles and disqualify them as lowly rebels, as criminals who are to be handed over to the police, to the state police, to the state security service. In the language of "pure science", these are the charlatans. They are denounced not only in the USA (the Reich case).

This becomes clearly visible even for the public in the judgement made of youthful rebels, who indeed are disqualified in West Germany as a "gang" of criminals (the Baader-Meinhoff gang), and as in "socialist" countries, so in the Soviet Union, where they like to accuse and condemn religious, political, spiritual dissidents as criminals, in many trials, even today.

Against this criminalization of the dissident who urges reforms in the state on the basis of his conscience and knowledge, civil rights campaigners work and appeal to "human rights". Even this appeal to human rights is not understood at all, psychically understood, in other continents and in parts of Europe (so indeed the Chinese language has not got a word for "the person, individual", for personal freedom, democracy etc.), in regions which have not participated in the 1,000-year process of developing human rights.

Human rights are based on the resistance struggles and the resistance rights of noble classes in England (the *ius rebellandi* in Poland and Hungary), on the struggle by free cities for their "freedoms", their *libertates*. They are based on the thinking of Calvinists in Switzerland, in Holland, in Scotland, on the thinking of nonconformist Italian humanists, on the theology of Spanish Dominican jurists (centred on Domingo de Soto and Vittoria), on the ideology and practice of Polish Anti-Trinitarians (the fathers of the Unitarians), of Dutch and English "Deists" and of half a dozen Free Church movements.

Of these the Baptists merit special mention, their right and their central wings. Their militant radical left wing was lost in the struggle for the Kingdom of God in Münster (religious movements often have more than two wings, like the cherubim and other archaic, mythical angelic beings). The passion narrative of the Baptists, who were murderously persecuted by all the great churches in Europe, forms a high point of the European passion. To it is related the suffering of the early Quakers.

It is indeed no accident that a scion of Baptist families is struggling so hard today for a global recognition of human rights, Jimmy Carter. People like to make fun of him in cynical, sceptical, hard-boiled Europe because this "old-fashioned" man is living in old-European traditions, in the belief in human rights.

It was nonconformists who first opened the slave question. Again and again the role of driving on the evolution, the humanization of man, and also the revolution fell to religious dissenters. They paid for it in the best, hardest currency there is, with their blood.

The thinkers, the ideologists of human rights in the 18th century round about the American Revolution and the French Enlightenment are the sons and heirs of rebels, of dissenters, of heretics of very different sorts. The president of the National Assembly, Rabaut-St-Etienne, is the son of the great pastor and leader of the Huguenot Église du Désert, who gathered many thousands round him in secret assemblies or services and inspired them.

Every old European society, church, institution, every European establishment right into the 20th century, each produces its own rebels, heretics and revolutionaries.

Back to our own time. It is not easy to be acknowledged as RHR today and to escape the criminalization, as in eastern Europe. In western Europe it is on the whole more easily done. The genuine rebel and revolutionary is generally not accorded any notice at all, is not acknowledged. The industry of the mass media and its experts put on show ersatz figures and ersatz achievements, the heroes of the western, of the thriller, of the horror production, as well as pop-singers and protest-singers (revolution as software) and youthful rebels who are quickly discovered and used by the publicity and fashion industry.

The rebel in "pure science", particularly in continental medicine but also in orthodox psycho-analysis, in national economics, in legal thinking is today mostly no less excommunicated than in former centuries, or is simply accused of heresy, as since the days of the first Bacon.

The great show – in television above all, but also in novels and science fiction stories – lives by the production of ersatz figures for the RHR and by romantic transfigurations and perversions of historical rebels, heretics and revolutionaries. So with the ghastly kitsch St Francis film, which out of this great rebel (rebel against his will) makes a mawkish wonder-boy. This is how they satisfy the demand of the masses for Robin Hood figures.

The supremacy of the superpowers, of their armies, their computer systems, their economic and political institutions, of their police systems and news machines and secret services is so great that nowadays genuine rebels and revolutionaries are often forced into the underground very early on; they disappear and collaborate in the underground with criminal elements and mafiosi of very diverse organizations, stretching out far beyond Europe to Japan, to South America.

We are also experiencing this today, a perversion of the revolution, of the revolutionaries, from above and below, and from the centre.

In the fires of the contemporary underground the rebel blends again with the heretic and the revolutionary, in the belief in salvation from destruction, in the belief in the birth of the new man, of the New Age from the fires of destruction, of persecution, of his own defeat. Suicide, conceived as a conscious act of liberation, already plays a significant role with Russian and Polish revolutionaries in the 19th and early 20th centuries, takes over a political function in the struggle, in the "total war", and is understood again today ideologically and practically as a weapon of the revolution. Some of the young assassins of Sarajevo 1914 were resolved on suicide, looked to Russian examples. Some young German women and men have rediscovered suicide as a political act for themselves. They have their roots in the evangelical youth movement, not all of them, but a nucleus.

In the battle against these terrorists the might, the superiority and a final impotence of the superpowers declares itself, a peculiar helplessness of men, not least in the battle against women (as already in the case of the 40 to 50 theologians who sat in judgement on Joan of Arc haughtily and helplessly), and of men who hold in their hands a potential for destruction that in 1974 already far exceeded the destructive potential of the bombs on Hiroshima and Nagasaki.

Compared with this potential for devastation, which today makes possible the great step forward – the great progress from the final solution of the Jewish question to a final solution of the human question – compared with the enormous destruction of human substance, human personality through the industrial large-scale operation, the destructive powers of these very individual rebels and revolutionaries appear small, childish, almost infantile.

In the RHR complex at least in Europe, in western Europe, prominent heretics fare best today. They occupy leading teaching chairs of the theological faculties in the Federal Republic of Germany and also stay in the public eye when their church decides against them. That is a great victory which Professor Martin Luther D.D. has impressively fought on behalf of his Catholic and Protestant heirs and successors.

For the truly significant heretic, the great expression of John Duns Scotus (who lies buried in Cologne) still holds even today, Scotus who understands man as an isolated being, and who speaks to, experiences, the person as *ultima solitudo*.

*Ultima solitudo*, a final loneliness, surrounds all great rebels, heretics, revolutionaries. It cannot be pierced or overcome by the lads, brothers, comrades, enemies who press against it – nor by all the inquisitions and all the historians and depth-psychologists who want to fathom the secret of their effect. This first and last loneliness shields them, surrounds them like an aura, a protective circle round their innermost centres of power, their "sources", which they break out of to overstep boundaries, boundaries of their society, their people, their time, not least the boundaries of their own first movement, grounding, revolution.

They are the transcending man, *homo transcendens*, the man who steps out beyond his boundaries, often blind, almost blind to dangers, to fatal threats. They see a vision which will never quite become reality, never quite real, which will never quite drown in the morass of the realities, of the efficiencies. It is this "*unreality*", this "exuberance", this bubbling quality which makes their vision undying. It dies in every attempt to "realize" it – in state, society, church, in closed systems of thought. But this vision can be born again, in young men, in old men, who let themselves be seized by it.

Europe's significant rebels, heretics, revolutionaries are the immortals of Europe (not the immortals of the Académie Française): Socrates and his spiritual son Plato who is a noble rebel; Thomas Muntzer – to jump 2,000 years – is alive again today in young German people, like a Tom Paine in young Americans.

One of the greatest heretical thinkers of the Roman Church, Meister Eckhart, preached to his anxious nuns, who daily had to fear being condemned as heretics by the Cologne Church (today this Church does not seriously dare to attack her heretic Heinrich Böll other than verbally), these glad tidings, "God is a God of the present."

Meister Eckhart, ecclesiastically condemned by John XXII's bull of 27 March 1329, in his writings consigned to the heap of failures by Pope Gregory XI and by Emperor Charles IV – with an imperial letter of 17 June 1369 – inspires Hegel and Schopenhauer, Karl Jaspers and C. G. Jung, and today inspires many restless young people in Russia, Poland, Hungary etc. and in Japan and in the USA. In symposiums there he is appointed helper and midwife for the delivery of a new man, who becomes completely free, unable to be destroyed by the terror of the superpowers which terrify today by their superiority and their impotence. (In the deep layers this resignation is related to Gandhi's satyagraha.)

In the 1st and in the 20th century after the birth of the young man from Galilee Europe swarms with restless spirits, with agitated people, with fanatics, who can, but not must, develop themselves in reflex to their personal, social, political, national situations as rebel, as heretic, as revolutionary. The hardest reactionaries and men of the Establishment are frustrated rebels, heretics, revolutionaries who have overpowered the fires of their own youth in themselves.

"Three in one are they, not to be separated." Goethe puts it like that looking at England in his *Faust*, "war, trade and piracy/Three in one are they, not to be separated."

Three in one are they, not to be separated, the rebel, the heretic, the revolutionary; they stem in Europe from one plant, from one paternal home. In their fight against their physical, spiritual, religious fathers they are fighting ultimately for this, for a rebirth of the father. This rebirth can be a terrible and terrifying incarnation. Stalin as a rebirth of Ivan Groszny, Ivan the Terrible (as already seen in the great Soviet film). This rebirth can be a mild, gentle incarnation, as in Poverello. Francis of Assisi as second Christ, as rebirth of the young man from Galilee, is at once so honoured, believed by his left-wing sons the radical Fraticelli, Franciscans who die at the stake, that they spurn the Roman supreme father as a murderer of the poverty movement, as a killer of Francis's glad tidings.

This thing will go on further then, as long as there are fathers, as long as there are sons, in Europe. The last sentences of the Old Testament hint at a solution to this monstrous problem. The prophet Malachi hints in his last sentences that the "Day of the Lord", that is the Last Judgement, the great destruction of sinful mankind, will perhaps not take place if first the fathers turn to the sons, their children! "Look, I will send you the prophet Elijah before the great and terrible day of the Lord comes. He will reconcile fathers to sons and sons to fathers, lest I come and put the land under a ban to destroy it." That is the greatest Utopia of European world history.

# 29

# *Europe beyond Europe*

## CHARLES BOXER

The great significance of European expansion during the last four centuries and the worldwide influences deriving from it, for both good and ill, need no elaboration here. Sixteenth-century Iberian chroniclers and 20th-century Marxist historians anticipate or recall the observation of Adam Smith in 1776: "The discovery of America and that of a passage to the East Indies by the Cape of Good Hope are the two greatest and most important events recorded in the history of mankind." Even nowadays, with men on the moon and with interplanetary travel in the offing, many people of all races and creeds would still be inclined to agree with the author of the *Inquiry into the Nature and Causes of the Wealth of Nations*. In so far as the European impact on Asia is concerned, K. M. Panikkar has analysed it admirably in his seminal *Asia and Western Dominance. A Survey of the Vasco da Gama Epoch of Asian History, 1498–1945* (London and New York, 1953). He defined the period 1498–1945 as characterized by the dominance of European maritime power over the land masses of Asia, and by the imposition of a commercial economy over communities whose economic life in the past had been based on agricultural production and internal trade. This process reached its peak with the industrial and technological revolutions between 1815 and 1914. Needless to add that the effects of European dominance over the New World were even more drastic, beginning with the catastrophic demographic decline of many of the Amerindian peoples in the 16th century. Africa and Australia were not basically affected by European penetration until the 19th century, if we except the development of the West African slave-trade to the New World by Portuguese, Dutch, English and French successively.

"What made them do it? I wish I knew", wrote Samuel Eliot Morison of the Iberian mariners, conquerors and settlers, who pioneered the great expansion of Europe overseas, which, above all else, marks off the medieval from the modern world. Despite his disclaimer of ignorance of their motivation, Morison supplied part of the answer himself; which is hardly surprising, since he wrote about them so perceptively. He went on to cite Bernal Diaz del Castillo (c. 1492–1581), a veteran of the conquest of Mexico, who avowed in his *True History* of that stupendous enterprise: "We came here to serve God and His Majesty, to bring light to those in darkness, and also to get rich, as all men desire to do." This troika in the service of God, the king and mammon, was certainly an important element in Iberian expansion overseas for several generations. Naturally, the relative importance of the three motives varied widely in accordance with the time, place and circumstances of the individuals or the groups concerned. At one extreme were self-sacrificing missionaries, vowed to the service of God and the king, typified by St Francis Xavier (1506–52), although clergy who placed the service of mammon alongside that of God were not exactly uncommon. In the middle, so to speak, were men who served without doing injury to either their conscience or their purse – both of these being fairly elastic. At the other extreme were the Portuguese *fidalgos* (gentry) who boasted that they had not come to "golden Goa" in order to gain honour, for they were born with that qualification, but merely in order to get rich.

It would seem to be axiomatic that a policy of expansion cannot succeed over a substantial period of time unless it is executed with full and confident determination. This, in turn, may involve disregarding, trampling upon or forcibly removing whoever happens to get in the way, if they decline to cooperate. This was indubitably the case with the Portuguese Crown, which spearheaded the vanguard of European expansion. When King Manuel I of Portugal jubilantly informed "the Catholic kings" (Ferdinand and Isabella) of Vasco da Gama's safe return in July 1499 from his voyage of discovery to India, he stressed that the prime motives of this daring undertaking were "the service of God our Lord, and our own profit". The "Fortunate King", as his subjects called him, or the "Grocer King", as the envious François I dubbed him, spoke for his predecessors and successors as well as for himself.

From the time of the Portuguese capture of Ceuta from the Moors (1415), the Crown was directly and heavily involved in the planning, financing and organization of the voyages and expeditions to Africa and Asia. The Crown also secured from the papacy a series of bulls and briefs, particularly those promulgated between 1452 and 1456, which gave the Portuguese the widest possible latitude in the employment of force against all non-Christian peoples who might prove actually or potentially hostile; and the Portuguese never hesitated to implement them as long as they had the power to do so. In fact, they sometimes tried to enforce their Crown's sweeping claim to the monopoly of "the conquest, navigation and commerce of Ethiopia, Arabia, Persia and India" (assumed by King Manuel in 1499), when it had no more relevance to real life than the English Crown's claim to the sovereignty of France and Jerusalem. Mazagão, the last Portuguese stronghold in Morocco, was not evacuated until 1769, although the garrison had not controlled an inch of ground beyond the range of their cannon for 200 years. In the mid-18th century the Portuguese authorities at Goa were still maintaining that no Asian shipping was allowed to navigate in the Indian Ocean without a passport (*cartaz*) supplied by them, although they avoided trying to enforce their absurd claim on any save those much weaker than themselves.

The Spanish Crown only belatedly came with modest financial help to Christopher Columbus in 1492; and the spectacular conquests of Hernán Cortéz (Mexico, 1519–22) and Francisco Pizarro (Peru, 1531–35) were achieved with a minimum of involvement by the Habsburg Emperor Charles V. But once the wealth and potential of these vast territorial acquisitions were realized, the Crown of Castile, under whose nominal aegis the conquests were made, lost no time in establishing effective control through the medium of a well-organized imperial bureaucracy and an ecclesiastical hierarchy. This process took longer in Peru than in Mexico; but by 1570 it was in full flower in all save the remotest frontier zones of Spanish America. Despite inevitable – and some avoidable – miscalculations and failings, the Crown of Castile contrived to control its vast American empire with a remarkable degree of success for some 250 years, even when Spain itself was torn apart by the First Peninsular War of 1702–13.

Similarly, the remarkable success of the Dutch East India Company in establishing a maritime empire over much of the Asian seas during the first half of the 17th century was largely due to the confident determination of its governing body of 17 directors (the *Heren Zeventien*, or the "Gentleman Seventeen"). Drawn entirely from the urban oligarchy which had the biggest say in the complicated governmental system of the seven "United Provinces of the Free Netherlands", these merchant-oligarchs were able, with state support when necessary, to prosecute both war and trade on a scale which dwarfed the efforts of their Portuguese, English and French competitors, for over half a century. By the end of the 17th century the English were beginning to catch up; and in the course of the 18th century they were able to overhaul their rivals. But this was due as much – or more – to the energy, drive and initiative of the private English traders in the east – originally stigmatized as "interlopers" – as to the conquests of "John Company" in its wars in Bengal and the Carnatic. As for the French, a Breton naval officer with over a quarter of a century's experience in Asia, wrote to an aristocratic Portuguese friend in 1722 that both the Dutch and the English deserved to have profitable colonies, because of the trouble they took over them. He added: "It is not necessary that plague should ruin the French colonies; our own irresponsibility is enough. What is the remedy for this? None. Witness the recent Mississippi disaster." Beauvollier de Courchant, governor of the island of Bourbon (now Réunion), when he penned this indictment, was unduly cynical. But it was true that lack of effective and steady government support at home, and the inability of the French colonial enterprises to attract sufficient capital investment from French merchants, accounted for the failure of abortive French colonies in Florida (1562), Brazil (1555–67), the Maranhão (1612–15) and elsewhere, and for the slow and stunted development of Canada (New France). The real success story of French colonial expansion under the Old Regime was the great economic development of the French West Indian sugar islands, particularly Guadeloupe and Martinique, during the second half of the 18th century. On the eve of the French Revolution these islands were producing far more than either Portuguese Brazil, or the British and Dutch West Indies, including Jamaica and Surinam respectively.

Once the seaways of the world had been opened to mankind as a result of the voyages of Columbus, da Gama and Magellan, 1492–1522, Europeans spread around the globe in a remarkably short space of time. By 1543 the Portuguese had reached Japan, and 20 years later the Spaniards were established in the Philippines. When Philip II of Castile became Philip I of Portugal in 1580–81, he was the monarch of a dual seaborne empire on which the sun never set, and which lasted till 1640.

Adequately to defend and colonize such a widely dispersed empire proved to be an impossible task; but gigantic efforts were made to do so with varying degrees of partial success, both before and after the union of the two Iberian crowns in 1580–1640. The population of mainland Portugal and its Atlantic islands probably oscillated around a million and a quarter for most of the 16th century. Of these, some 4,000–5,000 annually left for overseas, the great majority for "golden Goa" and the "gorgeous east" before c. 1580, and after that for Brazil. Those going to the east were mainly soldiers, with a sprinkling of missionaries, bureaucrats and merchants, young men in the prime of life. Most of the laymen who survived for more than a few years turned to trade and commerce as a full-time or part-time occupation. Very few women accompanied them on the outward voyage, probably never more than about 60 in any given year, usually less than half that number, and often none at all. A pilot familiar with "the State of India", as the Portuguese called their possessions between the Cape of Good Hope and Japan, observed (c. 1580) that this region was: "so vast and fertile, that no Portuguese there wishes to return home, except if forced to do so; since the land being so abundant and affording so many pleasures, they abandon their wives and children, and die there without wishing to see them again". An exaggeration, obviously, but one with a large element of truth. The Dutch governor-general at Batavia, Antonio van Diemen, said virtually the same thing when he informed his superiors in the Netherlands (1642): "Most of the Portuguese in Asia look upon this region as their fatherland. They think no more about Portugal. They drive little or no trade thither, but content themselves with the interport trade of Asia, just as if they were natives thereof and had no other country."

With the Dutch (1596–1663), the Omani Arabs (1650–1729) and the Marathas (1737–40) successively pulling Portugal's Asian empire apart, the inducement to emigrate thither in the Crown's service became progressively less. From the late 17th century convict-soldiers (degredados) supplied the bulk of the men leaving Lisbon for Goa and Mozambique. The number of ships dwindled to two or three a year and hardly any women at all went out after c. 1730. For three centuries only a small fraction (10 per cent?) of those people who left for the east ever returned, whether they went voluntarily or otherwise.

Portuguese emigration to Brazil was not for the most part directly organized by the Crown, save for limited times and places (Bahia, 1549; Pará, 1673; Santa Catarina, 1749). The voyage being much shorter and safer than the Cape route to India, the majority of emigrants went as private individuals and not in the service of the Crown. More women accompanied their menfolk, although never on the scale of the Spaniards, the English and the French in the New World. As the attractions of the "State of India" declined, so those of Brazil rose. The development of the sugar industry (c. 1570–1630), the repulse of a Dutch attempt to conquer northeast Brazil (1630–54) and the gold-rush in Minas Gerais (1698–1730) all contributed to spark successive waves of immigration. By the end of the 18th century Brazil's population was probably in the region of 2,250,000 souls (excluding "untamed" Amerindians). The population of metropolitan Portugal was then estimated at some 2,900,000. Both were still overwhelmingly rural societies, although Lisbon was a great city with a population of nearly 200,000.

By way of comparison, we may recollect that the infant United States in 1790 had still only some four million inhabitants. It was also an overwhelmingly rural society. No North American city numbered more than 50,000 inhabitants, and only six cities had more than 8,000. But Philadelphia, England's largest overseas port, on the eve of the American Revolution had grown from a small seaport of about 2,300 in 1700 to a thriving commercial centre of about 30,000 by 1776. The initial gold coinage dates from only 1795, whereas Portuguese India had its own gold coins from 1510 and Brazil from 1695. Great Britain, then in the first flush of the Industrial Revolution, had three and a half times the population of Portugal, and London a pullulating population of nearly a million. Thirty other cities had a population of over 10,000, seven of them over 50,000. Spain, with about the same total population as Great Britain, had 40 cities with 10,000 or more inhabitants, Madrid having about as many as Lisbon. The largest cities in Japan, China and India were certainly more populous than any in Europe, let alone any European colonial city.

Portuguese emigration to Africa, being for centuries virtually confined to unhealthy coastal regions and fever-stricken valleys, always contained a very high proportion of *degredados* and a minuscule number of women. The voluntary emigrants, whether they went east or west, came largely from the overpopulated Minho province of northern Portugal and from the Atlantic islands of Madeira and the Azores, which, although uninhabited when first settled in the 15th century, quickly outgrew their resources. These regions still furnish many emigrants, but they nowadays go to Venezuela, Canada and the USA, rather than to Brazil as they did until well into the 20th century. Since World War II, Portuguese emigration to France has overtaken all other destinations, clandestine emigrants alone numbering more than 100,000 in each of the years 1970–71. For most of the 19th and 20th centuries the Portuguese were very reluctant to emigrate to their own African colonies, preferring Hawaii, Guiana or Johannesburg, if they could not get into Brazil, Canada or the USA. Only after World War II did Angola and Mozambique begin to attract substantial numbers of settlers; and most of these have now left as a result of the collapse of the empire in 1974.

If Portugal ever since the Middle Ages has probably sent more emigrants overseas than any other European country, relatively speaking, Spain's contribution in remaking most of the New World in a European image is even more remarkable. Although Spain's population was probably something between six and eight millions during the 16th century, it seems that fewer than 2,000 people left annually for "the Indies", as the Spaniards termed America by preference for centuries. But after the conquest of Mexico and Peru, 1522–35, the bulk of these emigrants went to the healthy uplands of those regions – especially the former – for many decades. Their survival and reproduction rates were consequently much higher than those of the Portuguese in the fever-ridden tropical regions of Africa and Asia. Unlike the Portuguese Crown, the Castilian Crown (of which the Indies were legally a dependency) encouraged the emigration of wives and female relations to the New World, although it seldom went so far as to pay their passage. There was therefore a better balance between the sexes in so far as the emigrants were concerned. Both Spaniards and Portuguese tended to emigrate in groups from the same region and even the same locality when they went to the New World. Thus we find Basques prominent in the mining centre of Potosí in the high Andes, and also in the Philippine Islands. Minhotos from northern Portugal were foremost in the early colonization of 16th-century coastal Pernambuco and of 18th-century inland Minas Gerais in Brazil.

An early 19th-century political writer defined the British Empire as a system of outdoor relief for the upper classes. *Mutatis mutandis* that goes for all empires, but the middle and the lower classes benefited as well. Miguel de Cervantes (1547–1616), who once vainly applied for a government job in Mexico, observed in one of his novels that the Indies were the refuge and protection of the destitute and the vagrants of both sexes, even though few of them made good.

Apart from these social outcasts, to whom we shall return in a moment, there were lucrative jobs for the upper classes as viceroys, governors, bureaucrats, prelates of the Church (in Roman Catholic colonies), high court judges and sugar planters. For the middle classes, there were openings as merchants, farmers, physicians, notaries and advocates. Lower down the social scale, there was a variable demand for "cannon fodder" (soldiers and sailors) and for skilled workmen and artisans of various kinds. Unskilled labour, and at some times and places skilled labour, was often replaced by slave labour in the tropical African and American colonies, or by the very cheap labour which was available in monsoon Asia. In many places, of course, these various forms of labour coexisted. Goa and Macao contained many Negro slaves from East Africa, and Mexico and Peru had a large black slave population which supplemented the nominally free Amerindian wage labourers for over 200 years.

Apart from the people who emigrated voluntarily overseas, the "conquests", "colonies", "plantations" etc., as they were variously termed, were likewise regarded by several European governments as a suitable destination for social misfits and undesirables. The precedents in this, as in so many other respects, were set by the Portuguese. Their monarchs from the late 15th century onwards made a point of commuting death sentences to transportation for life overseas. Lesser crimes were frequently punished by shorter periods of exile. Elizabethan England's prime propagandist for overseas expansion, Richard Hakluyt the younger – though he took good care never to cross the Atlantic himself – urged this precedent on his compatriots in 1582. He pointed out that the Portuguese were successfully developing Brazil in this way. Colonizing North America with able-bodied jailbirds, he averred, would be more sensible than daily hanging them out of hand for petty thefts – "even twenty at a clap out of one jail, as was seen at the last assizes in Rochester". The English government did not follow this advice to any comparable extent until the last quarter of the 18th century, when not New England, but New South Wales became a dumping ground for convicts of both sexes.

Apart from criminals who were shipped overseas by order of the Crown or of the government, many individuals were sent overseas by their parents, families or friends, simply in the hope of getting rid of them. The "remittance man" is not just a 19th-century English phenomenon. Others, of course, were sent to the colonies in default of a suitable opening for them in the home country, particularly in the case of younger sons, and especially when they were illegitimate. In 18th-century Britain a frequent social pattern for "gentry" families with several sons was for the eldest to inherit the landed estate, and the others to enter the Church, the two services or the "Honourable East India Company". When someone was appointed to a high position in an overseas colony, it was common form for the new incumbent to take with him several poor relations who could be gratified with lesser positions. Thus a Portuguese priest, who was sent as Inquisitor to Goa in 1649, took five young nephews with him to place in the service of the Crown.

Inevitably, such emigrants, whether criminals or merely undesirables, were not necessarily well received at their various destinations. It was a constant (if often exaggerated) complaint of colonial governors from Macao in China to Lima in Peru, and from the Dutch Moluccas to Manhattan, that far too many people of the wrong sort were sent them. The directors of the English and French East India Companies all received similar complaints from their senior representatives in Asia. The members of the governing council of Netherlands Brazil complained in 1635 that the directors of the West India Company apparently regarded that (short-lived, 1630–54) colony as "a close-stool for voiding the dregs of Dutch society". The faeces rather than the faces of Europe. Contemporary critics of the Dutch East and West India Companies frequently alleged that the employees of those two great corporations were almost exclusively recruited from "the scum of the United Provinces", and from the lowest class of unemployed foreigners, chiefly Scandinavians and Germans. There were certainly very many of these men, who found service in the tropics, harsh and ill-paid as it was, better than the prospect of utter destitution in their homelands. But there were likewise many men from perfectly respectable families, and even sprigs of the nobility and gentry. By and large, one gets the impression that all the colonial empires of the Old Regime contained a pretty fair cross-section of the societies in their respective home countries, save only for the highest and wealthiest nobility. These exalted individuals had no inducement to go overseas save as viceroys or governors-general for a very limited period.

It is probably safe to say that the great majority of men who signed on with the Dutch, English, French and other East India Companies did not intend to spend all their lives in Asia, but intended to return to Europe, once they had made a fortune, or merely a modest competence, as the case might be. It is probably equally safe to assert that the majority did not return to end their lives in Europe, but died in the east, where the mortality rates for northern Europeans were very high, as we shall see below.

Rural poverty and land-hunger formed a sharp spur to emigration in many times and places, whether in 16th-century Spain and Portugal or in 19th-century Ireland. This was often complemented by the attraction of land overseas which could be had on very cheap terms, or even free, provided the emigrant agreed to cultivate or to farm it. The Spanish Crown tried early to foster settlement in the New World by land grants on generous terms. In much of English North America, land could be had virtually for the asking, as it could in early Dutch South Africa or in the interior of Portuguese Brazil. Scant regard was usually paid to the indigenous occupants, since it was tacitly or explicitly assumed the "civilized" European Christians had superior rights over "heathen savages". When it was thought necessary or desirable to make some formal agreement with the prior possessors of the soil, this was usually done by a token payment of trade goods, as the Dutch did at Manhattan and Cape Town. The recipients of these trifles seldom realized that they were thereby depriving themselves (in the eyes of the purchasers) of any rights over the lands concerned. The notion of individual possession of land was a marked European trait which contrasted strongly with the communal use of land which prevailed in many African, Amerindian and Australian societies. One of the strongest impulses to Iberian settlement overseas was the desire to live nobly (*à lei de nobreza*), as the nobility and gentry did at home. This was legally defined as living in one's own manor, with a household of servants (and/or slaves), a stand of weapons, and horses in the stables, without soiling one's hands by engaging in any form of manual labour or in retail trade. This ideal was not achieved by more than a fraction of those who strove for it; but the conviction that *el no vivir de rentas no es trato de nobles* (roughly, "only a *rentier* is a gentleman") permeated Iberian society for centuries on both sides of the Atlantic. The country squires and yeoman farmers of Old England had their counterparts in New England and Virginia. The sugar planters of the Caribbean, whether Spanish, Dutch, English or French, all shared with those of Brazil a conviction of their superior social status. This derived from their ownership and exploitation of the land, enabling them to indulge in a seigneurial way of life. The country houses of the nobility and gentry of the Old World had their — usually more modest — equivalents in the environs of Quebec, Richmond, Cape Town and Batavia from c. 1650 onwards.

Missionaries formed a clearly defined category of their own. Their motivation is patently obvious, at least for those of them who were sincere, as the great majority were. It is particularly well documented for the Society of Jesus, whose archives at Rome contain some 15,000 *Litterae Indipetae*, or letters from Jesuits all over Europe asking to be sent to the overseas missions, from 1540 to 1771. Some 2,000 of them specifically invoke St Francis Xavier as their exemplar. Many 16th-century pioneer Spanish missionaries who converted so much of Mexico in the wake of Hernán Cortéz's overthrow of the Aztec Empire, were inspired by millenarian convictions. The "Last Days", with the arrival of Antichrist and the Second Coming, were thought to be imminent. Hence the pressing need to convert multitudes of otherwise lost souls within a very short space of time. A rather similar attitude is to be found in some modern Protestant Fundamentalist churches, such as the Mormons and Jehovah's Witnesses. When transplanted to Black Africa, these creeds have given rise to indigenous variants, such as the prophetess Alice Lenshina and the Watchtower movement.

It is hardly necessary to recall that the desire to build a "New Jerusalem", a "City on the Hill" and so forth, was a prime motive with the Puritan settlers of New England. For the first time, whole families emigrated from western Europe on a massive scale. The proportion of women and children was far higher than with the Spaniards and Portuguese emigrating to the New World. French emigration to Canada was also on a family basis. On a much smaller scale, the emigration of French Huguenot refugees to the Cape of Good Hope in the 1680s provided that struggling colony with a better sexual balance than any other possession of the Dutch East India Company "of laudable and redoubtable name". By 1780 there were between 11,000 and 12,000 free burghers in the colony, of whom at least 3,000 lived in Cape Town. A contemporary visitor noted: "Although the first colonists here were composed of various nations, they are, by the operation of time, now so thoroughly blended together, that they are not to be distinguished from each other; even most of such as have been born in Europe, and who have resided here for some years, have, in a manner, changed their national character for that of this country." In other words, the formation of the Afrikaner people had begun. On the other hand, mammon, rather than God, was the prime motivation in the great gold-rushes, beginning with the Brazilian (1698–1720), and followed in due course by the Californian (1849), Australian (1850s), South African (1880s) and the Klondyke (1890s). In all of these, males were overwhelmingly predominant in the early stages. A more balanced pattern of emigration was evinced by the mass exodus resulting from the Irish famine in the mid-1840s; by the Jewish diaspora in the 19th century from central and eastern Europe; by the political émigrés from Europe after the failure of the 1848–49 uprisings. More than half of the 7,500,000 people who left the British Isles for North America between 1800 and 1875 were Irish. Political and religious motivation, as well as the desire to escape malnutrition and starvation, played a part in this human flood – the greatest trans-oceanic migration that mankind has ever made.

This was also the period when Australia and New Zealand were intensively settled by emigrants of British and Irish stock, although the number involved was much less than those crossing the north Atlantic.

Before turning from the motivation of those who left Europe for the wider world to a brief consideration of what they and their descendants did there, we may recall that many of the former either never reached their destination or else died shortly after their arrival. The death rate in the overcrowded carracks and galleons of the annual Portuguese East India fleets was seldom less than 20 or 30 per cent, and often much more. Over 30,000 men from outward-bound Portuguese Indiamen were buried on the unhealthy little coral island of Mozambique in 1528–58, apart from thousands more who died at sea. From 1604 to 1634 a total of 25,000 soldiers died in the Royal Hospital at Goa, most of them recent arrivals in the Indiamen. Of 326 Jesuits who embarked at Lisbon for the China mission between 1581 and 1721, no fewer than 127 died at sea, virtually all of them before they had reached Goa.

Other European nations, too, paid "the price of Admiralty", if not on quite the same stupendous scale. For the period 1620–1730, there was an average mortality of between 6 and 10 per cent on outward-bound Dutch East Indiamen; but this rose to between 10 and 23 per cent for the period 1730–75. The hospital at Batavia, "Queen of the Eastern Seas", which city had been a relatively healthy place before c. 1730, became virtually a mortuary thereafter. The death rate in the English convict-ships bound for Australia in 1787–1800 averaged almost exactly 10 per cent, despite the fact that – like the Dutch East Indiamen – they could call at the Cape of Good Hope for fresh provisions. In the "Great Migration" from Europe to North America during the 19th century mortality was often very high, despite the relative shortness of the Atlantic crossing. In 1847, admittedly the worst recorded year, 17,500 emigrants, 16 per cent of all who emigrated, died either in passage or on arrival. The hospital in 19th-century Quebec seems in some years to have rivalled those at 17th-century Goa and 18th-century Batavia as a virtual mortuary. The sobriquet of "White Man's Grave", given to West Africa for centuries, was the literal truth. The big changes for the better came successively with the advent of the steamship, the opening of the Suez Canal, the discovery of the germ theory of disease, and the therapeutic and pharmaceutical drugs developed in the late 19th and early 20th centuries. Only recently have scurvy, malaria, typhus, yellow fever, cholera, sleeping sickness etc. been tamed, if not yet completely conquered.

João de Barros (c. 1496–1570), the chronicler of Portuguese expansion, wrote prophetically in his *Dialogue in Praise of our Language* (1549): "The Portuguese arms and pillars placed in Africa and in Asia, and in so many thousand islands beyond the three parts of the earth, are material things, and Time may destroy them. But Time will not destroy the religion, customs and language, which the Portuguese leave in those lands." Barros was not far wrong. Long after the Portuguese empire in the east had shrunk to very modest dimensions, Portuguese continued to be the lingua franca of the ports and entrepôts of Asia until tardily replaced by English during the 19th century. In some regions of Africa, including Angola and Mozambique, it seems likely to survive the disintegration of the oldest European colonial empire. As the language of Brazil, its future in a vast area of South America is assured. If English now bids fair to become the nearest thing to a world language (instead of Spanish, as seemed likely in the 16th century), this phenomenon is partly due to the economic preponderance of Victorian Britain during the 19th century, and to the economic, cultural and technological preponderance of the United States since 1918.

The Christianity implanted by the Portuguese has also survived in many regions where once they dominated (Goa), or else merely traded (Vietnam). It seems likely to remain predominant in Brazil, despite the strong challenge from Protestant Fundamentalist sects, and also from Marxist-inspired beliefs, here as everywhere. Similarly, the Roman Catholicism implanted by the Spaniards still remains predominant in Spanish America and the Philippines, even if combined with elements of the pre-conquest indigenous beliefs in some regions. As regards customs, Alfred Russell Wallace, after visiting the Amazon region and some of the remotest islands of Indonesia in the mid-19th century, commented: "The Portuguese and Spaniards were truly wonderful conquerors and colonizers. They effected more rapid changes in the countries they conquered than any other nations of modern times, resembling the Romans in their power of impressing their own language, religion, and manners on rude and barbarous tribes." Just what João de Barros had claimed three centuries earlier. Barros, like all his well-educated Iberian contemporaries, was strongly influenced by "the grandeur that was Rome" and the imperial precedent which the Roman Empire afforded.

Although Calvinist missionary evangelism did not make the same impact overseas, or have the same whole-hearted government support which the Iberian missionaries received from their respective crowns, it should not be underrated. The intellectual life of the Dutch Republic can be characterized as permeated by a "dense fog of piety" (Simon Schama) generated by a "religion-saturated society" (Jan de Vries). Admittedly, this pious fog was considerably dissipated by the fierce tropical sun in maritime Asia. But its influence is clear if we compare the Dutch (VOC) and the English (EIC) East India Companies in their respective attitudes to Protestant evangelism among indigenous peoples. Whereas the attitude of the EIC was wholly negative, so that the London-based Society for the Propagation of the Gospel had to use the Danish territory of Tranquebar on the Coromandel Coast as the base of its operations, the Directors of the VOC always gave some positive support to Calvinist missionary activity in selected areas – Formosa 1624–62, Amboina after 1605, and Ceylon 1658–1796 – while always retaining a tight control over missionary personnel.

The VOC patronized the translation of the Bible and of numerous devotional works into various Oriental languages, including Malay, Malayalam, Sinhalese and Tamil, as well as into Portuguese, which was still the lingua franca for many European and Eurasian communities in the east. More particularly, the Company's Colombo Press printed many religious works in the last 25 years (1771–1796) of its existence. They included the whole of the New Testament and of the Pentateuch in Sinhalese, and of the Pentateuch in Tamil. By contrast, the early translations of the Bible, or portions thereof, into Chinese by Protestants in the sphere of the EIC had to be printed at "papist" Portuguese Macao (1814) and in Lutheran Danish Serampore (1815–22).

The French geographer, Vidal de la Blache, remarked that emigrants liked to carry their shells with them. They could hardly have done otherwise. Even those who left their native land because they were profoundly dissatisfied with it for religious, social or economic reasons, were usually anxious to retain familiar customs and *mores*. The degree to which they adapted themselves to new and often totally unexpected surroundings naturally varied widely according to time, place and circumstance. At one end were those who "went native" to a greater or lesser extent. These included: the Portuguese exiles (*lançados*) in riverine Guinea, who became completely Africanized save for retaining some vestiges of Christianity; the *Bandeirantes* of the Brazilian backlands; the French-Canadian *coureurs-du-bois*; and the Anglo-Saxon "Squaw-men" of North America. At the other end were those pioneers and settlers who disliked and despised – or else hated and feared – the indigenous peoples with whom they came into contact. "Manners they have none, and their customs are beastly"; "the only good Indian is a dead one". Attitudes which date from the 16th century, and are not extinct today.

Many pioneer settlers and their descendants resolutely tried to reproduce the life they had known – or been told about – in Europe. They retained European-style dress, food, housing, clothing and social attitudes even in the most unsuitable or incongruous surroundings. They would wear periwigs and velvet and scarlet cloth in the tropics. They would eat imported (and often very expensive and badly preserved) European provisions, such as dried codfish, wheaten bread and olive-oil in preference to local maize, rice, fresh fish etc., which were more cheaply and readily available. These also drank imported wines in preference to local varieties which could often be grown, as they were in Spanish Peru and Dutch South Africa. Dutch, English, Germans and other north Europeans transported and retained their heavy drinking habits in the tropics. When they could not afford the wines and beers which they imported on a massive scale, alike to the temperate zones of North America and to the torrid regions of the Caribbean and monsoon Asia, they swilled local substitutes such as Indian arrack, or Chinese and Japanese rice wine. Gin, brandy and other "strong waters" probably killed nearly as many north Europeans in the tropics as did malaria and dysentery. In any event, they certainly speeded the process, if only because the consumption of alcoholic liquors was commonly regarded as a remedy against the "miasmas and the night airs" which were wrongly suspected of causing fevers. Tobacco was a native plant of the Americas; but it was the Europeans who spread it around the world within a century of their first sampling "the divine weed" or the "hellish brew" as it was variously termed. Europeans were also responsible for transplanting, marketing and otherwise bringing into general use such items as tea, coffee and maize. They took their own preferences overseas with them, some of which likewise found universal acceptance. If Great Britain were to disappear beneath the waves tomorrow, her most lasting and widespread legacies would probably be Scotch whisky and soccer football. Both of these can be found in the uttermost parts of the earth, where the Kirk of Scotland and the Church of England have either never penetrated or else have failed to take root.

Considering the Eurocentric viewpoint of the great majority of missionaries for centuries, whether Roman Catholic or Protestant, it is surprising that they made as many converts as they did, particularly in countries like China and Vietnam, where they had no political power. Most missionaries, however long they spent in the mission field, and however fluent they became in the language of their indigenous flock, would have agreed with the Portuguese Jesuit in India, Fernão de Queiroz, who opined in 1688: "When these heathen came to explain what God is, then is seen the weakness of the human mind, especially when it is obscured by the vices of a nature corrupted and enfeebled by sensual appetites." Whatever their doctrinal differences, Roman Catholic and Protestants were alike convinced that the Holy Bible, on which the Church's teaching and world-view were based, was a divinely inspired work of universal validity for all times, for all places and for all peoples. Even when they found something admirable in indigenous cultures, they were prone to judge it by a European yardstick. Thus an early Jesuit missionary in the Philippines gave the following reasons for his appreciation of Tagalog: "I found in this language four qualities of the four greatest languages of the world; Hebrew, Greek, Latin and Spanish. It has the abstruseness and obscurity of the Hebrew; the articles and distinctions in proper, as well as in common, nouns of the Greek; the fullness and elegance of the Latin; and the refinement, polish and courtesy of the Spanish." High praise indeed from Padre Pedro Chirino (1557–1635), a product of the counter-Reformation and the high Baroque. Of course, there were always some individual exceptions. The Jesuits of the China mission who followed in the footsteps of Matteo Ricci (1552–1610) or those of the Indian mission in the wake of Roberto de' Nobili (1577–1656), with their toleration of the "Chinese Rites" and the "Malabar Rites" respectively, caused a "battle of the books" in the learned world of Europe, with Leibniz, Voltaire and others taking part. But the final decision of the papacy went against them in the 1740s – though belatedly reversed two centuries later. The Church of the counter-Reformation was also represented overseas by tribunals of the so-called and self-styled Holy Office of the Inquisition, through whose agency real or alleged crypto-Jews were burnt at the stake on occasion. The chief tribunals were established at Goa (1560) and Mexico City (1571), thus ensuring that one of the more unpleasant faces of Europe was reflected around the world for over 200 years. Europeans also exported their internecine religious quarrels overseas where Roman Catholics and Protestants usually retained a mutual dislike and mistrust for each other. This traditional tension gradually lessened in many regions with the spread of rationalism and deism during the 18th century.

J. H. van Linschoten, the Dutch secretary to the archbishop of Goa (1583–88), gave what can be regarded as a classic definition of imperialism, when he criticized the Portuguese in Asia for "their filthy pride and presumptuousness; for in all places they will be lords and masters to the contempt and embasing of the inhabitants". Little did Linschoten imagine that, when their turn came, the Dutch, the English and the French would behave in much the same domineering way, as the Spaniards were already doing in America. The flood-tide of European expansion in the 19th century reflected European arrogance and cocksureness at their height. Their conviction of innate moral and material superiority was shared by all classes, from drunken sailors on shore-leave to punctilious diplomats *en poste*. The Anglican bishop of Victoria (Hong Kong) lamented in 1860: "Europeans in every part of the world too often carry with them a contemptuous dislike of the aboriginal natives, and demean themselves with the air of a superior and conquering race even in countries where they are barely tolerated by the governing powers and are regarded (sometimes with the semblance of real truth) as inferior in civilisation. We must unlearn much of our East Indian pride of conquest and arrogant assumption of superiority of race before our phraseology or manners towards the natives will be a true reflection of the spirit and example of Christ." Perhaps so. But it was Japan's adoption of European armaments and her victories over China (1895) and Russia (1904–05), which gave Europe the first intimation that one day the tide might turn.

The British creation of India as a nation state has its origins in the change from the East India Company's rule (exercised in many ways, as the Mogul invaders and conquerors had done, according to Indian laws and customs) to direct control by the Crown and the home government. The legal system was fundamentally changed and reorganized according to the conceptions of 19th-century Europe. A colonial bureaucracy was created which necessitated the development of a large body of indigenous administrative personnel, although decades elapsed before Indians could aspire to reach the upper levels of the Indian Civil Service. Most important of all, a European system of education was introduced with English as the language of instruction. But India, even more than most other major civilizations, has always retained an enormous capacity to resist outside influences, or to absorb or deflect them, principally owing to the impermeable strength of the Hindu caste system. The present outpouring of nostalgic literature about the British Raj does not alter the fact that, with a very few exceptions, the British who went to India remained carefully segregated alien administrators, traders and soldiers – particularly after the traumatic uprising of 1857.

It is fashionable nowadays to write up the "resistance", "freedom" and independence movements which periodically or occasionally challenged European colonial control before the 20th century. They certainly existed, and they should not be belittled or ignored. But neither should we forget that the usual pattern was not fierce and unyielding opposition, save on the rugged – and ragged – frontiers of empire – the Araucanians in southern Chile, and the Pathans on the northwest frontier of British India etc. More usual, if less heroic, were varying patterns ranging from sullen acquiescence through relative indifference and reluctant cooperation to enthusiastic collaboration. European entrepôts in Asia, whether Goa and Batavia centuries ago, or Calcutta, Hongkong and Shanghai in more recent times, could never have flourished but for the large indigenous communities which preferred to live under European colonial rule rather than in the neighbouring regions still under the control of their kith and kin. Nor could the Spaniards have maintained themselves for so long in the Philippines, nor the Dutch in Indonesia, nor the British in India, but for the loyalty of the indigenous troops who served their colonial masters against their own compatriots.

Europeans were certainly well aware of the axiom "divide and rule" in the process of getting and keeping a colonial empire. But whether Cortéz in Mexico, Legazpi in the Philippines, Speelman in Indonesia, or Albuquerque, Dupleix and Clive in India, they merely exploited the deep-seated differences and rivalries which they found. The collaboration of some indigenous élites – if one may be excused this overworked term – with European intruders can only be briefly indicated here. The Spanish *conquistadores* and settlers used the Amerindian chiefs (*caciques*, *curacas* etc.) as intermediaries with the subjugated peoples. The Portuguese of "golden

Goa" relied heavily on Gujarati *Vanias* and on Saraswat Brahmins to keep the economy of their ramshackle "State of India" viable. The English in John Company's Bengal employed Banians and *Gumashtas* (salaried agents) to shake the proverbial "pagoda tree" until it could yield no more. The Dutch in Jan Compagnie's Java worked through the indigenous district rulers (later, officials) whom they termed "regents" after the regent oligarchs of the northern Netherlands. The ubiquitous Chinese *comprador* was indispensable to the European trader in 19th-century China.

The European concept of nationalism, with its stress on the doctrine of a national personality, and on the individuality of the nation-state, has also made a profound impression, particularly after the French Revolution and the Napoleonic Wars. We need only recall that Indian and Indonesian nationalisms, for example, were mainly the creations of western-educated or western-influenced cultural élites. European education can be regarded as the built-in destroyer of European imperialism and colonialism. For once this type of education was implanted among subjugated or dominated peoples, the seeds of dissatisfaction and resistance were likewise sown, however carefully the educational structure was framed to avoid this danger. The European concept of nationalism is also responsible for the perpetuation of the partition of Africa, the guidelines for which were laid down at the Berlin Congress of 1884–85, with a cavalier disregard of existing ethnic or tribal groupings. Yet these artificial boundaries are regarded as sacrosanct by modern successor states, such as Angola, Tanzania and Kenya.

We noted above that João de Barros was not far wrong when he claimed in 1549 that European cultural and religious influences would survive the passing of political empire. The peoples of the United States and of Latin America still retain indissoluble cultural and intellectual ties with Europe. Even if Christianity seems to be yielding to Marxism in some regions, this development can be seen as one European religion replacing another. The two Rhinelanders responsible for the lucubrations of *Das Kapital* might have been dismayed by some of the things done in their names by those who claimed to be their true heirs. So, perhaps, would the Twelve Apostles at the transformation of their essentially egalitarian and pacifist creed into the hierarchical and embattled variants of the Church Militant which flourished in Europe and the Americas for centuries.

# PART EIGHT

*Epilogue:*
*The Future of Europe*

# 30

# *The Future of Europe*

## EDWARD HEATH

What does the future hold for Europe? He would be a bold man who claimed to foresee that with certainty. Rather let us ask what the future *can* hold for our continent. It is that question which opens up such exciting prospects for Europe as well as revealing such daunting problems. The value of looking at the options open to us is that it can inspire us to make a choice and to exert ourselves to achieve our purpose. It is that constructive spirit which is most needed in Europe today.

For more than 35 years, since the end of World War II, Europe has enjoyed a sustained period of peace and western Europe an increase in its prosperity greater than any experienced before. It is true that our continent remains divided, both militarily and politically, between east and west, yet despite occasional power struggles, such as the test of strength over Berlin in the late 1940s, and the strain imposed by the continued growth of the military power of the Soviet bloc, a *modus vivendi* covering the *de facto* boundaries has been established. Western Europe is less cohesive than its eastern neighbours, consisting as it does of the members of the North Atlantic Treaty Organization, a member of the North Atlantic Alliance – to give France her proper technical status – those who assist the Alliance – such as Spain – the neutrals – such as Sweden, Switzerland and Finland – and the non-aligned Yugoslavia. Although the others maintain a working relationship with the eastern bloc it is the North Atlantic Alliance that provides the security for the whole of western Europe. That security is the basis for its future prosperity.

In the economic and political sphere the nine members of the European Economic Community have taken the first firm steps towards establishing a permanent unity. When the Coal and Steel Community was created in 1951 its founders used the economic means of putting these two basic industries under joint control in order to achieve the twin purposes of making it impossible for any member country, in particular, Germany or France, to wage war against another and, at the same time, steadily to improve the standard of living of their peoples so as to turn their faces away from Soviet communism. In these aims the Coal and Steel Community, now merged with EURATOM into the European Economic Community, has undoubtedly been successful. Whatever the risks may be in the future, so long as the Community is prosperous, it is impossible to visualize a situation in which its members would be at war with each other again. That scourge of centuries has been removed.

Moreover, the contrast between the democratic way of life of the Community and the authoritarian regimes of the East, emphasized by the superiority of the standard of living in the Federal Republic of Germany over the East German Republic, has undermined the natural and deep-seated German desire to see the reunification of their former territories. Again, it is difficult to visualize the West Germans abandoning all they enjoy in life in the Community to join up with their blood relatives in the East. Only in one set of circumstances could I picture that coming about. If the European Community were to show itself unable to deal with the problems of mass unemployment, which have struck the western world since the fourfold increase in oil prices from the OPEC countries in the autumn of 1973; if, as a consequence, Soviet influence through Euro-communism spread to the Channel; and if, as a result, the Community began to disintegrate, then there would be an immense temptation for the Germans to make their peace with the eastern bloc. This would offer them the possibility at the same time of reuniting their country. Painting this scenario clearly reveals how great the danger would be to the remaining democracies in Europe. Yet one has only to describe it to realize how improbable it is that such a situation would ever arise.

And why is this? I believe it is because we now have in Europe a new generation of young people who will never allow it to come about. Even in Yugoslavia, a non-aligned communist country west of the Iron Curtain, let alone in countries with so-called Euro-Communist Parties in their political organization, I think young people wish to maintain their prosperity and retain their national freedom. Properly led, they will make all the effort necessary to do so.

Today in Belgrade one cannot help being impressed by the rapid improvement in the standard of living that has taken place over the last 15 years. Equally one cannot fail to note the contrast between the life and colour of the city and the dull uniformity beyond the Iron Curtain. Although a communist country, Yugoslavia has been open to western investment on a large scale, has kept a considerable part of its agriculture outside of the Soviet system and has followed the style of the West much more than the East. The young people of Yugoslavia, tall, fit and full of vitality, wearing the ubiquitous jeans with brightly coloured blouse or shirt, are indistinguishable from their contemporaries in London, Paris, Bonn or Rome. Seeing this provokes a number of thoughts about the nature of our European society and its future. It is difficult to believe that the young Yugoslavs can want to lose their natural ebullient identification with the rest of their own generation in western Europe by finding the Iron Curtain pushed forward to envelop them and their families. Nor can they wish to see the strength they have gained from their national unity dissolved by the disorganization and disintegration of their still developing country. Given the choice, they must surely opt for a future working with their neighbours in the European Community, politically unaligned, but moving from their personal point of view more closely towards the way of life of the West. If this is so, their resistance to any attempt to break up or take over their country will be based on strong personal as well as national grounds.

I have said that young people today throughout western Europe share much in common, more so than in any previous generation. The same taste in clothes, in music, in entertainment, even in food and wine, is widespread among them. Nor is this surprising. Travel around Europe is easier and cheaper, comparatively speaking, than it has ever been before. All the barriers among the young are down. From whichever country they come, they can enjoy for themselves the experience of exchanging ideas with each other. In so doing they become, outwardly at any rate, more like each other. On radio they hear the same tunes and rhythms, on the television screen they see the same styles and fashions, they look at the same commercial advertisements for the products of the same transnational companies. Add to that the international chains of motels and hotels, all with similar furnishings and facilities, and we cannot be surprised at this common background for life in Europe today. No doubt it will continue to develop on these lines. Some will complain of the uniformity that it enforces. Others will welcome the easily recognizable standards it produces and the sense of security that goes with it. What many overlook is that it provides an infinitely greater variety of choice for the consumer than hitherto. Nor does this eliminate for the most part the older, more limited forms of local provision that have existed for so long. Indeed, in many towns and especially in country places people have become more determined, as a result of the general availability of the same wide variety of things, to maintain their own characteristics, whether in food or clothes, in architecture or the arts.

The oft-vented fear of being overwhelmed by dull uniformity is more often than not a fear of change in general rather than a fear of losing national or local characteristics in particular. After a certain point in life the desire to see things remain as they are, even though they are not satisfactory, simply because we have become accustomed to them, is deeply rooted in human nature. But change, as a result of more widespread information about other people's activities and the development of new technologies, is inevitable, if only because the younger generation for the most part regards what was good enough for their parents as not being good enough for them. This does not alter the fact that change can be brought about in a way which is typical of the local people or in keeping with their national tradition. A glance at the make-up of the United States, which recently celebrated its bicentenary, shows how the characteristics of particular groups, almost all from without its shores, are still maintained today. Even for the outsider it is the easiest thing in the world to tell the New Englander from the Southerner or the Mid-Westerner from those who live on the west coast, to say nothing of identifying the many different ethnic groups in Chicago and other great American cities. These are immediately recognizable despite the fact that they live in the country whose products are most uniformly spread not only over its own continent but across the whole world. How much stronger must be the roots of those who have not been transported into the New World but still live in their own countries, backed by centuries of tradition, many of them the oldest nation-states in Europe. There is little difficulty today in distinguishing a Berliner from a Bavarian, even less a Dane from an Italian. Nor in any time span we are considering for the future are these characteristics likely to disappear.

This does not mean that in the world of the creative arts we shall cease to influence each other. But this is no new phenomenon; it has been going on worldwide for centuries. Chinese porcelain of the T'ang and Ming periods influenced Persian craftsmen in the 14th and 15th centuries and later affected British colouring and design in the 18th and 19th centuries. Yet each maintained its own discernible characteristics. Many musicians have been influenced by the folk music of their own and other countries, Dvořák by that which he heard in the New World, Mahler by the peasant tunes of his own Austrian Alps, Vaughan Williams by the folk songs he heard and notated in the pubs of the English countryside, yet each of these were themselves part of the main stream of the musical development of their own countries. In literature the influence has been one rather more of content perhaps than of style. Words can become a barrier rather than a bridge. The individual aspects of language are such that it is often impossible to convey by translation all the colour and nuance of the original. This is because the writer is usually so deeply imbued with a style derived from his own background. On the other hand the ideas and progressions of thought, when powerfully expressed, can change the outlook of a large part of the continent.

It is perhaps in the field of pictorial art that the influence of one studio or school is most easily and widely detected. No one can doubt the all-pervasive effect of the Italian Renaissance, the inspiration of the Dutch School or the impact of the Impressionists on their immediate successors and even on their contemporaries. If we include in this category opera and ballet as the pictorial counterpart of music we can see how French opera in the 17th and 18th centuries, Italian and German opera in the 19th and British opera in the 20th have had a similar widespread effect. An outstanding example of this was the stimulant of the Diaghilev ballet at the beginning of this century which set the style for so much that was to follow in Europe. The early visit after World War II of the Bolshoi Ballet to London and other European capitals did the same. The result of these two remarkable artistic achievements was to encourage the growth of ballet in new contemporary forms, each rising from its own national background, rather than to produce an imitation, let alone a uniform copy, of the original artistic effort. Whereas in earlier times it may have required a deliberate act of exploration by scholars and travellers to find out what was happening in the creative arts, today the scope of the media is such, both verbal and pictorial, that we cannot fail to know how others are developing, we cannot avoid imbibing their thought processes and their visual techniques in our own work.

The institutional development of modern Europe appears to some to be along contradictory lines. In economic and political affairs the operative units have become larger. There are now two major blocs, the European Economic Community and COMECON, with a number of fringe countries related to a greater or lesser degree with each of them. There is in fact really no comparison between the highly organized European Community with its institutional basis and the loosely linked COMECON group. Nevertheless it seems to the people of Europe that their affairs, in politics, defence and economics, become more and more complex, requiring a larger and larger size of institution to manage them and thus appearing at times more and more remote from the people affected by them. They accept this intellectually, however much they revolt against it emotionally, because they appreciate that no individual European country can defend itself alone against the threat from the Soviet Union; because they realize that few countries have a market of sufficient size to be able to compete on their own with Japan or the United States; and because they know that security, politics and economics, peace and prosperity are indissolubly linked. All this makes them wish all the more to have a greater say in running those affairs closer and more familiar to them. Hence the pressure in parts of Britain, parts of France and parts of Spain for devolution, not necessarily in the same form, but for the same purpose as it already exists in the Federal German Republic and in Switzerland. This explains the growth all over western Europe of innumerable community groups and organizations. This is a healthy sign and much to be encouraged. I see nothing incompatible between the two objectives of creating and developing the institutions required to cope with the characteristics of modern defence, trade and industrial processes whilst, at the same time, encouraging grass-root activities among our fellow citizens which enable them to take part in discussing, and sometimes administering, their own local affairs.

Those who first created the European communities did so in the full knowledge that they were starting out on a new path. The Community, as they envisaged it, was not to be an enlarged nation-state, nor was it to be a replica of any of the existing federal systems. Even those who wished the ultimate outcome to be a federal system did not seek to copy the arrangement in North America or Australia. The organization embodied in the treaties involving an independent permanent commission to prepare and propose policies for decision by a governing body of ministers, after being debated by a representative assembly, was something quite new in international institutions. It is true that among its supporters were those who believed that at some future date a blueprint would be prepared for a political community, to deal particularly with foreign policy and the relations of the Community with the outside world, and also probably a defence community, which would give Europe a degree of independence from its major ally, the United States, which it had hitherto lacked. Today nobody believes that the Community will set about dealing with these problems in this way. Instead the last five years have shown that the Community institutions and the member states together have developed *ad hoc* arrangements to meet the new circumstances they are all facing.

Perhaps the most important of these is the regular four-monthly meeting of the heads of government known as the European Council. No provision for this is made in any of the treaties. Indeed when President Pompidou invited other heads of government to join him for a summit meeting in Paris in October 1972 there were some, among them many good Europeans, who challenged the right of heads of government to meet in this way and to lay the lines of development of the Community for the rest of the decade. At that meeting a decision was taken to reassemble in four years' time. Only a year later, after the oil crisis, heads of government realized that the business of the Community could not be carried on unless they met at least every six months. Now they do so every four months, combined with a considerable number of bilateral meetings.

Another important example is the start which has been made on formulating a common foreign policy at regular meetings of the ministers of foreign affairs. These developments spring from a pragmatic approach which can be described as typically British, but which has in fact been found by all its members to meet the real needs of the Community without involving it in the unnecessary doctrinal debates as to whether this should become a federal or a confederal entity. I am sure that it is this approach that will govern the future nature of our European institutions. A further impetus will continue to be given to this by the directly elected members of the European Assembly.

The application of Greece, Spain and Portugal for membership of the Community also clearly demonstrates that the Community is not a static organization but a means of creating an ever wider community in Europe. All three countries have recently moved from authoritarian regimes to democratic parliamentary systems. As such they are politically to be welcomed into the Community. At the same time, as the negotiations show, their admission provides considerable economic problems for the existing members. France and Italy will be confronted with competition in agricultural products, soft fruits, citrus and wine and the Community may well find itself with a surplus of these commodities. Some industries in the Community will face more competition, particularly in the field of textiles and other consumer goods, from the new members. Although this presents problems, the seriousness of which should not be under-estimated, it also provides the Community with opportunities for taking decisive action on new policies which will enable it to expand to 12 whilst, at the same time, accommodating the resources and the production of the additional Mediterranean countries. It will be an incentive to create an expanding economy which will effectively absorb the industrial products. It will bring about strong pressures to reorganize Mediterranean agriculture so as to reduce the surpluses of existing products and make the Community more self-supporting in other basic foodstuffs such as maize and soya bean. The fact that the Community will need to deal with these problems through properly thought-out overall policies will also support the impetus for Community action in other spheres.

One of the undoubted successes of the first 25 years of the Community has been the creation of a fresh relationship with the former colonial territories of the member states. This association, at first suspect to many of the developing countries outside the Community, has been widened since the enlargement took place in 1973. In many ways its nature has also changed. The Community has been able to finance development in these countries, consume their basic raw materials and foodstuffs, and at the same time provide a market for a growing quantity of their industrial products. In negotiations for fresh agreements, the Community may well be able to create precedents for the relations between north and south as a whole. One of the major preoccupations of the industrial West is the rapid fall in the exploration and mining of minerals because of political uncertainty about the stability of many developing countries and their future attitudes towards any investment made in them. This is bound to lead within a few years to world shortages of some basic raw materials. The problem is largely one of the relationship between the large transnational companies which carry out this form of investment and the governments of developing countries which feel themselves to be poor and weak in the face of these giants. An exciting prospect would be opened up if the Community were able to establish a *modus vivendi* between the transnational companies and the governments of developing countries which would be beneficial to both. In this, as in the past, the Community is aided by the fact that it is a new organization and of itself – as apart from its constituent members – has no colonial past to embarrass it.

The fact that the Community is making these attempts to ensure the supply of raw materials and to increase world trade in a liberal trading context does not exonerate it in any way from the effective use of its own resources. There is an interesting contrast in the comparatively small difference between the total domestic product of the United States and that of the European Community and the large gap between the achievements of the two economies. The United States is able to maintain a vast defence programme, including the continuing development of nuclear weapons, to carry out, rightly or wrongly, a number of huge space projects, and to support individual industries, such as civil aviation and computers which scoop the world pool. In Europe we have reached no such position. Can it be that in our continent too many firms and too many governments in too many countries are trying to achieve the same objective when in fact in modern conditions there is insufficient room for them all to do it successfully? In the private sector this requires the rationalization of our free-enterprise services which must be carried out by the firms themselves. In the public sector it requires concerted action by governments at the highest level to make decisions on a rational programme which takes into account overall each member's national interest. If, as a result, the Community were able to increase the scope of its industrial achievements it would at the same time be able to benefit its European neighbours by expanding its trade with them. Moreover it would have a broader base on which to secure its own defence. In the process it would enable Europeans to enjoy a richer, fuller life.

The ultimate result might well be a still greater disparity between the standard of living of western Europe and the Soviet bloc. The Iron Curtain might become more firmly entrenched than ever before. However well established a *modus vivendi* between the conflicting ideologies may become, it is difficult to visualize within a measurable time span a situation in which the COMECON countries develop liberal economies which will enable them to work as one within the European Community. However much individual members of the Soviet bloc wish to expand their trade with the rest of the world, to become members of international economic organizations and to give the impression of drawing closer to the members of the Community, they still internally maintain authoritarian regimes, completely unacceptable to the western democracies. Strangely enough the more liberal they appear in their outward stance to the rest of the trading world, the more illiberal their regimes seem to become internally. Nor can one yet see a situation in which the Soviet Union will be prepared to allow any of its satellites to move outside its orbit even though at times they may appear to stray somewhat from its path. This does not mean to say that western Europe, and in particular the Community, should not continue to expand trade with its eastern neighbours. We should help them to improve the standard of living of their people by providing them with modern technology and with large credits with which to support it, always providing that it is not of direct assistance to Soviet military strength. Although we may not be able to determine the time span in which a more liberal society can evolve behind the Iron Curtain, there is every reason to continue our efforts to open the windows through which the citizens of the eastern bloc can look out upon and communicate with the western world.

From Europe came the explorers, the navigators, the traders, the missionaries, who carried with them the values and traditions of centuries of western civilization. There followed an era during which the great powers, that is to say the European powers, tore all their own continent apart. Sometimes this originated in personal ambition or the desire for national domination; at others it was the result of trading rivalry or commercial conflict. Those days are now past. Europe has to play its part in maintaining its defence against the threat from outside its boundaries but it can devote more of its resources not to internal conflict but to the development of its people in the traditions and culture which have been its heritage over so many centuries. More than that. It can convey its values once again to the world, not by the sword but through friendly help and with the example of free peoples.

# INDEX OF NAMES

# ACKNOWLEDGEMENTS TO SOURCES OF PLATES

ALL FIGURES REFER TO
PLATE NUMBERS

Alinari, Florence, 21.
Art Institute, Chicago, 80.
Associated Press Ltd,
London, 95.
Bayerische Bibliothek,
Munich, 43.
Sir Alfred Beit, by kind
permission, 56.
Bibliothèque Nationale,
Paris, 20, 22, 26.
Bodleian Library, Oxford,
85.
British Library, London,
28.
British Museum, London,
1, 4, 6, 71, 3, 5 (photo
Michael Holford).
Central Press Photos,
London, 91.
Gerry Cranham, Coulsdon,
106.
Derby Art Gallery, 64
(photo Cooper
Bridgeman).
European Parliament
Audiovisual
Information,
Luxembourg, 107.

Frans Hals Museum,
Haarlem, 48, 50
(on loan from the
Rijkscollectie of The
Dienverspreide
Hague).
Giraudon, Paris, 24, 25.
Sonia Halliday, Weston
Turville, 97
Her Majesty the Queen,
reproduced by gracious
permission (copyright
reserved), 53, 57, 58, 60.
Hermitage, Leningrad, 66
(photo Giraudon).
John Hillelson, London,
103, 104, 105.
Michael Holford, London,
2.
Imperial War Museum,
London, 92 (photo
Cooper Bridgeman).
Jeu de Paume, Paris, 69
(photo Scala).
Kunsthistorisches
Museum, Vienna, 16.
Louvre, Paris, 31, 39
(photo Bulloz); 77
(photo Scala).
Bridgeman); 33, 59, 69
(photo Scala).

Magnum, Paris, 94, 98.
Museum, Greenwich,
100.
Maritshuis, The Hague, 45
(photo Scala).
Metropolitan Museum of
Art, New York, 7, 27.
Musée de l'Armée, Paris,
68.
Musée des Beaux Arts,
Brussels, 35 (photo
Scala); 40, 41.
Musée des Beaux Arts, Pau,
87 (photo Bulloz).
Musée de Lyon, 82.
Musée de Toulouse-
Lautrec, Albi, 88.
Musée de Versailles, 52
(photo Robert Harding
Assoc.); 65 (photo
Bulloz); 67 (photo
Cooper Bridgeman).
London,
Museo Nazionale, Naples,
13.
8, 11, 12 (photo Scala).
Museum of Fine Arts,
Boston, 76, 81.
National Gallery, London,
38, 46 (photo Cooper
Bridgeman),
National Gallery, Ottawa,
101.
National Maritime

Pennsylvania Academy of
Fine Arts, Philadelphia,
62, 63.
Ursula Pfistermeister,
Furtried, 30.
Prado, Madrid, 42 (Alvarez
Collection); 47 (photo
Scala); 51 (photo MAS,
Private Collection, USA,
102.
Public Records Office,
London, 18.
Pushkin Museum, Moscow,
89.
Radio Times Hulton
Picture Library, London,
74, 75.
Rheinisches
Landesmuseum, Trier,
13.
Ann Ronan Picture
Library, Loughton, 72.
Royal Archives, Windsor
Castle, 90.
Royal Geographic Society,
London, 23, 36, 61.
Royal Holloway College,
London, 78, 83 (photo
Cooper Bridgeman).

Scala, Florence, 9, 10, 14,
15, 17, 19, 32, 37, 108.
Staatliche Museum, Berlin,
34, 49, 70 (photo Scala),
73.
Staatsarchiv, Hamburg, 29.
Staatsbibliothek, Berlin,
84.
Städelsches Institut,
Frankfurt, 44 (photo
Cooper Bridgeman).
Städtische Galerie in
Lenbachhaus, Munich,
93.
Stedelijk Museum,
Amsterdam, 86, 99.
Tate Gallery, London, 79
(photo John Webb); 96.
Wallace Collection,
London, 55 (photo John
Freeman).

The Publishers have
attempted to observe the
legal requirements with
respect to the rights of the
suppliers of photographic
materials. Nevertheless,
persons who have claims
are invited to apply to the
Publishers.